SLOBODAN MILOSEVIC

and the Destruction of Yugoslavia

SLOBODAN MILOSEVIC

and the Destruction of Yugoslavia

LOUIS SELL

DUKE UNIVERSITY PRESS   *Durham & London 2002*

B
MILOSEVIC
S
2002

© 2002 Duke University Press
All rights reserved
Printed in the United States of America on acid-free paper ∞
Typeset in Trump Mediaeval by Wilsted & Taylor Publishing Services
Library of Congress Cataloging-in-Publication Data appear
on the last printed page of this book.

-m- 6/02 $35. -

Contents

Abbreviations

CSCE	Conference on Security and Cooperation in Europe
DOS	Democratic Opposition of Serbia
DS	Democratic Party
DSS	Democratic Party of Serbia
EC	European Community
EU	European Union
FBIS	Foreign Broadcast Information Service
FRY	Federal Republic of Yugoslavia
HDZ	Croatian Democratic Union
HV	Croatian Army
ICG	International Crisis Group
JNA	Yugoslav National Army
KDOM	Kosovo Diplomatic Observer Mission
KFOR	Kosovo Force
KLA	Kosovo Liberation Army
KOS	Counterintelligence Service
LCK	League of Communists of Kosovo
LCS	League of Communists of Serbia
LCY	League of Communists of Yugoslavia
LDK	League of Kosovo Democrats
NAM	Nonaligned Movement
NATO	North Atlantic Treaty Organization
OSCE	Organization for Security and Cooperation in Europe
RFE	Radio Free Europe
RRF	Rapid Reaction Force

SANU	Serbian Academy of Arts and Sciences
SDA	Party of Democratic Action
SDB	State Security Service
SDS	Serbian Democratic Party
SFRY	Socialist Federal Republic of Yugoslavia
SPO	Serbian Renewal Movement
SPS	Socialist Party of Serbia
SRS	Serbian Radical Party
UN	United Nations
UNPA	United Nations Protected Areas
UNRRA	United Nations Refugee and Relief Association

Chronology

April 1941	Nazi Germany attacks Yugoslavia
20 August 1941	Milosevic born in Pozarevac, occupied Serbia
October 1944	Belgrade liberated by Red Army and Tito's Partisan forces
28 June 1948	Yugoslav split with Stalin becomes public
January 1959	Milosevic joins LCY
1962	Milosevic's father commits suicide
1963	During debate on new constitution, Milosevic suggests country be named SFRY
1964	Milosevic graduates from University of Belgrade
14 March 1965	Milosevic marries childhood sweetheart, Mirjana Markovic
July 1965	Major political and economic reform introduces "market socialism" in Yugoslavia
July 1966	Hard-liner Aleksandar Rankovic forced out of office
1968	Demonstrations in Pristina
1971	Tito crushes Croatian nationalist "Maspok"
1972	Tito purges Serbian leadership; Milosevic's mother commits suicide
1974	Last, decentralized Yugoslav Constitution adopted
1975	Milosevic becomes director of Beogradska Banka
4 May 1980	Tito dies
1981	Demonstrations in Kosovo suppressed by military
1984	Milosevic serves on Krajger Commission

	on reforming Yugoslav economy; Milosevic becomes president of League of Communists of Belgrade
1985	Kosovo Serb leaders make contact with disaffected Serb intellectuals, around Dobrica Cosic
1986	Milosevic, with backing of patron Ivan Stambolic, becomes president of LCS; Memorandum of Serbian Academy of Arts and Sciences appears, decrying Serbia's position in Yugoslav federation
24 April 1987	Milosevic at Kosovo Polje first comes to public prominence, uttering words, "No one will beat this people again"
September 1987	Eighth session of LCS; Milosevic sidelines Stambolic
Summer 1988	Milosevic-inspired demonstrations across Vojvodina
October 1988	"Yogurt revolution" in Vojvodina; Provincial leadership overthrown by Milosevic-inspired mob; Seventeenth plenum of LCY; Effort to unseat Milosevic by some senior LCY officials fails
November 1988	Milosevic speaks at mass meeting in Belgrade
January 1989	Montenegrin leadership overthrown by Milosevic-inspired mob
February 1989	Yugoslav authorities introduce "special measures" in Kosovo
March 1989	Milosevic has Kosovo leader Azem Vllassi arrested; Under pressure, Kosovo Assembly adopts amendments to Serbian Constitution, restricting Kosovo autonomy; Demonstrations across province leave more than 100 dead according to some reports
28 June 1989	Milosevic speaks in Kosovo on six-hundredth anniversary of Serbian defeat at battle of Kosovo Polje
December 1989	Milosevic forced to call off "meeting of truth" in Ljubljana; Ibrahim Rugova forms LDK
January 1990	Final LCY Congress ends when Slovenes walk out
April 1990	Franjo Tudjman wins first multiparty elections in Croatia
May 1990	New Serbian Constitution

July 1990	Kosovo Albanians, under LDK influence, declare Kosovo an "independent unit" within Yugoslav federation; Serb Assembly adopts direct rule in Kosovo
September 1990	"Log revolution" in Serb-inhabited parts of Croatia
December 1990	Milosevic wins first multiparty elections in Serbia; Slovenia decides to leave Yugoslavia in six months
9 March 1991	Army puts down anti-Milosevic demonstrations in Belgrade
March 1991	Milosevic announces that Yugoslavia has entered its "final agony"
May 1991	Serb paramilitary massacre Croatian police in Borovo Selo
21 June 1991	Secretary of State James Baker pays one-day visit to Belgrade
26 June 1991	Slovenia leaves Yugoslavia, setting off brief intervention by JNA
7 July 1991	EC-brokered Brioni accord ends fighting in Slovenia; War is transferred to Croatia
7 September 1991	EC-led Hague peace conference opens
19 October 1991	Kosovo Albanians declare independence, but act is unrecognized by international community
November 1991	Serb referendum in Bosnia votes to create Serb autonomous regions in Bosnia
15 November 1991	Croatian town of Vukovar falls, after brutal JNA siege
2 January 1992	Vance agreement ends fighting in Croatia
February/March 1992	Referendum in Bosnia; Izetbegovic declares Bosnia independent
March 1992	Serb ethnic cleansing begins along Drina River in Bosnia
April 1992	United States and Europe recognize Bosnia as independent state
June 1992	Milosevic creates FRY; Dobrica Cosic chosen president and Milan Panic prime minister
August 1992	London conference on Yugoslavia
December 1992	Milosevic defeats Panic in questionable election
May 1993	Bosnian Serb assembly rejects Milosevic appeal that it adopt Vance-Owen peace plan for Bosnia

July 1994	Bosnian Serbs fail to accept Contact Group peace plan for Bosnia
August 1994	Milosevic announces blockade of all but humanitarian goods to Republika Srpska in Bosnia
May 1995	Bosnian Serbs take UN soldiers hostage
July 1995	Srebrenica falls; Serbs massacre several thousand Bosnian captives; London conference threatens bombing if Serbs attack Gorazde
August 1995	Croats launch "Operation Storm" and crush Serbian Krajina in one week; Two hundred thousand refugees flee to Serbia; After Serb mortar shell kills dozens in Sarajevo, NATO begins bombing Bosnian Serbs
September 1995	Combined Croatian-Bosnian offensive closes in on Banja Luka; U.S.-led diplomatic effort achieves agreement in Geneva on basic principles for Bosnian peace; Cease-fire in Bosnia
November 1995	Dayton Peace Agreement ends war in Bosnia
December 1996	Massive anti-Milosevic demonstrations begin in Belgrade
November 1997	Three masked KLA fighters appear at Kosovo Albanian funeral
February 1998	Serb police massacre Jashari family, setting off uprising in Kosovo
Summer 1998	Serb attacks send several hundred thousand Kosovo Albanians fleeing their homes
October 1998	Holbrooke agreement with Milosevic temporarily ends fighting in Kosovo
January 1999	Serb police massacre Albanians at Racak
March 1999	Milosevic rejects Rambouillet plan for Kosovo; Serb forces begin massive campaign of ethnic cleansing in Kosovo; NATO begins bombing Serbia
27 May 1999	Hague tribunal announces Milosevic indictment
June 1999	Milosevic accepts alliance terms for ending bombing; NATO enters Kosovo and Serb forces withdraw
September 2000	Milosevic loses FRY elections to DOS candidate Vojslav Kostunica
5 October 2000	Demonstrators in Belgrade seize assembly and television

6 October 2000	Milosevic announces his departure from office
December 2000	Milosevic's SPS defeated in Serbian elections, but is largest opposition party
31 March 2001	Milosevic arrested by FRY authorities
28 June 2001	Milosevic transferred to custody of the Hague Tribunal

Preface

In writing this book, I drew on experience gained during a total of almost eight years living and working in Yugoslavia, over the period 1974–2001, with the U.S. Foreign Service and the nongovernmental advocacy organization International Crisis Group (ICG). I was fortunate to have had the opportunity—while serving from 1974 to 1976 as a young vice consul in Zagreb—to observe Yugoslavia in its heyday. There is no point in romanticizing the past—Zagreb in those days was still living in a political deep freeze as a result of Tito's suppression of the Croatian national movement "Maspok." Croatian journalists and politicians sometimes felt they had to cross the street to avoid the potential danger of being seen talking to a U.S. diplomat. Nevertheless, the Yugoslavia of that era, when the generation of young Partisans who came down out of the hills with Tito at the end of the Second World War was beginning to leave the scene, was the most prosperous and tolerant Balkan state of its day.

Only a decade later, while serving at the U.S. embassy in Belgrade from 1987 to 1991, I watched as Yugoslavia—under the impulse of the aggressive nationalism unleashed by Slobodan Milosevic and his emulators in other republics—unraveled and plunged into war. A major motivation for this book is an effort to understand how the Yugoslavia that I and many other foreign observers knew and loved could have so quickly succumbed to barbarism. In 1995–1996, while serving as political adviser to European peace negotiator Carl Bildt, and in 2000, as the Kosovo director for ICG, I participated in a small way in international efforts to end the fighting let loose by Milosevic and to build a new, stable system in the region once called Yugoslavia—efforts that as I write these words in the summer of 2001, seem threatened by yet another round of conflict, this time in Macedonia.

Over the years, I had the opportunity to observe Milosevic at close quarters in numerous diplomatic meetings, including the Dayton Peace Conference. I also witnessed firsthand the events associated with Milosevic's rise to power, watching for example as Milosevic descended by helicopter like an avenging angel to speak before an estimated million Serbs on the six-hundredth anniversary of the Serb defeat by the Turks at Kosovo Polje. Sadly, I also saw the consequences of the wars that Milosevic first threatened in that speech, during visits to besieged Sarajevo in 1995 and residence there during the first year after Dayton, and in Kosovo after the 1999 war, whose loss played an important role in Milosevic's eventual downfall.

This book is intended to be a portrayal of Milosevic's political life and an account of the events that his aggressive pursuit of Serb nationalism helped set in motion. I have included some of my impressions of these events, even where they are not directly linked to Milosevic himself, in order to give a flavor of what the man wrought.

I have relied as much as possible on original sources, which for a work as contemporary as this one includes both Yugoslav and foreign media as well as the memoirs of Yugoslavs and foreigners who have dealt with Milosevic over the years. I also interviewed as many as possible of those who have had contact with Milosevic, including some of his former Yugoslav associates and my former diplomatic colleagues. Some of these individuals wished to remain anonymous.

Few things in Yugoslavia are as politically charged as language—as I learned in 1991 when an armed Croatian fighter threatened to kill me after he had complimented me on my Croatian, and I replied that I thought the language I was speaking was called Serbo-Croatian. I have continued that practice in this volume—although I hope readers will not react as violently—using standard Serbo-Croatian spellings for the names of people and places, primarily because those are the ones most familiar to me and, I believe, to most general readers. Except where I was able to draw on the excellent services of the Foreign Broadcast Information Service (FBIS)—whose downgrading and virtual starvation of funds constitutes one of the most egregious mistakes of the U.S. intelligence community in the late 1990s— I am responsible for translations from Serbo-Croatian sources.

Throughout the text, when I use the word Yugoslavia I mean the country which existed under a variety of names from 1918 to 1991. The so-called Federal Republic of Yugoslavia (FRY), formed in 1992, was an artificial creation of Milosevic, as demonstrated by the way in which he arbitrarily rammed through changes to its constitution to allow himself to run for president in 2000. The FRY had little in common with pre-1991 Yugoslavia, which despite its numerous problems was a functioning and—in many ways admirable—country. I prefer not to dignify Milosevic's creation by using the term "Yugoslavia" and when necessary to mention it I simply use the initials FRY.

I use the term "Bosnian" to pertain to the authorities in Sarajevo in 1992, after the collapse of Yugoslavia. In cases where the religious or ethnic element of this identity is important, I have used the term "Bosnian Moslem."

When I began this book, no biography of Milosevic had yet appeared in English. Two accounts of his life have since appeared in the interim—each excellent in its own way. I hope that my own account, attempting as it does to combine firsthand diplomatic and journalistic observation, together with as complete a scholarly covering of the contemporary sources as I could find, will also contribute something to the understanding of Milosevic the man and the events he precipitated.

There are a number of people and institutions I would like to thank for helping make this book possible. Those who read all or portions of this book in manuscript include Ambassador Warren Zimmermann, Carl Bildt, Dan Caldwell, John Treadway, Charles Ingrao, Oleg Levitin, Ken Dekleva, Graham Blewitt, Shaun Byrnes, David Austin, and Bruce Connuck. I owe special thanks to the Woodrow Wilson Center for Scholars, particularly its director Lee Hamilton, and Marty Sletzinger, the director of its East European Studies program, for a fellowship that made possible the beginning of the book. John Lampe, chairman of the Department of History at the University of Maryland and former director of the Wilson Center's East European program, encouraged me to apply for the Wilson fellowship and pointed me in the direction of a book on Slobodan Milosevic. Maria-Stella Gatzoulis and Christina Balis, research assistants at the Wilson Center, provided valuable assistance in tracking down materials for the book and helpful comments on its substance. The German Marshall Fund provided a grant which helped make possible a trip to Belgrade after Milosevic's fall. Cathy Zeljak, head of the Slavic, East European, and Asian reading room at the Gelman Library of the George Washington University provided access to a valuable collection of contemporary material. Judith Montgomery, associate librarian at Bowdoin College provided access to Bowdoin's library after I moved to Maine. I would also like to thank the University of Maine at Farmington, and particularly Rob Lively, dean of Arts and Sciences, and Waleck Dalpour, chairman of the Department of Social Sciences and Business, for providing me the opportunity to teach at the college level after I moved to Maine and thereby encouraged my continuing engagement in academic pursuits related to Eastern Europe and the former Soviet Union. James Hooper, a former colleague in the U.S. Foreign Service, offered me his own considerable insights into the diplomacy of the Yugoslav conflicts and also helped provide opportunities to work and travel in the former Yugoslavia after I left the State Department, which allowed continuing research and reflection on the subject of this book.

Finally, I would like to dedicate this book to my family: to my wife, Cathey, and my children, Laura, Andrew, and Elizabeth, who lived these events twice—in the original and in my subsequent attempt to recapture them on paper.

Whitefield, Maine
July 2000

Introduction

Epiphany

On the evening of 24 April 1987, in the shabby hamlet of Kosovo Polje, Slobodan Milosevic, then an obscure politician unknown even to most Yugoslavs, ordered a line of police to stop beating an angry crowd of Serbs. Counting on confrontation to publicize their claims of persecution by Kosovo's majority Albanian population, local Serb activists had gathered 15,000 people, who chanted slogans and pushed against the police cordon. When Milosevic arrived in a column of official vehicles, the crowd surrounded them and began to chant, "We want freedom!" Milosevic, according to some eyewitnesses, was in shock; never before had he seen such raw emotion and barely suppressed violence.

A line of police bundled Milosevic and Azem Vllassi—the young Albanian chief of the League of Communists of Kosovo (LCK) who Milosevic later jailed for fourteen months—into the "House of Culture." When stones began to clatter against the windows and sides of the building, local leaders begged Milosevic to intervene to prevent bloodshed. Milosevic hesitated; journalists standing next to him described him as pale and shaking. "How, where," he muttered. Vllassi told Milosevic to pull himself together, go to the window, and calm the crowd.

With Vllassi standing behind him, Milosevic spoke briefly. He urged the people to remain calm, select a delegation to enter the building, and present their grievances peacefully to the party leaders inside.

The events of that dramatic evening were televised throughout Yugoslavia. The words that Milosevic reportedly said to the police, "No one will ever beat this people again," became the trademark of the populist movement Milosevic led to power. Vllassi later said that Milosevic's actual words were more mundane—a simple order to the police to put aside the truncheons that were the preferred method of crowd control in Yugoslavia. No matter. A myth was created—of a Yugoslav politician who took the side of the people against the police.

A Star Is Born

Milosevic's appearance that evening in Kosovo Polje was actually something of an accident. Aware that trouble was brewing, Vllassi telephoned Ivan Stambolic, the president and most powerful figure in Serbia, and urged him to come personally to Kosovo. Stambolic, however, had spoken at a similar protest meeting in Kosovo the previous year and so, to his later regret, sent Milosevic, who had long been his protégé.[1]

But the demonstration in Kosovo Polje had not unfolded spontaneously. It was carefully orchestrated by a group of disaffected local Serb agitators, who for the past year had been working closely with nationalist intellectuals in Belgrade grouped around Dobrica Cosic, Serbia's leading novelist. Protest organizer Miroslav Solevic, a burly, linebackerlike figure who commanded wide authority among Serbs in Kosovo, had carefully stockpiled rocks for the demonstrators to use in pelting the police, confident that this would provoke a response that could then be used to embarrass party officials on the scene.

Milosevic, moreover, had actually visited Kosovo Polje four days previously. According to Vllassi, Milosevic—at the request of leaders in Belgrade and Pristina—met Soljevic and other local Serb activists at the Kosovo Polje school on 20 April to urge them not to carry out a threatened march on Belgrade. At the time, Milosevic seemed to be acting in accord with Stambolic's party line from Belgrade, which was to dampen down the agitation of the Serbs in Kosovo, while using their discontent—and signs of unhappiness in Serbia proper—to try cautiously to improve Serbia's standing within the complicated federal structure that Tito had bequeathed to Yugoslavia. But as he was often to do later in his career, Milosevic acted with a gambler's logic. Caution had no place in the strategy that began unfolding in Milosevic's mind about how to exploit the situation in Kosovo for his own benefit.

Just how much of that fateful 24 April evening in Kosovo Polje Milosevic had prepared and how much was spontaneous remains shrouded in mystery. Vllassi later said that he and other Kosovo Albanian party leaders were aware that the Serbs were planning to stage an incident. When he heard that Milosevic and not Stambolic was coming, Vllassi insisted that Milosevic meet first with the primarily Albanian leadership in Kosovo's capital, Pristina, to avoid the symbolism of the Serb leadership in Belgrade dealing directly with disaffected Serbs in Kosovo, which enjoyed autonomous status in Titoist Yugoslavia. But Milosevic found pretexts to delay his arrival in Pristina until late that night, after the Serb demonstration had begun, and went directly to Kosovo Polje.

Although Vllassi is convinced that Milosevic was in cahoots with the Kosovo Serb leaders, he also said that Milosevic seemed surprised and somewhat frightened by the size and militancy of the crowd. Until early in the morning, Milosevic—visibly shaken according to journalists on the scene—sat in the front row of the shabby House of Culture, listening to a parade of local Serbs describe incidents of mistreatment at the hands of their Albanian neighbors. When there was no one left who wished to speak, Milosevic took to the podium. Most of Milosevic's speech consisted of the usual Yugoslav Communist jargon, but at the end he improvised a few sentences that reflected the emotional intensity of the evening's events. He called on the Serbs to stay in Kosovo because "this is your country; your homes, fields, and memories are here." As he warmed to his subject, Milosevic raised the stakes: "Yugoslavia cannot exist without Kosovo. Yugoslavia and Serbia will not give up Kosovo."[2]

After the long night was over, Vllassi and Milosevic rode back to the airport in Vllassi's black Mercedes limousine. Vllassi, who had not spoken publicly the entire evening, said he was startled that Milosevic had not rebuked the racist sentiments toward Albanians displayed by many Serb speakers. Milosevic replied curtly that the Kosovo Serbs were a "tormented" people. Something had to be done to help them, Milosevic said, although he also promised—falsely as it later transpired—that he would work to prevent the problem in Kosovo from getting out of control.

Milosevic returned from Kosovo a changed man. As his Serbian biographer, Slavoljub Djukic, puts it, "In the spring of 1987, Milosevic first smelled glory." Before that, if Milosevic was distinguished for anything, it was his diligence in Communist administration. As the party boss of Belgrade, Milosevic was known among his subordinates as "Little Lenin" for his habit of barking out commands while striding about his office.[3] After that night in Kosovo, though, the one-time Communist apparatchik reinvented himself as a charismatic nationalist. Milosevic discovered how the raw, emotive force of nationalism could be used to mobilize popular energy in a way long lost to Yugoslavia's official ideology of self-management socialism. He also learned the power of his own words to set people in motion. Milosevic is by nature something of a recluse and loner. Yet over the next several years, he exploited his new persona to tragic effect.

The Strategy of Despair

Milosevic is often described as a brilliant tactician but a disastrous strategist—an apt characterization if one looks at the string of failures he led Serbia into. It also reveals, however, a certain misunderstanding of Milosevic's true objectives, which were to gain, expand, and finally, simply hang onto power. His hold on power was aided by the divisiveness, ineptness, and venality of, his domestic opponents. Milosevic also showed himself to be a shrewd manipulator of the international community, which over the years never seemed able to decide whether to treat the Serbian leader as the problem or the solution to the Yugoslav crisis. Milosevic skillfully exploited the media, and especially in the later years of his rule, did not shrink from utilizing the traditional tools of a Balkan tyrant, including the police baton and assassin's bullet.

To Kill a Country

Yugoslavia in the 1980s was a troubled but functioning multiethnic society. Its disintegration was not the inevitable product of long-standing ethnic hatreds, although these were present below the surface and helped give the Yugoslav wars their savage character. Yugoslavia did not die a natural death; it was murdered, and Milosevic, more than any other single leader, is responsible. In 1989, Milosevic forcibly suppressed Kosovo's autonomy and for more than a decade thereafter held it in the grip of a brutal police occupation. Tito's anonymous successors, lacking the Old Man's political skill as well as his ruthlessness, failed to stop Milosevic when they could have. The leaders of Yugoslavia's other republics, observing what Milosevic's rule had meant for Kosovo, concluded there was no place for them in a country that also included Milosevic.

The Yugoslav collapse was a homemade tragedy. In sharp contrast to most of Balkan history, outside powers did not play a major role in stimulating Yugoslav divisions nor did the crisis serve as a vehicle for serious conflicts among them, although there was plenty of bickering on the margins. Ironically, however, the relaxation of international tensions probably contributed to the collapse. Separatism in Slovenia and Croatia came more easily in the absence of the external threats that had united the South Slav peoples in the past. The end of the cold war robbed Yugoslavia of its special position between East and West, and diverted the attention of policymakers to other issues.

Milosevic pursued a careful and well-planned strategy, aimed first at winning supreme power for himself in Serbia proper and then at dominating all of Yugoslavia. He came perilously close to success. By 1989, Milosevic controlled the votes of four of Yugoslavia's eight federal units. Had Milosevic overturned one more republic, he might have achieved his goal of taking Tito's place, although Milosevic's rule would have been very different—and likely much shorter—than that of Tito's.

Milosevic failed because the Serb nationalism he used to propel his bid for power provoked counternationalisms in other Yugoslav republics. But one of Milosevic's most enduring traits is his resilience in the face of adversity. In early 1990, he embarked on a new strategy aimed at using armed force to create a separate Serb state, with the full knowledge that this would cause the disintegration of Yugoslavia and war.

Milosevic had plenty of accomplices in his plot against Yugoslavia. Franjo Tudjman—elected president of Croatia in 1990 in large part in reaction to Milosevic's aggressive Serb nationalism—undertook a number of provocative nationalist steps that he knew would arouse the fears of the Serb minority in Croatia. In Slovenia, a coalition of attractive young reformers, after winning power in Yugoslavia's first democratic election, embarked on a step-by-step strategy of separation from Yugoslavia, fully aware that their departure would lead to war in Croatia and Bosnia. The Slovenes were like the proverbial spectator in a crowded theater who cries "Fire!" and then dashes through a nearby exit, leaving the others to their fate. Alija Izetbegovic—who during the war became a courageous symbol of his Bosnian Moslem people's resistance to Serb aggression—must bear some of the responsibility for that conflict by championing Moslem nationalism without apparently having any strategy for handling its disastrous impact in multiethnic Bosnia.

Milosevic failed to achieve his objectives in war, despite careful preparations and the unleashing of the brutal tactic of ethnic cleansing. In pre-Milosevic Yugoslavia, Serbs lived in five of the country's six republics. Many Serbs nevertheless proved reluctant to fight for Milosevic's version of a Greater Serbia, popularized in the slogan, "All Serbs in One State."

International involvement and resistance by Bosnian and Croatian forces prevented Milosevic from simply annexing the territories that Serb forces carved out in Croatia and Bosnia in 1991 and 1992. But the international community—by its piecemeal approach to the conflict and failure to deal with the underlying causes, including Milosevic himself—also allowed Milosevic to escape the consequences of his own failures. After war broke out in 1991, a steady stream of European and U.S. diplomats trooped through Milosevic's office seeking his help in Croatia, Bosnia, and Kosovo. Milosevic reinvented himself once again, this time as a peacemaker.

The Yugoslav crisis did not come as a surprise. The U.S. embassy in Belgrade, where I served from 1987 to 1991, was warning at least a year before the conflict began that there could be no peaceful divorce in Yugoslavia. Our insight was not unique; diplomats and intelligence officials in the United States, Europe, and Russia understood that Yugoslav disintegration would almost certainly be accompanied by violence. After his belated June 1991 visit to Belgrade, U.S. Secretary of State James Baker aptly described the Yugoslav leaders as "sleepwalking into a car wreck."[4] The same could also be said of the international response to the Yugoslav collapse.

Over the decade that followed the Yugoslav split, hundreds of diplomats and thousands of soldiers from the United States, Europe, and Russia labored to return peace to the region; some gave their lives to that cause. With a few exceptions, though, the record of international involvement in Yugoslavia is one of failure and misplaced effort. There are many reasons for this unfortunate history, and a biography of Milosevic is not the place to pursue them all. In my view, the central reason that international efforts failed was that no nation felt its vital interests were at stake in Yugoslavia. This meant that the approaches all of the major players—the United States, Europe, and Russia—took to the conflict were shaped primarily by issues extraneous to Yugoslavia.

Possibly the single greatest overall conceptual fault—and one that continued to bedevil the international community even after Milosevic's fall in October 2000—was the failure to address on an equal basis the claims to self-determination of all the peoples that inhabited the former Yugoslavia. By insisting that the internal borders of the republics that constituted Yugoslavia must be maintained as the external borders of the new states emerging from the rubble of Yugoslavia's collapse, the international community denied to Serbs and Albanians—the peoples of Yugoslavia whose ethnic borders most deviated from the political ones—the independent nation-states that it granted to Slovenes, Croats, Macedonians, and Bosnians.

Ironically, it was Milosevic himself who was largely responsible for the unwillingness of the international community to give Serb claims a fair hearing. Milosevic argued that if Yugoslavia disintegrated, the Serbs—who were Yugoslavia's most numerous nationality—should have the right to live in one state with other Serbs. On the surface, the Serb assertion was not without merit, especially in Croatia, where Serbs—who constituted 12 percent of the population—could justifiably claim to be uneasy about living in a state led by Tudjman, who seemed less than committed to minority rights, flaunted Croat supremacy, and flirted with abhorrent symbols associated with the World War II Ustashi fascists who had slaughtered hundreds of thousands of Serbs.

But the Serb case was undermined by the aggressive methods Milosevic used to pursue it. While he claimed to want to preserve Yugoslavia, Milosevic was in fact pumping arms into the hands of the Serbs in Croatia and Bosnia, preparing an uprising that he knew would destroy Yugoslavia. Had Milosevic been willing to pursue Serb claims peacefully, through an honest referendum under international supervision, there is little doubt that Serbs in Croatia and Bosnia would have voted overwhelmingly in favor of joining Serbia. But the peaceful route to self-determination was not open to Milosevic as long as he was determined to hold onto Kosovo and its majority Albanian population by force.

Milosevic was central to the U.S. diplomatic effort that led to the Dayton Peace Agreement. The United States relied on Milosevic to deliver the Bosnian Serbs, and in the end, Milosevic obtained Bosnian Serb leader Radovan Karadzic's initials on the text by threatening to arrest him if he did not sign. U.S. diplomatic intervention in Bosnia in 1995, ironically, came as a lifeline to Milosevic, who in the summer of 1995 faced widespread popular unhappiness because of a combined Croatian and Bosnian ground offensive that sent two hundred thousand refugees fleeing into Serbia.

After Dayton, Milosevic retained his central role in the negotiating process as diplomats sought his help to keep the accord in Bosnia on track. But the international community neglected Kosovo, where it all began. Convinced after Dayton that they had been forgotten, Albanians finally began to fight back against the Serbs. A cycle of violence ensued, which led to the North Atlantic Treaty Organization (NATO) campaign of 1999.

Dayton, which seemed at the time a great triumph for Milosevic, actually sowed the seeds of his downfall five years later. Milosevic had expected that all sanctions on Serbia would be lifted after Dayton and he reacted with surprise and fury when he learned that the United States would retain the so-called "outer wall" of sanctions that blocked Belgrade's membership in the UN and international financial institutions. Shortly after returning from Dayton a deeply depressed Milosevic reportedly sought the advice of a long-time family physician and that period saw fundamental changes in his political and personal behavior. After Dayton, Milosevic relied more heavily on his wife, Mirjana Markovic, and a corrupt coterie that surrounded her. Associates found Milosevic increasingly withdrawn and morose as the decade progressed.

By mid-2000, a year after the failed war in Kosovo, support for Milosevic had evaporated. Overconfidence, bred from isolation and contempt for both the opposition and Serb people, led Milosevic to change the Constitution to allow elections months before any recourse to the polls was necessary. The Serb opposition—which almost to its own surprise managed to unite around one candidate, Vojslav Kostunica—and the United States—which provided major material and technical support to the opposition campaign—share the credit for actually bringing about Milosevic's downfall in October 2000, in a massive popular upheaval which combined elements of spontaneity with careful organization and determination, had it proved necessary, to use force.

On June 28, 2001, Milosevic found himself in a jail cell in the Hague—twelve years to the day after the nationalist campaign that brought him to power culminated in a speech before perhaps one million Serbs on the occasion of the six-hundredth anniversary of the Kosovo Polje battle, where the medieval Serbian empire lost its independence to the invading Ottoman Turks. Milosevic's transfer to the Hague revealed deep divisions in the coalition that had overthrown him but—despite fears of massive protest—it was greeted with relief by most Serbs, who were eager to get on with rebuilding a democratic and prosperous society to take the place of the politically, economically, and psychologically devastated country Milosevic left behind.

But Milosevic's legacy—in Serbia and throughout the former Yugoslavia—will take years to overcome and, in the immediate aftermath of his transfer to the Hague, the outcome is still uncertain. Much of war's devastation in Bosnia, Croatia, Kosovo, and Serbia itself remains to be repaired. Hundreds of thousands of refugees from Bosnia, Croatia, and Kosovo are still unable to return to their homes. Many people in the former Yugoslavia are working to overcome the consequences of the wars Milosevic helped unleash, but lasting peace remains an elusive goal, as demonstrated by the conflict that erupted in Macedonia in the spring of 2001.

Milosevic faces trial and likely lifetime imprisonment. No one can bring back the hundreds of thousands of dead or undo the consequences of the wounds, rapes, and other suffering he is responsible for. Justice demands that Milosevic pay for his misdeeds. Beyond that, Milosevic's trial should help the peoples of the former Yugoslavia begin to put behind them the awful consequences of his rule and seek a future of democracy and reconciliation.

It is my hope that this book, by explaining how Milosevic came to power, what he did with that power, and how the international community reacted to the challenges Milosevic posed, will contribute to the process of understanding, which is the first element of healing.

ONE

The Young Milosevic and the
Yugoslavia He Destroyed

Slobodan Milosevic was born on 20 August 1941 in the central Serbian town of Pozarevac, about seventy-five miles south of Belgrade, where his family had fled at the beginning of the Second World War. He comes from Montenegrin stock that traces its roots back to the time of the 1389 battle of Kosovo Polje, where the Ottoman Turks crushed the medieval Serbian Empire. One of Milosevic's later ancestors was Milos Markov, a noted Chetnik commander in the early eighteenth century who inspired a song about a hero killed by traitors and whose grave is said to be tended even today. Milosevic's paternal grandfather was an officer in the Montenegrin army. His father graduated from the Orthodox seminary in the ancient Montenegrin capital of Cetinje and served before the Second World War as a professor of Russian at the Theological Academy of the Serbian Orthodox Church in Belgrade. Both of Milosevic's parents were said to be Partisan sympathizers, although neither were apparently Partisan fighters. His mother, called by her uncle the most beautiful Montenegrin woman of her generation, was also said to be a devoted believer in Communism.[1]

Pozarevac is situated in Sumadija, an area of gently rolling hills and rich farms that is often described as the Serbian heartland. In 1804, a swarthy, illiterate pig dealer named Djordje Petrovic, later known as Karadjordje from the Turkish word for black, began the first Serbian uprising against the Turks in Sumadija. The thick oak forests that once covered Sumadija (the word *suma* means forest in Serbo-Croatian) also served for centuries as a haven for the *haidjuks*—forest outlaws who combined banditry with resistance to the Turkish overlords who ruled Serbia for almost five hundred years and whose exploits were recounted for centuries around the firesides of Serbian peasants.

In the nineteenth century, Sumadija formed the central core around which Serbian leaders gradually added territory won through a series of rebellions against the Turks and wars against their neighbors. Sumadija was also the center of the Serbian peasant culture that nineteenth-century intellectuals drew on to shape an image of Serbian national identity that highlighted folkways such as individuality, hospitality, sly good humor, and cheerfulness in the face of adversity—all important features of how Serbs see themselves today. But there was another, darker side to the Sumadija peasant heritage—narrow-minded, Serb-centered, primitive, and violent—that competed for the Serb soul. Throughout his career, it has been this atavistic side of the Serb character that Milosevic, the boy from Sumadija, has appealed to.

For the Milosevic family, like almost everyone else in Yugoslavia, the war years were probably a grinding and dangerous struggle for the basic necessities of survival. Hunger, disease, and violent death were daily occurrences even in areas like Pozarevac where there were no major battles. In October 1941, the Germans murdered several thousand civilians—including hundreds of schoolchildren—in the nearby town of Kragujevac and word of this massacre must have spread quickly to Pozarevac.

Like the rest of Yugoslavia, Serbia was the scene of a vicious civil war that went on underneath the German occupation. Sumadija was a center of the resistance movement known as the Chetniks. Led by a prewar Yugoslav army colonel named Draza Mihajlovic, the Chetniks were Serbian patriots whose strong anti-Communist beliefs eventually led them into fatal compromises with the occupying Germans, depriving them of Allied support and dooming them to defeat in the struggle for Yugoslavia's future.

The Chetniks saw their main enemy as Tito's Communist Partisans, who began their uprising against the Germans in the summer of 1941 by briefly seizing an arms factory in the town of Uzice, west of Pozarevac. Although the main Partisan forces were quickly driven out of Serbia—operating for most of the rest of the war in the more rugged, mountainous terrain of Bosnia, Montenegro, and Croatia—they returned to Pozarevac to stay in the fall of 1944 in the wake of the Red Army. Milosevic thus belongs to the generation of Yugoslavs who lived from the beginning of their conscious lives under the Communist regime founded by Tito.

By the end of the Second World War, Yugoslavia was a devastated land. At least one million Yugoslavs had been killed, most at the hands of fellow countrymen. Approximately half of the dead were Serbs, many slaughtered by the Croatian fascist Ustashi, who wiped out entire villages in their effort to eradicate the Serb presence from Croatia and Bosnia. Approximately 15 percent of Yugoslavia's prewar housing and 40 percent of its industrial facilities had been destroyed.[2] Allied bombing, resistance activities, and destruction by the retreating Germans had wiped out much of Yugoslavia's transportation and communication infrastructure. Poverty, hunger, and disease stalked the land when Milosevic was a small boy.

Foreign assistance meant the difference between life and death for many Yugoslavs, especially children of Milosevic's age. In the immediate postwar years, the United Nations (UN) distributed $415 million in humanitarian and economic assistance to Yugoslavia. The ubiquitous logo of the UN Refugee and Relief Agency (UNRRA)—found throughout Yugoslavia on sacks of food, crates of clothing, and vehicles—must have been among Milosevic's earliest memories. The United States contributed almost $300 million, or 72 percent of the UNRRA assistance, to Yugoslavia. Although the Communist authorities did their best to conceal it, most Yugoslavs knew the origin of the relief supplies reaching them. The memory provided a reservoir of grassroots goodwill toward the United States for decades. (Even thirty years after the Second World War, during our first tour in Yugoslavia, the mere sight of scrambled eggs on a breakfast plate was enough to cause every Yugoslav old enough to remember the postwar era to make a crack about "Truman eggs": the powdered eggs that formed a staple of U.S. food aid.) Whether Milosevic ever received any of the proverbial chewing gum from one of the three-hundred-strong U.S. relief mission is unknown, but he was probably aware of the Americans' presence and most likely saw them on some occasion.

Postwar Communism

The new Yugoslavia introduced by Tito and his youthful followers was distinguished by a fierce commitment to a militant brand of Communism. Partisans controlled the media, public administration, army, and police. Large economic enterprises were nationalized and a rigid, Soviet-style, centrally planned economy introduced.

The Partisans enforced a harsh retribution against their wartime enemies. In the spring of 1945, the Partisans killed perhaps as many as thirty thousand Ustashi, Croatian Homeguard soldiers, and Slovenian opponents, some of whom had been handed over by Allied forces. In 1946, Chetnik leader Mihajlovic was captured and executed, and in the period 1945–1946, perhaps one hundred thousand of his supporters were hunted down and killed.[3] Moslem opponents of the Partisans were also rounded up in Bosnia, including a student named Alija Izetbegovic, who was sentenced to three years imprisonment in 1946 for belonging to a group called the Young Moslems.

In 1948, the seven-year-old Milosevic may have heard his elders whispering in tones of awed and apprehensive disbelief about the defining moment in postwar Yugoslav history: the break with Josef Stalin. The Yugoslavs were prickly proud of their own independent path to power and quickly grew to resent the overbearing approach the Soviets took toward them. When the Yugoslavs presumed to differ with Stalin on a variety of domestic and diplomatic issues, the Soviets read Yugoslavia out of the Cominform, the organization established to coordinate Soviet hegemony over its new satellites in Eastern Europe.

For years the Yugoslav Communists had glorified Stalin, and sympathy toward the Soviet Union was widespread. "I will shake my little finger and there will be no more Tito," Stalin is reported to have said, but the Yugoslav police acted with their customary efficiency to forestall Stalin's finger wagging. Yugoslav scholars writing forty years after the split found that over 16,000 people had been arrested during the campaign against the Cominform, and another 55,600 had been officially registered as Cominform supporters and subjected to police monitoring.[4] Initially unable to believe that Stalin had truly turned his back on them, the Yugoslav Communists also tried to prove their loyalty by an aggressive pursuit of Stalinist policies at home, including a brief yet disastrous campaign of forced collectivization that must have hit the rural areas around Pozarevac hard.

Milosevic's father left his family after the Second World War, fleeing Pozarevac according to some in Belgrade because his background as a Russian language teacher led him to be suspected of pro-Moscow sympathies. Settling in a stone cottage in the Milosevic family homestead, near the remote hamlet of Tuzi, in the shadow of the desolate Komovi mountain range thirty miles north of the Montenegrin capital then known as Titograd, Milosevic's father was said to have been protected by the Montenegrin political leadership of the time. Whatever the reason for Milosevic's father's flight, he apparently never returned to Pozarevac and seems to have passed completely out of Milosevic's life—although in the last year of his rule Milosevic paid for his father's grave to be renovated with a new granite headstone.[5]

In its early years, Tito's Communist regime—despite its totalitarian ideology and early repressive actions—enjoyed genuine popularity in many parts of war-weary Yugoslavia. The Communists mobilized the population for a massive reconstruction effort, partly voluntary and partly through forced labor, that by 1947 had returned agricultural and mining output to almost prewar levels, well ahead of the rest of Europe. Partisan veterans, many themselves barely out of their teens, led youth brigades to rebuild destroyed ports, factories, and roads. In the immediate postwar years, Milosevic must have seen many of his older acquaintances joining these brigades and later probably participated in them himself. By the time Milosevic was old enough to join the youth brigades, however, their focus had shifted away from the critically needed reconstruction projects to propaganda exercises, such as the painfully accumulated piles of rocks arranged to display Tito's name, which can still be seen along some remote hillsides in Yugoslavia like the remnants an ancient civilization found amid the barren sands of a desert.

Romeo and Juliet

By the early 1950s, as the young Milosevic entered junior high school, life in Yugoslavia settled into a pattern of relative stability and prosperity. Yugoslavia in the 1950s experienced some of the highest growth rates in the world. Modern conveniences such as home appliances, tractors, and even a few private cars began to appear. Radio, film, and eventually television brought the outside world into areas such as Pozarevac, which only a generation earlier had still been shaped largely by the patriarchal traditions of Serb peasant culture.

Even as economic and social progress transformed Yugoslavia into something approaching a modern country, Communism retained its firm control over all essential elements of Yugoslav life. Marxist versions of politics, economics, and history were the only ones allowed in the educational system that molded the young Milosevic. The Partisan victory in World War II was ever present in stories, songs, and film. The contemporary world outside Yugoslavia was still treated in a mainly black-and-white fashion. Despite American economic and military assistance, which continued until the early 1960s, world capitalism led by the United States was portrayed as the enemy of all progressive humanity.

Milosevic's youth in Pozarevac passed unremarkably. His grades were good though not exceptional, but his seriousness and good behavior won the esteem of his teachers. In 1959, Milosevic joined the Communist Party while still in high school.

Uninterested in sports or other physical activities, Milosevic had few friends among his peers and seems to have been something of a prig. He generally sat in the front row of his class at school, and was noted for always wearing a white shirt and tie—definitely not standard behavior for boys in small-town Serbia. A former Milosevic classmate described the future president as a loner who spurned childhood pranks in favor of his books. "We called him 'Silky,'" said one such friend. "His mother dressed him funny and kept him soft. He had nothing in common with us. We could never get him to join in when we raided orchards or did other things that boys of that age do."[6]

Despite its seemingly uneventful beginnings in small-town Serbia, Milosevic's family history is steeped in tragedy. Both his parents ended their lives through suicide. After separating from Milosevic's mother, his father lived as something of a recluse in Montenegro. In 1962, Milosevic's father shot himself, possibly after the suicide of a pupil to whom he had given a low grade. Milosevic learned of his father's death while on a student trip to Russia and did not attend the funeral.

Years later, a remote Milosevic relative said there had been no shame in Milosevic's father's death. "One day he just decided to end his life. He didn't do it out of cowardice—I often heard him say how a fool lives as long as his destiny allows him."[7]

Ten years later, his mother also took her life under circumstances that remain unclear. She may have been lonely and dejected after the departure from home of both her sons or possibly she was affected by the suicide of her brother, a military intelligence officer.[8] A well-informed Western journalist reports that Milosevic's mother killed herself after a conflict with the human being who has been closest to Milosevic for most of his life—his wife, Mirjana Markovic.[9]

Milosevic met his future wife while both were attending high school in Pozarevac and he married her in 1965 shortly after his university graduation. From the beginning, the young Slobo and Mira had a relationship that went well beyond the casual schooltime romance. Often seen in public holding hands, they were called the "Pozarevac Romeo and Juliet." Until Milosevic's imprisonment in the Hague, they had never been separated since their youth, either romantically or politically. The only portrait in Milosevic's private office is of his wife, and when the couple are together, their affection for one another is obvious. "Unlike most men in the Balkans, he [Milosevic] has only slept with one woman in his life," said one Belgrade analyst who, like many at the end of the 1990s, believed that Milosevic's relationship with his wife was a key to understanding his behavior.[10]

Unlike Milosevic, who grew up in modest circumstances as the child of refugees, Mirjana Markovic comes from a family that was long prominent in the Pozarevac region. One ancestor was reportedly a lieutenant of Kara-djordje in his early-nineteenth-century uprising against the Turks. Born in 1942 in a war-time guerrilla hide-out, Markovic also comes from one of Ser-bia's leading Communist families. Her father, Moma Markovic, was a na-tional hero; her aunt, Davorjanka Paunovic, was Tito's secretary, mistress, and "the love of his life," according to some; and her uncle, Draza Mar-kovic, served as Serbia's Prime Minister. All his life Milosevic—according to those who have known both him and his wife—never lost the sense of be-ing a poor boy who had had the good fortune to enter into a family with a historic pedigree.

But Markovic also shares with her husband a similar tragic family back-ground. Her mother, Vera Miletic, helped organize the partisan movement in the Pozarevac region. But Miletic was later arrested by the Germans and, after being tortured, reportedly betrayed a number of partisan leaders in Belgrade. In his wartime memoirs, Markovic's father wrote that after be-having badly at the hands of the police, Miletic was executed by a partisan firing squad in the fall of 1944. Toward the end of his life, however, Moma Markovic in the circle of his family questioned whether his first wife had, in fact, cracked under police interrogation. Long-time associates of Mira Markovic say that she never believed that her mother had betrayed her comrades.[11]

Many in Belgrade believe that Mira Markovic's orthodox marxist views—she long insisted on being called "Comrade" and has been the driv-ing force behind two parties claiming to be successors to the Commu-nists—stem from her mother's unhappy history. Nebojsa Covic, mayor of Belgrade from 1994 to 1997, and later a prominent member of the coalition that overthrew Milosevic, says that Markovic "functions by trying to prove whether her mother betrayed [the Party] or not."[12] Even in her youth, Mar-kovic was attached to the ideal of pure Communism. For years she wore a silk rose in her hair, after discovering one in a photograph of her mother. She refused to join her powerful father in Belgrade and later recalled with disdain vacations on Tito's luxurious island retreat of Brioni, insisting that she could not wait to return to Pozarevac—and presumably to Slobodan as well.

Despite her infatuation with Milosevic, Markovic has always remained her own person. She retained her maiden name after their marriage, sup-ported by Milosevic, who said that he would "never have married a girl who would change her last name." Markovic began her career as a journalist at the prominent Belgrade daily *Politika*, but later became a professor of marxism at Belgrade University. By her own admission, Markovic has not had a single woman friend since high school. She is most comfortable among male friends, who she calls her "reference group." Markovic is vain about her appearance—in mid-1996, she underwent painful plastic surgery—and is said to be convinced of her attractiveness to men.

Markovic's ambition for Milosevic was evident from the start. According to one account, when she saw Tito's portrait displayed in a shop window, she told a school friend that one day Milosevic's portrait would be similarly displayed over the entire country.[13] Markovic played an important behind-the-scenes role from the beginning of Milosevic's career. She helped organize the "small Politburo" that orchestrated Milosevic's rise to power in the late 1980s and wrote many of his speeches.[14] Ten years later, as support for Milosevic dwindled, Markovic—surrounded by an odd assortment of retro-marxists and corrupt war profiteers—came to be viewed as the real power behind the throne.

The Inescapable Tito

Josip Broz Tito presided over Yugoslavia throughout Milosevic's youth and much of his adult life. Tito's photo, usually picturing him in his resplendent marshall's uniform, hung in every office, shop, and classroom throughout the country. (Milosevic's office in Belgrade had a portrait of Tito until 1991, when it was replaced by a picture of Mira.) Tito's travels and speeches were described with breathless adoration by the Yugoslav media and his word was law. Schoolchildren studied his life with reverence, and recited songs and poetry in his honor. The young Milosevic undoubtedly joined on many occasions with his schoolmates in singing songs such as "Comrade Tito, You Warm Us like the Sun." Milosevic, together with the rest of Pozarevac, was probably mobilized a few times to wave Yugoslav flags and cheer while the Marshall's motorcade or perhaps his famous "Blue Train" sped by.

A man of action rather than a deep thinker, Tito had an impatience for the subtleties of marxist dogma, which was probably beneficial for him and Yugoslavia. Although he never progressed beyond a grade school education and his only job outside the party was as a mechanic, Tito demonstrated a sure grasp for techniques of governance and the main directions of policy. His decision to stand up to Stalin and launch Yugoslavia on its path of independent development brought him wide popularity through the country, even among opponents of Communism. Once the initial harsh postwar years had passed, Tito showed tolerance for new ideas. In 1950, largely in order to distinguish Yugoslav socialism from the Soviet variety, he introduced the concept of self-management under which workers were supposed to own and manage their factories through autonomous workers councils. Self-management was the ideological centerpiece of the Yugoslav system that Milosevic grew up with. Behind the scenes, however, firm control always remained in the hands of the Communist Party.

Tito also enjoyed an almost Falstaffian appetite for the good things in life: flashy clothes, fast cars, luxurious appointments, and beautiful women. To this day, no one seems to have come up with an accurate count of the state residences, vacation resorts, and hunting lodges that were kept fully staffed and equipped waiting for a visit by him. These traits were carefully guarded from public attention while the Marshall was alive, but toward the end of the 1980s, media revelations about Tito's personal excesses were a major part of the assault on Yugoslavia unleashed by Milosevic and his imitators in other Yugoslav republics.

Tito's two greatest achievements occurred early in his rule, and they decisively shaped the Yugoslavia of Milosevic's youth. These were the re-creation of a united Yugoslavia in 1945 after its dismemberment by the Nazis, and his guidance of that state—after the 1948 split with Stalin—along a path of relative openness, tolerance, and prosperity. Tito's two greatest failings—his unwillingness to abandon one-party Communist rule as well as his failure to deal honestly and openly with the national question—ultimately made it possible for Milosevic to destroy the state Tito created.

Milosevic at the University

After high school, Milosevic left Pozarevac to attend the law faculty of the University of Belgrade, where he graduated in 1963 with a mediocre 8.9 (out of 10) average. (Milosevic's grades would have been higher had he not consistently obtained low marks in the required military training courses.) Milosevic's fellow students at the university remember him primarily for his buttoned-down seriousness and enthusiasm for politics. Becoming the head of the law faculty's Communist Party organization, Milosevic carried out his party work with efficiency and zeal. Milosevic had "a genius for party politics," recalls Nebojsa Popov, Milosevic's predecessor as student party head and later a prominent anti-Milosevic intellectual. Another university friend remembers party sessions held in the highly prized single room in the student dormitory that Milosevic received as a perk for his party position.[15]

Others, however, recollect Milosevic differently. A former Yugoslav official, who attended the university at the same time as Milosevic, recalls that many of the characteristics associated with the later Milosevic were already visible in his youth. According to the former official, Milosevic was regarded at the university as a typical young party careerist—a toady to those above him in the hierarchy and a bully to those below him in the pecking order.

At the University Milosevic had his first brush with Yugoslav high politics. In 1963, Yugoslavia changed its Constitution. The process was accompanied by public meetings around the country, where the masses were supposed to express their views on the new document. During a meeting at the law faculty, attended by some of the most senior officials in Yugoslavia—including Kiro Gligorov, who twenty-eight years later, as the first president of independent Macedonia, would successfully guide his republic's separation from the Milosevic-dominated rump Yugoslavia—the young Slobodan raised his hand to speak. The original draft of the 1963 Constitution established Yugoslavia as the Federal Socialist Republic of Yugoslavia. Milosevic suggested that the socialist character of the state would be better expressed if the first two words were reversed and the country called the Socialist Federal Republic of Yugoslavia (SFRY). Milosevic's proposal was accepted and eventually incorporated into the final version of the new Constitution.[16] Who could have suspected that twenty-five years later, the earnest young man would be responsible for destroying the country whose name he had suggested?

At the university, Milosevic also met the individual who had the most decisive influence on his early life. Ivan Stambolic, the nephew of Petar Stambolic, one of Serbia's most prominent partisan leaders, was already marked for a brilliant career. Something about Milosevic caught Stambolic's eye, and the two became fast friends at the university and after. Their families entertained together, and Milosevic became the godfather of Stambolic's children. For twenty years, Milosevic followed one step behind as Stambolic climbed the rungs of power in Serbia until they neared the top, at which point Milosevic unceremoniously pushed his friend off the ladder and scrambled to the summit himself.

Yugoslavia's Great Reform

Milosevic's adult career unfolded against the backdrop of the political, economic, and social processes unleashed by the Yugoslav reform program of 1965. Its basic thrust was to reduce the role of the state in the domestic economy and integrate the country more fully into the international market. Prices for Yugoslav goods were adjusted to reflect world prices —although not freed completely. Enterprises were given more latitude in business decisions and allowed to keep more of their hard currency earnings.[17]

These economic reforms were followed by major political changes, whose precipitating event was the fall in 1966 of Aleksandar Rankovic, Yugoslav vice president and long considered the most powerful person in the country after Tito because of his control over the secret police. When it became clear that Rankovic and his supporters were frustrating the 1965 reforms, Tito commissioned the army's intelligence service to conduct a covert investigation. Rankovic was sacked when the investigation turned up police wiretaps on many senior party officials, including microphones in Tito's office and, according to some versions, bedroom.

One result of the Rankovic affair was to dramatically reduce—although certainly not eliminate—secret police interference in the lives of Yugoslav citizens. Another outcome, little noticed at the time, was to have major consequences as Yugoslavia moved toward disintegration. By their reliance on the military intelligence service to investigate and break Rankovic's power, the Yugoslav authorities had, in effect, cast the military free from supervision by the secret police, traditionally one of the key levers of Communist civilian control over the military.

Rankovic's fall opened the way for changes in the Communist Party, renamed the League of Communists of Yugoslavia (LCY). The powerful, Soviet-style party secretariat was abolished. The executive committee, analogous to the Soviet politburo, was reduced in size and republican party chiefs were made ex officio members.[18] Tito still presided unchallenged over the party, but beneath him the effect was to reduce the powers of the federal LCY organization and increase the weight of the republican parties.

Economic performance soared in the years immediately after the 1965 reforms. Yugoslavia's gross domestic product (GDP) was almost 60 percent higher in 1970 than in 1960. Foreign trade grew. Millions of Western tourists visited the new hotels that opened along Yugoslavia's spectacular Adriatic coast, providing a source of hard currency earnings as well as reinforcing the country's openness and westward orientation. A new generation of managers, intellectuals, and politicians began to replace Partisan veterans in party, state, and economic institutions. This new generation—Milosevic's generation—was university educated and willing to take advantage of the new opportunities opened up by reform.[19]

Postreform Yugoslavia was an increasingly open society. Restrictions on the media were relaxed. A few sensitive themes remained—Tito, the role of the party, and nationalism—but Yugoslav newspapers and broadcast media became more straightforward in their domestic and foreign coverage. With most passport restrictions ended, foreign travel became common for the growing number of Yugoslavs who had the money to go abroad. Several hundred thousand Yugoslavs found more or less permanent employment in Western Europe. The hard currency they sent home was a major prop for the Yugoslav economy, and the access they brought to European life, customs, and fashions contributed to the country's increasing integration into the West.

Nevertheless, the balance sheet was not all positive. Inflation and unemployment became chronic problems. The importance of tourism and workers' remittances exposed the Yugoslav economy to the vicissitudes of international economic trends beyond Belgrade's influence. Economic and social imbalances between the developed Western half and poorer southern parts of the country accelerated. Despite massive transfers of investment resources during the postwar period, the Gross Material Product (GMP) of Yugoslavia's three least-developed regions, Kosovo, Bosnia, and Macedonia, fell further behind that of the developed parts of the country. By 1990, the gap in the GMP between the most-developed republic, Slovenia, and the least-developed region, Kosovo, had risen to an eight-to-one ratio.[20]

The reforms also failed to resolve the anomaly between Yugoslavia's growing prosperity and openness and the Communist Party's stifling monopoly of power. Limited experiments with allowing multiple candidates to run for local and republican positions in Serbia in 1967 were abandoned when the establishment candidates—representatives of the liberal leadership that led Serbia at the time—were generally defeated by hard-line opponents. In the most notorious example, a seat in southern Serbia was won by a flamboyant ex-general, who had joined the partisans from the Chetniks and still wore the trademark Chetnik beard.[21]

The reforms weakened the power of the party's central institutions, yet within each republic, the party retained its monopoly over all levers of political and economic power. The result was the frustration not only of political but also economic reform. Although banks and enterprises were supposed to operate on the basis of economic rationality, virtually all senior economic officials were, in fact, party members and republican party oligarchies had the final say in major economic decisions. What was changing, however, was that these decisions were increasingly being made on the basis of what each republic thought was best for itself and not necessarily for the country as a whole.

Conservative Retrenchment

In the early 1970s, a new generation of politicians swept into power in Croatia. Initial dissatisfaction with the amount of hard currency that Croatia was allowed to keep from the burgeoning foreign tourism along its Adriatic coast quickly expanded into broader unhappiness with Croatia's position in the Yugoslav federation. Intellectuals agitated for more attention to Croatian themes in language, literature, and culture. When Zagreb University students launched a strike in support of what had become known as the Maspok (Mass Movement), Tito sent police and military units into the Croatian capital. Purges removed the republican leadership and sent hundreds to jail, including a former general named Franjo Tudjman.

One year after his crackdown in Croatia, Tito moved against the liberal leadership in Serbia. The Serbs had earned Tito's ire by maneuvers that he believed could threaten the party's leading role in the economy, but many thought that Tito also acted to balance the repression he had meted out in Croatia. In Serbia, like Croatia, the result was to entrench a colorless, conservative leadership during the last years of Tito's rule and the critical transition period after his death.

Thoroughly alarmed by what seemed to be the undesirable results of reform, Tito pushed Yugoslavia back in a conservative direction in the mid-1970s. In 1974, Communist Yugoslavia got its fourth and final constitution, which turned the country into a decentralized confederation in all but name. Except for the military, federal institutions were stripped of most of their authority. All major legislative or executive branch decisions required the unanimous consent of the six Yugoslav republics and two autonomous provinces, which basically functioned as republics. Tito remained the country's president, but when he died, chief executive authority would pass to an unwieldy eight-member collective presidency where each federal unit had one vote.

The 1976 Law on Associated Labor created a similar decentralized structure for the Yugoslav economy. All enterprises and social organizations were subdivided into so-called Basic Organizations of Associated Labor (BOAL)—a total of 19,000 across the country—which were supposed to allow individual workers more opportunity to influence economic and social decisions. Factories were broken up into dozens or even hundreds of BOALS. The system was obviously unworkable from the beginning. Successful enterprise directors generally got their way on key decisions, but the complicated system wasted an enormous amount of time. It also reduced the incentive for investment by foreign firms, which often found it impossible to negotiate with Yugoslav business partners who themselves had to broker any deal with the BOALS in their own enterprises.

The system established by the 1974 Constitution and 1976 Law on Associated Labor constituted Tito's disastrous, final legacy. Yugoslavia in the mid-1970s had all the political, economic, and social preconditions to allow it to be the first Communist country to make a successful transition to a multiparty democracy. But Tito, unwilling to abandon the party's monopoly of power, chose decentralization over democracy. The cumbersome new system acted as a brake on political and economic progress. Since it could obviously function only through behind-the-scenes manipulation by the LCY, it contributed to a growing cynicism with existing institutions as well. The Yugoslav self-management system, in its early days at least, a source of pride and prestige, now became an object of derision. The word self-management became a synonym for everything shoddy, inefficient, and corrupt, especially in those few areas where private options existed. Self-managed medical personnel, repairmen, or restaurants were regarded as, and in fact generally were, inferior to their private counterparts.

Tito hoped that decentralization would reduce ethnic dissatisfaction by allowing each republic effective control over its own political and economic development. But Tito's decentralist approach actually increased interrepublic bickering and hence, by natural progression, sharpened ethnic differences. The increasingly public quarrels among republics encouraged tendencies within the majority national group in each republic to see opposing national groups in other republics as the enemy. Minority ethnic groups began to look to "their" home republic for protection. Although these trends were kept below the surface while Tito was alive, once he was gone they ripped the country apart.

The Young Professional
Milosevic's first job after graduating from the university was as the chief of the Information Service of the city of Belgrade, but he soon moved over to become deputy to Stambolic at the Belgrade firm Technogas. Milosevic took over as director of Technogas after Stambolic left in the 1970s, and when Stambolic became the president of the Serbian Chamber of Com-

merce, Milosevic found himself at the helm of Serbia's largest financial institution, Beogradska Banka. When Stambolic returned to politics, Milosevic followed there as well. In 1982, with Stambolic heading the Belgrade committee of the League of Communists—the largest and most important urban party organization in the country—Milosevic became the part-time chief of one of Belgrade's district party committees. Two years later, Milosevic returned to full-time political work, taking over the Belgrade committee when Stambolic left to become president of the League of Communists of Serbia (LCS).

Some who knew and worked with Milosevic in the early days of his career, when he was primarily concerned with economic matters, say he showed few signs in either his personality or his politics of what was to come. An economist, who moved with Milosevic from Technogas to Beogradska Banka, said that Milosevic worked hard at learning the business of banking but was not afraid to turn for advice to his professional staff. Borka Vucic, who was the deputy to Milosevic at Beogradska Banka for international operations and who is said to have masterminded the financial side of Milosevic's sanctions-busting operations in the 1990s, described Milosevic at Beogradska Banka as a "real businessman," who relied on her and other professionals for advice but who also brought a new breadth and vision to the bank. Vucic said that Milosevic assembled a good, professional team at the bank and that "he found it easy to learn the business of banking." Vucic, who even after Milosevic's fall clearly retained an affection for him, described the young Milosevic as "communicative, caring about people at the bank, and popular with his staff."[22]

Other friends of Milosevic in these early days describe him as convivial and relaxed. Milosevic and his wife went often to the theater and socialized with other members of the rising young Belgrade elite. Dogged later by speculation about excessive alcohol use, Milosevic was said to have been a moderate drinker in his early years. He generally started the evening with a brandy aperitif. Over dinner, he might help another couple polish off two bottles of wine. Markovic, however, was a teetotaler. Someone who knew Slobodan and Mira in the 1970s and 1980s before Milosevic became prominent, described him in company as a "typical Serb," that is, seeming naturally at ease, speaking freely, making jokes, and drinking a lot, although not to excess.

Milosevic's friends and colleagues also report that he showed no interest in women other than his wife. All senior Yugoslav officials had one telephone line on their desks that, because it bypassed their secretary, was called the "girlfriend line." A close colleague of Milosevic says that he never heard the line ring when it was not either his wife or children.

Friends and colleagues of the young Milosevic describe him as a proud and devoted father. Vucic said that Milosevic often talked about his children when he was president of Beogradska Banka and his children were in elementary school. He would brag about their achievements in school and would on occasion help them with their assignments. Vucic also said that Milosevic was proud when his wife, Mira Markovic, achieved her doctorate during his tenure as Beogradska Banka president. When Milosevic traveled abroad on banking business he would often buy books that Markovic needed for her studies. Mira, by contrast does not seem to have reciprocated with an interest in Milosevic's banking career. Vucic said she did not meet Markovic until years after Milosevic left Beogradska Banka. Unlike the wives of other senior Beogradska Banka officials, Markovic never attended receptions or other social functions organized by the bank.[23]

University colleagues of Markovic present a mixed picture of her and her husband. According to Milan Bozic, a professor of mathematics who first met Markovic in the late 1970s when she joined the prestigious Mathematics Faculty as a professor of sociology, as the subject of marxism was called in those days, Markovic was originally considered more important than her husband. Markovic came from an eminent Partisan family and therefore enjoyed the perks that went with political connections in Communist Yugoslavia, for example being able to take Slobodan and the children to vacations on the exclusive island retreat of Brioni, where Tito had his favorite summer villa. According to Bozic—who remained friendly with Markovic to the end and who rose to become Dean of the Mathematics Faculty in the 1990s despite the fact that he was also a prominent member of a leading opposition party—Milosevic was initially regarded as a member of the "economic nomenklatura," which had less prestige in Tito's Yugoslavia than the political elite. In these early days Bozic seldom saw Milosevic except when he would drop by the university to pick up his wife. Around this time, according to Bozic, faculty members took to calling Milosevic "Pinky" because of the flushed color of his skin—possibly a sign of the high blood pressure Milosevic was later said to suffer from.

Bozic said his first impression of Markovic was of someone very intelligent although perhaps somewhat hypersensitive. Other professors in the Mathematics Faculty, who became acquainted with Markovic later, describe her as "not very clever." One professor said that even in the 1980s Markovic displayed signs of the instability which became more pronounced later in life. This professor—somewhat younger than Markovic and a member of the opposition to Milosevic—described her as someone who "often had sad stories to tell" and as frequently crying at faculty meetings.

To some extent this somewhat condescending attitude toward Markovic may reflect the private disdain with which marxism and its professors were treated in the university and indeed throughout Yugoslav society. According to Bozic, Markovic stood out from the beginning because she was a convinced and vocal leftist. Most other professors, by contrast, simply did what they had to do to keep from running afoul of the party, while privately dismissing Socialist dogma. Ironically, according to Bozic, Milosevic in those days would sometimes poke gentle fun at his wife's leftist beliefs, asserting that his own experience traveling around the world as a banker had taught him that what Yugoslavia needed was more capital and less worry about capitalists.

Bozic and other professors who knew Markovic agree that she was generally popular with students. Some say that this was because she had a simple, straightforward style of lecturing without the large ego that often went with the prestigious position of professor in Yugoslav society. Other members of the university point out that one reason for Markovic's popularity may have been her reputation as an easy grader, a trait which she reportedly shared with many other professors of marxism who, knowing that they were teaching an unpopular and little-respected subject, tended to try to boost their popularity by giving their students high marks.

Like many urban Yugoslavs, the Milosevics retained their rural ties. They often returned to Pozarevac for the weekend, staying in the house that Markovic had grown up in. Milosevic maintained an affection for the relaxed, provincial ambiance of Pozarevac. On one occasion, friends recall Slobodan and Mira joining them for an informal dinner directly after returning from a weekend in Pozarevac. Dressed in jeans, an amused Milosevic told how he had been feeding chickens at their home in Pozarevac when a clutch of eggs hatched. The young chicks' first glimpse of the world was of Slobodan Milosevic leaning solicitously over them. Apparently mistaking him for their mother, the baby chicks clung for the rest of the weekend to the heels of the man later known as the "Beast of the Balkans."

Beginning of the End

On 4 May 1980, sirens wailed throughout Yugoslavia to announce Tito's death. Traffic stopped, people wept in the street, and the leading Serb and

Croat football teams walked off the field in Zagreb arm in arm with tears streaming down their faces. Initially, the succession mechanisms seemed to function smoothly. Yet under the surface, long-simmering economic, social, and political problems were growing more acute.

In the 1970s, a borrowing binge abetted by foreign banks awash with petrodollars kept the Yugoslav economy growing at an annual rate of 5.1 percent. By 1982, however, Yugoslavia's foreign debt reached the dangerous level of twenty billion dollars. The United States—under the lead of the U.S. Embassy in Belgrade and its ambassador, Lawrence Eagleburger—assembled an informal group of lenders known as the "Friends of Yugoslavia" that consolidated Yugoslavia's debt and put together a package of rescue loans by the International Monetary Fund (IMF) and the World Bank.

Action by the "Friends" staved off default and allowed Yugoslavia to remain a member in more or less good standing of the Western financial community. In order to obtain an IMF standby facility, though, Yugoslavia committed itself to a stringent program of economic retrenchment that included dinar devaluation, tight restrictions on credit, and a commitment to real interest rates at least 1 percent above the inflation level. Yugoslavia's exemplary record in carrying out the terms of the agreement brought a certain measure of financial stability. But there was a price to pay for this success. Any debate about why the international community failed to avert the Yugoslav catastrophe might begin by asking about the effect of encouraging an impoverished country to repay over one billion dollars in debt principal to Western creditors at a time of declining living standards among the population and a crying need for domestic investment.[24]

Yugoslavia's most serious problems were domestic. The system bequeathed by Tito was not working and everyone knew it. For the first time since the 1950s, rationing had to be introduced in the country for gasoline, electricity, and some food items. By 1985, unemployment in the social sector had risen to 16.3 percent. Real earnings declined by 25 percent between 1979 and 1985. Inflation passed 100 percent on its way to a hyperinflation that by December 1989, reached the level of 2,500 percent annually or 1.5 percent each day.[25]

The post-Tito Yugoslav elite proved incapable of dealing with the challenges facing the country. In 1983–1984, a commission headed by Sergei Krajger of Slovenia recommended a number of modifications to the existing Yugoslav economic system, intended to increase the role of the market and liberalize trade. But the Krajger recommendations left untouched the essentials of the "contract economy" introduced by the 1974 Constitution and 1976 Law on Associated Labor, and the commission never even came close to proposing an end to social ownership of the means of production.

Milosevic was a member of the Krajger commission, where he was among those most insistent on introducing a market-oriented economic system. Milosevic's position brought him into sharp conflict with conservative members of the commission, including Croatian ideologue Stipe Suvar, with whom Milosevic clashed again in 1988 when Suvar—by then president of the LCY—made the only serious effort to remove Milosevic from power. Another member of the Krajger commission, Slovene politician Milan Kucan, called Milosevic a "revisionist"—the ultimate Communist insult for someone who gets carried away by reform. Less than a decade later, Kucan, by then transformed into a political liberal, clashed with Milosevic as Kucan led Slovenia out of Yugoslavia.

But there was always one blind spot in Milosevic's supposed economic liberalism. Milosevic was never comfortable with the notion of private property. On the Krajger commission and later when he ruled Serbia, Milosevic always supported the primacy of state property. Whether grounded on the socialist teachings of his youth or ideological predilections of his wife, Milosevic's aversion to private ownership called into question the sincerity of his commitment to reform just as it later ensured his personal control over Serbia's major economic institutions.

When political bickering blocked implementation of even the modest recommendations of the Krajger commission, another commission was convened in 1985–1986 to consider changes to the Yugoslav political system. Headed by Croatian politician Josip Vrhovec, the new commission criticized the recommendations of its predecessor as incompatible with the socialist self-management system and consigned the question of multiparty democratic elections to a dismissive footnote. Instead, the Vrhovec commission, dominated by the republican elites who controlled Yugoslavia, concentrated on "democratizing the federation"—that is, on giving the republics even more rights.[26]

By the mid-1980s, the Yugoslav political system was locked in stasis while the economy continued to spiral downward. With Communism an increasingly obvious failure and democracy proscribed, the natural alternative in Yugoslavia was nationalism. All that was lacking was a demagogue willing to apply the spark of nationalism to Yugoslavia's explosive brew of political, economic, and social dissatisfaction.

Milosevic the Politician

In 1984, Milosevic returned full-time to Serbian politics, taking over from Stambolic as the president of the Belgrade party organization when his mentor became head of the Serbian party. Required by his new position to deal primarily with political matters, Milosevic soon displayed a devotion to socialist orthodoxy that had not been apparent when his primary focus was on economic affairs. In 1985, he supported a group of hard-line marxist professors—friends of his wife—in a campaign to retain the primacy of marxist ideology in the Serbian education system. Despite appeals from educators, parents, and liberal politicians to reduce the stultifying influence of marxism in the curriculum, Milosevic joined those who fought under the banner "return to marxism." Milosevic accused reformers, in what was later seen as the first trial of strength between hard-liners and reformers in Serbian politics, of "washing their hands" of socialism and warned that they should leave the party if they persisted in their course.[27]

Even in these early years some said Milosevic showed the characteristics that made him so dangerous a few years later. In the mid-1980s the Yugoslav authorities criticized the prominent Belgrade newsweekly *NIN*—considered by many the Yugoslav equivalent of *Time*—for being excessively liberal. Milosevic jumped heavily into the fray, saying after a visit to *NIN* that what was needed was not changes in the magazine's editorial policies but the replacement of the entire staff.

After Milosevic's fall from power, Petar Zivadinovic, a prominent political personality in Serbia in the 1980s who was exiled to the post of Yugoslav Ambassador to Paris after opposing Milosevic's climb to the top in Serbia, described Milosevic as "an ordinary party demagogue." According to Zivadinovic, Milosevic was "arrogant towards his subordinates, very cruel, disrespectful. But he was very forthcoming, pliant and even subservient to those above him in the party hierarchy." Even then, Zivadinovic said, "it was clear that he was power hungry." At meetings Milosevic was intent on impressing all present in order to promote his own ambition without ever disclosing what he really wanted or intended.

Zivadinovic also described some decisions of Milosevic in those early days that combined an apparent devotion to marxist orthodoxy with the populism that Milosevic used to boost his support among the masses a few years later. In the mid-1980s Milosevic took the initiative to tax the interest that Serbian citizens earned on foreign currency accounts. As an ex-banker, Milosevic was surely aware how the tax would discourage the inflow of much-needed foreign currency. The move was unpopular among the

Serbian elite, who traveled frequently abroad, but "from the demagogical point of view he scored big with the poorer strata of the population and the party leadership."[28]

Despite this record, in 1986, when Stambolic moved on to become president of Serbia, he decided that Milosevic should follow him as republican party boss. Up to this point, Milosevic had mainly been seen as Stambolic's loyal assistant. He enjoyed little respect within the party, where he was sometimes dismissively known as "little Sloba."[29] But Milosevic's behavior as Belgrade party chief had aroused the opposition of the Serbian liberals, and when his name was put forward to head the republican party, no less than seven opposing candidates took to the lists. Before the Serbian party met to decide the issue, Stambolic received numerous warnings about Milosevic from persons in the media, the university and the party apparat. The head of the Serbian Commission for Culture, Vladimir Jovicic, wrote that Stambolic should feel a sense of danger about Milosevic, who was clearly "planning something" after the election.

Aware of the opposition to his candidacy, in a private meeting Milosevic pleaded with Stambolic: "This is my last chance. There will not be another. Let me go through now or burn up." Stambolic suggested that the party allow—for the first time—multiple candidates in order to "simulate competition." When he heard this, Milosevic jumped as if he had been scalded, exclaiming, "No way. I don't agree. I want to be the only candidate!"[30]

Stambolic threw his support to the man he still considered his "right hand." In a two-day party meeting, Stambolic patiently wore down Milosevic's critics so that when the final vote came, it was—as always—unanimous. Subsequent voting for membership on the Serbian central committee showed the extent of the resentment over Milosevic's election. Milosevic received among the smallest number votes—1,281 out of a total of 1,354—of any new member. At the end of the session, Stambolic sought to allay concerns. Noting that in some circumstances what he called Milosevic's "brisk temperament" could be an advantage, Stambolic said that the Serbian party faced a decisive break with "opportunism, wavering, and verbalisms, a time of sharp cuts."[31] As he uttered these words, Stambolic probably did not imagine that he would be the first to fall victim to the political knife wielded by Milosevic.

In addition to Stambolic, Milosevic owed his victory to the support of the Partisan Old Guard—uneasy about the challenge posed by Milosevic's liberal critics—including Stambolic's uncle, Petar Stambolic, and Tito's last minister of defense, retired general Nikola Ljubicic. The day after his victory, Milosevic's first act was to drive 220 kilometers south to the mountain resort of Brezovica, where Petar Stambolic heard with satisfaction how the session had gone.[32] Another member of the Partisan generation, however, did not share the enthusiasm over Milosevic's election. Draza Markovic, Partisan hero and former Serbian prime minister—as well as Mira Markovic's uncle—told Ivan Stambolic that "history would never forgive this election. . . . Milosevic would destroy everything."[33]

Although Milosevic had always before moved in Stambolic's shadow, in his new position he quickly showed that he intended to be his own man. The first conflict between Milosevic and his patron came over the selection of a successor to Milosevic as head of the Belgrade party. Stambolic's choice was Dragisa Pavlovic, a genial and intelligent figure who had served as Stambolic's chef de cabinet. Milosevic opposed Pavlovic, who he believed had tried in the past to limit his access to Stambolic. Ignoring his opposition to multiple candidates against himself, Milosevic put forward several names to oppose Pavlovic. Milosevic's candidates lost, but the incident left a bad taste all around.

Some of Milosevic's early associates believe that after he became chief of the LCS—traditionally the most powerful post in the republic—his eyes opened to the possibility that he might rise to supreme power in Serbia and perhaps even beyond. Milosevic understood that the only man who stood in his way was his former friend and patron, Ivan Stambolic. And with Stambolic identified as the leader of the moderate reformers in the Serbian party, it was natural for Milosevic to cast himself as the standard-bearer of resurgent socialism—a position that he was more comfortable with anyway.

As Milosevic became more preoccupied with the struggle for power, he turned his back on the liberal economic advisers who had followed him from his days at Technogas and began to assemble his own team of conservative collaborators. They included younger members of the Serbian party who opposed Stambolic's liberalism, such as Borisav Jovic, Bogdan Trifunovic, and Zoran Sokolovic. Hard-line Belgrade University professors—associates of Milosevic's wife—such as Rados Smiljkovic already controlled a large bloc on the Belgrade League of Communists committee. Particularly important for Milosevic was the support of key figures in the Serbian media, especially Zivorad Minovic, the editor of *Politika*, Serbia's most influential daily newspaper. But Milosevic's closest adviser was his wife, Mira Markovic. She fueled Milosevic's ambitions, helped write his speeches, and participated in organizing his faction.

Stambolic, by now aware of the threat that his former assistant presented, blocked Milosevic's efforts to pack the LCS presidency with his own supporters. Milosevic's response showed the tactical dexterity that later became one of his political trademarks. He installed his own people at the head of party commissions dealing with social, economic, or political issues. In the past, these commissions had been sleepy sinecures, with the real political heavy lifting carried out by the central committee. Milosevic and his team used commission meetings—widely publicized in the media they controlled—to build a groundswell of support in the party and the public beyond.[34]

Quietly but unmistakably, the struggle for Serbia was beginning.

The Yugoslavia Milosevic Destroyed

The Yugoslavia that Milosevic destroyed was not inevitably doomed to disappear. Despite its deepening problems, Yugoslavia in the mid-1980s was a functioning multiethnic society. Few Yugoslavs either wanted or expected the country to disintegrate until shortly before the end. As late as April 1991, only two months before the outbreak of war, a poll in the Yugoslav daily *Borba* showed solid majorities in every Yugoslav republic except Slovenia for keeping Yugoslavia together in some form. And even in Slovenia, 40 percent of the poll's respondents still clung to the notion of Yugoslavia.[35]

In part, of course, the reluctance to contemplate the country's disintegration stemmed from fear of the bloodshed that almost all Yugoslavs and informed foreign observers understood would accompany the collapse. Despite Tito's efforts to suppress the historical record, the memory of Yugoslavia's ethnic bloodletting during the Second World War remained just below the surface of the country's collective consciousness.

In July 1987, I returned to Yugoslavia after an eleven-year absence. On the way to our new assignment in Belgrade, my family and I stopped in Zagreb to visit friends. The first evening in town, I walked from the magnificent prewar Hotel Esplanade, under the linden trees in the charming Zrinjevac Park, to Zagreb's central square, then still known as Square of the Republic. I found a crowd gathered around a fountain, newly installed on the site of a rediscovered historic well. A high-spirited group of young people began to throw not coins but currency into the fountain. People watched fascinated as ten, fifty, and one hundred dinar notes—once the equivalent of almost a month's salary, yet made almost worthless by Yugoslavia's rampant inflation—floated in the fountain. Attracted by the crowd, a young guitar player drifted over and began to play some songs with a mildly political content. Two police officers quickly hustled him away, roughly shoving aside a couple of other young people who remonstrated that the singer was doing no harm. A young woman standing beside me, watching these developments and still captivated by the bright crimson hundred dinar notes swirling in the luminous water—murmured almost to herself, "Red, like blood."

Blood was a word that came often to the lips of Yugoslavs in the years to come. That evening, I could not help remembering a comment made to me during the 1970s by one of the Yugoslav employees of the U.S. consulate general in Zagreb, an elderly Serb originally from the area that later became known as the Serb Krajina. When I asked him once how he got along with the Croatians who formed the majority of the consulate's staff of local employees, he said he experienced no problems with his colleagues as individuals, but added that sometimes when he looked into their eyes, he could not help recalling the blood that stained the hands of those responsible for the slaughter of Serbs during the Second World War.

There was more holding Yugoslavia together than the fear of violence, though. A definite sense of Yugoslav national identity existed, based on the many common experiences that linked Yugoslavs, from Macedonia in the south to Slovenia in the north. In his lyrical recollections of the shared experiences that united citizens of the lost Yugoslavia, the Slovenian poet Ales Debeljak called Yugoslavia "a many-colored carpet that allowed me to maintain contact with lands that were dramatically different from the Baroque Central European town where I grew up yet still be part of the same country."[36]

In Yugoslavia's last "normal" census, in 1981, almost 11 percent of the population identified themselves as either "Yugoslav" or "other"—that is, not one of the recognized ethnic groups. It is likely, moreover, that census data consistently underestimated the number of those who felt their primary allegiance to be to Yugoslavia rather than to one of the ethnic groups. The so-called national key, which assigned jobs within ethnically mixed republics and at the federal level based on ethnic balance, provided a powerful disincentive for people to declare themselves Yugoslav because by doing so they could lose the patronage of "their" republic or ethnic group. Mixed marriages were a common and apparently growing phenomenon, especially in cities and ethnically mixed areas. Within Yugoslavia as a whole, more than three million in a population of over twenty-two million were the children of ethnically mixed marriages or were themselves married to someone of a different nationality.[37]

Beginning in the 1960s, surveys showed that an increasing number of Yugoslav citizens, especially among the well educated and young, considered themselves to partake in some form of Yugoslav identity. An early 1970s' survey in Serbia found that 64 percent of high school students described their nationality as Serb and 32 percent as Yugoslav—a much higher figure for the latter category than was recorded in either the preceding or following censuses of 1971 and 1981. Among students in the elite "gymnasiums," the percentage identifying themselves as Yugoslav rose to 41 percent.[38] In a 1987 survey, 15 percent of Yugoslav youth declared Yugoslav identity and 36 percent showed a "preference" for it despite having declared another ethnic identity.[39]

Yugoslavs across the country shared many aspects of daily life and common culture. Consumer goods from all the republics circulated throughout Yugoslavia. Although each republic had its own media, the Communist Party ensured—at least until the end—that the news was broadly similar throughout the country. Television programs originating in one republic might be seen in other republics. Newspapers, popular fiction, and scholarly journals circulated freely. The entire country took pride in the 1961 Nobel Prize for Literature awarded to Ivo Andric, of a mixed Croatian-Serbian background in Bosnia, who served the prewar Royal Yugoslav government as ambassador to Germany and wrote with deep feeling about the intertwined fates of Moslems, Serbs, and Croats in Bosnia. Debeljak pointed out that the Serbian-Jewish writer Danilo Kis was the decisive influence on his generation of Slovene writers, the last to be reared in Yugoslavia.[40]

Yugoslavs also shared a common popular culture, heavily influenced by Western pop music and fashion, but drawing on traditional roots from across the country. In the 1970s, Sarajevo's White Button (Bjelo Dugme) became the first group to consciously employ folk traditions to create a distinctive Yugoslav rock sound that played to enthusiastic audiences around Yugoslavia. By the late 1980s, the most popular rock bands had countrywide audiences regardless of what republic they came from. The leading bands—White Button, Fish Soup from Belgrade, and Blue Orchestra from Zagreb—regularly did two-month tours covering sixty towns throughout Yugoslavia and their albums sold as many as five hundred thousand copies.[41]

Yugoslavs traveled widely throughout their country. Resorts along the Adriatic coast attracted a mix of tourists from all over Yugoslavia. Many Serbs bought summer homes along the Croatian Adriatic coast—often finding themselves dispossessed of their property after war broke out. In the early 1980s, Slovenes led the fight to block construction of a dam on Montenegro's spectacular Tara River, one of the last wild rivers left in Europe. In 1990, when my son and I made a three-day raft trip down the Tara, our guide was a Slovene, and along the way we shared the rapids with Montenegrins, Bosnians, and other Slovenes.

When Yugoslavs turned toward the outside world, their shared sense of identity was particularly evident. While traveling abroad, they tended to identify themselves to foreigners as Yugoslavs rather than Serbs, Croats, or whatever ethnic group they belonged to. Yugoslavs throughout the country rooted for the national sports teams and Olympic athletes. In the mid-1970s, I played on an amateur Croatian basketball team, where I was often amazed at the depth of the unhappiness my teammates sometimes expressed about developments in Croatia. But when a visiting U.S. basketball team played the Yugoslav national team—then the European champions—I was equally astonished to see some chanting "Yugoslavia" with the most vocal fans.

Tito's successful resistance to Stalin and the country's subsequent development of an independent, relatively tolerant form of marxism also contributed to the Yugoslavs' sense of belonging to something special that stood apart from their neighbors. Even the most anti-Communist of my Croatian friends expressed admiration for Tito's defiance of the Soviet Union. Debeljak writes how growing up in the late 1970s and early 1980s, his peers shared "the easy feeling that we didn't have it bad at all. We were different from our counterparts in the Soviet empire's East European satellites by way of the nonaligned politics of Tito, the great guru of the 'third way.'"[42]

Yugoslavia's independence, prosperity, and openness brought it into the mainstream of Western popular and intellectual culture. Members of Yugoslavia's rapidly expanding middle class might spend their vacations as easily in Italy or Spain as the Adriatic. Yugoslavs bought the records of Western jazz and rock groups, and they read the latest European and American authors, either in translation or the original obtained from bookstores in nearby Trieste, Vienna, or Munich.

Tito's nose-thumbing at Moscow and his sponsorship of the supposedly more humane self-management socialism made Yugoslavia the darling of the Right and Left in the West. Yugoslav writers, commentators, and professors could be found in prestigious universities from the Sorbonne to Harvard. Their articles appeared in popular magazines and weighty academic journals.

But modernization also bypassed much of what remained a very Balkan country. Not only were regional disparities large and growing but there were also major differences between rural and urban levels of development. As late as 1961, over one-third of those children over five years old were not attending primary school. Rates of illiteracy in the upland rural areas of Croatia heavily populated by Serbs ranged from 30 to 60 percent while 41 percent of Kosovo's population was still illiterate in 1961.[43]

The crisis of Communism undermined the sense of legitimacy in Yugoslavia as elsewhere in Eastern Europe. Declining economic performance and rising unemployment called into question the system's claim to provide relative prosperity for its citizens at the same time that it created a young underclass unable to find work at home or in Europe and susceptible to manipulation by demagogues. The collapse of the Soviet Union—whose tanks had sat for so long across the border in Hungary—eliminated the sense of an external enemy, which had always been among the most powerful factors for cohesion among the South Slavs.

For the last two decades of the country's existence, Yugoslav politicians and cultural leaders undermined many elements of shared identity in the critical areas of education, language, and culture. For fifteen years after the end of the Second World War, the country's leaders attempted to create a new sense of Yugoslav identity by imposing common socialist and partisan themes on the cultural and educational policies of all the republics. But in the early 1960s, as Yugoslavia moved away from the centralized Soviet model, the authorities abandoned the effort to create a common Yugoslav culture. As the political power of the republics grew, so too did efforts to emphasize their own distinctiveness in the fields of language, culture, and education. Tito crushed the political aspirations of the Croatian nationalist Maspok movement in 1971, but the Croatian educational program adopted three years later under the influence of the decentralizing 1974 Constitution stressed Croatian history and literature while providing significantly less information about the history and literature of other Yugoslav nations. Similar developments occurred in other Yugoslav republics.

In 1983, federal authorities, alarmed at the way each republic was highlighting its own culture and history at the expense of the other republics and Yugoslavia as a whole, proposed the establishment of a new core curriculum to ensure that students across Yugoslavia had a common fund of knowledge. Although there was broad support for the proposal—under which 50 percent of the curriculum would have been Yugoslav and 50 percent republican—the effort collapsed in the face of strong opposition from the Slovenian Writers Association, which characterized it as an unacceptable infringement of Slovenian cultural distinctiveness and sovereignty.[44]

Under the decentralized political system introduced by the 1974 Constitution, the locus of political power shifted to the republics. Yugoslavia's leaders failed to develop a true Yugoslav political culture despite the many ties that bound the country together. There were Yugoslav rock singers, sports heroes, and movie stars, but after Tito there was no such thing as a Yugoslav politician.

Yugoslavia's leaders continued to go through the rituals of the system established by Tito. The LCY central committee met regularly, adopted decisions, and then just as regularly, decried the failure of previous decisions to be implemented. One bland figure followed another in the annual rotations set out by the 1974 system for the positions of president and chief of the Communist Party that until Tito's death, had been held simultaneously by Tito. Few Yugoslavs could name these anonymous leaders, and fewer still cared about the men who, as Winston Churchill once said about an opponent, "had a lot to be modest about."

Waiting in the wings, however, was the first politician in Yugoslavia who not only understood that Tito was really dead but was prepared to act on the basis of that discovery.

TWO

The Rise of Milosevic

Milosevic "was like a heated stove" when he returned from Kosovo Polje in 1987. The emotional events of 24 April showed Milosevic the vulnerabilities in the balanced and technocratic approach that Stambolic was taking toward the issue of Kosovo. Milosevic, by contrast, had learned how to tap into the powerful passion that Kosovo aroused among Serbs. Bogdan Bogdanovic, the mayor of Belgrade from 1982 to 1986, says that Milosevic that evening first realized his power over crowds: "He came to realize he could govern by the use of the masses."[1] The Kosovo issue, with its central place in the Serb national psyche and powerful images of a beleaguered peasantry under assault by ancient enemies, was made for a demagogue, and Serbia was about to get one.

A sharper tone crept into Milosevic's public statements. At a June 1987 LCY plenum, Milosevic warned that unity in Kosovo was essential for peace in Yugoslavia—just a whiff of the threats of violence that he later made more explicit. Outside were other harbingers. In the park across the street from the Assembly building where the central committee was holding its session, Soljevic and about five hundred noisy Kosovo Serb protesters demanded admission. They were joined by a small group of Belgraders, led by Vojslav Seselj, a dissident who later became a notorious nationalist demagogue. As the party plenum progressed, the Serbian police issued exaggerated reports about the crowd's size and intentions. Heirs to a tradition of revolution and partisan warfare, the bureaucrats who now led the Yugoslav party peered out the windows and tried to decide what to do. Eventually, the young Croatian party leader Ivica Racan met the crowd and persuaded it to disperse. Sitting quietly while these events unfolded, Milosevic suddenly turned to Stambolic and hissed, "Why are you so afraid of the street and the people?"[2]

In early September, as Yugoslavs were returning from their summer vacations, an unexpected tragedy inflamed the political atmosphere in Serbia. A young Albanian conscript, Aziz Kelmendi, murdered four of his sleeping comrades with a stolen automatic weapon before fleeing and allegedly killing himself. There were several suspicious elements to the incident. In 1983, before his induction into the military, Kelmendi had been sentenced to fifteen days imprisonment for attempting to enter Albania illegally. Kelmendi's father, who was later sentenced for illegal possession of a pistol, was outside the Paracin barracks at the time of the shooting. The initial report of the Yugoslav National Army (JNA in its Serbo-Croatian acronym), issued a week after the shooting, made it appear as if Kelmendi—described as a misfit and loner—had a grudge against one of those he killed (a Moslem judging by his name) and then went berserk, spraying two rooms of sleeping soldiers with random gunfire.

Some weeks later, however, eight Albanian soldiers at the Paracin barracks were arrested and accused of helping Kelmendi. Although the soldiers claimed at their trial that their confessions had been coerced, they received jail sentences ranging from two to twenty years.[3] In his memoirs published long after the incident, Admiral Branko Mamula, who was Yugoslav defense minister at the time of the Paracin tragedy, writes that even after a detailed investigation, the JNA did not succeed in discovering Kelmendi's motivation. According to Mamula, Kelmendi was "behaving irrationally" at the time of the shooting and many facts pointed in the direction of a personal vendetta. Although the JNA concluded that Kelmendi was definitely an "Albanian nationalist, it uncovered no traces of ties to foreign émigré or terrorist organizations.[4]

Even though only one of Kelmendi's victims was a Serb, the Belgrade media cynically exploited the emotions aroused by the crime. On the evening of the killings, Zivorad Minovic, the editor of *Politika*, privately crowed that the incident came as if it had been made for the current Serbian situation.[5] *Politika* charged that Kelmendi had not acted alone and used the incident to launch a round of perfervid articles on the plight of Serbs in Kosovo. The Belgrade media dredged up incidents from nineteenth- and twentieth-century history to portray the Albanians as implacably hostile to Serbs. Contemporary Serbian villagers in Kosovo were reported to suffer from theft, harassment, and physical assault by their Albanian neighbors.

Serbian women, even nuns, were said to be the victims of frequent, politically motivated rape.

Two days after the shooting, I watched as perhaps 10,000 people turned the funeral of the Serbian soldier killed by Kelmendi—twenty-year-old Srdjan Simic from New Belgrade—into a nationalist demonstration. Senior JNA officers and the mayor of Belgrade presided over a dignified official ceremony in which one general implored, "Won't this tragedy be enough to teach us the importance of Brotherhood and Unity!" The crowd followed the funeral cortege in dead silence to the gravesite. (Some spectators complained that neither Stambolic nor Milosevic had bothered to attend.)

After a military honor guard fired three volleys in salute and as the casket was lowered into the ground, a man called out, "He died for us all!" A group of black-clad women from Kosovo—part of a contingent brought in to enflame the mood—began to keen hysterically. Some people sang the Yugoslav national anthem while others hissed "No Yugoslavia" and chanted "Serbia, Serbia." As the crowd broke up, a smaller group gathered around Rankovic's nearby grave and began to chant more pointed slogans, such as "Down with Azem Vllassi!" and "All Shiptars out of Serbia; Kosovo is Ours!" (Note: Serbs often use the word Shiptar as a derogatory term for Albanian.) A small group of police looked on nervously, but on this occasion there was no violence. As the crowd filed out, an attractive young blond put her arm around one of the watching police and said, "We know you are with us." The policeman replied, "Let us go down to Kosovo and we could solve the problem in a few months."

This was the first funeral for a victim of politically motivated violence and the first nationalist demonstration I attended in Yugoslavia, but it was not the last of either.

Serbia as Victim

By taking as his own the cause of Kosovo Serbs, Milosevic tapped into a broad vein of dissatisfaction among Serbs about their role in postwar Yugoslavia. Serbs believed that Tito's Partisans had drawn Yugoslavia's post–World War II republican borders in a manner intended to dilute Serb influence in the country as a whole. Yugoslavia's most numerous nationality, Serbs in 1981 constituted 36 percent of Yugoslavia's total population of 22.4 million. They lived in significant numbers in every Yugoslavia republic except Slovenia. After the Second World War, however, the borders of Serbia proper excluded several areas that Serbs had traditionally considered theirs by virtue of history or ethnicity. These included Macedonia, called "South Serbia" by the Serbs, and Kosovo, which Serbs considered to be "Old Serbia." Serbs, who remembered that in 1944 Tito had rejected a proposal by Partisan ideological chief Mose Pijade to form a special district out of the Serbian-inhabited areas of Croatia, resented that Serbia was the only republic to have autonomous provinces carved out of its territory.

In the 1980s, dissatisfaction with the virtually independent status of Serbia's two autonomous provinces, Kosovo and Vojvodina, became a lightning rod for discontent with Serbia's position in Yugoslavia. Although nominally part of Serbia, each autonomous province had its own independent representatives on all federal bodies. Vojvodina and Kosovo had their own internal governmental and party structures, yet they also participated with full voting rights in the Serbian equivalents. Major legislation or constitutional changes could not be adopted in Serbia without the consent of the provinces, giving them in effect a veto right over all of Serbia's most important policies.

Serbs also felt themselves under growing demographic pressure. In Bosnia, where Serbs had been a majority before the Second World War, their share in the republic's population had shrunk from 42.8 percent in 1961 to 32.2 percent by 1981. In Croatia, the Serb population never fully recovered from the Ustashi massacres. In the mid-1970s when my wife and I drove through the region, we saw that abandoned villages and churches still covered parts of Lika and Kordun where Serbs had been subjected to some of the most vicious attacks. By 1981, Serbs were about 12 percent of Croatia's population, and the areas where Serbs were concentrated were among the poorest in the republic.[6]

Serbs were also convinced that they had paid a heavy political price for the ethnic balancing act that constituted the heart of Tito's nationalities policy. Many Serbs believed that Rankovic's 1966 removal left no Serb at the top of the Yugoslav hierarchy to even out the Croatian Tito and his closest associate, the Slovene Edvard Kardelj. Many Serbs thought that Tito had undertaken the 1972 crackdown on the liberal Serb leadership of the time to balance his removal the year before of Croatian nationalist leaders.

Declining rates of growth and rising unemployment added to the sharpness of the political debate in Serbia, as it did in other parts of Yugoslavia. Serbia resented having to send a share of its wealth to the lesser-developed areas, especially when, as in Kosovo, the resources were either wasted or actually invested in things Serbs saw as inimical to their interests.

Nationalist Godfather

Novelist Dobrica Cosic was the godfather of Serbian intellectual opposition to Yugoslavia. Cosic's retiring manner and grandfatherly shock of white hair concealed a fierce resentment at what he believed to be Tito's suppression of Serbia's legitimate interests. A Partisan fighter in his youth, Cosic was expelled from the LCY in 1968 for a speech in which he asserted that federalism in Yugoslavia impeded modernization and encouraged the growth of conservative, local bureaucracies. In that speech, he was also the first to sound the alarm over the fate of Serbs in Kosovo, warning that in Kosovo Serbs "feel threatened, that there is pressure on them to emigrate, . . . that there is inequality in the courts and lack of respect for law and justice, that there is blackmail in the name of national identity."

In 1977, Cosic opened the nonparty intellectual uprising against Titoism with a speech to the Serbian Academy of Arts and Sciences (SANU in its Serbo-Croatian acronym) that attacked the Communists for suppressing those parts of Serbian history that did not accord with their ideology. Belgrade was seized in the mid-1980s by a dramatization drawn from Cosic's four-volume novel of Serbia in the First World War, *Time of Death*, which portrayed the heroic Serbian triumph over invading Austro-Hungarian troops in 1914. The play, *The Battle of Kolubarska*, was noteworthy for its positive portrayals of figures such as Serbian King Peter and his son Prince Alexandar, who had been ignored or treated as villains by the Communists. Performances were as emotional as a major sports event. Spectators cheered and often broke into tears, but they left feeling good about being Serbs—something they had not experienced for many years.

Cosic's play—and the novel from which it was drawn—dramatized a particular view of the Serbs about themselves that became prominent in the Serb nationalist upheaval inspired by Milosevic and that continued to affect the Serb view of their place in the world even after Milosevic fell from power. Cosic's characters share the belief that Serbs are a special people chosen by God and history to suffer for their own and other peoples' freedom. Early in the play, the narrator proclaims, "A long time ago the powerful Austro-Hungarian Empire resolved to crush the small nation of Serbia, a freedom-loving democratic country." The Serb commander at Kolubarska, General Misic, speaks to this Serb belief that they have often fought for others' interests when he links the battles the Serbs fought against the invading Austrians with the larger interests of Serbia's First World War allies. "At Valjevo we gave our lives for Paris and the French; on the Kolubara we defended the Dardenelles for the English; at Milovac we shed our blood for the Russians and the Ukraine. And on the Bacinac we've perished at the hands of our Croatian brothers, giving our lives for their freedom."[7]

A few years later, when Milosevic spoke to over a million Serbs in Kosovo at the commemoration of the six-hundredth anniversary of the Serbian defeat by invading Ottoman Turks, one of the banners I observed was, "Europe, Don't You Understand We Were Defending Your Freedom, Too?" Similarly, a prominent theme in the Milosevic propaganda arsenal was of an aggressive wave of Islam that threatened not just Serbs but also all of Europe. This notion that far from carrying out a policy of bloody aggression as most of the rest of the world saw it, Serbia in the 1990s was actually defending the interests of the Western world against an Islamic threat, penetrated deeply into the Serbian political psyche. It helps explain why even after Milosevic's fall so many Serbs continued to believe that the rest of the world had treated them unfairly.

For much of the postwar era, the intellectual community in Belgrade was split between Cosic's national dissent and a group of radical marxists centered around the journal *Praxis*, banned by the party in 1976. The *Praxis* group, whose most prominent representative was philosopher Mihajlo Markovic, attracted considerable support among left-wing circles in Europe and the United States for its efforts to present a humanist version of socialism. Cosic and Markovic, despite their ideological differences, were neighbors and close personal friends. Many evenings they walked together, and by the mid-1980s, the beliefs of the two men were also beginning to converge. In 1984, Cosic, Markovic, and other leading Belgrade intellectuals founded the Committee for the Defense of Freedom of Thought and the Press after the arrest of Vojslav Seselj, then an unknown young researcher, for an article in which he advocated the partition of Bosnia. Other cases that the committee took on included that of Alija Izetbegovic, later the first president of independent Bosnia, and Dobroslav Paraga, another human rights victim under Communist Yugoslavia who became a notorious Croatian extremist during the war with Milosevic's Serbia.

In the mid-1980s, the group of dissenting Belgrade intellectuals, who informally called themselves "the nonconformists," began to receive regular visits from the disaffected Kosovo Polje Serb activists. Kosovo Serb discontent, until then largely confined to isolated and poorly educated individuals, received a powerful intellectual and organizational boost. The Serbian intellectuals, for their part, acquired the foot soldiers they needed to turn their campaign against Serbia's position in Titoist Yugoslavia into a mass movement.

The results of this new alliance were not long in appearing. In January 1986, over two hundred prominent Belgrade intellectuals, including thirty-four academicians and six retired generals, signed a petition that in effect accused the authorities of treason in Kosovo. Taking as its starting point a 1985 list of grievances signed by two thousand Kosovo Serbs—which Cosic later acknowledged having inspired and helped write—the petition set forth a series of allegations that on later examination proved to be either untrue or highly exaggerated, including charges that old women and nuns were systematically raped, holy places were desecrated, and over two hundred thousand Serb inhabitants of Kosovo were forced to sell their property for a song and abandon ancient homesteads. All of these allegations were placed in the context of an ancient historical struggle between Serbs and Albanians whose most recent manifestation was supposed to be official toleration for the gradual surrender of Kosovo to Albania.[8]

In September 1986, the Belgrade tabloid *Vecernje Novosti* published excerpts from an even more sensational document: the draft of a memorandum prepared by SANU with the modest name "On Current Social Questions in Our Country." The first half of the SANU Memorandum was a relatively straightforward analysis of the causes and consequences of the political, economic, and moral crisis gripping Yugoslavia. The document warned that the 1974 Constitution had turned Yugoslavia into a loose confederation, that republican differences were blocking economic reform, and that billions of dollars in foreign credits had been wasted. The remedies that the authors of the Memorandum proposed—popular sovereignty, democracy, separation of powers, and human rights—were well outside the box for Yugoslavia at that time.

What really caught public attention, however, was the xenophobic second half of the Memorandum, which portrayed Serbia as the victim of a half-century conspiracy by Yugoslavia's Communists to keep it weak. Because of what it claimed was a predisposition to see Serbs as virtually genetically inclined toward hegemonism, Tito and his assistants, especially the Slovene Kardelj, were said to have constructed Communist Yugoslavia on the principle, "A weak Serbia means a strong Yugoslavia." The Memorandum also charged that Serbs in Kosovo were exposed to "physical, political, legal, and cultural genocide," and described the situation in Kosovo as Serbia's biggest defeat between the liberation from Turkey in 1804 and the Nazi invasion of 1941. Albanian "aggression" in Kosovo could only be stopped when the Serbian constitutional position in Yugoslavia was revised to give Belgrade full control over its autonomous provinces. The Memorandum concluded that if the problems it had raised could not be solved, Serbia might have to define its national interest for itself—that is, it would have to leave Yugoslavia.[9]

The appearance of the Memorandum caused a bombshell not only because of the hostility it displayed toward other Yugoslav nationalities but also because of the dangerous novelty of Serbs questioning whether Yugoslavia was the best solution for Serbia. Throughout most of Yugoslavia's history, it had been more common for smaller nationalities, especially the Croats, to advance separatist arguments on the grounds that Yugoslavia was simply a cover for a Greater Serbia. But if the Serbs began to move away from Yugoslavia, its days would be numbered.

The SANU Memorandum constituted the intellectual underpinning for Serbia's destruction of Yugoslavia. Its assertions on Kosovo and on Serbia's position in Yugoslavia were later incorporated almost word for word in the nationalist platform that Milosevic put into effect between 1988 and 1991. Similarly, the notion that Serbs were the victims of what the Memorandum described as an "anti-Serb coalition," became the basis for the Milosevic regime's approach toward the outside world. The Memorandum centered this supposed anti-Serb coalition in Zagreb and Ljubljana, but in subsequent years the Milosevic propaganda machine expanded its members to include virtually the entire world—the Vatican, United Nations, United States, and most of Western Europe. In Milosevic's hands, this notion of Serbia as victim became one of the regime's major psychological and political props, helping to rationalize why Milosevic's Serbia lurched from defeat to defeat, and why the longer he remained in power, the more extensive Serbia's list of enemies became.

The publication of the draft Memorandum aroused a storm of criticism in the Yugoslav media, but the reaction of the Serbian authorities was nuanced. Stambolic later alleged that a year before the Memorandum appeared, he had agreed that the SANU leadership should organize teams of specialists to study current social problems in Serbia.[10] Shortly after the Memorandum was leaked, however, Stambolic summoned the SANU leadership for a dressing-down. He said it was impossible to agree with the Memorandum's appeal that Serbs turn their backs on Yugoslavia, although he acknowledged that much of the "data" in the Memorandum was correct. Stambolic demanded a halt to further work on the Memorandum and insisted that the SANU leadership issue a public repudiation, which it refused to do.[11]

Milosevic, who had been installed by Stambolic as Serbian party chief shortly before the SANU Memorandum appeared, took a more cautious stance. The Belgrade party committee sharply criticized the Memorandum, but the Serbian party presidency, led by Milosevic, apparently never formally condemned it. On at least one occasion, though, Milosevic criticized the Memorandum in public. Asked about it in February 1987, Milosevic claimed that the League of Communists had adopted a clear position against the Memorandum, and called for members of the Academy to be held responsible for failing to stand up publicly and tell the authors of the Memorandum that it was "inadmissible to attack Tito and the revolution and to destroy Yugoslavia."[12]

In closed circles, moreover, Milosevic joined senior party officials, including Stambolic and Pavlovic, in an orchestrated campaign against SANU. At a meeting of the political "aktiv" of the Security Institute, a police training academy, Milosevic told the assembled police cadets that the "black nationalism" of the Memorandum would signify "the liquidation of our country's present system." He criticized the Memorandum for questioning Tito's legacy, and declaimed that Yugoslavia could "survive as socialist and federal only on the principles of Tito's policy."[13]

Milosevic was, nevertheless, not in the forefront of the critics of the Memorandum—a cautious approach that was fully in keeping with his strategy at the time. He was laying the groundwork for an attack on Stambolic from a position of strict adherence to socialist orthodoxy on the surface combined with a powerful, subliminal appeal to Serbian nationalism. He therefore could not embrace the Memorandum, which repudiated the entire Titoist legacy. Neither could Milosevic afford to openly attack the Memorandum's arguments on Kosovo, however, which formed the emotional backdrop for his assault on Stambolic. Once Milosevic had triumphed over Stambolic and taken complete power in his own hands, attacks on the Memorandum vanished from the Serbian media.

The Eighth Session: Milosevic Seizes Serbia

By the fall of 1987, Milosevic and Stambolic were heading for a showdown. Milosevic no longer bothered to consult with the Serbian president, and Stambolic found that he sometimes learned about Milosevic's initiatives from the media.

Amid a supercharged political and media atmosphere, Dragisa Pavlovic—the head of the Belgrade party organization whose election Milosevic had tried to block—gave Milosevic an excuse to strike. In early September, after the ugly nationalist tone that the Belgrade media adopted in the wake of the Kelmendi shooting had provoked attacks on some Albanian-owned shops in Belgrade, Pavlovic summoned newspaper editors to his office. Demanding that the media tone down its anti-Albanian rhetoric, Pavlovic angrily asked how many more Albanian shopwindows had to be broken to convince people of the danger of taking nationalism into the streets. He denounced the staged meetings of Kosovo Serbs in Belgrade and the hysterical tenor of the pro-Milosevic media as an unacceptable form of pressure, and warned against those who would use blood to lead people toward "imagined solutions."[14]

When he heard what Pavlovic had done, Milosevic was at home with his wife, and *Politika* editor Minovic. Milosevic was jubilant: "That's it; there's nothing more to wait for," he said. Markovic dictated an article to Minovic for the next day's *Politika*, charging Pavlovic with setting off a conflict between those who would defend and those who would ignore Serbia's interests.[15]

On 18 September, Milosevic convened a meeting of the LCS presidency to discuss "the matter of Dragisa Pavlovic." Milosevic and his supporters dredged up an obscure Belgrade media affair in which Pavlovic had downplayed a satirical attack on Tito by a student newspaper in order to accuse Pavlovic of disrespect for the late leader's memory. Pavlovic met the assault bravely, speaking six times in his own defense. Everyone understood, however, that Pavlovic's patron, Stambolic, was Milosevic's real target. On the second day of the proceedings, Milosevic informed the participants that he had just received information that turned the matter under discussion from the "unacceptable viewpoints" of Pavlovic to plots and the abuse of power by Stambolic. Milosevic announced that two days earlier, Stambolic had sent a letter defending Pavlovic to the Belgrade party committee, which Milosevic described as an improper effort to threaten a body that Stambolic did not actually belong to. At first, Milosevic claimed, he refused to believe that Stambolic could have taken such a step that, as Milosevic sanctimoniously charged, had "never before been seen in our League of Communists."

Despite the obvious hypocrisy of Milosevic accusing Stambolic of bullying tactics, the timing of his intervention proved decisive. Shortly thereafter, the LCS presidency voted eleven to five, with four abstentions, to accuse Pavlovic of resisting Communist unity, blocking the implementation of the party's program on Kosovo, and being insufficiently self-critical. Ominously for Stambolic, the party Presidency also drew attention to the failures of "other LC members in high positions."[16]

A week later, Milosevic assembled the LCS central committee to stage what amounted to a political show trial. In his opening speech, Milosevic attacked the "hooliganism" of those who criticized Tito, as if either Pavlovic or Stambolic—both longtime party functionaries—would have ever dreamed of doing so. For the next two days, in classic Communist fashion where words do not mean what they seem, ninety speakers trooped obediently to the podium to accuse Pavlovic and Stambolic of almost everything except what they were really guilty of—trying to block Milosevic's use of Kosovo and Serb nationalism to gain supreme power in Serbia.

Borisav Jovic, who served as Milosevic's hatchet man in the federal presidency at the time of the Yugoslav collapse, set the tone by accusing the two of "wrecking and splitting" the party and trying to smear its top leadership—that is, Milosevic. Zoran Sokolovic, later Serb interior minister, characterized the session as the beginning of an "antibureaucratic struggle"—apparently the first use of a term that later became a Milosevic trademark. In his concluding speech, Milosevic warned that it was unacceptable for Pavlovic to slow party policy on Kosovo, but at the same time he indignantly rejected charges of Serb nationalism, which he called "a snake in the entrails of the Serb people." When the session was over, the central committee voted—with eight against and eighteen abstentions—to fire Pavlovic and five others.[17]

Although Stambolic remained as Serbian president, his days were numbered. His image was cropped out of photos and nothing he said or did was deemed of sufficient interest to the Serbian people to appear in the media.

Toward the end of November, the Serbian member of the collective federal presidency, former Yugoslav Defense Minister Nikola Ljubicic, invited Stambolic to a private meeting with Milosevic and several supporters. Ljubicic claimed that the Serbian people had enthusiastically backed the session and contended that Stambolic should show he respected the people's will by resigning. Milosevic added that Stambolic was trying to provoke a split between party and state institutions, complaining, "Just think, he is accusing us of nationalism!"[18] Stambolic argued that to resign would be an implicit admission of wrongdoing and instead insisted that he be fired. On 14 December, he was, by a vote of six to one, with the Vojvodina and Kosovo representatives on the twelve-person collective Serbian state presidency joining Stambolic in abstaining.

What came to be known as the "eighth session" capped the first stage of Milosevic's ascent, in which he seized undisputed control of Serbia proper. The tactics that Milosevic used provided the first glimpse of the ruthlessness that he later displayed in a more violent form throughout Yugoslavia. In moving against Stambolic, Milosevic turned on one of his oldest friends, the man who had been his patron throughout his career. Once Milosevic decided to head out on his own, however, none of this counted. Rebuffing Stambolic's efforts to resolve their differences behind the scenes, Milosevic also reacted with icy indifference when his former friend attempted publicly to appeal to their previous relationship. Milosevic showed himself capable of exploiting personal weakness for political advantage as well. After Stambolic fell, the U.S. Embassy in Belgrade picked up rumors that Milosevic had threatened to use embarrassing pictures against Stambolic, who had a reputation as something of a ladies' man. Milosevic may also have threatened worse. According to Vukasin Stambolic, Ivan's elder brother, on the eve of the Eighth Session Milosevic told Ivan, "Why don't you kill yourself." After the political lynching was over, Milosevic threatened Stambolic, "You shall be dead."[19]

Milosevic and Stambolic represented two traditional poles in the postwar Yugoslav political debate. Stambolic took the tolerant view of Yugoslav liberals about what should be allowed under the broad umbrella of one-party rule. Under Stambolic, the Serbian media and political scene had become the most open and interesting in Yugoslavia. Nevertheless, Stambolic failed to come to grips with the rising dissatisfaction over Serbia's anomalous constitutional situation; nor did he show any signs of dealing with the economic failures of self-management. Milosevic initially drew his support from the conservative wing of the Yugoslav party. He jumped quickly to an aggressive and intolerant version of nationalism when it became clear that the tired verities of Yugoslav self-management socialism could no longer serve as a legitimizing basis for power. Stambolic, in short, was seeking to reform a system that was designed to make reform impossible; Milosevic, confronting the same dilemma, chose to destroy the system.

Stambolic, moreover, was handicapped in some quarters by his name. As the nephew and political heir of Petar Stambolic, who epitomized the young Partisan leaders who came out of the mountains with Tito and ruled Yugoslavia for forty years thereafter, Ivan Stambolic could not avoid being associated with the perceived failures of the old system. Liberals resented Petar Stambolic's role in Tito's 1972 purge of the reformist Serbian leadership. Conservatives saw the Stambolic clan as part of the post-Rankovic Serbian elite that, in their view, had handed Kosovo over to Albanian rule.

The relatively unknown Milosevic, by contrast, initially found it easy to be all things to all men. In the early stages of his rise, Milosevic successfully developed the image of a young, decisive, modern leader who would lead Serbia away from the shibboleths and stagnation of self-management socialism into a more dynamic and prosperous future. In a 23 October speech to the Belgrade party organization, Milosevic adopted a pose of honesty and practical problem solving that would have been refreshing had subsequent experience shown that he believed it. Describing Belgrade as it really was—dirty streets and breadlines at dawn—Milosevic urged the city's residents themselves to change things by reducing absenteeism and poor work discipline, and called on government and enterprise bureaucracies to reduce their huge administrative staffs. Milosevic said the LCY was suffering from the "disease" of a party in power, and the cure was to avoid high politics that the people cannot understand and focus instead on jobs, housing, health care, and schools.

The tactics that Milosevic used to come to power in Serbia provoked nervousness in Yugoslavia's two remaining federal institutions—the party and army—but Milosevic exploited personal rivalries and confusion about his real objectives to ensure their acquiescence. Milosevic's public endorsement of the old-time Titoist religion—under growing pressure in much of Yugoslavia—initially won him the support of some key conservatives. At the first meeting of the LCY presidency—the federal party's top body—after Stambolic had been humbled, Milosevic, without blinking an eye, depicted the eighth session as a mighty step in the consolidation of the LCY and a decisive stance against Serbian nationalism. The LCY president, Bosko Krunic from Vojvodina, asked dryly whether anyone had any questions and then closed the session. A year later, Krunic and the entire Vojvodina leadership were swept away by Milosevic-inspired mobs.

Yugoslavia's only other federal organization—the army—played an ambiguous role in the early stages of Milosevic's rise. The army was desperate to avoid being drawn into Kosovo, and some military figures hoped that the more decisive approach Milosevic promised there would lead to a quick resolution of the situation. Within Serbia, both Ljubicic and former Chief of Staff Petar Gracanin were key behind-the-scenes players in orchestrating Stambolic's ouster.

But Milosevic's aggressive brand of Serb nationalism also made the generals uneasy. As Milosevic began his rise to power, the minister of defense, Admiral Branko Mamula, ordered the JNA's much-feared Counterintelligence Service (KOS in Serbo-Croatian) to bug a number of high Serbian officials to discover Milosevic's intentions and identify his supporters.[20] In the fall of 1987, after Milosevic's humiliation of Stambolic at the Eighth Session, Mamula, according to his memoirs published long after the event, decided to go to the top federal and republican leaders with what amounted to a proposal to oust Milosevic. Just months before, at the time of the Paracin killings, Mamula and the JNA leadership had seriously considered military action to deal with the emerging sense of crisis in the country, including moves against the media, which the military saw as responsible for inflaming the public mood in a nationalist and antisocialist fashion. Now, Mamula and his colleagues suggested that Milosevic be brought to book for the "putschist" methods he used to edge out Stambolic. According to Mamula, the JNA found broad agreement among federal and republican leaders for its evaluation of the dangerous state of affairs in Yugoslavia. None of the leaders, however, were willing to support the JNA in a move against Milosevic.[21]

Yugoslav leaders had no enthusiasm for involving the conservative military bosses in politics. In September, after Mamula gave a stem-winding speech in which he cited the killings in Paracin as a sign that the leadership of the country was on the verge of losing control of events, he writes that he was summoned before a specially convened party-state commission to explain himself. The Slovene party leaders, moreover, understood perfectly well that if they consented to military moves against Milosevic, Slovenia would surely become the generals' next target.

In these early days of Milosevic's ascent, there was also a broad underestimation of the danger that he represented to Yugoslavia's future. Some Yugoslav leaders thought that Milosevic, who up to then had been chiefly noted for his commitment to orthodox socialism and had yet to fully display his nationalist colors, was the best person to combat the growing strength of nationalism among Serbian intellectuals. Many also saw Stambolic, with his strong Partisan connection, as the more dangerous Serbian figure. Hard-line Croatian party leader Stipe Suvar later commented that in the fall of 1987, he and his allies among the conservative wing of the party—including the Montenegrins Vidoje Zarkovic and Marko Orlandic who were soon to fall victim to Milosevic—believed that "the only thing that can save us is if Milosevic stops the attacks on Tito from those behind the 'memorandum' policy. And if Milosevic himself becomes captured by nationalism, it will be easier to stop him than Ivan Stambolic, who is the protégé of the Serb national elite and who is the one who started the SANU memorandum." Similarly, Krunic told the generals that he welcomed Milosevic's removal of Stambolic, who Krunic and other Vojvodina leaders thought was the driving force behind Belgrade's efforts to revise the Serbian constitution to reduce the autonomy enjoyed by Vojvodina and Kosovo.

Some members of the Yugoslav political elite also failed to recognize the degree of duplicity that Milosevic brought to politics. After Mamula spoke to the Slovene party leadership, then forming around a moderate liberal faction headed by Milan Kucan, Stane Dolanc, the Slovene representative on the collective federal presidency, telephoned Milosevic. A strongly conservative figure who at one time had been considered Tito's anointed successor, Dolanc at the time oversaw Yugoslav internal security forces. He could, if he had collaborated with Mamula, almost certainly have succeeded in removing Milosevic. Describing his conversation with Milosevic to Mamula, Dolanc said that on Kosovo, the Serb leader was "clean." Milosevic also promised Dolanc to support the selection of the reformist Croat, Ante Markovic, to become the new head of the Yugoslav federal government. Milosevic's later behavior showed his explanations to Dolanc on both Kosovo and Markovic to be wildly at variance with the truth.

Even in those early days, moreover, Milosevic displayed his capacity for careful planning, including use of the divide-and-rule tactics that characterized his subsequent march to power. Mamula said there was little support for Milosevic among the active-duty generals, but some retired generals who remained influential in the army and country believed that Milosevic, together with the conservative Suvar who was scheduled to become head of the LCY in 1988, could cooperate to "establish order" in Yugoslavia. Mamula also learned that Milosevic had gotten the head of the Yugoslav secret police, a young Croat named Zdravko Mustac, to persuade the leaders of the Croatian party to support Milosevic's tactics at the Eighth Session, in return for a pledge by Milosevic to use his influence among Serbs in Croatia to reduce criticism of the Croatian party leadership in the Croatian media.

Eventually, Mamula and his colleagues abandoned the effort to block Milosevic, concluding that they were simply "voices crying in the desert." Mamula retired in 1988—under circumstances that still remain unclear. At the time, some in Yugoslavia asserted that Mamula left because of charges—first raised in the strongly anti-JNA Slovene youth paper, *Mladina*—that Mamula had abused his position in a variety of ways, including using conscripts to built a luxurious villa on the Adriatic coast. In his memoirs, Mamula maintains that he retired because at sixty-seven, he was already over the mandatory JNA departure age of sixty-five. Mamula acknowledges, however, that his militant speech after the Paracin tragedy permanently soured his relationship with Yugoslavia's civilian leaders.[22]

Mamula's replacement, Veljko Kadijevic, turned out to be the last Yugoslav defense minister. An upright, conservative figure who ultimately played a tragically destructive role in Yugoslavia's collapse, Kadijevic was sympathetic to Milosevic yet he was also strongly attached to a united Yugoslavia. Kadijevic distanced the JNA politically from Milosevic until 1990, when the Slovene push for secession and the election of the nationalist Franjo Tudjman in Croatia eventually drove the JNA into the arms of the Serbs. But the heavy-handed response by Kadijevic and other JNA leaders to the swelling desire to break free from the straitjacket of one-party socialist rule did much to turn the demand for change, especially in Slovenia, into a rush for independence.

Milosevic Moves Out

After Stambolic's removal, the entire older generation of Serbian leaders was either fired or sidelined. Milosevic stood unchallenged in Serbia. It was still unclear, however, what Milosevic intended to do with his new power. Milosevic himself kept his distance from the noisy nationalist campaign his minions had unleashed in the media. During Mikhail Gorbachev's March 1988 visit to Yugoslavia, Milosevic—who toasted Gorbachev with the words, "In spite of all difficulties, which it meets on a daily and historical basis, Socialism is the most progressive society of our era"—was widely considered to have adopted a posture toward the reformist Soviet leader that was noteworthy for its toadyism and emphasis on socialist verities.[23]

By the summer of 1988 Milosevic was ready to expand his drive for power beyond Serbia proper. During a May LCY conference, Milosevic warned ominously that the party leadership had a duty to act in accordance with the wishes of the people; if it did not, the people would replace the leadership.[24] In the 1 July edition of the Belgrade weekly *NIN*, Milosevic made it clear who he had in mind—the leaders of Vojvodina and Kosovo. He accused them of seeking to constrain Serbia to the status of a second-class republic and announced his intention to ram through constitutional changes to cut back the autonomy of the two provinces.[25]

In early July 1988, Milosevic moved the issue into the streets—the first use of what later came to be called "street democracy," a tactic that Milosevic employed over the next year to overthrow the leaderships of three of Yugoslavia's eight constituent units. On a hot Sunday afternoon, a bare-chested Miroslav Soljevic led about five hundred Kosovo Serb activists in a march through Novi Sad, the usually tranquil capital of Vojvodina. Soljevic accused the Vojvodina leadership of working together with their Kosovo provincial counterparts to encourage Albanian separatism and mockingly challenged provincial party leader Sogorov to debate him. The authorities cut the power to Soljevic's loudspeaker system, a move that the protesters gleefully countered by plugging into a nearby, sympathetic apartment dweller's electric outlets. Police stood by but did not intervene, possibly be-cause a number of Novi Sad residents cheered and joined the Kosovo pro-testers.

A few days later, *Politika* published the transcript of an emergency meeting where the Vojvodina leadership had called Milosevic's actions an "open declaration of war." One member of the Vojvodina presidency, Djordge Stojsic, went to the heart of the matter: "In the beginning, we did not take Slobodan Milosevic seriously, but now if we do not muster enough strength to stop him in the League of Communists, who knows where it will end. . . . Milosevic identifies himself with Serbia, but what will hap-pen to those who think differently than he does."[26] In a Yugoslavia where most political differences were settled behind closed doors, the publication of the party's private discussion—which the pro-Milosevic Serbian press portrayed as a sign of the Vojvodina leadership's preoccupation with its own survival and indifference to the fate of Serbs in Kosovo—was an unprece-dented affront.

Milosevic chose Vojvodina as his first target because with a majority Serbian population, it was an easier nut to crack than predominantly Alba-nian Kosovo. But Vojvodina—which until 1918 had been ruled from Vi-enna—retained a sense of distinctness from the rest of Serbia that went be-yond the baroque architecture of its towns and churches. Vojvodina's native Serb population, called "Serbs from over the river" (*"precani srbi"*), nurtured an identity founded on a different history, a higher level of eco-nomic development, and a tradition of ethnic tolerance. Under Austrian control, the province had often served as a refuge for Serbs fleeing Turkish rule and some of the earliest writings by Serbian intellectuals had appeared there. For two hundred years, after its late-sixteenth-century flight from Kosovo, the seat of the Serbian Orthodox Church had been in the tiny Voj-vodina hamlet of Sremski Karlovac.

Underneath its tranquil provincial atmosphere, Vojvodina was vulnerable. The agriculturally rich province had suffered severely from the restrictive economic policies pursued by the Yugoslav federal government under Prime Minister Branko Mikulic. In the spring, Vojvodina's farmers drove their tractors into the streets to protest rising gasoline prices, which they claimed made plowing impossible. The leadership of the Vojvodina party, moreover, had a reputation for being among the most conservative and colorless in all of Yugoslavia. As in other multinational areas of Yugoslavia, the inclination of the Vojvodina party was to avoid potential problems by restricting public discussion—a tactic that worked as long as control from the top remained strong, but that encouraged an explosion of popular discontent once the firm hand was relaxed.

Milosevic also capitalized skillfully on divisions within the Vojvodina Serb community. At the end of the Second World War, Vojvodina's half-million-strong ethnic German community, which had inhabited Vojvodina for centuries, fled before the advancing Red Army. The victorious Partisans settled their supporters, often drawn from the primitive mountainous regions of Yugoslavia where Partisan backing was strongest, on the land the Germans left behind. The descendants of these so-called new settlers, who tended to view themselves as an economic underclass exploited by the province's *precani* elite, were among the most prominent figures in the demonstrations that spread throughout Vojvodina in the coming weeks.

The pattern was always the same. In the front row were the Kosovo Serb activists, many wearing traditional Serbian folk costumes and carrying pictures of figures from the Serbian past that the Communist regime had ignored, such as King Peter I, who ruled Serbia during the First World War, or the Montenegrin poet-prince Njegos. The banners the demonstrators carried quickly became icons in this new Serbian uprising, bearing slogans such as "Better Death Than Slavery" or "We Will Give up Our Lives, but Not Kosovo."

Milosevic's picture—striking with his trademark, flaring pompadour—was everywhere among the crowds. Demonstrators often chanted his name rhythmically for minutes on end or sang songs made up in his honor. Although Milosevic himself never appeared at the rallies, his support for them was obvious. In late July, he described the rallies as the essential quality of democracy. In a 6 September meeting of the Serbian party, Milosevic angrily rejected criticism of the demonstrations from outside Serbia, portraying the summer of 1988 as the moment when the patience of the Serbian people finally ran out.[27] Although the rallies were ostensibly arranged by a six-member Kosovo "organizing committee," official Serbian backing for the rallies was never in doubt. The Kosovo Serb activists were transported to the demonstrations in buses, whose cost was reportedly borne by enterprises in Serbia. The buses were frequently escorted by police vehicles from Serbia proper, which were subordinated to Milosevic's Serbian Ministry of the Interior and not to its Vojvodina counterpart.

As summer turned into fall, the so-called solidarity meetings grew in size and militancy, spreading from Vojvodina into Serbia proper. In early September, sixty thousand gathered at the steel center of Smederevo, and by the end of the month, three hundred thousand assembled in the southern Serb city of Nis. Many of the banners now assumed a more threatening tone: "Give Us Arms," "Death to Vllassi," and "Kill the Fascists." In early September, one local official caught the mood by orating, "We will consider as enemies those Albanians who continue to look on calmly at the suffering of their neighbors and will fight them with force if necessary."[28] On 25 September, the Serbian road show returned to Novi Sad. Now, however, instead of a few hundred people, seventy thousand gathered in the streets of the Vojvodina capital to demand the replacement of the provincial leadership.

Yogurt Revolution in Vojvodina

The appearance of militant Serb nationalism, on a scale that had not been seen in Yugoslavia since before the Second World War, and the clearly evident intention of Milosevic to use it to overturn the leadership of one of Yugoslavia's other federal units, set off political shock waves throughout the country. Slovenian party leader Milan Kucan warned that Serb nationalism, by threatening to turn Yugoslavia away from the European political mainstream, could lead the country's other nationalities to reconsider whether they wanted to stay in Yugoslavia.

Federal authorities also recognized the gravity of Milosevic's challenge. At a closed session of the LCY presidency, held just days after the 9 July demonstration in Novi Sad, Suvar criticized the incident so sharply that Milosevic is reported to have stalked out in anger. Later that summer, the LCY issued a statement on the Novi Sad demonstration that sought to strike a balance by criticizing the Vojvodina leaders for failing to meet with the demonstrators, but also called for a halt to further gatherings and an investigation into who was responsible for organizing them. On 20 September, with the scale and virulence of the protests expanding, the collective federal presidency, Yugoslavia's highest state organ, weighed in by warning of the consequences for Yugoslavia's security of holding any more demonstrations.

Finger wagging by the federal authorities had no effect. Tito's decentralizing reforms had stripped the federal LCY of real authority over its nominally subordinate republican branches. The state presidency had the legal authority to order the police or armed forces to take action against a domestic threat to order and in 1988, it took a cautious step in this direction by instructing KOS and its civilian secret police counterpart, the State Security Service (SDB), to investigate Milosevic and his followers.[29] But as the leader of a republican League of Communists organization, Milosevic stood at the pinnacle of party power in Yugoslavia. And unlike most of his colleagues in other party positions throughout Yugoslavia, Milosevic enjoyed genuine popular support. Only a few months before, with unease strong even in Serbia over the demagogic methods Milosevic had used to unseat Stambolic, a combined army and party effort to oust Milosevic might have worked. By the summer of 1988, though, Milosevic's combination of control over the levers of political power and use of mass meetings to build his personal popularity in Yugoslavia's largest republic made it unthinkable for the federal authorities to order the army or police to act against him. The inability of the Yugoslav federation to stop the Serbian offensive revealed the hollowness of the Titoist system and set the stage for the dissolution of the country three years later.

At a 30 September meeting of the LCY presidency, Milosevic and his Vojvodina counterpart, Milan Sogorov, engaged in a public slanging match that, in retrospect, may have triggered the Vojvodina leadership's downfall. After Milosevic had complained that Serbia must become a "real republic," Sogorov stepped up to the podium and bluntly told Milosevic that Vojvodina would never agree to the constitutional changes Serbia was demanding. Less than a week later, Sogorov and the entire Vojvodina leadership was gone—swept away by a massive demonstration that amounted to the first forcible overthrow of a legitimate Yugoslav government since the Second World War.

On 4 October, thirty thousand people, many of them factory workers, marched from the Vojvodina town of Backa Palanka to Novi Sad to protest efforts by the Vojvodina leadership to fire local officials who had supported the Serbian rallies. Obviously planned in advance, the demonstrators were led by a minor trade union leader of Hungarian nationality, Mihajlo Kertes, who was probably acting as an agent of the Serbian secret police and who later became a high official in the Milosevic regime. As the demonstrators marched toward Novi Sad, they were met by buses, cars, and even tractors to convey them to their destination. By evening, tens of thousands of people filled the square in front of the Vojvodina party headquarters, calling for the dismissal of the Vojvodina leadership and demanding Milosevic's presence. When Sogorov tried to speak, the crowd demonstratively turned their backs toward him.

The next day over one hundred thousand people converged on Novi Sad, scuffling with police cordons as they sought to break into party headquarters. The Yugoslav federal leadership, aware that behind the crowd stood Milosevic and Serbia, cast the Vojvodina leaders to their fate. Late in the evening of 5 October, the Vojvodina leaders appealed to the collective federal presidency to order the military to disburse the crowd. Some members of the presidency reportedly agreed with the Vojvodina request. The military hierarchy, however, took the position that it was not authorized to intervene in an autonomous province without the approval of the republican leadership, which of course, the Serbs had no intention of giving.[30] Similarly, the LCY abandoned the Vojvodina leaders. At an emergency meeting the morning of 6 October, the party presidency blamed the situation in Novi Sad on the bureaucratic methods and lack of self-criticism of the Vojvodina leadership, concluding that only the resignation of the Vojvodina leaders would restore the people's confidence.[31]

Nothing was left for the Vojvodina leaders but to appeal to Milosevic for mercy. With the crowd howling outside his office, Sogorov begged, "Comrade Milosevic, if you do not come to calm the people, we will all be killed." Milosevic said he would only come after the Vojvodina leaders had resigned. When Sogorov tried to postpone the inevitable by proposing a conference to discuss all outstanding problems, Milosevic replied coldly, "Your conference interests no one."[32]

In classic Stalinist fashion, it was the victims themselves who were required to proclaim their fate. At a 6 October session of the LCS presidency, which described the demonstrations in Novi Sad as "glorious and dignified," Sogorov confessed that the Vojvodina leadership had lost the trust of the people and announced that it would submit its resignation that evening. There were no casualties in Vojvodina's "yogurt revolution," so called because of the plastic packages of the pungent Yugoslav dairy product that the crowd seized from a nearby store and hurled at the Vojvodina party headquarters. Future upheavals would not be so peaceful.

Temporary Setback in Montenegro

Just one day after his success in Vojvodina, Milosevic struck the neighboring republic of Montenegro. Yugoslavia's smallest republic, Montenegro enjoyed traditionally close ties with Serbia. It was also in catastrophic shape economically. Over 100,000 of Montenegro's population of 550,000 lived below the poverty level, and unemployment was over 25 percent.[33] On 7 October, workers at the Radoja Dakic factory marched to the Montenegrin capital of Titograd, where by the end of the day 25,000 people had gathered in front of the party headquarters demanding the resignation of the republican leadership.

This time, however, Milosevic had overreached himself—albeit only temporarily. The Montenegrin leadership, backed now by the federal authorities, stood firm. Marko Orlandic, a leading member of the Montenegrin League of Communists, rejected the crowd's appeal for Milosevic's presence. "He can't help you," Orlandic said dismissively, a gesture that at the time earned him considerable praise in other parts of Yugoslavia, but subsequently proved to mark the end of his political career. Early in the morning of 8 October, Montenegrin police disbursed the demonstrators in Titograd. The police also broke up a column of workers marching to Titograd from the steel mill in Niksic, chasing several workers over a precipice to their deaths in the process. This action—the first time in postwar Yugoslavia that the police had actually killed protesting workers—caused widespread revulsion.

The Montenegrins' firm stand was bolstered by support from the federal authorities. The LCY presidency described the demonstration in Titograd as an attempted coup, and the state presidency made clear its willingness to authorize the use of force to back the legitimate republican leadership. The Yugoslav military, according to press reports, canceled leaves and mobilized reservists for possible action.[34] The head of the Yugoslav collective state presidency, Raif Dizdarevic of Bosnia, made a dramatic speech to the nation—the first by any president since Tito's death. Speaking in grave and measured tones, Dizdarevic warned of the danger posed by the spread of nationalism and threatened that further unrest could lead the presidency to impose emergency measures to preserve order. Nevertheless, the only specific corrective step that Dizdarevic offered was a promise to hold a series of meetings to try to reconcile differences among republican leaders.

The Seventeenth Plenum:
The LCY Fails to Remove Milosevic

Events in Vojvodina and Montenegro jolted Suvar into an effort to use a previously scheduled 17 October central committee plenum to oust Milosevic. Ambitious and intelligent, Suvar had made a reputation as an orthodox marxist when he supported Tito's 1971 crackdown on Croatian nationalism. In June, reformists in the party opposed Suvar's scheduled rotation into a regular, one-year term in the top LCY slot. In the balloting among LCY presidency members to choose the new party chief, which had always before been unanimous, Suvar had received several negative votes. At that time Milosevic had supported Suvar, but the two quickly broke when Suvar opposed the Serbian demonstrations in the summer of 1988.

The plenum was already scheduled to hold a secret vote of confidence on the LCY presidency and central committee, a grandstand move intended to revitalize public confidence in the party. Suvar slyly proposed that the heads of the republican parties, who served as ex officio members of the LCY presidency, be added to the confidence vote. Many believed that should Milosevic's name be put to a secret ballot, opposition from other republics would cause him to lose. After intense, behind-the-scenes maneuvering, Suvar's ploy failed. At the insistence of Slovenia—which opposed any move tending to increase the power of federal authorities in Belgrade—as well as Serbia, republican League of Communists chiefs were removed from the ballot.

Instead of dealing a blow directly to Milosevic, the LCY settled for public humiliation. When the central committee voted on the regular members of the LCY presidency—two from each republic—Dusan Ckrebic of Serbia, known as a strong Milosevic supporter, failed to receive the required majority. The other Serbian LCY presidency member, Radisa Gacic, who had opposed Milosevic at the Eighth Plenum when Stambolic was humbled, received a comfortable majority. After the vote, a visibly angry Milosevic insisted that Ckrebic not resign until the issue had been reviewed by Ckrebic's Serbian party "base," which shortly after the plenum duly voted its "unconditional support" for Ckrebic.

The so-called seventeenth plenum contained several gloomy portents for Yugoslavia's future. The quick collapse of Suvar's effort to remove Milosevic showed the impossibility of effective party action against a popular republican leader. With Tito gone, there was now no civilian leader capable of repeating his strikes against the Croatian and Serbian leaderships in 1971–1972. Moreover, by allowing Milosevic to ignore the central committee's vote against Ckrebic, the LCY revealed itself to be powerless even against an act of direct defiance by a republican party. Although the LCY is usually said to have died in January 1990 when the Slovenes walked out of its last congress, the seventeenth plenum marked its demise as any sort of real federal institution.

The role of the military in the events surrounding the seventeenth plenum is also interesting. During the summer and fall of 1988, the Belgrade rumor mill reported that Suvar was making special efforts to cultivate the military—a development that provoked some unease in view of his presumed ambition and hard-line reputation. In his memoirs, Mamula says that the JNA was prepared to support Suvar in "cleaning house" by changing party rules to allow all decisions to be made by majority vote, and then using that to remove both Milosevic and the Slovene leadership. But Suvar, who apparently did not trust Mamula's successor, Kadijevic, drew back from throwing in his lot with the military and settled for the hopeless attempt to remove Milosevic through a procedural trick.[35] Suvar, for his part, acknowledges that the JNA at the time was still maintaining its distance from Milosevic, but he also judged that it was not prepared to participate in any effort to remove the Serbian leader.[36]

The seventeenth plenum was generally regarded as a setback for Milosevic. After the vote against Ckrebic, the Serbian delegation held a gloomy internal meeting into the early hours of the morning, and Milosevic was uncharacteristically subdued at the plenum session the following day. Yet the Serbian leader quickly recovered his confidence. On 19 November, a rally in Belgrade that some observers estimated to include as many as one million people, served as the capstone to the previous summer's demonstrations in Vojvodina. Speaking for the first time at one of these Serbian demonstrations, Milosevic made it clear that his ambitions extended beyond Serbia. He described the Serbian program as leading to changes that should be implemented throughout Yugoslavia and, in closing, summoned the crowd to chant its support for "Socialist Yugoslavia, our country." Milosevic's rhetoric was laced with military metaphors, comparing the Serbs' current "battle" for Kosovo to earlier struggles against the Turks and Germans. His tone, at times, was truculent. He declaimed that Serbia did not frighten easily and that the Serbian movement could no longer be stopped by force.[37] Although the crowd was peaceful, the atmosphere was electric with anticipation. Participants turned on some foreign diplomats who did not respond with sufficient exuberance to Milosevic.

The demonstrators in Belgrade included the usual Kosovo Serb militants and enthusiasts in folk costumes carrying provocative banners. But the crowd included vast numbers of ordinary Serbs from all over the republic as well—young people, workers, and middle-class intellectuals. The size of the demonstration showed that Milosevic had captured the popular imagination—among Serbs at least—in a way that no other Yugoslav figure had done since Tito.

The demonstration was also a warning to the rest of Yugoslavia of the potential power that Milosevic possessed as the unchallenged leader of an aroused Serbia. No other leader in contemporary Yugoslavia could have come close to mobilizing such a vast number of people. Before the rally, officials in the nearby federal government building had seriously worried that Milosevic might direct the crowd to occupy their offices. In the end, however, Milosevic chose not to set the crowd in motion toward a specific goal. The overall message was nevertheless clear: Serbia was on its feet, and Milosevic intended to use it to reshape all of Yugoslavia.

Milosevic as Reformer

Two days after the monster rally in Belgrade, Milosevic chaired a conference to kick off what was depicted as a new program of economic reform for Serbia. The program Milosevic revealed had something in it for everyone—reforms to increase the construction of new homes, encouragement for small- and medium-sized enterprises, and radical changes to the education system. It also included a veneer of market measures, such as openness to foreign capital and bankruptcy for failing enterprises. Real change was limited. Though Milosevic denounced the "contract economy" established by the 1976 Law on Associated Labor, he also portrayed public ownership of the means of production and a continued emphasis on commodity production as the best guarantees for prosperity.[38]

By donning the garb of an economic reformer, Milosevic was trying to show the people of Serbia that his antibureaucratic revolution could bring them tangible economic benefits. Milosevic was also attempting to persuade the rest of Yugoslavia that there was something more to his message than Kosovo and Serb nationalism. With Yugoslavia's deepening economic crisis putting the federal government headed by conservative Prime Minister Mikulic under heavy pressure, Milosevic sought to use Serbia's central position in the country to push the economic reform debate in the direction of his brand of modest tinkering with the socialist system against the proposals for more radical market reform already appearing in Slovenia and Croatia.

Few were persuaded by the "kinder, gentler" Milosevic, largely because the bad old Milosevic kept breaking through. In January 1989, a new round of demonstrations erupted in Montenegro. The scenario for these events was virtually the same as the failed uprising in October. This time, however, the Montenegrin leadership—its authority undermined by economic troubles and popular revulsion against the deaths of the Niksic workers in November—collapsed as readily as had the Vojvodina leadership before it. A group of student radicals took over the diminutive republic, led by the thirty-three-year-old head of the party organization at Titograd University, Momir Bulatovic, and the even younger chief of the Montenegrin youth league, Ljubisa Stankovic. Montenegro's new leaders promised bold democratic reforms, but Bulatovic also made it clear that henceforth Serbia and Montenegro would be one family.

By the beginning of 1989, Milosevic had seized center stage in Yugoslavia. He controlled three of the country's eight federal units. He was by far the dominant political personality in a post-Tito Yugoslavia still largely ruled by gray bureaucrats. Despite efforts to cloak himself in Tito's mantle, Milosevic had asserted his determination not only to destroy the Titoist system but his willingness to use any means to do so. Milosevic's goal was clear: to dominate all of Yugoslavia. Yet he first had to gain full control of Serbia, which meant crushing the Albanian leadership in Kosovo.

THREE

Milosevic Takes Kosovo

I n Balkan history, as with statistics, it is possible to prove almost anything by choosing the right starting point. If you begin a discussion of
Kosovo in the fourteenth century, it is obvious—at least to Serbs—that
Kosovo was the heart of the medieval Serbian Empire and must remain,
now and forever, part of Serbia. Albanians concede nothing to the Serbs on
history—they claim descent from the ancient Illyrians, the pre-Roman inhabitants of the Balkan peninsula—but they also base their claim to Kosovo on demographics, pointing out that the population of Kosovo has been
predominantly Albanian for centuries.

One constant in Kosovo's history, however, has been the willingness of
its inhabitants to use violence to pursue their conflicting claims. In most
cases, it is wise to be cautious about explanations of Balkan conflicts as the
inevitable product of ancient hatreds. All too often such assertions have
served to rationalize the unwillingness of policymakers to get involved.
Yet if there is any part of the Balkans that qualifies as a hotbed of long-
standing ethnic animosities, it is Kosovo. Individual Serbs and Albanians
have often managed to live together in relative harmony, but every time
Kosovo has experienced a war, foreign occupation, or change of regime over
the past 150 years, whichever ethnic group benefited from the event has
acted against the other—often with great brutality.

Milosevic Takes the Offensive

Milosevic kept a low profile for several months after his return from Kosovo Polje in April 1987, while his supporters in the party and media quietly prepared the ground. Then, at a special meeting of the Serbian party

devoted to Kosovo in July, Milosevic returned to the attack. In a militant speech, he called for police to protect Serb women and children, and for special Serb-dominated courts to try Albanians charged with raping Serbian women. Responding to Stambolic's call for cool heads to allow time for economic growth, Milosevic shot back that "cool heads had not stopped rapes, humiliation, and emigration."[1]

Speaking the same day before a parallel session of the Kosovo party's central committee, the Kosovo party chief, Azem Vllassi, adopted a strikingly different tone. He made the obligatory bow toward criticizing Albanian nationalism and promised to implement a series of fifty specific tasks required by the LCY in its action program on Kosovo, such as purging textbooks of Albanian nationalism, installing road signs in both Serbian and Albanian, and ensuring equal treatment for both languages in the provincial administration and media. For the first time, though, Vllassi publicly took on the nationalism of the Kosovo Serbs. Vllassi warned that the Kosovo party would "not tolerate Serb nationalism, which is now operating in an organized manner in collaboration with circles and centers outside Kosovo." He pledged a "settling of accounts" with party members infected by Serb nationalism—a contagion he said was being imported from Belgrade.[2]

Over the next eighteen months, the thirty-nine-year-old Vllassi was Milosevic's most prominent opponent in the struggle for Kosovo. In the late 1970s, Vllassi caught Tito's eye as the leader of the Yugoslav Socialist Youth League. He rose rapidly in the Kosovo party hierarchy following a crackdown in the province after massive demonstrations in 1981. Vllassi enjoyed the backing of the Yugoslav leadership on the strength of his reputation as a Yugoslav-oriented Albanian who could pull the province away from the close ties it had developed to Tirana before 1981. Although he was intelligent and personable, Vllassi was distrusted by many Kosovo Albanians because of his youth and because he was seen as associated with the repressive measures carried out by the Yugoslav authorities after 1981.

Vllassi later said that by 1986, the Kosovo party leadership realized it could not simultaneously fight a war against Belgrade and its own people. The issue was no longer how to "normalize" Kosovo after the 1981 demonstrations, Vllassi said, but how to defend Kosovo's autonomy against a growing assault by local Serbs with the direct support of Belgrade.

In the summer of 1986, Vllassi sought to settle accounts with the militant Kosovo Serb agitators by arresting one of their leaders, Kosta Bulatovic. The resulting Serb protest brought Stambolic to the province to broker a compromise. Ironically, it was because of this visit that Stambolic decided not to go again to Kosovo in April 1987 and asked Milosevic to go in his stead.

According to Milosevic's former associates, Milosevic and Vllassi had earlier been friends, even dining together on occasion. Both belonged to the rising young generation of post-Tito Yugoslav politicians, liberal in a Yugoslav context yet also professed believers in Yugoslav socialism. But Vllassi's experience in watching Milosevic manipulate the Serb crowd the night of the 24 April demonstration in Kosovo Polje convinced him that Milosevic was dangerous and not to be trusted. Vllassi never again met Milosevic without a witness present. Milosevic "worked for the abolition of the autonomy of the province while I worked for its retention," Vllassi later told a foreign observer.[3]

Vllassi's basic strategy regarding Milosevic was to carry out federally mandated measures against Albanian nationalism while simultaneously moving against the Kosovo Serb activists, in the hope that faithfulness in carrying out party directives on Kosovo would earn him federal protection from the inevitable Serb response. His strategy failed because he was abandoned by both the Yugoslav federal authorities and other republics, such as Slovenia and Croatia, that had criticized Milosevic's tactics in Kosovo. Vllassi also underestimated the degree to which Milosevic was prepared to use any means, including violence, to achieve his aim of the total subordination of Kosovo. As late as 1988, when Vllassi saw the U.S. ambassador to Yugoslavia, John Scanlan, he seemed confident. Vllassi told Scanlan that his main differences with Milosevic were not legal but how to ensure the use of Albanian language and culture in a Kosovo that would remain part of Serbia. If that could be accomplished and there was no resort to force, Vllassi suggested that he understood the Serbs and could manage the situation.[4]

In September 1987, the Belgrade media's sensationalist exploitation of the Paracin murders and its "outing" of longtime Kosovo Albanian leader Fadil Hodza for an anti-Serbian slur brought Kosovo to the boiling point. At a private dinner in November 1986, Hodza had reportedly told a group of Yugoslav army officers that if the Serbs were so worried about the safety of their women, they should bring more Serbian waitresses to Kosovo who could double as prostitutes. When Hodza's remarks were leaked by the Belgrade media, a storm of protest erupted, including a carefully scripted demonstration by some one thousand Kosovo Serb women who called for martial law and shouted slogans such as "either freedom or military rule." Two days later, on 25 October, the federal presidency unexpectedly decided to send a detachment of special police to Kosovo "as a preventative measure."

The presidency statement announcing the dispatch of the special police took an evenhanded approach, blaming both the "intensified hostile activities" of Albanian separatists and the "organized activities" of Serb nationalists. Officials in the federal Ministry of Internal Affairs told me at the time that the dispatch of the police—done without consulting either the Serbian or Kosovo authorities—was primarily intended to warn off Milosevic. The special police patrolled in conspicuous locations around the province, but did not actually engage in any police operations. Their presence had a calming effect on the atmosphere throughout Kosovo and led to a marked decline in demonstrations by Kosovo Serbs. Unfortunately, it was the last time the Yugoslav federal authorities did anything to impede Milosevic in Kosovo.

Kosovo Realities

The territory that Serbs and Albanians were struggling over appeared, to an outside observer at least, as an unlikely prize. Kosovo is about the size of the state of Connecticut. Rugged mountains surround Kosovo, but most of the population is found in the gently rolling central plain, which at 1,200 feet above sea level is hot and dry in the summer and often covered by snow in the winter. Settlements straggle higgledy-piggledy across the plain, much of which is rough and scarred by erosion.

One of the most striking aspects of Kosovo villages, however, are the large walled compounds that many Albanian families build. Plain, whitewashed walls, often two-stories high, surround houses and farm outbuildings, where several generations and their livestock live together in close proximity. The dark and mysterious deeds supposedly concealed behind these walls formed a central part of the Serb demonology of the Kosovo Albanians, yet the custom is probably no more than a traditional response to the region's unsettled history, which the experience of recent years did nothing to discourage.

Kosovo's capital, Pristina, comprises a central core of shoddy, socialist-era high-rise office and apartment buildings, surrounded by densely packed, squalid slums, with a few lovely residential neighborhoods climbing the hills that encircle the town. Large, immaculate villas often stand next to crude dwellings made from roughly thrown together boards and sheets of corrugated metal. Dirt roads, where children and animals play together in the dust of summer and mud of winter, run only a few hundred yards from the center of Pristina.

Kosovo possesses some important deposits of metals and low-grade coal, but its most abundant resource is people. At 147 persons per square kilometer, Kosovo in the mid-1980s was the most densely inhabited region in Yugoslavia and possibly all of Europe. In 1985, the annual rate of natural increase among Kosovo Albanians was an astounding 2.5 percent—more than three times the Yugoslav average.[5] According to the 1981 Yugoslav census, of Kosovo's total population of 1,585,000 people, 77.5 percent were Albanian, 13.3 percent were Serb, 1.7 percent Montenegrin, and the remaining 7.5 percent various other minorities including Gypsies and Turks.[6] By 1991, despite a decade of efforts by Belgrade to increase the Serbian share of the province's population, Albanians had risen to approximately 90 percent and Serbs fallen to less than 10 percent.[7] Ninety-five percent of Kosovo Albanians are Moslem, and almost all of the remainder are Catholic. Religion has not, however, been a major factor in the lives of most Kosovo Albanians, who have traditionally displayed a relatively relaxed attitude toward the formalities of religious worship and a tolerance toward the religion of others. Islamic fundamentalism is virtually unknown in Kosovo.

Kosovo was the poorest region in the former Yugoslavia. In 1988, its per capita income was only 27 percent of the Yugoslav average. Kosovo's backwardness was reflected in a range of social indicators; infant mortality and the percentage of illiterates, for example, were both double the Yugoslav average.[8] Despite decades of assistance, the economic gap between Kosovo and the richer parts of Yugoslavia actually grew. In 1952, the per capita income of Slovenia, the most developed Yugoslav republic, was 4.1 times greater than that of Kosovo; by 1984, it was 6.1 times greater.[9]

Visitors to Kosovo in the 1980s were invariably struck by the large numbers of bored-looking young men lounging about in the main squares of every town and village—a visible sign of the unemployment that in Kosovo was three times the Yugoslav average. Yugoslav leaders did little to address the underlying cause of unemployment. They encouraged the growth of heavy industry, which had only a limited capacity to absorb Kosovo's rapidly expanding labor force, and neglected agriculture, which in Kosovo as the rest of Yugoslavia was chronically underfunded and hampered by legal disadvantages such as limits on the maximum size of individual holdings.

Facing dismal economic prospects at home, many Kosovo Albanian men sought work abroad. The export of the Kosovo Albanian workforce acted as something of a safety valve to reduce unemployment pressures, but it also brought with it new types of political and social tension. Some Kosovars were drawn into a highly developed Albanian criminal network that stretched from the Middle East and Turkey across Europe and into the United States. Hard data is naturally scarce on this topic, but Kosovo Albanians were said to be active in the smuggling of drugs and arms. In the late 1980s, Suvar, then serving as president of the federal LCY, told U.S. diplomats that 10 percent of Yugoslav citizens residing in France—of which a disproportionate number were Kosovo Albanian—actually made their home in jail.

Legal restrictions imposed by the Communist authorities on private enterprise meant that little of the money Albanians earned abroad could be used for productive investment in Kosovo. A certain amount went into the flashy cars that crowded the lanes of poverty-stricken Kosovo towns and villages twice each year, during the guest workers' traditional return for the new year and summer holidays. Money that did return to Kosovo was often used in ways that were perfectly legitimate, but that tended to increase the suspicion and resentment of the province's declining Serbian minority—for instance, to build walled living compounds or purchase Kosovo's most prized commodity: arable land.

The Serbian Myth of Kosovo

All nations shape their image of themselves, at least in part, on myth. For Serbia, the central myth is one of heroic struggle, often against hopeless odds, followed by betrayal and defeat, but also—eventually—rebirth and triumph. Like all national myths, the Serbian picture contains many exaggerations and downright falsehoods. Still, like all enduring national myths, it also contains a kernel of truth. Serbian history has its glorious passages. The Serbs were the first Balkan people to liberate themselves from Ottoman rule. The retreat of the Serbian army in 1915 across the frozen mountains of Albania after breaking out of encirclement by vastly superior German forces has been forgotten in the West, yet at the time it was hailed as a military exploit to rank with the march of Xenophon's ten thousand.

But it is the 1389 battle at Kosovo Polje—the field of the blackbirds—that lies at the heart of the way Serbs view themselves and their role in history. On 28 June 1389, a Turkish army led by Sultan Murad met a Serbian coalition under the command of Tsar Lazar. The Serb forces included a Bosnian contingent and Albanians—then still Christians. There are no eyewitness accounts of the battle, and much of what came to be believed about it stemmed from subsequent embellishments by Serbian mythmakers.

On the eve of the engagement, Lazar is said to have had a vision, offering him a choice between an earthly kingdom—that is, victory on the field of battle—and the eternal kingdom of Heaven—meaning death and defeat. Lazar chose the second option, and the Serb forces were duly defeated and Lazar killed—in part, according to legend, through the treachery of one of their leaders, Vuk Brankovic. The battle broke the power of the medieval Serb empire, thereby marking the effective end of Serb independence for almost five hundred years.[10]

The Turks eliminated the Serbian nobility, leaving behind a mass of illiterate peasants and a sprinkling of hardly better educated priests. Memories of the Kosovo battle, and indeed the whole concept of Serbia as a nation, were preserved through a remarkable tradition of oral folk poems. Passed on by generation after generation of illiterate peasant bards, the tales were collected in the early nineteenth century by Vuk Karadzic, the man most responsible for both the creation of the Serbo-Croatian language and development of the Serbian national identity. Vuk's tales embody all of the triumphs and horrors of Balkan history. In them can be heard distant echoes of Christian medieval chivalry, but after centuries of rendition by and to largely peasant audiences, just as prominent are fatalism, violence, revenge, and an almost anarchic resistance to authority.[11]

The Turkish conquest removed Serbia from the mainstream of European history for several centuries. Not until the end of the eighteenth century did Serbs begin to reenter European intellectual and political life. Serbia missed out on many of the intellectual currents that have shaped the Western tradition, including the Renaissance, Reformation, and Enlightenment. When Serbia reemerged, Europe was dominated by the romantic nationalism of the post-Napoleonic era. Nation building, in both the political and cultural sense, was on the agenda. Throughout the nineteenth century, Serb statesmen and intellectuals pursued the task of re-creating Serbia and expanding its territory through a combination of war, diplomacy, and terror that earned for Serbia the reputation of "the Piedmont of the Balkans." The softer edges of the European tradition, such as toleration, respect for individual rights, and the rule of law—whose importance is, of course, recognized by many Serbs—were nevertheless not central to the Serb experience as a nation.

In the nineteenth century, the cult of Kosovo was part of the raw material that Serbian intellectuals and government officials used to create a new Serbian national identity. In 1844, Serbian statesman Ilija Garasanin wrote the "Nacertanije" ("Draft" or "Blueprint"), which amounted to a secret strategy for the establishment of a Greater Serbia at the expense of the crumbling Ottoman Empire. Garasanin saw the new Serbian state as "building its foundation in the Serbian Empire of the thirteenth and fourteenth centuries, and the rich and glorious Serb history" that had been interrupted by the arrival of the Turks.[12] Throughout the nineteenth century, Serbia followed Garasanin's strategy in a gradual expansion southward from Belgrade. When Kosovo was finally reclaimed during the 1912 Balkan War against Turkey, the Serb peasant soldiers were said to have removed their boots as they walked across Gazimestan, the site of the ancient battle, because they were treading on soil that had been sanctified by the blood of their forefathers.

When the young American journalist John Reed—later famed for his eyewitness account of the Russian Revolution—visited Serbia during the First World War, he found the Kosovo myth still a powerful psychological force in the Serbian mobilization for war. His guides explained the ferocity of Serbian resistance to the invading Central Powers by affirming that every Serbian peasant soldier remembered that when he was a child, his mother had greeted him, "Hail, little avenger of Kosovo!" Reed also recounted hearing Serbian children in their geography lessons reciting the list of "Serbian lands in the order of their [still to come] redemption"—Bosnia, Hercegovina, and Croatia—an agenda for national expansion strikingly similar to that pursued by Milosevic almost a century later.[13]

The Communists—who deliberately downplayed the national histories of all the Yugoslav peoples—did their best to suppress the Kosovo myth in Serbia. It was revived in the 1980s by Cosic and the other ideologues of the Serb nationalist revolt when they saw how effectively images of the beleaguered Serb population in Kosovo could be manipulated to mobilize popular support for their campaign to overturn Communism in Serbia.

There is no evidence that Milosevic as a young man displayed much interest in Serb national traditions, but he later proved adept in using for his own purposes the political and psychological themes that underlie the Kosovo myth. The notion of unrequited sacrifice that lay behind the Serbs' belief that their ancestors fell in Kosovo in defense of the ramparts of Christian civilization—even though memory of their sacrifice had disappeared from European consciousness—lent itself to being exploited by Milosevic to explain why the country became an international pariah under his rule.

The tradition of Brankovic's treason, which endowed the Serbs with a long-ing for unity, forms the backdrop for the Serb national slogan, *"Samo Sloga Spasavaju Serbiju"* ("Only Harmony Can Save Serbia"). The four Cyrillic *S* initials of this slogan were ubiquitous in the Serbian nationalist graffiti of the 1980s, and the thought behind the slogan was effectively employed by Milosevic to portray his opponents as traitors. Finally, Lazar's fatal choice framed the Serbs' image of themselves as a nation of romantic visionaries, inclined to strive for the impossible ideal against every expectation of fail-ure—and failure is something that Milosevic's dismal record gave the Serbs plenty of opportunity to experience.

Serb Myth Meets Albanian Reality

As the Serbs expanded southward in the nineteenth century, their vision of Kosovo collided with the reality of the majority Albanian presence on the ground. Exactly when Albanians became the dominant nationality in Ko-sovo, like virtually everything else in the province's history, is disputed. Serbs almost certainly formed the overwhelming majority of Kosovo's pop-ulation at the time of the 1389 battle. For some time afterward, changes in the area's ethnic composition occurred gradually, as some Serbs moved north to Sumadija to escape Turkish exactions, while others converted to Islam and gradually lost their Slavic identity. In 1690, tens of thousands of Serbs fled Kosovo into present-day Vojvodina to escape Turkish reprisals af-ter a brief incursion by Hapsburg forces into Kosovo. The number who actu-ally fled in what the Serbs call the "Great Migration" (*"Velika Seoba"*) is uncertain—as is whether they left, as legend has it, in a column headed by Patriarch Arsenija. Nevertheless, it is clear that during the eighteenth cen-tury, growing numbers of Albanians began to occupy land in Kosovo left empty by war or flight. Only in the later half of the nineteenth century, however, do reliable population data for Kosovo emerge. In the 1890s, an Austrian study based on Ottoman statistics yielded a proportion of 72 per-cent Moslems and 28 percent non-Moslems, with most of the latter proba-bly Serbs.[14]

What happened in Kosovo during the first part of Turkish rule was, in short, a classic pattern of the victors taking the spoils. Yugoslav scholar, and former Partisan leader, Vladimir Velebit captures the consequences aptly:

> There is little doubt that the process of appropriating the possessions
> of the preexisting population created a deeply felt resentment be-

tween those who had lost their homes and their land and those who had profited from the conquest. This hatred was transmitted from father to son over many generations and it became a constant factor in the relationship between the Serbs and the Albanians. Inherent in this feeling was a strong desire to retake the lost areas if an opportunity appeared.[15]

In the late nineteenth century, Albanians experienced their own awakening in response to growing feelings of national consciousness among their Slavic neighbors and to the turmoil that accompanied the last years of the decaying Ottoman Empire. As Serb and Albanian national feelings developed, and as Belgrade expanded its rule southward, relations between the two peoples deteriorated. After 1878, the Serbs expelled thousands of Albanians from areas around Nis awarded to Belgrade at the Congress of Berlin. Serbs, for their part, began to flee Kosovo under the dual impetus of the attraction of living in their own nearby state and growing repression by the Turkish authorities. By the first years of the twentieth century, the Serb population of Kosovo had fallen to less than 25 percent.[16]

During the Balkan Wars of 1912–1913, Serbia conquered Kosovo, Macedonia, and also occupied much of what is now Albania proper before being forced to abandon it by the Great Powers. Albanians resisted the advancing Serbs even after the regular Ottoman armies had been defeated. The Catholic archbishop of Skopje estimated that Serb forces killed twenty-five thousand Albanians as well as carrying out thousands of forced conversions across what is now Kosovo and Macedonia. Lev Trotskiy, who covered the Balkan Wars for a Ukrainian newspaper, reported that around the village of Kumanovo, now in northern Macedonia, "entire Albanian villages had been turned into pillars of fire."[17]

During the interwar years, the Serbian authorities ruled Kosovo in a fashion that has been called "internal colonization." All leading positions were in the hands of a largely imported Serbian elite. Every effort was made to obstruct the development of Albanian national consciousness. All education was in Serbian, with the result that 90 percent of the Albanian population remained illiterate. On the eve of the Second Word War, only 2 percent of eligible Albanians were enrolled in secondary schools.[18]

The Serbs also tried to reshape the ethnic balance of Kosovo. Between 90,000 to 150,000 Moslems fled Kosovo between 1918 and 1941.[19] By 1940, approximately 18,000 Slavic families had been settled in Kosovo, many coming from impoverished areas of Bosnia and Montenegro, as a reward for services to Serbia during the First World War.[20] In 1937, Vaso Cubrilovic, who participated in the assassination of Archduke Franz Ferdinand but escaped execution because of his youth, drafted a plan calling for the systematic expulsion of hundreds of thousands of Albanians. Yugoslavia and Turkey agreed in 1938 to resettle up to 200,000 Albanians and Turks in Kurdish areas of Turkey—a plan that was never implemented because of the outbreak of World War II.[21]

After Yugoslavia's defeat in 1941, the German and Italian occupiers found enthusiastic collaborators among the Kosovo Albanians, who saw the new regime as a chance to settle scores with former Serbian overlords. Thousands of Albanians served in the Skanderbeg division that the Nazis set up after the Italian surrender in 1943. Serb colonists, exposed to official discrimination, violent harassment, and confiscation of their properties, fled Kosovo.[22]

Tito's policy of all-out resistance to the fascist occupiers gained little sympathy in Kosovo. Long after the war, Svetozar Vukmanovic-Tempo, Tito's commander in the southern Balkans, acknowledged that Kosovo Albanians, because of their "chauvinist hatred" of Serbs, did not join the national liberation struggle.[23] Another Partisan leader admitted that only a "few dozen" Albanians joined Partisan detachments, while an attempt to use Albanians as frontline soldiers against the Germans after the Partisans had seized Kosovo ended in disaster when the recruits killed their Serb officers.[24]

In December 1944, the Albanian nationalist front, Balli Kombetar, rebelled against the Partisans. The insurgents, initially numbering as many as fifteen thousand, were not defeated until the end of 1945. As late as 1946, the Yugoslav secret police estimated there were still fifty-five Ballist groups operating in Kosovo; they were only reduced to isolated remnants in the beginning of 1947.[25]

After the war, Kosovo became an autonomous region within Serbia, although its autonomy initially was only symbolic. Tito banned the return of the Serb colonists and also began the first large-scale program of primary education in the Albanian language in Kosovo's history. By the early 1960s, 85 percent of eligible Albanian children were enrolled in elementary schools.

Yet Serbs retained their dominant position in Kosovo. In 1953, Serbs who made up 31.5 percent of the province's population held 68 percent of the "administrative leading" positions. In the mid-1960s, only half of the party membership in Kosovo was Albanian, and few of those held leading positions.[26] Real power in Kosovo during the first two decades of Communist rule rested in the hands of the Yugoslav secret police chief, Alexandar Rankovic, the only Serb in Tito's inner circle. The Serbs, who predominated in the police and security forces, exercised their authority with a heavy hand. In 1954, a young man named Adam Demaci was arrested for being one of the leaders of the pro-Tirana Revolutionary Movement for the Unification of Albanians, beginning a cumulative total of twenty-eight years served in Yugoslav prisons, which earned for him the sobriquet, "the Albanian Mandela."

After Rankovic's 1966 dismissal, conditions began to change in Kosovo. In 1967, on his first visit to Kosovo in sixteen years, Tito said, "One cannot talk about equal rights when Serbs are given preference in the factories, even when they are disqualified, and Albanians are rejected, although they have the same or better qualification." After a 1968 demonstration by Albanian students highlighted tensions in the province, Tito allowed effective control of local affairs to pass to the Albanians. Albanian language and culture became predominant in administration, education, and the media, aided by hundreds of teachers brought in from Albania. By 1978, Albanians comprised two-thirds of the provincial party membership, and occupied most leading party and state positions. Police and security organs were said to be three-quarters Albanian.[27] The 1974 Yugoslav Constitution freed Kosovo from all but symbolic control by Serbia, making it a federal unit with a vote in all decisions equal to that of the six Yugoslav republics.

Perhaps the most visible changes were in higher education. The modernistic facilities of the new University of Pristina—founded only in 1970 and built largely with developmental funds from other parts of Yugoslavia—included a striking, multidomed library on a hill that dominated the capital's downtown area. By the end of the 1970s, approximately thirty thousand Albanians were enrolled in various higher education programs. Two-thirds of these, however, were in nontechnical fields.[28]

Unfortunately, little was done to address Kosovo's underlying economic problems. Per capita income declined in Kosovo from 48 percent of the Yugoslav average in 1954, to 33 percent in 1975, and 27 percent by 1980.[29] The dangerous result was the rapid growth of a new intelligentsia—imbued with a highly developed consciousness of its Albanian heritage—large numbers of whom could not find employment in the province's depressed economy.

Discontent, simmering just below the surface among both nationalities, centered on the anomalous position Kosovo enjoyed under the 1974 Constitution. Frustrated by the gap between the province's glitzy new superstructure and the enduring reality of its Third World poverty, Albanians continued to long for the status of a full Yugoslav republic.

As long as he was alive, Tito imposed a delicate balance of discontent on both groups. When the 1974 Constitution was being drafted, Mahmut Bakalli, who after the 1968 demonstrations became the first Albanian head of Kosovo's party organization, met with Tito. Bakalli made the political, economic, and cultural case why the new Constitution should give Kosovo the status of a full-fledged Yugoslav republic. The aging Tito listened carefully and with evident sympathy to the impassioned arguments of the young Albanian leader. Tito's reply, however, showed a Solomonic finesse. Tito said that Kosovo could have all the attributes of separate status that Bakalli had argued for, but that Serb resistance simply made it impossible for Kosovo to be called a republic.[30]

Serbs, on the other hand, saw the autonomy that the 1974 Constitution granted Kosovo as the first step toward its secession and unification with Albania. In 1976, Mira Markovic's uncle, Draza Markovic, put together the so-called "Blue Book," an unpublished document that cataloged all the grievances Serbia had with its contemporary position in Yugoslavia. At the top of the list was the constitutional status of Kosovo, which the authors insisted threatened the future prospects of the Serbian inhabitants of the province. At a closed meeting of the Yugoslav leadership on Tito's island retreat of Brioni to discuss the "Blue Book," generally considered the first attempt to undo the 1974 Constitution, Tito said, "That book must disappear," yet he took no steps against its authors.[31]

In the spring of 1981, rioting spread throughout Kosovo after police harshly suppressed a student demonstration. The Yugoslav authorities reacted strongly to this first incident of major unrest after Tito's death, which claimed eleven victims according to official figures, but hundreds more according to Western human rights groups and some Kosovo Albanian sources. A state of emergency was declared, troops were called in, and the province was closed to outsiders for several months. Bakalli resigned in protest over the dispatch of troops. He was later excluded from the party and subjected to two-years house arrest but the young protesters—some of whom became instrumental in founding the Kosovo Liberation Army (KLA) in the 1990s—fared much worse. More than two thousand Albanians were arrested, and thousands more were expelled from the party.[32]

The Serb Offensive Begins

The 1981 demonstrations were a turning point for both nationalities. Albanians grew increasingly resentful of a situation where young people could find themselves sentenced to long jail terms simply for uttering the words, "Kosovo Republic." Serbs, for their part, had been terrified by the specter of thousands of angry Albanians in the streets. Charges and countercharges of competing nationalist activities swirled about the province.

The case of Djordje Martinovic became a symbol for both sides. In May 1985, Martinovic, a fifty-six-year-old Kosovo Serb, was admitted to the hospital with severe internal injuries caused by having a glass bottle thrust into his anus. Martinovic claimed that two Albanians had perpetrated the act. The Belgrade media seized on the Martinovic affair as a particularly sensational example of the pressures facing Serbs in Kosovo. *Politika* charged that the individuals who allegedly attacked Martinovic belonged to an Albanian family who wanted to purchase land that Martinovic refused to sell.

The facts of the Martinovic affair remained murky. During an initial investigation in Pristina, Martinovic reportedly confessed to a JNA colonel that he had placed the bottle on the ground and impaled himself. When the investigation was transferred to the prestigious Military Medical Academy in Belgrade, an initial report found that Martinovic's injuries were not consistent with a self-inflicted wound. A second report, after a specialist from Macedonia had been added to the team, found insufficient evidence to determine the wound's origin. This finding was supported by the federal Justice Ministry, which said it could not confirm that Martinovic had been attacked. Although this was not reported at the time, the Yugoslav secret police and military intelligence also concluded that Martinovic's wounds were self-inflicted, which may be one reason why the federal authorities did not act and why the Serb authorities failed to pursue the case after they took over Kosovo.[33]

Milosevic, then serving as the chief of the Belgrade party committee, never commented in public about the Martinovic case. Nevertheless, it marked a turning point in the way the media in Yugoslavia handled ethnic issues, which directly contributed to Milosevic's ability to exploit the Kosovo issue two years later. Notes one scholar, "While most of the Yugoslav press had previously downplayed nationalism, the press after Martinovic trumpeted national conflict."[34]

The hyperventilating coverage of the Martinovic affair in the Belgrade media helped convince Serbs—even those not sympathetic to nationalism—that their brethren in Kosovo routinely suffered abuse at the hands of their Albanian neighbors. Mica Popovic, an artist and member of the group of nonconformist Belgrade intellectuals, provided a good example. In the 1970s and 1980s, Popovic was known for works that showed the unvarnished reality of socialism in Serbia. A 1974 exhibition of his works was closed when a painting depicting a dejected Yugoslav guest worker leaving for Germany in a typically crowded and dirty Yugoslav train was hung next to a picture of an elegantly dressed Tito and his wife meeting the Dutch king and queen. In 1985, Popovic produced a large, allegorical work based on the Martinovic case. A Serb peasant intended to represent Martinovic was portrayed being crucified on a cross hanging below a bottle, while a white-capped Albanian and a Yugoslav police officer stand indifferently beside the anguished figure of a watching Serb peasant woman. Despite its melodramatic character, Popovic's work was an effective symbol—not necessarily of what was really happening in Kosovo but of the collective psychosis about Kosovo that seemed for a period to grip otherwise-sensible Serbs.

Many of the Serb allegations about Kosovo were either untrue or highly exaggerated. There was little evidence of ethnically motivated crime. Kosovo had the lowest murder rate in Yugoslavia. During the period 1981 to 1987, there were five interethnic murders in Kosovo: two in which Albanians killed Serbs, and three in which Serbs killed Albanians.[35] Kosovo had the second-lowest rate of rape in Yugoslavia, and few rapes were committed by one nationality against another. Examination of many of the so-called forced land sales by Serbs to Albanians often revealed that the purchasers had paid handsomely for the land. There were also signs that the Albanian birthrate was beginning to follow patterns of decline typical of those in other developing societies—in 1947, it was 38.5 births per thousand people while by 1988 it had fallen to 29.[36]

Some of the Serb charges, however, had a core of truth. Given sufficient liquid lubrication, it was possible in the 1980s to find Kosovo Albanians who would privately agree with the Serbs that they intended to procreate their way to independence. Serbs in Kosovo sometimes did experience violence and intimidation. In 1988, I visited a Serbian village in Kosovo where the inhabitants described what appeared to be a campaign of intimidation, including the killing of livestock, burning of outbuildings, and the verbal and physical harassment of children as they walked to school through neighboring Albanian villages. The Serbs claimed that a nearby Albanian family was behind the attacks, said to be motivated by the desire to acquire their land, and discussions with the Albanians convinced me that there might be something to the Serb charges. International human rights monitors also found a clear pattern of official abuse in the failure of the Kosovo authorities to stop, or even seriously investigate—the pattern of intimidating assaults against persons and property that some Kosovo Serbs experienced.[37] In a mid-1990s' interview with a Western researcher, Kosovo Albanian leader Ibrahim Rugova admitted that some Albanians "did not behave as they should have" toward local Serbs during this period.[38]

Milosevic's response, though—a political takeover and military occupation of Kosovo—was out of all proportion to the nature and scale of the problems, and also failed to address the underlying causes of the conflict. One irony was that the Serbs charged the Albanians with activities in Kosovo that the Serbs themselves later carried out in a much more systematic and brutal fashion in Croatia, Bosnia, and Kosovo itself. Another irony was the fact that nothing Milosevic and his minions did in Kosovo was actually aimed at improving the plight of the province's downtrodden Serbs or enhancing their ability to live peacefully with their Albanian neighbors. Milosevic exploited the Kosovo Serbs and dropped them when they were no longer of any use to him.

Get Vllassi!

In July 1988, as the "summer of truth" was getting underway in Vojvodina, Milosevic issued his first threat of force in Kosovo. At the end of another heated session of the Serbian party on Kosovo, Milosevic warned that "state measures" would be needed to protect the legal and physical security of Serbs in Kosovo because "political means were not sufficient." Less than two months later, Milosevic sent the first Serbian police into Kosovo, ostensibly to protect Serbian villagers being harassed by Albanian neighbors. This unilateral Serb action constituted a direct challenge to the federal authorities. Having already looked the other way, however, while Milosevic used Serbian police to protect the "meetings of truth" in Vojvodina, the federal authorities did the same thing in Kosovo.

No sooner had Milosevic taken over Vojvodina and launched his first, unsuccessful probe into Montenegro, than the Serbs returned to the offensive on Kosovo. By now Vllassi—who had been replaced in a regular rotation as Kosovo party chief by Kacusa Jasari, but retained real power in his hands—was the particular focus of Serb hatred. During a joint party meeting in Pristina to discuss Fadil Hodja's alleged remarks about the moral character of Serbian waitresses, when Vllassi presumed to defend Hodja, Milosevic replied with a crude sexual insult to "the mother of one who defends someone who calls for the rape of Serbian women." Vllassi, saying that he would not respond in kind but that he would never forget the insult, walked out of the meeting and never spoke to Milosevic again.[39] At this distance, it is impossible to tell whether Milosevic's public display of spite was a calculated insult or simply an uncharacteristic outburst from the usually tightly controlled Serbian leader. It was, in any case, a telling sign of the emotions being aroused on all sides.

By moving against Vllassi, Milosevic helped radicalize the Kosovo Albanian population while also removing the most genuinely Yugoslav-oriented leader from the Kosovo Albanian party leadership. Yet even after Milosevic's assaults had transformed him into a martyr figure, Vllassi—in contrast to his successors—steadfastly refused to use the anger and resentment that the Serb campaign stirred up in Kosovo to stimulate counternationalism among the Albanian population.

Ambassador Scanlan saw the danger of Milosevic's hard-line stance toward Vllassi. Scanlan, who had known Milosevic since his days as a banker and who also knew Vllassi, went quietly to warn Milosevic that instead of firings and repression, he should be focusing on how to maintain the trust of the Albanians. When Scanlan stressed the importance of moderates like Vllassi, who believed in keeping Kosovo within Yugoslavia, Milosevic immediately tightened up, claiming that Vllassi had let the security situation deteriorate for everyone in Kosovo. When Scanlan persisted, noting that Vllassi enjoyed wide respect among Albanians, Milosevic dismissed the appeal out of hand. "There will be others," he said. "Vllassi has got to go."[40]

Bitter public polemics over Kosovo erupted in October 1988 at the seventeenth plenum when Serbs sought to have Vllassi and two other Kosovo party officials removed from office. In a militant speech, Milosevic said Serbia expected support from the rest of Yugoslavia for "its efforts to restore itself constitutionally." Implicitly challenging party leaders outside Serbia who might be inclined to back the Albanians, he asked who would "forbid Serbia to make itself equal to other Yugoslav republics?" Milosevic proclaimed that the Serb leadership enjoyed broad public support for its moves in Kosovo and warned that "the citizens of Serbia would not accept any tutelage" with respect to their rights in Kosovo. Vllassi, by contrast, called for "Yugoslav truth" to prevail in Kosovo and charged that the "self-proclaimed protectors" of the Serbs in Kosovo were actually aiming at the breakup of Yugoslavia—possibly the first time this accusation had been made toward Milosevic, albeit indirectly, at a public forum.[41]

The bitter disputes over Kosovo also revealed that Milosevic's drive to reassert control over the province was provoking incipient divisions within the senior levels of the military. JNA Chief of Staff Stevan Mirkovic, who led Yugoslav troops into Kosovo in 1981 and later joined Milosevic's wife in founding a marxist successor party to the LCY, observed that the situation in Kosovo could threaten Yugoslavia's security. General Nebojsa Tico, claiming that Albanian separatists were planning open rebellion in Kosovo, also charged that some Albanian reserve officers had been infected with nationalism and could not be trusted. By contrast, Yugoslav Minister of Defense Kadijevic took a more neutral position. He implicitly criticized Milosevic by warning against those who would seek to push military personnel toward narrow republican views or adopt stands not consistent with a Yugoslav orientation.[42]

On 17 November, Vllassi stepped down from the Kosovo party presidium, although he remained a member of the LCY central committee at the federal level. Serbian pressure, however, unified Albanians behind the provincial party leadership. When Vllassi's resignation was announced, three thousand coal miners marched to Pristina behind portraits of Tito and the Yugoslav flag, chanting, "We won't give up Azem." The next day, one hundred thousand Albanians assembled outside the provincial government headquarters.

The restrained behavior of the Albanians was in sharp contrast to the provocative sloganeering at the Serb demonstrations that Milosevic had orchestrated over the previous several months. The Albanians carefully refrained from shouting offensive slogans such as "Kosovo republic"—which was said to have triggered the police intervention during the 1981 demonstrations. The Kosovo leadership resisted the temptation to use the spontaneous Albanian demonstrations to build an Albanian nationalist backfire against the Serbs. For several days, Vllassi rushed from place to place throughout Kosovo, eventually persuading the demonstrators to return to their homes. Although the Yugoslav authorities did not, uncharacteristically, use force against the Albanians, federal Interior Minister Culafic flew to Pristina at the height of the demonstrations to let the Kosovo leadership know that if they did not succeed in getting their people off the street, the police would do it for them.

The Kosovo leadership's responsible behavior gained it only a temporary reprieve. In January 1989, after Milosevic had once again shown his strength by successfully overturning the Montenegrin leadership, the LCY central committee voted in a secret ballot to exclude Vllassi from membership. Visibly shaken, Vllassi made a dignified farewell speech remarking that the party's action had damaged the interests of Yugoslavia and appealing for an end to any further settling of accounts.

Serb Victory

The LCY's move against Vllassi showed that the Yugoslav federal authorities—thoroughly frightened by Milosevic's takeover of Vojvodina and Montenegro—were prepared to abandon the Albanians. Milosevic, ever alert to signs of weakness, stepped up the pressure. In a four-week period over February and March 1989, Milosevic crushed Kosovo's autonomy—at the cost of violent demonstrations that claimed the lives of over one hundred Albanians.

On 20 February 1989, four days before the Serbian assembly was scheduled to vote on constitutional amendments that would deprive the provinces of their autonomy, one thousand miners barricaded themselves underground in the Stari Trg mine. The miners demanded the rejection of the constitutional amendments; the resignation of Rahman Morina, the former provincial police chief who Milosevic had installed to head the province; and that both Milosevic and LCY President Suvar visit them underground. The next day, with thousands of Albanians demonstrating peacefully across the province, and shops and businesses closing in support of the miners, the new Kosovo leadership appealed to Milosevic and Suvar to come—a tacit acknowledgment that it had lost control of the situation.

Milosevic flew to Pristina in a helicopter. On arrival, he greeted a sparse crowd with one sentence in Albanian that he had memorized on the flight down: "Comrades, good day!" After this clumsy essay into conciliatory language politics—which the Albanians met with silent hostility—Milosevic drove to the JNA club in downtown Pristina, where he and Suvar addressed a group of Albanian political leaders. Milosevic's substantive remarks were unyielding. He called for the defeat of Albanian nationalism and urged Albanians to protect local Serbs. In words that only a few weeks later proved completely empty, Milosevic promised that the impending constitutional changes would not impinge on any Albanian political, language, cultural, or educational rights.[43]

Suvar took up the miners' challenge to meet them underground, but his insensitive remarks did nothing to calm the situation. He told them that they could not expect to gain their demands through unauthorized meetings—glossing over the fact that Milosevic had recently used just such tactics to overturn two Yugoslav leaderships. When the miners were unmoved by his oratory, Suvar concluded coldly, "I have nothing more to say to you."

By 27 February, it appeared that the Kosovo Albanians, against all odds, might win their confrontation with the Serbs. Dramatic pictures of the Stari Trg miners—some reportedly near death after a week underground without food or water—built up sympathy throughout Yugoslavia, which like other Communist countries had long considered miners the elite of the working class. Morina and the other newly installed Kosovo leaders, up to then viewed as Serbian puppets, submitted their resignations at an emotional meeting of the Kosovo party leadership, where sentiments of Albanian ethnic solidarity apparently overweighed the previous willingness to submit to Belgrade.

The next two days were decisive for Milosevic's takeover of Kosovo and, in retrospect, for Yugoslavia's continued existence as a unified state. With the assistance of conservative and frightened members of the Partisan Old Guard, Milosevic used mob pressure to intimidate the Yugoslav federal organs into giving him a free hand in Kosovo. The other Yugoslav republics allowed themselves to be bullied into casting the Kosovo Albanians to their fate. The consequence was the acceleration of centripetal force throughout the country, as Yugoslavs watched Milosevic's actions in horror, and fear grew in other republics that they might be next.

On 27 February, the collective federal presidency met again at the Serbs' request to deal with the situation caused by the resignation of the Albanian leaders. Under the chair of federal President Raif Dizdarevic of Bosnia, the presidency declared that "special measures" were being imposed in Kosovo and issued "work orders" requiring that strikers return to their jobs. The so-called special measures, which had no foundation in Yugoslav law, were a euphemism for a "state of emergency," a term that Dizdarevic said the presidency had avoided out of concern for the reaction abroad.[44]

The dispatch of troops to Kosovo provoked alarm in Slovenia, which had experienced its own confrontation with the Yugoslav military the year before. Speaking before a large crowd in downtown Ljubljana, Slovenian party chief Milan Kucan suggested that Albanians—who he called a threatened minority—were justified in opposing the amendments to the Serbian Constitution. He labeled the presidency's actions in Kosovo a "quiet coup." Kucan warned that Slovene Communists would "not take part in such a Yugoslavia"—marking the first time that a Slovene leader had made an implied threat of secession.

Meanwhile, a massive counterreaction developed in Belgrade. Slavoljub

Unkovic, the rector of Belgrade University, led several thousand students to an all-night vigil before the federal Assembly building. Other marchers came from the Belgrade industrial suburb of Rakovica, long a hotbed of pro-Milosevic, nationalist sentiment.

By the next day, several hundred thousand Serbs packed the square in front of the federal Assembly building. Large crowds also gathered in other Serbian cities. The Belgrade demonstrators put forward a long list of extreme demands, which had obviously been carefully crafted by the Serbian leadership. These included rescinding the resignations of the three Kosovo Albanian leaders, immediate adoption of the Serbian constitutional amendments, condemnation of Slovenian and Croatian leaders for their support of the Albanian "separatists," and suppression of the emerging non-Communist opposition parties in Croatia and Slovenia.

With downtown Belgrade paralyzed, the LCY presidency met to give its required approval to the emergency measures that the state presidency had adopted the previous day. Milosevic used the presence of the crowd to bully the frightened Yugoslav party leaders into giving him what he wanted in Kosovo. Referring to the explosive situation in Belgrade, he demanded that the LCY presidency promise "immediate measures" against the ringleaders of the Albanian demonstrations in Pristina. In the confused and fluid discussion that followed, the hard-line Macedonian representative, Jakov Lazeroski, remarked that the situation was bad all over Yugoslavia and he seemed—together with the JNA representative, General Petar Simic—to be seeking a state of emergency throughout the country. This, of course, was more than Milosevic bargained for. He wanted a free hand in Kosovo, not to have his own hands tied in Serbia.

While this discussion was unfolding, Dizdarevic attempted to placate the crowd, but its mood on that sunny and unusually warm early spring day was militant. "We want Slobo," the crowd jeered. Dizdarevic retreated inside the Assembly building, pale and obviously shaken. Returning to the party meeting, Dizdarevic passed on his sense of alarm: "The demonstration is becoming too big. We must calm things." Milosevic continued to insist that the protesters' demands be immediately accepted, but Kucan and Croatian party chief Ivica Racan refused. Racan, who undoubtedly recalled having been sent out to address a smaller gathering of Kosovo Serb demonstrators two years before, observed that if the party accepted Milosevic's advice, it would have to submit every future decision to a similar mass demonstration.

Milosevic resorted to direct intimidation. If the demonstrators were not given an immediate answer, he said he would not take responsibility for what would happen. Racan heatedly rejoined that he would never agree to blackmail, and Kucan, perhaps sarcastically, said that he would be willing to accompany Milosevic if he would go out to speak to the crowd. After more discussion, Milosevic accepted a compromise statement that did not mention arrests.[45]

But Milosevic had no intention of allowing the party to stop him from getting Vllassi's head. Around nine o'clock that evening, after many in the crowd had been waiting for more than twelve hours, Milosevic finally appeared on the steps of the assembly building. He confined his comments to the parameters of the statement agreed to earlier with the LCY leadership. The crowd, its bloodlust up, was still dissatisfied when Milosevic finished speaking. Thousands of voices called out, "Arrest Vllassi!" Milosevic gave them what they wanted. "Those who manipulated the masses will be punished and arrested. I guarantee you this," he said.[46]

Two days later, Vllassi was arrested at the home of his wife's parents, in the Bosnian town of Bijelina—which two years later was one of the first to experience ethnic cleansing at the hands of Serb paramilitary units. Vllassi and two leaders of the Stari Trg mine were arrested for "counterrevolutionary activity, destruction of brotherhood and unity, and destroying the economic base of the country." Six months after his arrest, when Vllassi's indictment was finally made available to his lawyers, it was found that the Serbs had also charged him with being the "moral author" of the deaths of twenty-four ethnic Albanians shot by Serbian riot police during the March 1989 demonstrations, even though Vllassi was actually in jail at the time.

The day after Milosevic's coup de main, Lazar Mojsov, a respected member of Yugoslavia's aging partisan generation who had served as president of the UN General Assembly in the 1970s, addressed a special session of the federal Assembly. Unreservedly backing the Serbian position on Kosovo, Mojsov claimed to have in his hand a sixteen-page report of a secret investigation ordered by the collective federal presidency into the activities of Albanian separatists in Kosovo. Mojsov charged that this investigation by federal, Serbian, and Kosovo secret police had determined that "people in important positions" in Kosovo were behind the demonstrations. He justified the imposition of special security measures in Kosovo by claiming that the police had only a few days earlier learned that "a group of Kosovo Communists" had prepared a three-stage plan that included strikes, demonstrations, and an "armed uprising" to prevent the adoption of the amendments to the Serb Constitution.[47]

Mojsov did not reveal the names of the Kosovo leaders allegedly involved in organizing the uprising, nor did he ever show the document from which he was supposedly reading. Even at the time, many questioned the authenticity of Mojsov's information. A month later, the Slovene representative on the collective federal presidency, Stane Dolanc, privately told the Slovene leadership that no such document existed. He claimed that Mojsov had not, in fact, been speaking on behalf of the state presidency but had undertaken his remarks on his own initiative, with encouragement from Minister of Defense Kadijevic.[48]

The Yugoslav federal and republican leaders turned their collective backs on the Kosovo Albanians, hoping that Milosevic would stop with Kosovo. They were wrong. The application of countervailing force was always the only way to stop Milosevic, as anyone who dealt with him eventually discovered.

On 23 March, the Kosovo Assembly gave Milosevic his final victory. With a Serb presiding and only six delegates opposed, the provincial Assembly approved amendments to the Serbian Constitution that gave Serbia control over Kosovo's security, judiciary, finances, and social planning. The province reverted to its traditional name of Kosovo and Metohija, and many provisions of the 1974 Constitution were declared null and void. On the Assembly floor, Serbian officials carefully monitored the votes of each Albanian delegate and, according to some reports, actually voted themselves. The few Albanian delegates who stood up to the Serbian steamroller paid for their courage by being expelled from the Assembly, dismissed from their jobs, and threatened with criminal prosecution.[49]

Demonstrations and Decapitation

On 28 March, the Serbian Assembly formally adopted the amendments. In a defiant speech, Assembly President Borisav Jovic exalted that it was up to those who have long lectured Serbia to "understand and accept the new, united Serbia." Jovic did not bother to repeat Milosevic's earlier assurances that the amendments would not harm the Kosovo Albanians. Instead, he warned that the Constitution would be "used without remission" against anyone who dared attack the integrity of Serbia.

As Jovic was speaking, crowds danced in Belgrade's streets singing, "Oh, Serbia, once divided in three, you will again be whole." In Kosovo, the mood was different. With Vllassi in jail and the existing provincial leadership regarded as quislings, there was no one to calm the situation. In the town of Podujevo, protesters and police fought a pitched battle in which 2 police officers were killed. After six days, the official toll of victims was 22 demonstrators plus the 2 police officers killed, and 222 injured. Unofficial reports of casualties, however, were far higher. Slovenian journalists claimed that as many as 140 Albanians had been killed, while Western journalists saw children as young as nine years old being treated in hospitals for gunshot wounds.[50]

Just before the Kosovo Assembly's vote, the Serbian authorities secretly detained 240 Albanian political leaders, business officials, and intellectuals. They were interrogated and held without charge for up to four months, under a hitherto secret provision of the Yugoslav code that was intended to allow the "isolation" of dangerous individuals during wartime. Conditions for those in isolation were brutal. Detainees in the southern Serbian prison in Leckovac, for example, were forced to run a gauntlet of guards who beat them with batons and truncheons, and were later beaten in their cells as well.[51]

Milosevic at Gazimestan

Three months later, on 28 June 1989—the six-hundredth anniversary of the Turkish victory at Kosovo Polje—Milosevic celebrated his own conquest of Kosovo before a throng of over a million from all over Serbia. The mood of the crowd as it waited for hours under a warm sun to greet Milosevic was triumphant. Gaily colored banners and flags waved in the breeze beside the ubiquitous posters of Milosevic and Tsar Lazar. Chants of "We love Slobo" and "Europe, don't you remember that we defended you!" filled the air. JNA units were deployed discretely around the perimeter of the site, but Albanians kept well away from the festivities.

Just when the crowd seemed to be getting impatient, Milosevic descended like an avenging angel by helicopter directly onto the site of the rally. An enthusiastic roar greeted him when he began his speech by welcoming the multitudes to what he described as "Kosovo—the heart of Serbia!"

Milosevic's relatively short speech was divided into two parts. In the first half, he evoked Serb nationalist themes to extol his own achievements. Noting that Serbia had lost the Kosovo battle because of "tragic disunity in the leadership of the Serbian state" and criticizing concessions Communist leaders had made at the expense of the Serb people, Milosevic trumpeted that "Serbia today is united and equal to other republics." In the second half of the speech, which sounded as if it was written by his wife, Milosevic suddenly switched tack and began to praise the virtues of ethnic toleration and socialism. As Milosevic lectured the crowd on how "the world is more and more marked by national tolerance, national cooperation, and even national equality," and called for equal and harmonious relations among the peoples of Yugoslavia, the gathering grew silent and almost restive. At the end, however, Milosevic brought the crowd back to cheering, whistling life when—for the first time—he raised the possibility of armed conflict in Yugoslavia. Six centuries after the Kosovo battle, he said, "we are again engaged in battles and are facing battles; they are not armed battles but such things cannot be excluded."[52]

Janez Drnovsek, the young, democratically elected Slovene who had recently taken Dizdarevic's place as president of the collective federal presidency, sat next to Milosevic during the ceremony. Drnovsek described Milosevic's mood as euphoric. During the opening phases of the ceremony, Milosevic kept looking back over his shoulder to see how many people had turned up. He and Kadijevic exchanged estimates, with the cautious defense minister guessing half a million, but Milosevic finally decided that one and a half million had come to hear him speak.[53]

As soon as Milosevic had finished speaking, he was whisked out of Kosovo by helicopter. The participants in the rally wended their way home through monumental traffic jams and followed out of the province by the sullen stares of Kosovo's Albanian inhabitants.

The Albanian Alternative

After Milosevic's decapitation of the LCK, new Albanian political groups appeared, taking advantage of the decision by the Yugoslav authorities to allow the formation of non-Communist political organizations. Many of these new groups grew out of existing organizations of intellectuals, such as the Kosovo Association of Writers, whose head, Ibrahim Rugova, quickly became the informal leader of what was known as the Albanian alternative. The Kosovo branch of the Association for a Yugoslav Democratic Initiative (AYDI)—the only organization of Yugoslav intellectuals founded on an avowedly all-Yugoslav and nonnationalist platform—became influential under the leadership of Veton Surroi, a young Rilindja reporter. Surroi's level-headed judgment, wry sense of humor, and good English soon made him one of the most prominent of the Albanian spokesmen.

One of AYDI's first initiatives was the circulation of a petition, "For Democracy, against Violence." Signed by over four hundred thousand Kosovars, this document played a crucial role in shaping the Albanian strategy of nonviolent resistance to Serb repression. In late 1988, I watched a courageous and energetic group of students, under Surroi's leadership, circulate the petition throughout the province, often literally under the guns of Serbian armored vehicles. Surroi and his young colleagues, who could sometimes be seen literally thrusting the petition in the faces of angry groups of Albanians gathered to oppose the Serb police, helped prevent Kosovo from exploding into hopeless violence as the Serb police tightened their grip on the province.

The Albanian alternative movement also brought a halt to the age-old practice of blood vengeance among Albanians. Intellectuals and students fanned out through Kosovo's rural areas to persuade feuding families to abandon this tradition, which Albanian researchers said had accounted for up to one hundred deaths a year in Kosovo and kept as many as twenty thousand Kosovo men confined to their homes for fear of retribution from their neighbors. In huge, open-air ceremonies, hundreds of feuding representatives forgave each other and promised to end the cycle of violence.[54]

Sometimes Albanian self-restraint would break down, and young Albanians would take on the Serbian police. In Urosevac in 1989, I witnessed a typical example as Albanians, sparked by reports that the police had arrested and publicly beaten several individuals, seized control of the center of town. They built barricades out of overturned cars and burning tires from behind which they hurled stones, metal debris, and an occasional Molotov cocktail at the Serb riot police who advanced on them behind clouds of tear gas. As the police took control of and dismantled one barricade, the Albanians would scuttle away and build another in the densely packed streets of the city center. By the time the police had cleared away all the demonstrators, there were dozens of casualties on both sides including, according to the Albanians, several dead protesters. Many houses and shops had their windows smashed, and thick columns of oily smoke rose into the sky.

Two days later, I joined a long column of mourners at the funeral of one of the young men reportedly killed by Serb police. Several thousand Albanians snaked through the village lanes in total silence to a nearby cemetery. Family members watched as the coffin, draped in the red and black Albanian national flag, was lowered into the ground. The crowd was disciplined and peaceful, yet its anger ran deep. At the end of the ceremony, the father of the victim and his other sons undertook one of the most sacred obligations in Albanian culture—swearing an oath, or *besa*, to exact retribution for the death of the young man. The Albanians might have agreed to end feuds against their fellow nationals, but this had not diminished their desire for revenge against their Serb oppressors.

Sometimes the confrontations were even uglier. Albanians described to me what happened after a column of Serb police vehicles was fired on by unidentified assailants and two police officers wounded. In response, Serbian armored vehicles drove into the nearby town of Malisevo and opened fire on unsuspecting passersby in the town center. No one ever established how many were killed in this incident, but days later blood still stained the street and the walls of many buildings bore the pockmarks of heavy machine gun bullets.

Rugova and the LDK

The League of Democrats of Kosovo (LDK), founded in December 1989 by Rugova, quickly became the real center of authority among Kosovo Albanians. If there are any heroes in the Yugoslav tragedy, Ibrahim Rugova is certainly one of them. Rugova was born in 1944. His father was a prosperous farmer who was killed by the Partisans toward the end of the Second World War. Rugova became a literary scholar, and in 1976, spent a year in Paris, where he began wearing the bright red scarf that later became his personal trademark.

A gentle and quiet-spoken man, Rugova seemed an unlikely antagonist to Milosevic. Yet Rugova possessed an iron determination to resist Serbian oppression. His choice of nonviolent tactics stemmed from a desire to avoid the bloodbath he knew would accompany any effort by the largely unarmed Albanians to oppose the Serbs through violent means. Rugova's approach, however, had nothing to do with passivity. He himself described it as "a war without arms."[55]

Rugova's objectives throughout his long years of struggle remained remarkably consistent and he never deviated from them despite pressure to do so by his international backers. While Yugoslavia still existed, Rugova insisted that Kosovo should have a status equal to all other Yugoslav republics. Once Yugoslavia had disintegrated, Rugova made it clear that Kosovo must become independent.[56] He called for Kosovo to be placed under an international protectorate as early as 1994, but at no time was Rugova ever willing to consider returning Kosovo to its status as a Serbian province.

Rugova's steadfast advocacy of nonviolent resistance to Serb oppression won him broad international support. But he made two important mistakes. The first was in refusing to participate in the Serb elections of 1990 and later. Despite repeated entreaties by U.S. Ambassador Warren Zimmermann, who replaced Scanlan in 1989, and lower-level diplomats including me, Rugova maintained that Kosovo Albanians would never again recognize Serbian authority and that he would not last a single day as Albanian leader if he agreed to join Serb elections.[57]

Although one can understand why Rugova and other Kosovo Albanians would resist any step that would indicate allegiance to a state that was abusing them so mercilessly, the absence of the Albanian voters was a gift that helped Milosevic retain power. One reason why Milosevic opposed the creation of multiple parties in Serbia was his fear that the Albanians in Kosovo would form their own party, which he told advisers would cause Serbia to "lose" Kosovo.[58] The results of the 1993 Serb parliamentary elections show how the Albanian boycott allowed Milosevic to win seats "on the cheap." Milosevic's Socialist Party of Serbia (SPS) won twenty-one seats from a total of 59,945 votes cast in the Pristina electoral district, one of nine in all of Serbia. In Belgrade by contrast, the SPS won sixteen seats on the basis of 255,071 votes.[59] Later, when support for Milosevic had fallen in Serbia, the failure of the Kosovo Albanian population to vote in Serbian elections helped Milosevic to use the province as a reservoir of phony votes to boost his by-then dwindling electoral support. A study of the voting patterns in the 1997 elections by the respected independent Serbian election monitoring group, Center for Free Elections and Democracy (CESID in its Serbo-Croatian acronym), compared the total estimated numbers of Serbs living in Kosovo election districts with the total number of officially recorded votes and concluded that perhaps almost 328,000 "phantom" votes could have been added from Kosovo.[60]

Rugova's second mistake, ironically, was in going too far in believing the international community and especially the United States—which had a special relationship with Kosovo because of its early advocacy of human rights in the province. From the beginning, a succession of Western diplomats—again including myself—encouraged Rugova to continue his policy of nonviolent resistance. But since the Serbs would never voluntarily relinquish control of Kosovo, Rugova's strategy only made sense if the international community were willing to force the Serbs to reach an aggreement on Kosovo acceptable to its majority Albanian inhabitants. And on this point, Rugova and his Kosovo Albanian compatriots experienced nothing but delay and disappointment. Once war broke out in the rest of Yugoslavia, Kosovo virtually disappeared from the pages of the media and hence from the labors of international peace negotiators. Not until Kosovo Albanians had finally decided "enough is enough" and begun to shoot back at their Serb oppressors did the international community actively reengage on Kosovo, although by then it was too late for a peaceful solution.

Albanian Resistance

As the Yugoslav crisis deepened, the Albanians sought to adjust political developments in Kosovo to the pace of the disintegrative processes elsewhere in Yugoslavia. On 2 July 1990, standing in front of the locked doors of the Kosovo Assembly building, 114 of the 127 Albanian delegates "annulled" their agreement the previous year to the changes to the Serb Constitution. By now firmly under LDK control the delegates declared Kosovo to be an "independent unit" within the Yugoslav community.

The Albanian declaration of independence from Serbia occurred on the same day that Slovenia adopted a sweeping Declaration of State Sovereignty. But there was a critical difference between Kosovo and Slovenia. Milosevic ruled Kosovo and he was determined to retain it, with or without the rest of Yugoslavia. During heated discussions on the collective federal presidency, the Serbs failed to gain agreement for a measure authorizing the use of the army in Kosovo "as a preventive measure." At one point in the debate, Milosevic asked angrily, "Is it really possible that around this table a question can be raised that runs something like this: Does Serbia have the right to protect its territorial integrity and constitutional order? We simply cannot discuss this question."[61]

Despite his failure to gain the presidency's backing, Milosevic responded decisively to the Albanian declaration. On 5 July, the Serb Assembly formally dissolved its Kosovo counterpart. All laws passed by the Kosovo Assembly were declared invalid, and the Serb Assembly assumed all legislative functions in the province.[62]

A year later, on 22 September 1991, as war raged in Croatia, Albanian Assembly delegates met secretly in Pristina to declare Kosovo an independent, sovereign state. In May 1992, the Albanians completed their construction of a separate but illegal Albanian political structure by holding multiparty elections for a new Kosovo Assembly. Rugova gained 99.9 percent of the votes in running unopposed for president, and the LDK won ninety-six out of one hundred single-member assembly seats.[63]

Apartheid

Beginning in 1990, the Serbian authorities created what amounted to a system of apartheid that excluded the province's majority Albanian population from virtually every phase of political, economic, social, and cultural life. On 5 July 1990, heavily armed special police stormed into the broadcasting facilities of Pristina Television and Radio in response to its favorable reporting on the declaration of republican status by the Kosovo Assembly. Albanian-language broadcasting was reduced to two, twenty-minute programs that regurgitated translations of the Serbian news. The next month, the major Albanian daily *Rilindja* was also shut down. Its workers were fired, and many were also reportedly evicted from their apartments.[64]

Tens of thousands of ethnic Albanian workers in government and public enterprises were dismissed from their jobs after a general strike in September, timed to coincide with the adoption of the 1990 Constitution. Other workers were fired because they refused to sign a Serbian loyalty oath or simply because they were Albanian. So-called emergency management teams consisting only of Serbs were established in many of Kosovo's most important enterprises, such as the Trepca coal mines.[65]

One of the most repulsive Serbian actions was to create conditions that led to the dismissal of virtually all Albanian education and medical personnel. In June 1990, Serbian medical workers demonstratively left Pristina's medical school hospital, saying that they no longer wished to work with Albanians. After the Albanian staff was fired, the Serbs returned. In August 1990, Serb military personnel surrounded another Pristina hospital; about forty-five doctors were handcuffed and taken in for questioning. When the Serbian authorities promulgated new regulations requiring all medical documentation to be written in Serbian, Albanian medical personnel unwilling or unable to comply were dismissed.[66]

No aspect of life in Kosovo was left untouched. The Albanian theater in Pristina was shut down because its director allowed an unauthorized photo exhibit in the lobby. The local film company was put under Serb direction, while the Albanian ballet was closed altogether. During the siege of Sarajevo, Serb gunners destroyed Bosnia's cultural and historical heritage by lobbing incendiary shells into the national library. In Kosovo, the Serbs accomplished the same task by theft. Albanian-language materials were removed from libraries across the province.

What Kosovo?

In 1990, Milosevic declaimed, "Every man in Serbia is ready to head for Kosovo if the terror is continuing there."[67] After his 1989 speech at Gazimestan, however, Milosevic did not visit Kosovo for another six years. Neither war nor peace, the situation in Kosovo was inherently unstable and inevitably destined for conflict. Serbs and Albanians were locked into irreconcilably opposing positions on the future of the province, and with every day of separate existence and every instance of police brutality, the gulf between the two communities became ever more unbridgeable.

FOUR

A New Tito?

With Kosovo subdued, Milosevic dominated four of Yugoslavia's eight federal units. Gaining even one more would give him a majority on the eight-member collective federal presidency—the country's highest executive body, which controlled key security decisions including the imposition of a state of emergency and the use of the military in domestic crises.

Belgrade at the time was practically bursting with speculation about Milosevic's next moves. It was widely believed that Milosevic intended to try to take control of the entire country. Many suspected that he saw himself as the successor to Tito. Mihajlo Crnobrnja, one of Milosevic's economic advisers, told the Western media that he had the clear impression Milosevic aimed to take up Tito's mantle. "That is his ambition," Crnobrnja said straightforwardly.[1]

In March 1989, the Belgrade weekly *NIN* published an article noting that the broad powers granted Tito under the 1974 Constitution had never been formally revoked. After Tito's death, the role of head of state was taken over by the collective federal presidency, where each republic and autonomous province had one representative. The provisions of the Constitution that specified the powers accorded to the individual president—although intended to apply only to Tito—remained officially on the books. *NIN* suggested that one person again be chosen to the post of president as a way to resolve the constitutional gridlock caused by the requirement for consensus on all major decisions. In case anyone missed the point, *NIN* juxtaposed the article with a laudatory review of a recently published collection of Milosevic's speeches.

Milosevic, however, faced a problem. So far, he had confined his noisy nationalist campaign to areas within Serbia or those—like Montenegro—closely linked to it by history and ethnicity. To expand his sway, Milosevic would have to act in republics where Serbs were a minority, such as Croatia and Bosnia, or where they were hardly present at all, such as Macedonia and Slovenia.

In Belgrade, Milosevic's henchmen openly discussed how they intended to exploit the weaknesses of other republics to achieve their master's goals. Bosnia, its traditional leadership discredited by recent scandals, was experiencing a political vacuum. Macedonia was economically dependent on Serbia and inclined to sympathize with Milosevic's stance on Kosovo because of worries about its own rapidly growing Albanian population. The Croatian party leadership was split internally between conservative and reformist wings, and was thus subject to pressures from the republic's Serb minority.

Slovenia, prosperous and ethnically homogeneous, had fewer vulnerabilities for Milosevic to exploit. Its liberal and Western-oriented population was repulsed by Milosevic's methods in Kosovo, which the Slovenes saw as inconsistent with their vision of democracy and as a possible portent of what could happen to them if Milosevic prevailed throughout Yugoslavia. In 1988, Slovene League of Communists President Milan Kucan had become the most popular politician in the republic by putting himself at the head of the resistance to the trial of three young Slovene journalists and a JNA warrant officer for leaking what appeared to be a JNA plan to intervene in Slovenia. Over the next year, the struggle for Yugoslavia became something of a battle between Milosevic and Kucan.

The Serbian Plan for a New Yugoslavia

Speaking at a Serbian party plenum on 12 April 1989, Milosevic announced his intention to continue the offensive after his triumph in Kosovo. "Nothing can stop us anymore," Milosevic boasted. Dismissing critics of his populist methods, Milosevic warned, "We do not have time to explain our policies in detail to everyone individually."[2] A month later, in a speech in Novi Sad where he introduced a new economic program, Milosevic sounded almost giddy, "Intoxicated by its victories, Serbia will not stand still."

He pursued his assault on the Yugoslav political system along three fronts. The first was an effort to replace the 1974 Constitution with a new document that would allow more efficient decision making at the federal level, but would also—by introducing the one-person, one-vote principle—

allow the Serbs to dominate the country's political life by force of numbers. Milosevic also tried to use the tactic of mass rallies, which had overthrown the leaderships of Vojvodina and Montenegro, against the Slovenes. His final line of attack was an effort to take over the LCY by amending its procedures to allow decisions based on majority vote. Milosevic's three-pronged strategy failed, but only narrowly. His offensive convulsed the Yugoslav political system, and added to the growing pressure in Slovenia and Croatia to leave Yugoslavia.

By 1989, Yugoslavia had been mired for several years in unsuccessful negotiations among the republics over minor changes to the 1974 federal Constitution. In a 9 May speech on his inauguration as Serbian president, Milosevic once again showed his inclination for bold solutions that leapfrogged over the day-to-day conventions of Yugoslav political life. Declaring that the edifice established by the 1974 Constitution was obsolete, Milosevic called for a new document that would replace the decentralized system bequeathed by Tito with a truly federal one where only a small number of issues would still require consensus among all republics. Toward the end of July, he laid out the main points of his proposed new Constitution. Economic, foreign, and defense policy would be the exclusive domain of the federal authorities. In the lower chamber of the bicameral assembly proposed by Milosevic, representatives would be directly elected on the basis of one person, one vote, and all decisions would be reached as a result of a simple majority. Each republic would have an equal vote in the upper chamber, and all decisions there would be taken on the principle of consensus.

There were some obvious lacunae in the Milosevic draft. It expressly rejected the concept of multiparty democracy and was vague on human rights. Its call for more referendums to decide important national issues was patently favorable to the Serbs. Sovereignty, moreover, would reside in the Yugoslav federation and not in the republics, thereby undoing at one stroke the basic principle of sovereign equality among the republics that Slovenia and Croatia claimed was the foundation of Yugoslavia.[3]

The proposed Serbian Constitution was nevertheless one of the more reasonable efforts to resolve the perennial Yugoslav debate over the distribution of power between the federation and republics. Its most glaring flaw was its source. The very fact of its introduction by Milosevic made it suspect in other republics. But even if the proposed new Constitution had been introduced by Thomas Jefferson, it would have faced a skeptical audience. Its adoption would have instantly reversed the decentralization that underpinned the power of the republican elites that had run Yugoslavia since Tito's death. Just as it is easier to make an omelet from an egg than to make an egg from an omelet, the experience of Yugoslavia showed that it was easier to create a decentralized system than to recentralize an already decentralized one, especially when there are good reasons to suspect the motives of the centralizer and when his opponents enjoy a veto over any changes.

As Milosevic was putting forward his plan for a new Yugoslav federation, the Slovenes advanced a competing future vision. In June 1989, Slovenia adopted a "Basic Charter," which was subsequently signed by virtually all the republic's citizens. Slovenes, according to the charter, wanted to live in a democratic state, founded on human rights and the sovereignty of the Slovene people. The charter contained only the most grudging references to Yugoslavia, noting that Slovenes would only live in a Yugoslavia that assured them sovereignty as well as "the permanent and inalienable right to self-determination," and would not stay in a country where they were subject to national or political hegemony.[4]

In September 1989, a major political and constitutional crisis erupted over amendments to the Slovenian Constitution that put the principles of the charter into practice. The amendments laid the groundwork for replacing socialism in Slovenia—by calling for the republic's legal system to conform to West European norms—and for the end of Yugoslavia as a united state—by claiming for Slovenia the right to self-determination and secession.

The Slovene amendments provoked major battles within the Yugoslav leadership. The Serbian representative on the collective federal presidency, Borisav Jovic, took the lead in condemning the amendments as inconsistent with the Yugoslav Constitution and as a first step toward secession. The Serbs were supported by all the other republics, which had no sympathy for the Slovene position, and feared being left behind in a Milosevic-dominated Yugoslavia if the Slovenes departed. Shortly before the Slovene assembly's vote, Kucan brought the republic's leadership to Belgrade for a private meeting with the presidency. During the heated discussion, Kucan rejected an appeal to delay the amendments, claiming that it would cause the League of Communists' political demise in Slovenia. When Jovic asked how the party had lost such standing in Slovenia, Kucan shot back that the fault lay with the two-year Serbian offensive against the Slovene leadership.[5]

With the Slovenes unyielding, Milosevic and Jovic attempted to persuade the military to intervene. Yugoslav Defense Minister Veljko Kadi-jevic shared the Serb view that the amendments were merely the first move toward secession. The military particularly objected to a provision that would allow Ljubljana to decide for itself how much it would pay toward the federal defense budget. During the meeting with the Slovene leader-ship, Jovic and Kadijevic had threatened to use "other measures at the dis-posal of the presidency" if the Slovenes did not back down.

After the meeting, Jovic attempted to turn the threat of military inter-vention into a reality by getting Kadijevic's agreement to military prepara-tions to block adoption of the Slovene amendments. An atmosphere of crisis spread across the country during the final days of September. The Ser-bian media unleashed an offensive against the amendments, and officially inspired demonstrations occurred in many Serbian cities. Rumors of im-pending military action were widespread. When Janez Drnovsek, the Slo-vene who headed the collective federal presidency, left the country to at-tend the opening of the UN General Assembly, Jovic convened a special session of the Council for the Protection of the Yugoslav Constitutional Or-der, a shadowy body that had the authority to order the use of the military in crisis situations. Drnovsek returned from New York without delivering his speech, to be present at the 26 September session of the Slovene Assem-bly that considered the amendments.

Yet nothing happened. The Slovene Assembly adopted the amendments unanimously, except for the votes of its military members, and the furor promptly subsided. Told by his lawyers that an intervention would be "on the borderline of constitutionality," Kadijevic decided not to move. Meet-ing together the next day, Milosevic and Jovic agreed that Kadijevic's inac-tion was "an enormous failure" that amounted to the beginning of the end for Yugoslavia. When Kadijevic unexpectedly showed up, the two Serbs tried, without much conviction, to persuade him to intervene if the Yugo-slav Supreme Court ruled that the Slovene amendments were inconsistent with the existing Yugoslav Constitution.[6] It was the first—but not the last—time that the Serbian leadership tried unsuccessfully to encourage a surprisingly cautious JNA to move against Slovenia or Croatia. Writing later, Drnovsek shared the Serbs' assessment that the Slovene amendments marked the beginning of the breakup of federal Yugoslavia. Drnovsek, how-ever, placed the blame squarely on Belgrade, claiming that what happened in Slovenia was "no more than a normal response to the undemocratic course of events in Serbia and specifically in Kosovo."[7]

With the military unwilling to act, Milosevic dusted off the tactic of street democracy to pressure the Slovenes. In November, the Kosovo Serb radicals, who had been quiet for some months, suddenly decided to hold a "meeting of truth" in Ljubljana on 1 December 1989, the anniversary of the founding of the first Yugoslav state in 1918. Citizens from all the towns in Serbia and Montenegro where rallies were held in 1988 were invited to join. At about the same time, Milosevic told foreign journalists that Serbia was "not indifferent" to the fate of Serbs living outside its borders—a clear warning to Croatia and Bosnia, with their substantial Serb minorities, that the Serbs were on the offensive again.[8]

Slovenia took the threatened Serb demonstration seriously. On 21 November, the Slovene daily *Delo* called the proposed rally "an act of civil war." Slovene police declared a ban on public movement and prepared to meet an invasion. On the walls of Ljubljana, graffiti appeared saying, "*Srbe na vrbe*," meaning "hang the Serbs on the willow trees" that lined the parks and riverbanks of the usually tranquil Slovene capital.

The federal authorities, as usual, were divided. Drnovsek failed to persuade a majority of the federal presidency to support a motion banning the Serbian rally. But the Yugoslav military, despite its anger at the Slovenes, was not eager to see Milosevic overturn yet another legitimate Yugoslav government. A few months earlier, Kadijevic had issued a sharp warning to feuding republican leaders—implicitly aimed at Milosevic and Kucan—stating that "no individual in Yugoslavia would be allowed" to "impose special interests" or the political schemes of one region at the expense of the national interest.[9] Now, when Drnovsek beseeched him for assistance, an angry Kadijevic twice called Milosevic to demand that the rally be canceled.[10] The federal police, even though they were headed by the Serb Petar Gracanin, also proved unhelpful, refusing to provide assurances that the demonstrators would be able to move freely to Slovenia.

The Kosovo Serbs canceled the rally, adding that the Slovenes had disgraced themselves by closing their border to Serbs who had only wanted to show them the picture of a Serb mother guarding her child from Albanian terrorists! On 1 December, a few dozen Serbs managed to rally in front of the small Orthodox church in Ljubljana, with a banner reading, "This is still Yugoslavia," before dispersing at the request of heavily armed Slovenian riot police. In Belgrade, Milosevic seems to have taken the failure hard. Jovic said he had to console Milosevic, who had seen his scheme unravel due to the unwillingness of Yugoslav federal authorities—even those basically sympathetic to the Serbs—to contemplate the use of force against the Slovenes.[11]

It is hard to know whether to consider the aborted Serb meeting in Ljubljana as tragedy or farce. The Serbs apparently never made any serious effort to arrange for the transport of large numbers of demonstrators across the three hundred miles between Belgrade and Ljubljana. In any case, it is difficult to see how they could have done so in opposition to the federal authorities, not to mention the Croats across whose territory the Serbs would have had to travel and who also deployed police to block the demonstrators. Drnovsek, nevertheless, asserts that after the threat of the meeting in Ljubljana, Slovenes no longer felt comfortable in Yugoslavia.[12]

The attempt to hold the rally in Ljubljana also shows how out of touch Milosevic could be with realities in other parts of Yugoslavia. The Serbian leader, who seldom traveled outside his own republic's sphere, apparently did not understand that the tactics he had employed against earlier victims in Vojvodina or Montenegro would not work in Slovenia, where the leadership enjoyed solid support from its own population.

Still, the incident reveals the depth of emotions on both sides. Serbia met the ban on the Ljubljana meeting by declaring a boycott on Slovene goods. The Slovenes responded by redirecting their economic ties westward. The two nations—traditional allies in the Yugoslav constellation—turned their backs on each other, a development that boded ill for the country's future.

Reform of the LCY: Back to the Future

Seizing control of the LCY was the final element of Milosevic's efforts to turn himself into the "new Tito." Milosevic sought to return the party to the hoary Leninist principle of democratic centralism—that is, unconditional submission to all decisions from the top. He ultimately failed—Milosevic could hardly have succeeded in something that went so obviously against the grain of history—but his efforts destroyed the party that had ruled Yugoslavia since 1945.

In some ways, the LCY never fully came to grip with the domestic consequences of Tito's 1948 split with the Soviet Union. The Yugoslav party veered for forty years between periods of relaxation—which inevitably went too far, at least in Tito's view—followed by periods of repression. The LCY's last conservative turn was ratified at the tenth party congress in 1974, when Tito reimposed top-down discipline but left only himself at the top.

After Tito's death in 1980, the LCY turned into a loose confederal organization at the national level. The party president was a figurehead, chosen on an annual rotational basis from representatives of the eight federal units on the collective party presidency. Decisions of the League of Communists presidency, in practice, required consensus of the eight as well. Within each republic and province, however, the League of Communists exercised unchallenged power through a combination of formal and informal mechanisms that varied in tightness from republic to republic.

By the late 1980s, the LCY's clear inability to deal with the country's deepening political and economic crisis led to a steep decline in its authority. Alternative political and social advocacy groups appeared, especially in Slovenia and Croatia. Strikes or other forms of worker protests were on the rise, even in conservative areas where there was as yet little organized political opposition.

One of the LCY's most damaging wounds was self-inflicted. Beginning with the seventeenth plenum in October 1988, the party allowed central committee sessions to be televised live. This well-intentioned effort to demonstrate the party's openness and accessibility boomeranged by allowing the entire country to view the petty wrangling among the party's republican elites. Yugoslavs watched, first in fascination and then in growing disgust, as meeting after meeting degenerated into verbal cat-fights. The aura of mystery and lingering fear that had accompanied the tradition of party secrecy vanished. The LCY's reputation—already low—evaporated.

Membership in the party began to fall in 1984 and it accelerated in 1988, especially among workers and young people, whose share in the party ranks fell by almost one-half in the 1980s from 33.1 percent in 1980 to 18.1 percent in 1988. Over six hundred thousand members left the party after 1983, with one hundred thousand leaving in 1989 alone. The decline was greatest in Slovenia, where only one in thirteen adult inhabitants was a party member.[13] The party's response was typically slow and bureaucratic. A reform commission established in 1987 quickly bogged down in fighting between two factions. A pluralist school, led by the Slovenes, wanted to expand the range of allowed political activity and, as time went on, was even willing to permit competing political parties. The second faction, led by the Serbs, paid lip service to pluralism, but was unwilling to give up the LCY's monopoly on power.

Milosevic's primary line of attack was a push to revise the party statutes to allow decisions to be taken on the basis of one-member, one-vote. In 1988, more than half the total party membership of slightly more than two million was in Serbia, Montenegro, and the JNA, and Serbs were also strong in the party organizations of Croatia and Bosnia. In effect, therefore, Milosevic was trying to use the numerical strength of the Serbs and their allies to take over the LCY.[14]

In April 1989, at a meeting described by the Yugoslav media as a "confrontation of polarized stands," the LCY handed Milosevic a major victory by agreeing over Slovene objections to hold an extraordinary party congress with the authority to amend the party's statutes. Delegates would be chosen on the basis of one for every two thousand members. Milosevic trumpeted that the rule of consensus would finally be abolished and that on the table at last was what kind of Yugoslavia would exist in the future. His puppets in Vojvodina—claiming that a special party congress was necessary because the "central committee and the presidency of the LCY have lost the confidence of the rank and file"—made it clear that what Milosevic really wanted was a purge of all party leaders opposed to him. Over Serbian objections, however, the date of the congress was deferred until the end of the year, to allow time for a commission headed by Milosevic's opponent Suvar to draft a new reform program.[15]

In October, Suvar's commission produced a torturously negotiated document to serve as a basis for discussion at the congress. With Communism crumbling across the continent, the LCY acknowledged the obvious: that "the existing model of Socialism" did not have a suitable answer to serious political and economic crises. The document suggested the right to organize political groups within—or outside—the official popular front organization, the Socialist Alliance, but added confusingly that "it was not necessary to reproduce the bourgeois political party" system. The Yugoslav federation, self-management, and the Communist Party's leading role were not to be touched.[16]

Events were rapidly moving beyond the control of the cautious bureaucrats who dominated the LCY, though. By the time the extraordinary congress met in January 1990, the Berlin Wall had fallen and Communist regimes had been swept away throughout Eastern Europe. In Slovenia and Croatia, the party organizations had responded to the events elsewhere in Eastern Europe by scheduling multiparty elections in their republics for the spring of 1990.

Milosevic, however, was not to be deflected from his chosen course by the collapse of Communism outside his own domain. Although he had risen to power on the crest of a nationalist wave, Milosevic remained committed to one-party socialism. As late as December 1989, he told the press, "If this so-called political pluralism is used as another term to supplant Yugoslavia and Socialism, then we in Serbia are against it." Dismissing the growing appeals for introduction of a multiparty system in words redolent of the radical leftism of his wife, Milosevic alleged that freedom of association existed in Serbia and said he was against "those forms of democracy that have become obsolete even in bourgeois society, which is itself looking for new forms of democracy."[17]

The LCY Commits Suicide

The fourteenth extraordinary congress, the final meeting of the Communist Party of Yugoslavia, under whose banner Tito's partisans had fought the Nazis and ruled Yugoslavia for forty-four years, opened at Belgrade's Sava Center on 20 January 1990. Aware that he could count on the delegations from Serbia, Vojvodina, Kosovo, Montenegro, and the army as well as many individual delegates from Macedonia and Bosnia, Milosevic was confident of victory, even though the Slovenes had already made clear they would not stay in a party dominated by Serbia. When the LCY president, Milan Pancevski from Macedonia, warned Milosevic that he had heard the Slovenes were preparing to walk out, Milosevic replied, "I don't believe it. Anyway, we can continue without them."[18]

The Serbian delegation and its supporters adopted an aggressive stance throughout the session, often jeering when the Slovenes spoke and regularly outvoting their proposals. By a lopsided vote of 1,156 to 169, the Slovenes lost their most important proposal: to transform the LCY into a league of equal and independent parties. The congress also rejected a compromise proposed by a group of Croatian delegates to split the LCY into a social democratic party and a Marxist-Leninist one.

Late in the evening of the third day, Kucan rose from his seat. Shaking Pancevski's hand, Kucan headed for the exit, followed by the rest of the Slovene delegation. Some of the Slovenes shed tears as they left—to the accompaniment of catcalls from the Serbian delegation. When the hapless Pancevski asked pathetically, "What do we do now?" Milosevic strode quickly to the podium. "I propose that the congress immediately decide to continue its work," he said in a voice brittle with emotion. On the floor of the conference center, meanwhile, delegates milled about in confusion, arguing heatedly with one another.

Out of the babble, Ivica Racan, the bearded young reformer who had taken control of the Croatian party only a few weeks earlier, claimed the floor: "I demand a break for consultations. If this proposal is not accepted, our delegation will not participate any more in the decisions of the congress." Looking relieved, Pancevski gaveled an adjournment.[19]

Milosevic saw his plans collapse during the break. Delegates from Bosnia, Macedonia, and reportedly, even some from Serbia—taken aback by what had just occurred—joined the Croats in blocking Milosevic's plan to continue the work of the congress without the Slovenes. After intense discussions, Pancevski returned to the podium and announced curtly that the congress would resume sometime in the future. In fact, the LCY never met again.

Milosevic usually keeps his public emotions under tight control, but the anger on his face as the congress escaped his grasp showed that he realized that the end of the party also meant the end of his efforts to dominate Yugoslavia.

Why Is This Man Smiling?

The predominant mood in the country as the LCY committed suicide seemed to be indifference. Drnovsek, Yugoslavia's first non-Communist president, went skiing while the party congress was meeting. One man, however, seemed particularly unperturbed by the evening's events. Amid the pandemonium at the Sava Center, a smiling Ante Markovic, Yugoslavia's last and greatest prime minister, said, "The Communist Party has died but Yugoslavia will continue to exist."

In 1990, Markovic became the most popular politician in Yugoslavia, and the only one with broad appeal across the entire country, by virtue of his success in reducing Yugoslav inflation from several thousand percent annually to below zero. Markovic appealed to those—still in 1990, probably a majority—who saw Yugoslavia's future as a united and democratic country. His objective was to transform Yugoslavia into a developed, Western-style democracy with a modern, market economy. To do this, Markovic sought to enhance the stature of the federal government by amending the Constitution to allow him to run in democratic elections at the federal level. On the economic side, his program aimed at reducing the state's role to that of a regulator, requiring Yugoslav enterprises to operate without subsidies in accordance with the laws of the market, and establishing an independent and financially sound banking system.

But the Yugoslav federal government that Markovic presided over was little more than an executive agent for the republics. When Markovic saw his hopes for constitutional changes doomed by republican objections, he tried to appeal over the heads of the republican leaders to the Yugoslav people directly. Unfortunately, he waited too long. Not until August 1990 did Markovic launch a new political party, the Alliance of Reform Forces, before an enthusiastic, multiethnic crowd gathered in a field in Bosnia. Limited in its access to media and swimming against the prevailing tide of nationalist euphoria, Markovic's party won only 50 out of 735 seats in the four republican elections it contested. The party did best in Macedonia—although even there it won only 9 percent of the vote—and in Bosnia—where it gained only 5 percent of the legislative seats although its total vote was higher.[20]

Markovic also attempted to set up a new, all-Yugoslav television network to provide a vehicle for his reformist views and an alternative to the republican broadcast networks, which had turned the Yugoslav airways into a battleground of poisonous ethnic hatred. Only in October 1990 was Markovic's JUTEL able to begin broadcasting nationwide, out of a studio in Sarajevo. Hostility by the republics prevented its news program from appearing until midnight, and in many parts of the country JUTEL could not be seen at all. Milosevic refused to allow "Markovic TV" to use Serbian broadcast facilities, which reduced JUTEL in the Belgrade area to transmitting from a mobile army transmitter truck parked on a hill overlooking the capital, as if it were an underground station operating in an enemy area—which in a sense it was.

Milosevic saw Markovic as his main enemy. As early as July 1989, after Markovic had been in office only a few months, the Belgrade press was forbidden to write positively about him.[21] By the beginning of 1990, Milosevic was simply refusing to implement key elements of Markovic's reform program in Serbia. Milosevic and Jovic—who had been Serbia's unsuccessful candidate for prime minister against Markovic—spoke of trying to dump Markovic after his first year in office and replace him with Minister of Defense Kadijevic.[22]

Milosevic claimed that Markovic's program unfairly discriminated against Serbia, which conducted a large proportion of its trade via nonmonetary clearing accounts with the Soviet bloc. In fact, Milosevic opposed Markovic because the prime minister's emphasis on private enterprise and the market threatened to knock away the economic underpinnings of Milosevic's rule. Although Milosevic had made a great public show of introducing market reform in Serbia, economics for Milosevic was always subordinated to politics, which for him meant retaining power at all costs. His economic program largely consisted of ensuring that all major economic institutions and enterprises were controlled by trusted subordinates who were prepared to allow him to skim off the resources he needed to finance whatever tasks he considered a priority at the moment.

Milosevic's hostility to Markovic deepened in 1990, as it became evident that the prime minister was the major obstacle to his plans to split Yugoslavia. During an August vacation excursion, the Serb leadership discussed what to do about the challenge represented by Markovic, who they described to themselves as an agent of the United States. The Serbs decided that the way to dispose of Markovic was to bring about a collapse in the functioning of Yugoslavia's federal institutions and then to "take things into our own hands."[23] Throughout the fall of 1990, this is just what Milosevic tried to do. In October 1990, Serbia introduced heavy customs duties against goods from other republics, which had the effect of ending Yugoslavia as a unified market. In December, the Serbian assembly decided to hold back its share of funds for financing the federation. It became known after the 1990 elections in Serbia that Milosevic had resorted to what amounted to the theft of Yugoslav federal resources to help maintain an artificial sense of prosperity in Serbia. During December, the Serbian authorities had simply helped themselves to approximately $1.5 billion from the National Bank of Yugoslavia, which was used to pay salaries and pensions in Serbia on the eve of the election.

FIVE

All Serbs in One State

By 1990, it was clear that Milosevic would not become Yugoslavia's second Tito. But Milosevic is nothing if not resilient, and within weeks of the collapse of the LCY he had come up with a new strategy—to unite all Serbs living in Yugoslavia under his rule, with the full knowledge that this meant breaking up Yugoslavia and war.

On 26 March 1990, the Serbian "coordinating committee" held a secret meeting. Coordinating committees, informal bodies that existed at all levels of the Yugoslav system, consisted of key officials who met in advance to work out party positions on issues before they were adopted by the organs nominally responsible for them. The Serbian coordinating committee—most likely chaired by Milosevic, but in any case fully under his control—decided to prepare Serbia for a future in which Yugoslavia no longer existed. If agreement could not be achieved on transforming Yugoslavia into what it called a more efficient federation, the committee decided that Serbia would seek to redraw Yugoslav borders to include Serbs living in Croatia and Bosnia in a new state. Since it was already obvious that Slovenia and Croatia wanted to move Yugoslavia in the opposite direction, toward a looser confederation, the decision amounted to a covert Serb decision to attack Yugoslavia. To be ready for upcoming events, the coordinating committee agreed to begin work on a new constitution, which could be used for an independent Serbian state.[1]

Two months later, Milosevic publicly launched his new attack plan. During a 10 May visit to the Belgrade industrial suburb of Pancevo, he drew directly from the language of the xenophobic 1986 SANU Memorandum to warn that an "anti-Serb coalition" was slowing Serbia's development as a state. In the current situation, which he compared to the crisis Serbia faced on the eve of the First World War, Milosevic proclaimed that "the interests of Serbia must be above all others." Appointing himself the guardian of Serbs throughout Yugoslavia, Milosevic warned that Serbia would "not sit with folded arms" if there were any kind of violence against Serbs living outside the republic. Milosevic, turning to the situation in Serbia itself, developed the theme of internal treason that later became one of the central elements in his stance toward his Serbian opponents. He charged that some of the new political parties emerging in Serbia after the LCY's collapse were prepared to trade with the territory as well as the political and economic independence of Serbia. "Some," Milosevic declaimed, "are even traitors of their people, demanding and obtaining financial and political support from outside Serbia in order to destroy its citizens by drawing them into mutual conflicts."[2]

Five days later, Milosevic's ally, Jovic, replaced Drnovsek as the president of the collective federal presidency. Jovic's militant inaugural speech, whose tone and substance contrasted sharply with the erudite and conciliatory language habitually used by his predecessor, amounted to a declaration of war against Croatia and Slovenia, which only the month before had elected postwar Yugoslavia's first non-Communist governments. In a widely remarked breach of protocol, revealing how the passions aroused by the Yugoslav crisis were eroding the common courtesies of political life, Jovic refused to offer the traditional words of thanks to his predecessor. The other members of the presidency looked in embarrassment around the table, until Suvar, who had taken over as Croatia's representative on the presidency after his term as LCY chief expired, rose to say a few words of appreciation to Drnovsek.

Two days after Jovic's harsh speech, people on their way to work in Belgrade noticed something unusual. The city's buses and trams, usually tightly packed at rush hour, were strangely empty. Small groups of uniformed men hurried along the sidewalks. Some wore their military blouse over tattered work pants, after apparently losing a battle to fit ample civilian stomachs into long-unused uniform trousers.

Waiting until Drnovsek stepped down as president, the Yugoslav military, under Jovic's order, had mobilized reserve units to seize control of the weapons maintained throughout the country by Territorial Defense forces—part of the strategy of guerrilla resistance that Tito had adopted after the 1968 Soviet invasion of Czechoslovakia. Only in Slovenia, where a portion of the republic's Territorial Defense forces refused to hand over their weapons, did the JNA fail. Nevertheless, over a million weapons were seized, mostly small arms, but also mortars, artillery, and a few armored vehicles. The republics had been disarmed, Jovic crowed.

On 25 June, Milosevic introduced the new Serbian constitution in a speech that made explicit his threat to use the Serbian populations living outside of Serbia proper to break up Yugoslavia. He claimed that Serbs preferred to remain in a united, federal Yugoslavia, yet added that the new draft constitution had been written to provide for the option of Serbia becoming an independent state. If other republics insisted on turning Yugoslavia into a confederation, Serbia might have no other option but to seek independence, in which case revising republican borders—which Milosevic described as purely administrative—would become "an open question." Milosevic's meaning was clear: if newly elected Croatian President Tudjman proceeded with his already declared insistence on loosening Yugoslavia's federal ties, Serbia would take over the areas in Croatia where Serbs lived.[3]

Only three days later, Milosevic and Jovic had a conversation that affirmed that even a year before Yugoslavia actually disintegrated, Milosevic was prepared to use armed force to carry out his threat to redraw republican borders. Jovic told Milosevic that he and Minister of Defense Kadijevic had discussed using the military to "expel" Slovenia and Croatia—minus its Serbs—from Yugoslavia. While Jovic and Kadijevic had worried about the constitutional procedures for such action, Milosevic showed no concern for such niceties. He suggested that Jovic persuade the military to "amputate" Croatia from Yugoslavia within a week. If the JNA insisted on majority support for the move from the presidency, this could be easily obtained by simply barring the two republics to be "amputated" from participating in the vote—on the grounds that they were interested parties to the decision![4]

We Can Outsmart the Boss

Milosevic's new policy brought him into contact with Dobrica Cosic and the Serb nationalist intellectuals. On March 25, the day before the Serb coordinating committee met, Milosevic had his first long meeting with Cosic, who told him that Yugoslavia had outlived its usefulness. Writing in his diary, Cosic described Milosevic as "an intelligent person, with a strong political will." He seemed to Cosic to be "the first Serbian Communist who has a conception of economics, communication, and development," but also an "autocratic personality" who was by type "a party organizational secretary." Cosic's evaluation showed a novelist's fine eye for character, but he also made the mistake, as have many others, that Milosevic could be used, saying "He has his own opinion but he is prepared to change it."[5]

Milosevic also paid a well-publicized visit to the SANU offices, thereby legitimizing the organization that had produced the infamous Serb nationalist Memorandum.[6] A few months later, when Milosevic formed the SPS, he attracted into the new party's leadership a number of intellectuals, including Antonije Isakovic, the leading figure behind the SANU memorandum, and Mihajlo Markovic, the *Praxis* leader who had gone over to the nationalist camp.

As party chief, first of Belgrade and then of Serbia, Milosevic was not known for taking a soft line toward intellectual opponents of the Communists. But in 1988 and 1989, as Milosevic's nationalist line took on a more anti-Tito cast, a process of mutual attraction began between him and the dissident Serbian intellectuals who over the past two decades had become increasingly critical of Serbia's position within Titoist Yugoslavia. The Serbian media began to open their pages to intellectuals who had sometimes been kept out of print for decades. Even Milovan Djilas, the most famous of all Communist dissidents in Yugoslavia, acknowledged a soft spot for Milosevic, telling the newsweekly *NIN* that, "Under Milosevic I got the possibility of publishing my books."[7]

Djilas had no sympathy for the nationalist substance of Milosevic's message but many of the intellectuals newly able to publish views in the media found that the nationalism unleashed by Milosevic was a powerful vehicle for supporting their own critique of Serbia's position under the Communists.

The Serb nationalist intellectuals supplied the verbal ammunition for the ethnic warfare that Milosevic's Serbia waged against Yugoslavia's other republics. They filled the pages of the Serbian media with articles on the "blank spots" in Serbian history that had been ignored by the Communists, most of which involved accusations of injustices or mistreatment experienced by Serbs at the hands of Yugoslavia's other nationalities.

Cosic and his friends also played a major role in organizing Serbs outside of Serbia. Cosic helped found the radical nationalist Serbian Democratic Party (SDS) in Croatia and Bosnia. As leader of the SDS in Croatia, Cosic chose the relatively moderate Jovan Raskovic, a genial, bearded psychiatrist from the rugged mountains that line the Dalmatian coast. In Bosnia, Cosic turned to another psychiatrist, a Sarajevo boulevardier with a modest local reputation for poetry, named Radovan Karadzic.

In September 1990 Jovic asked to meet Cosic, who told the seeming receptive president that there was "no longer any serious reason for the existence of Yugoslavia." Cosic said that he was not interested in the struggle for power in Serbia—thereby signaling his disinclination to oppose Milosevic in the upcoming election in Serbia. Cosic said he was more concerned with "the state of the Serbs," which he said should exchange territory with Croatia so that the number of Serbs who remained in Croatia would be equal to the number of Croats who remained in Serbia. Cosic said that many people were seeking his advice and informed Jovic, in this connection, that "ethnic maps of the Serbian space (*prostor*) were being worked out, especially in Bosnia and Croatia, to clearly show the territory where Serbs were in the majority. According to the account of the meeting that Jovic penned in his diary, Cosic described a long, half-moon slice of territory from Sibenik on the Adriatic coast across the mountainous Lika district in Croatia, western Bosnia along the Sava River, to Bijelina on the Drina River and continuing south along the Drina in order to split the Bosnian Moslems from the Moslems living in the Sandjak region of Serbia. "That is the future space of Serbia," Jovic concluded about this territory, which included virtually all of the areas that the Serbs seized in Croatia in 1991 and in Bosnia in 1992.[8]

The alliance between Milosevic and the Serb nationalist intellectuals, weighted with reservations on both sides, was destined to be only temporary. The intellectuals looked down on Milosevic as a provincial and an apparatchik. They believed they could exploit Milosevic's popularity and the organizational strength of his party, and then dump him when they had achieved their objective of a non-Communist Greater Serbia. After a four-hour private meeting with Milosevic in July, Cosic gave his friends an evaluation that was typical of the way the intellectuals underestimated the Serb leader. Cosic patronizingly described Milosevic as a politician who had his own views, but was also prepared to change them—implicitly to those of Cosic and the intellectuals.[9] Milosevic, for his part, recognized that Cosic—sometimes called "the second most popular figure in Serbia" —was a potentially dangerous rival who required careful handling. In December 1990, when Milosevic got around to holding multiparty elections —making Serbia the last republic in Yugoslavia to do so—many Serb opposition figures urged Cosic to run against Milosevic. To head this off, Milosevic offered Cosic the post of speaker of the Serbian Assembly, which he said Cosic could use to "teach us how democracy should be in Serbia."[10] In the end, however, the stubbornly independent and somewhat naive Cosic preferred to sit out the elections, much to Milosevic's relief.

Krajina

The area that Milosevic and Cosic had marked for separation from Croatia was traditionally called the "Military Border" ("Vojna Krajina"). The history of the Krajina was as fierce as its rugged terrain. The Hapsburgs gave its inhabitants autonomous rights in return for the obligation to maintain military units ready to repel marauding Turks. Many, but far from all, of the Krajina frontiersmen were Serbs, resettled by the Austrians in areas depopulated by the constant border fighting between the two empires.

In World War II, the region was the scene of brutal atrocities by the fascist Ustashi puppet state that the Nazis established in Zagreb. The number of Serbs killed or expelled by the Ustashi is a hotly disputed matter, but there is no doubt that hundreds of thousands of Serbs perished and that thousands more were expelled to German-occupied Serbia. The survivors, filled with deep hatred for the Ustashi, were a fertile recruiting ground for Tito's Communist Partisan forces—one reason why Serbs throughout the postwar era were overrepresented in the Croatian Communist Party and police. After the Allied victory in 1945, the Communists exacted a fierce revenge on the Ustashi and their supporters. Thousands were killed, their bodies often dumped in remote caves.

Even in the 1970s, thirty years after the end of the Second World War, the physical and psychological scars of conflict were evident in the Krajina. Deserted villages and ruined churches were scattered throughout the hills of the region. Dangerous memories lurked just below the surface. In 1974, the first of a total of eight years in which I lived in Yugoslavia, I found myself in a restaurant in an area populated by a mix of Croats and Serbs. As the evening wore on, and the quantity of empty bottles on the tables grew, people began to sing. It started innocently enough with folk songs they had all been taught in school. Eventually, though, one Croat began hesitantly to sing a Croatian national song. Serbs quickly replied with one of their own. Instantaneously, the tension in the air became even thicker than the cigarette smoke. Two police officers appeared within minutes. The singing stopped and people hurriedly disbursed, well aware that in Tito's Yugoslavia, such songs could lead to jail sentences. It was a small yet revealing glimpse into the dark underside of Yugoslavia's history and the futile efforts of the Communists to eliminate it.

The parts of Croatia claimed by the Serbs constituted several diverse regions. In many areas, the ethnic composition of the population was heavily intermixed, and Serbs were a clear majority in only a few regions. These border regions, taken together, had a total population in 1981 of almost one million, of which about 51 percent were Croats and 30 percent Serbs. Serbs constituted about two-thirds of the Krajina heartland, centered on the poor and thinly populated mountainous districts of Lika, Kordun, and Baranija. Serbs were seldom a majority in the rich agricultural lands and prosperous small cities that dotted eastern and southern Slavonia, on the edge of the lush Pannonian plain.[11]

Political traditions were not uniform among the Krajina Serbs. The Lika long remained a bedrock of solid Communist support. By contrast, in the northern Dalmatian regions of Obrovac and Benkovac, nationalist Chetniks had been strong during the war and here the agitation from Belgrade had its greatest initial effect.

Nor were the sentiments of the Krajina centered on national revenge, at least in the beginning. Throughout the borderlands, many inhabitants simply wanted to take advantage of the new political and social space opened up by the erosion of Titoist controls. In a visit to what became the Krajina in 1990, I found Croats and Serbs alike starting to rebuild the Catholic and Orthodox churches that had been particularly targeted by both sides during the Second World War, and whose reconstruction had been discouraged by the Communists. Decades of underbrush was being cleared away from the remains of shattered stone walls. Makeshift altars, covered with freshly cut flowers, stood amid the ruins, a testament to the power of memory and faith.

The Rise of the West: Elections in Slovenia and Croatia

In April 1990, Slovenia and Croatia held the first multiparty elections in Yugoslavia since the Second World War. In Slovenia, the non-Communist DEMOS coalition took over the republican government and began a quick-step march toward independence. The Slovene Assembly on 2 July adopted by an overwhelming margin a Declaration on State Sovereignty, which included a provision that Yugoslav laws would be valid in Slovenia only to the extent that they did not contravene the Slovene Constitution and laws. On 4 October, the Slovene Assembly annulled thirty Yugoslav federal laws on such important matters as defense, the economy, and the political system. Finally, on 23 December 1990, almost 89 percent of Slovene voters expressed support for independence, and three days later, the Slovene Assembly adopted a declaration calling for Slovenia to leave Yugoslavia in six months.

Slovenia's drive toward secession aroused consternation in the rest of Yugoslavia. Jovic called the Slovene actions illegal and threatened that the presidency would use all means at its disposal—meaning the military—to enforce federal legislation. The JNA blustered its own threats and at one point briefly occupied the headquarters of the Slovene Territorial Defense forces—only to find that the Slovenes had already emptied the building of anything useful.

Milosevic, on the other hand, realized that the secession of ethnically homogeneous Slovenia would give him a freer hand to lop off the Serb-inhabited parts of Croatia. As early as August 1990, Milosevic told the Slovenes he had no objection to Slovenia deciding on independence through a referendum.[12] In January 1991, shortly after the Slovene plebiscite on independence, Drnovsek sought out Milosevic, who calmly acknowledged the right of the Slovene people to independence. Throughout the confused events of the next six months, Milosevic never wavered from this course. In February, when Kadijevic said the JNA was considering military intervention, Milosevic welcomed the prospect of a move against Croatia, but said the generals should let Slovenia go.

Tudjman and his hard-line Croatian Democratic Union (HDZ) won an overwhelming victory in April 1990 in Croatia's first multiparty elections since the Second World War. A former Partisan who rose to the rank of general in the JNA, Tudjman served two jail terms for Croatian nationalist activity. In his election campaign, Tudjman demanded that Croatia be recognized as a sovereign republic in a new Yugoslav confederation, although he stopped short of advocating outright independence.

Tudjman's victory set off alarm bells among Serbs in Croatia, who resented the steps he took to reduce the numbers of Serbs found in the Croatian government, media, and police as well as his introduction of a new constitution that defined Croatia as the national state of the Croats. Tudjman's adoption of nationalist symbols that had also been used by the Ustashi aroused visceral fear among the populace of the Serb-inhabited Krajina, where memories of World War II massacres lay just below the surface, making the people there easy targets for Milosevic's Serb nationalist propaganda.

"Log" Revolution in Croatia

The nationalist euphoria that Milosevic released in Serbia in 1988 and 1989 was not long in spreading into the Serb-inhabited areas of Croatia. On 8 July 1989, a week after Milosevic had addressed a million Serbs at the six-hundredth anniversary of the Kosovo battle, a similar celebration was held in Knin, a railroad center in the hills above the Adriatic coast that later became the capital of the breakaway "Serb Krajina." In the officers' club of the local JNA garrison, Croatian and Serbian party representatives, together with Orthodox and Catholic priests, led several hundred people in a ceremony that began with the Yugoslav and Croatian anthems and ended with a hymn to the Serb patron, Saint Sava.

That such a celebration could be held at all, let alone in a military facility, was already a sign of the major changes welling up below the surface of the Croatian political landscape, which had been frozen into immobility since Tito suppressed the Croat nationalist Maspok in 1971. Even a year earlier, party leaders in Croatia would never have deigned to appear on the same podium with religious figures or to celebrate an event so intimately connected with the national history of one ethnic group.

Outside the hall, however, was an even more unusual—and ominous—celebration. Several thousand Serbs jammed the dusty streets of Knin—some from the area, and others brought there in a steady stream of buses and cars from other parts of Croatia and Serbia. Carrying Serb flags and decked out in the usual nationalistic paraphernalia of Serb folk costumes, Chetnik hats, and Serb royalist medallions, the crowd enthusiastically waved pictures and banners celebrating Milosevic. In contrast to the restrained festivities organized by the authorities, the crowd in the streets—which included a number of the "meeting makers" familiar to anyone who had seen the Serb nationalist demonstrations in Vojvodina, Montenegro, and Serbia itself—chanted such provocative slogans as "Freedom for Cyrillic," "Who represents us in Zagreb?" and "Slobodan Come Here! We are waiting for you!"[13]

For almost a year after this event, agitation percolated gradually through the Serb-inhabited areas of Croatia. In June 1990, Milosevic laid the political and military groundwork for a Serb insurrection in Croatia. Drawing on the weapons stocks of the Serbian police and Territorial Defense forces, Mihajlo Kertes, who had become a senior official in the Serb secret police after helping organize Milosevic's yogurt revolution in Vojvodina, began the covert shipment of arms into the Serb-populated regions of Croatia.

At the end of July, over one hundred thousand Serbs held the founding session of a new Serb assembly. Raskovic described the gathering as an "unarmed rebellion," but the mood of the crowd was probably better reflected in the frequent chants, "Kill the Ustashi!" The Serbs organized a referendum in August where Krajina inhabitants were said to have voted overwhelmingly to establish their own autonomous area in Croatia. During the voting, tensions rose dramatically when the JNA was reported to have forced down two helicopters carrying Croatian police officers to Knin. When Stipe Mesic, then serving as head of the Croatian parliament, called JNA Chief of Staff Blagoje Adzic to complain, Adzic claimed that flight controllers had simply directed the helicopters to return to base because they had not filed an approved flight plan. Nevertheless, Adzic warned that the military would intervene if there was any bloodshed, which in the context was clearly aimed at intimidating any efforts by Croatia to send its forces into the rebellious Serb areas, where armed and uniformed reservists had begun to appear in the streets.[14]

In late September, Serbs briefly occupied a number of local police stations in reaction to an order by the Croatian authorities that the weapons stored there should be handed over to the republican Ministry of the Interior. Aroused Serbs felled trees to block mountain roads leading through the region to the Adriatic coast and briefly besieged a group of Croatian special police. In a provocative gesture, Jovic received a delegation of Serbs from Croatia, and the next day the federal presidency adopted a one-sided statement calling on Croatia to remove its police from the area as well as rescind the measures that it said gave rise to fear and resistance from the Serbs.

After the "log revolution," Zagreb never completely regained control of the Serb areas. Local authorities began to answer to the self-proclaimed Serbian autonomous region of the Krajina. Milan Babic, a radical dentist who was then considered close to Milosevic, took over from the moderate and somewhat ineffectual Raskovic. Self-appointed armed guards swaggered through the region's dingy towns and villages. Some were local lowlifes and others had arrived from outside the region. Serb nationalist graffiti appeared on the walls of Croat homes, and some Croat-owned shops were smashed and looted. Croats began moving out of the region.

Six months after the meeting of the Serb coordinating committee, Yugoslavia was beginning to separate along ethnic lines.

Milosevic and Tudjman

The relationship between Serbia and Croatia was always the central factor in Yugoslav politics. In the upcoming years, the Yugoslav scene was to a large extent a duel between the leaders of these two republics. Milosevic and Tudjman generally seemed to get along fine in person. For instance, after Tudjman's death, his successor, Mesic, told journalists that he had discovered a secret "hot line" between the two men, although later reports seemed to call into question the existence of the link, which Mesic claimed had been installed in Tudjman's office by Serb specialists.[15]

Unlike Milosevic, Tudjman had a firm set of core beliefs that shaped his political behavior. These were a strong belief in Croatian nationhood and an almost messianic faith in himself as the symbol of the first independent Croatian state in one thousand years.

Tudjman was born in the hill country north of Zagreb, not far from Tito's birthplace—possibly one reason why later in life he found it so natural to take over the homes, resorts, and flashy uniform styles of the Communist dictator. In 1941, Tudjman joined the Partisans together with his father and brothers, and by the end of the war had risen to the rank of colonel in the political wing. After the war, Tudjman's father became the Communist head of Zagreb, but in 1946 he was found dead, reportedly from suicide, although later in his life Tudjman professed to believe that his father had been killed by the Communists.

As a military officer, Tudjman lived for almost twenty years in Belgrade. In sharp contrast to the reclusive Milosevic, who has few interests other than politics, Tudjman—at least in his younger days—was supposedly something of a bon vivant. Tudjman was a prominent member of the Yugoslav football establishment in Belgrade and by all accounts seems to have enjoyed his years in the capital of what later became his chief enemy. During his election campaign, Tudjman set off a minor tempest when he publicly used a Serbian expression for "good luck" rather than its Croatian equivalent—a sign of just how high nationalist fevers had mounted in Yugoslavia as well as an indicator of how closely intertwined its peoples were before the split.

Tudjman's opponents in the 1990 elections included the leaders of the 1971 Croatian nationalist Maspok and the reformed Communists under Racan, who fielded an attractive slate of young candidates. Croatian intellectuals derisively called Tudjman "our Milosevic." But the Yugoslav elections of that year were about the nation, not democracy. As far as many Croats were concerned, Tudjman's nationalist credo represented Croatia's best defense against the militant Serb nationalism unleashed by Milosevic. One of Tudjman's early advisers, Zvonko Lerotic, described the 1990 ballot as "formally a multi-party election but what it really amounted to was a plebiscite in which the Croatian people voted for Croatia."[16]

After the elections, Milosevic and Tudjman locked into a spiral of confrontation in Croatia. Tudjman initially sought to enhance Croatia's position within a united but more loosely organized Yugoslavia. Milosevic, however, had already determined to use the alleged plight of Serbs as an excuse to dismember Croatia. As Slovenia moved closer to secession, moreover, Tudjman was driven to declaring Croatia's intention to seek full independence rather than remain in a rump Yugoslavia dominated by Milosevic.

Bosnia was an area where Milosevic and Tudjman could see a certain convergence of interests, though. A major difficulty with Milosevic's strategy of including all Serbs under his rule was the awkward fact that Serbs did not live contiguously in one area of Yugoslavia; parts of Bosnia that were heavily populated by Croats and Moslems intervened between Serbia proper and the Serb-inhabited regions of Croatia and Bosnia that Milosevic had his eye on. For his part, Tudjman was obsessed by the threat supposedly posed by the Moslems of Bosnia and made no secret of his belief that the western half of Bosnia belonged by right to Croatia.

Dividing Bosnia, therefore, had obvious appeals to both leaders. According to Mesic, an enthusiastic Tudjman returned from his first meeting with Milosevic in the spring of 1991 with a map detailing the Serb leader's proposal to share Bosnia along the lines of a 1939 deal called the "Sporazum."[17] In June 1991, Milosevic and Tudjman, in Izetbegovic's presence, discussed dividing Bosnia into cantons—two for the Moslems, two for the Serbs, and two for the Croats.[18] Even as late as April 1999, during the NATO bombing of Serbia, Tudjman reportedly talked with a Croatian ally about the possibility of dividing Bosnia with Belgrade in order to give Milosevic "a victory which he could show the Serbs in exchange for the lost portions of Kosovo."[19]

Tudjman and Milosevic could never consummate a deal on dividing Bosnia because they could not agree on what to do in Croatia. Milosevic's 1991 offer to divide Bosnia was meant as a kind of consolation prize for giving up Serb Krajina. Tudjman was interested, but fears that he might be willing to engage in a "grand trade" of territory in Bosnia for territory in Croatia provoked a near mutiny among his supporters.

The Milosevic-Tudjman conflict was something of a tortoise-and-the-hare contest. With no firm beliefs, Milosevic was ever the artful improviser. Lighter on his feet than Tudjman in the thrust and parry of diplomatic negotiation, Milosevic failed over the long haul. After bringing war to half the Balkans, Milosevic casually dismissed the idea of a Greater Serbia when it proved beyond his ability to accomplish. Tudjman, or the other hand, seldom wavered in his determination to create an independent Croatia under his control. When he was weak, Tudjman maneuvered skillfully to obtain international support against the Serbs. When he was strong, Tudjman struck the Serbs with equal brutality although greater skill and decisiveness than Milosevic ever displayed.

All Serbs in One State : 119

Milosevic and the JNA

The JNA was the most formidable barrier that Milosevic and other republican leaders faced in pushing Yugoslavia toward disintegration. In a 10 July 1990 speech to Partisan veterans, JNA Chief of Staff Adzic sought to rekindle the flagging sense of Yugoslav national unity based on the victorious Partisan struggle during the Second World War. He affirmed that "Yugoslavia is not a slogan or an artificial creation that can be destroyed like a house of cards. Yugoslavia lies in the hearts and minds of millions of its citizens, and every inch of its territory is drenched with the blood of its patriots." Adzic warned, "We will not allow the SFRY to be cut up and disintegrate; nor will we permit our nations and nationalities to be pushed into a civil war."[20]

Senior JNA leaders had been directly touched by ethnic violence in the Second World War. Both of Adzic's parents were murdered by the Ustashi. Minister of Defense Kadijevic, a Serb from the rugged Imotski region of Dalmatia, had witnessed ethnic violence as a young Partisan soldier. Listening to these officers during meetings with U.S. officials in 1990 and 1991, it was impossible not to be impressed by their obviously sincere fear of the bloody ethnic war that both saw as the inevitable consequence of Yugoslavia's breakup.

As subsequent events showed, the JNA was correct in its fears of disintegration and civil war. The problem was that the cure the generals proposed—a return to the old-time socialist religion—was hopelessly out of step with the times and actually helped make the breakup more likely. Perhaps the best proof of the JNA's combination of accurate analysis of some of the dangers facing the country with an overall retrograde political stance can be seen from a secret document that its political directorate prepared and distributed to all officers toward the end of January 1991. According to versions leaked to the Yugoslav media, the JNA believed that socialism was not defeated in Yugoslavia and that the USSR would survive despite reform trends "leading to perdition." "Scenarists" in the West were said to be seeking to destroy socialism in Yugoslavia, even at the price of breaking it up. The document outlined three steps to solve the Yugoslav crisis: reform the economy, make the federal government structure more effective, and most important, it was said, transform the League of Communists–Movement for Yugoslavia (LC–MY)—a newly formed successor to the defunct LCY in which Milosevic's wife was a leading figure—into the main political force in Yugoslavia.[21]

Despite its profound unhappiness with developments in Yugoslavia, the

JNA could never bring itself to stage a coup. The JNA hierarchy was aware that one-sided intervention would split the army and thereby increase the risk of conflict. The cautious military leaders also had an intrinsic respect for forms of legality, which prevented them from acting without the constitutionally required approval from the presidency.

The Slovene member of the collective presidency, Drnovsek, crossed swords with the JNA leaders on many occasions, but nevertheless apparently ended up with a grudging respect for them. He described Kadijevic as "an intelligent and well-informed man," capable of surprising liberalism in his economic views as well as accepting the multiparty system as a rational and logical necessity of the times. Drnovsek concluded that what primarily motivated Kadijevic and his colleagues was a desperate desire to avoid developments they saw as driving Yugoslavia toward a repetition of the bloodshed of the Second World War, but that the only way they could conceive of doing this was through a solution that would leave Yugoslavia intact and socialism in power.[22]

Even though Prime Minister Markovic shared the JNA's commitment to preserving a united Yugoslavia, the military could never bring itself to back Markovic wholeheartedly because he also wished to transform Yugoslavia into a democracy. Gossiping with the Serb leadership during a vacation excursion on the Adriatic coast, Kadijevic labeled Markovic "a son of a bitch" and regretted that the JNA had, as he saw it, "saved" Markovic on several occasions.[23]

Before his rise to power, Milosevic never showed much interest in the military. Once Milosevic decided to seize power, he understood that he would need the army on his side. He lost no opportunity in 1987 and 1988 to make favorable references to then Yugoslav Minister of Defense Admiral Mamula. In the main, though, Milosevic opted for "discreet courtship"— avoiding any criticism of the army itself as well as discouraging it among his staff, associates, and the Serbian media.[24]

For its part, the JNA leadership had a complicated relationship with Milosevic. Many of the top military leaders were Serbs. Even before Yugoslavia's breakup, the JNA's penultimate chief of staff, General Stevan Mirkovic, who joined Milosevic's wife in the leadership of the LC–MY, glowingly described Milosevic to me as Serbia's "leader," using the word *vozd*, which Yugoslavs applied to Tito and Stalin.

Despite the sentimental factors pulling them toward Serbia, the JNA leaders had few illusions about Milosevic. In February 1990, the JNA initially resisted Milosevic's almost hysterical demands for military intervention against Albanian demonstrators in Kosovo, prompting a threat by Milosevic to publicly announce that Serbia's interests were not being protected. Later, after the JNA had agreed to move into Kosovo, Adzic lambasted Jovic for the Serbian policy of removing Yugoslav-oriented Albanian leaders such as Vllassi as well as for "mistake after mistake" with Croatia and Slovenia.[25]

Although the generals had reservations about Milosevic, they saw the leaders in the other republics as even worse. In the late 1980s, the JNA's ham-handed response to irreverent actions by young Slovene "alternative" groups, which questioned many socialist shibboleths and also attacked the generals on some specific military issues such as conscientious objection, helped radicalize Slovene opinion. The JNA was correct in its analysis of the dangers posed by Slovene secession, yet the military was unable to come up with any strategy for stopping it. As the Slovenes steadily chipped away at their ties to the Yugoslav federation, the JNA hierarchy discussed military intervention on several occasions, but could never make up its mind to move. In June 1990, Kadijevic told Jovic that the JNA was considering arresting Kucan, who Kadijevic claimed had once been a military intelligence agent, although like other threats of military action, this eventually trickled away into nothing.[26]

But it was Tudjman's HDZ regime, which the JNA viewed as a modern reincarnation of the murderous Ustashi, that really made the generals see red. Kadijevic and Adzic were both intelligent men, but during meetings with foreigners, when the subject turned to Tudjman and the HDZ, they seemed to lose all sense of perspective. After Tudjman's election, the JNA devoted most of its energies to an ultimately unsuccessful effort to unseat him, which had the inevitable countereffects of radicalizing the Croats and, in turn, driving the military step-by-step closer to Milosevic.

The JNA viewed Jovic's accession to the post of president in May 1990 as an opportunity to move against the offending republics. The 17 May seizure of Territorial Defense weapons was supposed to have been part of a much more sweeping military operation that never came off because the JNA got cold feet at the last minute. Throughout 1990, the JNA toyed with plans for military intervention. Kadijevic told Jovic in September that the JNA would be ready to intervene in Croatia and Slovenia in the fall, and in October, Kadijevic claimed that the JNA had drawn up a plan to "get rid of" one hundred people, after which "everything would be fine." By then, however, Jovic had lost patience with the JNA, which he viewed as vacillating and disoriented.[27]

The JNA's on-again, off-again plans for intervention were intended to hold Yugoslavia together as a united state, which by mid-1990 ran directly counter to Milosevic's aims. Despite its innate sympathy with the Serbs in Croatia and its anger at Tudjman, the JNA leadership was still unwilling to openly support the breakaway activities of the Croatian Serbs. At the end of September, the JNA refused to go along with Serbian appeals that it intervene to "protect" Serbs in Croatia during the log revolution. Kadijevic stubbornly refused Milosevic's demands as late as the end of January 1991 for military protection for the Serbs in Croatia, saying that he would not allow the military to be seen as "Serb."[28]

In early January 1991, the JNA attempted to force through the presidency a decision requiring the disarming of both the illegal Serbian paramilitary groups and the militarized Croatian police units that were being covertly armed with foreign weapons. Milosevic, not surprisingly, reacted with outrage to the JNA's proposal since most of the weapons in the hands of the Serbs in Croatia had been sent there from Serbian stocks. According to Jovic, Milosevic "blew his top" when Jovic reported to him that the presidency had agreed that both sides would turn in their weapons, prompting the usually loyal Jovic to ask Milosevic directly whether he wanted bloodshed over a matter that might be resolved peacefully. Three days later, Milosevic was relieved when the agreement collapsed. "Excellent," an excited Milosevic replied when told that the Croats had threatened to secede if their police weapons were confiscated. He told Jovic and Kadijevic that Croatian secession should be promptly accepted—provided that Krajina would be held onto militarily.[29]

Despite efforts at the top to maintain some semblance of evenhandedness, Tudjman's election victory persuaded a number of younger JNA officers to swing over to more active support of the Serbs. In the summer of 1990, a small group of military officers—including a young colonel named Ratko Mladic—began to meet informally over dinner to discuss plans for the future. The group, which reportedly came to be known as the Military Line (Vojna Linija), was said to have put together a plan—called RAM (meaning "frame" in Serbo-Croatian)—that included prepositioning weapons and ammunition, and creating underground organizations in areas of Croatia and Bosnia claimed by the Serbs. By 1990–1991, the United States was aware that groups in the military had secretly begun planning operations in Croatia and preparing maps of territory to be seized that roughly approximated the borders of the Krajina para-state that the Serbs carved out of Croatia the following year.[30]

The JNA reacted to the failure of its efforts to collect weapons in Croatia with what amounted to a public declaration of war on the Croatian leadership. It released a covertly prepared television film documenting the import of illegal weapons from Hungary and issued an arrest warrant for Croatian Defense Minister Martin Spegl, who was shown in the film discussing what appeared to be potential terrorist actions against JNA soldiers and their families stationed in Croatia. The JNA detained four low-level Croat police officials, but an incensed Tudjman—who had learned about the JNA film as he was returning from a tense presidency meeting in Belgrade—refused to hand over Spegl. From that point on, cooperation between the military and Zagreb was impossible, and escalating tensions pulled the military deeper into local conflicts in Croatia on the side of the Serbs.

On 2 March, Jovic sent JNA units into the Croatian hamlet of Pakrac after clashes broke out when 150 Croatian special police entered the town in a bid to regain control of the local police headquarters, which had been seized by police loyal to the Krajina Serb authorities. For the first time, there was a brief exchange of fire between the JNA and Croatian forces. The JNA interposed itself between Croatian police and local Serb forces at the end of March after a clash in the beautiful Plitvice Lake National Park left dead on both sides. In each incident, the JNA's intervention, although ending the violence, had the practical effect of leaving rebellious local Serbs in control of the terrain.

Multiparty Milosevic

Aversion to anything that smacks of genuine democratic choice is one of the most persistent legacies of Milosevic's Communist background. Milosevic fears the uncertainty inherent in elections because he cannot conceive of allowing anything to threaten his hold on power. During the 1990 elections in Serbia, when I visited the polling place just around the corner from Milosevic's home in the swanky Belgrade district of Dedinje shortly before Milosevic was scheduled to vote, I noticed that the ballot box, which was supposed to be sealed to prevent tampering, was actually open and hinged at the bottom. Apparently Milosevic's election managers did not want to risk the embarrassment of having the president lose in his own precinct, which could have easily happened in Dedinje, home to many of Belgrade's cranky intellectual and cultural elite.

Milosevic and his followers in Serbia were among the most resistant in Yugoslavia to allowing alternative political groups. In November 1989—

around the time the Berlin Wall was falling, and after Croatia and Slovenia had scheduled multiparty elections—several members of the Association for a Yugoslav Democratic Initiative, an antinationalist human rights group composed of intellectuals from around the country, were charged with disturbing the peace in Belgrade for holding a protest vigil against the staged elections of December 1989 in which Milosevic ran for president against several carefully selected nonentities. At that time, Ratomir Vico, a member of the Serbian party presidency, announced that Serbia in the future might consider allowing opposition political parties, but only if they were "socialist."

In June 1990, Milosevic abandoned efforts to re-create the LCY—six months after the Slovenes walked out of its last congress—and decided to form what amounted to a successor to the LCS, called the Socialist Party of Serbia (SPS). Milosevic's new party inherited all of the Communists' material resources, including buildings, bank accounts, and vehicles. Even more important, it took over the Communists' network of members in key media, governmental, and economic positions in Serbia.

In the same month that the SPS was founded, Serbia experienced its first opposition political rally, when as many as seventy thousand people gathered in front of the *Politika* newspaper office to protest Milosevic's media manipulation. The police dispersed the crowd with nightsticks after Milosevic's picture was burned on the pavement, leading many to ask sarcastically what had happened to the pledge that Milosevic made to Serbs at Kosovo Polje that no one would beat them anymore. Milosevic was taken off guard by the size of the demonstration and vehemence of its slogans. "Who are those people who gathered there?" he is reported to have remarked.[31]

Fifty-five political parties registered for Serbia's first multiparty elections, held in December 1990. Some of the parties tried to prove their credentials by taking the names of leading prewar political parties, such as the Radical Party led by Nikola Pasic, Serbia's prime minister during the First World War. For the most part, though, the Serbian opposition was a mélange of competing egos and unfulfilled ambitions. Some prominent Serbian intellectuals were rudely surprised when they found that towering academic reputations did not necessarily translate into electoral support. Others enjoyed the proverbial fifteen minutes of notoriety before dropping quickly back into obscurity—sometimes hurried on their way by the tactics of Milosevic's secret police. A well-known Belgrade attorney promised that I would be his first diplomatic guest after he became the next Serbian president. The attorney seemed to believe the elections a mere formality—until he vanished from the political screen after Milosevic's followers leaked material about his alleged sexual preferences.

Conspicuously absent from the Serbian political spectrum was a major party not tainted by extreme nationalism. In the prevailing atmosphere of national euphoria, most of the Serb opposition parties competed in trading accusations about which was the better defender of Serb national interests and which could invent the more extravagant examples of how the Serbian people had been victimized by the Communists, the Vatican, and world history in general.

The most prominent figure in the Serbian opposition was Vuk Draskovic, a former journalist who had made a reputation in the mid-1980s with historical novels that for the first time treated Tito's World War II Chetnik opponents with sympathy. Draskovic's unkempt hair and flowing beard made him look like a cross between a biblical prophet and Balkan bandit, but he was a fiery speaker and the only genuinely charismatic figure among the Serbian opposition. During a snowy rally in downtown Belgrade on the eve of the elections, Draskovic extravagantly predicted that Milosevic would suffer the same fate experienced a year earlier by Nicolae Ceauşescu in Romania.

Milosevic used all the financial, administrative, and media resources at his disposal against the opposition. The Serb media seldom referred to the activity of the opposition parties other than in derogatory terms. When protests from Cosic, among others, finally forced Milosevic to adopt an ostensibly more evenhanded approach, Belgrade Television allowed each party an hour of time to state its views. Major parties, such as Draskovic's Serbian Renewal Movement (SPO in its Serbo-Croatian acronym), shared the screen with fringe groups such as the Beer Lovers party, which many suspected of being government plants. In 1991, the head of Serbia Radio-Television (RTS) publicly acknowledged its bias during the elections. "We did a good job in the election campaign with regard to the SPS victory, and that is clear—I think that is clear, more than clear, to everyone."[32]

Milosevic also showed himself to be an effective campaigner. Leaving the opposition to squabble about who was the best Serb, and secure in the awareness that no one was going to challenge his own nationalist credentials, Milosevic shifted to the center. In a September speech in Pirot, Milosevic had the audacity to complain that Serbs were devoting too much attention to the past. But Milosevic never let his listeners forget who was really standing up for Serbia. In a November speech at the mining center of

Bor, he accused the opposition of "hiding in their mouse holes" while Serbia was being defended.

The results were predictable. Milosevic won 65 percent of the vote in the race for president. Draskovic, his closest competitor, took only 16 percent. Milosevic's sps won an overwhelming 196 of the 250 seats in the national assembly. Draskovic's spo was the largest opposition party, with only 16 seats. Markovic's Alliance of Reform Forces gained only 2 percent of the vote, marking the effective end of the prime minister's political hopes.

After the election, Milosevic said that he expected mutual accusations and hatred to disappear from the media, and with only slightly more realism, also urged political parties to clean the streets of their posters and other detritus of the campaign.

In some respects, Milosevic's victory was less substantial than it first appeared. Although there was no doubt of Milosevic's personal popularity, the sps gained less than half of the total votes cast. The party owed its overwhelming win in the Assembly to the first past the post electoral system and the broad distribution of its votes throughout the country—a result of the organization and voter recognition it had inherited from the old League of Communists. The opposition, by contrast, was divided and its strength tended to be concentrated in a few areas. Two-thirds of the seats taken by the opposition came from multiethnic Vojvodina—with its large Hungarian minority—and in downtown Belgrade—with its concentration of middle-class, well-educated voters.[33]

Milosevic also benefited from the patriarchal and conservative traditions that underlay Serbia's political culture. For example, Draskovic once described meeting a Serbian peasant who expressed great enthusiasm for him. Draskovic thanked him for his support, and the peasant replied that as soon as Draskovic became president, he would be sure to vote for him! Milosevic also skillfully manipulated the anxiety about the future that was everywhere in Serbia, as in the rest of Yugoslavia. The sps slogan, "With Us There is No Uncertainty," highlighted the notion of stability and continuity.

The Final Agony Begins

As 1991 began, Milosevic's drive to destroy Yugoslavia moved into high gear. Throughout the spring of 1991, while Milosevic was publicly mouthing support for a united, federal Yugoslavia, what he was actually doing was undermining Yugoslavia every way he could.

Milosevic found an ally in the Slovene leadership, well on its way to creating the first truly democratic state in the Balkans, but also locked into a trajectory for secession in June 1991. The Slovenes dragged in their wake Tudjman's Croatia, which was unwilling to stay in Yugoslavia without Slovenia, although also painfully aware that the smoldering rebellion the Serbs were preparing in Krajina—with the growing cooperation of the JNA—would burst into flames as soon as Croatia followed Slovenia out the door. Caught in the middle were Bosnia and Macedonia, unwilling to remain in a Milosevic-dominated rump "Serboslavia," but also unable—as yet—to contemplate independence.

On 24 January, the tacit Serb-Slovene alliance became explicit. After Kucan met Milosevic in Belgrade, the two republics issued a joint statement asserting that self-determination should be respected for all nations in Yugoslavia. Serbia acknowledged the right of the Slovene people to follow their own path. Slovenia conceded that Yugoslavia should respect the right of the Serbian nation to live in one state. The import of the agreement was clear. Milosevic announced his readiness to let Slovenia leave Yugoslavia, while the Slovenes gave Milosevic carte blanche to create a Greater Serbia out of the wreckage.

The Croats were furious, understanding full well that they were the real targets of Milosevic's deal with Kucan. On 12 February, the Croatian and Slovenian leaderships met at the charming castle of Otocec, on an island surrounded by the green and swiftly flowing Krka River, to try to repair the damage. Afterward, Tudjman told the press that if Yugoslavia disintegrated, Croatia and Slovenia had agreed to seek international arbitration. Tudjman announced four days later that Croatia "cannot remain in Yugoslavia without Slovenia." His statement had the effect of penciling war onto the Yugoslav calendar of upcoming events for 25 June, the day that Slovenia—now to be accompanied by Croatia—had announced its secession.

Republican Presidents Try to Save Yugoslavia

During February 1991, the leaders of the country's six republics began a series of meetings aimed at coming up with a compromise solution on the future structure of a new Yugoslavia. The first round was held in Sarajevo on 22 February. At its conclusion, Alija Izetbegovic—a Moslem who two months earlier had been chosen Bosnia's president after the republic's first multiparty elections—made an optimistic-sounding statement. Since neither the federal solution favored by the Serbs nor the alliance of sovereign states favored by Croatia and Slovenia had prevailed, Izetbegovic said there would be a new approach: an asymmetrical federation. Slovenia and Croatia would, if they wished, maintain loose ties with the four remaining republics that would be linked in a new federation.

Three days later, Izetbegovic had to backtrack. Criticized by Moslem hard-liners for seeming to signal a willingness to remain in a rump Yugoslavia, Izetbegovic announced that a sovereign and independent Bosnia was a prerequisite for an asymmetrical federation. If Slovenia and Croatia left Yugoslavia, Izetbegovic said, Bosnia would have to decide its future status through the republican Assembly or a referendum. Since it was already clear that Serbs would not voluntarily stay within an independent Bosnia, Izetbegovic's statement meant—in the Rube Goldberg structure of Yugoslavia—that war was also inevitable in Bosnia. Only the date of its outbreak remained to be decided.

In another harbinger of future conflict, after the talks in Sarajevo, Milosevic visited Radovan Karadzic—apparently the first meeting between the two men. Although Milosevic made no statement to the press, Karadzic was characteristically open and effusive. The Bosnian leader said he had given Milosevic a mandate to represent Serbs in Bosnia and gushed, "We are amateurs; perhaps talented, some even brilliantly talented amateurs. Only Slobodan Milosevic is a real statesman who could lead the country."[34]

Over the next three months, the Yugoslav republican leaders met in a series of lakeside, seaside, and mountain resorts, whose beauty and diversity was a silent testimony to the richness of the country its leaders were in the process of destroying. Milosevic continued to insist throughout the meetings on a more efficiently organized federal structure for Yugoslavia, which he knew the Slovenes and Croats would never accept. The latter two republics, for their part, held firm to the concept of an asymmetrical confederation, which was unacceptable to Serbia and probably unworkable in any case.

The two opposing camps also differed in what they wanted to do if the talks failed. Slovenia and Croatia said that if there were no agreement on a future Yugoslavia, they intended to secede and form sovereign, independent states within their existing republican borders. The Serbs, by contrast, insisted that any republic that wished to secede must hold a referendum to determine whether members of other Yugoslav nations living there wanted to remain part of the seceding republic or retain their links with Yugoslavia. The Serbs also maintained that members of a minority in one republic should have the right to hold their own referendum—to avoid being outvoted by the majority nation in the seceding republic. Since Slovenia was ethnically homogeneous—and Milosevic had in any case already told the Slovenes they could go—what the Serbs were saying was that if Croatia and Bosnia wished to leave Yugoslavia, Serbs in those two ethnically mixed republics had the right to vote their preference in separate referendums.

On the surface, the Serb position had merit. The model that the Serbs proposed for a federal Yugoslavia was a much more sensible structure than either the decentralized hybrid bequeathed by Tito or the awkward constructions proposed by Slovenia and Croatia. It provided for a democratically elected, bicameral Yugoslav federal assembly, with one chamber elected on the principle of one-person, one-vote, and a second in which republics would be represented equally and certain key decisions taken on the basis of consensus.

There was also some justice with respect to the Serb position on self-determination. If Croats and Slovenes were seeking for themselves the right of self-determination, why should Serbs not have the same right? The Serb argument was especially strong in Croatia, where the Serb population could justifiably claim to be uneasy about living in an HDZ state that flaunted Croat supremacy, and flirted with abhorrent Ustashi symbols and sympathies.

But the Serb case was undermined by the aggressive methods Milosevic used to pursue it. Had Milosevic been willing to allow an honest referendum under international supervision, there is little doubt that Serbs in Croatia and Bosnia would have voted overwhelmingly in favor of joining Serbia. The international community, which in the early days of the Yugoslav crisis had little sympathy for Tudjman's Croato-centric rhetoric or Izetbegovic's flirtations with Islamism, would have been hard-pressed to reject Serb demands to create a new state if they had been expressed through a peaceful and honest vote.

But the peaceful route to self-determination was not open to Milosevic as long as he was determined to hold onto Kosovo by force. Milosevic was not prepared to grant Kosovo Albanians the same right to live in their own state that he demanded for Serbs in Croatia and Bosnia. Kosovo, the generator of the crises that led to Yugoslavia's disintegration, was thus also the source of the ethnic wars that followed.

March 9 Rally in Belgrade

On 9 March 1991, Vuk Draskovic led an opposition rally that briefly turned downtown Belgrade into something approaching a war zone, beginning a dramatic week that shook Milosevic's hold on power more dangerously than ever before. To defeat the challenge, Milosevic persuaded the JNA to send tanks into downtown Belgrade—the first time that the clatter of steel treads on pavement had been heard in Yugoslavia's capital since the Second World War—and issued what amounted to an open declaration of war on the rest of Yugoslavia.

The authorities banned the rally, which was organized to protest the blatant manipulation of the media during the Serb election campaign, and deployed police on the roads outside Belgrade to turn away out-of-town contingents. Yet the police did nothing to block thousands of people from walking into the center of town, a suspicious lapse that led some to conclude later that the Serbian authorities had actually wanted the rally to go forward to stage a provocation.

On that sunny spring morning, I watched as the rally began with several thousand demonstrators milling about Belgrade's Republic Square shouting anti-Milosevic slogans and singing long-banned Chetnik songs. In the background could be heard the low rumble of diesel engines, but when Vuk appeared on the balcony of the National Theater overlooking the square, a huge roar of approval went up from the crowd. Shortly after he began speaking, columns of helmeted riot police, backed by armored vehicles and water cannons, emerged from several side streets and pitched into the throng without warning or provocation. As powerful streams of water swept the crowd from several directions and tear gas drifted across the square, the police advanced behind their shields, the dull thud of truncheons slamming against human flesh and bone audible over the noise of the melee.

Far from retreating, the crowd fought back with vigor. Many of the tough-looking young men who stood in the front ranks of the demonstrators had brought clubs or other weapons with them. Senior figures in Draskovic's SPO, who maintained close contacts with the Belgrade criminal underworld, had recruited these hard-nosed "political activists," many of whom later joined the paramilitary Serbian guard that Draskovic sent into the fighting in Croatia.[35] With their leader shouting from the balcony, "Charge the Bastille!" Draskovic's followers seized water hoses and used them to sweep the police off their feet, while others stripped them of their riot gear and sometimes their weapons. Police cars were smashed and set ablaze, and some demonstrators attempted to immobilize armored vehicles by jamming chairs and tables snatched from nearby open-air restaurants into their treads.

By midday, central Belgrade belonged to Vuk. One large group of demonstrators moved toward the headquarters of Belgrade Television, where the staff was issued automatic weapons—never used—as a police cordon managed to keep the protesters at bay. Draskovic led another group into the Serbian Assembly building, from where he challenged Milosevic to meet him and threatened to form a "government of national salvation" that evening. Demonstrators overturned buses and trolleys to serve as barricades. In the streets around central Belgrade, the smoke from burning vehicles mingled with clouds of tear gas. Shopwindows were smashed and some demonstrators helped themselves to the goods on display.

Late in the afternoon, I was standing at one of downtown Belgrade's major intersections, watching a group of young demonstrators enthusiastically overturn and torch an abandoned police car. Down a hilly street about two hundred yards away, a small group of police watched with apparent indifference. Suddenly and without warning, they dropped to their knees and began to fire automatic weapons. As bullets zipped overhead, the crowd scattered in a panic, shouting, "They're shooting at us; they're killing us!" A young student nearby clutched his throat and fell, mortally wounded, to the ground. Blood splattered across the pavement.

As darkness fell, a hard-core remainder shouted angry slogans as they marched past the Ministry of Defense building, but it looked as if the demonstration was winding down. Dozens of JNA armored vehicles suddenly appeared and hundreds of fresh riot police moved in behind them, beating anyone in their path, including me when I tried to stop police from beating a young woman who had fallen to the pavement. Draskovic was arrested inside the assembly building, and within a couple of hours the streets of Belgrade were quiet.

For the first time facing a serious public challenge—and possibly believing that Draskovic might actually intend to carry out his threats to dispatch him and his wife the same way that the Ceauşescus had left the scene in Romania—Milosevic panicked. He telephoned Jovic, who was out of town for the weekend, to plead for military intervention, even though subsequent events showed there were plenty of riot police on hand to disburse the diminished crowd that remained in the streets at the end of the day. Initially unwilling to send in troops without the agreement of a majority of the presidency, Kadijevic became more amenable when the protesters rallied in front of the Ministry of Defense building. Jovic quickly telephoned other members of the presidency, gaining the approval of all but Drnovsek and Mesic. The tanks went in, and Milosevic promised to cover the formalities by sending in a written request in the morning.[36]

Once the military had acted and the streets were cleared, an obviously shaken Milosevic made a brief televised statement, calling on Serbs to oppose the forces of "chaos and madness." He said that Serbian forces would act within their constitutional powers to prevent violence, but made no reference to the tanks that people could see with their own eyes on the streets of the capital.

The next day, parents with children in hand gazed at the armored vehicles parked in front of the national assembly and other key buildings. Young conscript soldiers sat atop them in obvious embarrassment. In the afternoon, without further explanation, the soldiers started their vehicles' engines and drove away.

Milosevic seemed to have weathered the storm. Yet that evening, several thousand University of Belgrade students fought their way through a contingent of riot police guarding the bridges over the Sava River and occupied one of the city's central squares. The students demanded the resignation of the minister of the interior and top officials in the Serbian media, the opening of the media to all points of view, and the beginning of a transition to true democracy. For the next several days, central Belgrade hosted something similar to a 1960s' era political happening. Music blared from speakers set up on the square, and a steady stream of intellectual, artistic, and political personalities urged the students to keep up their nonviolent protest. Many orators recalled nostalgically their own generation's 1968 protest, when thousands of students had occupied the University until Tito sent in the police to expel them. More ominously for Milosevic, the Belgrade media began to report that sympathy for the students was growing among the workers in the Belgrade industrial suburb of Rakovica—who had earlier been among the most prominent foot soldiers in Milosevic's antibureaucratic revolution.

Milosevic was forced to compromise. Draskovic was released from jail, and both the minister of the interior, Radmilo Bogdanovic, and the head of Belgrade Radio-Television Zivorad Minovic, resigned.

In addition, Milosevic met with a delegation of the student demonstrators. It was one of the few times in his career that Milosevic entered into an event that he could not be certain in advance of controlling. Just as he had in Kosovo Polje, however, Milosevic turned in a virtuoso performance, combining equal doses of defiance and apparently sincere apology. He appeared unfazed when one of the students—to loud applause—called for his resignation. Milosevic promised an investigation into the police violence at the start of the demonstrations, compared himself favorably to Tito in

1968 by saying that he would not make promises to the students only to allow them to be broken later, and declaimed that if anyone ever caught him speaking less than the truth to Serbia he would immediately resign. When one student asked cheekily what had happened to the promise he made in Kosovo Polje in 1987 that no one would beat Serbs again, Milosevic replied that the pledge still stood, but that the Serbian people must be protected from "anarchy." At the end of the three-hour meeting, it was Milosevic's turn to receive a standing ovation. Any danger to his rule from the students was over.

"Are We Arrested?"

Being forced into the position of having to send tanks into the streets of Belgrade embarrassed the JNA and seems momentarily to have shaken the military hierarchy free from its chronic indecision. Between 12–15 March, the JNA summoned the members of the Yugoslav presidency for several pressure-filled meetings, demanding in effect that the country's top civilian leadership give the army a green light to stage a coup. Although Jovic supported the military, Milosevic had reservations about the JNA's plans. He had long since come to regard the military's efforts to hold Yugoslavia together as quixotic and possibly dangerous. Milosevic also knew the military still harbored reservations about him; months later, Adzic told Milosevic he regretted not having arrested him when it would have been possible to have done so.

On 12 March, Jovic summoned the members of the presidency to the palace of the federation on the banks of the Danube River, where they were brusquely loaded into buses and driven in the company of armed soldiers to the Ministry of Defense headquarters building in downtown Belgrade. "Are we arrested?" asked the new Croatian representative on the presidency, Mesic, who knew the drill, having already done time for Croatian nationalist activity.

At the ministry, a grim-faced Kadijevic greeted the presidency members. He described Yugoslavia as being on the brink of civil war and demanded that the presidency adopt a number of tough measures, including introducing a state of emergency throughout the country, increasing the combat readiness of the JNA, dissolving all paramilitary formations, holding a referendum in those republics that had decided on secession, and agreeing on a new constitution and multiparty elections to establish a parliamentary democracy in the remainder of Yugoslavia within six months.[37] Jovic was the only member of the presidency to express unqualified backing for introducing a state of emergency. Even Milosevic's supporters from Montenegro, Vojvodina, and Kosovo waffled. Facing a near solid front of opposition, the JNA withdrew its request for a state of emergency, yet continued to insist on all of the other proposed special measures. This proposal failed when only the four members from the Milosevic-controlled parts of the country supported it.

Kadijevic flew secretly that night to Moscow, where he asked Minister of Defense Dmitri Yazov whether the Soviet Union would protect Yugoslavia from Western intervention if the military intervened. The Soviets, who had troubles of their own, said the West would not intervene but declined to discuss military assistance.

After returning from his fruitless trip to Moscow, Kadijevic and Adzic summoned Milosevic and Jovic. According to Jovic, Adzic asserted, "We are going to stage a military coup." Kadijevic said that the JNA would mobilize to depose both the presidency and Markovic's federal executive council and ban the federal assembly from meeting. The military would then impose a deadline of six months for an agreement on Yugoslavia's future. Republican leaders would be removed if they got in the JNA's way. Jovic had no objections to the JNA's plans. He stated that he would resign if the presidency did not approve the JNA's renewed proposals, in order to give the military room to act. Milosevic listened to Kadijevic's presentation in silence, but on the way out, told Jovic enigmatically that if he resigned, he would not take Jovic's place on the presidency as he was obliged to do under the Constitution.

The sessions of the presidency continued for two more days. Jovic took an extremely aggressive position, at one point expressly calling for a military coup by maintaining that the deadlocked presidency was unable to carry out its constitutional function of commanding the armed forces and asking the military leadership to draw the appropriate conclusions. He also warned that if the army's hands were tied, the Serbian people—who Jovic falsely described as lacking arms—would appeal for the creation of a Serbian army and that the Serbian leadership would not prevent this. Other republican leaders were less aggressive than Jovic, but equally unyielding on substance. Drnovsek portrayed Slovenia as already both de facto and de jure detached from the Yugoslav federal system. He also tried to buy off the JNA by holding out the possibility that Slovenia would resume financing its share of the federal military budget. Mesic warned that if the military's proposals were adopted, Croatia would declare a general mobilization.

As the squabbling proceeded, the military leaders—despite the threatening tone they adopted, especially toward Mesic and Drnovsek—also seemed almost pathetic in their appeals for some kind of resolution. Kadijevic at one point pleaded that Slovenia and the other republics stop dragging out the process of disintegration and reach a decision on the country's future in fifteen days. When Kadijevic later commented that "the prime minister" had told him that Slovenia simply could not secede, Drnovsek at first did not understand which prime minister Kadijevic had in mind, while Jovic snarled, "Leave Markovic out of this." By then, each republic was too committed to its own path to give any consideration to the interests of the united Yugoslavia federation that Markovic represented. Neither, apparently, did anyone discuss the military's proposals for multiparty, democratic elections in six months. Given its track record, no one had any confidence in the JNA's commitment to democracy, and in any case, the debate in Yugoslavia was over the rights of nations to go their own way and not over the democratic rights of individuals.[38]

On 15 March, after three days of fruitless discussion by the presidency, Kadijevic growled angrily yet mysteriously that the JNA would assess the situation and draw the appropriate conclusions. That evening, in an emergency nationwide address, Jovic carried out his part of the bargain. He announced that he had decided to submit his resignation from the presidency, saying hypocritically that he did not want to be an accomplice in the breakup of the country.

Two days later, Jovic and Milosevic were once more summoned to Kadijevic's office. The JNA leaders told the Serbs they had decided that taking emergency measures without presidency approval risked provoking armed resistance in Croatia and foreign intervention, thereby signaling their retreat from the military coup they had promised only a few days earlier.

Jovic was seething. He pointed out to Kadijevic that he had resigned in order to give the military space to carry out its plans and that the generals must have realized before they discussed a coup that they would have to overcome resistance in Croatia. Milosevic's only question to Kadijevic—to which he received an affirmative response—was whether the military would protect the Serbian authorities if the opposition resorted to violence.[39]

Milosevic understood that the JNA's retreat removed the last obstacle to his preparations for breaking up Yugoslavia. After Jovic resigned from the presidency, Milosevic spoke to the Serbian people. Declaring that "Yugoslavia has entered into the final phase of its agony," Milosevic ordered the mobilization of Serbian police reserves and announced that additional Serb police forces would be created. Calling on all political parties in Serbia to cooperate with the authorities, Milosevic promised the defeat of "the anti-Serb coalition now hovering over our country." He concluded with words intended both as a reassurance to the Serb population and a warning to the JNA: "There is no need for emergency measures in Serbia."[40] Years later, Kadijevic acknowledged that after the fateful March presidency meetings, "it was definitely clear that from then on it would be hard to preserve Yugoslavia in her existing borders and those who wanted Yugoslavia in those borders were not making the decisions."[41] It was now Milosevic who would be giving the orders and Kadijevic who would follow them.

On 5 April, in a meeting with Milosevic and Jovic, Kadijevic and Adzic agreed that in the future, the JNA would take armed action to halt Croatian moves against local Serbs without waiting for approval from the hopelessly paralyzed presidency. In other words, the JNA no longer recognized an obligation to act under the direction of the country's legally constituted authorities and would instead begin to coordinate its actions with the Serbian leadership. As Jovic said, Serbia and the JNA had "crossed the Rubicon."[42]

On 16 March, meeting secretly with the leaders of Serbia's districts, Milosevic issued what amounted to an order to prepare for war. Milosevic claimed that the situation in Yugoslavia had changed after the dramatic events over the past few days. It was obvious that Serbia could not achieve what Milosevic said had been its objective of a strengthened Yugoslav federation. On the table now was the question of the borders of the new state that would be left behind after Slovenia and Croatia separated. "And," noted Milosevic, "borders, as you know, are always dictated by the strong and are never dictated by the weak." Milosevic described the steps he was taking to increase Serbia's military preparedness, and proclaimed that Serbia's new forces would be used to "defend the interests of our republic and also the interests of the Serb people beyond Serbia." Milosevic made it clear that he expected Croatia to secede along with Slovenia, and that when it did, he would ensure that Serbs in Krajina would simultaneously leave Croatia and join a new, smaller Yugoslav federation dominated by Belgrade. Milosevic claimed to want a peaceful solution to the crisis, but he warned that "if we have to fight, then we will fight. But I hope that there will not be too many people who want to fight with us. Because if we don't know how to work or manage the economy well, at least we know how to fight well!"

There was a subtext to Milosevic's remarks: his intention to use the climate of crisis he and Jovic had whipped up to deflect the attention of the

Serb people from the challenge to his own position that had unfolded with the 9 March demonstration and subsequent student protest. Milosevic laid out for the local leaders a vision of Serbia under assault by a hostile coalition of world powers. He claimed that a united Germany, supported by "big American capital," was aiming to put itself at the head of a new Europe that was in some mysterious fashion also seeking to restore the Austro-Hungarian monarchy. This odd coalition had already, according to Milosevic, established puppet regimes in Slovenia and Croatia, and was aiming to dismember Serbia by joining Kosovo with Albania and detaching Vojvodina and the Sandjak. Getting to the point, Milosevic contended that the demonstrations in Serbia over the previous week had been part of an international strategy to destabilize Serbia. There should be no party conflicts when Serbia's interests were at stake, Milosevic intoned. He provoked a round of applause when he ended the session with an appeal for "harmony," an allusion to the traditional Serbian fear of disunity that supposedly caused the Serbs to lose the battle of Kosovo and was embodied in the slogan seen everywhere in Serbia at the time, "Only Harmony Can Save Serbia."[43]

Borovo Selo: The Horror Begins

By spring, the Danube River border area between Serbia and Croatia had become a caldron of tension as the Serbs began to carve out zones of control intended to link Vojvodina with Krajina, which had already passed out of Zagreb's hands. The Serbian Ministry of the Interior continued to pump arms into the region, and now groups of paramilitary thugs began showing up to use them. Drawn from the dregs of Belgrade's criminal and psychopathic underworld, these booze-swilling, gap-toothed paramilitaries strutted about with shiny new weapons, often to the dismay of the local Serb population. After the incident at Pakrac, for example, a group of local Serbs had visited the U.S. embassy in Belgrade to complain that the fighting had been provoked by armed outsiders of both nationalities, and to plead with the United States to lean on Belgrade and Zagreb to stop the dispatch of more such lowlifes.

In mid-April, Gojko Susak, an émigré restauranteur who later became Croatian minister of defense, fired three missiles into the Serb village of Borovo Selo near Vukovar. On 1 May, the Serbs responded in a manner that finally stripped away the belief, until then retained by most Yugoslavs, that a descent into the savage ethnic violence of the past was impossible in the last decade of the twentieth century. Serbian irregulars, who had swarmed into Borovo Selo after Susak's attack, ambushed a group of Croat police officers, killing as many as fifteen. Horrified Yugoslav journalists who visited the scene shortly after the incident later recounted how the Serb "victors," toasting their success at a local watering hole, had described with savage, drunken glee torturing and then killing captive Croatian police officers.

Borovo Selo set off a wave of fear and hatred throughout the region. Driving nearby the next day, my family and I encountered a roadblock established by armed Croatian villagers. Asked what had happened, the Croats replied that the Serbian village down the road harbored a large number of armed "Chetniks" and they feared for their lives. Proceeding on our way, we encountered a similar roadblock outside the Serb village. When I asked why they had set up barricades, the Serbs replied that their lives were in danger from hundreds of armed "Ustashi" that had appeared in the Croat village we had just left and they expressed surprise that we had escaped unscathed.

The stage was set for the war that Milosevic had always known would accompany his plans to break up Yugoslavia.

SIX

Milosevic at War

Although Milosevic did not come to international prominence until the end of the 1980s, his own experience with the world outside Yugoslavia began much earlier. Milosevic's first recorded travel abroad was in the early 1960s, when he visited the Soviet Union with a student delegation. In the early 1970s, as director of Technogas, Milosevic must have had numerous contacts with the Soviet Union, a major supplier of natural gas to Yugoslavia.

In the late 1970s, when Milosevic served as director of Beogradska Banka, Serbia's largest financial institution, he traveled to the United States at least once a year to attend the annual meetings of the IMF and World Bank as well as to meet with the heads of major U.S. commercial banks. Milosevic appeared at ease in the world of international high finance, according to colleagues close to him at the time. He developed a good knowledge of English along with a solid working relationship with senior international and U.S. bankers. In 1982, John Scanlan, then serving as deputy assistant secretary of state for Eastern Europe and Yugoslavia, first met Milosevic—affable and seemingly comfortable with the vocabulary of international finance—working the crowd at a 1982 meeting of the U.S.–Yugoslav Chamber of Commerce in Dubrovnik.

Borka Vucic, who as vice president for International Operations at Beogradska Banka traveled with Milosevic on many of his foreign banking trips, said that Milosevic took special interest in international banking. Vucic claimed that at Beogradska Banka Milosevic tried to orient the bank's business toward the United States. She described Milosevic as instrumental in the acquisition by the Yugoslav national airline, JAT, of U.S. jet aircraft and engines and as having visited the headquarters of Boeing in Seattle and McDonnell Douglas in California. According to Vucic, Milosevic had only rudimentary English when he arrived at Beogradska Banka but he quickly improved. She described Milosevic as having "a talent for languages."[1]

When Milosevic reentered the world of Serbian politics, his financial excursions abroad ended, but he continued to try to capitalize on the reputation he had earned as an economic moderate. His team of advisers, including young, reform-oriented economists such as Mihajlo Crnobrnja, later Yugoslav ambassador to the European Community (EC), and Slovenian Professor of Economics Juri Bajec, actively worked the diplomatic and journalist circuit. When Scanlan returned to Belgrade as U.S. ambassador in 1985, he thought that Milosevic—by then serving as head of the Belgrade party committee—seemed like a breath of fresh air in comparison to other, hide-bound party functionaries.[2] In the late 1980s, as Milosevic first came to the attention of the international media, Lawrence Eagleburger, U.S. ambassador to Belgrade in the late 1970s when Milosevic was at Beogradska Banka, also recalled Milosevic as a liberal reformer.

As Milosevic's noisy, nationalist campaign unfolded, however, his efforts to portray himself as a reformer became increasingly threadbare. He turned away from his liberal advisers and relied for economic counsel on the so-called "national economists," including Kosta Mihailovic, who had written the strongly dirigiste economic section of the 1986 SANU Memorandum. Milosevic's relations with the United States became particularly difficult as his actions in Kosovo brought more human rights criticism from Washington.

In 1991, as Yugoslavia's slide toward war attracted the personal attention of high-level international statesmen—most of whom at that stage regarded Milosevic as primarily responsible for the crisis—Milosevic's international contacts were often contentious despite the personal charm that even then sometimes surprised unwary foreign visitors. After his June 1991 visit to Belgrade, U.S. Secretary of State James Baker concluded that meeting Milosevic was like talking to "a wall with a crew cut."[3] European negotiators who met with Milosevic in the early phases of international intervention into the Yugoslav crisis found him even harder to deal with. In August 1991, after Milosevic refused to attend a negotiating session aimed at brokering a cease-fire in Croatia, Dutch Foreign Minister Hans van den Broeck—then serving as chair of the EC troika—was provoked to state publicly, "We pity people who have such leaders."[4]

The End of Yugoslavia's Special Role

Milosevic's emergence onto the center stage of world politics in the late 1980s coincided with international developments that changed the way the outside world treated Yugoslavia. Ever since Tito's 1948 break with Stalin, the West had supported Yugoslavia's independent, liberal version of Communism. The end of the cold war, however, deprived Yugoslavia of its special strategic role, at the same time that dramatic developments elsewhere, such as German reunification and the Gulf War, absorbed the attention of international officials around the world.

The changing international environment had a particularly significant effect on the U.S. approach toward Yugoslavia. Throughout the postwar era, the United States and Yugoslavia enjoyed a special relationship. Although they seldom mentioned it, Yugoslav officials knew that on several occasions, the United States had provided a possibly decisive margin of assistance to Yugoslavia in standing up to the Soviet Union. Americans living or traveling in Yugoslavia generally got a friendly reception—it seemed that almost every Yugoslav had a cousin somewhere in the United States. Within the U.S. Foreign Service, Yugoslavia was regarded as a plum assignment because of its pivotal place in the Communist world.

Still, there was also something of a love-hate element to the U.S.–Yugoslav relationship. Yugoslavia's influential place in the Nonaligned Movement (NAM) often prompted it to make harsh criticisms of U.S. policies around the world, but Yugoslav officials tended to react with wounded pride if the United States presumed to question developments in Yugoslavia. Belgrade's NAM ties also led it into questionable connections with radical Palestinian terrorist groups. On one occasion, for example, Belgrade detained and then released noted terrorist Carlos the Jackal, causing a sharp crisis in U.S.–Yugoslav relations. During my tenure at the U.S. embassy in Belgrade, a Palestinian terrorist supply network was discovered in Yugoslavia, including a large cache of the deadly Semtex explosive. Yet in the final analysis, the United States was never willing to push these contentious issues to the point where they might appear to undermine U.S. willingness to support an independent Yugoslavia against the USSR.

Warren Zimmermann's arrival as the new U.S. ambassador to Yugoslavia in 1989 marked a change in the ground rules of the U.S.–Yugoslav relationship. Zimmermann prepared for his new assignment by seeking out Eagleburger, now serving the Bush administration as deputy secretary of state. The two agreed that the traditional cold war approach toward Yugoslavia no longer made sense amid the revolutionary transformations sweeping Europe. They decided that when Zimmermann arrived in Belgrade, he would take the position that although Yugoslavia remained important to the United States, it was no longer unique either in its independence from the Soviet Union or its relatively open political system. And Yugoslavia's human rights problems, which the United States had tended to gloss over during the era of cold war competition, could no longer be ignored. The United States would maintain its traditional mantra of support for Yugoslav unity, independence, and territorial integrity, but as a sign of the growing concern about prospects for Yugoslavia's future, Zimmermann got himself instructed to add that the United States would only support Yugoslavia's unity in the context of progress toward democracy and would strongly oppose unity maintained by force.[5]

Zimmermann's forthright assertions that the United States expected Yugoslavia to honor its human rights commitments shocked some Yugoslav officials. His new approach also brought him into direct confrontation with Milosevic.

Shortly after Zimmermann arrived in Belgrade, the Serbian leader invited foreign ambassadors to participate in the commemoration of the six-hundredth anniversary of the Kosovo battle. Unwilling to be "a prop in Milosevic's theatrical performance," Zimmermann declined the invitation and his gesture was followed by most European ambassadors. (The Turkish ambassador, however, told Zimmermann that as the representative of the winning side in the battle, he had an obligation to be present.)[6] Incensed by the Western boycott and blaming Zimmermann personally for it, Milosevic refused to meet with the U.S. ambassador for almost a year after his arrival. Milosevic's tantrum was a telling sign of the Serbian dictator's difficulties in dealing with independent criticism. It had no impact on U.S. policy and, if anything, enhanced Zimmermann's stature, especially in the rest of Yugoslavia. Years later, after Milosevic had become more adept at dealing with foreign diplomats, he separately told European negotiator David Owen and U.S. diplomat Richard Holbrooke that refusing to meet Zimmermann had been one of his biggest mistakes.

Milosevic's reaction to Zimmermann was an early sign of the ambiguous and shifting approach Milosevic has taken toward the United States. During his trips to the United States as a banker, Milosevic was said to have been impressed by the efficiency of U.S. institutions and the pragmatism of the American character. In power, Milosevic had a split view of the United States. He tended from the beginning to view the United States as one-sidedly critical of the Serbs and excessively sympathetic to Albanians. Toward the end of the 1990s, as Milosevic's isolation deepened, and as he came under the growing influence of his wife, Milosevic's views on the United States sharpened. He vilified Washington during the war with NATO over Kosovo as a world bully, and his propaganda machine drew explicit parallels between the United States and Nazi Germany.

At the same time, though, Milosevic was fascinated by America's position as the world's most powerful nation. Throughout the Yugoslav crisis, Milosevic generally preferred to deal with the United States rather than other, less-powerful international actors—even those nominally more sympathetic to Serbia. In late August 1991, on the eve of Serbia's acceptance of EC negotiator Lord Carrington's proposed conference on Yugoslavia, a senior Milosevic adviser tried to interest the United States in taking the lead on the crisis. The adviser told U.S. diplomats that Milosevic had little confidence in the EC because it had not required either Croatia or Slovenia to carry out their commitments under the Brioni accords. The United States, by contrast, had no territorial claims on Yugoslavia and would be a preferred mediator for Serbia.

The World Rediscovers Yugoslavia—but Too Late

A major irony of the Yugoslav crisis was the fact that the country, which played a greater role during the cold war than its size or intrinsic importance would warrant, found itself shoved to the diplomatic back burner by the end of the cold war just when it needed international attention the most. Despite repeated pleas by the U.S. embassy in Belgrade for greater engagement by Washington, Secretary of State Baker did not visit Yugoslavia until 21 June, less than a week before Slovenia had pledged to secede. In one day, Baker met twice with Prime Minister Ante Markovic, with the presidents of each of Yugoslavia's six republics, and with Ibrahim Rugova, the leader of the Kosovo Albanians. Baker and his entourage shuttled through the cavernous halls of Belgrade's federation palace for ten hours, from the office of one Yugoslav republic to another. Each was decorated with its own distinctive ethnic art, but inside each the U.S. diplomats found the same unwillingness to alter rigidly staked-out internal positions.

Baker's meeting with Milosevic was the most contentious of all. His basic message to Milosevic was the same as to all the other quarreling Yugoslav leaders: the United States believed that Yugoslavia should be transformed into a democratically renewed union and that unilateral acts or violence must be avoided. Baker warned the Serbian leader that the United

States viewed his policies as the main generator of the Yugoslav crisis. If Milosevic persisted, the United States along with the rest of the international community would reject any Serbian claims to territory beyond its borders and Serbia would become an international outcast for a generation. Milosevic stuck to his well-rehearsed script, denying the existence of human rights violations in Kosovo and disclaiming territorial ambitions. Although Baker found Milosevic on first appearance to be "a friendly charmer in a well-tailored suit," in the end he doubted that he had had any effect whatever on Milosevic or his other Yugoslav interlocutors.[7]

Drole de guerre in Slovenia

Five days after Baker left Belgrade, Slovenia left Yugoslavia. Although both the Serbs and the JNA had previously told the Slovenes they could go, Ljubljana's secession triggered a brief, confused conflict. The Slovenes won through the skillful use of their Territorial Defense forces to harass lumbering JNA columns composed of confused, frightened, and sometimes unarmed conscripts, and by their even-more-skillful manipulation of the media to create the impression of a plucky Slovenian David standing up to a brutal JNA Goliath.

At the time of the conflict in Slovenia, it was widely thought that Milosevic supported the army's use of force. It fact, the opposite was true. Five days before the war, the Serb and Montenegrin leaderships—believing Slovene secession to be inevitable—agreed to demand that the JNA "conduct a redeployment of the military along the new Serbian borders of Yugoslavia." When the Serbs and their Montenegrin fellow travelers met the military leadership, they found to their surprise that Kadijevic, possibly swayed by Baker's resolute stand in defense of a federal Yugoslavia, was urging them to help Markovic save Yugoslavia. The Serbs—who had long since lost any interest in Yugoslavia or Markovic and who thought they had brought Kadijevic into their camp—were stupefied.[8]

On 27 June, the day JNA units seized Slovenian border posts, Milosevic and Jovic again insisted that the military pull back to the future borders of the Greater Serbian state they intended to create. A week later—with the JNA now facing defeat in Slovenia—the pair demanded that the JNA bomb Slovenia—to raise military morale, frighten Croatia, and appease the Serbs—and then immediately withdraw to a line in Croatia that would cover the territory where Serbs lived. Otherwise, Milosevic and Jovic warned, they would lose in Serbia, which would lead inevitably to the military's collapse. Kadijevic now agreed that a pullout from Slovenia was inevitable, but begged pathetically for help in organizing a "For Yugoslavia" rally—in Sarajevo—to encourage JNA soldiers, who were deserting in droves.[9]

The Hour of Europe Comes—and Goes

The descent of the Yugoslav crisis into open warfare coincided with a new feeling of European self-confidence. The end of the continent's cold war divisions and the tighter institutional arrangements of the Maastrict treaty convinced European political leaders that the old continent was finally in a position to play a role in international diplomacy commensurate with its already strong economic clout. In early July 1991, Dutch Foreign Minister van den Broeck visited Washington shortly after the Netherlands assumed its six-month position as the president of the EC Council of Ministers. Van den Broeck breezily told skeptical yet relieved U.S. officials that the United States had done a good job in the Gulf War, but that Yugoslavia was part of Europe, and thus Europe would take the lead in solving its own crises.

Europe's peacemaking diplomacy ran into trouble from the start. The EC helped end the fighting in Slovenia at a meeting of Yugoslav leaders held at Tito's luxurious island retreat of Brioni, but the practical effect of the Brioni accord was to ratify Slovene independence and transfer the war to Croatia. During the talks in Brioni, the Slovene Drnovsek and the Serb Jovic quietly agreed on pulling the JNA out of Slovenia. On 18 July, Serbia and its satellites joined Slovenia in ramming the withdrawal decision through the presidency, over the objections of Ljubljana's erstwhile Croatian allies as well as Bosnia and Macedonia, which knew that they were next on Milosevic's list of victims.

Brioni represented a triumph for the policy that Milosevic had been pursuing for more than a year. With Slovenia out of Yugoslavia for all practical purposes, Milosevic was free to turn his attention to Croatia. A few days after Brioni, Ambassador Zimmermann found Milosevic "burbling with triumph." He blithely declared, "Who cares?" when asked what would happen if Yugoslavia broke up. By reiterating that Yugoslavia's republican borders were purely administrative and subject to change, Milosevic made it clear that he still intended to carve up Croatia. Milosevic also noted expansively that he would have no objection if the Croatian population in the Bosnian region of Hercegovina joined Croatia, revealing that the division of Bosnia, which he and Tudjman had already discussed on at least two occasions, remained very much on his mind.[10]

War for Real in Croatia

After its humiliation in Slovenia, the JNA was spoiling for a fight in Croatia. Over the summer of 1991, the JNA, assisted by Serb paramilitary units, launched attacks over an area that included one-third of the Croatian territory. In Dalmatia, Serb forces reached the outskirts of the major Adriatic ports of Sibenik and Zadar. At the other end of the border Serbs besieged Osijek, located on the edge of the Panonian plain. Heavy fighting devastated the approaches to Karlovac, an ancient garrison town that had been the headquarters of the Hapsburg military border and was only a thirty-minute drive along a modern superhighway from Zagreb. In between, the entire region dissolved into a confused, swirling pattern of violence that pitted village against village and neighbor against neighbor.

Croatian President Tudjman seemed surprised and disoriented by the outbreak of fighting, even though it had obviously been looming for months. In June, Baker found Tudjman almost cavalier about the danger from the JNA. Tudjman claimed that as a former general, he knew the JNA and was confident it would never attack Croatia.[11] Even as late as a 30 July 1991 session of the Croatian supreme state council, Tudjman said, "I am certain that [General] Kadijevic will not attack Croatia . . . because I have guarantees!"[12]

By August, however, Tudjman was telling European visitors, "We are being beaten and we know it." Toward the end of the month, Tudjman told Ambassador Zimmermann that he would have no alternative but to declare total war if the JNA persisted in its attacks. He pleaded with the United States to join European efforts to stop Milosevic.[13]

Two things saved Tudjman and Croatia. Most important was the ability of the Croatian military leadership—a combination of JNA veterans and eager amateurs—to put together an effective fighting force in the midst of the Serbian offensive. The other factor was EC diplomatic intervention. By insisting that republican borders be considered state boundaries and subject to change only by the consent of all concerned parties, the EC established conditions, which meant that Milosevic could create a Greater Serbia only through military victory—something he was unable to do. The EC approach, however, also contributed to future problems in other areas of Yugoslavia by failing to address the issue of ethnic minorities in Bosnia and Kosovo, who found themselves on the wrong side of the new international borders.

Milosevic looked with suspicion on intervention by the EC because he considered—not without reason—that some of its members were partial toward Slovenia and Croatia. In addition, Milosevic seems to have taken a personal dislike to some of the European officials initially involved in the EC's peacemaking efforts. His meetings with van den Broeck sometimes degenerated into angry exchanges, and on some occasions he simply refused to meet European representatives.

On 1 September, after six hours of intense, closed-door squabbling, EC diplomats finally succeeded in gaining Serbian agreement to a plan that combined a cease-fire, disbanding paramilitary forces, returning the JNA to its barracks, and an international peace conference under EC auspices. Prospects for the agreement's success seemed limited, however. Fighting continued to rage throughout Croatia, and after signing the accord, an obviously angry Milosevic sat stone-faced and silent. Refusing to applaud or raise a glass to the EC-brokered pact, Milosevic tried to plow his way through the throng of assembled diplomats and journalists until van den Broeck cornered him and politely insisted that Milosevic toast the agreement he had just signed. Milosevic took a reluctant swallow of orange juice and then began an oration on the subject of the Serbs as the victims in the war in Croatia. The Dutch foreign minister cut him off, raising his glass to all those who had been killed and reminding Milosevic that most of these had been Croats.[14]

Carrington, a former British minister of defense and secretary general of NATO, opened the EC peace conference on Yugoslavia on 7 September in The Hague. Milosevic and Tudjman exchanged bitter accusations. The Serb leader claimed that the Croatian authorities had used "ruthless discrimination and state terror" against Serbs, while for his part, Tudjman accused Serbia of waging a "dirty undeclared war" for over a year. Showing no signs of changing the line that had driven Yugoslavia into war, Milosevic warned that only the external borders of Yugoslavia were untouchable; republican borders were purely administrative and thus subject to alteration. For good measure, Milosevic added that the EC should confine its role in the talks to providing unbiased mediation; Yugoslavs would sort out their problems themselves.[15]

Milosevic suffered a rude surprise at a mid-October meeting of the Hague conference when Montenegro—his heretofore loyal satrapy—announced its agreement with the Carrington plan. Visibly astonished, Milosevic was overheard by EC mediators telling Montenegrin President Momir Bulatovic as they left the hall that he would be fired or, according to other diplomatic observers, hanged.[16] After returning to Belgrade, Milosevic sent

Jovic to Podgorica, the Montenegrin capital, with an admonition that if Bulatovic did not recant, Milosevic would ensure that he was overthrown. Bulatovic resisted for two days, insisting that if Serbia was unwilling to fully mobilize for war against Croatia, the European peace proposals should be accepted. Eventually, Serbian pressure prevailed, and Bulatovic sent the EC a message—dictated by Milosevic—retracting his apostasy.[17]

As winter approached, developments on the battlefield pushed the combatants toward a halt in the fighting. Vukovar, which had been under siege by the JNA and Serbian irregulars for three months, finally fell on 15 November. Unable because of low morale and desertions to capture the city quickly through infantry attack, the JNA shelled Vukovar into submission while the inhabitants, Croats and Serbs alike, huddled in their basements. By the end of the siege, over 2,300 civilians had died and thousands more were wounded. The JNA expelled the city's remaining Croatian inhabitants after Vukovar's capitulation. Several hundred wounded Croatian defenders were removed from the makeshift hospital and disappeared—probably murdered—which led to the indictment of several JNA officers for war crimes in 1995.

At about the same time, the JNA also stepped up its shelling of the historic walled city of Dubrovnik, on the Adriatic coast. Dubrovnik had no military significance, and the shelling was probably intended as a warning to Croatia of what could happen if it continued the war. In his memoirs, Kadijevic claims that Dubrovnik was shelled because Serb forces ignored his orders to keep out of artillery range of the city.[18] According to Zimmermann, the only figure who pretended that there was any military objective in Dubrovnik was Milosevic, who claimed that the attack was justified because of foreign mercenaries holed up in the city.[19]

Vukovar marked the end of the Serb offensive. Kadijevic says in his memoirs that the JNA's original objective in the war was to completely defeat Croatian forces and cut Croatia in half by occupying a line from eastern Slavonia—Zagreb—and Knin and on to Zadar and Split on the Adriatic coast. This plan failed, Kadijevic admits, because of "the half successful mobilization and the organized desertion in the reserve components of the JNA."[20] After the fall of Vukovar, Serb forces in western Slavonia were pushed back by a Croatian offensive that drove fifty thousand Serb inhabitants out of the area and cut the link between Belgrade and Krajina. During this battle, only one and a half of the necessary five Serbian brigades reported for duty.[21]

Milosevic as War Leader

On 7 July, two weeks after Slovenia and Croatia declared their independence, Milosevic made his first public remarks about the war engulfing Yugoslavia. Denouncing "all those who are bent on persecuting the Serbian people," he said Slovenia could leave Yugoslavia, but demanded that the JNA protect the six hundred thousand Serbs living in Croatia. Warning that Serbian Territorial Defense forces were well armed and ready, Milosevic concluded that "the Serbian people have throughout their history never waged wars of conquest but have always been victorious when fighting for their own freedom."[22]

Milosevic's militant public posture was accompanied by vicious propaganda against Croatia in the Serbian media. Serbian television news routinely opened with reports of Croatian attacks on what were usually described as innocent Serb villagers. Atrocities by Croatian forces were standard fare; one horrific, four-hour prime-time documentary featured footage of victims with their eyes gouged out and brains sliced open. Serbian media portrayed Tudjman's Croatia as the successor in philosophy and action to Pavelic's World War II fascist puppet state. On one occasion, Belgrade Television showed a clip of Pavelic meeting Hitler, followed immediately by shots of Tudjman shaking the hand of German Chancellor Helmut Kohl.

After his 7 July speech, Milosevic was rarely seen in public. He gave few interviews and seldom appeared on television. Milosevic engaged in none of the ceremonial activities that wartime leaders usually consider important to maintain public morale and enhance their own political stature. Throughout the years of war in Yugoslavia, Milosevic never visited Serb forces at the front or wounded soldiers in the hospital, nor did he meet Serbian refugees driven from their homes by the fighting that he himself had been so instrumental in unleashing. A loner who is uncomfortable in situations that he cannot control, Milosevic may well have avoided such popular gestures because of the risk of some kind of spontaneous, critical behavior by those who he would meet.

Milosevic's odd behavior as the invisible war leader—so different from the charismatic public persona he adopted during his rise to power—reflects deep insecurities within his personality, but it also includes an element of practical political calculation. He understood that the war in Croatia, and those that followed in Bosnia and Kosovo, were unpopular with most Serbs. Despite the JNA's advantage in numbers, organization, and heavy weapons, once armed conflict began, it turned out that few Serbs were willing to fight for Milosevic's vision of a Greater Serbia. In some places, entire units of several thousand soldiers deserted their posts and returned home; other mutinous units jeered high-ranking JNA officers sent to try to calm them. By late September, one of Yugoslavia's most respected military commentators said publicly, "The response to mobilization has been getting poorer and poorer. They lack conscripts. Nobody wants to go to this war."[23]

Milosevic had little interest in military matters, and hardly bothered to hide his contempt for the indecision and professional incompetence of the JNA generals—at the same time that he refused to provide them with the resources they said were necessary to finish off Croatian resistance. As early as 12 September, Kadijevic told the Serbian leadership that the military could not fight the war in Croatia with the forces at its disposal. On 24 September, Kadijevic, who seemed to Jovic to be "confused, almost lost," said the military would lose the war unless there was a successful mobilization, and Serbia and Montenegro assumed full responsibility for financing the war. Kadijevic bluntly asked Milosevic a few days later why he had never expressed public support for the military and mobilization. At one meeting, tension became so high that Kadijevic threatened to come to Belgrade "with guns in hand to settle scores with those who are responsible."[24]

Milosevic never developed the kind of staff structure usually required to lead a nation in war. There is no evidence, for instance, that Milosevic had a personal military aide. As early as the summer of 1991, Milosevic exhibited the pattern of isolation from his own government that later turned him into a virtual hermit-leader. Mihajlo Markovic, vice president of Milosevic's SPS, told Western reporters that Milosevic's staff consisted of a single secretary and several advisers, most of whose offices were not even in the same building as the president's. One Western diplomat who visited Milosevic in late August 1991, at the height of the military and diplomatic activity around the war in Croatia, said Milosevic "seemed to be glad to have someone to talk to."[25] Eight years later, on the eve of war in Kosovo, Milosevic reportedly began phoning to ask old chums from high school to drop by, claiming that he was bored.[26]

There is little doubt that had Serbia been able to use all of the human and military resources at its disposal in 1991, it could have defeated Croatia. But Milosevic lacked the political vision and resolution to be a stirring wartime leader. He never told the Serbian people what he wanted them to fight for in Croatia or anywhere else, which made it impossible to rally public support for the military effort when difficulties arose. Without any core beliefs or values other than his own political survival, Milosevic was simply incapable of arousing lasting conviction or sustained sacrifice on the part of others.

Despite his detached public posture, there is no doubt that he either initiated or approved major military policies and actions during the war in Croatia. Vasil Tuperkovski, the Macedonian representative on the Yugoslav federal presidency, said in the summer of 1991 that Milosevic "totally controlled" Serbian forces fighting in Croatia and could enforce a cease-fire there any time he chose. On 8 August, even as the Serbian leadership was debating its response to a European-proposed cease-fire in Croatia, Milosevic insistently demanded of Kadijevic "when and whether the military will finally begin the definitive showdown" with the Croats.[27] He was reported to be in daily contact via a special phone with Serbian Minister of Defense Tomislav Simovic; in one case, Simovic telephoned Milosevic while the Serbian leader was in The Hague for the EC conference on Yugoslavia.[28]

Germany Rams through Recognition

In December, with Milosevic still refusing to accept Carrington's peace plan, and with public opinion increasingly outraged by Serb excesses at Vukovar and Dubrovnik, Germany told its EC colleagues that it intended to unilaterally recognize Slovenia and Croatia by Christmas if the EC had not done so before then. Britain, France, and most other EC members opposed the German position, but on 16 December, in an acrimonious late-evening session, Foreign Minister Hans Dietrich Genscher strong-armed the EC into announcing that it planned to recognize the two republics as independent states in January.

The day after the EC decision, Carrington, who had advised against recognition, met Tudjman, Milosevic, and Slovene President Kucan in the Austrian city of Graz, just across the border from Croatia. Carrington found Tudjman so elated that he had lost any interest in a cease-fire agreement. An angry Milosevic, by contrast, insisted that the EC step aside and let the UN take the lead in peace diplomacy. About the only thing that all three Yugoslav leaders could agree on was that the EC decision had made war in Bosnia virtually inevitable. (Tudjman, however, could not resist adding that the time was also ripe to divide Bosnia.)

Genscher and other advocates of recognition have contended that Milosevic's acceptance of the Vance plan only two weeks after the EC move shows that it succeeded in halting the fighting in Croatia. Recognition was undoubtedly an important message to Milosevic that the international community would not allow him to carve up Croatia and annex the Serb-controlled bits to Serbia proper. Yet Milosevic had already absorbed that message in the Carrington negotiations. On 2 November, six weeks before the EC recognition decision, Milosevic and Jovic agreed among themselves that it was time to call a halt to the fighting. Most of the territory in which Serbs constituted a majority—except for western Slavonia—was under Serb rule, and the Serb leaders knew they had to do something to head off the JNA's ever-more-insistent demands for full mobilization, which the Serb population would never support. Political bankruptcy and military exhaustion, not EC recognition of Croatia, were the primary factors leading the Serbs to seek a mediated halt to the fighting in Croatia.[29]

Ironically, EC recognition was probably more effective in persuading Tudjman to overrule his advisers who sensed the possibility of Croatian military victory than in stopping Milosevic from continuing the war. By December, Croatia had mobilized two hundred thousand troops that unlike their Serbian counterparts, were highly motivated to fight. They were also becoming better equipped thanks to shipments from abroad and the capture of military stores from some JNA garrisons in Croatia. The Croatian commander on the Slavonian front claimed that his main problem was not in sending soldiers into battle but rather in stopping them.[30]

Zimmermann movingly describes meeting Croatian Chief of Staff Antun Tus—a former JNA air force chief who did not join Croatian forces until the spring of 1991—shortly after the fall of Vukovar. When Zimmermann commiserated with him over the loss, Tus silently lowered his head to the maps on the table and rested it there for several seconds.[31] Two months later, Tus was suggesting to Tudjman that Croatia had developed sufficient strength to conduct offensive actions against the Serb Krajina fastness.[32] Tudjman, however, understood that continuing the conflict after recognition risked losing international support, which Tudjman knew was still the best guarantee of Croatia's independence.

The UN Steps In

As the EC stumbled toward failure, the UN, whose humanitarian agencies were heavily involved from the beginning of the crisis, became more engaged at the political level. In early October, UN Secretary General Boutros Boutros Ghali appointed former U.S. Secretary of State Cyrus Vance as his personal envoy to Yugoslavia. As it became clear that Carrington's plan for an overall Yugoslav settlement was going nowhere, Vance and his deputy,

U.S. Ambassador Herb Okun, took the lead on negotiations aimed at achieving a durable cease-fire and laying the foundation for a political settlement.

Vance found a receptive climate in Belgrade as he began his mission. On 9 November, the Serb-dominated rump Yugoslav presidency formally requested that UN peacekeeping forces be deployed in what it called the "border zone" between the Serb and Croatian territories. Vance's personal style of tact and patience was also crucial to the ultimate success of his mission. A careful listener, Vance developed a good working relationship with both Milosevic and Kadijevic without diminishing his own impartiality or authority. In early January 1992, for example, Vance bluntly warned Milosevic that any recognition by Belgrade of Krajina's independence would bring an end to the peace process, an injunction Milosevic heeded for the rest of the conflict.

Shortly after Germany announced its recognition of Croatia and Slovenia, Vance—at the urging of the UN—undertook a last-ditch, ten-day effort to achieve a cease-fire in Croatia before what many feared could be a wider war there as well as in Bosnia. After an intensive round of shuttle diplomacy, Milosevic announced on 31 December that he had no objections to the Vance plan. The cease-fire was signed on 2 January 1992, in Sarajevo by Croatian Defense Minister Susak and the senior JNA officer in Croatia, who had to be flown in from his besieged Zagreb headquarters in a Croatian aircraft.

One reason Vance succeeded was that, unlike the EC, he was able to offer the parties an international peacekeeping force on the ground. The modalities of the force's deployment required careful negotiation, however. The Serbs wanted the peacekeeping force deployed along the confrontation line, which would have effectively partitioned Croatia. Zagreb wanted the force deployed only along the border with Serbia, which would have left Serb communities unprotected. The solution was the "ink blot" approach, which provided for UN forces to be deployed in four so-called UN Protected Areas (UNPAS) that covered ground held by both sides. Other elements of the Vance plan, intended as the military precursor to a broader political settlement, included the complete withdrawal of JNA forces from Croatia and the disarmament of all forces within the UNPAS, which neither side ever carried out.

A second major factor in Vance's success was his recognition of the importance of securing the safe withdrawal of JNA forces from the besieged garrisons in Croatia. According to Okun, Kadijevic told Vance, "On the day that I have the promise that the last soldier will be withdrawn from the garrisons, this war will end." Persuading Tudjman to allow the JNA troops to leave was difficult—the Croatian president's advisers were telling him that capture of the stockpiled JNA weapons could decisively shift the military balance in Zagreb's favor—but when Tudjman finally agreed on Christmas Day to allow the JNA to depart, "the deal was half done."[33]

After Belgrade and Zagreb had agreed, it still remained to gain the approval of the Krajina Serbs, who correctly saw the Vance plan, which recognized the Serb-held territories to be part of Croatia, as the beginning of a sellout by Milosevic. According to Jovic, all of the negotiations over the Vance plan were initially handled by Milosevic personally. When he failed to persuade the hard-line Krajina Serb leader Milan Babic to agree to the Vance plan, Milosevic "completely lost his nerve." Jovic contends that he "took the baton" from Milosevic and, with the aid of General Adzic, who headed the JNA after Kadijevic's resignation, managed to persuade the Krajina Serbs to drop their objections to the plan although they were still unwilling to publicly endorse it.[34]

Once the agreement of all the parties to the conflict had been secured, it was the international community's turn to cause problems. Because of U.S. objections to its initial $90 million price tag, the UN Security Council did not vote for a resolution authorizing a scaled-back peacekeeping force for Croatia until late February 1992. This, in turn, meant that significant numbers of UN peacekeepers did not arrive on the ground until the spring. By then war had erupted in Bosnia, which made both sides even more reluctant to surrender their weapons, and diverted international attention and UN resources from the political settlement that was supposed to follow the Vance agreement. The pattern of this incident—the international community pushing the UN into ambitious commitments without providing sufficient resources to get the job done—would be repeated on numerous occasions over the next three years of the UN's involvement in Croatia and Bosnia.

Bosnia Comes Apart

As an uneasy peace settled over Croatia, attention turned to Bosnia—Yugoslavia's most diverse republic. According to the 1991 census, Moslems constituted approximately 44 percent of the population, Serbs 31 percent, Croats 17 percent, and a mix of "Yugoslavs" and some smaller minorities the remaining 8 percent. Like Croatia, Bosnia was a bitter ethnic battleground during the Second World War. Fascist Ustashi Croats slaughtered Serbs in Bosnia, but Serbs and Moslems also engaged in bitter internecine strife. Tito's Partisans suppressed all of the warring bands with their usual efficient brutality, yet in the postwar era, the Communists presided over a remarkable upsurge in Bosnia's economic, educational, and cultural development. Ethnic barriers began to break down. Sarajevo experienced a social and cultural transformation, symbolized by hosting the 1984 winter Olympics.

Bosnia's postwar Communist leaders, well aware they were sitting on top of an ethnic volcano, turned the republic into Yugoslavia's most rigid and politically conservative structure. Any deviation from accepted Yugoslav political norms was severely repressed, especially if it involved a whiff of nationalism. Positions throughout the republic were parceled out among the three ethnic groups based on what was known as the "national key." The practice was intended to foster concord through ethnic balance, but an unintended consequence was to discredit the entire system, as Bosnia's increasingly sophisticated middle class saw how merit was often less important than ethnic identity in obtaining jobs or other benefits.

The wave of Serbian nationalism triggered by Milosevic hit Bosnia— like Croatia—during a time of political transition. A 1987 financial scandal at the Bosnian firm Agrokomerc led to the resignation of the Bosnian member of the collective federal presidency and the arrest of the firm's flamboyant director, Fikret Abdic. The Agrokomerc affair, which discredited Bosnia's old-line Moslem political families, was followed by a series of revelations about corrupt activities by other members of the Bosnian elite. When the Bosnian Croat Branko Mikulic, the successful organizer of the 1984 Olympics, became the first Yugoslav prime minister to resign under pressure, the rout of the traditional Bosnian elite was complete.

Bosnian Elections

Bosnia's first multiparty elections, in November 1990, revealed the republic's division along ethnic lines. Three overtly ethnic parties—the Party of Democratic Action (SDA), led by Izetbegovic, the SDS, led by Karadzic, and the Bosnian branch of Tudjman's HDZ—won 84 percent of the seats in the Bosnian legislature. The two parties that attempted to appeal across ethnic lines—the Communists and Prime Minister Markovic's Alliance of Reform Forces—won only 5 and 6 percent, respectively, of the assembly seats, although they took as much as 20 percent of the vote at the local level.[35]

As in Croatia, the nationalist parties in Bosnia owed their victory in large part to Milosevic's injection of aggressive Serb nationalism into the republic's political life, which helped trigger the rise of counternationalisms in the other two nationalities. The campaign was marked by a singular absence of debate over any issue other than nationality. Accusations of collective guilt against other ethnic groups and the revival of prejudice followed the rekindling of long-suppressed memories from Bosnia's turbulent past.[36] The result was an election based primarily on fear. Many Bosnians, even those who looked with suspicion on the nationalist parties, nevertheless held their nose and voted for "their" ethnic candidate lest they be outvoted by neighbors who would vote for "theirs."

Despite the emotions unleashed by the election campaign, after the balloting was over, the leaders of the three national parties—in traditional Bosnian fashion—divided the republic's leading positions among themselves. Izetbegovic became president, after Abdic—who had outpolled him in the race for the Moslem member of the collective presidency—decided to return to his Agrokomerc fiefdom in northwest Bosnia, where he would lead a dissident Moslem faction during the upcoming war. Momcilo Krajisnik of the SDS became president of the assembly, and the Croat Jure Pelivan was chosen as prime minister.

In the postelection period, Izetbegovic, Karadzic, and leading members of the opposition could often be seen chatting together amid the plush, red velvet decor of the Austrian-era coffeehouse at the Evropa Hotel in downtown Sarajevo. Their efforts at cooperation, however, were fragile and short-lived. Little more than two years after the elections, Serb incendiary shells smashed into the Evropa, leaving only a concrete frame to mark the place where Sarajevans of all ethnic groups had met for generations to sip strong Turkish coffee and even stronger Serbian plum brandy.

Bosnian Leaders

Milosevic's primary adversary in Bosnia, Izetbegovic, was twice arrested by the Communists for Islamic activity. Izetbegovic's modest demeanor concealed a determination to return the ways of Islam, suppressed during the postwar Communist era, to Bosnia's Moslem population. When he founded the SDA in March 1990, Izetbegovic leaned on former cell mates and others who were similarly inclined toward an identity defined largely in terms of Islam and sought a dominant role for Moslems in Bosnia's public life.

Izetbegovic was best known before he began his political career for his *Islamic Declaration* (*Islamska Deklaracija*). Written in 1970—when the prospect of an avowed Islamic party taking power in Bosnia seemed remote—the *Declaration* describes a society organized on Islamic principles and law, which Izetbegovic stressed must include toleration for other religions and respect for minorities. Yet Bosnia's non-Moslem population might legitimately ask what a society led by Izetbegovic had in store for them when he also called for the creation of a Moslem federation from Indonesia to Morocco or advocated that the media be entrusted only to people of deeply Islamic faith.[37]

Even more than Milosevic, Izetbegovic lacked a strategy for dealing with the events and emotions that he helped set in motion. He never seemed to have any idea how to accommodate a religiously mobilized Moslem nation into multiethnic Bosnia or how to deal with the reaction that he knew would inevitably appear among Serbs and Croats to his own use of Islam as a political force. Put more simply, Izetbegovic had trouble with arithmetic. Since Moslems constituted only a plurality in Bosnia, they could not by themselves dominate it. And if ethnicity were allowed to become the primary determining factor in politics, Serbs and Croats could always cooperate to overpower the Moslems.

Izetbegovic's behavior throughout the crisis of Yugoslavia's disintegration reflected this dilemma. During negotiations among republican leaders in the spring of 1991, Izetbegovic and his Macedonian colleague Kiro Gligorov tried desperately to find some compromise formula that would allow Yugoslavia to survive. Once Yugoslav disintegration became inevitable, Izetbegovic seemed lost. On some occasions, he flirted with the notion of remaining within Milosevic's rump Yugoslavia, but he was always pulled back by opposition from hard-liners within his own party. In October 1991, Izetbegovic told Ambassador Zimmermann that partition was one solution to the Bosnian conundrum, but then went on to demonstrate how difficult it would be to come up with borders that made sense.[38] Finally, in early 1992, Izetbegovic allowed the international community to push Bosnia into declaring itself independent, even though he was well aware the Serbs would use this as a pretext for war.

The Serb standard-bearer in Bosnia, Karadzic, seldom wavered from the path of confrontation. Born to poor peasants in Montenegro in 1945, Karadzic graduated with a degree in psychiatry from the University of Sarajevo. Karadzic was a well-known member in Sarajevo's cosmopolitan cultural elite before the war. He published four volumes of poetry and dabbled in various small business ventures. Exuberant and convivial by nature, Karadzic was also prominent in Sarajevo's highly developed café society, with a noted fondness for gambling.

There was a darker side to Karadzic's personality as well. Like many others, Karadzic became involved in student politics in 1968 and was expelled from the Communist Party. But he was also ostracized from the student movement on suspicion of being a police informer. In 1985, he served eleven months in prison for fraud and misuse of public funds. Themes of exile, death, destruction, and return to a forsaken homeland pervade Karadzic's poetry from the beginning, but his last volume, published in 1990 and titled *The Black Fable* (*Crna Bajka*), revealed an obsession with themes of blood and violence. Zimmermann, who met with Karadzic on numerous occasions as Bosnia slid toward conflict, found that although Karadzic had a soft voice and an outwardly friendly manner, his conversation was peppered with words such as "war," "genocide," and "hell," and he had a deep-seated hostility, amounting to racism, toward Moslems, Croats, and other non-Slav groups.[39]

Bosnia Slides toward War

Throughout 1991, events steadily pushed Bosnia toward confrontation. In February and May 1991, the SDA tried to obtain assembly approval for a Bosnian declaration of sovereignty, but was defeated by the combined opposition of Serb and Croatian delegates. In October 1991, the SDA tried again. This time, with war raging in Croatia, the Bosnian Croats went along. In his speech to the Assembly, Izetbegovic acknowledged that seeking sovereignty carried with it the risk of conflict. Karadzic made the same point in typically extravagant fashion, warning that the vote would put Bosnia on "the same highway to hell and suffering that Slovenia and Croatia are traveling."[40] The aim of the SDA hard-liners who pressed for the vote appeared to be to make impossible any deal that would allow Bosnia to remain within a Milosevic-dominated rump Yugoslavia. The Serbs, for their part, responded by organizing a November 1991 referendum, in which virtually all Serb voters agreed that Serbs in Bosnia should join a Greater Serbia that included Serbia proper and Krajina.

Serbs in Bosnia formed autonomous districts in areas they claimed and the Croats followed, setting up their own administrations in the Neretva River valley and along the Sava River border with Croatia. Extremists gained ground everywhere. In July, the Serb mayor of the eastern Hercegovinian city of Trebinje, a former truck driver and self-proclaimed poet, told visitors that Bosnia's breakup was inevitable. "We have hated each other for one thousand years and now we are allowed to say it openly," was his comment on the current political situation. Three weeks later, Hasan Cengic, then head of the SDA, said there was no longer any possibility of negotiating a peaceful solution with the Serbs.

As the fighting in Croatia drew to a close, it was clear to all observers that it was only a matter of time before violence broke out in Bosnia. In the summer of 1991, the JNA began to transfer arms to the Bosnian Serbs and these efforts were stepped up after the November 1991 Serb referendum.[41] Many Bosnian Serbs—over ten thousand according to Moslem estimates—who had fought in Croatia were allowed to return to Bosnia with their arms after the fighting there ended. The JNA also transferred troops to Bosnia. At the end of November 1991, members of the EC monitoring mission estimated that the JNA had a total of one hundred thousand regular and reserve troops in Bosnia. Two JNA corps had been deployed in the Trebinje and Neretva area, where they were well positioned to seize key internal communication routes and assist the local Serb populations. The behavior of reservists attached to these JNA forces—frequently drunk and often insulting to the local non-Serb population—did much to raise ethnic tensions and increase resentment against the JNA.

Milosevic's Options in Bosnia

In Bosnia, unlike Croatia, Milosevic tried to camouflage his involvement. In December 1991, correctly anticipating that international recognition of Bosnian independence would make it difficult for the JNA to operate openly there, Milosevic insisted—over initial objections by Kadijevic—that JNA forces in Bosnia be staffed only by Serbs from Bosnia.[42]

From the very beginning of the Yugoslav crisis, Milosevic had made clear his intention to include the Serbs of Bosnia within the borders of the new state he aimed to carve out of the ruins of Yugoslavia. Yet, the approach that Milosevic took to accomplishing this objective differed in Bosnia as compared to Croatia. In Croatia, Milosevic encouraged the "amputation" of the Serb-inhabited regions even a year before the Yugoslav collapse. Milosevic's initial preference in Bosnia, however, seems to have been to keep the entire republic, or at least the non-Croatian parts of it, within a rump Yugoslavia that he could dominate. During the secret 16 March 1991 meeting with Serb district leaders in which he issued a call to war in Croatia, Milosevic also described the Moslems of Bosnia as having no interest in leaving Yugoslavia. He said Slovenia and Croatia were bent on secession, but claimed to want for the Moslems a "tolerant, cultured, and I would say civil, neighborly, and friendly relationship" with the Serb people.

Although Bosnian Moslems might well question Milosevic's lyrical depiction of the alliance on offer, many Moslems seriously considered whether remaining in some kind of connection with Belgrade might be preferable to the conflict that all understood would be the inevitable result of separation. In the summer of 1991, Adil Zulfikarpasic, the wealthy scion of one of pre–Second World War Bosnia's most illustrious aristocratic families and the leader of a small Moslem political party, met in succession with Karadzic, Izetbegovic, and Milosevic to seek an arrangement that would allow Bosnia to remain within a confederal Yugoslavia. According to Zulfikarpasic, Milosevic was initially surprised by Zulfikarpasic's proposal, but then enthusiastically thanked him for "finding a way to avoid catastrophe." Zulfikarpasic got Izetbegovic to discuss his plan with Milosevic, although Izetbegovic claimed to have heard nothing new when they met. Later, leaks about Zulfikarpasic's plan, probably inspired by SDA hardliners, led Izetbegovic to repudiate the deal.

There remain many questions about both the shape of the deal Zulfikarpasic proposed and the motives of the various players. Zulfikarpasic portrayed the arrangement as a "confederation or a union of states" that would have a common currency and its own defense forces.[43] Zulfikarpasic also may have made the agreement contingent on Croatia remaining part of Yugoslavia or on Milosevic giving Sandjak to Bosnia. Subsequently, a senior adviser to Milosevic told U.S. diplomats that Milosevic had offered the Bosnians status as a sovereign republic in a new, federal Yugoslavia, with guarantees of full internal autonomy. The new federal government would have responsibility for economic, defense, and foreign policy, but Bosnian interests would be protected by having a bicameral legislature where decisions in the upper chamber could only be reached on the basis of consensus among the republics.

At the time, the initiative was seen as an effort to divide the Bosnian Moslems, which indeed was probably one of Milosevic's motives in meeting with the well-meaning but naive Zulfikarpasic. ("I believe Milosevic," Zulfikarpasic told the press after meeting the Serb president—an assertion that put Zulfikarpasic in a rather select group.)

In January 1992, after the Vance agreement had ended the fighting in Croatia, Milosevic held out a public olive branch to the Moslems, suggesting that "a common and equitable life" would be in the interests of both Serbs and Moslems in Bosnia. On 21 January, the Serbian government issued an appeal to Bosnia and Macedonia to stay within what remained of the Yugoslav federation. At about this time, Zimmermann found Milosevic's rhetoric about the plight of Serbs in Bosnia to be more subdued than it had been about their fellows in Croatia.

By late February, though, Milosevic's tone had stiffened. Declaring that

Serbs in Bosnia could "neither be threatened nor separated against their will," Milosevic said any decision on Bosnia would have to be based on consensus among its three constituent peoples.[44] Since he was speaking only days before a referendum on Bosnian independence, which the Serbs had already said they would boycott, Milosevic's demand for consensus amounted to a rejection of the approach that Izetbegovic was taking—with the support of the United States and Europe. Milosevic also told Zimmermann that he would not object to Bosnian independence but insisted that Serbs should control the 64 percent of Bosnia's territory he claimed they occupied. Pursuing what Zimmermann sarcastically described as a new, "clean hands" strategy, Milosevic also maintained that he did not know Karadzic well and that "Serbia has nothing to do with Bosnia. It's not our problem."[45]

Milosevic's claim of noninvolvement in Bosnia was a lie and his assertion that Serbs controlled the majority of the republic's land belonged to the realm of nationalist mythology. Moreover, at the same time that Milosevic held out the possibility of a deal with the Moslems, the Serbs also continued to explore the possibility of partition with the Croats. In February, Karadzic met in Graz with a senior Tudjman adviser and the two issued a statement that seemed to indicate considerable common ground on the subject of Bosnia.

By the beginning of 1992, however, developments on the ground in Bosnia and within the international diplomatic community outside of Yugoslavia were starting to outrun the ability of Milosevic—or anyone else—to control them. International outrage with Milosevic had reached the point where no one was willing to take seriously any hints by him at compromise.

Bosnia: Referendum Plus Recognition Equals War

In early 1992, events in Bosnia were driven by the interplay between overlapping and sometimes conflicting international efforts to resolve the problem and the growing determination of all three ethnic groups to pursue their own objectives, even at the price of conflict. The Badinter commission, established by the EC to determine whether the Yugoslav republics met the criteria for international recognition, decided that "the will of the peoples of Bosnia-Hercegovina to constitute the Socialist Republic of Bosnia-Hercegovina [SRBH] as a sovereign and independent State cannot be held to have been fully established." The commission added that this decision could be reviewed if appropriate guarantees were provided, "possibly by means of a referendum of all the citizens of the srbh without distinction, carried out under international supervision."[46]

Unfortunately, conditions in Bosnia had long passed the point where all three ethnic groups could voluntarily agree to participate in joint action of any kind, and the international community never even tried to follow the commission's recommendation that the referendum be internationally supervised.

On 25 January, the Bosnian assembly debated the holding of a referendum. The discussion centered on whether an agreement on regional structures among the three ethnic groups in Bosnia should precede or follow the referendum. Karadzic and sda vice president Cengic agreed that a proposal for regionalization should be worked out, after which the referendum would take place within a specified time. "Never were we closer to agreement as at this time," Karadzic said to the applause of the delegates. After a pause in the assembly's work, Izetbegovic shot down the incipient agreement when Karadzic suggested that the commitment to regionalization be incorporated into a constitutional amendment before the referendum was held. After the Serb delegates withdrew in response, the decision to hold the referendum was adopted by the votes of the Moslem and Croatian delegates.[47]

The 29 February–1 March Bosnian referendum produced predictable results. Some 63 percent of all voters in Bosnia supported independence, almost exactly the outcome that would be expected if all Moslems and Croats voted yes—as they had been advised to do by their political and religious leaders. Virtually all Serbs boycotted the referendum, as Karadzic and the sds had ordered. On 3 March, Izetbegovic declared Bosnia independent, and one month later, the United States and Europe formally recognized Bosnia as an independent country, even though the referendum met none of the conditions required by the Badinter commission.

In Sarajevo the day of the referendum, Okun advised Izetbegovic to begin acting as if Bosnia were independent, but to avoid a formal declaration. Aware of the sensitivity the jna had displayed to the fate of its blockaded garrisons in Croatia, Okun asked Izetbegovic what he intended to do about the jna garrisons spread throughout Bosnia, including in downtown Sarajevo.[48] Izetbegovic replied that when Bosnia proclaimed its independence, the jna would become an occupying army and he would demand its departure. He had no answer to what would happen if the jna ignored the order.

As Bosnia moved toward the referendum and its preordained outcome, the international community displayed the divisions and inconsistencies that plagued its efforts there for the next three years. Observing what appeared to be an inevitable slide toward war, the EC began to get cold feet about the approach it had helped set in motion by recognizing Croatia and Slovenia. The United States, by contrast, which had refused to follow the EC's lead on recognition of the western republics, now began to press for recognition of Bosnia, reducing the prospects—low as they might be—that continued negotiations could head off conflict.

On 14 February, EC-sponsored peace talks opened in Sarajevo under the chair of Jose Cutileiro of Portugal, which had taken over from the Netherlands as EC president. On 18 March, all three ethnic groups agreed "as a basis for further discussions" to a set of "constitutional principles" that would have turned Bosnia into an independent state composed of three constituent units based on national principles and taking account of economic, geographic, and other criteria. The parties also agreed, according to Cutileiro, to a map showing how the division of Bosnia into ethnically based constituent units would be accomplished, but this agreement was later repudiated by the Croats—who insisted on more territory in central Bosnia—and even if the agreement had gone forward, it would probably also have also been rejected by Karadzic because it gave the Moslems more land than the Serbs were prepared to allow.

The first of a long series of failed international efforts to bring peace to Bosnia, the Cutileiro plan had a number of shortcomings. Most noteworthy, of course, was the fact that the prewar ethnic geography of Bosnia did not lend itself to neat ethnic divisions. Had it been implemented in the absence of a strong international peacekeeping force, it would almost certainly—like the Vance-Owen plan that followed it a year later—have encouraged land grabs and ethnic cleansing on all sides. Nevertheless, the Cutileiro plan would have established a more effective Bosnian central government and probably resulted in less of an ethnically divided state than the accord agreed to at Dayton, after three years of war and brutal ethnic cleansing. In retrospect, it is a tragedy that the Cutileiro plan was not adopted, but by then the tide of events was running too strongly in the opposite direction.

In early February, the U.S. embassy in Belgrade told Washington that Bosnia was on the verge of war. The embassy recommended U.S. diplomatic recognition as a tactic that might stave off conflict by increasing Western pressure on Milosevic and Karadzic. Even if it failed in that, recognition would pave the way for Bosnia's admission into the UN, while allowing the United States to deal with Bosnia as a state and provide assistance directly. Washington, which had not followed the European lead in recognizing Croatia and Slovenia but was moving to recognize the independence of the former republics of the USSR, bought the embassy's recommendation. On 11 March, Secretary Baker, in Brussels for consultations with the allies, reached a private understanding that the EC would recognize Bosnia on 6 April, to be followed shortly thereafter by the United States. In Washington, however, U.S. officials were already backgrounding the press that President Bush had decided to recognize Bosnia.[49]

European diplomats claimed that the U.S. decision on recognition undermined negotiations on the Cutiliero agreement, for which they purported to have Milosevic's backing.[50] This is doubtful. At the very moment that the United States announced its decision, the JNA and Serb police were shipping weapons into Bosnia and otherwise preparing for the Serb offensive that unfolded there only a few weeks later.

Nevertheless, while recognition did not, by itself, cause the fighting in Bosnia, it helped push both Serbs and Moslems along already existing paths toward war. It reduced incentives for the Moslems to agree to the ethnically driven Cutiliero plan, which was in any case repugnant to their integralist vision of Bosnia. It also increased Sarajevo's hope, perhaps its only consistent strategy throughout the war, that someday the United States would come to its rescue. Conversely, recognition increased the Serb proclivity to go for a military solution in Bosnia—an option for which they were already well prepared.

War Begins in Bosnia

In the last week of March, fighting erupted at several spots along Bosnia's fractious ethnic divides. The JNA, together with paramilitary bands from Serbia and the Bosnian Serb forces, launched what was clearly a long-planned and well-coordinated offensive in early April that aimed to seize control of eastern Bosnia. By the middle of April, the Serbs had taken six major towns along the Drina River. After only one month of fighting, the UN estimated that over five hundred thousand people—12 percent of Bosnia's prewar population—had been displaced.[51]

The fate of Visegrad, the site of a long Turkish stone bridge and the model for Nobel Prize-winning novelist Ivo Andric's *Bridge on the Drina*, was typical. JNA troops and paramilitaries surrounded the town, which before the war had been 63 percent Moslem and 33 percent Serb. On 14 April, under a creeping barrage laid down by JNA mortars and 122 mm rockets, Serb forces advanced to the center of Visegrad. The paramilitaries, many drunk and their vehicles blazoned with traditional Serb slogans, carried out the dirty work of flushing out houses in advance of the regular troops, but a JNA colonel was identified by Western journalists as being in overall charge of the operation. According to the UN, after Visegrad was captured on 13 April 1992, the JNA broadcast a message instructing residents who had fled into the surrounding hills and forests to return to their homes, and guaranteeing their safety. The JNA then blocked the roads out of Visegrad, and its soldiers assisted paramilitaries in taking away Moslems whose names appeared on a master list.[52] In Belgrade, JNA Chief of Staff Zivota Panic made no effort to hide the Serbian military's role in Bosnia. On the day that Visegrad fell, he threatened to step up the offensive, claiming that the army was acting to repel attacks on the Serbian people by Moslem and Croat militias.[53]

Ethnic Cleansing

Initiated and practiced most extensively by the Serbs, what came to be known as ethnic cleansing was carried out by all sides in the Bosnian conflict. Ethnic cleansing in Bosnia was not merely an eruption of ancient hatred and irrational violence, although once it got going, cleansing generated plenty of both. Serbian ethnic cleansing followed a clear strategy, planned well in advance and executed with ruthless precision. Its basic objective was to establish ethnically pure, Serb-dominated territory, covering the 65 to 70 percent of Bosnia that Serbs claimed as theirs by virtue of demographics, economics, or history. Cleansing was also intended to establish Serb domination over key geographic, economic, and military features; set up lines of communication; and create corridors linking Serbia proper with Serb-controlled territory in Bosnia and Krajina.

A study by the UN special rapporteur for human rights in the former Yugoslavia, Tadeusz Mazowiecki, of the Serb takeover of the northwestern Bosnian town of Prijedor revealed the careful planning and advance preparation that accompanied Serb ethnic cleansing. Six months before the outbreak of war, Serbs began building their own parallel administration in Prijedor, an ethnically mixed region that was the site of some of the most notorious Serb concentration camps. In early 1992, the Serbs seized control of the television tower atop nearby Mt. Kozara, blocking the reception of programs from Sarajevo and Zagreb. Limiting programming to the hate-filled offerings of Serb television in Belgrade and Banja Luka undoubtedly played a crucial role in creating the proper psychological climate for what followed. Before the seizure of power, JNA soldiers withdrawn from Croatia were used to control the access roads to Prijedor. Simo Drljaca, the SDS official in charge of the takeover, had 1,775 men and 13 police stations under his command, and when the order to move came on the night of 29–30 April was able to seize power in Prijedor in half an hour with virtually no casualties.

After the takeover, non-Serbs were isolated, forced to wear white armbands, and subjected to abuse and attacks by local Serbs, who were given to understand they could prey on their neighbors with impunity. Over six thousand non-Serbs incarcerated in the Omarska concentration camp experienced beatings, hunger, and killings. Most women and children were expelled, but some were interned in the Trnopolje camp, where rape and other abuses were common. The Serbs singled out Moslem community leaders, such as local politicians, intellectuals, and religious leaders, for special attention. Mosques and Catholic Churches were destroyed to eliminate the physical traces of non-Serb culture, and over 47,000 homes belonging to non-Serbs were destroyed. By June 1993, the total number of those killed or expelled in the Prijedor area reached 52,811. Virtually all of the Moslems and over half of the Croats who had lived in Prijedor were gone.[54]

Milosevic's Two-Tier Game

Once the war in Bosnia began, Milosevic played what diplomats in Belgrade at the time called a two-tier game. He denied any territorial pretensions in Bosnia, committed himself in public to UN peace efforts, and even, in private meetings with Ambassador Zimmermann, acknowledged that the Serb minority in Bosnia was not under any serious threat of persecution—a charge he had used to justify Serbian intervention in Croatia. As Bosnian Serb forces, with the active assistance of Belgrade, were executing long-prepared plans for carving out an exclusive Serb zone across much of western and northern Bosnia, Milosevic labeled accounts of Serb aggression a world conspiracy against Serbia. He denied the existence of paramilitary bands in Serbia, and for good measure, said that none of this nonexistent force had been sent to Bosnia.[55]

As pressure mounted, Milosevic maneuvered to head off international action—especially economic sanctions, which he feared most of all. On 23 April, Milosevic gave his personal approval to an EC-brokered truce in Bosnia, and the British and French ambassadors in Belgrade were assured by a senior Serb official that no Serb irregulars would be allowed to cross into Bosnia. (A member of the Serbian opposition said Milosevic looked "ashen" after he met with the EC delegation.) The next day, Belgrade Television reported that Dragoslav Bokan, the commander of the paramilitary group White Eagles established by former dissident Seselj, who only a week earlier had participated in the assault on Visegrad, had been arrested. Arkan, the notorious paramilitary leader, was reported to have gone "on vacation."[56]

Further cosmetic moves followed. At the end of April, Karadzic dropped his insistence that the Serbian-controlled territories in Bosnia become part of Serbia proper. On 5 May, the Serbian authorities stated they were formally relinquishing control over military units in Bosnia. Announcing that all citizens of Serbia and Montenegro would be withdrawn from Serb forces in Bosnia within fifteen days, the authorities said they "no longer had any legal grounds to make any decisions regarding military issues in Bosnia and Herzegovina."

Milosevic's bobbing and weaving did not prevent Serbia from being subjected to the toughest economic sanctions since the Gulf War. At the same time, however, a subtle change came over the international community's approach to Milosevic. "Like it or not, Milosevic has become a part of the peace process," a Western diplomat remarked in Belgrade. Another diplomat added, "It's ironic but as far as the peace effort is concerned, Milosevic has become a source of stability."[57]

By 1992, even as Serb ethnic cleansing rolled across Bosnia, the international community began to view Milosevic as key to solving the crises unleashed by the collapse of Yugoslavia. Diplomats looked for the solution to the Bosnian conflict not in Sarajevo or Karadzic's mountain fastness of Pale but in Belgrade with Milosevic. Although this was not an unreasonable assumption, in view of Milosevic's role in instigating the crisis, working with Milosevic to achieve peace inevitably brought international negotiators into a false position. Milosevic expected to be rewarded for supporting the activities of international negotiators, even as Belgrade continued to provide crucial military and economic support to its clients in Bosnia and Croatia. The arsonist was enlisted to extinguish the fires that he himself had created.

SEVEN

Milosevic and the Politics of Power

What Makes Slobo Run?

By nature a private person, Milosevic never speaks candidly in public about himself and seldom unbends in private even to the small circle of people who have at times been close to him. Milosevic seems to have been a rather normal young professional of the Yugoslav self-management type in his early days. The careerism and toadying that some saw then did not distinguish him from thousands of others making their way up the Yugoslav political ladder.

Former officials who worked and socialized with Milosevic early on believe that his personality began to change in the mid-1980s, when he first sensed that instead of clinging endlessly to Stambolic's coattails, he might achieve supreme power himself. Milosevic's Serbian biographer, Slavoljub Djukic, concludes that Milosevic "completely changed at the end of the 1980s." At that time, "the sky opened before him and he convinced himself that God had sent him to lead the Serbian people to great victories."[1] Djukic also contends that Milosevic never succeeded in liberating himself from the memory of the adulation that swept over him as he rode to the top on a wave of Serb nationalism at the end of the 1980s. In 1992, when Milan Panic, who Milosevic asked to become federal prime minister, expressed surprise that Milosevic was willing to give up control of this position, Milosevic replied, "My function is not important, Milan. For Serbs I am a kind of Homeini."[2]

Almost all who have known or worked with Milosevic agree that power is what motivates him. But there is something curious about Slobodan Milosevic and power. Over the course of his thirteen-year career at the top, Milosevic did not seem intent on using power for any of the conventional purposes. He was not interested in what he could do with power for his country. Nor, at least until the end, was he concerned with using power to destroy his opponents. Unlike his wife, Milosevic did not seem to be vindictive toward vanquished political foes or even, judging by his friendly behavior toward Tudjman at Dayton, particularly resentful toward those who bested him.

Milosevic, in fact, was not very good at using power for anything other than keeping it. He did not use power to build up Serbia's military or economic might—quite the reverse. Under Milosevic, Serbia lost four wars and became one of Europe's poorest states. Neither did Milosevic have any grand conception of what he intended to accomplish as leader of Serbia, nor any "dream" that he sought to share with the Serbian people.

Although Milosevic exploited nationalism to come to power, he may be telling the truth when he denies—as he consistently does—being a nationalist. For the first twenty-five years of his professional life, Milosevic appeared to be a typical Yugoslav Communist apparatchik. He dropped Communism and embraced Serb nationalism in the late 1980s to fuel his own rise to power, but nationalism for him was just a tool. Milosevic dropped nationalism just as quickly when it became inconvenient to his efforts to cultivate the image of a peacemaker. Toward the end of the 1990s, in the run-up to his failed war in Kosovo, Milosevic again adopted a public posture of virulent Serb chauvinism combined with a bizarre version of Third World anti-imperialism, but that was the desperate ploy of a cornered man and no less a pose than any of his earlier political postures.

Milosevic seemed detached from the day-to-day routine of governance, which evidently bored him. All of the foreign statesmen who dealt with Milosevic noted how much time he had to devote to long negotiating sessions often followed by even longer banquets. Aides to Milosevic told foreign visitors that Milosevic was not a reader and did not like to wade through long reports. These aides said Milosevic relied primarily for information on oral briefings and a "situation report" he received every morning. Milosevic seldom met with members of his own government, who could go months without ever speaking to their nominal chief.

Sometimes, Milosevic seemed to go out of his way to flaunt his distance from officials who were responsible for the ordinary affairs of government—especially those who had little to do with the security and diplomatic issues that preoccupied him during his last years in office. In early 1999, when NATO commander General Wes Clark was pressing Milosevic to allow Louise Arbour, the Hague tribunal chief prosecutor, into Kosovo, Milosevic turned to Serb President Milan Milutinovic, saying the necessary instructions should be issued to allow her to come as a tourist, and then with a kind of dismissive tone and gesture asked, "What's the name of our justice minister?"[3]

Milosevic was also uninterested in the ceremonial trappings of power. The uniforms, bands, and elaborate protocol that have so attracted some other Balkan rulers—for example, Tito and Tudjman—seem completely alien to Milosevic's personality. On those rare occasions when Milosevic appeared in public or spoke to the nation, he invariably wore a plain business suit. When he traveled about Belgrade, it was in a small and rather unobtrusive motorcade, with fewer sirens and police outriders than, say, the secretary of state in Washington, D.C.

Although his family amassed great wealth during his rule, Milosevic himself does not appear to have been motivated by money. His personal lifestyle was rather modest, despite Milosevic's enjoyment of expensive Scotch and cigars. Milosevic appropriated some of the villas that Tito had in Serbia, but he seemed to use them mainly for official purposes and as hideaways in his increasingly reclusive lifestyle. In public, at least, Milosevic displayed little fondness for the trappings of wealth—the expensive cars, flashy clothes, luxurious villas, and beautiful women—that made Tito in some ways such a human figure.

There is little evidence in the public record, Milosevic's scanty remarks about himself, or the observations of foreign visitors that Milosevic had special interests of any kind. When Milosevic would unbend during dinners with foreign visitors, he seemed to enjoy casual political chitchat and would often gossip about Yugoslav or foreign participants in the peace process. But he seldom, if ever revealed much interest in other matters, such as sports, entertainment, literature, or any other common area of human endeavor.

Take away Slobodan Milosevic's interest in power and the man is pretty much a cipher.

Two Milosevics?

Milosevic's reticence about himself and economical approach to the truth make his an elusive personality to get a handle on. Djukic, who devoted fifteen years to the study of Milosevic and his family, concluded shortly after Milosevic was deposed that "the more I think about Milosevic, the less I understand."[4] Warren Zimmermann, the last U.S. ambassador to Yugoslavia, suggested—only partially in jest—the existence of two Milosevics. Milosevic One was a hard-liner and belligerent, while Milosevic Two was affable and always looking for reasonable solutions.[5] Foreign negotiators, who almost uniformly noted Milosevic's charm, intelligence, and excellent English, generally saw Milosevic Two—at least until the 1999 war in Kosovo. A good listener, Milosevic could be an engaging host with a real talent for repartee—a tactic for putting visitors at their ease, which sometimes also worked to disarm the unwary. Milosevic could display a genuine sense of humor, too.

On some occasions, however, the mask of confidence and self-possession that Milosevic usually showed foreigners slipped away. In September 1995 while NATO was bombing the Bosnian Serbs, Carl Bildt, the international community's first High Representative for Bosnia, found Milosevic so distracted that he seemed to be on the verge of losing control.[6] Near the end of the Dayton conference, when it appeared that no agreement would be reached, Milosevic turned desperate. He pleaded with the United States not to give up its efforts to wring out an additional 1 percent of territory from the Bosnian delegation, and some noticed tears in his eyes when an agreement finally fell into place.[7] To some extent, of course, the distinction also reflected the different ways Milosevic dealt with foreigners and other Yugoslavs. Bildt notes that during the difficult negotiations in June 1996 over Karadzic's role in Bosnia, Milosevic turned suddenly to the Bosnian Serb vice presidents, Biljana Plavsic and Nikola Koljevic, and barked out instructions to them in a manner and tone very different from that he had just been employing with Bildt himself.[8]

Milosevic is by nature a loner. After the carefully organized wave of demonstrations in the late 1980s had passed, Milosevic reverted to character. Throughout the thirteen years of his rule, he never held a press conference. Milosevic seldom spoke directly to the Serbian nation, even in times of crisis. Not until six weeks after NATO began bombing Serbia in 1999, for example, did Milosevic emerge from seclusion to make a brief public appearance to award medals to members of the armed forces.

Milosevic allowed only a few, carefully chosen and clearly subordinate individuals regular access to him. He preferred to surround himself with yes men and does not deal easily with criticism. In the late 1980s, I accompanied a delegation of U.S. religious figures to a meeting with Milosevic, who waxed long and eloquent about how the United States was wrong to prop up Albania, as he said, to be an unsinkable aircraft carrier against Serbia. At the end of the meeting, I told Milosevic politely that his understanding of U.S. policy was wrong. Clearly not used to hearing that kind of remark—at least in Serbo-Croatian—Milosevic stepped back almost as if he had been struck, a look of horror came over his face, and an aide quickly moved him away.

Liar, Liar

One of the few constants in Milosevic's personality is mendacity. Although this is not an uncommon trait in the Balkans, few political leaders share Milosevic's capacity not only for lying but also for actually appearing to believe their own lies. Ivor Roberts, the British chargé d'affaires in Belgrade during the war in Bosnia, remarks that whenever Milosevic says, "To be perfectly honest," his interlocutors should pay particular attention to what follows.[9]

In 1997 NATO Secretary General Javier Solana accused Milosevic of infiltrating Serbian secret police into Bosnia and taking payoffs. Milosevic denied the assertion but backed off and changed the subject when Solana looked into his eyes and said, "Yes, you are lying," after Milosevic asked angrily whether Solana was calling him a liar. Milosevic later acknowledged to Solana that "Yes, you are right, I was lying. But this is normal, everyone does it."[10]

U.S. psychiatrists, who have studied Milosevic closely describe him as having a "malignant narcissistic" personality. They see Milosevic as "strongly self-centered, vain, and full of self-love." He is also completely indifferent to almost anyone or anything else around him. A malignant narcissist such as Milosevic creates a core personality for himself and then shapes his own perception of the world to fit that personality. According to this analysis, Milosevic is actively in touch with reality, but also has a high capacity for ignoring or altering information that conflicts with his own view of himself in the world. Milosevic understands what is really going on, he knows that his own depictions of events that diverge from reality are lies, but at the same time he believes so strongly in his own lies that he sometimes gives the appearance of crossing the line into unreality.

With malignant narcissists such as Milosevic, the truth is part of their own self-deception. The narcissist's core personality is a sham, and to give up portions of its truth would be to reveal the sham at its very center. This, for instance, may be one reason why Milosevic has always been so sensitive on the subject of Kosovo and why he so often uttered such obvious lies about Kosovo—even when he knew the falsehood could easily be detected. In an interview conducted by the pro-Milosevic TV Palma two months after losing power, Milosevic asserted that from 1987 to 1997, no one was killed and no one was arrested in Kosovo.[11] When he made this statement, Milosevic was certainly aware that over the period he mentioned, there had been hundreds of deaths and thousands of arrests in Kosovo. Milosevic also understood that the truth about Kosovo had long been known to international observers and was also becoming known to Serbian audiences with the collapse of the media monopoly that Milosevic had maintained while in power. But his career and power were built on Kosovo, so to give it up or acknowledge the truth—even when common sense or political realities dictated that he do so—was hard. Former Russian Prime Minister Viktor Chernomyrdin, who met Milosevic five times during the negotiations over ending the 1999 war in Kosovo, found that it was most difficult to persuade Milosevic to accept terms for ending the war because Milosevic genuinely considered NATO "an aggressor and murderer," and Milosevic himself "was confident that he didn't do anything wrong with Kosovo."[12]

People with Milosevic's type of personality frequently either cannot or will not recognize the reality of facts that diverge from their own perception of the way the world is or should be. In an interview with the *Washington Post* at the end of 1998, Milosevic first denied the existence of ethnic cleansing and then claimed that he had condemned its use in Bosnia by all ethnic groups. Asked whether he had any regrets or had made any mistakes, Milosevic first appeared not to understand the question but then concluded, "I have a clear conscience."[13] In the TV Palma interview, when the question of his accountability before the Hague tribunal came up, Milosevic again replied, "My conscience is completely clear."[14] For Milosevic, it was as if the hundreds of thousands of victims—the dead, wounded, raped, and the refugees—simply did not exist.

Sometimes, of course, the divergence between the reality of the world as it is and the world as Milosevic wanted it to be grew too great for him to handle comfortably. Throughout his career, there were reports that Milosevic was subject to periods of depression, which sometimes led to his disappearance from public view for prolonged periods. During the 1988 New Year's holiday period, a vehicle in which Milosevic was riding was part of a traffic accident. Rumors circulated in Belgrade that the car had flipped over after tires had burst, possibly because of an accident or possibly because of an attempt on Milosevic's life. Whatever the truth of the incident, Milosevic was seldom seen in public for several months after the accident even though his injuries were described as superficial. In 1993, aides to the then president of the Federal Republic of Yugoslavia (FRY), Dobrica Cosic, told

European negotiator David Owen that Milosevic was "in one of his periodic phases of deep depression and indecision" after the Bosnian Serb assembly rejected the Vance-Owen peace plan despite a personal appeal by Milosevic to adopt it.[15]

Milosevic is also reportedly subject to fits of anger when events do not go his way. During the massive public demonstrations in Belgrade over the winter of 1996–1997, Milosevic was said to have trashed his own office in rage. According to NATO intelligence sources, he behaved similarly in 1999 when it became clear that the war in Kosovo was going badly.[16]

When malignant narcissists such as Milosevic occupy positions of power, they have the capability to manipulate people and even entire nations to meet their own twisted worldview. Milosevic was a user of people throughout his career. He had few friends, and his allies were always transient, embraced when they were useful and cast aside when their utility had passed. Other than his wife, few people remained close to Milosevic through the various phases of his political life. Milosevic generally got others to carry out his political dirty work, but when he was directly involved, it was with striking personal coldness. After the eighth session, Milosevic reacted with icy indifference when the deposed Stambolic tried publicly to appeal to their former friendship. Several years later, at a meeting of the SPS where some of those who had helped remove Stambolic were themselves dismissed, Milosevic simply read out the names of those to be axed without any explanation or thanks for past service.

A callous user of people, Milosevic sometimes seems to have no conception of the human consequences of his actions nor any hesitation in turning for help to those he has victimized. A few months after Milosevic dumped Stambolic, the latter's daughter was killed in a traffic accident. Milosevic attended the funeral, as if nothing had happened between him and his former mentor, and seemed surprised when Stambolic's wife refused to greet him. Years later, after Milosevic had been arrested and found himself in a Serbian prison hospital, he asked Dobrica Cosic to use his influence with new FRY President Vojslav Kostunica to allow Milosevic to remain in the hospital and not have to return to his Serbian jail cell. Milosevic seemed completely oblivious to the incongruousness of appealing for assistance to Cosic, whom he had used and then crudely dumped as FRY president years earlier.[17]

Milosevic is, in fact, a master of betrayal. The list of politicians with whom he has collaborated and then betrayed includes almost everyone who has at one time worked closely with him. It began with his mentor and closest friend, Stambolic, but it continued through political associates such as Jovic and Cosic, nationalist ideologues such as Karadzic and Seselj, and officials who have played important roles in executing the policies Milosevic set in motion, such as army Chief of Staff Momcilo Perisic and secret police head Jovica Stanisic.

Yet Milosevic took betrayal beyond the individual level. He consistently betrayed the interests and lives of the Serbian people. Milosevic exploited the Kosovo Serbs in his march to power, then cynically turned his back on them once their rabble-rousing became an embarrassment. Even though he armed the Croatian Serbs and encouraged them to rebell against Zagreb as part of his campaign to destroy Yugoslavia, he displayed no sign of sympathy—let alone remorse—in 1995 when Tudjman drove virtually all of the two hundred thousand Krajina Serbs from their homes.[18]

Two Wounded Souls

Milosevic's wife, Mirjana Markovic, played an important role both in Milosevic's system of rule over Serbia and in the psychological defenses Milosevic built against the awkward intrusion of the world of reality. U.S. psychiatrists described them as "two wounded souls" because of their similar background of family tragedy. Markovic is the only individual who consistently remained close to Milosevic, both in the political and personal sense. Djukic believes that "in order to explain his [Milosevic's] personality, it is first of all necessary to explain the personality of Mira Markovic."

Ivor Roberts labels Markovic's influence over Milosevic as "invariably baleful."[19] Djukic points out that members of Milosevic's regime feared Markovic much more than her husband.[20] In the late 1990s, as Serbia sank deeper into international isolation, Milosevic fell increasingly under the sway of Markovic's anti-Western foreign policy views and obscurantist domestic agenda. Vindictive to those who she comes to believe do not wholeheartedly share her views of what is best for Milosevic and Serbia, Markovic's unpredictable reactions are typical of people unable or unwilling to hold back their anger.

Perhaps not surprisingly for someone who still believes in the victory of orthodox Marxism-Leninism, Markovic's grasp on reality is sometimes said to be tenuous. During the 1997 anti-Milosevic demonstrations, she was reportedly hospitalized for deep depression at Belgrade's military hospital. Markovic sometimes attacked her nurses, according to one account, because she was convinced they were part of a plot against her. A few days after Milosevic's defeat in the September 2000 FRY elections, Markovic was said to have suffered a nervous breakdown that required heavy sedation.[21]

Despite Markovic's hard-line marxist views, there is a dreamy, almost otherworldly quality to her personality, which comes through in her writings. For several years in the mid-1990s, the Belgrade magazine *Duga* published her diary. At a time when war was raging in Bosnia, Markovic saw fit to inform the Serbian public about her musings on such matters as the flight of a butterfly. Markovic shuns public appearance, seldom straying beyond a narrow circle of family, friends, and cronies. Despite her image as the Lady Macbeth of Serbian politics, the few Westerners who have met Markovic have often remarked on her fragility and vulnerability. A well-informed Western journalist who met Markovic in 1996 was struck by her mousiness and the way her eyes vibrated "like a scared animal."[22] A diplomat quickly backed off serious discussion when it became clear that Markovic was out of her intellectual and emotional depth dealing with anything more substantive than the repetition of clichés.

But there is also, apparently, an uglier side to Markovic's personality. Media accounts linked her and her associates to some of the unexplained political murders that became an increasingly prominent feature in the final years of Milosevic's rule.

According to Milosevic's Serbian biographer, Slavoljub Djukic, "It is impossible to understand Milosevic or his wife unless you speak to their doctors." Djukic said that doctors have described both individuals as traumatized personalities who bear wounds from their childhood. Over the years they have constructed a very unusual relationship that reflects in many ways the scars that they carry from their youth.

Well-informed Serbian journalists, who have spoken at length to a doctor who treated the Milosevic family for years, say that the doctor described a highly dysfunctional family. According to these sources Milosevic—whose only serious chronic ailment was said to be high blood pressure—is the most normal member of his family. His wife, Mira Markovic, suffers from severe schizophrenia and often has only a tenuous grasp on reality. She is also said to be a hypochondriac who would often tell her doctors that she was ill with previously unknown diseases that only she could get. She would fly into a rage and become insulting if her doctors said that her health was satisfactory. The Milosevics's daughter, Marija, was described by these sources as "even sicker than her mother." Their son, Marko, was said not to be ill but rather a "simple criminal," whose violent and self-centered behavior was explained by the fact that since becoming a teenager "he was basically brought up by his bodyguards."

According to the doctor, Milosevic and his wife had a "very abnormal relationship," one of unusual dependency on Milosevic's part and superiority and exploitation by his wife. Milosevic was said by these sources to be completely devoted and unnaturally tied to his wife. According to Djukic, Milosevic had an unhealthy relationship with his wife. "Milosevic has had a deep love for his wife but he had to pay for his love."[23]

Although Markovic—according to everyone who has had any contact with her—apparently met Milosevic's devotion with love and faithfulness on her part, she also apparently took a certain advantage of Milosevic's dependency on her. According to the doctor, when Markovic was in one of her periodic fits of depression she would sometimes criticize Milosevic to his face. She would say that he was not competent to run the state, not very intelligent, and incapable of thinking deeply. On these occasions Markovic often highlighted her own supposed status as an intellectual who read books—an activity Milosevic apparently seldom engaged in—and who, unlike her husband, was capable of understanding great ideas. Milosevic was said never to reply to these sallies by his wife.

Markovic was always an important behind-the-scenes influence in Milosevic's political career—she helped orchestrate Milosevic's campaign against Ivan Stambolic and reportedly wrote many of his speeches. In the mid-1990s, however, Markovic began to play a more overt role in Serbian affairs. To a certain extent what may have happened is the classic example of a middle-aged woman, her children leaving home and no longer demanding as much attention, seeking out a second career. The prominent political role Markovic's family had played in Titoist Yugoslavia and her own exaggerated conception of her abilities probably made it seem utterly natural for her to move more openly into the political process. Indeed, the doctor noted that after Markovic founded her own political party—JUL—her hypochondria decreased.

As Markovic became more openly involved in politics, Milosevic—who never had much interest in the humdrum business of daily government—began to withdraw from political activity and even, according to many Belgrade insiders, to a certain extent from active contact with the world itself. As the 1990s progressed, Milosevic relied on an ever narrower circle of advisers—most of whom gained their entrée into the inner circle through their contacts with Mira and JUL.

Aleksandar Tijanic, who in the middle of the decade served Milosevic as Serbian Minister of Information and after the fall of Milosevic surfaced as a media adviser to President Kostunica, said that Markovic's influence varied depending on the issue. "In some things she had more influence than he did and in some things not."[24]

In the mid-1990s, Markovic used her influence to drive out of the SPS and the government a group of nationalist-inclined officials who had been close to Milosevic since he rose to power, including former Praxis figure Mihajlo Markovic, the director of Radio-Television Serbia (RTS), Milorad Vucelic, and former *Politika* director Zivorad Minovic. According to Belgrade insiders, Markovic was particularly hostile to those who developed close personal relationships with Milosevic, in ways that threatened to sidestep her own influence over Milosevic. The teetotaling Markovic was reportedly particularly hostile to the rabidly nationalistic and hard-drinking writer Branislav Crncevic—a close Milosevic connection in the late 1980s and early 1990s—whose boozy sessions with her husband she thought improper in both a political and a personal sense. Markovic's aversion to flamboyant nationalists also extended to Bosnian Serb leader Radovan Karadzic. According to Tijanic, when Mira picked up the phone at home once in the mid-1990s to find Karadzic on the other end of the line she frostily ordered him never to speak to Milosevic at home again.

Milosevic seemed insensitive to growing resentment that Markovic's expanding influence caused among his associates. In 1997, according to one Belgrade insider, Milosevic offered the position of president of Serbia to Nebojsa Covic, who had resigned as mayor of Belgrade during the massive street demonstrations against Milosevic beginning in 1996. Covic, according to this account, said he would accept but only if Milosevic would promise that his wife would not interfere with his business as president the way she had when he was mayor. As an example of the kind of influence he wished to avoid, Covic cited attempts by Markovic to pressure him to turn over a tennis court in the prestigious Belgrade suburb of Dedinje to the control of her JUL party. According to this account, Milosevic withdrew the offer when he heard Covic's condition and never spoke again to Covic—who later emerged as one of the more prominent members of the opposition coalition that overthrew Milosevic—a good example of the way in which Milosevic's dependency on Markovic acted to undermine his base of support among the Serbian political elite.

Players in what became the Milosevic-Markovic court camarilla—or what one Serbian observer called "an Oriental sultanate without the harem"—sometimes risked becoming caught up in cross-cutting currents between the two spouses. Tijanic, for example, says that Milosevic never forgave him for an article he wrote criticizing Milosevic after the removal of Ivan Stambolic. Mira tried to reconcile the two and brought Tijanic into the government but this only made matters worse. According to Tijanic, Milosevic did not like it when other men had close relations with Markovic. He could become jealous and see other men as potential rivals—not as lovers of Markovic, something about which neither Milosevic nor anyone else apparently had any suspicion—but as rivals for closeness and attention from the only woman in his life.

Markovic's involvement in politics did not, unfortunately, lead to any improvement in the quality of the top officials around Milosevic. Markovic used JUL to help her gain in the rivalry with the SPS for influence over Milosevic but, for the most part, JUL leaders consisted of corrupt war profiteers, smugglers, and gangsters. In part this reliance on corrupt advisers who made their way through flattery was due to the tendency of both Milosevic and Markovic to close their eyes to the reality of the world around them. According to Tijanic, Mira was "only weakly in contact with reality." Neither she nor Milosevic really liked people, he said, and both lived "in an autistic relation with the world around them, like Forest Gump."

Markovic's increasingly visible influence went in tandem—probably partly as cause and partly as consequence—of a change in Milosevic's personality and a decline in his interest and engagement in the affairs of governance that many Serbian insiders claim to have observed beginning in the middle of the 1990s. Milorad Vucelic said that the Milosevic of the mid-1990s was a different person than the man he first met early in the decade. According to Vucelic, in the beginning Milosevic was "charming, elegant, and gracious." At that time he showed no signs of the "hardness and arrogance" that later characterized his behavior toward those around him. Vucelic—who described Markovic as "cunning, crafty, perverted, and evil"—said that "beginning in 1995 Markovic began to control Milosevic and in the last year she ruled Serbia through him." Vucelic, like many others, also points to the almost unnatural quality of the devotion that Milosevic gave his wife. "He simply served her," is how Vucelic described it.[25]

Milosevic's dependency on Markovic and her cronies increased his isolation from former friends and associates in the Serbian elite and also contributed to a growing sense of detachment from the world of reality that many noted in Milosevic's last years. The longer Milosevic was in power the more isolated he became is a common observation among many Belgrade insiders. According to Tijanic, both Milosevic and Markovic began to consider themselves "like gods." Vucelic remarked that, "Milosevic lost contact with reality because he was surrounded by people who would only tell him what he wanted to hear and then he began to believe what he wanted to hear."

Toward the end Milosevic thought he was much more secure than he actually was, according to many insiders, and this sense of complacency may have contributed to the relative ease with which Milosevic fell under pressure of street demonstrations in October 2000. Aware that those at the top did not want to hear bad news, Serbian police in the second half of the 1990s routinely underestimated the size of demonstrations against Milosevic. This behavior apparently contributed to the failure of the Serbian authorities to deploy sufficient police in the streets to handle the demonstrations of October 5.

The Accidental Charismatic

In the first years of his rule, Milosevic gave a good imitation of being a charismatic leader. In the heady days of his climb to power, Milosevic developed a short and to-the-point speaking style that was consciously intended to distinguish his speeches from the jargon-filled orations of Yugoslav politicians before him. Milosevic capitalized on the discredited nature of self-management to promise the Serbian people an "antibureaucratic revolution" that would, in some fashion Milosevic never really explained, sweep away the poverty, corruption, and pettiness that for years had seemed to steadily narrow the horizons of life in post-Tito Yugoslavia.

At the height of Milosevic's ascent, the Slovenian daily *Delo* provided a penetrating analysis of the new style that Milosevic seemed to have brought to the Yugoslav political scene. Noting that Milosevic was clearly not a born speaker, that his delivery was somewhat rapid and he seemed more accustomed to reading his speeches than to ad-libbing, *Delo* nevertheless observed that Milosevic was something new in Yugoslavia. Milosevic had "stepped out of the bounds of the Communist jargon of our politicians. . . . His speeches contain no long and involved sentences whose meaning is grasped by the listener only after he has worked his way through five or six subordinate clauses." Milosevic's speeches were delivered in short and simple sentences. They were filled with comparisons and slogans that could be easily understood by everyone. *Delo* showed that even at that relatively early date, it had fully grasped the essence of Milosevic's new approach to Yugoslav politics: "Milosevic's speeches are not intended for discussion; they are a demonstration of power and determination."[26]

There was also an element to Milosevic's appeal that defied rational analysis. The former Communist bureaucrat had somehow made himself over into the symbol and voice of the Serbian people. On 4 October 1988, thousands of workers from the Belgrade industrial suburb of Rakovica marched to the square in front of the Yugoslav assembly building. They booed a series of hapless Yugoslav officials sent out to calm them and refused to leave until Milosevic appeared. Like a small-town revivalist, Milosevic led the workers through a staccato refrain of promise and response, holding out a vision of prosperity, political reform, and an end to "counterrevolution" in Kosovo. At the end of his speech, he paused dramatically then concluded, "And now, everyone to his task." The crowd replied as one, "We believe," and disbursed.

Milosevic appealed to traditional Serbian themes as well—buried but not forgotten underneath the surface of Communism—including the glorification of heroic leaders and the yearning for unity against perceived outside enemies. As the logjam of Communist rule was starting to break, Milosevic sensed a longing in the Serbian people for new certainties, and he gave it to them in an ideology that glorified the Serbian past and also attacked the nationalisms of the other Yugoslav peoples as anti-Serbian, revanchist, and genocidal. Milosevic's manipulation of nationalist themes did not separate him from his rivals in other Yugoslav republics who also found nationalism the most convenient alternative to Communism. What distinguished Milosevic was his success in using the concept of external threats to Serbia to tar opponents with the brush of national treason, a device that forced most of the opposition to adopt the nationalist agenda—but in even shriller tones—allowing Milosevic, in turn, to portray himself as a moderate.

Milosevic's appeal to Serb national themes found a ready audience in the peasant proletariat that flooded into Belgrade and other Serbian cities after World War II. In 1948, Belgrade's population was 385,000, but by 1981 it had grown to 1.4 million. In 1971, less than 39 percent of the city's population had been born there. Many of these newcomers ended up in the crowded and shoddily built housing complexes that ringed Belgrade, where they suffered from crime, alcohol abuse, and other ailments common to an urban underclass. Many maintained close ties with their native villages, often returning home to help with the harvest and sometimes even bringing a few farm animals back with them to their city apartments. In the 1980s, it was not uncommon in the autumn to see pigs strung up for slaughter outside high-rise apartment complexes on the outskirts of the city. These urban peasants of the Belgrade industrial suburbs formed ready cannon fodder for Milosevic's "street democracy."

Media Mogul

Control of the media was one of the most consistent elements of Milosevic's rule. Milosevic and the inner circle around him used state television and major print organs, especially those in the Politika publishing house, to create a climate of public opinion aimed first at discrediting Milosevic's rivals in Serbia and then at mobilizing mass support for Milosevic's aggressive campaign to expand his control outside of Serbia proper. Milosevic discovered early on that the most effective way to manage the media was not by formal censorship but by putting them in the hands of unscrupulous journalists who were prepared to slavishly follow his line and who would not shrink from appealing to the lowest instincts of the mob. Milosevic also intervened directly with editors to ensure that media organs reported the news exactly as he wanted it portrayed. The last U.S. ambassador to Yugoslavia, Zimmermann, learned that in the late 1980s, Milosevic met every day with the head of Belgrade Television. Zimmermann also once overheard an editor silence a journalist protesting over changes to a story by saying, "That's the way the boss wants it."[27] When the Serbian Krajina fell to Croatia in 1995, Milosevic summoned the heads of the major Serbian media organs and gave them explicit directions on how to slant their coverage of the disaster.[28]

Milosevic's close attention to the news was often uncomfortable for those he put in charge of the media. Vucelic, RTS director in the mid-1990s, traces his break with Milosevic to the fall of the Serb enclave of Western Slavonija to a Croatian offensive in May 1995. When RTS reported the event in a short statement eighteen minutes into its regular evening news program, Vucelic—who says he was away at the time—called Milosevic and labeled the scanty coverage "shameful," which provoked an angry quarrel. In August 1995, when Belgrade television showed pictures of massive columns of Serb refugees fleeing into Serbia from the Croatian offensive that crushed Krajina, an angry Milosevic telephoned Vucelic and demanded that he end such coverage. According to Vucelic, Milosevic yelled into the telephone that he was supposed to be running "Serbian television, not refugee television," and that if he wanted to show pictures of tractors—on which many refugees were fleeing—he should run footage of farms in Voj-vodina.[29]

Vucelic's story shows how Milosevic paid particularly close attention to television, which he knew was the chief source of information for the majority of the Serbian population. According to one well-informed Belgrade journalist, a chief editor of the Serbian evening news program recounted how as soon as the program was over he would sit back at his desk and begin to look apprehensively at the telephone. When it rang it would be Milosevic on the line, who would chew him out for what he considered mistakes on the just-concluded news program. After these uncomfortable conversations, which often included strings of profanity from Milosevic, the editor said his shirt would be drenched with sweat.

In the hands of Milosevic's creatures the media proved an astonishingly effective vehicle for molding public opinion. When Milosevic moved against Stambolic in 1987, he had not succeeded—despite intense efforts—in gaining a secure majority on the central committee. His supporters, therefore, turned to the media—exploiting incidents such as the Paracin murders and exaggerated claims of harassment experienced by Serbs in Ko-sovo—to create a climate of public hysteria that made it virtually impossible to oppose the Milosevic juggernaut. During the Milosevic-inspired demonstrations in the summer of 1988, the news editor of Radio-Television Serbia, Branko Mihajlovic, got instructions to inflate the numbers of the protesters and to emphasize the chants and posters that glorified Milosevic while ignoring those of the more extreme nationalists. By contrast, Serb television attempted to discredit the 9 March 1991 demonstrations against Milosevic—running pictures of the grief-stricken family of the police officer killed during the demonstrations, but ignoring the student who was also killed and labeling the protests a violent attempt to overturn the legitimate government of Serbia.[30]

In a media environment where 60 percent of the population got their only information from the regime-dominated evening television news and only a small minority regularly read newspapers of any kind, it proved easy to manipulate public opinion. Polls showing shifting popular attitudes to the 1993 Vance-Owen peace plan for Bosnia reveal this process. A poll taken on 9 April 1993, when the regime opposed Vance-Owen, found that 70 percent of Serbs were against the plan. An identical survey, taken on 27 April after the regime had come out publicly in support of Vance-Owen, found that only 20 percent opposed the plan and 39 percent supported it.[31]

The regime also used its control of the media to foster a xenophobic,

Serbia-against-the-world attitude. While the news produced a steady diet of glorification of Serbian themes and vilification of its enemies, popular culture was reshaped to bolster the regime's appeal to the most violent and primitive sides of human nature. After the outbreak of war in 1991, positive references to the United States or Europe vanished. Violent action films—ironically, often from Hollywood—were the only foreign shows allowed. Turbo-folk music, a hard-driving and hypnotic combination of hard rock and simplistic Serbian folk themes, flooded the airwaves. The urbane and well-traveled Yugoslav intellectuals who had led Belgrade's public and cultural life before the war disappeared from view, replaced by fanatics, mystics, and charlatans. Milosevic and his circle "dumbed down" an entire society to make it more malleable to their political objectives.[32]

For most of his rule, Milosevic tolerated a limited number of small independent media, which served as safety valves for opposition intellectuals and window dressing to counter foreign charges of repression. In the late 1980s, *Borba*, the central organ of the LCY—in effect, the Yugoslav *Pravda*—reinvented itself as an independent and nonnationalist alternative paper. *Borba* became the leading Belgrade daily opposed to Milosevic after Yugoslavia's collapse. *Vreme*, founded in 1990 as Yugoslavia's first privately owned newsweekly, continued throughout Milosevic's rule as the most consistent and courageous center of print media opposition to Milosevic. In the mid-1990s, several small opposition papers appeared, generally funded by maverick business figures. Two small independent stations—TV Studio B and Radio B-92—provided a broadcast media alternative.

But Milosevic was careful to confine the alternative media to the fringes of public attention. Independent newspapers had their supplies of paper limited and were denied access to newsstands controlled by the major, regime-dominated publishing houses. As a result, independent papers were generally only available at a few places in downtown Belgrade and were usually sold out by midmorning. Their readership was generally confined to a small number of intellectuals who were already committed to opposing the regime and to foreign journalists and diplomats. Independent television and radio outlets were denied access to government-controlled relay towers, and their signals reached only a few areas in Belgrade.

Beginning in 1994, Milosevic began to cut back on even the small space earlier allowed the independent media—a process of "salami slicing" whose timing often seemed linked to developments in international negotiations. Milosevic moved to take over *Borba* at roughly the same time that he broke with the hard-line Bosnian Serb leaders and when the official media, obviously acting under instructions, began to downplay nationalist themes. The move against *Borba* seemed intended to eliminate a source of embarrassing questions about the shift in policy. Milosevic shut down Studio B in early 1996, apparently calculating—correctly as it turned out—that the central place he had assumed in the U.S.-led Dayton peace process would limit the scope of international protests. In the spring of 1998, as the deteriorating situation in Kosovo began to draw increasing foreign attention, Milosevic moved to close many of the independent local radio stations. In the fall of that year, at the same time that a U.S. team under the leadership of Richard Holbrooke sought a diplomatic settlement in Kosovo, Milosevic used a drastic new Law on the Media to close or levy heavy fines against several independent broadcast and print media outlets.

Milosevic's moves against the independent media also reflected the growing influence of his wife, who was apparently much less tolerant than her husband of personal attacks, and concern on Milosevic's part that as his own domestic position weakened, the heretofore relatively marginal independent media was expanding its reach and influence. In 1996 and 1997—in part thanks to foreign funding support—independent radio stations opened in seventeen towns beyond Belgrade. According to Veran Matic, the respected editor-in-chief of B-92, the largest independent broadcast outlet, in those years "we became a real force in an area which Milosevic had previously considered all his own—the Serbian countryside and small towns outside Belgrade." At the same time the first large-circulation independent daily newspapers appeared. *Blic*, backed by German investors and *Dnevni telegraf*, founded by Slavko Curuvija, combined an opposition political message with sensationalist coverage of daily events, expanding their readership beyond the elitist circles to which the opposition print media had formerly been confined.[33]

One Man's Economy

Control of the economy was another pillar of Milosevic's rule. At the start of his tenure in power, Milosevic liked to describe himself to foreigners as a banker. But Milosevic was a Yugoslav self-management banker, which had about as much relation to real banking as alchemy has to chemistry. Under socialist Yugoslavia, banks functioned as a way for the government to move resources among favored enterprises, and Milosevic always retained this vision of the Serbian economy as the milch cow for his own ambitions. In 2001, Nikola Zivanovic, the young, Western-educated investment banker who took over as chief of Beogradska Banka from Borka Vucic after Milosevic's fall, said that few at the bank remembered Milosevic's tenure as president twenty years earlier but added, "from what I have heard he was a good banker for that time." Zivanovic noted, however, that "a good banker in a socialist country is not the same thing as a good banker in a market economy."[34]

In any case, Milosevic's experience as a banker does not seem to have been at all beneficial for the Serbian economy. In the 1990s, a combination of economic mismanagement, the burden of war, and the effect of international sanctions plunged Belgrade's economy into disaster. By 1998 GDP had fallen to $17.4 billion, about 56 percent of its level in 1989, the last more or less normal economic year before the dissolution of Yugoslavia. Over the same period industrial production fell by almost 64 percent while official unemployment went up from 17.9 percent to 25.1 percent.[35] Confiscation by the authorities—supposedly to finance the war effort—two rounds of hyperinflation, and a mid-1990s pyramid scheme combined to eliminate the savings of the middle class and reduce the bulk of Serbia's urban population to destitution.

Despite Serbia's poverty, Milosevic always found a way to use his control of the country's economy to ensure that resources were available to him and his supporters to keep the system functioning, fight the wars, and reward family and friends. In the late 1980s, Milosevic utilized this control to finance his new SPS political party and deny funding to the opposition. Milosevic later drained Serbian economic institutions to support the war in Croatia and Bosnia. In 1997, he reportedly used the proceeds from Serbia's first major post-Dayton international business deal, with an Italian telecommunications company, to pay pensions and salaries across Serbia in order to counter growing support for the opposition.

Another measure of the economic cost of the Milosevic regime is the tremendous growth in expenditures on the police, which Milosevic used to maintain himself in power. Over the period 1994 to 1999 the share of police expenditures in the state budget rose from an already high figure of 15.13 percent to 27.91 percent. In its last years, particularly, this increase came largely at the expense of expenditures in education and science.[36]

Within Milosevic's administration, state-controlled financial institutions were as important as the security forces. They acted as sources of money as well as channels for diverting funds to recipients, both within Serbia and overseas. Beogradska Banka, formerly headed by Milosevic, was at the heart of this network. Documents from a Beogradska Banka subsidiary made available to the media after Milosevic's fall described about one hundred credits, some of which apparently went to benefit members of the Milosevic family, while others were apparently funneled through regime officials or supporters to finance activity crucial to keeping Milosevic in power.[37] Among recipients of such funds were Mihajlo Kertes, who after his role supplying arms to Serbs in Croatia and Bosnia became federal customs director. After Milosevic's fall, Kertes said money channeled through him was used to finance the SPS and other illicit activities. "They always wanted more, more for pensions, more for the army, more for health care, more for social peace. More for more," Kertes told the Belgrade media.[38]

Milosevic's heist of about $1.5 billion worth of state funds from the Yugoslav National Bank at the end of 1990 caused outrage throughout Yugoslavia, and helped accelerate the drive to secession in Slovenia and Croatia. But according to Mladjan Dinkic, long prominent in the anti-Milosevic opposition and appointed as chair of the National Bank after Milosevic's fall, the abuse of the state economy controlled by Milosevic for his own purposes began as early as 1989, with the diversion of the approximately $100 million in dinars and hard currency donated by patriotic Serbs to Milosevic's "National Bond for the Rebirth of Serbia," much of which found its way into the hands of Milosevic supporters. Milosevic froze all savings in hard currency in 1991 as war unfolded, which allowed the state to seize around $4 billion. Much of the money diverted in this fashion later found its way into the hands of the pro-Milosevic elite, either for private purposes such as the purchase of apartments, flashy cars, and expensive vacations, or for use by the Milosevic regime in such activities as financing imports needed to evade sanctions and supporting the wars in Croatia, Bosnia, and Kosovo.[39]

According to media accounts and interviews with members of G-17, a group of economists associated with the opposition that overthrew Milosevic in 2000, Borka Vucic was at the center of the Milosevic financial empire. In 1988 Vucic, facing retirement at Beogradska Banka, opened a branch of the bank in Cyprus, long a haven for off-shore financial operations. Over the nine years she remained in Cyprus, Vucic's operation reportedly became the financial linchpin of Milosevic's sanctions-busting operations, which also provided the foundation for Milosevic's wartime economy. Dozens of Serbian companies had branches in Cyprus and billions of dollars moved in and out of Belgrade's accounts on the island.

A sprightly, grey-haired septuagenarian, Vucic was likened by Western bankers to Rosa Klebb, the doctrinaire opposing spy chief in Ian Fleming's James Bond spy novels. "She single-handedly raised more funds than anyone for Yugoslavia," a U.S. banker with extensive experience in the area later told the media.[40]

The scale of the Milosevic illicit financial operation was staggering, especially considering the impoverished state of the Serbian economy. After Milosevic fell from power the media reported that U.S. Treasury investigators had concluded that at least one billion dollars had been spirited out of the country by Milosevic associates and flowed through banks in Cyprus to other destinations. "It is apparently the money which the former regime had transferred to Cyprus in the course of the 1990s," Dinkic told a news conference.[41]

According to Suzanna Mrkic, chief executive of G-17 Plus, "Vucic was the key person in the transfer of funds to Cyprus." Most of the money was shipped to Cyprus in cash, stashed in suitcases, bags, and any other device in which money could be sent undetected. In Cyprus, Vucic reportedly served as both the record keeper and as the manager of investments. But Vucic left few traces of her activities, reportedly memorizing most of the records of the illicit financial transactions. "You just can't imagine what facts and figures she kept in her head," Mrgic commented.[42]

Vucic, for her part, staunchly denies any wrong-doing. She admitted with a smile to having a good head for figures but asserted that all transactions involving Beogradska Banka in Cyprus were carried out in writing and in full accord with Serbian and Cypriot laws and that repeated audits had confirmed that all of the bank's activities were proper. "I did not get a single dollar from Belgrade as capital," Vucic claimed, but she added proudly that when she left, Beogradska Banka in Cyprus had a capital value of 60 million dollars, a success which she attributed to her own experience of forty years as an international banker.[43]

The money that moved through Cyprus was the foundation of a wartime economy that allowed Milosevic to keep his armies and defense industries functioning despite the sanctions. A small number of state-owned enterprises and trading companies organized the shipment of the illegal goods. Progress, a huge state trading company, had a lock on trade with Russia, especially gas imports. Jugopetrol, the Communist-era oil monopoly for Serbia, organized the import of oil and gasoline from Russia, Libya, and other sources. Once in the illegal pipeline, the oil moved into Serbia through a variety of routes: up the Danube, via Albania and across Lake Skadar, and even from supposedly hostile Croatia.

As the bulk of the Serbian people sank into poverty, a new class of flamboyantly wealthy smugglers and mafiosi took center stage in Belgrade's economic, political, and social life. Some members of this new class got their start from goods stolen during ethnic cleansing operations in Bosnia or Croatia. Arkan, for example, opened a chain of stores specializing in imported luxury goods. Many of Milosevic's leading political associates also had their hands in the till, according to media reports. The speaker of the Serbian parliament, Dragan Tomic, headed Jugopetrol, where he reportedly profited handsomely from the illicit oil that flowed into Serbia during sanctions. Serbian Prime Minister Mirko Marjanovic made millions selling wheat that had been acquired cheaply from Serbian farmers during sanctions on the international market at a high price.[44]

During the 1990s, Milosevic and his team used the Yugoslav socially owned system of agricultural supply and fuel companies to maximize control over the largely private farmers in the rich, grain-producing region of Vojvodina. The regime forced farmers to obtain necessary supplies such as seed, fertilizer, and fuel from state-controlled enterprises at relatively high prices, and then to sell the output of their fields to state-controlled mills at low prices. The difference went in the till of the Milosevic machine, either to support the war and sanction-busting effort or into the pockets of the officials involved.[45]

Milosevic certainly benefited personally from the web of illicit financial transactions made possible by his control of the Serbian economy. Shortly after his fall from power, for instance, he was reported to be building a villa worth £2 million in the prestigious Belgrade suburb of Dedinje.[46] Nevertheless, as noted earlier, Milosevic seems to have been motivated primarily by power and not wealth. The same cannot be said, however, for other members of his family. Milosevic's brother, Branislav, the Serbian ambassador to Moscow, played a central role in organizing Serbian trade with Russia.[47] But the most avaricious member of the Milosevic family turned out to be Markovic. She had always cultivated the image of a dreamy intellectual, but turned out to have a surprisingly strong appetite for wealth for someone devoted to Marxist-Leninist orthodoxy. After Milosevic's fall, details of Markovic's decidedly nonmarxist lifestyle began to surface, including allegations that she had given a "tip" worth £165,000 to her hairdresser in order to redecorate her chrome- and marble-lined salon.[48]

Beginning in mid-1994, Markovic presided over the creation of a new political and economic ruling elite loosely organized around her JUL party, but in fact motivated primarily by lust for loot and depending for the satisfaction of that need on access to regime favors dispensed by Markovic. According to one story, when Markovic created her new party, she asked friends what organization had lasted the longest. The answer was the Mafia, which one friend pointed out had ensured the absolute loyalty of its members by providing financial benefits and protection as well as the certainty that betrayal would be repaid with death. "I like that," Mira supposedly said. "We are going to use these principles for our organization."[49] Whether this story is true or not, the sentiments behind it aptly describe the "rabble of war profiteers, smugglers, and criminals" that constituted the circle most closely connected with JUL and increasingly with Milosevic.

JUL took over the top floors of the skyscraper in New Belgrade across from the city center that was formerly the headquarters of the LCY. Membership in the party became the best ticket to political advancement and economic wealth. Because of her diligence in dispensing favors to those whose hard-line political views and loyalty to the Milosevic clan pleased her, Markovic came to be known as the "Mother Theresa of profiteers, fawners, and lackeys."[50]

After Milosevic's fall, former JNA Chief of Staff Stevan Mirkovic, who was allied with Markovic in founding the short-lived successor to the LCY, the LC–MY, portrayed the connection between politics, crime, and illicit financial dealings that characterized Markovic's empire from the first. He described the formation in the spring of 1991—as the LC–MY party was getting underway—of the firm Komet, an organization that combined black marketeering, commercial enterprise, and paramilitary muscle. According to Mirkovic, Komet was intended to provide both financing and security for the LC–MY. Komet's first director, Miodrag Tomasevic, was close to Markovic, and the firm's offices were located in the old LCY headquarters building across the river from downtown Belgrade. Initially, all of the LCY dues, which continued to be deducted from the pay of JNA officers even after the party's collapse, went into Komet's coffers. From the beginning, though, Komet also disposed of large sums of money whose source was uncertain even to Mirkovic. Komet hired former employees of the Yugoslav secret police as guards for the LC–MY and also, reportedly, for a number of other government and private institutions. As well, Komet amassed an arsenal of several hundred weapons, including automatic rifles and pistols. According to media accounts, some of Komet's activities included beating opposition activists and breaking up opposition demonstrations. Serbian journalists and lawyers also asserted that Komet, together with JUL official and Markovic friend, Slobodan Cerovic—then the Serb minister of tourism—may have played a role in the murder of opposition journalist Slavka Curuvija, who was shot under mysterious circumstances shortly after the NATO bombing of Serbia began in 1999.[51]

Members of the Milosevic entourage used Markovic's vanity and socialist sympathies to their own financial and political advantage as well. The Yugoslav media described how the Karic brothers—Kosovo Serb businessmen who founded Serbia's largest private bank—staged a Potemkin book launching to celebrate the publication in Moscow of a Russian edition of a book by Markovic that was supposedly a best-seller, but was in fact largely given away or pulped. The Karic brothers used Markovic's presence at the promotional event to gain access to high levels of the Russian government and society, including Russian Orthodox Patriarch Aleksei II, who was one of the few world leaders to visit Milosevic in Belgrade during his last years in power. The event pandered to Markovic's notion of creating an anti-U.S. alliance among ex-Communist states while helping the business connections of the Karic brothers, whose offices in Moscow reportedly took on something of the status of a second FRY embassy.[52]

Milosevic's children, too, demonstrated a proclivity for using their father's position for financial gain. His daughter, Marija, according to the media, received an unsecured loan worth $446,000 to finance Studio Kosava, the radio and television station she began in the mid-1990s.[53] Milosevic's son, Marko, was the most notorious of the clan. Although Marko never managed to finish high school, he was dispatched while still in his early twenties to head an export-import firm in Athens, where he became infamous for his flamboyant lifestyle, which included a stint as a race car driver. "Daddy got mad after the first 15 cars I wrecked, but after that he stopped paying attention," Marko told one of his friends.[54] After leaving Athens, Marko returned to the family homestead in Pozarevac, where he presided over a quasi-criminal commercial network that included duty-free stores, a discotheque, and a "Bambi Park" for children, whose opening shortly after the end of the NATO bombing, Marko claimed, showed his concern for future generations in Serbia.[55]

After Milosevic's fall stories began to surface that Marko and his associates—and possibly even Slobodan Milosevic himself—may have been involved in drug smuggling and other crimes. Germany's foreign intelligence agency charged in a secret report leaked to the German media that Milosevic placed more than $100 million in foreign accounts and was involved in drug trafficking. "Numerous hints let us recognize Milosevic and his entourage as an organized crime structure, engaged in drug trade, money laundering, and other crimes," the German newsweekly *Bild* quoted the report as saying. Lydia Rauscher, the spokeswoman for the Federal Intelligence Service, broadly confirmed the newspaper's account: "Such a fortune cannot have been amassed by legal means." Many of the Milosevic millions, according to this source, were made from cigarette smuggling and black-market currency deals. Allies of the former president and Marko were granted concessions that allowed them to circumvent normal customs duties. The intelligence report also asserted that Milosevic controlled accounts in other nations, which was presumably one reason why the Swiss authorities froze one hundred bank accounts linked to Milosevic and his associates around the time of his fall.[56]

No Alternative

Milosevic was an odd kind of dictator. Although in some ways the last of Europe's Communist rulers, his was generally a "soft" authoritarianism—at least until shortly before the 1999 war with NATO. Aleksa Djilas, a noted Belgrade intellectual and the son of famous Communist-era dissident Milovan Djilas, noted with some irony that Milosevic was probably the only ruler in Yugoslavia's history never to have banned a book.[57] The midnight knock on the door was not, by and large, a feature of Milosevic's rule in Serbia. (In Kosovo, of course, Milosevic's rule had a different character; there, political prisoners numbered in the thousands and police violence was routine.)

Control over the media, economy, and organs of state power were essential elements in Milosevic's political longevity. But Milosevic's strategy for survival went beyond these typical features of authoritarian rule. In what has been variously called by Serbian political analysts "decivilization" or the "destruction of society," Milosevic pursued a policy aimed at impoverishing not just the economic but also the intellectual and social fabric of Serbia in order to eliminate the very capacity for independent alternatives to emerge.[58]

Since many of the middle-class professionals and intellectuals who were hardest hit by the decline in the Serbian economy were already convinced Milosevic opponents, the regime lost little sleep over their plight. The appearance of a new class of corrupt war profiteers, who owed their wealth and positions to their personal ties with the regime, on the other hand, created a powerful new social group with a direct interest in the regime's continued survival. The shrinking economy dominated by a small number of enterprises or trading companies that were either owned by the state or depended on it for their access to money or goods, made it even easier for the regime to tighten its control over people's daily lives. Access to jobs, new housing, utilities, and scarce consumer goods increasingly depended on the regime or the criminal underclass that now dominated Serbia.

According to a 1994 poll, about 82 percent of the Serb population spent more than 50 percent of their earnings on food alone, while 45 percent reported spending between 66 to 100 percent of their income on food.[59] These economic hardships aroused anger—which regime propaganda attempted to direct toward the West and especially the United States—but they also fostered apathy. Forced to expend more and more physical and mental energy for their day-to-day survival, people simply did not have the time or strength left over to oppose the regime.

A perceptive 1999 sociological study of Milosevic's Serbia attempted to answer the question of how Milosevic had managed to survive in view of the unbroken string of failures he had brought to the Serbian people. Its answer was that the Milosevic regime survived not by mobilizing opinion in its favor—that possibility was long since gone—but by closing off "alternative avenues of information, expression, and sociability." Aware that it could no longer count on active support from the majority of Serbs, the regime acted not only to destroy alternatives but to make it impossible for the Serbian population even to conceive of any alternative to Milosevic. According to this analysis, "habituation, resignation, and apathy" were the main props of the Milosevic regime.[60]

EIGHT

Man of Peace

B y the middle of 1992, Milosevic faced trouble on several fronts. Serb forces controlled one-third of Croatia and over half of Bosnia, but antiwar sentiment was growing at home. Ethnic cleansing had aroused world condemnation, and on 30 May, the UN Security Council imposed the first economic sanctions against Serbia. Gradually tightened over the next two years, the sanctions—together with mismanagement by Milosevic's followers—had a severe impact on the Serbian economy. Milosevic resorted to the printing press to finance the heavy burdens of supporting Serbia's bloated state structures, maintaining the military on a war footing, feeding almost half a million refugees, and subsidizing the Serb para-states in Croatia and Bosnia. By the end of 1993, Serbia had achieved the dubious distinction of equaling inflation in Weimar Germany in 1923, up until then the highest in Europe.[1]

London Conference

The 26–27 August 1992 London Conference on the Former Yugoslavia ended the EC's sputtering efforts to mediate the Yugoslav crisis. The conference issued a statement of principles—respect for human rights, compliance with the Geneva Convention, and sanctity of borders—that might have provided a sound basis for ending the conflict in Yugoslavia had anyone paid the slightest attention to them.

The London conference, which unfolded as dramatic pictures of the emaciated inmates of Serb concentration camps in Bosnia were flooding the world media, resounded with criticism of Belgrade. Eagleburger, the head of the U.S. delegation, set the tone: "It is the Serbs who are most guilty today of crimes . . . and it is the Serbs who face a spectacularly bleak future unless they manage to change the reckless course their leaders chose."[2]

Milosevic was an unhappy man at the London conference. The reason had less to do with international criticism than the outspoken behavior of Milan Panic, the Serbian-American businessman Milosevic had appointed as prime minister of the FRY, the union of Serbia and Montenegro that Milo-sevic had created to buttress his claim to be the successor to the old Yugo-slavia that Milosevic himself had done so much to destroy. Ten days before the London conference, Panic—intent on demonstrating his distance from Milosevic—sent a letter to the UN Security Council rejecting "the barbaric practice of ethnic cleansing in any form" and renouncing territorial claims on the FRY's former Yugoslav neighbors. At the conference, Panic reported the arrest of five people for ethnic cleansing and declared that he was pre-pared to bring to justice any FRY citizen involved in such activity.[3]

British Prime Minister John Major, who chaired the London conference, described Milosevic as glowering from the second-row seat behind the ta-ble, to which Panic had relegated him. At one point, when Milosevic tried to respond to a question posed by Major, Panic told him to "be quiet." Later, the two nearly came to blows in a cloakroom over Panic's decision to accept language in the conference communiqué critical of Serb nationalism.[4]

Lord Owen Has Plans

The London conference appointed former British Foreign Secretary David Owen as special envoy to the former Yugoslavia. Shortly before the confer-ence, Owen had publicly called for air strikes against Serbia and his ap-pointment was seen as heralding a more vigorous approach to international peacemaking. Over the next two years, Owen crisscrossed the region, meeting countless times with all the warring parties. Assisted by a small team of capable advisers drawn largely from the British Foreign Office and the UN bureaucracy, Owen came up with a series of plans to end the conflict in Bosnia. As soon as a plan was shot down by one or, more frequently, all of the warring parties, the indefatigable Owen was on the road again with another.

Owen had no illusions about Milosevic. In his memoirs, he acknowl-edges Milosevic's ruthless pursuit of power for its own sake and tendency to regard individuals as disposable. But Owen also believed that Milosevic saw cooperation with international diplomacy in Bosnia as an opportunity to jump off the tiger's back of nationalism and concluded that the Serbian leader "stayed true to that strand of his policy from then onwards."[5]

Over the next three years the international community pursued a variety of fruitless efforts to bring peace to Bosnia. Milosevic sought to give the impression that nationalism and a Greater Serbia were the farthest things from his mind. Much of this, of course, was for foreign consumption, but it was true that things had not developed entirely to Milosevic's liking in the Serb-held areas outside of Serbia proper. Milosevic had given up on the prospect of incorporating Krajina into Serbia. The most he probably expected to achieve in Croatia was that the division might eventually settle into a de facto, permanent partition and that he could maintain some form of protectorate over the Serbs in eastern Slavonia, which borders on Serbian Vojvodina.

Milosevic and the Serb media under his control had also stopped talking publicly about incorporating Serb-held areas of Bosnia into Serbia. Over the next three years, Milosevic signed onto a variety of peace plans that provided for the Republika Srpska—the name Bosnian Serbs had given their statelet—to remain within a separate Bosnian state. But Milosevic never expected these jury-rigged Bosnian creations to last long and anticipated that Serb-held territory in Bosnia would eventually join Serbia.

In November 1993, Milosevic held the first of a series of secret meetings with Tudjman's chief foreign policy adviser, Hrvoje Sarinic. As later described by Sarinic, who admits he was surprised by Milosevic's openness, the Serbian leader laid out his private views on how to settle the crisis. Milosevic—who over the years made a habit of disparaging all of his Serb allies—called the Krajina Serb leaders "crazy" and "guaranteed" that his aim was not to unite Krajina with Serbia, which he said would be a "big mistake."[6] Milosevic was not, however, willing to act on these words either then or, to his subsequent regret, ever.

Bosnia was the problem Milosevic most wanted to address and he made it clear that his preferred option was to divide Bosnia with Tudjman: "I tell you openly that only with the Republika Srpska in BH [Bosnia-Hecegovina], which sooner or later will become part of Serbia, we will resolve 90 percent of the Serb national question the way that Tudjman resolved the national question of Croatia with Herceg-Bosna."[7] Milosevic said he had nothing against the international option for Bosnia then on the table—a loose union of the three ethnic groups—but he observed cynically that such a union would not last long. Sarinic concluded that Milosevic was primarily concerned with two problems: the effect of sanctions on the Serbian economy and the danger of Islamic fundamentalism in the Balkans, especially in Kosovo, which Milosevic consistently called a "huge problem."[8]

While Milosevic struggled to evade the effect of international sanctions on the Serbian economy, Tudjman was becoming increasingly confident in Croatia of eventual victory over the isolated Krajina Serbs. Tudjman's great fear with respect to Krajina was the obverse of the Serbs' only hope—a Cyprus-style partition. He waited with growing impatience as the UN failed to achieve a political settlement, largely because neither side was ever willing to seriously consider a plan—called the Z-4 plan because it had been developed by four ambassadors in Zagreb—for granting Krajina broad autonomy within Croatia.

Unlike Milosevic, Tudjman never lost control of his own creations. The Bosnian Croats always remained firmly under Zagreb's thumb, and were willing to agree to almost any Bosnian settlement as long as it left them holding the territory along the interior of the Adriatic coast and the Neretva valley they had seized at the beginning of the war. Tudjman's paranoia about Islamic fundamentalism was, if anything, even greater than Milosevic's and he never lost the itch to divide Bosnia. But as the United States became increasingly sympathetic to Sarajevo, Tudjman switched his strategy on Bosnia from partition to one of using Croatia's geographic proximity and growing military might to dominate that part of Bosnia not held by the Serbs.

The Bosnian Moslems—the weakest party militarily—had the most ambitious objectives, which is one reason why international negotiators found them so difficult to deal with. The Bosnian authorities, led by Izetbegovic and the SDA, consistently sought a settlement that would preserve Bosnia as a unitary state, with the most powerful central government that the traffic would bear. They hoped that their numerical advantage, aided by an outflow of Serb and Croatian populations to their respective home republics, would eventually enable them to dominate Bosnia. Aware that Europe lacked the military muscle and political will to resolve the Bosnian problem itself, and convinced—with good reason—that they enjoyed little sympathy among many Europeans, the Bosnians' basic strategy was to draw the United States into the war on their side. Until this happened, the Bosnians had to walk a fine line between obstructing international peace efforts that threatened their vision of themselves as the rightful rulers of Bosnia and not going so far as to provoke the international community—on which they relied for military protection and humanitarian supplies—to throw up its hands and leave Bosnia altogether. This strategy of aggressive victimhood made the Bosnians infuriating diplomatic partners—a difficulty that was compounded by the uneasy awareness among most internationals that the Bosnians were, in fact, the victims of Serb aggression that the international community had failed to stop.

Interlude: "Slobodan, When Are You Leaving?"

In June 1992, Milosevic invited Cosic to become the president of the FRY, hoping to shield himself from mounting criticism by installing the popular writer in this largely ceremonial position. Only two months earlier, Cosic had written Milosevic a sharp private letter in which he warned of the demoralization that war and Milosevic's economic policies had brought to Serbia and concluded that "Slobodan Milosevic, with all his unarguable capabilities, cannot any longer lead the national policies of Serbia." Cosic's letter, however, contained no criticism of the ethnic cleansing that Milosevic's minions were even then unleashing in Bosnia. The correctives that Cosic proposed—compromise with the opposition, ties with Serbs in Bosnia and Croatia, and convening prominent Serbs to discuss the situation in Kosovo, which even then Cosic acknowledged was heading toward loss or war—revealed the continued preoccupation of Milosevic's critics with the national issue, to the neglect of democracy.[9]

Cosic was surprised when, shortly after he wrote this letter, Milosevic offered him the job of FRY president. Milosevic even accepted all of Cosic's conditions for the new job—early elections, an independent government of specialists, a new constitution, and a flexible international policy—none of which, of course, Milosevic had the slightest intention of actually carrying out.

In June 1992, Cosic, who had been expelled from the LCY by Tito in 1968 and had led the assault of the Serbian intellectuals on Tito's legacy, found himself sitting at the huge desk in Belgrade's Federation Palace that had originally been made for Tito. Cosic's first act was to convene the four-member rump presidency left over from Yugoslavia's collapse, but the members—before they vanished forever from the Yugoslav scene—confessed they had nothing to do and no suggestions to offer. Cosic next telephoned the head of military intelligence and army chief of staff, both of whom figuratively snapped to attention when they heard the voice of their new president on the line, yet seemed somewhat startled when Cosic confessed he had not called for any special purpose other than to request a meeting. When the meeting was held, the elderly head of the federal police, Petar Gracanin, put everyone to sleep with a long, droning presentation. It was an inauspicious though symbolically apt beginning for the indecisive Cosic.[10]

The man that Milosevic chose to serve as FRY prime minister, the energetic and aggressively self-confident Panic, was an entirely different character. Born in 1929 in Belgrade, Panic fled Yugoslavia in 1955 while a member of Yugoslavia's bicycling team. He made a fortune in the United States as the founder and director of the pharmaceutical firm Galenika.

Unlike Cosic, Panic had a clear agenda: to get rid of Milosevic. Panic arrived in Belgrade in early June 1992 and his first question to Milosevic was, "Well, Slobodan, when are you leaving?" He told Milosevic that only his departure would make possible the lifting of sanctions, and promised that if Milosevic stepped down, he would ensure that he received a U.S. visa and would find him a job in a U.S. bank. Milosevic described Panic's idea as "fantastic," but he apparently did not completely reject the idea. Panic's adviser, former Ambassador Scanlan, and Milosevic's surrogate, former *Politika* head Dusan Mitevic, cooperated on a letter that contained the terms on which Milosevic would agree to leave office.

Unfortunately, Panic was promising more than he could deliver. Two days after this meeting with Milosevic, Panic met Secretary of State Baker in the clear plastic "bubble" of the U.S. embassy in Helsinki. Panic told Baker that relaxing sanctions would help his efforts to remove Milosevic, but Baker pointed out that sanctions relief would require specific actions, no matter who was in charge of Serbia, including a democratic solution in Kosovo and the withdrawal of Belgrade's support for the Bosnian Serbs. Baker, however, concluded on a positive note: we want you to succeed, and "as one American to another," I admire your courage. Panic left the meeting upbeat, yet others around Panic were less certain about the degree of Washington's support.

When Panic returned to Belgrade, he found Milosevic having second thoughts. Milosevic claimed he had to consider the interests of the Serbian people who had elected him. He also expressed annoyance with remarks Panic had made in Helsinki to a Serbian journalist—that Milosevic would need the assistance of prayer if he got in Panic's way. Milosevic refused to sign the letter that Scanlan and Mitevic had prepared, and a few days later he told Panic to act as if the entire incident had never happened.

It is hard to imagine Milosevic ever voluntarily surrendering power, but participants in the exchange believe that Milosevic was not just feigning interest. Later, Panic said the incident had taught him never to believe anything Milosevic said. In Belgrade, though, it was widely believed that Milosevic's wife had intervened to stiffen her husband's resolve.[11]

Despite this setback, Panic continued to pursue his aim of removing Milosevic. He put together a cabinet dominated by Milosevic foes, keeping the post of minister of defense for himself. But Panic, unless he could count on firm international backing, was playing from a weak hand. The constitutional authority of the FRY government was limited. Real power remained firmly in the grasp of Milosevic, who controlled the Serbian government, media, and special police. Serbs, moreover, never fully accepted Panic as one of their own. In his first speech to the assembly, Panic's Serbian language was painfully awkward, making it easier for Milosevic to portray him as a U.S. puppet. Panic also appeared disorganized and erratic and his penchant for frank speaking sometimes needlessly offended people who should have supported him.

Immediately after his humiliation at the London conference—Milosevic decided to remove Panic. At the end of August, Assembly delegates belonging to Milosevic's SPS and the Serbian Radical Party (SRS) of Vojslav Seselj—who had capitalized on the reputation he made as a paramilitary leader in Croatia and Bosnia to found a radically nationalist party, and who throughout most of his political career served as a willing cat's-paw for Milosevic—demanded a vote of no-confidence in the prime minister. Milosevic's move against Panic set off turmoil in the assembly and the country. Cosic threw his support to Panic as did delegates from Montenegro. Panic was not cowed, and his supporters among the Belgrade students began to organize street demonstrations. When Milosevic entered the assembly building, he was greeted by jeers from crowds gathered outside, probably the first time this had happened to him since his rise to power five years earlier. Milosevic agreed to call off the vote in the Assembly if Panic would keep his supporters out of the streets.[12] Panic had won, but Milosevic's retreat was only temporary.

In early October, Milosevic and Panic had their last meeting—a long boozy session at Milosevic's office in the Serbian presidency building in downtown Belgrade. Neither man pulled any punches, in a relationship that by now had descended to the level of mutual hatred. Panic told Milosevic that as minister of defense, he would order the military to arrest Milosevic. Milosevic, in reply, advised "his friend, Milan," not to be present when the generals came because Milosevic would have them arrested and probably shot. Panic reminded Milosevic of his earlier agreement to resign, and Milosevic retorted that he had never signed anything and had no intention of leaving. At one point, Panic later told associates, the conversation became so intense that Milosevic pulled a pistol from his desk, handed it to Panic, and challenged that if the prime minister wanted so badly to get rid of him, he should just shoot him. Panic, probably wisely for his own safety, declined. As Panic and Mitevic—who had been summoned to read the text of the letter he and Scanlan had drafted in June—were leaving, Panic asked what Milosevic meant by the meeting. "He declared war on you," Mitevic said prophetically. "Then we will wage war," Panic replied, with a confidence that turned out to be misplaced.[13]

Panic's first move was to hold a series of meetings with Zivota Panic (no relation), the chief of staff of the army. Both Panic and Milosevic were well aware that the army harbored potentially dangerous resentments against Milosevic. Associates of Prime Minister Panic believe that the military was sitting on the fence and would have been willing to support Panic against Milosevic if the prime minister had received a clear sign of support from Washington. U.S. diplomats in Belgrade at the time, however, contend that Chief of Staff Panic was under Milosevic's thumb, and that Prime Minister Panic was deluding himself by thinking that he might get the army to move against Milosevic.

Milosevic met Panic's challenge with his usual decisiveness. On 19 October, while Panic and Cosic were out of the country, Milosevic sent an AK-47–toting Kertes, who Panic had publicly fired as deputy minister of the interior during the London conference, to seize control of the federal police headquarters. Some of Panic's associates urged him to respond by calling out the military to remove Kertes, yet Panic did not want to be responsible for bloodshed in the streets of Belgrade. Instead, he telephoned the military to ask what was going on, but Chief of Staff Panic told the prime minister to sleep on it.

According to some accounts, there was considerable support for Cosic within the military, and one commander of an elite unit even offered through indirect channels his own support to regain the building by force.[14]

In the end neither Panic, Cosic, nor the military did anything. Not naturally a man of action, Cosic visited the headquarters of the General Staff in downtown Belgrade and demanded, "Milosevic must go. Generals, I am waiting and expect your answer."[15] But the generals were silent. Divided and demoralized by Milosevic's purges, the military was unwilling to risk moving against Milosevic—who took the precaution of parking a small force of police armored vehicles outside the military barracks near Belgrade as a warning. The result was a public humiliation for Panic and the subjugation of the last center of armed force in Serbia not under Milosevic's control.

The final showdown between Milosevic and Panic came in the December 1992 elections for Serbian president. The Serbian opposition greeted the event with its usual display of divisiveness. In early November, a broad range of opposition parties came together in a new coalition to contest the election, only to have the incipient alliance fall apart within a few days over a rivalry between Draskovic and Zoran Djindjic, a rising star in the Serb opposition firmament, who had taken over control of the Democratic Party (DS) from its founder, Vojslav Kostunica. Despite repeated urgings by Panic and others, Cosic declined to run against Milosevic, citing poor health and his desire to remain above the political fray as the president of all Serbs regardless of party affiliation. With the Serbian opposition hopelessly divided and Cosic unwilling to sully himself with electoral politics, only Panic was left to challenge Milosevic. Later, Cosic acknowledged that his biggest mistake was in not running for president, telling me that, "I am aware that I bear responsibility before my people for not entering into a political struggle with Slobodan Milosevic."[16]

Panic and his advisers recognized that it was an act of desperation for Panic, who had lived in Belgrade for less than six months, to run against Milosevic. Panic nevertheless threw himself into the campaign with his characteristic energy. He campaigned actively in the working-class suburbs of Belgrade, where opposition intellectuals seldom entered, and when officials in Nis refused to meet him, he held an impromptu rally attended by over ten thousand enthusiastic supporters. Panic was buoyed by signs that support for Milosevic was flagging. When Milosevic visited Cacak, he was greeted by whistles and cheers of "We want Panic." U.S. pollsters brought in by Panic told him that their soundings showed he could win a free and fair election.

But Milosevic, of course, had no intention of allowing any such thing. His campaign presented Serbian voters with a Manichaean choice between patriots and traitors, treating Serbia's isolation from the world as a badge of pride. Calling Panic "a coyote and a bandit," Milosevic's media deployed all of its dirty propaganda arsenal against him. The media ignored Panic's energetic, U.S.-style campaign, featuring press-the-flesh visits to towns, villages, and peasant homes throughout Serbia, while every act of Milosevic and his supporters was treated as a major state event.

Panic's best hope for success was in persuading Serbs that he was the only person capable of ending Serbia's international isolation. Panic, however, was not supported by the West, and his associates maintain that this failure played a critical role in his defeat. On 17 November, the UN actually toughened sanctions, which was interpreted in Serbia as a slap at Panic. SPS leader Mihajlo Markovic commented, "Whatever we do we are punished. This gives people reason to think that Milosevic was right because Panic got only a tightening of sanctions."[17] The Bush administration rebuffed appeals by associates of Panic that it issue a statement of support and authorize aid to Panic's campaign from private U.S. groups specializing in assistance to democratic elections, which the United States had provided in many other election campaigns in the ex-Communist world and which the United States supplied on a massive scale to opposition groups in the September 2000 elections that brought Milosevic down.

United States officials have acknowledged reluctance to go to the mat on behalf of Panic, in part because they were unable to deliver all he was asking and in part because of doubts about Panic himself. Senior U.S. officials later described Panic's plea that sanctions be lifted as "unsaleable politically," in part because they were worried about the awkwardness of having to reimpose sanctions if Panic lost the election to Milosevic—as U.S. officials fully expected him to do. According to a senior State Department official who occupied a key advisory position at the time, "Our perception was that Panic was a flake and that Milosevic could have him for breakfast whenever he wanted."

Despite the handicaps Panic faced, election day exit polls showed the two rivals running neck and neck. Yet, when the results were announced, Milosevic was said to have gained 2.6 million votes to only 1.6 million for Panic. In the simultaneous elections for the Serbian Assembly, Milosevic's SPS won 1.5 million votes, while—in a major surprise—Seselj's hard-line nationalist SRS won over one million votes. Together, the two parties controlled 104, or 70 percent, of the Assembly seats. There was little doubt that Milosevic had used his control over the local authorities and police to intimidate voters and manipulate the count. Vuk Draskovic described the elections as "rigged to the last degree," while international observers characterized them as "seriously flawed."[18]

Zoran Lucic, of Belgrade's respected independent election monitoring organization, The Center for Free Elections and Democracy (CESID in its Serbo-Croatian acronym), believes that although Panic probably did lose the election, the real results were much closer than the one million vote victory Milosevic claimed.[19] Many Belgrade observers believe that Milosevic was in real trouble and that if Cosic had run against him Milosevic might have lost.

What is certain, however, is that Milosevic, having weathered the storm, moved decisively to end possible future threats. On 29 December Panic was dumped by a no-confidence vote in the FRY Assembly. A few months later, Cosic—by then no longer necessary to Milosevic—followed Panic out of office after he was unconvincingly accused of plotting with military leaders.

The Clinton Administration Arrives

Shortly after Panic's ouster, Bill Clinton entered the White House. During his campaign, Clinton had advocated the use of air power against the Serbs and lifting the arms embargo to allow the Moslems to fight Serb ethnic cleansing. In office, though, the Clinton administration found its ability to act in Yugoslavia constrained by the same realities that had affected Bush. There was a critical difference in the way the Bush and Clinton administrations approached the Yugoslav issue, however. Senior officials in the Bush administration decided early on that Yugoslavia did not touch vital U.S. interests and that there were no solutions to the conflict that could be effectively advanced by the United States. Whether the Bush administration was sincere in these premises or was simply sheltering behind them to avoid involvement in what was seen as a no-win issue remains a matter of debate. But the Bush administration consistently avoided military involvement in Yugoslavia and allowed others—first the EC and later the UN—to take the lead in Yugoslav diplomacy. The policy provoked dissent, but as Eagleburger once remarked, it never got above the fifth floor of the State Department—that is, above the desk officer level.

The Clinton administration, by contrast, could never make up its mind on Yugoslavia. Clinton's instincts on Yugoslavia were sound, but his interest was only sporadic and primarily aimed at ensuring that Yugoslavia did not divert attention from domestic matters. The administration itself was riven by high-level disagreements on Yugoslavia. Vice President Al Gore and Madeline Albright, as U.S. ambassador to the UN and later secretary of state, consistently advocated a tough line against the Serbs, while the Pentagon under Clinton was no more eager for U.S. military involvement than it had been under Bush.

In February, new Secretary of State Warren Christopher sought a briefing from the Pentagon on the military implications of involvement in

Yugoslavia. When Christopher asked what would be required to bring stability and peace to Bosnia, the briefer—a three-star army general—replied that it would take a field army of at least four hundred thousand soldiers. Participants in the policy debates of the time believe that the military habitually exaggerated the difficulties and forces needed to act in Yugoslavia, but according to a senior State Department official present at the meeting, "All the color drained out of Christopher's face when he heard this reply."

In late April, after an intensive series of interagency meetings, the Clinton administration came up with a new policy toward Bosnia that came to be called "lift and strike." The United States would propose that the arms embargo, which had severely constrained the lightly armed Bosnians, be lifted and that NATO be prepared to carry out air strikes against Serb forces who would probably move against the Bosnians before new arms could reach them. There were, however, real questions about both the substance of the new policy and depth of the administration's commitment to it. In May, Christopher went to Europe, not as is usually the case, to inform key allies about a policy decision that the United States had already made, but as he later characterized it, to take a "more conciliatory approach, laying the proposal before our allies, describing it as the only complete option on the table, and asking for their support."[20]

The new U.S. approach, which Owen derided as "lift and pray," ran into a buzz saw of opposition. British Prime Minister Major told Christopher that his government would fall if he put the proposal before Parliament, while French President François Mitterand, although recognizing the "morality" of the U.S. approach, said Serb retaliation would pose too great a risk for French soldiers serving with the UN in Bosnia. In Moscow, President Boris Yeltsin and Foreign Minister Audrey Kozyrev claimed that the U.S. proposal would derail ongoing peace negotiations.[21] Russian Minister of Defense Pavel Grachev shocked the United States by saying that if the lift-and-strike policy were implemented, Russia would provide military assistance to the Serbs.

The U.S. ambassador to Great Britain at the time, Raymond Seitz—who described Secretary Christopher briefing the British officials on lift and strike with "all the verve of a solicitor going over a conveyance deed"— wondered whether Clinton might be using the proposal as a device to avoid action in Bosnia by creating a situation in which the president could tell Congress that "he had proposed a bold plan to salvage Bosnia but the Allies wouldn't let him do it." Christopher, for his part, says he recommended that the United States go ahead with lift and strike despite European opposition.

When Christopher returned to Washington, however, he found that there had been a "sea change in attitudes." President Clinton had become more pessimistic about prospects for reconciliation in Bosnia, reportedly from reading *Balkan Ghosts*, Robert Kaplan's account of his travels through the Balkans on the eve of the Yugoslav collapse—from which the president was said to have concluded that foreign intervention would be unlikely to resolve Balkan quarrels based on ancient ethnic animosities. Regardless of the possible effect of the president's evening reading, European opposition to lift and strike reinvigorated the U.S. military's arguments against the use of armed force in Yugoslavia. Lift and strike trickled away into the back-of-the-briefing-book never-never land of unimplemented policies.[22]

Vance-Owen

While the Clinton administration was wrestling itself to the ground over Bosnia, Owen had come up with a new plan to settle the conflict. On 2 January 1993 in Geneva, he presented Milosevic, Tudjman, and the warring parties a package that included constitutional proposals for a decentralized Bosnian government, a map dividing Bosnia into ten provinces, each dominated numerically by one or the other of Bosnia's three ethnic groups, plus a multiethnic Sarajevo.[23] The Serbs complained that the map, which Owen says provided for Serb-dominated cantons covering 43 percent of Bosnia or far less territory than the Bosnian Serbs controlled at the time, required them to give up too much land. The Bosnians, by contrast, contended that the Owen map simply ratified the results of ethnic cleansing.

By the end of January, after intensive negotiations in Geneva and in Yugoslavia, Owen thought that Karadzic had been told by Milosevic to sign and that a deal was close. In his memoirs, Owen says he is convinced that Karadzic would have signed if Izetbegovic had not been encouraged by some in the Clinton administration to hold out for a better deal. Owen's skepticism about the U.S. approach was confirmed after a "disillusioning" 1 February meeting with Christopher where he found it "painfully apparent that the Secretary of State knew very little about the detail of our plan."[24]

In early March Milosevic visited Paris, where President Mitterand told him that if the Vance-Owen map were accepted, sanctions would be lifted as soon as technically possible. Owen notes that after this meeting, he detected a marked change in Milosevic's attitude.[25] This is hardly surprising since, on the face of it, the French president was offering to lift sanctions—always Milosevic's most sought-after objective—without any linkage to good-faith implementation let alone Serbian actions in other areas, such as Kosovo.

On 25 April, two days before tough new sanctions that would close Serbia's borders to all international trade and freeze its financial assets abroad were due to take effect, Milosevic, Cosic, and Montenegrin President Bulatovic sent what Owen calls a "somewhat peremptory" letter urging that the Bosnian Serb assembly accept Vance-Owen. Not until a 2 May meeting in Athens, after Milosevic, Greek Prime Minister Konstantin Mitsotakis and Russian Deputy Foreign Minister Vitaliy Churkin had argued with Karadzic through the night, was the Bosnian Serb leader "bullied" into signing—but he insisted that the deal be confirmed by a vote in the Bosnian Serb assembly in Pale. The assembly rejected Vance-Owen on 6 May by a lopsided vote of fifty-one to two with twelve abstentions despite a personal, on-the-scene appeal by Milosevic that it be accepted.

Milorad Vucelic, director of Radio Television Serbia (RTS) and SPS vice president, who was with Milosevic in Pale, said the Serb leader strongly supported Vance-Owen and genuinely believed it was a good deal for the Bosnian Serbs. After the Pale Assembly nixed the deal—the first time any Serb institution had expressly rejected a public appeal by Milosevic—Vucelic described Milosevic as "angry, nervous, and upset." In a fury, Milosevic lashed out at the delegates, charging that "never has such a small number of irresponsible Serbs made such a fatal decision for the Serb people." According to Vucelic, Milosevic primarily blamed Assembly president Momcilo Krajisnik for the rejection because Krajisnik halted the Assembly proceedings after Milosevic's speech to allow for lobbying against the deal.[26] The next day, when a still angry and tired Milosevic telephoned Owen, he claimed that Bosnian Serb commander Ratko Mladic had swung the vote by using the delay to show delegates a map of Serb-held areas in Bosnia that would be lost if the Vance-Owen plan went into effect.[27]

The U.S. approach to Vance-Owen—a combination of skepticism and on-again, off-again support—contributed to growing transatlantic differences over Bosnia. At the end of March, U.S. pressure had persuaded the Bosnians to agree to Vance-Owen, although they retained doubts about the map. Six weeks later, as efforts to pressure the Bosnian Serbs to sign onto Vance-Owen were at their height, Christopher was touring European capitals with the new U.S. option of lift and strike. During a briefing on 6 May for the EU troika, Christopher dismissed Vance-Owen as a failure, which infuriated Owen, who saw the results of months of patient negotiating slipping away.

The disarray in Western ranks deepened as the United States, only a few days later, began to back away from lift and strike. On 18 May, Christopher testified to Congress that Bosnia was a European problem. At a hastily convened meeting on 22 May foreign ministers of the United States, Europe, and Russia effectively disassociated themselves from Vance-Owen by agreeing to a joint action program, which proposed forming "safe areas" in Bosnia and, for the first time, called for creating an international court to try Yugoslav war criminals.

The fiasco over Vance-Owen had disastrous consequences in Yugoslavia. In Sarajevo, which felt justifiably let down by the United States, resentment toward the outside world deepened. Fighting between Moslems and Croats, which had begun in October 1992 and intensified in the spring of 1993 after a Croat ultimatum to the Moslems to vacate areas the Croats contended were assigned them under Vance-Owen, intensified. Only the Bosnian Serbs were pleased. Isolated in their tiny mountain fastness of Pale, the Bosnian Serbs' megalomaniac belief in their ability to defy the world with impunity received a powerful boost.

After his fall from power, Milosevic portrayed Vance-Owen as a tragic missed opportunity that would have allowed the Serbs to end the fighting in Bosnia on significantly better terms than they received two years later in Dayton.[28] Milosevic's disappointment was obvious even at the time. Not only had the prospect of sanctions relief vanished but for the first time Milosevic's legendary ability to sway Serb opinions had experienced a public failure. After Milosevic returned from Pale, aides to Cosic described Milosevic to Owen as being in one of his periodic phases of depression.[29]

As time passed, however, it became clear that the Vance-Owen plan was a watershed for Milosevic. Owen depicted Milosevic's decision to publicly pressure the Bosnian Serbs as the moment when Milosevic formally gave up the notion of a Greater Serbia.[30] Milosevic's private remarks to Sarinic show that this was not completely accurate, but the stature that Milosevic won through his public engagement on behalf of Vance-Owen dramatically changed his relationship with the international community. After April 1993, Milosevic successfully reinvented himself as a peacemaker. A succession of international negotiators trooped through Milosevic's office over the next three years seeking his support for a variety of peace plans in Bosnia and Croatia. Milosevic skillfully played on the anxieties of international negotiators for someone who could "deliver" the recalcitrant Bosnian Serbs, to transform the way he was perceived from nationalist rabble-rouser to the linchpin of the peace process.

He also drew important lessons about the U.S. role. Although the United States had failed to engage effectively in resolving the Bosnian conflict in 1993, Milosevic saw clearly that the United States could frustrate meaningful action by any other power. Milosevic continued to participate in the diplomatic process under Owen, but with diminishing expectations of success. In future Bosnian negotiations, it was only when the United States took the lead—in the so-called Contact Group plan of 1994 and Dayton negotiations in 1995—that Milosevic fully committed his own personal prestige to the process.

Milosevic the Negotiator

In the early years, most of Milosevic's negotiating sessions with foreigners were held in his private office on the second floor of the Serbian presidency building. Large and sparsely furnished in Yugoslav apparatchik style, Milosevic's office contained a huge desk that generally appeared devoid of paperwork. Serbian genre art hung on the walls of his outer office. Milosevic smoked thin cigarillos and he generally started a meeting with a Vilamovka, his favorite Serbian brandy, often followed during the course of the discussions by several glasses of scotch. He always seemed to have plenty of time for prolonged conversations with his foreign visitors. Milosevic was seldom interrupted by telephone calls or importunate aides seeking a decision on some pressing domestic matter.

In later years, many of Milosevic's negotiating sessions were held at Karadjordjevo, a former hunting retreat for Tito located about an hour outside of Belgrade. Sessions there tended to be long and usually ended with a traditional Balkan meal of roast lamb. Most of the negotiations concerning the Kosovo conflict of 1998–1999, however, occurred in Belgrade, perhaps because these talks tended to be more contentious than earlier negotiations or because by then international negotiators had begun to tire of the boozy, cholesterol-rich pleasures of Karadjordjevo.

As a negotiator, Milosevic was quick, self-confident, and operated almost entirely on his own. He was accompanied at many meetings only by his trusted amanuensis, Goran Milanovic, who never spoke except to answer some whispered command. On those occasions when Milosevic was accompanied by senior officials, there was never any doubt who was alpha Serb. Even after Pale had humiliated Milosevic by rejecting his plea to agree to Vance-Owen, U.S. negotiator Ambassador Charles Redman observed that as long as Milosevic was present, he spoke for the Serb delegation with no sign of objection by Karadzic or other Pale Serbs.[31] U.S. diplomats who met frequently with Milosevic in later years remarked that Milan Milutinovic, who as foreign minister and later president of Serbia was often the only other Serb to sit at the table beside Milosevic, was hesitant to speak in Milosevic's presence and would sometimes find himself cut off abruptly by Milosevic when he made a joke or minor comment.

Milosevic had a dismissive attitude toward other Serbs, especially those who attempted to stand up to him. During the run-up to the Dayton negotiations, when U.S. negotiator Holbrooke asked Milosevic about "your friends from Pale," Milosevic replied angrily, "They are not my friends. They are not my colleagues. It is awful just to be in the same room with them for so long. They are sh—."[32]

Milosevic seldom spoke from a prepared text and never seemed to take notes or refer to papers to refresh his memory. He spoke with foreigners in his competent though accented English, which includes a workmanlike grasp of swear words. "Bull. . . " is one of his favorite phrases of dismissal. Milosevic has a quick and retentive mind with a sure grasp of the details of complex negotiations as well as a memory that can reach back over years of earlier talks. Ignoring these characteristics could be dangerous for inattentive negotiators.

Unlike many of his counterparts in the Balkans, however, Milosevic's typical style as a negotiator—at least until the Kosovo conflict of 1998–1999—was not to be obstructionist but a problem solver. Ivor Roberts, the British chargé d'affaires in Belgrade during the war in Bosnia, found that "Milosevic knew how to aim for the maximum but to settle for second best if he judged that a sufficiently large 'critical mass'—a favorite Milosevic phrase—of positive elements had been assembled."[33]

Milosevic's intelligence, command of the English language, and grasp of details made him a formidable negotiating partner. General Wes Clark, NATO military commander during the 1999 war in Kosovo and one of the two or three international figures who spent the most time with Milosevic over the last years of his rule, had the following to say: "I've spent hundreds of hours dealing with Milosevic. He's a very shrewd, forceful, tough, wily negotiator. He's not afraid to make bold decisions, and he's not afraid to use force. He plays by his own rules and he has his own standards of rationality."[34]

Even for those who were nominally sympathetic to him, Milosevic could be a difficult negotiating partner. Former Russian Prime Minister

Chernomyrdin, who played a key role in the negotiations with Milosevic that led to the end of the 1999 war, recounted how trying it was to bring Milosevic around to accepting the need to compromise with NATO. Chernomyrdin described how Milosevic "would jump up, tear the papers, thrust them, go out, and come back again. It was hard."[35]

Milosevic often used mood swings and displays of temper as a negotiating tactic. Holbrooke observes that Milosevic could switch moods with astonishing speed, possibly to keep others off balance: "He could range from charm to brutality, from emotional outbursts to calm discussions of legal minutiae. When he was angry his face wrinkled up but he could regain control of himself instantly."[36] Similarly, German General Klaus Naumann, who accompanied Clark on many of his meetings with Milosevic in 1998 and 1999, explains that "Milosevic is a man who changes from an attitude of extreme friendliness; he can be so nice you feel like you should cuddle into the arms of a big bear and feel happy, and suddenly he is shifting gears and he can get very angry."[37] During the Dayton negotiations while Milosevic was engaging in a casual and seemingly friendly conversation in a garden with Holbrooke, Clark, and Holbrooke's deputy, U.S. Ambassador Chris Hill, Milosevic suddenly changed moods completely. His voice rising with anger, he began to shout, "Mr. Holbrooke, I've had enough. I've given my concessions. Now it is time for your Moslem friends to make concessions. But you are not man enough to do this. You don't have the ba— to tell them what to do. If you want war, let there be war, but you are not man enough."[38]

Milosevic varied his behavior depending on the nationality of his interlocutor. When the United States was taking the lead in the peace process, Milosevic adopted a polite yet somewhat patronizing tone toward European diplomats. But he would criticize U.S. negotiators or negotiating positions when he thought that would be congenial to the ear of European diplomats. With Americans, Milosevic was often scornful of Russians, while during his meetings with Russians, Milosevic practically never had a good word to say about the West.

A Russian source observes that Milosevic's favorite game was to divide states and politicians into "good guys" and "bad guys"—categories that Milosevic was capable of shifting quickly and sometimes without obvious reasons. In meetings with Russian officials, Milosevic usually referred to Westerners as either "very bad" or, at best, "not half bad." One day Milosevic would tell the Russians that Holbrooke, the U.S. diplomat who took the lead in negotiating the Dayton agreement with Milosevic, was his enemy, and the next day it would be Albright, U.S. ambassador to the UN and later secretary of state, who would be opposed to Holbrooke as a "bad person."

Milosevic had a sense of self-confidence, and his tactical flexibility gave him an ease in negotiations that none of the other Yugoslav leaders possessed. In 1993, during a difficult stage in negotiations on the British aircraft carrier *Invincible*, Milosevic took up a blue pencil, and with Karadzic looking over his shoulder, he went confidently to the map and began to draw lines indicating possible territorial solutions that even Izetbegovic later admitted to be reasonable. Other Yugoslav leaders seldom took this kind of initiative. Unwilling themselves to run the risk of proposing specific negotiating outcomes, they generally preferred to let internationals make initiatives that they could either reject or claim they had been forced to accept by outside pressure.

Milosevic understands power relationships and is most flexible when his partner holds critical cards. Roberts notes that Milosevic was "apparently reasonable, particularly when you held a major trump card in the shape of sanctions in your hand."[39] As Holbrooke commented at Dayton, "Standing up to him [Milosevic] is key; he respects people who act as tough as him." Milosevic is also capable of Balkan duplicity. Holbrooke told Christopher during Dayton that Milosevic has often lied outright about factual data or changed his position after we thought we had locked something in."[40]

The United States Returns to the Fore

On 5 February 1994, a mortar shell fell into Sarajevo's central market, killing sixty-eight people and wounding over two hundred. The outrage generated by this particularly horrifying incident provoked a new round of international diplomacy, which led to the highly publicized arrival in Sarajevo of a battalion of Russian peacekeepers, the withdrawal of heavy weapons, and the halting of Serb shelling. The 1994 market massacre also brought the United States back to the fore of the Bosnian diplomatic process.

The groundwork for the new U.S. activism was laid in January 1994 when Secretary Christopher had a disastrous series of consultations on Yugoslavia with U.S. allies. French President Mitterand and Foreign Minister Balladur pressed the United States to lean on the Bosnians to accept Owen's current plan, warning that if a settlement was not achieved soon, the Europeans would withdraw their forces from Bosnia. On the plane home, Christopher told his team that the United States had to find some way to deal with the corrosive effect Bosnia was having on alliance relationships.

Immediately after the mortar attack, State Department Undersecretary Peter Tarnoff and the U.S. envoy for Yugoslav negotiations, Ambassador Redman, flew to Europe with a mandate from the White House to engage the United States actively in the search for peace. The United States had no preconceived plan other than to get involved and encourage the Moslems to be more receptive to a solution, but the signs of U.S. leadership were immediately apparent. After a sober, nine-hour session of the North Atlantic Council—marked by unusual U.S. and French cooperation—NATO threatened air strikes unless all heavy weapons around Sarajevo were placed under UN observation.

On 11 February, while UN troops were struggling through heavy snow in the hills around Sarajevo to monitor the withdrawal of heavy weapons, Redman met Karadzic and described the new U.S. role in the peace process. Seemingly taken aback by the rapid pace of events, Karadzic shook his head occasionally but listened almost without words. Strangely, he concluded by telling Redman, "I'm glad you're here."

On 17 February, a tired Milosevic told diplomats that Owen's current plan was flawed and that he welcomed the new U.S. role in the peace process. Milosevic said he was working with Russian special envoy Churkin to get the Bosnian Serbs to withdraw their heavy weapons, but worried that if the Serbs did so, the Bosnians might use their numerical advantage in infantry to overrun Serb defenses—not an unreasonable concern since UN troops reported that one of the first Bosnian responses to the eventual cease-fire was to advance their trenches toward Serb lines. Later, the commander of UN forces in Bosnia, British General Michael Rose, found Milosevic seeming to enjoy his role as mediator. Milosevic promised to pressure Karadzic, yet he also insisted that the Bosnians would have to accept compromises on the complete demilitarization of Sarajevo.[41]

Both sides had complied with NATO's demands by 2 February. General Rose marked the cease-fire by strolling between Serb and Moslem lines, which no one had been able to do for the past two years. For a few brief weeks, something approaching normal life returned to Sarajevo.

Once the immediate crisis around Sarajevo had been defused, the United States moved to end the fighting between Bosnians and Croats, which had led to some of the worst atrocities of the war, including the destruction by Croat artillery of the graceful Turkish bridge in Mostar—the symbol of prewar Bosnia. In late February, Bosnian and Croatian commanders concluded a cease-fire and mutual disengagement of forces, which both agreed would allow them to turn their attention to the real enemy, "the Serb aggressor."[42] On 18 March in Washington, following several weeks of negotiation at the U.S. embassy in Vienna, Izetbegovic, Tudjman, and the Bosnian Croat leader Kresimir Zubak signed an agreement creating the Moslem-Croat Federation in Bosnia.

The federation pact ended the fighting between Moslems and Croats, but there was an element to the accord that was not visible at the time: Washington's tacit agreement to allow Iran and other Moslem countries to expand covert arms supplies to the Bosnians. On 28 and 29 March, U.S. Ambassador to Croatia Peter Galbreath, on orders from Washington, told the Croatian authorities that he had "no instructions" in response to a Croatian request for Washington's views on a proposal the Bosnians had made to allow Iran to expand covert arms shipments via Croatia. As Galbreath and Redman, who was present for the second meeting, told congressional investigators two years later, the Croats understood the U.S. position to be an implicit authorization to go forward.[43] Over the next eighteen months, the arms supplies to the Bosnians together with growing military cooperation between the Bosnians and Croats, gradually shifted the military balance in Bosnia against the Bosnian Serbs.

The Contact Group Plan

The increased activism of the United States and Russia in the Bosnian peace process reinforced the need for a new diplomatic mechanism. In April, the Contact Group was formed, consisting of the United States and Russia, Great Britain and France as the two leading troop-contributing nations in Bosnia, and Germany as the EU chair during that period. (When Germany's six-month tenure at the EU helm expired, it remained in the Contact Group, much to the dissatisfaction of other European nations, especially Italy.) Although Owen stayed on the job for another year, the Contact Group became the focus of international diplomacy in Yugoslavia.

The formation of the Contact Group came at a low point for Milosevic. Negotiations were stalled, the Serbian economy was spiraling downward, and his relations with the Bosnian Serbs were worsening. Milosevic chafed at not being involved in the U.S.-led negotiations that created the Federation. He worried that the Moslems and Croats, having settled their differences, might turn militarily on the Bosnian Serbs. But he also saw possibilities for a political breakthrough if the Bosnian Serbs were allowed the same kind of confederal ties with Serbia that the Federation had with Croatia. In late March, Milosevic told Owen that he did not oppose the Federation but would like to follow it with an overall Bosnian settlement. In April, however, during a new crisis caused by Bosnian Serb attacks on the Moslem enclave of Gorazde, Roberts found Milosevic to be "subdued and listless." Frustrated that the increasingly aggressive course pursued by Mladic was threatening to call down retaliation on him and also sensing that the European-led negotiating track under Owen was becoming irrelevant, Milosevic insisted that he would not participate in the peace process unless offered the prospect of sanctions relief.[44]

In late May, the Contact Group met in the French lakeside resort of Talloires, near Geneva, to hammer out a new proposal. The heart of what came to be known as the Contact Group plan was a map giving 51 percent of Bosnian territory to the Federation and 49 percent to the Serbs. It also included an agreement on cessation of hostilities as well as constitutional arrangements for a loose union between the Federation and the Republika Srpska. The Contact Group map, which had primarily been worked out in negotiations between Redman and the Bosnians, was highly favorable to Sarajevo. The Bosnians were allowed to retain their isolated enclaves along the Drina River and control the strategic town of Brcko, which had the effect of splitting the Republika Srpska in two.

Karadzic's first reaction was to call the Contact Group map "humiliating" and deliberately designed to elicit a Serb rejection. Milosevic, by contrast, saw it as a chance to resume the long-stalled peace process and obtain a lifting of sanctions. On 12 July, *Politika* urged the Bosnian Serb leadership to "come to their senses" and accept the plan, which it said gave the Serbs more territory than they would have gained under Vance-Owen. Other voices out of Belgrade were less helpful. The Bishops Conference of the Serbian Orthodox Church pontificated that Serbs should "rather lose more life than betray the present or future fate of our nation," and in mid-July, Patriarch Pavle visited Pale to lobby for the plan's rejection.

On 18 July, the Bosnian (Moslem) and Federation assemblies approved the Contact Group plan in an emotional debate that left little doubt that the Bosnians would prefer to continue the war to victory rather than accept a negotiated outcome. Izetbegovic described the plan as "unjust," but said there was no realistic alternative to its adoption. He added that he expected the war to continue—a sign that the Bosnians expected the Serbs to reject the plan, which together with its U.S. authorship, was probably a major reason why Sarajevo had accepted it. Other speakers said that agreeing to the plan would allow the Bosnian army time for preparations to take back all of Bosnia—a sentiment that was met by calls of "Banja Luka [the largest Serb-held city] will be ours."

Milosevic met in Belgrade with Karadzic and other Serb leaders the day before the Assembly voted on the plan, but unwilling to risk a repetition of the public humiliation he had suffered over Vance-Owen, he did not travel to Pale to lobby personally. Karadzic took an ambivalent position on the Contact Group plan. In his speech to the Assembly, which was greeted by sustained applause, Karadzic said that if the Serbs accepted the plan they would face "slaughter and chaos," but if they rejected it they would face an escalation of fighting. The Serb Assembly's response to the plan—which with characteristic flair for the histrionic Karadzic unveiled from a sealed pink envelope at a meeting with the Contact Group in Geneva on 21 July—was that the map "could in considerable measure serve as a basis for settlement" even though it needed more work. Pale also sought more information on the constitution and status of Sarajevo, access to the sea, and a schedule for lifting sanctions. Since the Serbs had been given the plan on a take-it-or-leave-it basis, all the members of the Contact Group, including Russia, interpreted the response as a rejection.

Milosevic reacted vigorously to this second Bosnian Serb trashing of a peace plan that he had endorsed. Toward the end of July, Roberts found Milosevic "seriously engaged and animated"—a transformed man from his lackluster performance at the beginning of the year. Describing Karadzic as sick and "hot for war," Milosevic promised to put the squeeze on Pale.[45] Shortly thereafter, in a front-page interview in *Politika*, Milosevic publicly took the offensive against Karadzic and the Pale leadership. Four days later, after Contact Group foreign ministers had pledged to introduce a UN Security Council resolution relaxing sanctions on Belgrade if the Bosnian Serbs accepted the Contact Group plan, Milosevic broke off all relations with the Pale leadership and announced the closure of Serbia's border with the Bosnian Serb territories to all traffic except humanitarian goods.

Milosevic spent the second half of 1994 pursuing his quarrel with Karadzic and burnishing his international reputation as a peacemaker. On 9 September, Milosevic made a major speech—by then a rare event—in which he emphasized the fairness of the Contact Group plan and mentioned the word peace fifteen times. But there was no peace between Belgrade and Pale. In his 4 August speech announcing the blockade, Milosevic attacked the Bosnian Serb leadership for including "war profiteers . . . people whose conscience is not clear and who are afraid of peace." The

Milosevic-controlled media accused Karadzic and Krajisnik of having made £6 million by selling cars stolen from the ruined Volkswagen plant that straddled the front lines in Sarajevo. Milosevic, who had questioned Mladic's sanity during the Serb attack on Gorazde in April, began to meet regularly in Belgrade with the popular Bosnian Serb commander. It was widely rumored in Belgrade that during one such secret meeting, Milosevic had offered Mladic a senior position in the FRY military if Mladic would abandon the Bosnian Serb forces.[46] In the early months of 1995, Milosevic told Roberts that Mladic was seriously considering Milosevic's suggestion that Mladic take over the reins of government in Pale.[47]

Although Milosevic's anger with the Pale leadership was real, there were limits to the extent he was prepared to pressure the Bosnian Serbs. The "Drina blockade" was never a formidable barrier to the Bosnian Serbs' obtaining the supplies they needed. After he was ousted from power, Milosevic portrayed the barrier as "a clever political maneuver so as to reduce the severity of the sanctions" and said it was "never a real blockade."[48]

Over the year that Milosevic maintained the restrictions on supplies to the Bosnian Serbs, U.S. intelligence described numerous instances of evasion, including mobile military bridges apparently being stationed in places along the Drina where they could be used to provide a temporary crossing point for the covert provision of supplies to the Bosnian Serbs. U.S. intelligence and international monitors also discovered what appeared to be numerous instances of unauthorized supply flights between Serbia and Bosnia.

In the summer of 1995—at Carl Bildt's behest—I spent two weeks traveling almost every inch of the border between the Serb-held portions of Bosnia, Serbia, and Montenegro, where by then international inspectors had been monitoring the blockade for almost a year. At the official border crossing points, where international inspectors were permanently present, the blockade was generally functioning as it should. Traffic in unauthorized items was mostly limited to small-scale smuggling. On one afternoon, for example, I watched as a Bosnian peasant woman repeatedly trundled a wheelbarrow containing two cases of beer—just below the authorized amount—across a bridge that was closed to all but pedestrian traffic.

More significant evasion of the blockade was clearly occurring along those stretches of the border—which snaked for several hundred miles through some of the most rugged terrain in the Balkans—where the international presence was limited to sporadic patrols. Along parts of the Drina, in many places no more than a couple-hundred-yards wide, so much gasoline and oil was being smuggled across in small boats that the banks of the river reeked of petroleum. In the Montenegrin mountains, I watched one evening with the aid of a night-vision scope while small trucks and peasant wagons made their way along tiny tracks that crossed the border. In a more serious vein, I also found one site unguarded by international monitors—where the Yugoslav authorities appeared to be using the cover of darkness to drive trucks across the broad tops of a dam that spanned the river between Serbia and Bosnia.

Despite the porosity of the blockade, the international community rewarded Milosevic by lifting sanctions on Serb participation in international sporting and cultural events as well as allowing international air carriers to resume flights into Belgrade. These moves did not make much difference to the economy but they reduced the sense of isolation from the outside world, which had been one of the most unpleasant effects of the sanctions for many Serbs.

And even the economy no longer seemed such a basket case. In January 1994, Dragoslav Avramovic, the new head of the National Bank of Yugoslavia and a former World Bank economist, announced an anti-inflation program strongly reminiscent of the one Yugoslav Prime Minister Markovic had introduced in 1989. Old dinars were replaced by a new, "super" dinar that was fully backed by hard currency reserves and pegged to the deutsche mark at a rate of one to one. Within a few months, Avramovic had reduced inflation from an annual rate of 310 million percent to zero.[49]

The Serbs' traditional talent for operating outside the system—*na levo*, or on the left—also helped mitigate the effect of the sanctions. The expanding class of smugglers, black marketers, and mafiosi was becoming increasingly adept at sanctions busting. Foreign goods filled the shelves of Belgrade stores that had been bare only a year earlier. Thanks to a well-developed smuggling network up the Danube, across the Adriatic, and even through supposedly hostile Croatia, gasoline was cheaper in Serbia than in most European capitals. Traffic jams returned to Belgrade, and drivers found that lines were shorter and the service less surly when buying from the private vendors who sold gasoline at almost every major intersection than it had been at socially owned gas stations before the war.

In early November, diplomats found Milosevic confident and upbeat. He asserted that things were going well and that the forces of peace, among which he presumably included himself, would prevail. Milosevic urged the United States to stick with the Contact Group plan and dismissed the latest European peace initiative.

He took a similarly confident tack in a 12 December meeting with Sarinic—their first in over a year. Milosevic claimed to have in his pocket forty-three of the fifty-one delegates to the Bosnian Serb Assembly needed to overturn Karadzic and gain Pale's agreement to the Contact Group plan. Once this happened, Milosevic expounded with assurance, a new round of negotiations could begin. Changes could be made to the map, with the Bosnian-held enclaves along the Drina going to the Serbs and the Bosnians gaining compensation in the west. The Bosnian Serbs would also be allowed to enter into a confederation "or some other form of ties" with Serbia proper. Only when the conversation turned to the economy did Milosevic's mood darken. Noting that during his ride into Belgrade from the military airport at Batajnica he had seen homes without lights and gasoline being sold out of wine bottles beside the road, Sarinic accused Milosevic of leading his people back into the Middle Ages. Milosevic replied simply, "I know," and lapsed into a long, uncomfortable silence.[50]

Drift and Appeasement

The failure of the Contact Group plan marked the nadir of international diplomacy in Bosnia. The plan remained theoretically on the table, but with the Contact Group nations having committed their prestige to Serb acceptance, there was little room for further negotiation. The Serbs brushed off threats by Britain and France that UN forces might be withdrawn from Bosnia if the stalemate continued. A final layer of complexity was added in July to the international mess over Bosnia when UN Secretary General Boutrous-Ghali sent a letter to Contact Group nations complaining that he was not being kept informed and warning that if the Contact Group plan were accepted, the UN should withdraw and implementation be entrusted to NATO.

The peace process halted while the world waited for sanctions and Milosevic's blockade to bring the Bosnian Serbs to their senses. Sanctions, meanwhile, had taken on a life of their own. A sizeable bureaucracy had grown up charged with enforcing and monitoring the effect of the sanctions. With the backing of senior officials in the White House and influential members of the U.S. Congress, this apparatus was quick to criticize any move toward flexibility as undercutting the sanctions' effect.

The situation on the ground in Bosnia was, if possible, even worse than the diplomatic tangle. The Bosnians could hardly conceal their relief when Pale rejected the Contact Group plan. By the end of July, Izetbegovic was telling diplomats that Bosnian approval of the plan could not be assumed indefinitely.

Toward the end of 1994, the Serb response to a failed Bosnian military offensive brought the situation in Bosnia to the verge of international collapse. Sarajevo used the lull in fighting connected with the Contact Group plan to capture the stronghold of Moslem maverick Fikret Abdic at Velika Kladusa, in northwest Bosnia. Emboldened by this success, the Bosnians attacked Serb forces from the nearby safe area of Bihac—a clear violation of UN rules. The Bosnians initially seemed on the verge of breaking out of the Bihac pocket, but in mid-November a Serb counterattack, aided by forces from Krajina, drove the Bosnians back to the outskirts of Bihac. The Bosnians appealed for international rescue, while a confident Karadzic proposed to Tudjman the division of Bosnia along an east-west axis, with Krajina Serbs being resettled in Bosnia. This scheme, Tudjman mused to foreign diplomats, might be acceptable since Washington had prevented Croatia from intervening militarily to aid the Bosnians around Bihac. Milosevic told Roberts that Karadzic had ordered the capture of Bihac, but that Mladic had promised Milosevic he would not enter the city.[51] As Milosevic was speaking, however, new air defense equipment was appearing in Bosnia that could only have come from Belgrade, despite Milosevic's proclaimed blockade.

NATO attempted to deter the Serbs by striking their air base at Udbina, near Bihac. In response, the Serbs took 165 UN peacekeepers hostage, even though NATO had deliberately limited its strikes to cratering the runway. U.S. demands for additional air strikes met an angry allied rejection. Instead, Brussels issued a weak communiqué calling on all parties to exercise restraint. NATO had blinked.

Differences over Bosnia brought relations within the NATO alliance to their worst point since the 1956 Suez crisis. Over the Thanksgiving weekend, President Clinton's national security adviser, Anthony Lake, drafted a memo that, in effect, declared NATO unity to be more important than Bosnia and argued that "since the stick of military pressure is no longer viable," it should be abandoned. With the Allies unwilling to endorse additional air strikes unless the United States was willing to commit its own troops on the ground in Bosnia, which the Clinton administration considered politically impossible, Washington concluded that the only way to end the conflict in Bosnia and preserve harmony in NATO was to accommodate the Serbs.[52]

As a first step, the administration pressured the Bosnians to abandon their military offensives, most of which had ended disastrously anyway and had by the winter largely run out of steam. The administration also decided on moves intended to bring the Bosnian Serbs back to the negotiating table over the Contact Group plan, which obviously meant new concessions to Pale, which would be even less likely to accept the original version of the plan once it realized that NATO was backing away from its earlier threats of force. The concessions involved territorial modifications to the Contact Group map, allowing constitutional links between Pale and Belgrade—and balancing links between the Bosnian Croats and Zagreb—and reestablishing contacts with the Karadzic regime in Pale.[53] After Redman, then U.S. ambassador in Bonn, visited Pale in early December, Karadzic said that he might consider accepting the Contact Group plan now that he understood it could be modified.[54] Shortly thereafter, ex-President Jimmy Carter, in a surprise visit to Bosnia, negotiated a four-month cease-fire and was said to be preparing a new peace proposal as an alternative to the Contact Group plan.

There was a whiff of Munich in the air around Yugoslavia.

NINE

Dayton

Milosevic had reason to be cautiously satisfied at the beginning of 1995. In January, diplomats found him upbeat and confident of eventually gaining Bosnian Serb agreement to the Contact Group peace plan. He claimed that a growing number of Bosnian Serb deputies were ready for a compromise involving a swap of Serb-held areas around Sarajevo in return for control of the Moslem enclaves along the Drina.

In the spring, Britain and France—anxious to extricate themselves and their troops from an obviously failing UN mission in Bosnia—came up with a new approach. Called "Plan B" to distinguish it from the Contact Group plan, which still remained theoretically on the table, the latest initiative involved getting Milosevic to recognize Bosnia within its internationally acknowledged borders and tighten his embargo on supplies to the Bosnian Serbs in return for relief from economic sanctions. But the talks stalled over Milosevic's insistence that sanctions be "lifted" rather than "suspended," and whether Bosnia would be recognized as a "union" of two entities, as the Serbs wanted, or a "state" that the international community was offering. Throughout the spring of 1995, a series of allied negotiators visited Milosevic to sweeten the deal, in a process that one U.S. diplomat likened to offering to sell a house at successively lower prices: "Why should he buy now and agree to a peace plan when he knows that in a few months he's going to get a better deal?"[1] In April, Milosevic felt confident enough to threaten that he might end the embargo if a satisfactory deal on sanctions had not been reached by August, the first anniversary of his break with Pale.

The Balance Shifts

Despite Milosevic's show of assurance, under the surface the military and political balance in Yugoslavia was shifting against Serbia—its economy in shambles from international sanctions and internal mismanagement, and its population demoralized by years of war and hardship. Croatia, by contrast, was growing in military power and diplomatic assurance. Tudjman and his advisers used the three years after the Vance cease-fire to build the Croatian army into a modern, professional force that included significant inventories of armor and artillery. Although Tudjman's "Croatian Army" remained smaller than that of Milosevic's "Yugoslav army," Zagreb's growing military power far outclassed its Croatian Serb opponents in numbers, training, and morale.

Similar changes were also underway in Bosnia. Once a ragtag collection of isolated bands, the Bosnian military had developed a rudimentary command and communications structure that for the first time, allowed it to engage in coordinated, large-unit operations. After a year of U.S.-tolerated covert arms shipments and training from Iran and other Moslem countries, Bosnian forces were well supplied with infantry weapons and mortars even though they remained woefully deficient in armor and heavy artillery. The turnaround in military capabilities infused Bosnian political leaders with growing confidence in their ability to prevail militarily over the Serbs and a corresponding disinterest in the peace process. In January, Izetbegovic told diplomats that Sarajevo intended to use the respite of former President Carter's just-concluded four-month cease-fire to organize and train its military. If the Bosnian Serbs did not accept the Contact Group plan, the Bosnians would take the offensive in May.

While their enemies gained in strength, trends were running in the opposite direction for the Bosnian Serbs. Although Milosevic and the Serb military made sure that the Drina blockade did not seriously affect the Bosnian Serb military, the diminished flow of civilian goods reduced already low standards of living and economic performance. Increasing numbers of Bosnian Serb men left, either to seek more favorable economic prospects or avoid military service. The population of the Serb-held areas of Bosnia may have dropped as low as five hundred thousand, less than half the prewar totals.[2]

The improving capabilities of its opponents confronted the Bosnian Serb military with a serious challenge. Serb forces relied on their superiority in heavy weapons, communications, and transport to offset the Bosnian numerical advantage but with the weapons and maneuverability of their opponents improving, the Serbs were hard-pressed to defend a front line that snaked through hundreds of miles of rugged terrain. The Bosnian forces began offensive operations in March, two months before the cease-fire negotiated by President Carter expired, and by May, Karadzic told UN officials that the Bosnian Serbs could not sustain a prolonged low-intensity conflict. If the fighting continued, he threatened that Pale would go for a military solution. Karadzic called the Bosnian enclaves along the Drina a time bomb waiting to explode. He predicted Bosnian efforts to break out, and in an ominous warning of what was in store for Srebrenica and Zepa, said that if that occurred the Serbs would not respect the enclaves' status as so-called safe areas.

A Different Milosevic

Although Milosevic seemed confident and even cocky in his dealings with international negotiators, he showed a different side of his personality in a resumed series of secret meetings with Tudjman's adviser, Sarinic, over the winter and spring of 1995. In January 1995, Sarinic found Milosevic prepared to give up almost anything to end sanctions, but also existing in a fantasy world where he tried to convince Sarinic—and seemingly himself—that he was not to blame for what had happened in Yugoslavia. Milosevic reminisced about prewar visits to Dubrovnik and hoped that a quick settlement in Croatia—which he promised that year—would allow him to return. A month later, by contrast, Milosevic was "dissatisfied, angry, disappointed, and even frightened" by the UN's unwillingness a few days before to relax sanctions in return for the continuation of Milosevic's blockade against the Bosnian Serbs.

In a March 13 conversation, Milosevic told Sarinic he would not insist that Serbs in Croatia have the legal status of a "constituent nation," which meant the Serbs could be considered a "national minority"—something Milosevic had refused to accept at the time of Yugoslavia's collapse. Sarinic saw this as Milosevic's first acknowledgment of the defeat of his Greater Serb policy in Croatia. In a 21 April meeting, Sarinic found Milosevic charming and full of jokes, but also—intentionally or not—leaving the impression that he was in a "very difficult, almost hopeless situation." Milosevic tried to buy time by proposing a secret meeting with Tudjman in Russia, where they would resolve outstanding differences without interference by other powers.

Ten days later, Tudjman launched Operation Lightning—seizing the isolated Serb-held zone in western Slavonia in a two-day blitzkrieg. As the operation was winding down, an agitated Milosevic telephoned Sarinic demanding that Croatian planes stop attacking Serb refugees. When Sarinic coolly inquired whether Milosevic was prepared to remove the Krajina Serb leaders—who at that moment were firing surface-to-surface missiles into Zagreb—Milosevic angrily hung up, shouting that Sarinic knew he had not installed the Krajina Serbs and could not remove them. The Croats drew important lessons from this incident, noting that Milosevic did not lift a finger to help the Serbs of western Slavonia but displayed acute sensitivity to the potential impact that renewed flows of Serb refugees could have on his domestic political standing.[3]

The sense that time was working against the Serbs—which Milosevic was careful not to show to international negotiators—also led to an effort by Milosevic to cut a deal directly with the Bosnians. In March 1995, after Milosevic put out feelers for talks in Russia, Izetbegovic sent a trusted emissary, Muhamed Filipovic, to meet Milosevic in Belgrade. As Izetbegovic described the meeting to foreign diplomats, Milosevic proposed a four-point plan for ending the conflict, which included Bosnia's division into a union of two entities, each with the right of confederation with its ethnic neighbors. Serbs would be a "constituent nation" in Bosnia, so that no significant question could be resolved without their consent, and there would be land swaps in which the Serbs would give up territory around Sarajevo in return for a widening of the vulnerable Brcko corridor between the eastern and western portions of Serb-held territory in Bosnia. Except for Brcko, Milosevic achieved many of these objectives at Dayton a few months later.

In discussions that spring with British chargé d'affaires Roberts, Milosevic left the impression that it was the other parties who were seeking separate negotiations without the international community. "To hell with the foreigners. We can only solve this problem ourselves," is how Milosevic portrayed the messages allegedly conveyed by the Bosnian and Croatian emissaries. Milosevic, nevertheless, expressed confidence that he could easily settle Bosnia's problems in direct talks with Izetbegovic, who he described as having a "grand vizier" mentality.[4]

Facing International Failure in Bosnia

In the spring of 1995, Britain and France, the two leading troop-contributing nations to the UN in Bosnia, let it be known that they intended to withdraw their soldiers before the next winter if a political settlement was not achieved. The prospect of a UN withdrawal forced NATO to accelerate its operational planning for assisting the UN's departure, to which it had been committed for over a year. NATO military planners in Brussels produced a massive document, known as Op Plan 40104, that would have involved approximately sixty thousand troops—half of them from the United States—and required up to six months to carry out. The NATO operation, potentially the largest military undertaking in Europe since the Second World War, was also a prescription for political disaster, as everyone who looked into it recognized. Not knowing how the parties would react, NATO had to plan for all eventualities including a fighting retreat under attack by some or all of the warring parties.

The failure of international diplomacy in Bosnia was also changing the political equation in the United States. Capitalizing on widespread sympathy among the U.S. public for Sarajevo and sensing a target of opportunity in the 1996 presidential campaign, Republicans stepped up their criticism of the Clinton administration's Bosnia policy. Sentiment in Congress was building in favor of ending U.S. adherence to the embargo on the supply of arms to the Bosnian Moslems—an action that Britain and France promised would lead them to pull their troops out of Bosnia. Horrified policymakers saw themselves headed toward a slow-motion, but seemingly unstoppable train wreck. Having ruled out the use of U.S. troops to impose a Bosnian settlement, the United States faced the prospect of committing its forces to pull out a failed UN mission—an operation fraught with the risk of casualties and certain to leave Bosnia embroiled in worse conflict.

Last-Gasp U.S. Negotiations

As summer approached, Washington launched a last-ditch effort to achieve a settlement before hostilities spun out of control. Deputy Assistant Secretary of State Robert Frasure—a skilled and patient negotiator who combined intelligence, good humor, and fundamental decency—visited Belgrade several times in May 1995. Milosevic, who at one point had refused even to discuss Plan B with senior European diplomats, proved more amenable when he thought the United States was behind the negotiations. On 18 May, after three days together at Karadgordgevo, Frasure and Milosevic reached agreement on a deal involving the phased suspension of sanctions on nonstrategic goods and the import of sufficient oil to meet civilian needs in Serbia, in return for Milosevic's agreement to recognize Bosnia in its prewar borders and tighten up the embargo on the Bosnian Serbs. Suspension of all sanctions would follow once Pale agreed to the 1994 Contact Group plan.[5]

Coming out of his talks with Milosevic, Frasure described him as "learning very quickly how to be a statesman. Look at him like this: he's a Mafia boss who's gotten tired of doing drugs in the South Bronx and so he's planning on moving to Palm Beach and getting into junk bonds."[6] Behind Frasure's typically witty comment was an equally typical insight that few seemed to have grasped at the time: Despite his surface display of confidence, Milosevic badly wanted an agreement and was prepared to sacrifice the interests of the Bosnian Serbs to get one.

Frasure's agreement was repudiated in Washington. Hard-liners objected to the one-year suspension of sanctions and the provision requiring a vote by the UN Security Council to reinstate them, which in practice put Russia in a blocking position. Frasure was sent back with a new U.S. proposal to allow sanctions to be reimposed by one Security Council member—meaning the United States—which was unacceptable not only to Milosevic but every other Security Council member as well. Seemingly unfazed, Milosevic said he was prepared to wait until Washington had greater faith in him, but also promised that he would continue peace negotiations only with the United States.

Carl Bildt Replaces Owen

Former Swedish Prime Minister Carl Bildt, who had replaced Lord Owen as the chief European negotiator for Yugoslavia in early June, was entrusted with picking up the pieces. The boyish-looking Bildt was intelligent and hardworking; he also possessed a talent for getting quickly to the heart of an issue. Coming from neutral Sweden, Bildt had little experience in multilateral diplomacy and had not developed the habit of deference to Washington, which some U.S. diplomats—especially in the post–cold war era of U.S. geopolitical predominance—seemed increasingly to expect.

When I was asked by the State Department to serve as Bildt's deputy, State Department officials told me that Washington had decided to back Bildt as the international community's chief Yugoslav peace negotiator. Within two months, however, a combination of Bildt's unwillingness to take direction from Washington and his slowness in reacting to the changed circumstances in Bosnia—which pulled the United States back into a leading role in the peace process—led to growing differences between Bildt and the United States.

After several rounds of negotiations, Bildt reached agreement with Milosevic on a revised package on 19 July. The deal included Milosevic's pledge to recognize Bosnia within its international borders, and the implementation of the Contact Group plan by establishing Bosnia as a union of two equal and balanced entities—the Federation and the Republika Srpska, each having the right to establish "parallel special relationships" with neighboring countries. The territorial settlement would be based on the fifty-one to forty-nine parameters of the Contact Group plan, which by now had assumed sacrosanct status for all sides. There was also a side agreement negotiated between Bosnian Serb commander Mladic and UN commander Rupert Smith on reopening land access to Sarajevo. Bildt reduced the length of sanctions suspension from one year in the Frasure agreement to nine months, but fended off ex-banker Milosevic's strong arguments that Serbia's financial bank assets be unfrozen. On the reimposition issue, Bildt basically split the difference between Washington and Belgrade by allowing it through a simple majority vote of the five-member UN Security Council. This approach meant that the United States alone could not reimpose sanctions, but neither could Russia and China block it.

By the time Bildt reached his agreement with Milosevic, the situation in Bosnia had changed dramatically. Now it was Milosevic who was in a hurry. No longer was he speaking archly of waiting until Washington came around. International outrage was building as the details of the Serb massacre of Bosnian prisoners in Srebrenica began to trickle out. Milosevic told Bildt he wanted to use television, a trusted weapon in the hands of his media henchmen—to mobilize support for overturning Karadzic and then move quickly to an international peace conference.[7]

Bildt presented his agreement to Contact Group foreign ministers in London the evening of 21 July at a private meeting held immediately after a contentious, day-long conference of all international participants in the Bosnian drama had resulted in the British hosts issuing a warning of renewed bombing if the Serbs continued their attacks on Bosnian enclaves along the Drina River. U.S. Secretary of State Christopher refused to go along with Bildt's agreement. Showing how Srebrenica, coming on top of a string of other failures in the region, had rubbed emotions raw among all those dealing with Bosnia that fateful summer, the usually dour Christopher—to support his arguments that the Bildt package gave too much to the Serbs—urged all present at the meeting to remember a picture recently flashed around the world of a young woman refugee from Srebrenica who had hanged herself. German Foreign Minister Klaus Kinkel also expressed reservations, pointing out that the Bosnians were victims and there were limits to how far the international community could push them. France and Russia enthusiastically accepted Bildt's agreement, but without U.S. support it was dead on arrival.

Bildt was naturally disappointed. Against great odds, he had accomplished what he had been asked to do. Nevertheless, it should have been clear that after Srebrenica, any deal that appeared to reward Milosevic was politically impossible. Bildt's obstinate although understandable defense of his agreement irritated Christopher, who appeared as unfamiliar with the plan's details as he had two years earlier with the Vance-Owen plan, and marked the start of the U.S. evolution away from Bildt. Although Christopher told Bildt after the meeting that he thought Washington might be willing to go along in a few weeks, the fast-moving pace of events swept Bildt's plan away.[8]

The UN Collapses in Bosnia

Even as Frasure negotiated with Milosevic in May, the Bosnians began offensive operations around Sarajevo. Shortly thereafter, Croatian forces began an offensive up the Livno Valley in western Bosnia. The Serbs responded by stepping up the shelling of Sarajevo and other Bosnian cities. On 25 May, Rose's successor as UN commander in Bosnia, British General Rupert Smith, called in air strikes against a Serb ammunition dump in Pale. The Serbs countered by taking over four hundred UN peacekeepers hostage. Televised images of UN soldiers handcuffed to potential NATO bombing targets brought home to viewers throughout the world the failure of the UN mission in Bosnia.

Milosevic reacted sharply to the hostage crisis, which he recognized had the potential to derail his strategy of cutting a deal with the United States. Meeting diplomats at the end of May, Milosevic said NATO air strikes had made the Bosnian Serbs "blind with emotion and anger." Milosevic claimed to be advising Mladic to return Serb heavy weapons to their UN collection centers, and to meet with General Smith and his Bosnian counterpart, General Delic, to calm the situation. Milosevic took a stronger approach with Roberts. He described the hostage taking as a humiliation for all Serbs and said he was dispatching the head of his secret police, the trusted and discreet Jovica Stanisic, to Bosnia. As Milosevic told Roberts, "Stanisic will tell Karadzic that I will have him killed if he doesn't release the hostages. He knows I can do it."[9]

The initial international reaction to the hostage crisis, by contrast, was one of disarray and finger-pointing. UN Secretary General Boutros-Ghali, who had long been unhappy about the UN role in Bosnia, argued that the UN should either withdraw or sharply redefine its mission. With the lives of their soldiers at stake, London and Paris angrily rejected U.S. calls for additional air strikes, but also beefed up their forces in Bosnia by deploying a Rapid Reaction Force (RRF) of artillery units backed by two mobile brigades. As a symbol of their potential war-fighting role, the RRF soldiers did not wear the traditional UN "blue helmets" and their vehicles retained their combat camouflage paint instead of the highly visible UN white.

Despite the tough talk, the White House made it clear to journalists that the president had not changed his opposition to the use of U.S. ground troops in Bosnia. In Brussels, NATO stepped up its withdrawal planning and NATO military officials let it be known that a decision to pull out the UN would have to be made soon if the operation was to be completed before winter. After prolonged internal negotiations, the RRF was deployed under a limited mandate that included operation under both the UN's command and existing UN rules of engagement.

The hostage crisis was resolved through negotiations of unusual murkiness and complexity even by Balkan standards. According to Roberts, the hostages were released after Milosevic agreed to a Bosnian Serb request for urgent military spare parts.[10] One study of the Bosnian conflict notes that hostages were freed after the UN command announced on 10 June that it would "strictly abide by peacekeeping principles until further notice," which amounted to effective agreement to the Serb demand that the UN renounce the use of force.[11] The United States also dispatched Frasure to Belgrade, where he worked with Milosevic to gain the hostages' release and the resupply of the blockaded UN garrisons. Separately, Paris sent General Bertrande de la Presle, a former commander of UN forces in Yugoslavia, to negotiate with Mladic for the hostages' release.

The resolution of the hostage crisis provided the occasion for further international bickering. U.S. officials suspected that France had promised to block additional air strikes in return for the release of the hostages, which Paris denied.[12] European officials, meanwhile, expressed concerns that the United States—determined to avoid being dragged into military confrontation—would give away too much in talks with Milosevic.

Renewed Fighting in Bosnia

On 15 June, the long-suffering residents of Sarajevo watched in jubilation as Bosnian infantry swarmed up the hills that ringed the city behind a barrage of exploding mortar shells. On the other side of town, Bosnian forces struggled through the ruins of a massive prewar Volkswagen plant in an effort to link up with a column fighting its way out of the highlands to the west of the city. Elated Bosnian forces briefly cut the mountain road leading to the

Serb capital of Pale, while street fighting was reported in the Serb-held suburb of Ilijas, whose capture would break the siege by opening up the road to Tuzla. On 18 June, however, the Serbs counterattacked. Serb heavy artillery, including some weapons seized from UN peacekeepers, smashed the attacking Bosnian infantry. The ring around Sarajevo remained unbroken.

The Serbs responded to the Bosnian offensive by stepping up their shelling of Sarajevo and completely closing off all access to the city. Worse was soon to come. In early July, Serb forces began to advance on the Bosnian-held enclave of Srebrenica, a small town tucked away in a steep valley near the Drina River, which the Bosnians had managed to hold since the beginning of the war. The UN declared Srebrenica a safe area in 1993, and its war-swollen population of approximately fifty thousand Moslem refugees was supposedly protected by a battalion of Dutch peacekeepers. In fact, neither the lightly armed Dutch troops nor the Bosnian soldiers in Srebrenica—forced by the international community to surrender the few heavy weapons they possessed when Srebrenica became a safe area—were any match for the heavily armed Serb forces that controlled the hills around the town. On 11 July, Mladic announced that he was giving Srebrenica as a "present to the Serb nation."

After the surrender, Srebrenica's women and children were placed on buses and driven to Tuzla. Some of Srebrenica's men surrendered to the Serbs immediately. Others were killed or captured while fleeing through the wooded hills toward Moslem-held territory in central Bosnia or even, in some cases, across the Drina into Serbia. Virtually all of the men captured by the Bosnian Serb forces were executed. The Red Cross registered 6,546 missing persons from Srebrenica, most of them presumed murdered.[13]

Milosevic and Srebrenica

The capture of Srebrenica was a carefully planned and skillfully executed military operation. The Serbs brushed aside feeble Bosnian resistance, and the killings that followed were handled promptly and with a grim thoroughness. Mladic, who was on the scene part of the time, bears most of the responsibility. Karadzic had long been threatening action against the Drina enclaves, and he and other members of the Bosnian Serb civilian leadership must also have been aware of and approved the operation. The Serb military leadership in Belgrade, which throughout the war provided essential backup to the Bosnian Serb military, almost certainly helped in planning and supporting the attack on Srebrenica. A knowledgeable journalist reported that Chief of Staff Momcilo Perisic gave Mladic explicit permission in early July to attack Srebrenica.[14] Other journalistic accounts allege that U.S. intelligence overheard Perisic planning the attack with Mladic.[15] Throughout the war, Belgrade provided Bosnian Serb forces with specialized military units and individuals, and according to an authoritative study of the Srebrenica massacre, U.S. intelligence sources believe that armored units from the Yugoslav army were involved in the attack on the enclave.[16] Shortly after the fall of Srebrenica, I witnessed Serb special police sweeping the Serb side of the Drina River border area south of the enclave for stragglers.

On 12 July, the day before Srebrenica fell, Milosevic exploded, "Why blame me!" when diplomats warned that they would look to him to bring the Serb offensive to a halt. Yet throughout the Srebrenica crisis, Milosevic was in direct personal contact with Mladic. On 14 July, as Serb forces were combing the Moslem men out of the hills and sending women and children away in buses, Bildt met Milosevic and Mladic together during the final stages of negotiations over his package. The Swedish negotiator, who believes "there were limits to what he [Milosevic] could get Mladic to accept," observed Milosevic alternating between begging and trying to give orders to Mladic.[17]

There is no doubt that Mladic was a stubbornly independent personality, and that Milosevic could not simply issue instructions to Mladic and expect to have them automatically obeyed. Milosevic's prolonged and ultimately unsuccessful efforts to entice Mladic into conducting a coup against Karadzic the previous winter show the limits of his influence over the Bosnian Serb commander. On the other hand, Mladic had clearly broken with the Pale civilian leadership by the summer of 1995, and according to Roberts, "Mladic seems to have preferred to take his instructions from Belgrade rather than from Pale at this stage of the war."[18]

During that summer, Mladic has been depicted as being "on a perpetual high" psychologically. At an emotional celebration of the anniversary of the Kosovo battle shortly before the attack on Srebrenica, Mladic appeared to identify himself and the Bosnian Serb people with Tsar Lazar and the Serbs of the battle.[19] UN officials who met Mladic during the summer described him to me as excited and sometimes almost feverish, but at the same time fully capable of rational, controlled behavior. Some speculated that his mood had been affected by the recent suicide of his daughter.

Despite the undoubted difficulty of dealing with someone like Mladic, whether as ally or subordinate, there is no doubt that Milosevic was aware of what was happening in Srebrenica and that he had the ability to compel

Mladic to stop—although whether he could have done so in time to have prevented the massacre is uncertain. Bosnian Serb forces depended on Belgrade for essential supplies, and there is no particular reason to believe that the FRY military would not have obeyed an order to use this lever against the Bosnian Serbs. Later in the summer, Milosevic's loyal ally Montenegrin Prime Minister Bulatovic, calling the Bosnian Serb military "lunatics," told diplomats that the FRY military was prepared to intervene to silence Bosnian Serb guns that had resumed shelling Dubrovnik. Milosevic could also, of course, have ordered Stanisic to simply arrest Mladic, who was a frequent visitor to Belgrade that summer. Milosevic's reported use of Stanisic to threaten Karadzic with assassination during the hostage crisis reveals the lengths he was prepared to go to enforce his will in matters of real importance to him, although moving against Mladic would have been much problematic because of the general's immense popularity among Serbs.

Both the United States and Bildt urged Milosevic to use his influence to stop the Bosnian Serbs' attack, and warned that the capture of Srebrenica would have negative consequences for the peace process.[20] But there was considerable confusion around Srebrenica in the days immediately after its fall. UN officials knew that the Serbs were separating male prisoners from the women and children, and within days of the city's fall refugees appearing in Tuzla began to report atrocities committed by the Serb forces. Yet the UN also knew that thousands of Bosnian men had escaped Srebrenica's surrender and were fleeing through the hills. Not until after a U.S. U-2 spy plane photographed what appeared to be fresh mass graves near the Srebrenica football field on 27 July, almost two weeks after Srebrenica fell, did conclusive proof of the scope of the Serb crime appear.[21]

After Srebrenica, Milosevic was urged to pressure the Bosnian Serbs to provide information and access for humanitarian personnel. No effort was made to hold him accountable for the massacre, though. By then Milosevic was central to the process of negotiation by which the international community hoped to bring the Bosnian nightmare to a close. In the summer of 1995, moreover, as Washington groped for a new approach to the Bosnian quagmire, some were arguing for redrawing the Contact Group map, which had left the isolated Drina River enclaves in Bosnian hands, to give the authorities in Sarajevo more defensible borders. In this context, the fall of Srebrenica and the smaller enclave of Zepa had simplified the ethnic map of Bosnia and thereby made a diplomatic settlement easier to achieve. An unnamed senior U.S. official noted, "While losing the enclaves has been unfortunate for Bosnia it's been great for us."[22]

The Sarajevo That Milosevic Wrought

The failure of the much-heralded Bosnian summer offensive, followed quickly by the loss of Srebrenica and Zepa, brought the situation in Sarajevo to a new low. The surrounding Serb forces shut down the airport and closed off all land routes. Access to the city was possible only by a narrow and dangerous dirt road leading over rugged Mt. Igman that was exposed to Serb gunfire in its last kilometer, and then through a cramped and dangerous tunnel under the airport's runway.

Serb shelling increased in intensity, its timing and location seemingly intended to maximize the terror effect on the population. Seasoned Sarajevo hands noted that the shelling was generally most heavy at 11:00 A.M., when people were doing their meager shopping; at 7:30 P.M., when those who had access to some kind of power were listening to the news; and at 11:00 P.M., when people were trying to go to sleep. In many parts of the city, electricity, gas, and water service had long since collapsed. Sarajevans lived in a bizarre combination of medieval darkness and primitive sanitary conditions, surrounded at the same time by the ruins of what had once been one of Yugoslavia's most pleasant cities.

As visitors to Sarajevo—few in number at that time—emerged from the no-man's-land around the airport, they were greeted by spray-painted graffiti on the wall of a ruined apartment building saying, "Welcome to Hell." Everything about Sarajevo then confirmed the accuracy of the inscription. The only traffic was white-painted UN vehicles that careered quickly down the empty streets, their occupants uncomfortably aware of the gunsights undoubtedly trained on them from the low hills that loomed only a few hundred yards above "snipers' alley." At night, guests of the Holiday Inn—possibly the only one of that chain whose front desk featured a sign advising clients to avoid walking through the center of the lobby because of the danger of snipers—could watch the two sides exchange gunfire across the narrow Mlijecka River only a few yards away. The heavy whoosh of what, to my untrained ear, sounded like outgoing rockets from Bosnian positions would inevitably be followed soon thereafter by incoming mortar rounds from Serb positions in the nearby hills.

Many of Sarajevo's public buildings, such as the National Library with its priceless prewar manuscript collection, had been deliberately targeted by Serb gunners and stood along the streets as burned-out ruins. Almost every pane of glass in the city had been shattered, replaced either by wooden boards or heavy plastic wrap marked with the ubiquitous blue-and-white UN logo. With no place to go, residents mostly stayed indoors, especially on days of heavy shelling. The empty streets and sidewalks of Sarajevo were covered with jagged holes in the pavement where Serb shells had fallen. Surrounded by rings of smaller holes left by flying shrapnel, they were called "Sarajevo flowers." From the angle of the gouges in the pavement, it was possible to tell with fair accuracy where the shell had been fired from. Often, Sarajevans could also recall just who had died when that particular flower exploded.

After three years of war Sarajevo had experienced other, less visible but probably more permanent changes. Sarajevo's prewar population of 450,000 had fallen to 280,000, and half of the current inhabitants were Moslem refugees from Serb cleansing. The influx of impoverished and embittered rural refugees changed the character of once cosmopolitan and sophisticated Sarajevo. More women could be seen wearing scarves; Islamic forms of greeting became common. Feelings of abandonment by the West encouraged many to turn to Islam for spiritual comfort—a trend encouraged by the large and well-funded relief operations run by Iran, Saudi Arabia, and the Gulf States.

Years of failed international promises had left many Bosnian officials angry and embittered. The justice of their complaints, even if often delivered with an unsettling shrillness, made meeting with them especially painful during that grim summer of 1995. Sometimes, however, an incident occurred that cut through the rhetoric and allowed a visitor to sense the strain on the Bosnian leaders. Once, when Bildt was meeting Bosnian officials in Izetbegovic's large though tattered office, two Serb shells exploded in the square behind the building. The sound was deafening, and the impact reverberated through the building and the bodies of those in the meeting. Conversation ceased, and in the silence that followed the second explosion, Izetbegovic looked to the ceiling and said almost to himself, "While we are talking, people are dying."

After three years of siege, people no longer believed in the possibility of international assistance or the promises of their own government. As Bildt and I waited to see Izetbegovic, officials close to the Bosnian president described an incipient sense of panic hanging over Sarajevo. Rumors circulated through the city that the Serbs would soon attack, repeating on a larger scale what they had just done in Srebrenica. Sarajevans whispered of Serb commandos slipping down into the city at night from the surrounding hills in order to prepare for the final assault. At the beginning of the war, the Bosnian authorities had imposed a ban on leaving the city—a kind of administrative siege in reverse. Now, anyone who could devise a convincing excuse to leave, or pay the required bribes, was trying to get out. Sarajevo Mayor Tarik Kupusovic—an island of decency and good sense amid the madness of war—was blunt. "Sarajevo could not survive another winter of war," he told every visitor.

For the Sarajevo that Milosevic had wrought it was the darkness before the dawn, but at the time no one knew.

Toughening International Response

Coming so soon after the humiliation of the UN hostage crisis, the massacre at Srebrenica triggered a swelling demand for tough action against the Serbs. How to stop them continued to divide the international community, however. France proposed to introduce a brigade of its troops to defend Gorazde, the last remaining Bosnian enclave along the Drina, but only if the United States was willing to provide Apache helicopters, which Washington refused to risk. In turn, the French rejected the U.S. proposal that Gorazde be defended by air strikes alone. The British thought that Gorazde should be abandoned and ordered the small British special forces unit in the enclave to slip out. Russia, meanwhile, continued to oppose military action of any kind.

On 21 July, Great Britain hosted a meeting of all the major participants in the international intervention in Bosnia. After a day of speeches and discordant wrangling in the corridors, the British issued a statement that condemned the Serb seizure of Srebrenica and Zepa, warning that an attack on the remaining Bosnian-held enclave of Gorazde would be met with "a substantial and decisive response." Separate press conferences by other participants showed that the differences continued. U.S. Secretary of State Christopher, flanked by Secretary of Defense William Perry and Chair of the Joint Chiefs of Staff John Shalikashvili, asserted that an attack on Gorazde would be met by a "significant air campaign." Russian Foreign Minister Kozyrev and Defense Minister Grachev issued a separate statement opposing any use of air power.[23] The French foreign minister added to the confusion by revealing to the public Bildt's agreement with Milosevic and urging that negotiations continue along that track.

The London conference marked a turning point in the ponderous evolution of the international ship of states toward a more forceful response in Bosnia, but there was also a certain element of posing in its outcome. The allies drew a line in the sand around Gorazde, yet it was a line the Serbs had no intention of crossing. Although Mladic had earlier boasted that the Serbs would capture all Bosnian enclaves by the fall, UN forces in Bosnia detected no preparations around Gorazde for a Serb offensive. The day after the London conference, moreover, Belgrade media, citing "sources close to the Bosnian Serb army," said that Mladic did not plan to attack Gorazde. At the same time, a Serb attack on Bihac—which began on 24 July—passed without Western response. After London, NATO was all dressed up to bomb, but for over a month its warplanes went nowhere.

Tudjman to the Rescue

While the international community continued to dither over air strikes, military action of a much more decisive kind unfolded near Bosnia. On 4 August, Croatia launched "Operation Storm," a massive invasion aimed at recapturing all of the areas of Croatia seized by the Serbs in 1991, except for a strip of territory in eastern Slavonia that was considered too risky to attack because of the proximity of powerful FRY forces in adjoining Vojvodina. The Croatian offensive was preceded by an artillery barrage on the Krajina capital of Knin, which according to the UN commander, killed many civilians. Knin fell in less than twenty-four hours, and within a week the jubilant Croatian forces had occupied Krajina entirely. Almost all of the region's two hundred thousand Serb residents fled—hastened on their way by looting, burning, and physical attacks from the advancing Croatian forces.[24]

Some time after the Croatian offensive, I drove across what had once been Krajina. The usual detritus of ethnic war in the Balkans—abandoned houses with their roofs ripped off and interiors burned out—was visible at the edge of the former front line and along some of the main roads. Graffiti left by both sides plastered many walls. On one was a crudely painted picture of a tiger, showing that Arkan's Serbian thugs had been there. Another proclaimed with misplaced hope, "Mladic will defend us forever!" Croats had painted in black the name of Croatia's World War II fascist leader Ante Pavelic on some of their houses. In towns where a few of the Croats expelled by the Serbs in 1991 had begun to trickle back, some houses had been painted with a more practical appeal: "Don't destroy; owned by a Croat."

Deeper into Krajina the signs of fighting vanished, replaced by simple emptiness. Village after village was completely deserted. Dust sifted through open windows and doors banged in the wind. Many of the houses had been looted, but others seemed to have been too poor to bother. Behind a few houses, tattered remnants of washing fluttered forlornly on lines. Few Croats had lived in this barren Serbian heartland before the war, and with the Serbs gone, it seemed likely to remain uninhabited for a long time.

Did Milosevic Cut a Deal with Tudjman?

Krajina's rapid collapse and Belgrade's failure to intervene caused considerable speculation that Milosevic had secretly agreed to allow Tudjman to crush the rebellious Croatian Serbs. The evidence available does not seem to support the notion of an explicit deal but it definitely reveals Milosevic's complete indifference to the fate of the Krajina Serbs.

In early 1995, after Tudjman threatened to force the UN out of Croatia, the FRY foreign ministry formally warned the major powers involved in Yugoslavia that no government in Belgrade could allow a Croatian takeover of Krajina. In late February, Milosevic told the Finnish head of the international monitoring mission along the Drina that he did not believe Tudjman would be so stupid as to start a war in Krajina because Tudjman knew that he would support the Croatian Serbs if they were attacked.

Over the rest of the year, however, Milosevic adopted a head-in-the-sand approach toward Krajina. He complained about the pigheaded intransigence of the Krajina Serb leadership to anyone who would listen and attempted to build up the supposedly more moderate Krajina Prime Minister Mikelic as a counter to Babic. But Milosevic never used the economic and military levers he possessed to force the Krajina Serbs into negotiating seriously with Zagreb. On 2 August, Babic, who met U.S. Ambassador to Croatia Galbreath in Belgrade in a desperate effort to head off the imminent Croatian attack, intimated that Milosevic had all along encouraged Knin to reject the Z-4 plan for an autonomous Serb entity within Croatia. Babic is not necessarily the most reliable witness; he was obviously seeking to shift blame for the impending catastrophe away from himself. Nevertheless, it is clear that Milosevic did not actively seek an agreement in Croatia but rather hoped somehow to freeze the situation long enough to allow the de facto partition to become permanent.

By the end of July, with Croatian preparations for an attack obvious and journalists returning from Krajina reporting that the Serb leadership was "in a panic," Milosevic finally bestirred himself. He informed the United States and other countries on 30 July that the Croatian Serb and Bosnian Serb militaries had agreed to halt their offensive on nearby Bihac, which the Croats were citing as a justification for attacking Krajina. Milosevic implored the United States to stop the impending Croatian offensive in order to allow a resumption of the Z-4 talks. Yet he refused to meet with U.S. diplomats on 2 August to receive a message urging him to ensure that the Krajina Serbs negotiated seriously at a last-ditch session held under UN auspices the following day in Geneva.

No mention of a deal over Krajina appears in Sarinic's record of his conversations with Milosevic. To the contrary, Sarinic's account reveals natural anxiety in Zagreb about how Belgrade would respond. Not until the evening of 3 August, only a few hours before the Croat guns opened fire, did the Croatian leaders relax, after a statement from the head of the Serbian state television that they interpreted as a sign that Milosevic "would not hurry to the assistance of the Serbs beyond the Drina."[25]

Milosevic's initial reaction to the Croatian offensive reinforces the impression that he was detached from the reality of events on the ground in Krajina. On the day the Croatians attacked, Milosevic told Bildt, who happened to be in Belgrade at the time, that Tudjman had made an expensive mistake and predicted that the Krajina Serbs would hold out for twenty years. Similarly, Milosevic told RTS director Milorad Vucelic, who had a short separate meeting with Milosevic during the talks with Bildt, that the Krajina Serbs were holding fast at all but a few points and that they would surely defeat the Croats.[26] In actuality, the resistance of the Krajina Serbs—supposedly the toughest of all Serb fighters—lasted less than a week.

Milosevic heard the news of Knin's fall at a government retreat where he was relaxing with his wife and his wealthy businessman crony, Bogoljub Karic. When Milosevic was informed over the phone, he did not seem surprised or particularly horrified, remarking, "Imagine, those fools withdrew!" The next evening, Milosevic met separately with the military, the SPS leadership, and trusted newspaper editors. According to those present, Milosevic did not appear disturbed. He attributed Knin's fall to failures by Martic and Karadzic, and the order went out to the Serb media to follow this line in its reporting of the catastrophe.[27]

The Croats and Moslems Continue the Attack

Like the fall of a single boulder that triggers a larger avalanche, the Croatian success released a snowballing pattern of military and political setbacks for Milosevic. Only intervention from a seemingly unlikely source—Washington—saved Milosevic from further disasters that had they been allowed to proceed unchecked, might well have loosened his hold on office that summer.

In early August, while the fighting in Krajina was still underway, Croatian officials informed the United States about joint military operations with Bosnian forces that had been agreed to at a meeting in late July between Tudjman and Izetbegovic. What Croatian Foreign Minister Mate Granic and Defense Minister Susak basically laid out was a plan to end the war in Bosnia through military victory by the fall. After mopping up Krajina, the Croats intended to send fifteen to twenty-five thousand soldiers to the assistance of the Bosnian V Corps in Bihac to allow it to capture Prijedor. Meanwhile the Croatian Army, in cooperation with Bosnian Croat forces, would continue its advance through western Bosnia until Drvar and Jajce had been captured. Following that, Croat and Moslem forces would cooperate to push the Serbs beyond artillery range of Mostar and Dubrovnik. Finally, the Croats said, they would be prepared to open a corridor to Sarajevo—with U.S. assistance.

Additional military pressure on the Serbs fitted well with the new U.S. diplomatic initiative that was emerging at that time. Washington's only concern was that the new allies might go too far. Accordingly, it warned the Croats and Bosnians not to push their military operations to Prijedor or Banja Luka, whose fall the United States feared might force Milosevic to send FRY troops into Bosnia. This was a line that Washington adhered to throughout the fall. The United States wanted to use the joint Bosnian and Croatian offensive to push the Serbs back and force them into a compromise settlement. It was not, however, prepared to see the Serbs crushed completely. Washington wanted a quick solution in Bosnia—not a catastrophic defeat for the Serbs, which would undermine the strategy of relying on Milosevic to deliver the Serb side of an agreement and might also set off further upheavals that would keep the Balkans churning indefinitely.

Krajina Refugees Unsettle Serbia

A few days after Krajina's collapse, I watched the first of approximately two hundred thousand refugees entering Serbia, after fleeing 250 miles across northern Bosnia. Driving west out of Belgrade, our party ran into the first groups of refugees trekking incongruously down the deserted superhighway that before the war had linked Yugoslavia's capital with Western Europe. At the border with Serb-held Bosnia, the scene was a nightmarish vision of the human impact of defeat. Backed up as far as the eye could see were tens of thousands of people fleeing in every imaginable conveyance: buses, trucks, cars, tractors, and horse-drawn carts. Old people, families with young children, and soldiers mingled in one massive column of misery. Women cried, children played among the slow-moving vehicles, and men stared in vacant exhaustion down a road they knew led nowhere.

Most of the refugees had been traveling for over a week; some had been attacked by Croatian warplanes on the way. All had precipitously abandoned their homes, grabbing whatever they could carry before the Croatian soldiers arrived. What was striking was how little the Serbian authorities had done to receive the refugees, even though the arrival of the slow-moving columns could have been predicted several days in advance. Police collected weapons and a few harassed Red Cross officials tried to register names, but otherwise no provisions seemed to have been made to help the refugees. After they crossed the border, the refugees simply kept on going like a medieval migration of peoples inching slowly across the lush, late summer Serbian landscape.

When I returned a few days later they were still coming. For almost a week the flow continued, day and night. Sometimes as many as one thousand people an hour passed, for a total of over fifty thousand at this one border crossing point alone. By the time of my second visit, the authorities had begun some minimal efforts to help. In one tent, a few overworked doctors and nurses provided simple medical treatment. Water trucks had been parked in a nearby field and small quantities of food were being distributed to children. As before, though, the local Serbs stood in their front yards and watched the seemingly endless lines of refugees flowing by them in silence and with expressions that seemed to range from indifference to hostility. When I joined international border monitors in donating blood for the relief of the refugees, it was considered so unusual that I found myself being interviewed on Serb television.

Talking to the refugees provided some revealing insights into the psychological realities of ethnic warfare. Few of the refugees had actually witnessed the arrival of Croatian troops into Krajina. Most had fled before the invaders showed up, well aware of the fate that awaited them if they remained. None of these refugees mentioned it, but all of them understood that it was payback time, that the victorious Croats would exact revenge for what Serbs had done to the Croatian inhabitants of Krajina in 1991.

Physically exhausted, the refugees also seemed resigned to their fate. These Serbs were abandoning the rugged, mountainous borderland where their ancestors had lived for hundreds of years. Few ever expected to return. Nevertheless, they showed surprisingly little anger toward the Croatians or toward me as an American, even though all were convinced that the United States had helped the Croats militarily. But that was war, and in war one expected nothing good from the enemy. The refugees reserved their anger for their own authorities who had abandoned them and most of all for Milosevic, who they were convinced had betrayed them.

Not even Milosevic's efficient propaganda machine could hide the spectacle of this defeated horde from the rest of Serbia. After entering Serbia, many of the refugees evaded police barricades set up to divert them away from the capital and plodded slowly along the highway that runs through the center of Belgrade. Anger and humiliation swept the country. At a soccer match, fifty thousand fans chanted, "Slobo—You have betrayed Krajina." Friends found a despairing FRY Prime Minister Radoje Kontic drinking in his office, after his children told him, "Pi . . . on your prime ministership."[28]

A history of Serbia in the 1990s reports that "a sense that the Serbs were undergoing a national catastrophe of apocalyptic proportions informed public discourse during the late summer of 1995."[29] Many in Belgrade expected trouble for Milosevic, especially if the setback in Croatia was followed by further defeats in Bosnia. Mihajlo Markovic, the well-known intellectual who was soon to be unceremoniously dumped as vice president of Milosevic's SPS, told me at the time that the disaster in Krajina had affected Milosevic's psychological state. Markovic said that Milosevic was drinking more heavily, becoming even more reclusive, and was increasingly reliant on his wife and a narrow circle around her. On the walls in Belgrade, graffiti appeared that captured the bleak mood: "Pair off in twos: dead, hungry; dead, hungry."

On 12 August, Sarinic had his first meeting with Milosevic since the fall of Krajina. Characteristically, while Krajina refugees were still pouring through Belgrade and Serbs everywhere were trying to come to grips with the consequences of their worst defeat since 1941, Sarinic found Milosevic isolated in a secret mountain hideaway far from Belgrade. It was a different Milosevic that Sarinic met, however. Gone were his jokes, smiles, and charm. Milosevic had lost the self-confidence and "triumphalism" that Sarinic thought had marked his behavior before "Storm." Now, Sarinic noted with spiteful self-satisfaction, Milosevic often punctuated his remarks with "I don't know," "I have no idea," and "I can't." Milosevic never mentioned Storm directly, but he began by telling Sarinic that "the situation (in Serbia) is very difficult and I will soon be unable to control it."

Milosevic's substantive proposals showed the combination of tactical dexterity and strategic blindness that had always been his hallmark— punctuated by a new sense of desperation. He began by demanding what he knew the Croats would not grant—that the Serb refugees be allowed to return home—and added—after refusing to discuss the subject for years— that now the Serbs would be satisfied with the status of autonomy within Croatia. Sarinic contemptuously dismissed these sallies. By contrast, Milosevic and Sarinic easily agreed that a political settlement in Bosnia should be based on dividing the country into two entities. Milosevic pleaded for a meeting with Tudjman where he said they could quickly resolve all problems without the international community. As they were leaving, a depressed Milosevic tried to convince Sarinic that he had always fought against ethnic cleansing, but he failed to respond to Sarinic's barbed retort.[30]

This must have been one of Milosevic's darkest hours—but help was on its way.

The U.S. (Diplomatic) Cavalry Rescues Milosevic

If events in Yugoslavia at the end of the summer looked bad to Milosevic, at the beginning of the summer they hardly seemed any better in Washington. As disaster followed disaster in Bosnia, the administration was flayed by Congress, the media, and the public.

With the various elements of the U.S. national security bureaucracy firmly dug into opposing positions over Bosnia, an initiative to break the deadlock could only come from the top. In June, President Clinton's national security adviser, Tony Lake began to put together what he called the "Endgame Strategy"—an effort to sidestep entrenched bureaucratic positions by defining where the administration wanted to be in six months on Bosnia and only then deciding how to get there. In early August, after Congress had passed a bill requiring the United States under certain conditions to lift the arms embargo on the Bosnians—which U.S. allies had already said would lead them to pull the plug on the UN mission—the president sent Lake and his Endgame Strategy to Europe. Lake won allied approval relatively quickly—the allies had for years been begging for U.S. engagement on Bosnia and, according to Gen. Wes Clark, who accompanied Lake to Europe, the new U.S. willingness to commit 25,000 troops to help implement an agreement was key.[31] After allied support had been obtained, the task of negotiating an agreement with the warring parties was passed to Holbrooke. Bildt, who only two months earlier had been told he would have U.S. support as the lead negotiator, was casually elbowed aside.

The Endgame Strategy consisted of seven points, most drawn from previous peace plans. These included: a comprehensive peace settlement based on the core principles of the 1994 Contact Group plan; mutual recognition of Croatia, Bosnia, and the FRY in their international borders; a united Bosnia consisting of two entities, the Moslem-Croat Federation and Serb-held territories; territorial division between the two entities based on the Contact Group fifty-one to forty-nine proposal, but with revisions to reflect recent changes of territory on the battlefield; and an end to all economic sanctions once the agreement had been implemented.[32]

Nevertheless, the two most important elements of the U.S. initiative did not appear on paper. The first was the U.S. determination to achieve a Bosnian peace settlement that year. The second was Washington's willingness to use force to persuade the Serbs to agree.

Milosevic was initially dismissive of the U.S. diplomatic initiative, describing it to Bildt in August as "undeveloped ideas based on insufficient knowledge."[33] Even as late as 4 September, Milosevic told Sarinic that the United States was simply "lulling" the Moslems and understood nothing. He again proposed that he and Tudjman resolve all outstanding problems without international participation, with each taking "its part" of Bosnia.[34]

Despite Milosevic's predictably snide insinuations to non-Americans, the U.S. diplomatic initiative came as a lifeline to him. Throughout the late summer and fall, the Croatian-Bosnian ground offensive rolled Bosnian Serb forces steadily backward. By the end of August, Croatian forces had captured most of eastern Bosnia, and by the middle of September, they were knocking on the door of Banja Luka, the only major city still held by the Serbs. Had the Croatian-Bosnian forces been allowed to proceed as far as possible, they would certainly have retaken all Serb-held territory in eastern and central Bosnia, and in the opinion of some informed observers at the time, might well have swept all the way to the Drina River and expelled the Serbs completely from Bosnia. In either case, the result would have been a catastrophe for the Serbs as well as Milosevic personally. A second major defeat in less than two months accompanied by another and probably even larger wave of refugees would have further inflamed tensions in Serbia, and might have fatally weakened Milosevic.

Milosevic was careful to hide his anxieties from international negotiators, but early in the process he took a step that showed how badly he wanted an agreement. On 30 August, during the Holbrooke team's second visit to Belgrade, Milosevic surprised the Americans by pulling out a paper in which the Bosnian Serbs basically signed over their negotiating rights to Milosevic.[35] During the previous week, Milosevic had convened two secret meetings of the political and military leadership of Belgrade and Pale, in the presence of Patriarch Pavle. In an agreement signed the day before the U.S. team's arrival, the Bosnian Serbs agreed to completely harmonize their approach to the peace process with that of the FRY leadership—that is, with Milosevic. The Bosnian Serbs also agreed to a joint delegation on which—in the case of disagreement—Milosevic would have the deciding vote. Bosnian Serb Vice President Nikola Koljevic told Roberts that Pale had gone along with Milosevic highjacking the Serb negotiating team because "we had no choice."[36]

Milosevic's coup was a major boost for the U.S. diplomatic effort. A week earlier, in a twelve-point peace plan intended to set the stage for negotiations, Izetbegovic had demanded that Milosevic be the only Serb negotiator. Izetbegovic was no friend of Milosevic, but he understood that since the May 1993 Vance-Owen agreement, the Bosnian Serbs had blocked one proposed peace deal after another. In a secret meeting with Bildt to discuss possible territorial settlements only a few days before, the Bosnian Serbs had shown such unrealistic expectations—seeking major parts of Sarajevo, a corridor to the sea, possession of the Sarajevo airport, and the takeover of the Gorazde enclave—as to make an agreement with them seem highly unlikely.

NATO Bombing

On 28 August, five mortar shells slammed into Sarajevo's central market, near the site of the similar tragic attack in February 1994. This time, thirty-seven people were killed and ninety wounded. As with the previous incident, the Serbs immediately disclaimed responsibility—almost as though their guns had not been shelling Sarajevo for more than three years—and Serb military sources in Belgrade spread the word that it was the work of a Moslem splinter group.[37] Among some UN officials in Sarajevo, it had become almost an article of faith that the Bosnians provoked incidents of violence in order to stimulate sympathetic media coverage of their plight. Such suspicions had been heightened a few months earlier when a French military investigation allegedly found conclusive proof that Bosnian snipers had fired on their own people. Some UN officials were also convinced they had observed Bosnian forces covertly firing from positions near the city's Kosevo hospital in a cynical effort to exploit the shock value when the media flashed pictures around the world of the Serbs shelling the hospital in response.

This time, however, there was little question about the perpetrators. By the next day, UN forces in Sarajevo had "concluded beyond doubt" that the mortars were fired from Serb territory. The UN investigation, briefed to the Security Council on 13 September, was based on analysis of the impact site by teams from several countries, observations of UN soldiers on duty at the time of the incident, and data from a British artillery tracking radar unit that had been installed in an old Turkish fort overlooking the city after the February 1994 incident. Analysis of the impact craters and the observations of UN soldiers showed that the five mortar rounds came from southwest of the city, while data from the British radar indicated that they were fired from a range of 1,550 to 3,500 meters. Since the distance from the impact site to the confrontation line between Bosnian and Serb forces in the direction from which the shells were fired was 1,050 meters, it was obvious that they had originated within Serb lines. UN investigators also found a tail fin from a 120 mm mortar whose design matched those used by the Bosnian Serbs near the impact point of the round that caused most of the casualties.[38]

Two days after the market shelling, NATO began a bombing campaign against Bosnian Serb air defense, command and control, and communications facilities. NATO avoided targets in populated areas that might cause civilian casualties and also stayed away from major military targets, such as ammunition dumps and troop concentrations. When the operation ended two weeks later, a total of 3,515 sorties had been flown, delivering over 1,026 high-explosive munitions on 48 Bosnian Serb targets.[39] Possibly more damaging militarily to the Serbs than the bombing—and certainly uplifting to the spirits of the besieged people of Sarajevo—was the impressive barrage of over 500 shells that the mortars and heavy artillery of the Anglo-French RRF launched from its positions atop Mt. Igman against Serb guns ringing Sarajevo. Serb artillery never again fired on Sarajevo.

In addition to air defenses, NATO bombing targeted the Bosnian Serb communication and transportation systems, which had been key to the Serb ability to move troops and heavy weapons rapidly to points threatened by their numerically superior opponents. The bombing complicated the Bosnian Serb capability to move forces from the eastern part of Bosnia, where they had been concentrated in summer during the attacks on Srebrenica and Zepa, to the western part of Bosnia, where they were needed to defend against the combined Bosnian and Croatian offensive.[40]

The psychological effect of the bombing may well have been at least as great as the military's impact. Already reeling from Croatian and Bosnian ground attacks, the Serbs now faced the prospect of adding the world's most powerful military alliance to their foes. UN military commanders in Bosnia at the time believed that the psychological shock of 12 September cruise missile attacks on Banja Luka, although they did little lasting military damage, and the destruction of some of the bridges across the Drina, on which the Bosnian Serb forces depended for resupply from Serbia, convinced the Serbs that they might well be the target of a wider air war with more devastating consequences.

The NATO bombing also had a noticeable effect on the psychological state of the Serb leaders. On 12 September, just before the bombing ended, Bildt found Milosevic "distracted—obsessed by the thought that the bombing was about to destroy everything and in no condition to discuss anything else."[41]

The bombing seemed to have an effect on Mladic's psychological state, too. On 4 September, UN Commander French General Bernard Janvier received a bizarre message from Mladic. In a long and at times nearly incoherent letter—a faxed copy of which I helped translate for Bildt in the incongruous setting of an open-air restaurant beside the Bay of Naples—Mladic complained that the Serb people were being forcibly isolated from the world, charged that the NATO bombing was more brutal than that of the Nazis against Belgrade in the Second World War, and threatened UN personnel. The contents and tone of Mladic's message raised serious questions in the minds of those who read it about the Bosnian Serb commander's grasp on reality.

On 13 September, Milosevic set up a meeting in Belgrade between the U.S. diplomatic team and Karadzic and Mladic. Milosevic said the situation on the ground needed "calming" and proposed a cease-fire throughout Bosnia followed immediately by an international peace conference. This was an obvious sign of weakness on Milosevic's part, and Holbrooke rejected it in order to give the Bosnian and Croatian forces more time to advance even though Washington, not to mention other world capitals, would likely have welcomed Milosevic's proposal. Instead, after a shouting match with the Bosnian Serbs, Milosevic obtained Pale's agreement to a more limited U.S. proposal, involving the withdrawal of Serb heavy weapons from around Sarajevo along with the opening of the Bosnian capital to air and land transportation. After the document was signed, the mercurial Karadzic told Holbrooke, "We are ready for peace," while a dejected Mladic looked "utterly spent."[42]

Breakthrough in Geneva

On 19 August, three members of the U.S. negotiating team—Frasure, Defense Department official Joe Kruzel, and National Security Council staffer Colonel Nelson Drew—were killed when the armored vehicle they were riding in rolled off the narrow dirt road over Mt. Igman, on the way into Sarajevo. The tragic deaths of the three officials, all of who enjoyed the sincere respect of their colleagues, deepened the determination of the remaining members of the U.S. team, which continued its shuttle diplomacy even as NATO bombs were falling. In early September, the U.S. team won Milosevic's and Izetbegovic's approval for a set of basic political principles to govern Bosnia's future. Formally ratified at an 8 September foreign ministers meeting in Geneva, the "Agreed Basic Principles" were the political breakthrough that made the Dayton agreement possible.

The essence of the Geneva deal was that the Serbs swallowed the necessity of remaining within Bosnia while the Bosnians conceded the existence of a separate Serb entity. The U.S. approach, which took as its starting point the 1994 Contact Group plan, included many points that the warring parties had already agreed to at various times over the previous three years of international diplomacy. Under Holbrooke's leadership, the great achievement of the capable and persistent U.S. negotiating team was to get all three parties to agree simultaneously on the basic elements of the deal and then make them stick by that agreement long enough to end the fighting, flesh out the details, and construct a peace settlement.[43]

Considering how badly the Serbs were being knocked about at the time —on the ground by the Croatian-Bosnian offensive and from the air by NATO—they did not do badly by the Geneva deal. On the symbolic front— always important in Yugoslavia—Milosevic succeeded in preserving the Serbs' name for their entity, the Republika Srpska. The Bosnians strongly objected to this provision out of a fear, later confirmed in practice, that allowing an explicit link between ethnicity and territory would reinforce the prospects that the unfolding settlement would create a de facto partition among the three ethnic groups. The Serbs, in turn, had to give up the notion that Bosnia would be a "union" of the two entities—a point they had won in the 1993 Invincible package and the Bildt deal, and that they liked because it implied a virtually invisible central government.

The Bosnians objected most strongly of all to the requirement that they give up the name under which their state had been recognized in 1992. It would now be called simply Bosnia and Herzegovina instead of the Republic of Bosnia-Herzegovina. To the pragmatic Americans, this change seemed to be of little import when placed next to a deal that preserved Bosnia as one state and brought peace to the region. The Bosnians, however, understood that abandoning the prewar name meant the symbolic end to any hope that Bosnia might someday be reconstituted a unitary state as it had been before the war—which the Moslems could eventually hope to dominate through force of numbers. Still, the Bosnians won agreement that the new state would continue the legal existence of the old one—something they had long been seeking because it would allow them to maintain their existing representation in international organizations such as the UN.

The Geneva agreement set the negotiating dynamics for the rest of the Dayton process. Even though he did not attend the Geneva meeting, Milosevic made all major Serb decisions himself, bringing along the Bosnian Serbs primarily by ignoring them. In the Geneva agreement, Milosevic achieved most of the basic Serb interests as he saw them: securing the existence of a separate Serb entity within Bosnia, whose territory would reflect the sacrosanct fifty-one to forty-nine division, that would also have the right to a separate, special relationship with Belgrade. As for the rest, he settled for the best that the traffic would bear given the military situation on the ground and political realities within the international community.

Aware of their long-term weakness vis-à-vis their more powerful Serb and Croat neighbors, and divided internally, the Bosnians were never really convinced that their own best interests would be met by a political settlement instead of the military victory that seemed so tantalizingly close in the fall of 1995. The United States, therefore, had to play the role of enforcer toward the Bosnians that Milosevic played with the Bosnian Serbs. The U.S. team basically came up with solutions that it considered would meet Bosnian interests and were sellable both in Washington and to the Serbs, then obtained Bosnian agreement through a combination of patient diplomacy followed in the end by the requisite degree of arm twisting. As for the Croats, Tudjman made it clear from the outset that his primary interest was in using a deal over Bosnia as leverage to obtain an agreement providing for the return of eastern Slavonia to Croatia.

The Geneva meeting also confirmed the subordinate role the non-U.S. members of the international community would play throughout the Dayton process. Bildt, nominally cochairing the conference with Holbrooke, did not see the text of the agreement the U.S. team had hammered out until midnight of the evening before the conference began. He had few objections since it was immediately apparent that the U.S. draft, aside from a few innovations such as a Commission to Protect National Monuments that was said to be significant to the parties, was largely drawn from previous negotiations. It constituted a sound basis for final agreement, provided the Bosnians could be brought along—which as other members of the Bosnian peace process had understood for at least two years, could only be made to happen through pressure from Washington.

The Contact Group was prepared to accept almost any text that offered the prospect of ending the long Bosnian nightmare. At a meeting of Contact Group diplomats just before the set-piece Geneva ceremony, however, some participants seemed not fully reconciled to their appointed role as Greek chorus. When a member of the German delegation began to raise substantive questions about the draft, Holbrooke intervened to note that every word had been tortuously negotiated and any changes could cause the whole deal to come unglued. "This document is a done deal," Holbrooke said, adding that Serb Foreign Minister Milan Milutinovic had told him that he would have to telephone Milosevic if even one word were altered. Holbrooke's intervention, despite being recognized as an accurate reflection of the diplomatic state-of-play, provoked Russian Deputy Foreign Minister Igor Ivanov to ask whether the United States had any objection to a few questions aimed at trying to understand the text before he signed it.

Dayton

As Milosevic was leaving for Dayton, one of his senior advisers told diplomats that the most important element of Milosevic's strategy was simply to gain an agreement; its elements were secondary. Milosevic's remarks at the opening session of Dayton made his position crystal clear. Noting that the bulk of the groundwork had been completed in Geneva and other preparatory meetings, Milosevic said all that needed to be resolved in Dayton were territorial and implementation issues as well as the lifting of sanctions.[44]

Milosevic did most of his negotiating alone, assisted on some occasions by Foreign Minister Milutinovic. He engaged personally only on those issues that he considered key, such as the map. On a few issues that he saw as secondary, such as the constitution, Milosevic allowed the Bosnian Serbs to participate actively in the negotiations. For the most part, though, the Pale delegation, headed by Assembly President Momcilo Krajisnik—seized by NATO troops in 2000 and sent to the Hague tribunal as an accused war criminal—wandered forlornly about the grounds of the compound or sat by themselves in the restaurant seeking information from delegates they considered sympathetic. When Holbrooke showed Milosevic angry letters from Krajisnik demanding to know what was going on, Milosevic flipped them into the wastebasket, saying, "Pay no attention to those guys. I'll make sure they accept the final agreement."[45]

From the beginning of the conference, Milosevic adopted a confidant, charming, and seemingly carefree demeanor, almost as if he were the gracious victor dispensing terms to defeated opponents. Milosevic quickly established a favorite table at the Wright-Patterson Officers Club, where he spent hours eating, drinking, and generally giving the appearance of a genial and contented host. He sometimes showed a lighter side of his personality. On one occasion, a well-lubricated Milosevic amused European delegates with a wickedly clever series of imitations of the voices and mannerisms of the various international negotiators who had come his way over the years. Milosevic occupied a first-floor suite across the courtyard from Holbrooke's and Bildt's rooms, and both noted that the light was often on in Milosevic's room until the small hours of the morning.[46]

Milosevic's relations with other Yugoslav representatives were mixed. In his first meeting with Tudjman, Milosevic jovially hailed his Croatian rival as Franjo. Tudjman, in return, called him Slobo—something no member of the Serb delegation ever did to Milosevic's face. Bildt remarked that Milosevic and Tudjman had a common bond at the conference: neither cared much for the future of Bosnia and each sought to shape the agreement in ways that emphasized the separate interests of their own ethnic group.[47] Milosevic's relationship with the reserved Izetbegovic seemed more distant. Milosevic often called the Bosnian leader Alija, which had a somewhat patronizing connotation in the Yugoslav context where the Bosnian leader's obviously Moslem first name was frequently used sarcastically to stress the supposed influence of Islamic fundamentalism in Bosnia. But Holbrooke records one bizarre conversation between the two men, during a dinner in the Wright-Patterson Air Museum, in which Milosevic called Izetbegovic "brave" and both men expressed surprise that the war had gone on so long.[48]

The Croats at Dayton regarded themselves as the victors and behaved accordingly. Tudjman had little interest in the details of the settlement in Bosnia. At one point, he told Bildt that the best way to get an accord would be to negotiate a broad framework agreement and then deploy NATO to impose the remaining details. Midway through the conference, after an hour of shouting at each other in the parking lot, Milosevic and Tudjman resolved the eastern Slavonia issue by agreeing to a phased, two-year transition period for the region to revert to Croatian rule.[49]

Milosevic and Tudjman also agreed to a swap of territory in which Croatia would surrender control of the Prevlaka Peninsula, which commands the entrance to the major FRY naval base in Montenegro's Bay of Kotor. In return, Milosevic promised the Croats some of the mountainous hinterland behind Dubrovnik, from which the Serbs had shelled the historic city. Milosevic was unconcerned about dealing away territory that belonged to the Bosnian Serbs, but the arrangement fell through after Tudjman returned home to face a firestorm of opposition to ceding any part of Croatian territory.

The Bosnian Croats' primary concern was to ensure that they were left free to run their own zones of control along the coast, up the Neretva Valley, and in central Bosnia. During negotiations over the constitution, they often teamed up with the Serbs to keep the institutions of the central government as weak as possible.

The hardest negotiations in Dayton were with the Bosnians. Their delegation was internally divided; midway through the conference, Izetbegovic and his deputy, Haris Silajdzic, stopped speaking to each other, and Bosnian Foreign Minister Muhamed Sacirbey was plotting against Silajdzic, according to Holbrooke. Although both Milosevic and Tudjman—for different reasons—wanted an agreement at Dayton, it was not clear until the very end whether Izetbegovic shared this objective.

In what Bildt called a "de facto alliance between Sarajevo and Capitol Hill," the Bosnians always negotiated with an eye toward critics of the Clinton administration's Bosnia policy. Former Reagan administration Defense Department official Richard Perle spent several days at the conference, helping the Bosnians toughen language on the responsibilities of the NATO implementation force. The Bosnians also brought in a number of U.S. legal specialists. In one meeting I attended on the constitution, all but one of the members of the Bosnian negotiating team were Americans.

Milosevic argued hard for issues he viewed as important, but in the end he was always willing to ride roughshod over Bosnian Serb interests when he considered it necessary. Milosevic's decision to give away most of the areas around Sarajevo held by the Serbs is a prime example. The U.S. team brought to Dayton a proposal, drawn from earlier Bosnian peace plans, to make Sarajevo a separate district, governed jointly by representatives of all three ethnic groups. Halfway through the conference—just one day after a discouraged Holbrooke told Secretary Christopher that the choice at Dayton was between "closure and closing down"—Milosevic surprised his U.S. negotiating partners by saying that the district model was too complicated. "Izetbegovic has earned Sarajevo by not abandoning it. He is one tough guy. It's his."[50]

As well, Milosevic agreed to other key territorial concessions, including allowing the Bosnians a land corridor to Gorazde and returning the politically important town of Orasje, along the Sava River, to the Bosnian Croats. On the last day of the conference, two days after the United States had given its "final, final" ultimatum, Milosevic—saying that he would "walk the final mile for peace"—proposed to defer for one year settling the status of the contested city of Brcko, which sat astride the narrow Posavina corridor linking the eastern and western halves of the Republika Srpska.[51]

On only one issue did Milosevic threaten to bring the agreement down. When he discovered that the map then on the table would give the Bosnian Serbs only 45 percent of Bosnian territory, Milosevic angrily accused U.S. negotiators of having tricked him. "Abandoning 49:51 is just impossible," he told Bildt. "Give me something! Steppes, rocks, or swamps—anything will do."[52] To resolve the problem, Milosevic agreed that the Bosnian Serbs would be assigned possession of a lightly populated, hilly region south of Banja Luka—called the anvil because of its odd appearance on the map—that had been captured and cleansed by the Croats during the final days of their offensive in Bosnia.

At the last minute, Milosevic's cavalier treatment of the Bosnian Serbs almost caused Dayton's collapse. Not until an hour before the signing ceremony did Milosevic share with the Bosnian Serbs all the details of the final settlement, including the map showing the areas around Sarajevo he had given away. When they saw what Milosevic had done, the Bosnian Serbs exploded. Krajisnik angrily refused to sign and issued a public statement repudiating the deal. The unwillingness of the Bosnian Serbs to sign on the dotted line was a major problem since the U.S. military had based its plans on having an agreement acceptable to all of the parties, not one that might require it to fight its way into Bosnia. Milosevic told the U.S. team not to worry and promised to deliver a copy of the Dayton agreement signed by the Bosnian Serbs to the U.S. embassy in Belgrade within ten days.[53]

One can only imagine the tenor of the discussions on the Serb plane during the long flight home from Dayton. British chargé d'affaires Roberts was at the airport when the Serb delegation returned. An upbeat Milosevic made a rare public statement praising the agreement while the Bosnian Serbs trailed off the plane at the end of the procession, looking "bedraggled, crushed, and defeated."[54] Milosevic immediately summoned Karadzic to a meeting at a villa near Belgrade, obtaining his initials on the agreement by threatening to arrest him and the rest of the Bosnian Serb leadership if they did not comply, he later told diplomats.

A New Man

Milosevic had good reason to be satisfied as he returned home from Paris on 14 December after the official signing of the Dayton agreement. The accord gave the Serbs most of what they wanted in Bosnia, even if the stubborn Pale leadership failed to acknowledge it. The Serbs had their own ministate, with its own political institutions and laws, protected by its own armed forces and police. Srebrenica and other ethnically cleansed towns and cities remained in Serb hands. The agreement guaranteed refugees the right to return home, but no one seriously expected Moslems or Croatians to try to exercise this right in territories controlled by the Serb leadership that had expelled them in the first place. Although the Serbs had been forced to remain within a single Bosnian state, the central government was weak and each of the three ethnic groups enjoyed the practical right of veto over major decisions.

It was also true, of course, that the Republika Srpska as established by Dayton made little geographic or economic sense. Its people were impoverished and its economy had ceased to exist. The Serbs angrily resented the requirement that they surrender control of the suburbs around Sarajevo, and three months after Dayton, almost one hundred thousand Serbs fled these territories rather than live under Bosnian rule. But Milosevic had long since demonstrated that he cared little for the plight of individual Serbs. By settling in homes abandoned by Moslem refugees in Srebrenica and other ethnically cleansed areas along the Drina River, the Serb Sarajevo refugees actually helped cement Bosnia's ethnic partition.

On the international front, Milosevic had good reason to feel satisfied as well. President Clinton had praised his contribution to peace and Milosevic was firmly ensconced in his role as guarantor of the Dayton agreement. UN sanctions against Serbia were lifted at the end of November. Europe rushed to resume diplomatic and commercial relations with Belgrade.

Despite his seeming triumph at Dayton, Milosevic—say Serbs who knew and worked with him—returned from the peace conference a changed man. According to well-informed sources in Belgrade, sometime after returning from Dayton Milosevic sought a meeting with his family's long-time personal doctor. For five hours Milosevic vented his frustrations and feelings. According to this source, Milosevic was "lonely and depressed" at Dayton. He complained about being kept in "isolation" and was described as especially "desperate" about the long separation from his wife, who did not attend Dayton—although he gave little evidence of these feelings to foreign participants in the talks. The doctor, who treated the Milosevic family for over ten years, described Milosevic after Dayton as a "destroyed person"—more withdrawn from the affairs of state and as more absentminded in his personal behavior.

There seem to be two reasons for the changes in Milosevic's personality and behavior after Dayton. One was the growing influence of his wife and her use of that influence to replace many of Milosevic's long-time associates with her own mediocre and corrupt cronies. The second factor was Milosevic's disappointment with the lack of benefits for him and for Serbia from what he viewed as his cooperation with the United States in achieving peace in Bosnia.

Even before Dayton, criticism from his wife was causing a decline in the influence of some who had been with Milosevic since his rise to power, such as Borisav Jovic, Mihajlo Markovic, and Milorad Vucelic. Persons close to Milosevic at the time report that Mira Markovic did not like many of these figures because they tended to think of Milosevic as an equal and made the mistake of treating her as simply the wife of Serbia's leader and not as the strong political figure in her own right that she considered herself to be.

Mihajlo Markovic was the first to discover the dangers of opposing Mira. In 1994 he engaged in a public debate with her in the pages of *Borba*, in which he criticized her decision to form the JUL party as tending to divide the forces of the Left and to weaken Milosevic's own SPS, of which Mihajlo Markovic was then vice president. At an SPS meeting in the summer of 1995 participants applauded Mihajlo Markovic when he described the leaders of JUL—accurately—as some of the most corrupt war profiteers in Serbia. Milosevic responded that Mihajlo Markovic was wrong although everyone was entitled to his own opinion—words to which Milosevic's own behavior soon gave the lie.

While Milosevic was away in Dayton, this behind-the-scene struggle for influence came to a head. Figures close to Mira Markovic at the time say that she disliked the nationalism of those in the faction around Jovic and Mihajlo Markovic, which she called the "Chetniks." According to one of the leading figures on the losing side, Mira persuaded her husband that in his absence her opponents—Jovic, Mihajlo Markovic, and Vucelic—had tried to mount a coup against him. In November, shortly after his return from Dayton, Milosevic held a meeting of the Main Board of the SPS. He rose and said coldly that all of the offending individuals were "dismissed" without a word of explanation and still less of thanks for past services.

Milosevic's move, in effect, provoked a split in the SPS from which it never fully recovered. Many of the party's more talented people followed those purged out of its ranks or reduced their activity to the minimum necessary to keep their jobs. As the SPS became less influential, Milosevic began to rely more on his wife's JUL party—a collection of hidebound supporters of prewar Socialist Yugoslavia, crooks, and careerists that had never enjoyed a shred of popular support. Most Serbian observers of Milosevic believe that his isolation from reality and growing sense of paranoia began around this time.

The second factor affecting Milosevic's changed behavior after Dayton was the disappointment he experienced with its results on the plane of international diplomacy. When Milosevic returned from Dayton he had spent several months at the epicenter of world diplomacy. He had been courted by a series of Western diplomats, treated by the United States as a virtual partner in the process, and in the end thanked for his contribution by Western political leaders from President Clinton on. It was, in its own way, the diplomatic equivalent of Milosevic's heady experience atop the wave of popular adulation that accompanied his rise to power in the late 1980s.

According to many Belgrade observers, one reason for the split in the SPS was that many of the figures purged by Milosevic had opposed his cooperation with the United States in the Dayton peace process. Milosevic, for his part, tended to dismiss these critics as primitives who did not understand the advantages that would accrue to Serbia from the expected end of its international isolation and its cooperation with the United States and other Western nations. According to Vucelic—one of the losers in the struggle—Milosevic after his return from Dayton "considered that he was the friend of America and of Europe."

Milosevic after Dayton expected to remain at the center stage of world diplomacy and to continue to be treated as the valued partner of the United States and the rest of the Western world. The result was something different.

Milosevic's first and major disappointment was over sanctions. After the peace agreement in Bosnia was concluded, multilateral trade sanctions contained in a series of UN Security Council resolutions were lifted. But the United States did not end its so-called "outer wall" of sanctions, which prevented Serbia from joining international organizations such as the UN and the OSCE and, more importantly, kept it out of international financial institutions such as the IMF and the World Bank, which limited the trade and investment that would come to the devastated Serbian economy.

The practical result, as far as Milosevic was concerned, was irritatingly contradictory. International negotiators and U.S. diplomats continued to demand his assistance in resolving problems with the Dayton accords. But Serbia and Milosevic personally still found themselves treated as pariahs by the international community. And although the Hague Tribunal in the mid-1990s had still not indicted Milosevic for war crimes—which many felt he richly deserved—the announcement that the tribunal had issued sealed indictments for accused war criminals it did not name in public made foreign travel problematical for Milosevic and a number of other senior Serbian figures.

Milosevic felt betrayed and said so loudly to many domestic supporters and international visitors.

The effect seems to have been twofold. First, Milosevic became less trustful of the international community, especially of the United States, and less inclined to take international objections into account in his own behavior in such areas as Kosovo. Second, Milosevic seemed to those closest to him to become increasingly apathetic and disengaged from the daily affairs of state. This disinterest increased—according to many Serbian observers—after the massive street demonstrations against Milosevic's rule in the winter of 1996–1997. According to Tijanic, after Dayton and the demonstrations of 1996–1997, Milosevic experienced a sense that "everything was beginning to fail." Milosevic seemed "tired" of ruling. Tijanic also recalled that Mira Markovic said sadly that her husband in that era "was not the old Slobo." According to Vucelic, "When I returned to government in 1997 I saw an old, tired man." Vucelic adds that after 1997 Milosevic often spoke of his desire to leave politics, claiming that he would retire in 2000 when his mandate as FRY president expired.[55]

It seems likely that the post-Dayton disconnect over sanctions occurred partly as a result of misunderstandings and partly because U.S. statesmen did not always highlight the full complexity of U.S. sanctions, which included measures based on UN Security Council resolutions and other measures imposed by the U.S. Congress. In discussions with its allies before Dayton, the United States consistently tied the lifting of the outer wall of sanctions to Kosovo. Whether this point was made to Milosevic with equal consistency in the run-up to Dayton is unclear. Bildt, who took over the "sanctions lift" talks with Milosevic from U.S. envoy Frasure in the spring of 1995, focused his discussions with Milosevic on the terms for lifting the sanctions imposed by the UN. As a European, it was natural for Bildt not to discuss sanctions that Washington had unilaterally implemented, but the United States let Milosevic know that it supported Bildt's efforts, so it would have been natural for Milosevic to have concluded that the offer on the table included lifting all sanctions.

A review of the public record of the Dayton process seems to support the notion that the Serbs had some reason to expect that all sanctions would be lifted in return for Belgrade's cooperation in bringing about a Bosnian settlement. In his memoirs, Secretary Christopher points out that on the first day of Dayton, Milosevic bemoaned the effect of sanctions on the Serbian economy, which Christopher says, "Gave me the chance to tell him the sanctions would stay in place until he initialed the peace agreement."[56] As Holbrooke explains in his memoirs, the "seven points" that constituted the heart of the U.S. proposal to end the Bosnian conflict included "the full lifting of all economic sanctions," which arguably would mean participation in international financial institutions.[57] Even members of the U.S. negotiating team profess uncertainty as to what Holbrooke told Milosevic about sanctions, and Holbrooke's memoirs are silent on this point. Bildt believes that Milosevic left Dayton convinced that all sanctions would be lifted. In a television interview after he lost power, Milosevic alleged that "the Dayton Agreement lifted sanctions on us. . . . But then, two months after the sanctions were lifted [by a UN Security Council resolution] the U.S. thought up the so-called external wall of sanctions."[58]

Milosevic could not, however, legitimately claim to be completely in the dark about the outer wall. His diplomatic missions in the United States kept Belgrade fully informed about executive branch and congressional actions with respect to sanctions, including the fact that the United States had introduced a number of sanctions of its own, which went beyond those adopted by the UN. Members of the U.S. delegation to the Dayton conference expressly told Milosevic about the outer wall at a dinner held toward the end of the conference in the officers club—Milosevic's favorite haunt during the conference—hosted by Holbrooke and attended by senior Treasury and State Department officials. Yet some participants in the dinner wonder whether Milosevic, who seemed most interested in the effect on Serbia of the lifting of the UN measures, fully understood the U.S. message about its own unilateral sanctions.

The Happening of the People

In November 1996, a coalition of opposition parties known as Zajedno (Together) defeated the ruling party in local elections in many parts of Serbia. When the regime reacted by annulling the results in a number of cities, a group of students gathered and began to pelt government buildings with eggs. The students were joined by opposition leader Draskovic, who proclaimed that Milosevic had overthrown the Vojvodina government in the 1988 yogurt revolution and now the people would oust him in an "egg revolution."

A coalition of students and Zajedno leaders organized massive public protests. Every afternoon for three months, tens of thousands of protesters marched through the streets of Belgrade, whistling, banging pots, and shouting defiance at the regime. Milosevic branded the demonstrators as traitors and set the police to harass them, but he did not dare to crush them by force because of the sympathy the protesters had evoked through much of the country. The demonstrators met Milosevic's restrictive steps with imaginative countermoves of their own, urging supporters to drive into the middle of Belgrade and create monumental traffic jams, for example, when the police blocked the protesters' march route.

The protests also provoked cracks in the ruling coalition. In January 1997 Nebojsa Covic the pro-Milosevic mayor of Belgrade resigned and went over to the side of the opposition. Even more ominous for Milosevic were signs of sympathy for the protesters among the military and security organs. Police on the streets were sometimes seen fraternizing with the protesters, and a delegation of students met with Chief of Staff Perisic, who reportedly promised that the military would not allow itself to be used against the demonstrators.

One element of Milosevic's genius for retaining power was his ability when under pressure to make tactical concessions that over the longer run act to defeat his enemies. In February 1997, Milosevic agreed to reinstate the results of the November local elections, but he claimed to be acceding to the demands of an Organization for Security and Cooperation in Europe (OSCE) commission headed by former Spanish Prime Minister Filipe Gonzales, thereby sending a message that the opposition demonstrations had been in the service of foreign powers. Milosevic also cleverly divided the protesters by conceding to Zajedno on the local elections while ignoring the demands of the students, who were forced to continue their demonstrations alone for another month until they won the dismissal of the rector of the University of Belgrade.

Once installed in their local offices, the opposition immediately showed the wisdom of Milosevic's Fabian tactics. Conflicts within Zajedno emerged over the allocation of local offices, which in Serbia's socialist-paternalist system also meant lucrative control over local business and government facilities.[59] In the summer of 1997, Zoran Djindjic, the head of the Democratic Party (DS), was deposed as mayor of Belgrade by supporters of

Draskovic's SPO. Draskovic and his formidable wife, Danica, quickly installed themselves as the rulers of the Belgrade patronage machine and began a process of moving closer to Milosevic that eventually ended in Draskovic joining the government.

Milosevic had weathered the challenge from the streets, yet he soon faced a new and even more dangerous one in the region of his first triumphs—Kosovo.

TEN

Milosevic Loses Kosovo

uropean statesmen who rushed to put out the flames of war in Slovenia and Croatia in the summer of 1991 paid little attention to the smoldering conflict in Kosovo—a pattern of Western neglect that prevailed for most of the decade. Kosovo Albanian chieftain Rugova was not invited to the July 1991 EC-sponsored Brioni conference of Yugoslav leaders, which ended the fighting in Slovenia and launched Europe's efforts to seek a broader Yugoslav settlement. The Brioni Joint Declaration effectively consigned Kosovo Albanians to remaining within Serbia, by establishing the principle that the right of self-determination was limited to Yugoslav "peoples." Under Yugoslav practice, Albanians were not considered a "people" or a "nation" (the Serbo-Croatian word *narod* means both) but were consigned to the lesser status of a "nationality."

During the Hague conference in the fall of 1991, the EC chief negotiator, Lord Carrington, attempted to deal with Kosovo by adopting an idea Milosevic put forward that certain regions in Yugoslavia be granted "special status." Milosevic had in mind the Serb-populated zones of Croatia and Bosnia, but Carrington also tried to apply the concept to Kosovo, Vojvodina, and Sandjak. Using as a model the Austrian-inhabited Alto Adige area of northern Italy, the Carrington plan provided "a special status of autonomy" for areas where a nation or ethnic group formed a majority. But Milosevic never had any problem denying to Kosovo Albanians the same rights he demanded for Serbs in Croatia and Bosnia. He insisted that application of the concept be limited to Krajina, which he claimed was undergoing a "second genocide." Carrington—in a vain attempt to keep Milosevic on board—excluded Kosovo.[1]

The Badinter commission, created in late 1991 to resolve legal issues connected with the disintegration of Yugoslavia, also avoided the issue of Kosovo. Concerned that disintegration in Yugoslavia could have undesirable consequences in the USSR and aware that many European states had their own areas of ethnic unrest, Badinter limited the right of self-determination to the six Yugoslav republics on the grounds that they were sovereign, founding members of the Yugoslav federation. Badinter dismissed pleas by Albanians that Kosovo's position as one of the eight federal units in Yugoslavia, as demonstrated by Kosovo's separate membership on the collective presidency and other Yugoslav institutions, entitled it to be considered for independence on the same basis as the six republics.[2]

Rugova was allowed to be present during the August 1992 London conference, but was forced to watch the proceedings on closed-circuit television from an adjoining room. At the conference, newly appointed FRY Prime Minister Milan Panic met Rugova and took a number of steps to try to move the Kosovo issue off square one. Against Milosevic's wishes, Panic agreed to allow a CSCE observer mission to operate in Kosovo. The London conference also established a special working group on Kosovo, chaired by Gerd Ahrens, a German diplomat who spoke fluent Serbo-Croatian. This group met six times between September and December 1992, producing a joint Serb-Albanian statement on returning the divided Kosovo educational system to a normal situation, but the agreement collapsed after the Serbs arrested the rector of the Albanian underground university.[3]

Later, Panic offered to make Kosovo a third republic, equal to Serbia and Montenegro, within the FRY. By this time, however, the Albanians were unwilling to consider anything short of independence and, in any case, it is doubtful that Panic enjoyed sufficient authority in Belgrade to have actually carried through on his offers had the Albanians accepted. Rugova similarly rebuffed Panic's pleas that the Albanians put up candidates for the December 1992 Serbian elections, although the votes of the 1.8 million Kosovo Albanians could have made a major contribution toward defeating Milosevic. Years later, Blerim Shala, editor of one of Kosovo's leading papers and a prominent Albanian political figure, told me that Kosovo Albanian leaders at the time had been surprised not to have received more Western pressure to participate in the 1992 elections. Had such pressure been stronger, Shala said, the Albanians might have taken part in the vote.

Christmas Warning

The outbreak of war in Slovenia and Croatia in 1991, followed by Bosnia in 1992, put Kosovo on Washington's foreign policy back burner, where it stayed for most of the rest of the decade. U.S. diplomats continued to travel to Kosovo, encouraging Rugova to persevere in his path of nonviolent resistance and, with less success, consider alternatives for Kosovo other than complete independence.

Almost the only instance of a U.S. initiative on Kosovo between 1991 and 1998 was the "Christmas warning" issued by the lame-duck Bush administration in December 1992. On Christmas morning, Bob Rackmales, the U.S. chargé d'affaires in Belgrade, received an urgent and unexpected message from Washington. Rackmales was instructed to seek one-on-one meetings that day with Milosevic and Serb military Chief of Staff Zivota Panic to convey what was known in diplomatic parlance as an "oral message" from President Bush.

Milosevic listened, as he generally does in such situations, quietly and with intense concentration when Rackmales met him later that day in his private office in the Serbian presidency building. There were four parts to the U.S. message, which Rackmales was instructed to read verbatim, without any changes. The first three dealt with Bosnia, warning that the United States was prepared to respond forcefully if the Serbs violated a UN no-fly zone in Bosnia or if UN forces were attacked or relief efforts interfered with. Milosevic understood the seriousness of the U.S. message both from its content and its unusual Christmas Day timing, but his responses to the points on Bosnia were routine, possibly because over the past few months Bosnia had become such a familiar topic of diplomatic conversations.

His reaction was different to the final point, regarding Kosovo, which read in its entirety: "In the event of conflict in Kosovo caused by Serbian action, the U.S. will be prepared to employ military force against Serbians in Kosovo and in Serbia proper."[4] Milosevic said in apparently genuine puzzlement that it was quiet in Kosovo and wondered why anyone would think that he would have anything to gain by starting something there. He did not respond substantively to the U.S. threat of force—the first ever in the Yugoslav crisis—but Chief of Staff Panic, who Rackmales met immediately after seeing Milosevic, reacted more sharply. Panic denied any intention to use the army in Kosovo, although he blustered that the Serbs would resist a U.S. attack and that Serbia's "friends," the Russians, would help.

A few weeks after meeting Milosevic, Rackmales traveled to Kosovo, where he delivered a parallel message to Rugova. The United States said it supported Rugova's policy of nonviolent resistance, yet it emphasized that if the Kosovo Albanians attempted to take advantage of the U.S. warning to Milosevic by starting violence of their own, the U.S. threat of military action against the Serbs would not apply. Rugova acknowledged that there were some "hotheads" on the Albanian side that he did not control but said he understood that if the Albanians tried to start an armed uprising in Kosovo, there would be a bloodbath, which he was committed to avoiding.

Former senior State Department officials and intelligence community analysts explained the warning by saying that U.S. intelligence picked up indications that Milosevic might intend taking advantage of the interregnum between the November 1992 U.S. election and the Clinton inauguration in January to ethnically cleanse Kosovo. These indications included the movement of paramilitary forces and additional police units into the province along with what appeared to be the creation of new logistical and command networks capable of supporting the deployment of even larger forces. The actions appeared similar to what the Serbs had done to prepare for their campaign of ethnic cleansing in eastern Bosnia in the spring of 1992. There were divisions in the U.S. intelligence community about the significance of the Serb moves, but against the backdrop of the controversy over alleged recent "intelligence failures," such as not recognizing indications that the Iraqis were preparing to invade Kuwait, the preponderance of opinion in the intelligence community was to alert policymakers that Milosevic might be up to something nasty in Kosovo.

With Serb ethnic cleansing in Croatia and Bosnia fresh in the public mind, and convinced that U.S. credibility was on the line, the Bush administration felt it had to react strongly. Senior Bush administration officials drew a distinction between Bosnia, where they said no vital U.S. interests were threatened, and Kosovo, where violence could easily spread into Macedonia or Albania and could, from there, also draw in neighboring members of the NATO alliance such as Greece or Turkey. According to this analysis, Bush sent his warning to Milosevic because he was concerned that "Belgrade might think that the example of U.S. restraint in Bosnia would apply as well in Kosovo."[5] Former officials have also said that the warning was intended to disabuse Milosevic of any notion that the recent deployment of U.S. peacekeeping troops into Somalia would divert U.S. attention away from Yugoslavia and provide a window of opportunity for him to act in Kosovo.

The Christmas warning was controversial at the time and has remained so until the present. Years later, one senior State Department official who at the time of the Christmas warning was a key adviser on Yugoslav affairs, said that the Christmas warning "could better be explained by a psychologist than a political observer." Like many State Department officials at the time he said he was "angry" about the Christmas warning, asking why the United States had threatened to do in Kosovo what it had refused to do in Bosnia.

He also noted that the possible military obligations with respect to Kosovo that were contained in the Christmas warning were treated quite differently from the possible military actions in Bosnia that the Bush Administration had earlier considered and rejected. With respect to military action in Bosnia there had been major fights within the administration as to the pros and cons of different alternatives, for example bombing Serb artillery positions around Sarajevo. Meanwhile, with respect to the possible military actions in Kosovo, the official indicated, "No planning was done whatsoever. No options were discussed, no assets moved, nothing." The Christmas warning was also never subjected to senior interagency scrutiny, as were other major policy options in Yugoslavia.

In any case, it is hard not to see the Christmas warning, at least to some extent, as a Parthian shot in Milosevic's direction by senior Bush administration officials. Several had served in Yugoslavia earlier in their careers and had ground their teeth in frustration as the Yugoslav tragedy unfolded without, in their view, being able to engage U.S. power to stop it. Now they took a last opportunity to threaten Milosevic, even though they knew they would not be around to enforce the warning.

The U.S. action came as a surprise to most observers of the Kosovo scene. The U.S. mission in Belgrade had not picked up any information about a possible Serb move in Kosovo and saw no reason why Milosevic would want to open a new front there at the same time war was raging in Bosnia. The Russians, usually well-informed on developments in Yugoslavia, were also surprised when I was instructed to inform them about the U.S. message a few days after Rackmales's démarche.

Whether the Christmas warning actually deterred Milosevic from violent action in Kosovo will remain in the category of historical might-have-beens, at least until the United States releases the information that provoked the démarche. Despite his initial surprise, the ever resourceful Milosevic quickly found a way to use the U.S. move for his own purposes. Within hours, the administration—which had intended to keep the warning secret—found itself embarrassed when the Serbs handed copies of Washington's message to U.S. allies, who had not been consulted in advance.

Milosevic and Kosovo: Does He Really Care?

Kosovo was always Milosevic's hot-button issue. Whenever Kosovo came up, Milosevic, usually a charming and graceful host to foreign negotiators, showed a different face. According to Ambassador Zimmermann, Milosevic "was unyielding, emotional, pugnacious, and full of invective for its Albanian inhabitants" on Kosovo.[6] Lord Owen, who developed a good working relationship with Milosevic over Bosnia, found that raising Kosovo always introduced a jarring note: "Over Kosovo the polite mask sometimes broke and we would be in an ugly confrontation."[7]

Later in the decade, as international pressure increased over Kosovo, visitors found Milosevic even more passionate and unyielding on Kosovo. German General Naumann, who as the chair of the NATO military committee accompanied NATO Commander Clark to Belgrade for several meetings with Milosevic in the run-up to the 1999 war, found that "as soon as you mentioned Kosovo in a way which may have triggered the thought in his mind that he may lose Kosovo one day, he got very emotional. He told us, I don't know how often, that Kosovo is really the cradle of Serb culture and religion."[8] Clark, for his part, described Milosevic as "excessively emotional about the Albanians. He gave his set platform speech about how bad these people were. . . . It was a dehumanization of another group. It's a straight incitement to ethnic cleansing."[9]

Despite the intensity of his reaction whenever the subject came up, Milosevic's views on Kosovo always seemed one-dimensional. Zimmermann observed that on Kosovo, "Milosevic painted a picture without shadings." Milosevic could wax eloquent on the benefits that Kosovo Albanians supposedly enjoyed under Belgrade's benevolent rule and insist with a straight face that there were no human rights violations in Kosovo even as Serbian police were shooting down the province's Albanian inhabitants. He would claim that Kosovo had "always" been Serbian, ignoring the fact that Albanians had also lived in Kosovo from time immemorial, that its population then was almost 90 percent Albanian, and that for five hundred years it had been part of the Ottoman Empire.[10]

Sometimes Milosevic gave the impression—whether true or as a tactical device—of being unaware of what was actually going on in the province. In the late 1990s, a U.S. diplomat, who unlike Milosevic traveled frequently to Kosovo, used his meetings with Milosevic to provide what amounted to political briefings on the true state of affairs in the province. Milosevic generally listened courteously, but never gave any sign of changing his opinion. In 1998, Ambassador Kai Eide, the Norwegian representative to the OSCE, visited Kosovo during the 1998 Serb offensive against the KLA. Eide watched from the roof of a house in the hills around Pristina as Serb jets swooped so low over the city that the faces of the pilots could be seen. Returning to Belgrade, Eide described the incident to Milosevic and told him that heavy-handed Serb military tactics were alienating the Kosovo population. Seemingly surprised, Milosevic called a senior Serb military officer and, when Eide's information was confirmed, ordered the buzzing stopped.[11]

Milosevic also showed himself capable of keeping his feelings in check on those rare occasions when he discussed Kosovo with Albanians. Mahmut Bakalli, a former Communist leader of Kosovo, participated in a 1998 meeting of Albanian leaders with Milosevic. Bakalli said Milosevic met the group at Belgrade's White Palace in a "relaxed and smiling" mood. He listened carefully for two hours while the members of the Albanian delegation set out their views on Kosovo, including the need for independence.[12]

Milosevic's cardboard-cutout depiction of Kosovo also reflected some elements, possibly only partly conscious, of self-deception. The U.S. diplomat thought that Milosevic had a great capacity for convincing himself of the truth of whatever he wanted to believe even when most evidence ran the other way. "I want this thing to be true and I want to persuade you that it is true so therefore it must be true," is how the diplomat said Milosevic's mind sometimes seemed to work.

To some extent, Milosevic's views on Kosovo seem to have been shaped by attitudes of antipathy and fear toward Moslems as a whole. As he was leaving Dayton, Milosevic told a senior member of the U.S. negotiating team that one good thing about the experience was that the United States would now finally understand how difficult it was to live with Moslems. During an early 1991 meeting between Milosevic and Tudjman, as part of his efforts to persuade Tudjman that the solution to the Yugoslav crisis lay in the creation of a strong federation, Milosevic showed Tudjman an analysis that if Yugoslavia broke up, five hundred thousand descendants of Moslems who had fled Yugoslavia since its creation in 1918 would come flooding back into the region. According to Stipe Mesic, who participated in the meeting as Croatia's representative on the collective federal presidency, both Milosevic and Tudjman seemed to take the preposterous argument seriously.[13]

Many who have discussed Kosovo with Milosevic found that he shared the racist views of Albanians that are common in Serbia and indeed throughout Yugoslavia. In October 1998, after Milosevic had agreed—under the threat of a NATO bombing—to a deal allowing two thousand foreign observers into Kosovo, he exploded before Clark. With his voice rising and his face "choleric," Milosevic yelled, "But general, we know how to deal with those murderers and rapists. They are killers, killers of their own kind, but we know how to deal with them and have done it before. In 1946, in Drenica we killed them, killed them all." When Milosevic was challenged, he calmed down somewhat, acknowledging, "Well, of course, we didn't [kill them] all at once. It took several years." Clark described Milosevic's performance on this occasion as, "Like watching a Nuremberg rally."[14]

Despite the political importance of Kosovo for Milosevic, there is little proof that he actually cared much for the province. Milosevic was as coldly unemotional about the inhabitants of Kosovo—both Albanian and Serb—as he was about any other human beings. He seems to have visited Kosovo only once after his famous speech on the six-hundredth anniversary of the battle of Kosovo Polje. After he had suppressed Kosovo's autonomy and cowed its Albanian population into submission, Milosevic made few efforts to channel investment to Kosovo or undertake any other measures to improve the dismal standard of living, even for the province's Serbian population. By the mid-1990s, the Serbs of Kosovo—bitterly aware that Milosevic had used them during his climb to power and then cast them aside—broke with Milosevic and became among his severest public critics.

Standoff: Kosovo before Dayton

After war began elsewhere in Yugoslavia, Milosevic took care to ensure that the Kosovo Albanians would not be emboldened to try to open a new front. Arms were distributed to Kosovo Serbs and the military demonstratively beefed up its presence. In August 1991, the JNA commander in Pristina warned publicly that if violence broke out in Kosovo, the JNA would not repeat its "mistake" in Slovenia.

Through most of the 1990s an uneasy standoff prevailed in Kosovo. Serb police maintained Belgrade's authority through periodic arrests, beatings, and other forms of intimidation, but on a day-to-day basis the Serbs tolerated many activities of the Albanian parallel state. Although the Serbs blocked meetings of political institutions such as the shadow Parliament, its commissions in such areas as education, finance, and health acted under the surface throughout the Albanian community. Nor did the Serbs stop the LDK from collecting what amounted to taxes—Albanians in Kosovo and abroad were supposed to contribute 3 percent of their income to the "shadow" government.

Despite the efforts of the Albanians to maintain a semblance of normality, the quality of life deteriorated sharply in most areas. The official economy in Kosovo more or less ceased to exist after the massive firing of the Albanian workforce in the early 1990s. Unemployment in Kosovo was estimated at 70 percent, while earnings from regular employment accounted for just 10 percent of total Kosovo income in 1996. According to the Mother Theresa organization, by 1994 over 370,000 people, or about 20 percent of the Kosovo population, were dependent on humanitarian aid.[15]

Milosevic, however, had good reason to be satisfied with the way things were turning out in Kosovo. By the end of 1993, repression and declining living standards had combined to induce an estimated four hundred thousand Albanians to leave Kosovo—a phenomenon that Albanians called "silent cleansing." Demonstrations, almost a monthly occurrence in the late 1980s and early 1990s, had practically ended. In mid-1993, after he ousted Panic and Cosic, Milosevic ejected the CSCE Kosovo monitoring mission, which had proved embarrassingly effective in reporting Serb human rights violations. In late 1994, Milosevic told diplomats that Kosovo was fully under control and predicted no trouble there.

From the Albanian point of view, by contrast, the situation in Kosovo had become what Vllassi—who returned to a law practice in Pristina after his 1990 release from a Serb jail—labeled "stable but desperate." Almost all informed observers, including Albanian moderates, foreign journalists, and the U.S. mission in Belgrade, warned that continued inaction by the United States would allow Milosevic to maintain repression without significant extra cost and virtually guarantee an eventual explosion from the increasingly desperate Kosovo Albanian population.

In mid-1994, Kosovo Prime Minister Bujar Bukoshi began to distance himself from Rugova. Since Bukoshi, from his exile in Bonn, controlled the collection of funds from the Albanian diaspora, the dispute reduced the LDK's ability to support the institutions of the parallel state and also complicated Rugova's effort to maintain his political base. Toward the end of 1994, Bukoshi told diplomats that frustrations were growing over the U.S. push to achieve a settlement in Bosnia without including Kosovo. He warned that Kosovo could explode at any time.

The first sign of opposition to Rugova in Kosovo itself came at an LDK Congress in June 1994, where Rugova was overwhelmingly reelected president, but a radical faction composed primarily of people who had been arrested after the 1981 demonstrations took control of the fifty-five-member executive board. The radicals urged greater reliance on confrontational tactics such as strikes and demonstrations, but they were silenced—at least for the moment—when Rugova's respected deputy, Femi Agani, challenged them to go into the villages and see what would happen if they tried to confront the Serbs.

In the spring of 1995, Rugova told diplomats that he was starting to worry about maintaining calm in Kosovo. He explained that a previously unknown group that he called the Movement for National Liberation, undoubtedly a precursor to the KLA, had begun to circulate flyers calling for an uprising.

Kosovo and Dayton:
Absence Does Not Make the Heart Grow Fonder

In the run-up to Dayton, Milosevic—aware that Bosnian Serb military setbacks left him in a weakened bargaining position—worked to keep Kosovo out of the Bosnian peace process by dangling the prospect of positive moves after a Bosnian settlement. In mid-September, Milosevic told British Foreign Secretary Malcolm Rifkind that he had a number of new ideas on Kosovo, which he intended to implement after a Bosnian peace had been achieved. One measure Milosevic described was the introduction of a new chamber in the FRY Parliament, which he said would represent the interests of the Kosovo Albanians and other non-Serbs. As the Serb delegation was leaving Belgrade for Dayton, a senior adviser told diplomats that Milosevic had in his pocket a contingency plan for Kosovo autonomy, but that he would only offer it at Dayton if the subject was raised, to avoid getting Kosovo entangled in sanctions relief. Since Kosovo was not a subject of negotiation at Dayton, Milosevic apparently never unveiled this mysterious plan.

In seeking to keep Kosovo out of Dayton, Milosevic was knocking on an open door. The United States and Europe, fed up with years of failure in the Balkans and deeply worried about the corrosive impact Bosnia was having on the NATO alliance, wanted nothing more than a quick settlement in Bosnia. Many Western diplomats involved in the peace process had bruises from previous encounters with Milosevic over Kosovo, and none had the slightest intention of allowing a seemingly quiet Kosovo to put at risk a Bosnian settlement that, at long last, seemed to be within reach. A senior member of the U.S. negotiating team said that trying to add Kosovo to the Dayton negotiating agenda would simply have been "a bridge too far."

Shortly before Dayton, the United States broke the news to Rugova, explaining that it was focusing on Bosnia because continuation of the conflict there would destabilize the entire region. If Milosevic cooperated in reaching a Bosnian settlement, Serbia would gain some sanctions relief, but the United States would not forget Kosovo and would retain leverage through such things as the normalization of Serbia's relations with the rest of the world. Rugova was disappointed, yet he recognized that he had no alternative to continued reliance on Washington.

In September 1995, visiting Kosovo on behalf of Carl Bildt, I met Rugova in the small wooden building near the center of Pristina that had formerly been the seat of the Kosovo Writers Association and now served as the LDK's headquarters. In the years since I had last been there, Rugova's office had acquired some of the accoutrements of the information age, including a fax machine and a computer, but it was still a surprisingly modest facility for a movement that despite its quasi-underground status, constituted the most respected authority for almost two million Kosovo Albanians.

Rugova spoke with his usual quietness, although there was no concealing the toughness of his message or the depth of his concern for the situation in Kosovo. He insisted, as he always did in conversations with foreigners, that independence was the only acceptable long-range outcome for Kosovo, but he was realistic enough to recognize that this could only come in stages. Rugova said he understood why the international community was focusing on Bosnia, yet he warned that advocates of violence in Kosovo would gain the upper hand if Albanians came to believe that international preoccupation with Bosnia meant that they would continue to be left to Milosevic's tender mercies.

Although dissatisfaction with Rugova's aloof leadership style was already causing discontent among the Kosovo elite, his undiminished stature among the Albanian people was still evident. When Rugova entered a restaurant in downtown Pristina, every guest would rise and stand silently by their chair until Rugova took his own seat. For the Albanians, this was a mark of respect for Rugova as a man and as their president, and also a silent act of defiance to the Serbian authorities, whose flak-jacketed special police would watch the display impassively from armored cars parked at nearby intersections.

Other Kosovo leaders thought that Albanians might eventually agree to remain in some kind of enhanced autonomous status within Serbia, but only provided that Serb police were completely withdrawn and the situation was monitored by a hefty foreign presence. Both Surroi and Vllassi had been in contact with Belgrade intellectual opponents of Milosevic, and both saw some hope for a foreign-mediated dialogue with the Serbs. But despite these glimmerings of optimism, both Surroi and Vllassi were deeply worried about Kosovo's future. The Serb and Albanian communities lived in hermetic isolation and a spark could set off violence at any time. Surroi, the son of a Yugoslav diplomat who had grown up speaking fluent English, Spanish, and Serbo-Croatian in addition to Albanian, noted that his own children, who attended one of the Albanian "parallel schools," had almost no opportunity to mix with their Serbian counterparts or speak the Serbo-Croatian language.

Although the Serbian police presence was a constant reminder of Kosovo's occupied status, I was also struck by the explosion of small-scale economic activity in both the Albanian and Serbian communities. After Milosevic fired most Albanians from their jobs in the "official" Kosovo economy, many opened small, privately owned shops, restaurants, and other businesses. Large new homes had appeared in many Albanian villages, often with a late model Mercedes or bmw parked nearby. Both the Albanian and Serb communities seemed to be sharing in the new developments. The Serbian hamlet of Kosovo Polje, in the late 1980s a dirty and dilapidated outpost, now sported a number of spiffy new shops and small hotels.

But these signs of prosperity were on the surface only. Poverty remained widespread. On the Albanian side, much of the surface prosperity stemmed from remittances sent home by the several hundred thousand Kosovo Albanians who had fled to Western Europe to escape the repressive Serb occupation. The origins of some of the money in both communities probably would not bear too close a scrutiny. Kosovo Albanians, despite their political problems with the Milosevic regime, were deeply involved in the Serbian sanctions-busting efforts, some of which passed through Kosovo from Albania and Montenegro. Sanctions busting and cigarette smuggling, together with the proceeds of ethnic cleansing in Croatia and Bosnia, undoubtedly lay at the root of the newfound prosperity of Kosovo Polje, which had become the informal headquarters of Arkan's Tigers and other Serb paramilitary groups. Still, the new developments seemed to offer some hope for the future. Albanian shopkeepers complained bitterly about arbitrary exactions by the Serbian authorities, but they also acknowledged correct business relations with Serbian suppliers. And one Albanian leader told me about a different kind of tie. Rich Albanians, he said, often used the private hotels in Kosovo Polje as places to meet their mistresses, well aware that there was little chance that Albanian friends or relatives would observe them in the Serbian hamlet.

Kosovo after Dayton: The Lid Blows Off

In 1995, a then unknown young man in Pristina heard the news of the Dayton Peace Agreement. He reacted with anger and, as he later told me, decided then that only through armed struggle could Kosovo be liberated from its Serb occupiers. Three years later, the world heard of the young man, Hashim Thaci, when the KLA that he then led unleashed a guerrilla war that eventually pulled NATO into the first war in its history.

For Kosovo, Dayton was the Rubicon between war and peace. Dayton convinced most Albanians that the world would never honor the promises diplomats had made over the years to require Milosevic to restore justice and human rights to the province. It also undermined the influence of America's chosen champion in Kosovo, Rugova. As a KLA fighter later recounted for Western journalists, "The so-called pacifist way failed and finally Albanians were convinced that they had to organize armed resistance. . . . From 1996 we had some movements or groups who didn't approve any more Rugova's peaceful way."[16]

In December 1995, shortly after Dayton, Rugova made what had become an annual pilgrimage to Washington. Secretary Christopher told Rugova that following the deployment of NATO troops to Bosnia, the United States would insist that Milosevic begin a dialogue with the Albanians and would maintain the outer wall of sanctions until Kosovo's autonomy was restored. Rugova returned to Kosovo proclaiming that Kosovo was at the top of Washington's foreign policy agenda, but many Albanians were more skeptical. Foreign observers visiting Kosovo shortly after Dayton found many fearing that Kosovo would be forgotten in the euphoria after a settlement of the Bosnian conflict. Discontent was also growing with Rugova. Many Albanians grumbled that after five years, there was nothing to show for his policy of peaceful resistance.

For two years after Dayton the United States and the rest of the international community essentially ignored Kosovo. In early 1996, the EU resumed political and economic relations with the FRY, which meant that Europe acknowledged Kosovo as part of Serbia. The United States successfully pushed Milosevic to allow it to open a one-person cultural center in Pristina, but high-level attention to Kosovo soon vanished.

The few voices calling for more international engagement in Kosovo, such as Bildt—who in addition to his position as high representative in Bosnia also retained a role as the EU negotiator for the former Yugoslavia —were essentially ignored. In 1996, Bildt and a small team of European diplomats put together a package of modest measures intended to make the climate more propitious for dialogue, including the release of up to eighty Albanian political prisoners; allowing Albanians to use the Pristina sports stadium, from which they were excluded under the Serb apartheid regime in Kosovo; and cooperation between Albanians and Serbs on practical measures such as education.

But without high-level backing, Bildt's efforts were ignored by all sides. Serb Foreign Minister Milutinovic in August 1996 told a British diplomat working with Bildt to forget about dialogue. When the time came, in about fifteen to twenty years according to Milutinovic, Kosovo would be divided, at which point the Albanian rump could declare itself independent. Kosovo Albanians, for their part, said they were uninterested in "magnanimous gestures" by Milosevic, which they feared he would use to raise his stature with the international community.

Bildt's efforts were also dismissed by both Europe and the United States. Bildt suggested that German Ambassador Martin Lutz, who had taken over from Gerd Ahrens as the chief European contact for Kosovo, be made a special EU representative and lead a renewed push for a Kosovo settlement. Bildt's proposal was blocked in the EU by the Dutch, who feared that human rights envoy, Max van den Stoel, a Dutchman, would be undercut. The United States, in any case, had no interest in allowing the Europeans to take the lead in Kosovo; as one senior U.S. diplomat explained, the EU was "morally bankrupt" because of its recognition of the FRY. In June 1996, when Bildt suggested a coordinated U.S.-European push on Kosovo to U.S. Secretary of State Christopher, the response was deafening silence.

Lost Window

In Kosovo, Milosevic and Rugova were locked in divergent positions: the one offering only a fictitious autonomy and the other insisting on complete independence. There were almost no attempts to get the two together for a serious effort at resolving their differences. Beyond the leaders, though, there were enough signs of moderation on both sides of the ethnic divide to suggest that if Dayton had been promptly followed by a major, U.S.-led diplomatic offensive, it might not have been too late to broker a compromise settlement in Kosovo. As late as mid-1997, non-LDK leaders such as Surroi,

Vllassi, Bakalli, and even the hard-line former political prisoner Adem Demaci were advocating solutions that amounted to less than full independence. Perhaps most remarkably, in December 1996, Demaci—a veteran of twenty-eight years in Yugoslav prisons—sent a public message of support to protesting students in Belgrade, saying, "We were right to love you, Serbian people."[17]

There were also some signs of flexibility on the Serb side. Although the vast majority of Serbs continued to believe that Kosovo should remain under Belgrade's control, the militant nationalism of the late 1980s had disappeared. A newspaper poll showed that 70 percent of Serbs opposed having close relations sent to fight in Kosovo.[18] When I visited Belgrade with Bildt in 1995, friends in Serbian opposition parties, including a then relatively unknown party leader named Vojslav Kostunica, recognized that Milosevic's policies had led to a dead end in Kosovo. Serb intellectuals, including those close to Cosic, were meeting with Albanian counterparts in an effort to find common ground. One option some Serbs were considering, Kostunica told me, was the partition of Kosovo with the predominantly Serb-populated north of the province, together with the areas around Serb monasteries and other historical sites, remaining part of Serbia and the rest of Kosovo being allowed to go its own way. In June 1996, the president of SANU, Alexandar Despic, caused a sensation when he said that the overwhelming Albanian demographic superiority in Kosovo meant that it was time for Belgrade to consider a "peaceful and civilized" secession of the region. At the end of 1997, Patriarch Pavle mirrored Demaci's action by sending a conciliatory letter to protesting Albanian students, condemning the actions of provincial police and equating the struggle of Serb and Albanian students.[19]

Unfortunately, there was no serious international diplomatic engagement in Kosovo until the return of violence in 1998—when it was too late. National Security Council Adviser Lake's 1995 Endgame Strategy, which set in motion the process leading to Dayton, did not deal with Kosovo at all—a telling sign of the headlines-driven approach that the Clinton administration always brought to Yugoslavia. Until the province began to heat up in 1998, the Clinton administration conducted no formal policy review of the situation in Kosovo.

After Dayton, the Clinton administration, facing reelection at the end of 1996 and acutely conscious that Bosnia was virtually its only foreign policy accomplishment, concentrated its Balkan diplomacy on ensuring that nothing happened to cause the Bosnian settlement to come unglued. Milosevic was seen as crucial to this effort, a posture that reduced the administration's interest in taking on Milosevic in Kosovo.

Europeans also preferred to keep Kosovo on the back burner. Toward the end of the Dayton conference, when it appeared an agreement might be reached in Bosnia, I told Bildt that one of his earliest priorities, as the chief European negotiator for the former Yugoslavia, should be to undertake a major initiative aimed at achieving a solution in Kosovo. Hearing this, a senior British diplomat interjected strongly that such a move would be an unnecessary and dangerous diversion from implementing a Bosnian agreement. Although it was obviously important to ensure full implementation of the Dayton Agreement, the failure to follow Dayton with an equally strong diplomatic push in Kosovo virtually guaranteed an explosion there.

The most important reason for international inattention to Kosovo, however, was the surface calm prevailing there, which allowed crisis-driven policymakers the luxury of turning their attention to seemingly more pressing matters. A U.S. ambassador in a nearby country later said that for two years after Dayton, he repeatedly told Washington of the danger brewing in Kosovo yet never succeeded in eliciting any interest from senior officials. In May 1997, as Bildt was stepping down, he warned about the dangers of the United States and Europe failing to work together to devise a strategy for resolving Kosovo, but his prophetic remarks were ignored.[20] Even in March 1998, when NATO Commander Clark warned his Pentagon superiors after a visit to the region that escalating violence required a strong diplomatic and military initiative in Kosovo, the response he received was that Washington could not deal with any more problems.[21]

In the two years after Dayton, the most important initiative in Kosovo came not from governments but from a private foundation. At the end of the Dayton conference, when a senior member of the U.S. delegation advised Milosevic to take advantage of the aura of peacemaker he had won at Dayton by taking immediate action to resolve Kosovo, Milosevic nodded in agreement and said his first step would be to revive plans for an agreement with the Albanians on education. A year later, on 1 September 1996, Milosevic and Rugova signed a framework agreement providing for the return of Albanians to the regular Kosovo school system. Called the Rome agreement because it had been brokered by the Italian Catholic group Communita di Sant' Egido, the deal was basically a replay of the agreement that German diplomat Ahrens had achieved in 1992. It proved to be equally stillborn. Serbs insisted that the Albanians would have to return to the regular Serbian educational system, while the Albanians claimed the accord should allow their students to use regular school facilities under their own, separate curriculum.

Half Measures and the Rise of the KLA

The spring of 1997 brought a sea change to Kosovo as Albanians began to meet Serb repression with armed resistance of their own. The agent of the Albanians' resistance was the KLA, a shadowy and loosely organized collection of groups that only gradually coalesced as its struggle with Serb security forces evolved.

Support for the KLA came from several directions. Young people jailed after the 1981 demonstrations, who began leaving prison in the early 1990s, just as Milosevic was suppressing the last remnants of Kosovo's autonomy, were early KLA supporters. Radicalized by their brutal treatment in Serb prisons and facing few prospects in the Kosovo to which they returned, these 1981 veterans formed a reservoir of hard men willing to risk their lives to take on the Serbs. Former Albanian police officers who had been fired or arrested as the Serbs took over Kosovo were another important source of resistance fighters because of their previous training in the use of weapons. Local elders and clan leaders, initially strong backers of Rugova's LDK, became more sympathetic to armed resistance as discontent grew with the apparently endless prospects of Serb repression.

Disappointment with U.S. policy was also a crucial factor in the rise of the KLA. Describing Dayton's impact, a senior KLA leader later said, "We all felt a deep sense of betrayal. . . . We mounted a peaceful, civilized protest to fight the totalitarian rule of Milosevic. . . . The result is that we were ignored."[22]

Developments in Albania in 1997 contributed to the rise of the KLA as well. The Socialist government of Fatos Nano, which took over Albania in the summer of 1997, backed away from the support that the government of Sali Berisa had given to the Kosovo Albanians and to Rugova personally. After Nano met Milosevic during a November 1997 Balkan summit at Crete, he said publicly that Kosovo was an internal affair of Serbia and that the solution was to be found in granting Kosovo Albanians basic human rights not autonomy.[23] Among Kosovo Albanians, Nano's words helped encourage a growing conviction that they would have to depend on their own efforts for liberation.

The social and political meltdown in Albania in the spring and summer of 1997 gave Kosovo Albanians for the first time the means to conduct an armed resistance. Many of the reported one million small arms plundered from Albanian arsenals ended up in the possession of Berisa's Democrats or criminal gangs, and from these sources a significant quantity eventually made its way into Kosovo. Berisa's mountainous northern Albanian home district took on the character of a KLA rear base.

Precisely when the first armed resistance began in Kosovo remains a matter of some dispute. In 1991, a group of Albanians in the rugged Drenica region of Kosovo—the area that Milosevic later cited to Clark as a successful example of post–World War II Serb suppression of Albanian rebels—blocked Serb police from entering a village. A few shots were fired and the surprised Serb police withdrew. The Albanians were led by Adem Jashari, a local headman who later became a KLA guerrilla leader. Demaci described this incident to me as the first appearance of what later became the KLA. He claimed the KLA's armed struggle began in 1993, but acknowledged that its activities in these early days mainly involved actions against "Serb spies"—that is, Albanians who allegedly sided with the Serbs.[24] Ramush Haradinaj, a prominent KLA fighter, wrote later that he entered Kosovo in 1994, armed and feeling then that he was a member of the KLA.[25]

Some Kosovo Albanian former police and military personnel received weapons training in Albania in 1993, but the first significant armed actions did not occur until early 1996, when for the first time there were parts of Kosovo where Serb police could not enter. The Albanians stepped up their attacks on Serb police and civilians over the next year and a half. On 28 November 1997—observed by Albanians as Flag Day—three armed men in black ski masks appeared at the funeral of Albanians killed in a skirmish with Serbian police. To the cheers of twenty thousand mourners, they proclaimed that the KLA was the only force fighting for the liberation of Kosovo. The next month, in the first public statement issued by the KLA "General Headquarters," the guerrillas threatened Serb "occupiers" that they would face increasing resistance and—warning against continued Western reluctance to deal with the KLA—said the movement would accept no agreement on Kosovo's status that it had not been a party to.[26]

In February 1998, Kosovo finally boiled over into a full-fledged insurgency, after Serb police killed Jashari and perhaps as many as fifty members of his family, including women and children, in an attack on his home in the village of Prekaz.[27] Shortly before the incident, U.S. diplomat Robert Gelbard had met with Milosevic, who he publicly praised for having shown "goodwill" and "a significant positive influence" by backing a supposedly moderate faction in the Bosnian Serb hierarchy led by Acting President Biljana Plavsic and Prime Minister Milorad Dodik. The United States rewarded Milosevic with a modest relaxation in sanctions, including granting U.S. landing rights to JAT airlines and allowing the FRY to open a consulate in New York.[28]

Immediately after meeting Milosevic, Gelbard traveled to Pristina, where he told Kosovo Albanians to avoid provocations and recognize that Belgrade was their government. He condemned the recent killing of three Serb police officers in a KLA ambush, saying, "I consider these to be terrorist actions, and it is the strong and firm policy of the U.S. to fully oppose all terrorist actions and all terrorist organizations."[29]

Gelbard's statement was apparently intended to demonstrate U.S. support for the moderate policies of Rugova and also to show Milosevic that the United States had no sympathy for armed resistance in Kosovo. But it revealed a lack of sensitivity to the years of violent Serb repression, which had called the KLA into being, and was seen as explicitly taking the Serb line, which condemned all resistance by Kosovo Albanians as terrorist.

Gelbard has been accused of essentially giving a green light to the Serb massacre in Prekaz, but this goes too far. During his February meeting with Milosevic, Gelbard reportedly warned him against escalation in Kosovo and publicly pointed his finger at the Serb side as responsible for most of the violence in Kosovo.[30]

The Serbs, moreover, needed no encouragement from the United States to go after the Jashari clan. They had long been aware of Prekaz's role as a center of armed resistance and had probably been planning action against Jashari for some time. Demaci told me that shortly before the fatal attack he had advised Jashari to leave his home, which was located almost in the shadow of a Serb police post, because of the obviously looming threat of a Serb blow, but that Jashari ignored his warning.[31]

The International Community Returns to Kosovo

The escalating violence in 1998 finally drew the international community back into Kosovo, but its belated efforts were weakened by divisions among the United States, Europe, and Russia, as well as by a reluctance to recognize the depth of Albanian determination never to voluntarily live under Serb rule. As the crisis turned to conflict, Kosovo—like Slovenia and Croatia in 1991—was supposed to be a European show, yet in the end it was once again the United States that took the diplomatic and military lead. Washington's response to Kosovo, however, was complicated by an unwillingness to back its diplomatic efforts with armed force and by a lingering nostalgia that the conflict in Kosovo, like Bosnia, could be resolved by dealing with Milosevic.

For Milosevic, though, there was a crucial difference between Kosovo and Bosnia. In 1995, Milosevic had been only too happy to cooperate with the U.S. diplomatic offensive in pressing the Bosnian Serbs to conclude an agreement. But Milosevic was well aware that any deal on Kosovo would reduce, if not eliminate, Serbian control over the province, which by the end of the 1990s was virtually all that he had left to show for a decade of disastrous rule. "Kosovo is not Bosnia. Kosovo is my head," Milosevic growled to a U.S. diplomat who saw him in early 1998 for the first time since the Dayton negotiations.

But Milosevic had not lost his deft diplomatic touch. Throughout 1998, he proved remarkably adept at keeping the level of violence in Kosovo just below the threshold sufficient to trigger international intervention. "A village a day keeps NATO away," was how one Yugoslav diplomat cynically described the Serb strategy.[32]

Milosevic also showed himself equally adept at maneuvering among the various diplomatic players he faced. After the Prekaz massacre, the administration sent Gelbard to Belgrade to warn against further violence. Armed with photographs of dead and mutilated bodies, Gelbard told Milosevic that "you have done more than anyone to increase membership in the KLA. You are acting as if you are their secret membership chairman."[33] An infuriated Milosevic reportedly responded by refusing to meet Gelbard again.

Kosovo's renewed prominence on the international agenda—together with Milosevic's unwillingness to meet Gelbard—drew the architect of the 1995 Dayton agreement, Richard Holbrooke, back into the diplomatic picture.

Holbrooke brought a new approach to the Kosovo crisis. As described by Ivo Daalder, director for European affairs at the National Security Council during the Dayton talks, Holbrooke—whether by request or because of his forceful personality—took the position that "the way to solve this problem is to deal directly with Milosevic. I'm the person who can deal with Milosevic. I've done it at Dayton. I'll do it again."[34] A senior U.S. official said Holbrooke at the time described Milosevic as a "serviceable villain," who could deliver a deal in Kosovo as he had in Bosnia.

Through 1998, Holbrooke and an able team of Dayton veterans sought to end the fighting by orchestrating threats of air strikes and promises of sanctions relief with Milosevic, and by painful efforts to forge a unified position among the fractious Kosovo Albanians. But by May 1998 when Holbrooke returned to the fray, the situation in Kosovo, thanks to years of neglect by the international community, was on the verge of spinning out of control. "The Kosovo issue in 1998 was as close to unsolvable as any I have seen," Holbrooke later commented.[35]

Kosovo, like Palestine, is that hardest of all international disputes to resolve—one in which two sides, their populations intermixed, each claim the same territory, and in which each has a certain amount of validity to its arguments and good reason to distrust the other. The diplomatic obstacles in Kosovo were enormous. There was no overlap between the positions of the two sides. By 1998, all Kosovo Albanians, whether they supported Rugova or the KLA, insisted that Kosovo must become an independent state. But Milosevic could not afford to give up Kosovo voluntarily, even if he had wanted to. The situation was complicated by the difficulty in finding a negotiating partner who could speak for the Albanian side. By 1998, Rugova's position in Kosovo was weakening under the combination of armed assault by the Serbs and pressure by the KLA. For its part, the KLA remained fragmented, suspicious of the outside world, and uncertain whether it was willing to subordinate its armed struggle to a strategy of diplomatic cooperation.

The international community was also confused and divided over strategies as well as the means to achieve them. Unwilling to contemplate independence for Kosovo—the only solution that could satisfy the vast majority of the province's population—the international community limited itself to seeking to bring the two sides together for a dialogue whose final objective was never fully defined, but that was focused on an outcome—broad autonomy for Kosovo—that was unacceptable to both sides. International diplomatic efforts in Kosovo were also undermined by the reluctance of all players, the United States and Europe alike, to use force in a way that made sense militarily, and yet was linked to realistic and achievable political goals.

From the start of the crisis the international community, including the United States, seemed mesmerized by Milosevic. Everyone agreed that the solution could only be found through Milosevic, but whether that was to be achieved by working with or against him was unclear. Everyone agreed that Milosevic only understood the language of force. Even Holbrooke, the leading advocate of seeking a deal through negotiations with Milosevic, later pointed out that "Milosevic only responds to the use of force or the absolutely incredible [credible?] threat of the use of force."[36] But no one seemed to know, or even to think seriously about, how much force would be enough. Most important, the alliance failed to think through its military and political options if Milosevic did not respond to the threat of force or to the limited bombing NATO leaders initially believed would be enough to compel him to deal on Kosovo. NATO, in short, had no "Plan B."

In the end, it seemed as if the international community, preoccupied with its own internal disputes and despite its fixation with Milosevic, did not take him seriously. When Milosevic said Kosovo was "his head," he knew what he was talking about. Kosovo's significance to his own survival meant that Milosevic was prepared to go to war with the most powerful military alliance on the planet, something that few seem to have expected.

Negotiations Begin

Holbrooke described the initial objective of his involvement in Kosovo in May 1998 as "not to get an agreement but to start a process going."[37] In May 1998, Holbrooke announced the first-ever meeting between Milosevic and Rugova. But the results proved disappointing. Moreover, as a reward to Milosevic for meeting Rugova, the United States prevailed on the Contact Group to relax the sanctions on foreign investment that it had painfully agreed to only a few days earlier. The U.S. move weakened Rugova's already crumbling position in Kosovo and also confused allies, with its apparent flip-flops between threats and rewards to Milosevic.[38]

Rugova was accompanied by several prominent Kosovo Albanian leaders, including his deputy Femi Agani, Surroi, and Bakalli. No KLA representative attended. Milosevic met the group at Belgrade's White Palace in a relaxed and jovial mood. For two hours each of the Albanians spoke in turn, with Rugova going last. All of the Albanian participants said that Kosovo had to become independent, although they also acknowledged that after independence, some kind of residual ties could be considered. Milosevic listened silently and attentively. In reply, Milosevic neither accepted nor rejected a dialogue on independence, confining himself to platitudes about the need for a just and stable solution in Kosovo, and then warning his visitors, "Don't forget, I'm surrounded by Serb chauvinists," a typical Milosevic disclaimer that his Albanian guests received with justified skepticism.

Other signs indicated from the beginning that Milosevic was not serious about dialogue with the Albanians. At the start of the meeting in Belgrade, Milosevic joked that Bakalli should show them around the White

Palace since he probably knew the place better than Milosevic in view of all the time he had spent there with Tito. That night television news pictured Rugova standing beside Milosevic and laughing. Rugova was reacting to Milosevic's witticism about Bakalli's familiarity with the White Palace. What viewers in Kosovo saw, however, was Rugova standing beside Milosevic with a grin on his face—an obvious effort to undermine Rugova.[39]

To get Rugova to meet Milosevic, Holbrooke had promised a later meeting with President Clinton, which occurred in Washington at the end of May 1998. Rugova warned that without direct U.S. intervention, Kosovo was headed for war, and pleaded for an increased U.S. presence. Much of the meeting, however, was reportedly spent discussing mineralogy in Kosovo and Arkansas after Rugova—an avid rock collector—presented Clinton with a piece of quartz from Kosovo. President Clinton reportedly deflected Rugova's pleas for a U.S. presence in Kosovo, but according to Surroi, who also participated in the talks, the president told them that "Bosnia should not be repeated and will not be repeated."[40]

At this stage in the crisis, Washington was desperately eager to avoid any form of military commitment in Kosovo. The Clinton administration, shortly after taking office, had reaffirmed the validity of the Christmas warning issued in 1992 by President Bush. But Washington remained deeply divided about the use of armed force, which according to Daalder's well-informed "insider" account of the diplomacy around the Kosovo war, meant that "it was very clear from the moment that violence started that the Christmas warning was off the table" as far as Berger, Clinton, and other senior administration officials were concerned.[41]

While the U.S. diplomatic effort was getting underway, the increasingly confident KLA expanded its presence in Kosovo, eventually establishing control of the major east-west road linking Pristina with Pec, a town near the border with Albania that is also the seat of the Serb Orthodox Patriarchate. In central Kosovo the KLA established its own capital in Malisevo, the main market town of the province's poorest county. There, uniformed KLA soldiers performed police functions, the KLA took over the administration of the town and surrounding countryside, and cars even began to sport KLA-issued license plates. The KLA's increasingly overt presence and growing control of the province's major lines of communication posed a threat to Milosevic's grip on Kosovo.

In June, Serb security forces unleashed a major offensive, sweeping KLA roadblocks off the province's main roads and driving the young guerrilla force back into the villages. The Serb army and police then teamed up to work their way methodically through one part of Kosovo after another, turning their attention first to the Drenica region, home to most of the top KLA leadership. While the military generally remained in the background, providing artillery or tank gunfire support where necessary, the Serb special police units assaulted villages one by one, driving out their inhabitants, and often killing, looting, and burning. Moving from one valley to another, Milosevic's clear aim was to eliminate or drive into the hills the poorly armed and trained KLA units as well as to send a strong message to the Albanian population about the costs of supporting the KLA.

Milosevic's brutal offensive also grabbed Western headlines. With 250,000 Kosovo Albanians driven from their homes, the United States and its allies came under growing pressure to act.

Yeltsin and Milosevic

Worried by the prospect of Western intervention into Kosovo and also seeking to demonstrate that Moscow remained a diplomatic player to be reckoned with, Russian President Yeltsin invited Milosevic to Moscow on 16 June 1998, just two weeks after Clinton's meeting with Rugova. Russia had long had an equivocal attitude toward Milosevic. Yeltsin's first foreign minister, the liberal and Western-oriented Andrey Kozyrev, developed a good personal relationship with Milosevic, which he hoped would counter Belgrade's sympathetic contacts with Russia's Communist-oriented parliamentary opposition. Kozyrev's successor as foreign minister, Yevgeniy Primakov, met Milosevic several times in his previous capacity as chief of the External Intelligence Service (SVR)—the KGB's foreign successor. Primakov opened a special link between the SVR and its Serbian equivalent in 1993 as a reward, Primakov claims, for accepting Russian advice to support the Vance-Owen peace plan for Bosnia. Unlike Kozyrev, who never raised Kosovo with Milosevic, Primakov as foreign minister took a more activist approach on the subject. Over a third of Primakov's first visit to Belgrade as foreign minister in May 1996 was devoted to Kosovo—to the Serbs' surprise. Primakov says that he warned Milosevic to pay attention to the explosive situation developing in Kosovo but that Milosevic ignored him, possibly, according to Primakov, because Milosevic had simply gotten used to ignoring any advice he did not wish to heed or possibly because he thought the importance the United States attached to his assistance in implementing the Dayton agreement would allow him to keep Kosovo away from international attention.[42]

By the summer of 1998, however, Kosovo had returned to the headlines and Milosevic saw his visit to Moscow as a chance to enlist Russian support against Western involvement in Kosovo. Russian sources believe that Milosevic placed "big hopes" in Yeltsin. Milosevic seemed to have somehow convinced himself that Yeltsin had good feelings toward Serbia and Milosevic personally, but that "the right information" was not getting through to Yeltsin. So Milosevic tried hard to "convey the truth" directly to the Russian president.

But Moscow failed to provide as much as Milosevic hoped, and the Serb leader was visibly disappointed when he realized how little Yeltsin cared for Serbia. Yeltsin, in fact, never liked Milosevic personally. In the latest volume of his memoirs, Yeltsin describes Milosevic as "one of the most cynical politicians I have ever dealt with."[43] Yeltsin told Milosevic there was no chance he would be invited back for a full-fledged state visit, something Milosevic wanted badly, until the situation in Kosovo calmed down.

Russian involvement, moreover, came with a price. Yeltsin told Milosevic unequivocally that he could not rely on Russian support in the conflict if he ignored advice from the Kremlin.[44] Yeltsin used the visit to obtain Milosevic's agreement to allow Russian, U.S., and EU diplomatic observer missions in Kosovo. The Russians saw the missions as evidence that they had the clout to get Milosevic to agree to something that the West had been seeking since Milosevic's 1993 expulsion of the CSCE observers from Kosovo. The Russians also hoped that the deal would help hold off deeper Western involvement, including the possibility of military action.

From Milosevic's perspective, he was playing the same kind of diplomatic shell game with the Russians that he had played so successfully in the past with a host of Western negotiators—and would do so in the future. What was needed in Kosovo was not observers but a political settlement and the means to enforce it. Milosevic knew this as well as the Russians did. By allowing the observer mission to be created Milosevic continued his tactic of small, step-by-step concessions in order to deflect heavier pressure for more meaningful moves. He knew that the Russians—like previous international visitors—desperately wanted to be able to report to the media and to their public back home that they had received something—anything—from Milosevic. Accepting the small missions with vague guidelines and no enforcement powers bought time and deflected the threat of more serious outside involvement.

Nevertheless, what came to be called the Kosovo Diplomatic Observer Mission (KDOM) may have helped moderate the behavior of the Serbian security forces in Kosovo. The presence of the missions raised the stakes for

Milosevic by bearing witness to the actions of the Serbian forces. Although the observers often found themselves powerless to prevent tragedy, the courage and dedication displayed by individuals in all three elements of KDOM helped save the lives of numbers of Kosovo inhabitants, both Albanians and Serbs.

NATO Dithers

Throughout the summer of 1998, Holbrooke's deputy, Ambassador Chris Hill, struggled to put together negotiations between the Albanians and the Serbs on Kosovo's future. This task proved difficult because Milosevic, on the one hand, continued to reject foreign mediation, while the Kosovo Albanians, on the other hand, were divided among themselves about both objectives and who should represent them.

U.S. officials began to meet with KLA representatives in June 1998, but the United States continued to view Rugova as its chief negotiating partner on the Albanian side and resisted including the KLA in the negotiating process. Despite these difficulties, Hill announced in early September that Milosevic and Rugova had agreed to work toward an interim agreement that would provide Kosovo substantial autonomy within the FRY and defer a decision on Kosovo's final status for three to five years. This potentially promising move, which represented the core of the later Rambouillet agreement, went nowhere primarily because both Serbs and Albanians at that stage were more interested in achieving results on the field of battle than at the negotiating table. The KLA challenged Rugova's right to speak on behalf of the Kosovo Albanian people and rejected the idea of deferring independence. Milosevic, for his part, never demonstrated any intention of discussing autonomy for Kosovo in a serious fashion, and his armed forces continued their offensive against the KLA.

As the conflict in Kosovo unfolded, world leaders responded with a series of warnings and appeals, none of which had any effect in deterring Serb actions. In June 1998, NATO—against the advice of its military experts, who saw it as a hollow exercise—conducted an air operation involving the flight of eighty aircraft over Albanian and Macedonian territory within fifteen miles of the FRY border. Intended to demonstrate NATO's capability to project air power into the region, the exercise may well have also shown Milosevic just how reluctant the alliance leaders were to actually use their power. General Naumann later assessed that Milosevic "rightly concluded that the NATO threat was a bluff . . . and finished his summer offensive."[45]

NATO leaders, conscious of the damage done by the alliance's absence in the early stages of the Bosnian conflict, wanted NATO to play an active role in the Kosovo crisis. When NATO defense ministers authorized the June air exercise, they also publicly directed alliance military planners to develop a full range of military options to halt the repression in Kosovo and create the conditions for serious negotiations. NATO Secretary General Solana stated that if the conflict in Kosovo continued, "nothing is excluded." By early August, NATO military planners had dutifully put together plans for eight or nine military options including a ground invasion of Kosovo, the use of troops to enforce a peace settlement, and various types of air campaigns.

But NATO's ability to act was hampered by an unwillingness to step up to the military implications of involvement. Despite Solana's tough talk, alliance civilian leaders—at the insistence of the United States—quietly shelved all options that involved ground troops. Even air options were constrained by alliance preoccupation with avoiding excessive use of force. Throughout the next year, NATO had three guiding principles: avoid casualties to its own forces, avoid collateral damage to Serb forces and civilians, and bring any conflict to a quick end. As Naumann later remarked, NATO leaders did not want to fight a war in which Serbia would be destroyed and brought to the negotiating table as a defeated country but instead preferred to use military measures to convince Milosevic to negotiate a peaceful solution.[46] In short, NATO planned and fought its war in the Balkans to change Milosevic's mind.

Holbrooke's October 1998 Agreement with Milosevic

Despite the tough talk from Brussels, Serb forces in Kosovo continued their brutal offensive against Albanian civilians. On 30 September, the *New York Times* reported a Serb attack on the village of Obrinje, running a gruesome front-page photo of an Albanian civilian with his throat cut. Holbrooke said later that this story, published on the day of a White House meeting to discuss Kosovo, helped galvanize the mood of senior U.S. officials. Washington decided to send Holbrooke back to Belgrade with a threat to Milosevic of a phased air campaign if Serb forces did not end their offensive.

Holbrooke's visit grew into what he described as a "mini-Dayton," a twelve-day negotiation that included fifty hours of face-to-face talks with Milosevic. Holbrooke's efforts had two thrusts. The first was to put in place a verification system on the ground in Kosovo to monitor Serb behavior. The second was to craft an interim political agreement between Serbs and Kosovo Albanians, based on the approach Hill had announced the previous month.

Holbrooke portrayed Milosevic as "cocky, confident, and cool most of the time." U.S. Lieutenant General Michael Short, NATO's joint air force component commander and a part of the Holbrooke team, was surprised when Milosevic on their first meeting asked, "So you are the man who is going to bomb me?" Short responded that he had B-52 bombers in one hand and U-2 reconnaissance aircraft in the other, and the choice of which to employ was up to Milosevic. Later, Milosevic asked Holbrooke, "Are you crazy enough to bomb us over these issues we're talking about in that lousy little Kosovo?" Although Holbrooke assured Milosevic that the United States was "just crazy enough to do it," it soon became clear that Milosevic was stalling. On 7 October, Holbrooke reported to Albright, "This guy's not taking us seriously." After three days of talks, Holbrooke left Belgrade in uncharacteristic silence while a defiant Milosevic denounced threats of NATO air strikes, which "jeopardize the continuation of the political process." Serb authorities began to prepare people for war, including cleaning out World War II–era bomb shelters.[47]

On 10 October, after a long and emotional discussion, the North Atlantic Council—NATO's highest permanent political body—approved "activation orders" that allowed NATO Commander Clark to begin air strikes ninety-six hours after determining that the Serbs had not complied with NATO's demands. What Holbrooke called this "credible threat" seems to have changed Milosevic's attitude. On 13 October, Holbrooke emerged from a two-hour meeting to announce that Milosevic had agreed to the withdrawal of Serb forces sent to Kosovo for the 1998 offensive and the deployment of international monitors to the province.[48]

Holbrooke said the October agreement achieved more than he had expected. It provided for two thousand unarmed OSCE observers, withdrawal of the Serb police forces that had committed the worst atrocities against the Albanian civilian population, and required no concessions by the Albanian side in return.[49] The agreement probably helped reduce the fighting in Kosovo. The deployment of OSCE monitors, in addition to the U.S., Russian, and EU teams already present in Kosovo as a result of Milosevic's agreement with Yeltsin, also encouraged Albanian refugees to return home and modestly enhanced confidence against an immediate resumption of the atrocities.

Nevertheless, the October agreement contained some major flaws. It was vague on the terms of the withdrawal of Serb forces from Kosovo, ambiguous about the verification authority of the monitors, and lacked any means of enforcement. The absence of any requirement for reciprocal actions by the KLA was a problem as well. Albanians did not participate in the October talks and the agreement included nothing on Kosovo's political status—although U.S. officials told the media during the talks that Milosevic was ready to agree to a unilateral statement granting limited autonomy to ethnic Albanians in the areas of local government, schools, and policing, and promising a full review of the province's status in three years' time.[50]

The key mistake in October, according to senior officials involved in the talks, was Washington's unwillingness—thanks to congressional and Pentagon opposition—to consider the use of U.S. troops on the ground in Kosovo to enforce the agreement.[51] In Brussels on his way to Belgrade Holbrooke complained to NATO commander General Wes Clark that U.S. Secretary of Defense Cohen "warned me that under no circumstances was I to offer NATO ground troops as peacekeepers."[52] Preoccupied with the unfolding Monica Lewinsky scandal, the Clinton administration found it difficult to offer the leadership necessary for decisive action. One of the president's key political advisers later told the media, "I hardly remember Kosovo in political discussions. It was all impeachment, impeachment, impeachment. There was nothing else." Former senator Bob Dole, a longtime advocate of Kosovo in the U.S. political process who visited the region in September 1998 on behalf of the Clinton administration, also said he thought "a lot of attention was diverted" by impeachment. "It was all consuming" and Kosovo "may have been one of the casualties."[53]

After Holbrooke left Belgrade, Generals Clark and Naumann accompanied NATO Secretary General Solana to Belgrade to sign that part of Holbrooke's deal authorizing NATO verification flights and to nail down the withdrawal of Serb forces from Kosovo. They found Milosevic defiant. He initially denied that the Serb units that NATO insisted be withdrawn were actually in Kosovo, but when Clark—backed up he says by Serb Chief of Staff Momcilo Perisic—presented evidence of their presence he retreated, saying, "OK, we have such a unit. It will be withdrawn."

Five days later, with the Serbs still dragging their heels, Clark flew down again for another set of talks with Milosevic. At one point, with Milosevic still resisting, Clark asked to see him alone. "Look, Mr. President," Clark said. "Get real. You have to pull out your forces and if you don't there is an activation order. And if they tell me to bomb you, I'm going to bomb you good. You don't want to get bombed so get those forces out." Clark's straight talk finally brought Milosevic around. After one more visit to Belgrade and an all-night negotiating session between Clark and Naumann and Serb generals on the details of the agreement, Milosevic committed himself to some specific obligations, including the withdrawal of four thousand police and excess heavy weapons as well as advance warning of new deployments. Even then, however, Milosevic tried to evade responsibility. When the text of the agreement was presented to Clark for his signature, the NATO general exploded when he noticed that Milosevic's name was not present. After this outburst, Milosevic relented and signed as well.[54]

Milosevic and the KLA Prepare for War

Both Serbs and Albanians treated the October 1998 agreement as an opportunity to catch their breaths and prepare to renew the conflict in the spring. Milosevic used the atmosphere of crisis to put the country on a war footing, consolidate his own internal position through a sweeping crackdown on the independent media, and purge politicians and leaders of the army and police who questioned his hard-line stance on Kosovo.

Milorad Vucelic, who returned to the regime in 1997 after being fired by Milosevic as RTS director in 1995, described Milosevic as "elated and euphoric" over the agreement with Holbrooke. Milosevic characterized the deal to Vucelic as "the biggest victory ever for the Serbian people." Vucelic said Milosevic thought he had solved Kosovo and at the same time would be able to return to the good graces of the United States, which would allow him to resume the central role in international diplomacy he had come to enjoy so much.[55]

Less than twenty-four hours after Holbrooke left Belgrade, Milosevic shut down two independent newspapers—accused by Minister of Information Vucic of "fomenting defeatism, panic, and fear"—and also banned the rebroadcast by independent radio stations of news from Radio Free Europe, BBC, and Deutsche Welle. At the University of Belgrade, Milosevic stepped up a campaign started in the spring of forcing out professors who were not members of his wife's hard-line JUL party.[56]

The crackdown provoked sharp criticism of the U.S. focus on Milosevic by Serb opposition and media figures. "They have abandoned us here," Goran Matic, the head of the largest independent news service, Radio B-92, said of the Clinton administration. Milosevic "is very good at creating a xenophobia inside the country and using that as an instrument to step down on any kind of democratic process," said Milan Protic, a Serb historian who briefly became Belgrade's ambassador to the United States after Milosevic's fall. "Virtually the only time Milosevic appears on television in Serbia is during the visits of foreign dignitaries, when he is filmed sitting in an armchair in front of a bowl of flowers, listening sphinx-like to his important visitors. People here watch him and think: 'If the international community supports him, who are we to oppose him?'" said Protic.[57]

Vucelic, who noted sourly that, "Whenever Milosevic thought he had achieved a big success, he fired someone," was himself fired in October after the agreement with Holbrooke, together with secret police chief Jovica Stanisic and army chief of staff Momcilo Perisic. Stanisic, who had headed the Serbian secret police since Milosevic's rise to power, had become privately critical of the direction in which Milosevic was taking Serbia and especially of the malign influence on the country of the corrupt cabal around Milosevic's wife, Markovic. Along with Stanisic, a dozen top operational officers of the security service were forced into retirement or removed. Stanisic was replaced by a senior police officer, Rade Markovic, a loyalist of Mira Markovic's JUL party.

During the summer of 1998, Perisic kept the army out of direct involvement in the Kosovo fighting. He made no secret of his unhappiness with Milosevic's policies when discussing Kosovo with other senior officers. The last straw for Milosevic came on 20 October when Perisic took his critical views to the public, telling the Belgrade daily *Blic* that politicians, not the army, were responsible for the conflict in Kosovo. Perisic added that "there are very few politicians" who are willing to admit that they cannot solve the problem and make way for those who can."[58]

In what was taken by many observers as a sign of Milosevic's slipping authority, both Stanisic and Perisic issued public statements criticizing their firing. Stanisic, who despite his involvement in supporting ethnic cleansing also enjoyed a reputation among Serbs for professionalism, released a dignified statement pointedly noting that throughout his tenure, he had always carried out the policies of the Serbian president—that is, Milosevic.[59] Perisic was more blunt. "I was replaced without consultations, in an inadequate and illegal way," the general said.[60]

Milosevic's moves were widely seen as due to the increasing influence of his wife, Mirjana Markovic. On October 19, journalists Aleksandar Tijanic and Slavko Curuvija, both once close to Markovic, published an open letter to Milosevic in the Belgrade weekly *Evropljanin*. The piece charged that Milosevic, perhaps "tired of responsibility for ruling the country" was unaware that "a group which had come out on top in the wars waged in the royal palace" had introduced a de facto state of emergency in Serbia. Without saying so directly, the two authors charged that the clique around Markovic—a small circle of about one hundred families that controlled the economy and the country—was destroying Serbia. They warned that Milosevic would be personally responsible for the consequences of what would inevitably be a short-lived period of such rule.

After the appearance of the open letter, which cost *Evropljanin* a $240,000 fine and confiscation of its property, Curuvija met Markovic. As he described it, the meeting with Markovic ended abruptly after Curuvija "told her that everything her husband had done was dramatically bad and that he had to do several things to save Serbia. If you don't stop what's going on, the end will be bloody, and that many people will be killed and maybe some will be on hanged on the Terazije" [a central square in Belgrade].[61]

Shortly after NATO began bombing Serbia, Curuvija was murdered by unknown assailants after a pro-Milosevic paper accused him of supporting the air strikes. Many believed from the beginning that there was an official connection in the Curuvija killing, and these suspicions seemed to be confirmed after Milosevic's fall in October 2000 when the Belgrade Fund for Humanitarian Law received a copy of an official document reportedly showing that Curuvija was being shadowed by the secret police, but that minutes before the killing his tails were ordered to withdraw. Belgrade media figures and lawyers for the Curuvija family also accused Slobodan Cerovic, an official of Markovic's JUL party and the Serb minister of tourism, of being behind the killing, with the possible involvement of the quasi-criminal commercial security firm Komet, which had long links to Markovic and her political activities.[62]

In Kosovo, the KLA took advantage of the breathing space offered by the October agreement to regroup—precisely what Milosevic had told Clark they would do. The Serb summer offensive had struck a heavy blow against the still-emerging KLA. Serb generals told Clark in October 1998 that they were just two weeks away from eliminating the KLA, and this assessment may not have been far off the mark. Haradinaj, one of the KLA's leading commanders, admitted that the Serb "September offensive had inflicted heavy losses on us" and called the Holbrooke agreement "life saving for the KLA." Agim Ceku, the KLA chief of staff during the 1999 war, later said, "The cease-fire was very useful for us."[63]

At the end of November, the KLA celebrated its first public appearance of a year earlier. Instead of a brief appearance by three masked men, however, this time about one hundred armed and uniformed KLA fighters stood at attention while a KLA commander vowed to continue the fight until Kosovo became independent. In nearby Drenica, where the Serb crackdown on the Jashari clan had set off the summer's fighting, three hundred new recruits were inducted into a KLA unit named after the dead clan chieftain.[64]

By Christmas 1998, the Holbrooke deal was starting to unravel. Low-level fighting was occurring all across Kosovo. Serb troops were returning in violation of the October deal, and the KLA had reestablished its own positions across the province.

Soon after the new year, the lid finally blew off. On 17 January, international monitors discovered the bodies of forty-five Albanians brutally murdered by Serb forces near the village of Racak. Visiting the scene shortly after the Serb attack, the chief of the OSCE monitoring mission, U.S. diplomat William Walker, called the massacre an "unspeakable atrocity" and concluded that he would not "hesitate to accuse government security forces of responsibility."[65]

Immediately after the Racak massacre, Clark and Naumann were once again dispatched to try to badger Milosevic into ending the violence. Since NATO had not authorized any new threats or warnings, Clark says that he and Naumann were sent to Belgrade without any specific instructions. On the plane to Belgrade, Clark and Naumann drew from a NATO press release to formulate three demands of Milosevic: allow Hague tribunal Chief Prosecutor Louise Arbour into Kosovo to investigate the Racak massacre, permit Walker—who Milosevic had ordered out of the country—to stay, and insist that Milosevic uphold his October promise to reduce Serb forces.

The two NATO generals found Milosevic belligerent and "extremely stubborn." After a long and evasive conversation in which Milosevic first said Arbour could not come to Kosovo at all and then said she could come but only as a "tourist," with the right simply to "observe" the Serbs' own investigation into Racak, Clark finally said to Milosevic, "Look, Mr. President, don't keep stringing us along. Be honest." Milosevic replied, "OK, Arbour can't come." Equally unyielding yet even more angry when the discussion turned to the behavior of Serb forces at Racak, Milosevic shouted, "This was not a massacre. This was staged. These people are terrorists." When Clark, summing up the results of the six-hour conversation, said he would have to tell NATO that Milosevic had rejected all of his demands, Milosevic erupted. "You are a war criminal. You are the ones who threaten with your bombs and missiles," he yelled. As for Walker, Milosevic said there was a Serb government decision requiring him to leave because he had violated the rules of diplomatic behavior and had "disgraced Serbia."

Nevertheless, during a refreshment break, Serb Prime Minister Miluti-novic predicted to Clark that Milosevic would eventually concede on Walker since Milosevic had tied his stand to an order of the Serbian government. Milosevic could, therefore, back down without being seen to have repudiated his own word.

The evasive stance that Milosevic took on Arbour and Walker during his meeting with Clark was a typical example of Milosevic's negotiating tactics. Under pressure, he agreed to allow Arbour to visit, but at the same time he refused to grant conditions that would give the visit any meaning. He kept "boxing in his agreement with conditions and evasions," Clark explains, because he believed that he could string the alliance along without significant cost to himself. Milosevic's anger was also partly tactical. Milosevic was genuinely angry but "if he did not want to be angry he would not have acted the way he did," Clark maintains. The bottom line according to Clark was that Milosevic thought he had little to fear from NATO warnings. Clark observes that "like most bullies, Slobodan Milosevic is a coward," and concluded that Milosevic "got angry at us because he thought he could kick the sh—out of us without any serious penalty."[66]

After Racak, a consensus emerged within the Clinton administration in favor of a more decisive approach. State Department spokesman James Rubin turned up the public pressure, asserting, "Milosevic has been at the center of every crisis in the former Yugoslavia over the last decade. He is not simply part of the problem—Milosevic is the problem."[67]

The new policy involved a subtle shift away from the Holbrooke approach of using the threat of force to compel Milosevic to negotiate a deal on Kosovo. After Racak, Secretary of State Madeline Albright put together a new strategy, drawing on a proposal submitted by U.S. Ambassador to NATO Vershbow the previous summer, under which both sides would be presented with an ultimatum to accept by a date certain an interim deal that would establish Kosovo as an international protectorate with a NATO force on the ground to implement it.

Rambouillet: Milosevic Defies the World

Outrage over the Racak massacre triggered a new round of international diplomacy. On 6 February, talks began under U.S., European, and Russian auspices at Rambouillet, an elegant, fourteenth-century chalet about thirty miles outside Paris. Rambouillet was billed in public as a European version of Dayton, with France and Britain taking on the facilitator's role that Holbrooke had assumed in Ohio—although the French hosts promised a better kitchen for the international delegates than the unvarnished American fare at Packy's, the air base's sports bar restaurant.

In fact, the quality of the cuisine was not the only difference between Rambouillet and Dayton. Rambouillet unfolded against a very different set of circumstances than had prevailed in Bosnia in 1995. Neither the Serb nor the Albanian side believed itself to be facing military defeat, as the Bosnian Serbs were in 1995. Neither side, therefore, was willing to compromise its incompatible objectives. Moreover, there were no real negotiations in Rambouillet—at least between Serbs and Albanians. The international community brought to Rambouillet a plan that the sides were given a one-week deadline—subsequently extended—to accept. In one way, however, Rambouillet was similar to Dayton. Despite pretension at making Rambouillet a European show, the draft agreement was written by the same group of U.S. diplomats and lawyers who had crafted the Dayton accord, and most of the diplomatic heavy lifting was done by the United States.

Before Rambouillet, in an obvious effort to dilute the influence of Kosovo's majority Albanian population, the Serbs had been seeking to boost the prominence of the minorities in Kosovo, such as Gypsies and Turks, even though they constituted only 2.29 and .52 percent, respectively, of the province's population.[68] The Serb plan for Kosovo, for example, included giving a special parliamentary chamber to six different minority groups. Members of the U.S. team that drafted the Rambouillet agreement characterized their text as an effort to meld this Serb concept of national communities with the Albanian insistence that Kosovo remain a single territory under one administration. As a member of the U.S. team described it, "The local Serbs could deal with Belgrade while the Albanians could say that they ran Kosovo."

The draft agreement reaffirmed the existing borders of Kosovo and the territorial integrity of the FRY, which retained authority for the monetary, taxation, customs, foreign, and defense policies of Kosovo. Under this umbrella, Kosovo would "govern itself democratically" through its own executive, legislative, and judicial authorities. Each of Kosovo's national communities would also be allowed to establish its own democratic institutions to provide for such matters as education, health, and the preservation of religious and historical sites. On the critical issue of security, the Yugoslav military would be limited to a total of 2,500 border guards and support personnel along Kosovo's external border. Within one year, all Serbian police were to be out of Kosovo and replaced by a new local force.

Milosevic did not go to Rambouillet—another key difference with Dayton—possibly because he was worried that his name might be among the list of sealed indictments in the files of the Hague war crimes tribunal or perhaps because he had already decided that there was no way he could reach agreement on terms acceptable to himself.

The Serb delegation, headed by Deputy Prime Minister Nikola Sainovic, seemed barely interested in the negotiations at all. According to participants in the talks, the Serb delegation spent most of the daylight hours strolling around the beautiful Rambouillet gardens and partied in the evening. On one occasion, the Albanians complained to their foreign hosts that the Serbs had kept them awake until the early hours of the morning playing the piano and singing nationalist songs.

In contrast to the Serbs, the Albanian delegation in Rambouillet included most of Kosovo's major figures: Rugova and his deputy Agani; Prime Minister Bukoshi; anti-Rugova political figures, such as Rejep Cosia; respected journalists such as Surroi and Shala; and for the first time on the international scene a representative of the KLA, in the person of Hasim Thaci, the head of the guerrilla group's political directorate. The Albanian delegation suffered from deep personal and political divisions, which reflected the uncertain situation on the ground in Kosovo, where the position of Rugova and his party, the LDK, was being steadily undermined by the KLA. Many local LDK leaders, unhappy with Rugova's unwillingness to endorse the uprising against the Serbs, were switching over to support the KLA or other armed groups, including a faction called the FARK that was funded by Bukoshi and conducted its own guerrilla campaign against the Serbs independent of the KLA and Rugova.

At the beginning of the talks, Surroi, Shala, and other delegation members not associated with Rugova's LDK—possibly believing they could control the twenty-nine-year old KLA leader—joined with KLA delegates to select Thaci as the head of the Albanian team. Those involved have stated that Rugova himself did not object to the choice of Thaci. Nevertheless, the move further undermined the authority of Rugova, who was described as withdrawn and intimidated by the KLA—not surprising since elements within the KLA were widely suspected of being behind the assassination of two of his close aides in the weeks before the conference.[69]

The basic U.S. game plan at Rambouillet was to pressure the Albanians into accepting the draft agreement, then use the threat of NATO air strikes to compel Milosevic to sign. Most Western negotiating energy was thus focused on the Albanians and, in practice, Thaci, who obstinately refused to abandon independence for Kosovo as a final objective. To meet Thaci's insistence on a referendum to determine Kosovo's future status, the United States added a carefully crafted provision in which "the will of the people" was one of a number of factors to be considered by an international meeting that would be held after three years to determine a mechanism for a final settlement in Kosovo. Albright also produced—but did not sign—a letter that indicated the United States would regard this formulation as "confirming the right of the people of Kosovo to hold a referendum on the final status of Kosovo after three years."[70]

Nevertheless, after two weeks the conference seemed near collapse when Thaci—encouraged by Demaci, who did not attend Rambouillet—resisted intense pressure to sign, including personal appeals by Clark and Albright. At one point Albright telephoned Demaci in Pristina entreating him to drop his objections, only to be told—not entirely unreasonably—that "a single telephone call could not solve such a bloody and serious problem." Demaci's stubborn behavior provoked a member of Albright's entourage to complain, "Here is the greatest nation on earth pleading with some nothing balls to do something entirely in their own interest . . . and they defy us the whole way."[71] Only a last minute appeal by Surroi and U.S. negotiator Ambassador Hill "to look inside their hearts" brought KLA agreement to a face-saving formulation of signature after a two-week consultation with "people" back home.

Obtaining Albanian consent to Rambouillet was also facilitated by the KLA's continued military weakness vis-à-vis the Serbs. Civilian members of the Albanian delegation told their KLA counterparts they would be prepared to stall the talks indefinitely if the KLA thought it could win the war on the battlefield, only to hear in reply that the KLA had ammunition sufficient only for a few weeks of hard fighting.[72]

In the interval between Rambouillet and the scheduled resumption of the talks in Paris two weeks later—with the Albanians signaling that they expected to be able to sign—attention shifted again to the Serbs. Relays of Russian, European, and OSCE diplomats failed to budge Milosevic.

The United States again sent Holbrooke into the breach. Members of the U.S. team that accompanied Holbrooke to Belgrade found that Milosevic misunderstood key elements of the Rambouillet plan, but his main sticking point was something the United States was not prepared to compromise on: the presence of NATO troops in Kosovo to enforce the deal. On Holbrooke's departure, Milosevic issued another defiant statement that "attempts to condition a political agreement on our country's acceptance of foreign troops . . . are unacceptable."[73]

When the Kosovo diplomatic cast reassembled in Paris on 15 March the Serbs were almost contemptuously defiant. In the view of one European participant, "Milosevic had clearly instructed Milutinovic not to conclude this or any other deal." The Serbs submitted changes to the accord that amounted to revising an estimated 70 percent of the text.[74] On 18 March, the process came to its by-then inevitable end: the Albanians signed the agreement, the Serbs refused, and the conference gloomily adjourned.

After Paris, Holbrooke returned to Belgrade for one last meeting with Milosevic. Holbrooke found Milosevic's attitude different from October 1998 when Holbrooke had also brought him an ultimatum on bombing. Then, "with the bombers on the runway," Holbrooke described Milosevic as "sweating." In March, by contrast, Holbrooke found Milosevic to be "cool and almost contemptuous" about the bombing. Wanting to make sure Milosevic had no misunderstanding about the scale of the threat he faced if he did not go along with the Rambouillet accord, Holbrooke depicted the planned bombing as "swift, severe, and sustained," terms he had cleared in advance with the Pentagon.

The next morning, just before leaving for the airport, Holbrooke saw Milosevic alone. Holbrooke sensed an atmosphere of resignation. "You're a great country, a powerful country," Milosevic said. "You can do anything you want. We can't stop you." At the same time, Milosevic continued his defiance to the end. "Go ahead and bomb us," he told Holbrooke, "but you will never get Kosovo." Holbrooke asked, "You understand that if I leave without an agreement today, bombing will start almost immediately?" Milosevic replied, "Yes, I understand that." Holbrooke pressed once more, "You're absolutely clear about what will happen when we leave?" Sitting by himself in an empty palace filled with paintings and other treasures left behind by Tito and previous rulers of Yugoslavia, Milosevic answered quietly, "Yes. You will bomb us."[75]

Why Did Milosevic Reject Rambouillet?

There has been considerable speculation about why Milosevic rejected Rambouillet despite the certainty that this would plunge him into conflict with the most powerful military alliance in the world. By March 1999, Milosevic had developed what some diplomats in regular contact with him called "a bunker mentality." Holbrooke characterized his final meetings with Milosevic, on the eve of the bombing, as "the most bleak and the least engaged that we've ever had."[76] Some portrayed Milosevic as extraordinarily out of touch, surrounded by mediocre aides, and living in a world of complete unreality. "He only wants to believe what he wants to believe," said chief European negotiator Wolfgang Petritsch. "He is not ready in any way to engage even in a meaningful discussion about alternatives and what can be done. He never refers to any of the issues that are of real relevance."[77]

Milosevic was also hearing optimistic evaluations from his own armed forces. Shortly before the bombing, Milosevic told U.S. negotiators that the Serb military claimed it could wipe out the KLA in one week. "Possibly he believed it," one U.S. diplomat concluded sadly. General Clark later commented, "Milosevic kept saying to me, 'We just need seven days to wipe out the Kosovo Liberation Army.' He absolutely failed to see that this kind of movement does not work that way."[78]

Milosevic may also have been demonstrating the kind of mulish fatalism that is all too familiar to anyone who has negotiated in the Balkans. On the eve of the NATO bombing, Milosevic told Hill, "You are a superpower. You can do what you want. If you want to say Sunday is Wednesday, you can. It is all up to you." When Hill explained that NATO would begin bombing, Milosevic shot back: "Anyone who does that—bomb—is going to spend the rest of his life on a psychiatric couch." Hill found the words extraordinary, coming from someone so consistently destructive throughout his political career, and concluded that for Milosevic, the symbolism of being seen to stand up to foreign pressure was apparently more important than the substance of the proposed deal.[79]

Holbrooke suggested three possible reasons why Milosevic rejected Rambouillet. Milosevic had undoubtedly paid close attention to Desert Fox, the seventy-two-hour British and American bombing campaign in December 1998 against Saddam Hussein in Iraq, and thought that he could survive something similar. Second, according to Holbrooke, was the possible leak of information about NATO's bombing plans. "He may have seen the bombing list and realized that it was light," Holbrooke said. Finally, in Holbrooke's opinion, Milosevic may have concluded that he had no chance of reaching an acceptable agreement and would just have to risk the bombing, which he believed he could survive, and wait for something better to turn up.[80]

Holbrooke's final point is key. Milosevic's rejection of Rambouillet was not the irrational act of an isolated and paranoid individual. Rather, it was part of a carefully considered strategy, one that was based on a realistic estimation of Serb military capabilities vis-à-vis the KLA, a brutal plan of action in Kosovo itself, and a close evaluation of likely alliance behavior in the event of war that, at least in the beginning, was not far from the mark.

Milosevic thought that he could outlast NATO in a duel of wills. In March, he told German Foreign Minister Joschka Fischer, "I can stand death—lots of it—but you can't."[81] Milosevic had years of familiarity with international waffling over Yugoslavia. He was well aware of the divisions within the international coalition—being replayed in the media even as NATO bombers were warming their engines. If he simply hunkered down and waited, Milosevic almost certainly expected that the alliance unity would crack and he would be presented with a new offer—as indeed he was, although in a different context than Milosevic anticipated. In an interview with a Western news agency during the war, Milosevic provided a revealing insight into the way his evaluation of Western leaders shaped his own thinking. "Your leaders are not strategic thinkers," he noted. "Short-term quick fixes, yes. They said let's bomb Yugoslavia and then figure out what to do next. Some said Milosevic would give up Kosovo after a few days of aggression from the air." But NATO "miscalculated."[82]

One factor that was not crucial in Milosevic's rejection of Rambouillet was the existence of so-called Annex B. This document, which would have provided NATO personnel, vehicles, and aircraft with unimpeded access to all FRY territory, is sometimes cited as being tantamount to a NATO occupation and therefore a reason for Belgrade's rejection of the accord. Yet the annex was actually a Status of Forces Agreement (SOFA), which U.S. and NATO forces generally prefer to have in areas where they operate, largely for legal reasons. A similar, though less sweeping SOFA was part of the Dayton package. Annex B was included in Rambouillet because at the time NATO was still considering the possibility, which it later abandoned, of supplying its peacekeeping forces in Kosovo from Western Europe across FRY territory. At the time of Rambouillet, Serb negotiators did not raise Annex B as an obstacle to signing; they had much more fundamental objections to the presence of NATO troops in Kosovo at all, let alone to their supply across Serbia proper. In June 1999, NATO decided not to include a SOFA in the military-technical agreement it negotiated with Serb forces at the end of the war. Ironically, by 2000, Serb authorities were actually insisting that NATO conclude a SOFA with them.

Mutual Miscalculation

NATO went to war with Serbia convinced that a relatively short bombing campaign would be sufficient to bring Milosevic back to the negotiating table. After extensive interviews in Washington, allied capitals, and at NATO headquarters, the authors of a comprehensive study of the war in Kosovo concluded, "There was widespread consensus that Milosevic would give in after just a few days of bombing." As Secretary Albright said on national television the night the bombing started, "I don't see this as a long-term operation." Many believed that Milosevic knew he could not win a war against the world's most powerful military alliance and that he needed a short NATO bombing campaign in order to show the Serbian public that he had no alternative to agreeing to the alliance's terms.[83]

One reason for this miscalculation on how Milosevic would react to the bombing was a fundamental misreading of what had happened in Bosnia in 1995. After Dayton, it became an article of faith among many U.S. officials that NATO bombing had driven the Serbs to the negotiating table. Milosevic, however, did not accept Dayton because of NATO bombing. Rather, he embraced the U.S. diplomatic process to save Bosnian Serbs from the victorious Croatian-Moslem ground offensive. Two elements were important: the prospect of military defeat on the ground and a U.S. diplomatic plan that offered the Serbs much of what they could, by then, realistically hope to achieve in Bosnia. In Kosovo, neither of these elements was present. President Clinton publicly ruled out the use of ground troops on the first day of the war, and the diplomatic plan on offer—involving as it did the de facto loss of Kosovo—had little attraction for Milosevic.

With the use of ground troops ruled out, the threat of bombing was the only military tool left at the alliance's disposal. Over the last year of the Kosovo crisis, though, Milosevic developed a sangfroid on bombing that sometimes astonished his Western interlocutors, but probably came naturally to someone like Milosevic who for years had watched the international community tie itself in knots over air strikes in Bosnia that seldom rose to the level of nuisance raids. According to Vuk Draskovic, who served as deputy prime minister during the crisis, "Milosevic absolutely did not expect to be bombed by NATO, or if it did bomb, it would only be for two or three days, just to save face and say it had done something."[84]

Milosevic's refusal to be intimidated by bombing precipitated an extraordinary scene during the negotiations that led up to the October 1998 Holbrooke agreement. During a ceremonial dinner in the presence of the entire U.S. and Serbian teams, Holbrooke impressed on Milosevic that if he did not agree to the U.S. proposal, he faced the prospect of massive bombing, and that the authority to launch NATO's warplanes had already been passed to alliance commander Clark. Milosevic replied that he fully understood alliance plans for bombing Serbia were all set. Then, Milosevic leaned back, took a long pull on his after-dinner cigarillo, and said, "Yes, Dick, I understand, but I'm sure that the bombing will be very polite." When General Short strongly interjected that there was no such thing as "polite bombing," Milosevic replied with a sneer, "Yes, I understand, but I'm sure the Americans will bomb with great politeness."[85]

Despite its seeming "what-me-worry" nature, Milosevic's evaluation of the alliance's posture on bombing in March 1999 was not far from the mark. NATO went into the war with a relatively limited air attack plan: a one-volume "Master Target File" containing only 169 approved targets across the entire country. (It ended with more than 976 targets, filling six volumes.)[86] NATO began the bombing campaign against Serbia with 350 planes, less than it had deployed in October the previous year and only about 10 percent of the air force armada assembled for the 1991 war against Iraq. General Short, the leader of the alliance air campaign, said that as planning for the operation proceeded, he was continually instructed, "You're only going to be allowed to bomb two, maybe three nights. That's all Washington can stand, and that's all some members of the alliance can stand."[87] In his memoirs NATO commander Clark describes some members of the alliance as interested in a pause in the bombing almost as soon as it began.[88]

Belgrade also apparently had inside information about alliance military planning, as Holbrooke's remarks suggest. During the Kosovo war, U.S. officials told me they believed Milosevic may have been aware of NATO's bombing plans, attributing the leaks at the time to "traditional friends of Belgrade" in the alliance. A year later, Pentagon spokesman Kenneth Bacon confirmed that security leaks at the beginning of the Kosovo air war enabled the Serbian military to gain key information about NATO missions and targets. Bacon said NATO had concluded that the Serbs somehow gained access to portions of the air tasking order, NATO's blueprint for its bombing missions, probably when parts of the order were sent by fax from NATO headquarters in Brussels back to home capitals.[89] General Clark writes that in October 1998 a French officer at NATO headquarters gave key portions of the air operations plan to the Serbs.[90]

Political disarray was also evident at the start of the campaign. NATO launched its conflict with Serbia without any agreed-on war aims. When after a few days it became clear that Milosevic was not going to back down quickly, there was great confusion within the alliance. In his address to the American public announcing the bombing, President Clinton stated three objectives: "To demonstrate NATO's seriousness of purpose, . . . to deter an even bloodier offensive against innocent civilians in Kosovo, and if necessary, to seriously damage the Serb military's capacity to harm the people of Kosovo." Within a week, as Milosevic let loose a massive campaign of ethnic cleansing, it was obvious that NATO was failing in all of these areas.

Support for the bombing campaign was soft in the leadership and publics of many NATO nations. In the second week of the war, U.S. Secretary of Defense Cohen said that one of the air campaign's goals was to "make him [Milosevic] pay a serious substantial price" for the ethnic cleansing then unfolding in Kosovo—language similar to what the United States had used in justifying its raids on Iraq. Not until early April, after intense internal negotiation, did the alliance agree on five conditions for ending the bombing campaign. These conditions—all of which NATO achieved at the end of the war—provided a fixed point around which members of the alliance could rally and proved critical to maintaining alliance cohesion as the war progressed.

"Operation Horseshoe"

The most significant element of Milosevic's strategic response to NATO was in Kosovo itself, where his plans were brutally straightforward. As soon as the OSCE and diplomatic observer missions were withdrawn from Kosovo, several days before the bombing began, Serb forces launched a massive campaign of ethnic cleansing, aimed not only at shifting the demographic balance in Belgrade's favor but also—by driving hundreds of thousands of desperate Albanians over the border into the fragile neighboring states of Macedonia and Albania—at threatening the Western allies with the destabilization of the entire Balkan peninsula. Milosevic's effort came uncomfortably close to success, yet what he failed to understand was how public revulsion to his war against Kosovo Albanian civilians would reinforce NATO solidarity and determination to see the war through to a favorable conclusion.

Before the bombing began, Austrian intelligence officials presented their U.S. counterparts with a chilling document. Called "Operation Horseshoe," it was described by U.S. officials as a comprehensive and detailed operational military plan for the cleansing of Kosovo that laid out the movement of Serb units on a day-to-day basis. Its final objective was apparently to undo centuries of history and reclaim possession of Kosovo for

Serbs, as can be seen from Western media reports that "Operation Horse-shoe" drew on Vaso Cubrilovic's 1937 pamphlet advocating the mass expulsion of Albanians from Kosovo.[91]

Milosevic himself gave NATO officials indirect warning of his intentions in Kosovo. When Clark and Naumann met Milosevic after the Racak massacre, the Serb leader made a remark that Naumann, in retrospect, considered an indication that Milosevic had already decided to expel Albanians from Kosovo if war broke out. In the course of what Naumann described as a "very emotional" discussion about Kosovo's role as the cradle of Serb culture, Milosevic said "he was fully aware that the greater fertility of the Albanians had changed the demographic balance over time and that for that reason he had to find a solution that the Albanians could not outnumber the Serbs once again."[92]

Only a few weeks after the onset of the NATO bombing campaign, Milosevic's plans in Kosovo seemed to be fully on track. A State Department report estimated that over seven hundred thousand Kosovo Albanians had fled Kosovo into camps in neighboring Albania or Macedonia. Within Kosovo, an additional six hundred thousand Albanians had been forced out of their homes, where they struggled to survive in isolated forests and mountain valleys.[93] Milosevic seemed to be well on his way to accomplishing what generations of Serb ethnic engineers had only dreamed of: turning Kosovo into an Albanian-free zone.

A comprehensive study by the respected ICG, based on interviews with thousands of Kosovo citizens in the year after the war, provides a chilling picture of what the report calls "a campaign conducted against the Kosovar population as a whole, intended to terrorize them into submission and expel them from the province." The report found that several days before the NATO bombing began, Serb military and police forces aided by paramilitary groups launched attacks in a number of Kosovo locations—which involved the shelling of towns and villages—followed by the forced eviction of their Albanian inhabitants. After the bombing started on 24 March, attacks by Serb forces "reached a new level of intensity." Thousands of witnesses from many parts of Kosovo reported homes shelled, livestock killed, and property burned or stolen. "The standard format for these attacks involved killings, beatings, sexual assaults, and other forms of physical and mental abuse." In some areas, the Serbs initiated their campaign of violence, intimidation, and harassment by focusing in on local political, intellectual, and religious leaders. In other areas, they targeted the entire population at once. Serb cleansing occurred in rural areas as well as cities. Serb forces began violently expelling Albanians from the elite Dragodan neighborhood in Pristina soon after the war began. In Pristina and other cities, Serbs herded large numbers of civilians to the railroad station and onto cattle cars for the trip to Macedonia or Albania.[94] By the end, approximately twelve thousand people had died in the war that Milosevic launched against the civilian population of Kosovo, although a definite number will never be determined in part because of Serb efforts to cover up the results of their atrocities—for example, by trucking some bodies into Serbia for secret disposal—where they were discovered after Milosevic's fall—and by reportedly incinerating bodies of their victims in furnaces in the metallurgical complex at Mitrovica in northern Kosovo.[95]

The Tide Shifts

After about a month in which the world was transfixed by the horror of the barbarous campaign unleashed by Milosevic and gripped by frustration at its inability to stop it—in part because of restrictions imposed by the United States and some other NATO members on NATO military activity due to the concern over casualties—the tide of political and military conflict began to shift against Milosevic. Former Russian Prime Minister Chernomyrdin, appointed by Yeltsin as a special envoy to Milosevic, described a change that came over Milosevic as the war progressed. In the beginning, according to Yeltsin's account, Chernomyrdin found Milosevic defiant. He acknowledged that he could not win but also asserted that he could not lose either. At times, notes Yeltsin, Milosevic even asked Chernomyrdin to handle the negotiations in such a way that NATO would start ground operations against him even sooner. Later, however, Milosevic's tone changed and "he asked to stop the war."[96]

Moreover, as the war progressed, there were signs that Milosevic was feeling the heat. Citing "deep, deep" intelligence sources, a senior NATO official said the Yugoslav leader had been losing his temper in his office, screaming at aides, and throwing military documents into the air in despair.[97] In mid-May, Milosevic took what was for him the practically unprecedented step of publicly acknowledging Serb casualties in a conflict and expressing gratitude for the sacrifice of those who fell. Awarding promotions to police officers on the eve of Security Day, Milosevic said, "During this struggle, many members of police and security forces died courageously. Their sacrifice is a shining example of bravery and devotion to one's people and fatherland."[98]

The unexpected firmness in alliance support for the bombing was undoubtedly an unpleasant surprise to Milosevic. In addition, by the second week of April, the alliance had coalesced around a set of objectives for the war that were tougher on Milosevic than the Rambouillet accord he had rejected. The conditions the alliance imposed as a price for ending the bombing—the departure of all Serb forces from Kosovo, the return of all Albanian refugees, and the introduction of a peacekeeping force under NATO auspices—meant the loss of Kosovo, which Milosevic fully understood would also threaten his hold on power in Serbia. The leaders of the alliance held fast to these objectives, despite considerable pressure at times to relax them. In the end, this firmness ensured Milosevic's defeat.

The growing intensity of the NATO air campaign contributed to Milosevic's discomfiture as well. The number of aircraft involved and number of sorties flown steadily increased as the war continued, as did the effectiveness of the NATO attacks against both tactical and strategic targets. By 20 May, NATO had destroyed about one hundred Serb aircraft and about 75 percent of its fixed SAM sites. NATO attacks against Serb infrastructure were growing in scope, damaging the Serb ability to support the war and undermining civilian morale. Belgrade downed only two NATO aircraft during the entire war, which sapped Serb morale and prevented the backlash of concern over allied casualties on which Milosevic had counted to undermine the coalition against him.[99]

The KLA strengthened considerably in the war's second month. At the end of May, the United States estimated that the KLA had fifteen to seventeen thousand troops in Kosovo and five thousand in Albania, a tripling of KLA might since the beginning of the war. KLA forces were also better equipped, thanks in part to the flow of funds from the Albanian diaspora. As the KLA grew stronger, Serb forces in Kosovo had to concentrate to take them on, which in turn, opened them up to more effective attacks by NATO warplanes. Haradinaj later wrote that "we benefited from the air raids while the NATO pilots benefited from our firing line, which forced the Serb forces to be exposed.[100]

Toward the end of April Milosevic began a "peace offensive"—releasing three U.S. soldiers captured by Serb commandos in Macedonia, reducing the flow of refugees into neighboring states by closing Kosovo's borders, and ordering refugees within Kosovo to go home—sometimes at rifle point, and announced that Serb forces in Kosovo—which had supposedly completed operations against the KLA insurgents—would begin a partial withdrawal. Milosevic also began to signal his conditions for ending the war, including a reduction of Serb forces in Kosovo, provided NATO drew down its forces in neighboring Macedonia and Albania, and the return of FRY citizen refugees—a condition that seemed intended to ensure that most refugees could not, in fact, return since many had been deprived of their identity documents by Serb forces.[101]

Another element in Milosevic's peace offensive was a bizarre incident in which an obviously uncomfortable Rugova was shown on television meeting in Belgrade with Milosevic. Although there was no sound accompanying the video images, Rugova was said to have called for a negotiated solution in Kosovo as well as for Albanian refugees to return to their homes, "to live together and cooperate."

Milosevic staged the incident with Rugova in order to divide and demoralize the Albanians while also confusing the international community about the proper avenue to peace in Kosovo. Anyone who knew Rugova, however, understood immediately that only severe pressure could have induced him to meet Milosevic under those circumstances. A few weeks later, a German reporter who had remained hidden in Pristina during the early phases of the war, described how she had been in Rugova's house when Serb police entered and took Rugova away by force.

After the war, Rugova said that he had no choice but to go to Belgrade. He labeled himself a "hostage," and said his children had been threatened and only survived through what he called "discipline." Rugova contended that Milosevic had pressed him strongly, but had "nothing to offer" except to suggest that the two could make a deal on Kosovo. Rugova rejected Milosevic's proposition, asking how there could be any agreement when Kosovo had been turned into a "national park," by which Rugova apparently meant empty land.[102]

The War Ends

On 2 June, Chernomyrdin and Finnish President Martti Ahtisari, representing the international coalition fighting the war against Serbia, presented Milosevic with an ultimatum. Ahtisaari read to Milosevic a ten-point document, the product of a month's difficult negotiations between NATO and Russia, which had only been completed that same morning, in talks at the German Foreign Ministry's mountaintop retreat of Petersburg, overlooking Bonn.

Milosevic, who according to Ahtisari behaved "throughout the meeting politely and in a dignified manner," listened carefully and then asked Chernomyrdin to speak. A few days earlier, Chernomyrdin had told Milosevic that if he did not accept the coalition's terms he would face not only intensified bombing but also the threat of a NATO ground invasion and that, in those circumstances, Russia could do nothing to help him. Now, according to Ahtisari, "Chernomyrdin stood loyally with me." After reading a copy of the paper Ahtisari had brought, Milosevic asked what was necessary to end the bombing, to which Ahtisari replied that he would have to accept the conditions in the paper and begin to withdraw his forces from Kosovo. After seeking some additional clarification—for example, asking why the deal was considered under Article VII of the UN Charter, which allowed the use of force to ensure compliance, Milosevic asked if Ahtisari and Chernomyrdin were authorized to negotiate. "Can anything in this proposal be changed?" he inquired. Ahtisari replied in a serious tone, "This is the best offer that you will get" but also added that the essence of the proposal was that Kosovo remained a part of the FRY although under limited sovereignty.

Ahtisari's and Chernomyrdin's first meeting with Milosevic ended inconclusively. Ahtisari spent the night in Belgrade's official guest villa, watching the red tracks of antiaircraft fire seeking out NATO aircraft prowling overhead. The next morning, after first treating Ahtisari to "his version of Kosovo," Milosevic said, "I accept the proposal as a peaceful proposal." Ahtisari replied, "This is the first step toward peace," and Milosevic lit up a cigarette. (During the previous day, he had smoked more than half a pack, according to one of Ahtisari's aides.)[103]

In a speech announcing the end of the war, Milosevic told the Serbian people, "We did not give up Kosovo." Although Milosevic was obviously trying to conceal the extent of his setback, in fact the deal he accepted to end the war was an improvement in some respects from the deal he rejected at Rambouillet. Like Rambouillet, the June 1999 agreement provided for an interim administration in which Kosovo was described as having substantial autonomy within the FRY. But the mechanism for reviewing Kosovo's final status after three years, including the referendum that was the key element in gaining Albanian acceptance to Rambouillet, was gone. Interim administration of Kosovo is entrusted to the UN, which gave nations sympathetic to Milosevic a voice in running Kosovo. More important, once the deal was codified in a UN Security Council resolution, any change in Kosovo's status would have to be approved by the Security Council, where Serbia's friends could block Kosovo's independence. The day after Ahtisaari read his ultimatum, Chernomyrdin apparently returned to see Milosevic alone, helping persuade Milosevic to agree by pointing out that he could seek to "supplement" parts of the deal when it came before the UN Security Council.[104]

Despite Milosevic's efforts to sugarcoat the deal, however, in practice it meant Serbia's loss of Kosovo, at least for the time being. Milosevic was forced to accept the entry into Kosovo of a NATO-led international security force, which had been his primary objection to Rambouillet. And unlike Rambouillet, the agreement required the prompt withdrawal of all Serb military and police forces with only a small number (hundreds not thousands) allowed to return at a future time of NATO's choosing. Also unlike Rambouillet, the agreement transferred to the UN all governmental authority in Kosovo, which although nominally still under Serb sovereignty, in fact became an international protectorate. All political arrangements in Kosovo, which Rambouillet spelled out in considerable detail including a guaranteed role for the Serb community in Kosovo, were left for the UN to decide in the future. Kosovo Serbs showed their understanding of the agreement's consequences by voting with their feet. Within a few weeks, half of the prewar Serb community had fled, hurried on their way by revenge attacks from the hundreds of thousands of Albanian refugees who came flooding joyously back into the province as soon as Serb forces left.

Behind closed doors, Milosevic—at least initially—did not try to hide that the deal had been forced on Serbia. "A few things are not logical, but the main thing is, we have no choice," Milosevic told the Serb Assembly. "To reject the document means the destruction of our state and nation." Milosevic was seconded by his wife. "This is not a surrender of the state but of a wrong policy," she said, to the surprise of some participants who had viewed her as more hawkish than her husband.[105]

But the decision to end the war did not come easy to Milosevic. Ahtisari reports that Milosevic twice tried to get him to brief the Assembly about the deal NATO was offering, which Ahtisari refused to do. Draskovic said that when Milosevic brought the deal to the Assembly "he seemed very bad, crushed." Despite efforts to present himself as "still strong," Draskovic said it was obvious that "Milosevic was very afraid of the possible continuation of the war if the Assembly rejected the plan."[106]

According to accounts later provided by Serbian insiders to Western correspondents, Milosevic had first himself to be persuaded by close aides that if he did not accept this deal, a worse one would follow. Milosevic then had to overcome opposition in the military. Ahtisari said the military leaders were unable to hide their "disappointment and shock" when Milosevic accepted the deal.

Milosevic accepted the alliance offer because the strategy he had adopted at the beginning of the war was not working, and he realized that he faced significantly higher military and political costs if he continued the war. Despite his boast to General Clark before the war that "Kosovo is more important than my head,"[107] Milosevic decided to try to cut his losses and go for the best deal he could get, confident that if he did not agree to the alliance terms, he would face more military and political pressure, thereby causing him not only to lose Kosovo but also quite possibly his hold on power in Serbia proper.

The ability of the NATO alliance to maintain its solidarity in support of the bombing was certainly a critical factor in his decision to seek an end to the war. The leaders of the nineteen NATO nations, despite their diverse range of interests and views about the war's objectives and how to fight it, all eventually agreed that the war simply had to be won. Aware that failure against Milosevic could cause the end of NATO, all members recognized that their interest in continuing the alliance was greater than any differences they had over a tin-pot Balkan dictator. The need to maintain alliance solidarity thus cut two ways in the conflict. On the one hand, it restricted the range of available military options. NATO military officers often chafed at the various political restrictions placed on their actions, which from a strictly military point of view undoubtedly complicated the conduct of the war. On the other hand, recognition of the stake that the alliance had in prevailing also meant that no nation was inclined to push tactical differences to the point where they could threaten NATO's ability to continue the war.

Milosevic's remarks both to the assembly and after his fall from power make it clear that the prospect of a significant escalation in NATO bombing was a major element in his decision to accept the international offer. When he carried the international community's final position to Belgrade on 2 June, Ahtisaari explained to Milosevic that if he refused the deal, NATO was prepared to attack a much broader range of targets—including the remaining bridges across the Danube, the power and heating systems, and the telephone network. With summer and good flying weather ahead, Milosevic was unwilling to see Serbia's economic, transportation, and communications infrastructure bombed into rubble over the coming months.

Another factor in Milosevic's decision to seek an end to the conflict was his awareness that by early June, NATO was moving toward a decision on invading Kosovo. Chernomyrdin told Milosevic during a visit to Belgrade on 27 May about NATO's likely ground attack plans, and one State Department official directly involved in Kosovo said that Milosevic "gave in because he understood that the United States and Wes Clark were prepared to destroy him if he continued the war."

On the first day of the air war, President Clinton promised in a television address from the Oval Office, "I do not intend to put our troops in Kosovo to fight a war." But on 18 May, the president took advantage of a rose garden photo opportunity to say pointedly that "all options are on the table." Shortly thereafter, NATO commander Clark was back in Washington for well-publicized consultations with the joint chiefs of staff on beefing up the U.S. military presence around Kosovo. Later, it became known that Clark— who chafed at the political constraints on allied military operations and was also skeptical that bombing alone would bring Milosevic to the table— had come with a plan to invade Kosovo from Albania using a total of 175,000 troops including up to 120,000 Americans.[108]

The KLA's growing strength was also a factor in Milosevic's decision. He realized that NATO's increasing close cooperation with the KLA meant that over time, the Albanians, if not able on their own to defeat the Serbs, would certainly be able to inflict more Serb casualties. In late April, the Central Intelligence Agency (CIA) and U.S. special forces in Albania began meeting with the KLA in Tirana and at a secret operations center in the border town of Kukes, to exchange operational intelligence information and discuss how to turn the KLA into a light infantry force that would be "at the enemy's rear blowing up bridges," said one U.S. official involved in the planning. Toward the end of the conflict, NATO aircraft reportedly inflicted heavy losses on Serb forces besieging KLA fighters on a mountaintop near the Albanian border.

As time progressed, and the bombing became more intense and casualties increased in Kosovo, the war's unpopularity grew in Serbia. In explaining what he called NATO's miscalculation in starting the war, Milosevic said that NATO failed to understand that "we are willing to die to defend our rights as an independent sovereign nation."[109] In fact, it was Milosevic, isolated in his Dedinje villa—at least until NATO destroyed it—and surrounded by his wife and her cronies, who miscalculated. Serbs, it was becoming clear, were no more eager to sacrifice their lives for Milosevic's schemes in Kosovo than they had earlier been in Croatia or Bosnia.

Despite the patriotic rush many Serbs experienced at the beginning of the conflict, the war in Kosovo was not popular and Milosevic knew it would become even more of a political burden as casualties increased. Indeed, Milosevic had almost as great a political problem with casualties as did the United States. Superior Serb firepower drove the KLA out of the villages, but neither the Serb military nor the police showed a strong desire to follow them into the woods or hills where ambush and casualties would be more likely. One U.S. official with much diplomatic and military experience described Kosovo as a "virtual war" on both sides. He noted that the conscripts and reservists who made up the regular Serb forces were not eager to be in Kosovo, and the only Serbs who really showed any enthusiasm for fighting the Albanians were the thuggish paramilitaries.

Toward the end of May, hundreds of Serb reservists were reported to have left Kosovo, fought their way through military checkpoints, and returned to their homes in the southern Serb towns of Krusevac and Aleksandrovac after hearing radio reports that police had violently dispersed demonstrations by women protesting the arrival of coffins containing the bodies of several local soldiers. Weariness with the war was also evident in Belgrade. Attendance at the daily rock concerts, begun shortly after the war started as a sign of solidarity, dwindled from ten thousand to a few hundred. Heavily promoted nighttime rallies on Belgrade's bridges, sponsored by Mira Markovic's JUL party, came to a halt.

Some international officials have speculated that Milosevic's indictment as a war criminal—announced on 27 May only days before Ahtisaari and Chernomyrdin flew to Belgrade—helped induce Milosevic to accept the alliance's June ultimatum. Others have taken the opposite view: that the indictment may have stiffened Milosevic's resolve. In announcing the indictment, Chief Prosecutor Arbour said it raised "serious questions about [Milosevic's] suitability to be guarantors of any deal."[110] Chernomyrdin was reportedly unhappy about the effect of the indictment on negotiations with Milosevic and suspicious about its timing.[111] U.S. State Department officials apparently tried to persuade the tribunal to delay the indictment out of concern that it could complicate the negotiations to end the war. In his memoirs, General Clark writes that "some in the Pentagon and the White House" were unhappy about Milosevic's indictment but that he believes it hardened European resolve to see the conflict through to a successful conclusion.[112]

Milosevic, for his part, must have seen the indictment as a sign of growing international determination not just to defeat Serbia but to remove him from the scene. This could have increased his desire to cut a deal quickly in hopes of forestalling something worse and then finding some way to sidestep the indictment in the future—not an unreasonable prospect looking at the way the international community ignored the indictment in the months after Milosevic fell from power. Alternatively, Milosevic could have viewed the indictment as one of those factors that argued for resistance until the bitter end. Milosevic never referred to the indictment in connection with ending the war, and it clearly did not stop him from agreeing to the alliance's terms.

Russia's Ambiguous Role

Russia also played an important, although somewhat ambiguous, role in persuading Milosevic to accept international terms. When Chernomyrdin told Milosevic that NATO would use ground forces if the air campaign failed and that Russia would not stand in NATO's way of pursuing the war to victory, the message, according to some accounts, was crucial. "We knew that when the Russians came in with this plan that was it," said one official close to Milosevic. "We knew that the carpet bombing of Belgrade would start the next day after we refused, so what was the choice?"[113]

But Russia's role in the early stages of the war was much less supportive of the alliance. At the beginning of the war, Yeltsin rejected Clinton's appeal that Russia back the bombing, arguing instead that it was possible to find a way to deal with Serbia without war.[114] Some officials also believe that the Russian military helped stiffen Belgrade's resolve to stand up to NATO bombing threats by pointing out how ineffective Soviet air power had been against the mujaheidin insurgents in Afghanistan. A month into the conflict, however, Yeltsin changed tack. During NATO's fiftieth anniversary celebrations in April 1999, Yeltsin telephoned Clinton and suggested that Chernomyrdin take on a mediating role, apparently out of concern over the damage that the conflict might cause to Russia's relationship with the United States.

Milosevic also sought to use the Russian involvement to bolster his own position. He proposed that Serbia become a member of the union then being worked out between Russia and Belarus.[115] Not until the end of May, when Yeltsin personally ordered his negotiator to find a solution, did the Russians agree to the key point that there could be no halt to the bombing until Milosevic agreed to pull all his forces out of Kosovo.

But Moscow also played a less benign role in the Kosovo endgame. On June 12, while Russian and U.S. officials were still negotiating terms of Moscow's participation in the Kosovo peacekeeping force, called KFOR, and despite promises that Russian troops would not move until agreement was reached on this question, Russian peacekeeping troops from Bosnia unexpectedly entered Kosovo. With the clear connivance of Belgrade, the Russians drove hell-for-leather to the Pristina airport, arriving before KFOR troops could get there from nearby Macedonia.

Russian negotiators told their American counterparts that they intended to secure access to the Pristina airport and General Ivashov, the lead Russian military representative, said straightforwardly that, "within six hours of your [NATO] deployment, we are going to the north and take the sector we want."[116] United States intelligence warned that paratroopers in Russia appeared to be making preparations for boarding transport planes at the same time that Russian government officials sought permission for aircraft to fly from Russia across Eastern Europe to the former Yugoslavia. State Department officials blocked this effort to reinforce by air the Russian contingent at the Pristina airport by prevailing on intervening countries to deny overflight privileges to the Russian aircraft.

There remains considerable uncertainty about what the Russians were about. Even after Milosevic agreed to the Alliance terms for ending the bombing, Moscow continued to contest NATO's role in Kosovo. Some State Department and Pentagon officials speculated to me that the Russian move was part of a deal Moscow cut with Milosevic and the Serb military to unilaterally carve out a Russian zone in Kosovo, behind which the Serbs could have maintained their own rump administration—as indeed Belgrade still did two years after the end of the war in the divided Kosovo city of Mitrovica and the northern part of Kosovo bordering on Serbia proper. According to this theory, the Russian move would have allowed Milosevic to salvage something from the wreckage of his failed Kosovo policy and also allowed Moscow to create, in effect, its own zone of control in the Balkans.

Ahtisari, citing information "from various sources," has a similar view. He writes that the Russian move to the Pristina airport was part of a much bigger plan than appeared at first glance. "There are reasons to suppose," he says, that the Russian and Serbian militaries had reached agreement that Russian forces would take control of Pristina and the northern part of Kosovo, in order to make it possible, if Kosovo became independent in two or three years, for Belgrade to retain a large part of the province, which it could settle exclusively with Serbs. Ahtisari believes this scheme could explain "the surprising ease" with which Milosevic accepted the plan he offered on June 2, as well as the delays that Milosevic and the Serb military threw up in subsequent days during the negotiations in Macedonia over a Military-Technical Agreement governing the terms of KFOR's entry into Kosovo.[117]

In his last volume of memoirs, Yeltsin writes that he was asked on

4 June to authorize in writing the dispatch of Russian paratroopers to Pristina—that is, almost a week before they actually appeared. Yeltsin notes that he approved the plan to show that Russia had won a "moral victory in the face of the enormous NATO military."[118]

In Yeltsin's account, the Russian move is portrayed as a symbolic gesture of political defiance to the West. Yet the small contingent of Russian forces that arrived in Pristina—so isolated that they had to be fed by surrounding NATO troops—was clearly intended to be the precursor to a larger force flown in from Russia.

Strobe Talbott, deputy secretary of state during the war, asserted that the theory that Milosevic cut a deal with the Russians does not "hang together." What happened, according to Talbott, was that the Russian military "jumped the gun, I think quite deliberately, in order to establish as it were a reality or new facts on the ground, so that it would be in a stronger position to bargain for what it wanted, which was a Russian sector." After Milosevic had accepted the deal offered him by Ahtisaari and Chernomyrdin, Talbott was in Moscow negotiating with Russian Foreign Minister Ivanov and National Security Adviser Putin—who a few months later unexpectedly took over from Yeltsin as president—on Russia's role in the NATO-led Kosovo Force (KFOR) that would occupy the province after the Serbs left. Talbott described how his talks with Ivanov and Putin "came to a fairly abrupt halt" after it became clear that Russian forces were moving through Pristina toward the airport, contrary to assurances that Ivanov and Putin had given him that the movement of Russian forces out of Bosnia was simply the predeployment of forces for their peacekeeping mission and that they would not enter Kosovo before agreement was reached on the terms of their participation in KFOR.[119]

The Russian move set off a major row within the Alliance. In his memoirs, NATO Commander General Wes Clark says that as soon as it became clear that the Russians were moving toward Pristina, and after receiving authorization from NATO Secretary General Javier Solana and from his U.S. military superiors in Washington, Clark ordered British General Sir Michael Jackson, commander of the NATO peacekeeping force then preparing to move into Kosovo, to seize the airport before the Russians arrived. Jackson had a plan to take the airport using troops to be airlifted by helicopter, but he also pointed out the danger that a NATO force could be cut off and get into a confrontation with the Serbs who still controlled the airport and with the Russians after they arrived. With Russian Foreign Minister Ivanov telling Secretary of State Albright that the Russians would not enter Kosovo and that the move of the Russian military was "a mistake"—an assertion that General Clark characterized to me as "a lie"—Washington decided not to fly in NATO troops. That evening the Russian force that had left Bosnia in the morning entered Pristina on their way to the airport and was received jubilantly as heroes by the Serb population of the Kosovo capital.

British forces arrived at the airport the next day but were denied entrance by the Russians. With Moscow still seeking overflight permission for its military aircraft from countries on the way to Kosovo, Clark—with Washington's backing—ordered that the runways be blocked, using U.S. Apache helicopters from Albania or British armored vehicles on the scene. General Jackson refused Clark's order and—in a private conversation that quickly leaked to the media—told Clark, his nominal superior, "Sir, I'm not starting World War III for you." With London supporting Jackson and Washington unable or unwilling to overrule, British troops moved to cut the roads leading to the airfield, leaving the small Russian contingent isolated.[120] Whether blocking the runways would have provoked an armed response from the heavily outnumbered Russian force is debatable but, in the event, isolating the Russians—together with continued U.S. diplomatic pressure to deny Moscow's overflight requests—proved sufficient to prevent the Russians from reinforcing their contingent and from carrying out whatever plans they may have made with the Serbs in Kosovo.

As NATO forces rolled across Kosovo—followed shortly thereafter by Serbs fleeing Albanian revenge—it appeared that Milosevic had not only lost his gamble to hold onto Kosovo but that he might also lose his hold on power in Belgrade. But Milosevic brushed aside initial efforts by the divided opposition to capitalize on the loss of Kosovo to overturn him. In retrospect, however, the loss of Kosovo, together with the sense of isolation and humiliation that spread through Serbia after its unsuccessful war against a coalition of all the major Western powers, provided the essential political and psychological backdrop for the successful efforts of the Democratic Opposition of Serbia (DOS) to overturn Milosevic in October 2000.

ELEVEN

War Criminal

On 27 May 1999, the Hague tribunal announced that Milosevic and four other senior Serb civilian and military officials had been indicted as war criminals. Milosevic—on the basis of his position as president of the FRY—was accused of planning, preparing, and executing a campaign that resulted in the expulsion—accompanied by killings, abuse, and theft—of over 740,000 Kosovo Albanians. Milosevic and the others were also accused of complicity in the murder of over 340 named individuals killed by the Serbs in the spring of 1999.[1]

Milosevic was overdue for indictment as a war criminal. The tribunal had long been investigating him in connection with the wars in Croatia and Bosnia, but allegedly had difficulty in establishing a chain of command authority that would run from Milosevic to Serb forces in Croatia or Bosnia. According to Deputy Prosecutor Graham Blewitt, "Everybody knew Milosevic had the real power over the Bosnian Serbs but his de jure power was very difficult to establish."[2]

The crisis in Kosovo, by contrast, allowed the tribunal to focus on Milosevic's responsibility for actions occurring on territory legally under his control and committed by military and police forces clearly subordinate to him. The tribunal's investigation into possible crimes in Kosovo began in 1998, but it did not really shift into high gear until after the January 1999 Racak killings. Toward the end of March, as NATO began bombing Serbia, Arbour told the Tribunal's team that the time had come to indict Milosevic—and fast.[3]

The announcement of the indictment only days before Milosevic accepted international terms for ending the Kosovo conflict led to considerable speculation that its timing was politically motivated. Responding to such charges, Arbour said that "as soon as the tribunal had a substantial case that would hold up in court," the decision was made to issue the indictment.[4] Nevertheless, it is apparent that concerns about how Milosevic's criminal accountability might be handled in the endgame diplomatic negotiations around Kosovo played a role in the timing of the indictment.

Arbour visited Washington, London, Bonn, and other major capitals in the weeks before the indictment was issued. One reason for her trip was to seek information from governments bearing on the indictment. Arbour also, however, seems to have sought some kind of policy context for the tribunal's action against Milosevic. She described the message she got from governments during her visit to capitals as "totally ambiguous." Although Arbour made it clear that she would not base her actions as prosecutor on the desires of governments, she also came away convinced that the governments she consulted "did not have a clue" about what should be done with respect to indicting Milosevic.[5]

Senior tribunal officials acknowledged that one reason for the timing of the indictment was the worry that the diplomatic negotiations over ending the bombing could have included a deal allowing Milosevic to escape his responsibility for war crimes. Blewitt said that in the middle of the NATO air campaign, Arbour "had reason to fear that an amnesty was being prepared for Milosevic." The tribunal was "outraged" at this prospect and believed that issuing the indictment against Milosevic, for which there was a "water-tight case," would stop such arrangements.[6]

Arbour was somewhat more cautious about whether there had been any prospect of a deal to allow Milosevic to escape criminal responsibility. In one sense, she pointed out, there should have been little concern that someone would try to give Milosevic a "golden handshake." Only the UN Security Council, which had established the Hague tribunal, could make a legally binding deal allowing Milosevic or any other individual to evade responsibility before the court. But Arbour also worried that in the negotiations over ending the war, there "could have been some effort to work out a deal to allow him [Milosevic] to depart to some secure location beyond reach of the court." Arbour said she had "no specific information"; still, during the negotiations with Milosevic, there "was an element of risk" that one would be offered "as I was informed had happened in Bosnia."[7]

After the indictment had been approved by one of the tribunal's judges, public announcement was delayed for three days to give time to warn UN and other international personnel who might be endangered as a result. The tribunal also used the interval to inform key governments about the impending indictment, which came as Chernomyrdin, Talbott, and Ahtisaari were meeting at Stalin's former dacha near Moscow for the beginning of what proved to be the climactic round of negotiations over terms to be presented to Milosevic for ending the bombing.

According to Talbott, Chernomyrdin was "more than a little suspicious about the motivation" for the indictment and wondered whether its timing "wasn't someone trying to sabotage his diplomacy."[8] Tribunal officials said that some countries tried to use the tribunal's heads up about the impending indictment as an opportunity to negotiate its terms. Other countries, including the United States according to Blewitt, wanted to delay announcing the indictment for a time in order to allow the peace negotiations to be completed. But Arbour maintained that delay was impossible given the relatively large numbers of officials around the world who had been informed. By the third day after the indictment had been secretly issued, news organizations were on the verge of breaking the story and further delay would have been impossible.

There is also considerable controversy about the sources of the information that the tribunal used to indict Milosevic. The tribunal has its own investigative capability and, by early 1999, was well placed to bring an indictment against Milosevic, in Blewitt's view, although some holes remained. During the NATO bombing, "these gaps were filled in by evidence that we thought relevant and could be used in a court of law. At that stage, the indictment was issued."[9]

Blewitt was coy about the origin of the information used to fill the gaps in the tribunal's knowledge, but one source may have been documents captured by the KLA. According to Western press accounts, "hundreds of documents" found in Kosovo by the KLA and turned over to NATO may have provided evidence linking Operation Horseshoe "to Serb army generals and police commanders all the way up to President Slobodan Milosevic." A NATO intelligence officer told Western correspondents that the documents helped show that "it was organized from the top and the plan went like clockwork."[10]

U.S. officials claimed that the impulse for indicting Milosevic had come from Washington. According to U.S. officials and former intelligence analysts, early in 1999, as the fighting in Kosovo intensified and the international community began to prepare for the Rambouillet conference, the United States became more active in seeking to tie Milosevic to war crimes in Kosovo. The small war crimes intelligence review unit that had been established in the State Department's Bureau of Intelligence and Research in 1996 was given a boost: the number of its analysts and urgency of its task were both increased.

After the NATO bombing campaign began in March 1999, this pressure intensified. Intelligence analysts with a specialty in war crimes reviewed a number of satellite photos of Serb operations in Kosovo that had formerly only been seen by military intelligence analysts primarily interested in information relating to Serb military operations. When the war crimes analysts scrutinized these same photos, it was suddenly, "Bingo." They observed pictures of regular army units, militarized police of the Ministry of Interior, and paramilitaries traveling in convoy together in areas where ethnic cleansing of Albanians had occurred. These photos demonstrated that the paramilitaries, responsible for much of the dirty work against Albanian civilians, were operating jointly with military and police units—whose chain of command ran directly to Milosevic. This was precisely the kind of evidence needed to indict Milosevic on the basis of "imputed command responsibility" for either being responsible himself for ordering the ethnic cleansing in Kosovo or for failing to take measures to stop it when he had the power to do so.

Hague tribunal sources, however, deny that the United States provided the information on which the Milosevic indictment was based. They claim that the United States actually gave the court very little that was not openly available and that what Washington did supply consisted largely of videotapes of Milosevic speeches, which in any case, arrived too late to be of use. Arbour reportedly told a U.S. diplomat that the materials confirming the indictment, seen only by the judge, included none of the last-minute material provided by the United States. She said at the time that when the trial takes place and the evidence comes out, "History will know who had it and who gave it to us. I think some people will be put to shame for taking credit."[11]

Nevertheless, Arbour acknowledged that after the NATO bombing began in March 1999, the flow of intelligence information to the tribunal increased. Even then, however, problems persisted. Most of the information the tribunal received was part of the NATO public relations campaign against Milosevic. Blewitt complained that it often took the tribunal days or weeks to get satellite photos that CNN obtained almost as soon as the shutter clicked. Over time the flow of information improved, but the tribunal still tended to receive information only after its own investigations had turned up material pointing in one direction or another. The bottom line, according to Blewitt, was, "We thought we were being manipulated."[12]

Some have charged that one reason Milosevic was not indicted earlier was that the United States and other nations did not transmit intelligence information at their disposal about Milosevic's role, possibly in order to avoid compromising their ability to work with him to achieve a diplomatic settlement in Bosnia. U.S. officials denied this charge, and some noted the difficulty in sorting through and verifying the large amount of intelligence information that the United States had collected over the years in the Balkans, most of which was not specifically aimed at the subject of war crimes.

The tribunal has procedures that allow it to receive and protect classified information for use in its investigations, but senior tribunal officials expressed considerable frustration over the quality and timing of information that governments provided the tribunal. Although the United States and Great Britain, the Western world's two largest collectors of intelligence information, regularly turned over information to the tribunal, there were definite limits to what governments were willing to share. Not all information, moreover, was valuable for the tribunal's purposes. Intelligence information is generally gathered for military or political purposes; it does not have to meet standards of proof required in a court of law. Intelligence and defense analysts also approached the issue of sensitive material differently than did the court. The intelligence community is secretive by nature and not used to routinely sharing data, especially when such information could end up in a public trial. Yet the tribunal needed raw data and information about its origin—something that intelligence agencies the world over, concerned about protecting their sources and methods of collection, are extremely reluctant to share. Arbour acknowledged, therefore, that the intelligence agencies "were not lying in their own eyes when they saw themselves as having been incredibly open." Arbour nonetheless felt that from an investigatory perspective, the material the court got from intelligence sources was "pretty modest."[13]

Important new sources of information opened up for the tribunal after Milosevic fell from office in October 2000 and even more after he was detained, first in a Serbian jail on charges of abuse of office in March 2001 and, finally, in June 2001 in the Hague. According to Western media accounts, paperwork handed over to the tribunal from two key ministries in Belgrade, telephone calls made by Milosevic and his advisers that were picked up by U.S. intelligence, and testimony from a senior Serbian officer questioned after Milosevic's fall, allowed war crimes investigators to establish that

Milosevic ordered the bodies of hundreds of civilians murdered in Kosovo to be dug up, driven to Belgrade, and reburied to conceal atrocities carried out early in the conflict. According to these sources, Milosevic ordered the removal of murdered civilians during a 30 March 1999 meeting at his presidential palace, telling Nikola Sainovic, his key subordinate for Kosovo policy and Minister of the Interior Vlajko Stojilkovic that, "All civilians killed in Kosovo have to be moved to places where they will not be discovered." In what was reportedly called "Operation Clean Up," the bodies of people killed by Serb forces in Kosovo—men, women, and children—were exhumed, driven to Serbia in trucks, and secretly reburied—in rivers or lakes, on special police bases, and in at least one case in a subsequently re-filled bomb crater under a Serbian highway.[14]

By mid-summer 2001, the Serbian media reported that investigators had located reburial sites containing up to seven hundred bodies. Some Serbs who had been drafted by the authorities for the grisly job of hiding the bodies were deeply disturbed by what they had experienced and were said to be cooperating with Serbian and Hague tribunal authorities. Publication in the Serbian media of stories about the discovery of the bodies was also playing an important role in forcing ordinary Serbs to confront the consequences of the crimes committed by Milosevic and his henchmen in their name.

Nevertheless, although the tribunal has a wealth of evidence to support the charges against Milosevic, key pieces of evidence establishing legally credible links between Milosevic and the killing, raping, and looting will be "complicated and challenging," according to Western media accounts based on contacts with tribunal insiders shortly after Milosevic's transfer to the Hague. A key member of the chief prosecutor's office said that "there is no classic paper trail" and the real chain of command "may not be the same as that is written on paper." According to this source, "it is not necessary to show that Milosevic ordered killings" but it must be shown that "he had actual control over commanders, that he knew the atrocities were happening, and that he did nothing to stop the crimes or to punish the perpetrators."[15]

Croatia and Bosnia

Another question that arose was why Milosevic had not been indicted years earlier for the actions of Serb forces in Croatia and Bosnia. The tribunal's 1995 indictments of Bosnian Serb leader Karadzic, for example, were also based on his responsibility as president and party leader for the killing and persecution of Bosnian Moslem and Croat civilians. If the Bosnian Serb leader could be indicted in 1995 for his command authority, it was natural to wonder why the same standard was not applied to Milosevic for crimes Serb forces committed in Croatia and Bosnia.

There was plenty of information available to show Serb police and military units acting in close concert with paramilitaries in areas where war crimes violations had occurred. Western correspondents as far back as the war in Croatia had reported this kind of activity. It had undoubtedly also been observed over the years by international civilian and military monitors, including the European Community Monitoring Mission, (ECMM), the white-clad "ice cream men" who were deployed throughout war-torn Yugoslavia beginning with the conflict in Slovenia in June 1991, as well as the verification missions deployed in Kosovo in 1998.

Former U.S. intelligence analysts have said that as the United States reviewed its intelligence records, it was unable to find a "smoking gun" that would directly link Milosevic to the actual commission of war crimes in Bosnia or Croatia. Even without access to sensitive intelligence material, however, it had long been clear that Milosevic was responsible for the ethnic cleansing and other crimes committed by Serb forces in Croatia and Bosnia, as he was in Kosovo. There is no doubt that Milosevic either initiated or approved major military moves during the war in Croatia. Colonel Veselin Sljivancanin, indicted in 1995 by the Hague tribunal for war crimes, contended that Zivota Panic, the JNA commander in charge of the siege of Vukovar, told him that the directive to shell the city was an "order from Dedinje"—the Belgrade suburb where Milosevic lived. Sljivancanin also claimed that it was "a very popular politician" who ordered the execution of wounded prisoners after Vukovar fell.[16] Sljivancanin had an obvious interest in trying to deflect blame for his own actions. Nevertheless, there is no reason to doubt his allusions to a chain of command that stretches back to Milosevic.

JNA forces, directly subordinate to Milosevic, were involved in the seizure and subsequent cleansing of the Bosnian towns along the Drina River in the spring of 1992. Western journalists frequently observed JNA officers acting in command during the assaults. A detailed study of the cleansing along the Drina, prepared by the Boltzmann Institute for Human Rights in Vienna on the basis of interviews with hundreds of survivors, concludes that "the attack on Zvornik was planned, coordinated and directed by the former JNA." The role of the JNA included assigning experienced officers to the area before the attack; stationing tank, artillery, and infantry units in the region in preparation for the attack; and supporting the activities of paramilitaries by barrage fire from artillery and tank units intended to terrorize the local population. The study also determined that JNA forces in the area, although nominally subordinated to JNA authorities in Tuzla, were probably commanded directly from Belgrade during the attack on Zvornik.[17]

Frustrated tribunal officials asserted that the absence of an indictment against Milosevic for crimes committed by Serb forces in Croatia and Bosnia was not for lack of trying. They noted that information in Western press stories or Yugoslav "insider accounts," such as the diaries of former Milosevic henchman Jovic, were useful in pointing the direction for the tribunal's own investigations, but were not by themselves sufficient to be used as evidence in a court of law. When Hague investigators approached the sources of this kind of information—Western journalists or former officials—some were cooperative, but others proved unwilling to help or changed their stories when confronted with a request to testify on behalf of the tribunal.[18]

Milosevic and the Serb Paramilitaries

Milosevic also bears responsibility for crimes in Croatia and Bosnia that stem from his connections with the Serb paramilitaries that carried out many of the worst atrocities. The war in Croatia marked the first use of the paramilitary bands that subsequently became an ugly feature of all the Yugoslav wars. Generally organized around a widely known leader or political party, their members were often drawn from the roughest elements of the Serbian criminal underworld—motivated as much by the thrill of violence and the prospect of loot as by attachment to the Serbian cause. The paramilitaries quickly earned a fearsome reputation for murder, rape, and other forms of savagery.

There is no doubt that the paramilitaries functioned as one piece of Milosevic's carefully planned strategy to create a Greater Serbia. Two of the most prominent paramilitary warlords, Zeljko Raznjatovic, known under his nom de crime as Arkan, and Vojslav Seselj, a onetime dissident turned nationalist demagogue, were particularly closely associated with Milosevic. In the spring of 1992, Milosevic observed that of all the opposition leaders, "I value Seselj the most . . . since he is most consistent in expressing his political views."[19]

Seselj, the more politically prominent of the two, fell in and out of public favor with Milosevic over the years—his status depending, at least in part, on the image that Milosevic wished to portray both at home and abroad. Arkan, however, seemed to hold a special place in Milosevic's affections. In 1991, Serbia's Milosevic-controlled media gave Arkan and his forces extensive and positive coverage, even going so far as to allow recruiting ads to appear on Belgrade television. After the spring of 1992, when international pressure became too great, Milosevic cut back his open signs of support for the paramilitaries. Nevertheless, during a secret meeting with Tudjman adviser Sarinic on 12 November 1993, Milosevic tacitly admitted that Arkan was acting under his control. When Sarinic asked Milosevic about Arkan, Milosevic replied with a laugh, "Someone has to carry out part of the business for me, too."[20] Two months after he lost power—and eighteen months after Arkan had been gunned down in a Belgrade hotel— Milosevic in a long television interview called the late paramilitary figure "a patriot." Milosevic also described how he had rejected a personal plea by U.S. Secretary of State Albright to arrest Arkan, despite urging that he do so from some of his advisers, who saw the move as an easy way to curry favor with Washington.[21]

In the 1970s and 1980s, Arkan had gained a reputation as a bank robber in Western Europe and reportedly also as an agent of the Yugoslav secret police responsible for attacks against émigré opponents of the Yugoslav regime. Arkan returned to Belgrade in 1986 and opened a fashionable sweetshop located across the street from the Red Star football stadium. During this period, Arkan was often seen at football games in the company of senior Serbian officials, such as Minister of the Interior Radmilo Bogdanovic. The Serbian Volunteer Guard, better known as the Tigers, which Arkan founded in October 1990, took as its nucleus a gang of fanatical young supporters of the Red Star team known as Delije.[22]

Ironically, Arkan's mobilization of the Belgrade soccer hooligans was originally encouraged by the authorities to counter Seselj's influence among them. Tall, bespectacled, and slightly stoop-shouldered, Seselj had a ready way with words that made him a prominent figure among the dissident intellectual fringes of Belgrade society in the late 1980s. During his imprisonment, though, he was reported to have been savagely beaten and, according to friends, raped.[23] Seselj's prison experience left its scars on his personality and, some said, his mental balance. It also presumably left Milosevic with a hold over Seselj through Milosevic's control of the police records of Seselj's time in prison.

Unlike Arkan, Seselj initially seemed to operate outside the approval of the Serbian authorities. In the spring of 1990, Serbian authorities publicly rebuked Seselj for threatening the Gypsy street musicians who frequented Belgrade's central walking street. Seselj was sentenced to another spell in prison in the fall of 1990 for efforts to organize volunteers to support the Serbs in Knin, but he quickly reemerged after apparently striking a deal with the authorities. By the spring of 1991, his paramilitary supporters, who went under the name White Eagles, were widely known among the armed groups operating in the Serb-controlled parts of Croatia.

A group within the Serbian secret police played the key role in arming and organizing the Serbian paramilitaries as well as supervising their role in ethnic cleansing in all of the Yugoslav wars, from Croatia in 1991 to the end of the war in Bosnia in 1995. The group was reportedly led by SDB chief Stanisic and included his deputy Kertes, Radovan Stojicic (known as Badja, the Serbo-Croatian name of cartoon sailor Popeye's brawny opponent), and Frank (Frenki) Simatovic. The chain of command from the SDB group to Milosevic was clear in both a legal and personal sense. Most of the group's members hailed from Vojvodina and had first come to prominence during Milosevic's takeover there. All reported to the president through Stanisic, who was known as the "second most powerful man in Serbia." After Milosevic fired Stanisic in 1998, Stanisic released a statement noting that while in office, the police under his authority had "linked its activities and responsibilities primarily to the institution of the Serbian president."[24]

In Bosnia and Croatia, Serbian police—under the direction of Milosevic's henchmen Stanisic, Kertes, Badja, and the rest—armed and directed the paramilitary forces that led the violence against the civilian population. Arkan's Tigers and Seselj's White Eagles were especially important in the ethnic cleansing along the Drina and in northern Bosnia. At the beginning of the fighting in Bosnia, Arkan himself reportedly personally directed the intimidation and expulsion of Moslems and Gypsies from Bijelina and Janja. The Tigers played a significant role in the takeover and cleansing of such towns as Zvornik, Bijelina, Bratunac, Prijedor, and Foca. According to UN experts, Seselj's Chetnik forces were also actively involved in war crimes in Bosnia. On 17 May 1992, for example, Seselj's forces entered Divic near Zvornik, where they looted and pillaged Moslem property for nine days.[25]

The paramilitary leaders often spoke of their ties to the Serb authorities. Seselj, who over the years alternated between periods of opposition and allegiance to Milosevic, said that his forces began cooperating with the authorities in 1991: "Our first contact with the police was in the summer of 1991. Then we began to receive arms directly. The first man who we had such contacts with was Kertes. And during this time it was Kertes who was most in evidence."[26] Likewise, Serbian rebel leader Simo Dubajic from Croatia claimed that he had received arms from the Crvena Zastava arms factory in Kragujevac before the fighting broke out and that he had coordinated closely with senior Serbian police officials, such as Bogdanovic, Kertes, and Stanisic.[27]

Seselj also cited the central role of Milosevic himself in the support he received from Serbian authorities. In Seselj's words, "Thanks to the cooperation and alliance with Milosevic, our impact on the war was exceptionally great. . . . We received from him weapons, uniforms, buses, and a barracks in Bubanj Potok [near Belgrade] where we trained our volunteers."[28]

Like Seselj, Arkan emphasized that he and his forces were subordinated to Serbian authorities and Milosevic in particular. "Let us understand each other," Arkan told an interviewer. "We are not just talking about paramilitary units. Every member of those units must, first of all, be responsible to the Serbian people, and must respect the parliament and the president of the republic."[29]

Seselj also alleged that "Milosevic . . . took complete control for good" over the operations at the time of the April 1992 assault on Zvornik. According to Seselj, Milosevic on numerous occasions directly requested that Seselj's paramilitary bands be deployed to certain areas that were occupied by Bosnian Serb forces.[30]

In October 2001 the Hague Tribunal—finally—indicted Milosevic for war crimes in Croatia. Tribunal officials also said that another indictment covering Milosevic's crimes in Bosnia and including charges of genocide would be released before Milosevic's trial. According to the Croatian indictment, Milosevic as President of Serbia, between at least August 1991 and June 1992, led a "joint criminal enterprise" that included the murder of hundreds of individuals, the deportation of at least 170,000, and the imprisonment of thousands of others under inhumane conditions. The twenty-one-page indictment amounts to a summary of the actions that Milosevic undertook to destroy Yugoslavia and to fight the subsequent war in Croatia. The indictment accuses a number of former associates of Milosevic of being co-conspirators, including former President Borisav Jovic, Defense Minister Kadijevic, and paramilitary leaders Arkan and Seselj. Among the atrocities that the indictment mentions specifically are the 1991 sieges of Dubrovnik and Vukovar and the torture and murder of approximately 255 patients taken from the hospital after Vukovar fell.[31]

TWELVE

The End

The loss of the war in Kosovo left Milosevic isolated and almost desperate, according to some close to him. The president of Mira Markovic's JUL party later acknowledged to Western reporters that "the regime was in a significant panic, unsure of what to do."[1] There was air of whistling in the dark in Milosevic's speech to the Serbian people announcing the end of the bombing. He attempted to cast the war as a victory and went out of his way to praise the army, which he called "invincible."[2] In the weeks after the end of the war there were clear signs of divisions within the ruling coalition. Milosevic's longtime ally and financial backer, Bogoljub Karic, resigned, as did Prime Minister Mirko Marjanovic. Rumors swept Belgrade about the loyalty of Serbian President Milutinovic and Zoran Lilic, another longtime Milosevic supporter.

The loss of the war in Kosovo continued the decline in Milosevic's popular support that had begun with the setbacks in Krajina and Bosnia. In the weeks following the war's end, reservists and their families demonstrated in towns across southern Serbia. In Krusevac, a town where up to eight thousand men had been mobilized for Kosovo, reservists blocked roads and trains and demonstrated in front of City Hall. In Leskovac, twenty thousand reservists looted the home of the local chief of the SPS. During an August football match, sixty thousand spectators took advantage of a power failure to chant, "Slobo, you sold out Kosovo!" and "Slobo leave!"[3]

A poll conducted during the last week of September 1999 provided dramatic evidence of Milosevic's waning support. Seventy-two percent of those polled disapproved of Milosevic's job performance and 67 percent thought he should resign immediately. More than one-third of those polled thought Milosevic should be delivered to the Hague war crimes tribunal.[4]

Rebound

In August 1999, Milosevic summoned his closest supporters to a secret meeting to put an end to the incipient rot in the ruling coalition and map out a strategy for survival. As participants later described the session to Western journalists, Milosevic said the main task was to get through the winter, week by week, month by month. He demanded that "our companies must provide help" with reconstruction, implying that it was time for those who had made money from their coziness with the Milosevic clan to pony up. Milosevic also made clear his expectation that the international coalition against him would fragment and that eventually he would be able to resume his accustomed role with international leaders. The world would change, Milosevic told his supporters. Elections would bring new presidents in the United States and Russia, which could be expected to choose someone more nationalist and closer to Serbia. Milosevic portrayed the world as tired of U.S. hegemony and expressed confidence that Europeans would understand that the region needed Serbia. Just hang on. He would outlast them, was Milosevic's message.[5]

The results of Milosevic's strategy were soon apparent. In mid-August, he formed a new government based on his own SPS, his wife's JUL, and Seselj's ultranationalist SRS. At the end of September, police forcibly broke up opposition street protests in Belgrade, thereby showing Milosevic had no intention of allowing a repetition of the 1996–1997 "Happening of the People." NATO commanders in Kosovo began to report increasing signs of covert support from Belgrade for the Serb-controlled section of Kosovo north of Mitrovica.

Milosevic's first major postwar speech set out a strange combination of fairyland unreality, vilification of the opposition as foreign lackeys, and mobilization of Serb pride for standing up to NATO "colonialism." Speaking in Leskovac in early October, Milosevic asserted that the "vast majority" of facilities destroyed by NATO bombing had been rebuilt—something the Serbian people could see with their own eyes was false if they simply looked at the downed bridges across the Danube or walked along some of the main streets in downtown Belgrade. In a sentence that had the ring of having been crafted by his wife, Milosevic claimed that during the war in Kosovo, Serbs "had greeted their deaths with a song on their lips." Milosevic called the opposition "cowards, blackmailers, and toadies" who were committed to plunging Serbia into a civil war that would lead to colonization from outside by those with German or Anglo-Saxon names.[6]

The heavy security that accompanied Milosevic's speech—seldom present during the long-ago days when Milosevic promised crowds of up to one million Serbs an antibureaucratic revolution—revealed the isolation of the regime. Before he arrived, the streets in Leskovac were cleared by the police and twenty thousand selected spectators, including many children, were bused into the city center from outlying villages. As Milosevic entered town, police stood every fifty meters along his route.

After the war in Kosovo, aware of the military's unhappiness with his handling of the conflict and of its importance for his own survival, Milosevic cultivated the armed forces in a way that he had never done before. In late July, he paid an unusual formal visit to army headquarters, where he met with Minister of Defense Ojdanic—a fellow indicted war criminal—and called the military the guarantee of Serbia's independence and "long-term stability."[7] In October, shortly after his Leskovac speech, Milosevic decorated an elite parachute unit for defending Serbia's "sovereignty, territory, independence, and constitutional order."

After the Hague tribunal indictments, the top military leadership had little choice but to support Milosevic. In July, Ojdanic publicly warned the opposition that the army could move against them. Ojdanic told *Politika*, "It is the task of us all now to preserve the stability of the country, because there are many sold souls, Western vassals, who want to take power by force and take the country into a new catastrophe."

Below the most senior levels, however, discontent with Milosevic was widespread in the military. Lower-level officers had long resented Milosevic's lack of financial support for the army, and now they seethed over his bootless policy of launching them into a war with NATO and then forcing them to withdraw from Kosovo without—in their view—having been defeated. Officers had been seen sympathizing with protesting reservists, and former generals were among the most prominent of Milosevic's public opponents. In late July, former chief of staff Perisic, who was reported to have been under house arrest during the war with NATO, called publicly for Milosevic's ouster: "The current state leadership must be removed by political means, and the people should be taken along the path of civic and democratic programs, and not those of hatred and violence." Perisic took particular aim at Markovic, charging that her party had penetrated into all Yugoslav institutions, including the army after his departure, through "usurpation, blackmail, and fear."[8] Another former general, Vuk Obrado-vic, who headed the Social Democratic Party, declared on the day the end of the bombing was announced, "Slobodan Milosevic is finished."—an assertion that proved accurate although premature.

Circling the Wagons

Milosevic, however, did not regard himself as finished. Early in 2000, he moved to eliminate the remaining vestiges of independent media. In March, police invaded the offices of Studio B, a Belgrade television station run by Draskovic and the country's largest broadcast outlet not under Milo-sevic's control. Police beat personnel on the scene, smashed some equipment, and took other essential items. Other independent outlets were hit with heavy licensing fees by the Serbian authorities in order to drive them out of business.

A new feature of Milosevic's strategy was the growing public promi-nence accorded his wife. On the eve of the war in Kosovo, she sought to rally public support by describing the "small Serbian nation" as under attack by the United States, which she called the "biggest bully at the end of the twentieth century," and compared U.S. policies to those of the Third Reich.[9] After the war, Markovic continued the same theme, telling an interviewer that the conflict had arisen because Serbia had the temerity to stand up to the "already obvious plan for having the world ruled by a single will and a single interest."[10] In late October 1999, Markovic made an un-usual public foray into high-level government business, participating in an official delegation to discuss the dispute between Serbia and the breakaway republic of Montenegro. Markovic's behavior—as depicted by the Monte-negrin media—perhaps explained why she had heretofore kept so assidu-ously out of visible public business. She was reported to have begun the meeting with a one-hour "hysterical fit," in which she said, "We were bombed, you were not, and you do not care. We are under sanctions, you are not, and you do not care," and then stormed out before the Montenegrins could reply.[11]

Another new and even uglier feature of Milosevic's post-Kosovo sur-vival strategy was the growing level of violence against regime opponents and infighting within the regime itself. In early October, Draskovic was lightly injured, and his brother-in-law and two bodyguards killed, when a truck suddenly swerved into the car in which they were riding. Draskovic fled to Montenegro and angrily charged the Milosevic regime with trying to kill him—an accusation that gained additional credence in the summer of 2000 when a sniper took a shot at Draskovic.

On January 16, notorious paramilitary leader Arkan, who had finally been indicted for war crimes during the NATO bombing of Serbia, was assassinated by three masked men as he walked with his family through the lobby of Belgrade's luxurious Intercontinental Hotel. It was widely assumed in Belgrade that the regime was responsible for Arkan's murder—a notion given some credence by reports that Arkan had been in touch with the Hague tribunal. "He knew his shelf-life was limited and he was flirting with the Hague," a source with close knowledge of the Serbian underworld told Western journalists.[12]

Setting the Stage for Political Suicide

In July 2000, seemingly confident that he had weathered the loss of Kosovo, Milosevic began the process that just four months later would lead to his own downfall. The Milosevic-dominated FRY Assembly rubber-stamped changes to the Constitution, intended to allow Milosevic to prolong his hold on power in Belgrade almost indefinitely. In a two-hour, virtually secret session, and with little debate or opportunity for review by constitutional experts, the Assembly amended the Constitution to provide for the election of the FRY president by direct popular vote rather than by the Assembly, as had previously been the rule, and to reduce the role in the FRY of Montenegro, whose government under Prime Minister Milo Djukanovic had split with Milosevic and—with the support and encouragement of the United States and other NATO members—was running Montenegro as virtually an independent entity. At the end of July, after the Assembly approved legislation that gave Milosevic the option to run for two more four-year terms, he scheduled elections for 24 September, even though his current term did not expire until July 2001.

Milosevic prepared for the election in what had become his usual fashion, moving against the country's few remaining independent media outlets and seeking to intimidate potential opponents. Essential equipment was stolen from radio and television stations in the cities of Nis and Pancevo; a Radio Free Europe correspondent was assaulted by police in front of his wife and children; and the publication of three Belgrade daily newspapers was undermined by a mysterious, lingering shortage of newsprint. Two dozen judges who refused to follow the government's orders were ousted from their positions, while Information Minister Matic

charged several independent media organs and a respected journalist, Lil-
jana Smajlovic, with taking orders from the CIA.[13] Milosevic had himself
proclaimed a "national hero" by the military, and his campaign appearances focused on his supposed success in rebuilding Serbia after NATO's
1999 bombing.

The decision to hold early elections nevertheless betrayed signs of
haste. Many speculated that the timing of Milosevic's move was influenced
by an awareness of looming economic difficulties. On the eve of the elections, Miroljub Labus, the chief macroeconomist with the influential G-17
group of independent economists, told the Western media that "this economy is on the verge of a great crisis. September was the last month for the
government to hold these elections."[14] A month later, after Milosevic fell,
when G-17 economists obtained access to the country's financial records
they found the situation was even worse than expected. Only $250 million
remained in official state reserves, much less than needed to support the dinar and prevent a new round of inflation.

There was another possible explanation for the early timing of the elections. Many in Belgrade noted that the elections coincided with the date of
Milosevic's 1987 victory over Stambolic at the Eighth Session. They speculated that Milosevic's wife—known to believe in astrology and the power
of favorable signs—had decided that date would also be a good one for her
husband to turn to the Serbian voters.

There were also some signs of disarray within the Milosevic camp. Public opinion polls continued to show low levels of popular support for Milosevic. In early July, media reports—apparently based on contacts with
members of Milosevic's SPS and his wife's JUL party—hinted that Milosevic
had offered former secret police chief Stanisic three-months tenure as Serbian interior minister, after which Stanisic could become president of Serbia or the FRY. Former information minister and Markovic adviser Aleksandar Tijanic claimed that a faction in the SPS was urging Milosevic to rely
on Stanisic to oversee a transitional period as he stepped down from
power.[15] Reports of divisions within the ruling coalition seemed to be confirmed when a number of leading figures in JUL, such as Dragan Tomic and
Dusan Matkovic, were not included on lists of candidates for the elections,
and by the failure of many prominent Milosevic supporters, including his
longtime aide Milutinovic—then serving as president of Serbia—to participate actively in the campaign. Evidence began to appear of a split between
Milosevic and Radical party leader Seselj, an unprincipled bellwether fig-

ure whose behavior was always a sign of which way the political winds were blowing.

In the months before Milosevic's decision to hold early elections, reports had appeared in the Western media of apparent efforts by some in the West to cut a deal with Milosevic that would allow him to step down from office and escape arrest by the Hague tribunal. The *New York Times* reported in June that the Clinton administration was exploring the possibility with NATO allies and Russia that Milosevic and his family would be allowed to leave Serbia with guarantees of their safety and that their financial assets would be untouched.[16] Other reports had Greek politicians seeking to broker a deal in which Milosevic would agree not to run in elections and private U.S. intermediaries putting out feelers of a Milosevic offer to create a new government with Draskovic in place of Seselj.[17] None of these reported deals panned out, and it is still difficult to determine how much substance there was to them. It is possible, however, that the timing of Milosevic's decision to seek early elections was influenced by the failure of these feelers and a consequent recognition on Milosevic's part that his best strategy was to hunker down for a long period at the helm of power in Belgrade.

Whatever his motives in calling the elections, as the campaign unfolded through an unusually hot and dry autumn, it soon became clear that Milosevic had miscalculated. Much to the surprise of everyone—including themselves—most of the fractious Serb opposition managed to unite around Kostunica, a little-known constitutional lawyer with impeccable anti-Communist, and nationalist, credentials.

Kostunica: Milosevic's Soft-Spoken Opponent

Born in Belgrade in 1944, Kostunica graduated from the University of Belgrade Law Faculty in 1966, earning a master's degree in 1970 with a thesis titled "The Political Theory and Practice of the Constitutional Judiciary in Yugoslavia." Four years later, he was fired from his job as a lecturer at the Law Faculty for his criticism of Tito's 1974 Constitution, which turned Serbia's autonomous provinces of Kosovo and Vojvodina into virtually separate republics, thereby diminishing Serbia's stature within the Yugoslav federation. In 1989, Kostunica helped found the Democratic Party (DS), whose name was intended to link it symbolically with the interwar party of the same name—founded by the prominent Croatian Serb politician Svetozar Pribicevic—that was devoted to the notion that Serbs and Croats constituted one people, and that had drawn its primary electoral strength from Serbs in Croatia.[18]

Unlike most members of the Serb opposition, Kostunica was never a member of the LCY, nor was he ever a particularly strong supporter of Yugoslavia. He belongs to that strand of the Serbian national tradition that views Serbia's future not in a union of south Slav peoples but rather in a Greater Serbia that would include all Serbs in the Balkans. Kostunica—who translated the *Federalist Papers* into Serbo-Croatian—describes himself as a Western liberal, with a belief in free speech, an independent media and judiciary, and the rule of law. In 1992, Kostunica broke away from the DS— whose leadership was taken over by Djindjic—to form the Democratic Party of Serbia (DSS) in a dispute largely driven by Kostunica's insistence that the Serb national issue should enjoy equal prominence with democracy on the political agenda.

When the fractious and personality-driven leaders of the Serb opposition looked for a candidate in the 2000 elections, it was Kostunica's unassuming nature that helped him become the choice to oppose Milosevic. Kostunica had few negatives, and unlike most other opposition leaders, who over the years had managed to find ways to profit from their political connections, Kostunica was seen as clean and uncorrupted. An outspoken critic of the 1999 bombing and known for his deep attachment to Serbian national issues, Kostunica could not be successfully tarred as a "NATO puppet" by the Milosevic regime.[19]

Kostunica began a campaign of retail politics, driving all over Serbia to shake hands, hold rallies, and appear on the local news. The election had not gone very far when it became clear that Kostunica's reputation for integrity had struck a spark, symbolized by his campaign slogan, "He Can Look You in the Eye"—a sharp contrast to the feeling most Serbs had about Milosevic. In the beginning of September, an opinion poll showed that 52 percent of Serb voters would back Kostunica and only 31 percent Milosevic.[20]

As Milosevic's ratings slipped, the official media stepped up its crude attacks on Kostunica. One pro-regime poster spread widely through Serbia in the closing stages of the campaign showed Kostunica as a puppet Pinocchio figure standing in front of a NATO flag. While the official media largely ignored Kostunica except to attack him, Milosevic's remarks were featured on the evening television news as well as spread across the pages of *Politika* and other pro-regime papers, usually with highly inflated figures for the number of people who had attended his tightly choreographed rallies.

As the campaign progressed, even uglier phenomena emerged. In late August, Ivan Stambolic—Milosevic's former mentor and rival—disappeared while jogging near his home in Banovo Brdo, a hilly district on the outskirts of Belgrade. Eyewitnesses said that Stambolic had been bundled into a white van as he was resting on a park bench in the area. Although no explanation was put forth for Stambolic's disappearance, few doubted that the Milosevic regime was behind it. In the weeks before his disappearance, Stambolic had begun to speak out publicly against Milosevic. Speculation was spreading within some Belgrade intellectual circles about Stambolic as a possible successor to Milosevic, in part because many saw the opposition as divided and lacking credibility. In an interview on Montenegrin television, Stambolic described Milosevic as a "master of consuming and reproducing chaos" who was doomed to disappear in a civil war. In language similar to what journalist Curuvija had used shortly before he also disappeared, Stambolic said, "At the end he must be destroyed, most people are against him and they will get him. He will never go in peace."[21] Stambolic had an unpublicized dinner in Paris a few weeks before his disappearance with former Macedonian President Kiro Gligorov and former Kosovo leader Vllassi, hosted by a Serbian émigré businessman, at which the subject of Serbia and the Balkans after Milosevic was discussed.

Aware of the tide running against them, Milosevic and his wife hit the hustings themselves—a sure sign of the anxiety felt by the usually reclusive pair. Three days before the election, for the first time ever in his tenure as Serbian leader, Milosevic made two campaign appearances in a single day. In rallies in Belgrade and Montenegro, he delivered slashing attacks on the opposition, calling them "rabbits, rats and even hyenas" who wanted to turn Serbia into a "permed poodle" and had "the loyalty of dogs" to the NATO masters "who bribe and pay them." Milosevic mocked Djukanovic as someone who would surrender Montenegro's independence, leaving its traditional musical instruments and costumes reduced to museum exhibits "for American stars and British spinsters to see after they swim free on the beaches of Sveti Stefan," a famous Montenegrin resort where Djindjic had reportedly spent the 1999 war, after receiving warning that his life might be in danger. For the first time openly campaigning with her husband and running for a seat in the FRY Parliament, Markovic made her own contribution to the debate by dividing Serbia into patriots and traitors, calling voters to a defense against "evil Western neocolonialism," and labeling the opposition "mental retards."[22]

Despite the vigor of his invective, the tone of Milosevic's remarks and the tightly controlled character of his campaign appearances only served to reinforce how out of touch he had become with ordinary life and people. Milosevic stopped in Montenegro for only thirty-five minutes at a FRY military air base, and in Belgrade he spoke at the central sports hall, where access was limited to fifteen thousand well-dressed supporters. Milosevic's attacks on the opposition for abusing Serbia's children through "sects, intelligence organizations, terrorist groups, and the narco-mafia" must have rung hollow to most Serbs at a time when Milosevic's police were beating young activists even as flashy criminals with links to the Milosevic regime flaunted their wealth and outrageous lifestyle against the backdrop of the deepening poverty of most ordinary Serbs.[23]

The Opposition Gets Serious

Kostunica's campaign benefited from a number of factors that previous opponents of Milosevic had not enjoyed. Most important was the unity that the traditionally fractious Serbian opposition displayed throughout the campaign. Although Vuk Draskovic and Seselj ran separate campaigns against Milosevic, fourteen opposition parties came together in a coalition called the Democratic Opposition of Serbia (DOS). Many DOS members were uneasy about Kostunica's nationalism—one prominent DOS figure had formerly called Kostunica "a saloon fascist"—but once the campaign got underway the coalition pulled together until victory was achieved.

The independent media also played a major role in the opposition's victory. Veran Matic, editor-in-chief of B-92, said he tried to create an atmosphere of impending victory, "a mood that the time has come when the people will rise up and be decisive." Despite the Milosevic regime's May 2000 seizure of B-92's studios in downtown Belgrade, its young journalists continued to work from a number of makeshift, semiclandestine studios in apartments through Belgrade. B-92, which Matic described as operating "on the brink of illegality," sent its radio news out of Serbia via Internet, from which it was beamed back into the country through a variety of means including foreign radio stations, which the regime often jammed but which B-92 would then shift to another frequency. B-92's television news was smuggled out of Serbia on tape by courier, usually to the Republika Srpska in Bosnia, whose pro-Western prime minister, Milorad Dodik, was an important source of support to the opposition.[24]

The DOS coalition also benefited from several years of grassroots political activity by democratic, nongovernmental organizations (NGOs) throughout Serbia. NGOs became particularly important after the failure of the 1996–97 demonstrations in Belgrade, which at the time many saw as confirmation of the inability of opposition political parties to mount a credible challenge to Milosevic. NGOs concentrated on grassroots democratic consciousness-raising in the towns and countryside outside of Belgrade, in an effort to undermine Milosevic's support in areas of his traditional strength. Milenko Dereta, the president of the Citizens Association for Democracy and Civic Education, pointed out that this kind of activity, by showing the previously apathetic Serbian population that there was an alternative to the current regime, helped pull the rug out from under Milosevic even before the election campaign began. "Simply organizing an NGO or participating in an activity sponsored by an NGO was important in showing people it was possible to take control out of Milosevic's hands," he observed.[25]

The most influential of the NGOS was the student activist group Otpor, which means resistance. Otpor was created in October 1998 during what one of its leaders, Slobodan Homen, called a "particularly dark period in Serbia" caused by Milosevic's strong moves against the independent media and the university at the same time that the U.S. administration was making negotiations with Milosevic the center of its efforts to seek a solution in Kosovo. After the NATO bombing, Otpor, which up to then had been concentrated in universities, began to branch out into southern Serbia and rural areas. By the time of the election, Otpor had over eighty branches throughout Serbia including an active one in Milosevic's hometown of Pozarevac.

Otpor's young activists—most were university or even high-school aged—concentrated on demonstrative actions, such as putting up anti-Milosevic posters or graffiti, which often provoked a brutal police response. Otpor's clenched fist symbol appeared on walls, tee shirts, and posters throughout Serbia and its slogan "He's finished" became the opposition's rallying cry. Otpor activists suffered over four thousand detentions, but repression only increased the determination of its members and the prominence of its role across the country. Less concerned than their elders about police action against jobs or family, young people were not easily intimidated by the police. The viciousness of the police action and the virulence of the Milosevic regime's propaganda actually helped Otpor and undermined the regime. The Milosevic media called Otpor "NATO infantry" but as Homen observed, "How could my parents believe that I was a foot soldier for NATO?"[26] In September 2000, after five Otpor activists in the southern Serbian town of Vladicin Han were hung from the ceiling and severely beaten by drunken policemen, another Otpor adviser described how counterproductive police repression proved to be. When parents "saw their kid taken to a police station and tortured Gestapo-style just for wearing an Otpor tee-shirt it became more personal."[27]

Kostunica himself had little sympathy for Otpor, which he accused of relying on "dubious" funding. "He does not like us and we do not like him," is how Homen described the relationship. But Otpor, like other members of the democratic opposition swallowed their doubts and focused on Kostunica's integrity and ability to defeat Milosevic. "Kostunica is someone who will obey the law and that is enough for me," Homen said.

Despite these differences, a close adviser to Kostunica acknowledged the new president's debt to Otpor. He told me that Otpor played "an enormous psychological role" in dispelling fear. "If their children were courageous enough to suffer police beatings for their beliefs then it would be shameful for their parents not to be willing to face the same thing" is how he described the situation.

The opposition to Milosevic also exploited less orthodox ways of undermining the regime. A famous eighteenth-century Serbian prophecy, called the Kremicka Procanstvo, predicted that wars in Serbia would end when the country was ruled by someone who had the same name as the village where he was born. Independent media, therefore, helped spread across Serbia the information that Vojslav Kostunica was born in a village named Kostunica.

Milosevic's foes also benefited from a comprehensive, $77 million program of U.S. assistance. In June 2000, the United States opened an unusual "off-shore" embassy in nearby Budapest to carry out as many as possible of the reporting and assistance tasks that would normally have been done by the U.S. Embassy in Belgrade—still closed after the 1999 NATO bombing. When Milosevic decided to schedule elections later in 2000, a team of U.S. diplomats, foreign assistance officials, and representatives of nongovernmental organizations was available to apply in Serbia the lessons learned in successful efforts to aid democratic opposition groups in overturning authoritarian regimes in a number of other Eastern European countries.

The United States provided assistance at several key junctures of the opposition's campaign to unseat Milosevic. In the beginning, U.S. advice and polling data helped convince veteran opposition figure Zoran Djindjic, the leader of the Democratic Party (DS) and the most prominent figure in the DOS coalition, that his image among the Serbian people contained too many negatives and that he should step aside in favor of the lesser-known Kostunica. During the campaign, U.S. polling data helped keep the DOS on message and—by showing the dramatic rise in voter support for Kostunica and the DOS—bolstered the opposition's confidence during a campaign in which it was virtually shut out of the official media and many of its activists were beaten and detained by the police.

Some opposition figures, noting that Milosevic received about the same number of votes in 2000 as he had during his previous election campaigns, said that the U.S.-assisted get-out-the-vote effort—aimed particularly at anti-Milosevic younger voters—provided the opposition with its margin of victory on polling day. But "probably the most important thing the U.S. did was in helping design and implement the opposition's parallel vote count," according to a senior U.S. diplomat. Here, the United States provided the opposition with the resources and training to capitalize on a Milosevic mistake. In the 2000 election, unlike previous ones, every polling station was required to post the results of its election night vote count at the same time that it passed these results on for tabulation higher up the chain of election officials. On election day an independent Serbian election organization, The Center for Free Elections and Democracy (CESID), together with the DOS, which was allowed to have one representative on the election board in each polling place, managed to cover about 80 percent of the 10,000 precincts in Serbia. They transmitted the results to centers in Belgrade through telephone, courier, and the Internet—a complicated and redundant system intended to foil police harassment. As a result, the opposition knew by the early hours of the morning—probably before Milosevic himself—that it had won a convincing victory. Possession of this accurate and independent vote count gave the opposition the confidence it needed to resist Milosevic's subsequent efforts to steal the election. In the words of a senior U.S. diplomat, the opposition "could stand up and say they had a book with the results for each polling station."

DOS political figures were reluctant to discuss U.S. assistance—Kostunica, indeed, spent a good part of the campaign lambasting the United States. But independent media figures and leaders of the numerous and sophisticated Serbian NGOs, which provided much of the grassroots organizational effort in the campaign, were less inhibited. Matic pointed out that with Milosevic controlling almost all of the economic levers in Serbia, U.S. assistance allowed the independent media access to resources that would have been difficult to obtain otherwise.[28] Homen noted that "if you want to blanket the country with one million posters, someone has to pay for it."[29]

Dereta said, "All our actions were funded by the Americans" and only a small amount of assistance came from the Europeans. He pointed out that the flexible and trusting approach that U.S. advisers brought was critical. The U.S. did not try to dictate schemes to the Serbian opposition but rather allowed other Eastern Europeans to describe what had worked in their countries. Dereta also noted the practical importance of seemingly small and unglamorous measures such as U.S. funding for the translation and publication of a book, "From Dictatorship to Democracy"—a manual of nonviolent resistance to authoritarian regimes. Dereta described the book as "the bible of the opposition's resistance activities."[30]

The Regime Crumbles

On election day, the voters of Serbia decisively repudiated Milosevic. Thanks to its election monitoring arrangements, the opposition knew by 2 A.M. that Kostunica had won a convincing victory with, at that stage, 56.8 percent of the votes, compared to 34.2 percent for Milosevic. "A first-round victory is certain," Kostunica declared. "Dawn is coming to Serbia." More than twenty thousand people gathered in central Belgrade on the night of the election for a concert and rally to celebrate Kostunica's victory.[31]

But Milosevic refused to concede defeat. When Nikola Sainovic brought the bad news that Kostunica was heading toward victory, Milosevic, according to press accounts, reacted with fury. He grabbed Sainovic—long one of his leading henchmen in Bosnia and Kosovo—by the moustache, and told him to go and reverse the results. SPS officials initially asserted that Milosevic was leading by 45 to 40 percent. When it became clear that claims of an outright Milosevic victory would lack credibility, the Milosevic-controlled Central Election Commission shaved just enough votes away from Kostunica to contend that he had failed to gain the required 50 percent of registered voters.

After the election, Milosevic's party and police machine, which had ruled Serbia virtually unchallenged for thirteen years, began to crumble from within. "The defeat is too obvious to be denied," a former SPS official told the press. "They didn't expect such poor results. Even a small defeat is a problem for Milosevic. Now it's hard for him to find a way out without creating a crisis inside the system."[32] Patriarch Pavle greeted Kostunica as the president of the country, and called on him and his supporters to take power in a "dignified fashion and on the basis of results, which show that he has the confidence of the people to whom he belongs."[33] Officials within Milosevic's SPS party began to panic, sensing the end of their long, comfortable, and lucrative rule. Local SPS officials in party meetings throughout the country expressed fear over the impending opposition victory. Many said they did not want to be seen as hostages to Markovic's tiny and despised JUL party. Some senior SPS officials called on Milosevic to recognize that Kostunica had won the first round of the presidential elections.[34]

Even more dangerous for Milosevic were signs of neutrality among the army and police. Chief of Staff Pavkovic, who shortly before the election had referred to Milosevic as "brave, decisive, and especially visionary," said at the end of the month that the army would respect the choice Serbs made in the presidential elections. In the industrial city of Kragujevac, a group of police officers were reported to have gone to the local offices of Otpor and put its trademark clenched-fist badge on their uniforms. In Valjevo, sixty miles southwest of Belgrade—and long known for being a "Chetnik" town—when the police received orders to arrest four local opposition leaders, the local commander held a secret vote with his men and decided against the arrests.

Visitors to Milosevic's hometown, Pozarevac, sensed the fear gripping the regime and his family. Milosevic's son, Marko, and his armed followers had long kept Pozarevac in a kind of reign of terror. In May, a teacher was attacked and charged by the police with attempted murder after he stepped in to defend some students who were being beaten by Marko's thugs. A few days before the scheduled runoff, Marko sought out the teacher to apologize and asked the opposition "not to be rude to my family."[35]

Isolated within the heavily guarded White Palace, Milosevic and Markovic seemed unable to comprehend what was happening. On 2 October, as the date for the scheduled run-off election approached, Milosevic made his first televised address to the Serb people since the end of the Kosovo war. Using scare tactics, Milosevic asserted that a vote for the opposition would lead to the dismemberment of Serbia and the extinction of its national identity. He claimed that the opposition's real leader was not Kostunica but DS chief Djindjic, who "could not hide his cooperation" with NATO—an allusion to Djindjic's flight to Montenegro during the 1999 war. In remarks that must have sounded ironic to his listeners, but that reflected the depth of his and his wife's isolation from daily life in Serbia, Milosevic warned that a victory for the opposition would lead to an increase in poverty and crime.

After the speech, Milosevic summoned Pavkovic and the head of the secret police, Rade Markovic, to prepare a crackdown. But Pavkovic and Markovic replied that there was a revolt simmering within the army and police, and that officers could well switch sides if ordered to intervene against the opposition. Sources present at the meeting said later that Milosevic "looked like he was going to die," while his wife went into hysterics and had to be given a tranquilizer injection.[36]

Disregarding advice from their Western backers, Kostunica and other opposition leaders refused to participate in run-off elections, which they charged would simply legitimate Milosevic's fraudulent manipulation of the first round. Instead, the opposition called for an escalating series of protest meetings throughout Serbia. The first, held on a chilly night in Belgrade, was disappointing, drawing perhaps forty thousand people—far fewer than the two hundred thousand or more who had turned out a few days earlier to celebrate Kostunica's election victory. The response was stronger in opposition strongholds such as Kragujevac, Cacak, Nis, and Novi Sad, where protesters filled town squares and blocked major highways. In some places, official television and radio stopped regular programming in a sign of support for the protests. Some formerly pro-Milosevic media organs, including Belgrade's influential daily, *Politika*, began to report relatively objective and straightforward news, including accounts of the activities of the opposition.[37] Striking miners at the Kolubarska coal field south of Belgrade defied threats of arrest and appeals by Pavkovic to return to work, and in the first public sign that Milosevic was losing control of the situation, police sent to break up the strike stood aside as a crowd of several thousand from all over Serbia arrived to support the miners.

The Fall

The climax came on 5 October. The opposition had given Milosevic a deadline to resign by 3:00 P.M. or face massive demonstrations aimed at bringing the entire country to a halt. On the day of the deadline a huge crowd, including large contingents from opposition strongholds such as Cacak, Kragujevac, and Nis, converged on the center of Belgrade. In the space of only a few hours, the crowds—overcoming police tear gas and some shots, but suffering in the process only one, accidental death—seized the assembly building and the headquarters of the official television network. When the relatively small numbers of police fled, in some cases handing their weapons over to the demonstrators, and the army refused to intervene, control of Belgrade passed over to the opposition. That evening, seeming almost astonished by his own success, Kostunica greeted a jubilant crowd with the words, "Good evening, liberated Serbia."

On television it appeared as if Milosevic had been overthrown by a massive and spontaneous popular demonstration, but accounts by media and opposition leaders later revealed that what had occurred was a combination of careful organization and spontaneity—and one whose result was not certain until many hours after Kostunica made his triumphant speech. The rebellion included meticulous planning, selection of targets, penetration of the police communications system, and the inclusion in the ranks of the demonstrators of an oganized "shock unit," composed of former soldiers and policemen, well-armed and cold-bloodedly resolute.

This time, indeed, the opposition's mood and intentions were in stark contrast to the two previous occasions when Serbs took to the streets in massive protest against Milosevic—on 9 March 1991 and the winter of 1996–97. After thirteen years of Milosevic's disastrous rule and secure in the knowledge that it had won a legitimate victory in the September elections, DOS was prepared, if necessary, to use force to overturn Milosevic. On September 26 as DOS began planning its campaign of post-election moves against Milosevic, its leaders voted "that in any conflict with the organs of public order equivalent measures would be used to those that are used against us." In a pattern that would continue on the day of the demonstration and beyond, the only DOS leader to oppose this decision was Vojslav Kostunica.

Like a massive tree that begins to rot from within, the defenders of the Milosevic regime were wavering in their willingness to use force against the people even before the demonstration began. At 6 P.M. on October 4, just twelve hours before the first columns of demonstrators began to move, Zoran Djindjic met with Mihajlo Ulemek, known as "Legija," who had taken over from "Frenki" Simatovic as commander of the dreaded red-beret police "Special Operations Unit," responsible for much ethnic cleansing throughout the Milosevic wars and also his first line of defense when the time came to crack Serbian heads. Summoning Djindjic to a meeting in an armored jeep, "Legija" told him that the police had received orders to use "extreme measures" against the demonstrators. When Djindjic asked him what he intended to do, "Legija" replied that if the demonstrators would not shoot at his police or attack their headquarters, his men would not intervene. Later, Djindjic acknowledged, that when he heard these words, "A stone fell from my heart," because "the 'Red Berets' frightened him most of all."[38]

After the demonstrations were over and Milosevic had fallen, it became clear that the police were poorly prepared for the massive crowds and psychologically reluctant to intervene against the people on behalf of Milosevic. Isolated in his Dedinje villa and surrounded by nonentities who only told him what he wanted to hear, Milosevic in his last days apparently took almost no measures to defend himself against the largest popular challenge he ever faced. The Serbian government did not meet on October 4 and there was apparently no comprehensive plan to deal with the demonstrations. On October 5, approximately 3,650 police were available in Belgrade, a figure that included all regular police on duty in the city at the time—which police officials acknowledged was insufficient to handle a crowd of at least several hundred thousand people. The police, moreover, were wavering in their support for Milosevic even before the demonstrations. After Milosevic had fallen, secret police chief Rade Markovic said, "After the elections, an awareness that Milosevic had lost entered the heads of the police."

Zoran Djindjic, the former mayor of Belgrade who broke with Milosevic at the time of the 1996–97 demonstrations and operating out of an informal command center in the headquarters of the Democratic Center Party of Nebojsa Covic, played the most important role in coordinating the October uprising. Kostunica apparently kept his distance from the operational details. Two days before Milosevic fell, when Otpor leader Slobodan Homan told Kostunica that Otpor would have over fifty thousand activists in the streets and asked for instructions on what do, Homan said he received no answer.

The architects of the uprising set as their objective the taking of targets that symbolized some of the most prominent and hated aspects of Milosevic's rule: the Assembly, where Milosevic had once addressed a crowd of over a million enthusiastic supporters, and where three years earlier demonstrators had for months fruitlessly banged pans and blown whistles against the regime; the official television building, against which Draskovic's 9 March 1991 demonstration had crashed unsuccessfully; the headquarters of Milosevic's despised SPS; and Radio B-92, the popular independent station that had been seized earlier in the year previously by the authorities.

Some of the tactics and associates used by the opposition in overturning the regime had earlier been employed by Milosevic himself. Djindjic recruited Captain Dragan—one of the most notorious Serb paramilitary leaders, accused of orchestrating many atrocities during the 1991 conflict in Croatia—to take control of Studio B television station and the state customs house, key centers of media power and finance. On the night before the uprising, Dragan spirited about 170 armed men into the building. Once the demonstration got underway the next day, Dragan's men used two anti-tank rocket launchers to intimidate police guards, who they released after confiscating their weapons.

Provincial cities south of Belgrade provided many of the shock troops used in the storming of the Assembly and television building. At 7:30 in the morning of October 5 Velimir Ilic, the tough-talking mayor of Cacak led approximately ten thousand people in a column of 230 trucks, 52 buses, and hundreds of private cars on the one hundred mile trip to Belgrade. Shouting "victory or death" as they left, the Cacak demonstrators included a number of heavily armed men with prior military or police experience. According to accounts Ilic gave the media, he had earlier established contact with sympathizers in the police who provided him with inside information about police activities. "We knew every order coming from the Interior Ministry," he said. "We knew what they were planning. We saw their faxes." Ilic maintained that his contingent was determined to stay in Belgrade until they had brought Milosevic down. On the way, they swept through several police barricades set up to halt them. In one incident, the police reportedly stood aside when a demonstrator slapped the blockade commander in the face and challenged his officers to open fire.

Slobodan Homon of Otpor later described this as the decisive moment of the October 5 demonstrations. "When Ilic broke through the police barricades on the way to Belgrade, he broke the fear among the Serbian people."

At about noon demonstrators began to appear in front of the Assembly. At first police used tear gas and batons to chase the crowd across the street into Pioneer Park, the former gardens of the royal palace before the Second World War and the place where Kosovo Serbs had gathered in the late 1980s for the demonstrations that helped propel Milosevic to power. As the crowd swelled into the tens and then hundreds of thousands the outnumbered police were squeezed back against the steps of the Assembly.

The battle for the Assembly, which began at about 3:30 P.M., was over in thirty minutes. Ilic had brought along his own armored support—a bulldozer driven by a construction worker named Ljubislav Djokic. When the police again resorted to tear gas, Djokic raised the blade on his machine and lumbered forward, smashing through concrete flower box barriers and breaking several large windows, into which other demonstrators threw Molotov cocktails. As flames licked the Assembly building, the police radioed for reinforcements, only to hear that police in other parts of the city were laying down their weapons. Police fired rubber bullets and stun grenades, but as the crowd kept coming, they called their superior and asked permission to leave. They received orders to use "all possible means" to fight back, but instead, the commander removed his side arms, the unit put down its weapons and riot gear, and left the building.

While some demonstrators began to loot the Assembly, in the process tossing into the street election ballots reportedly already marked for Milosevic, others headed for the television building. Djokic drove his bulldozer four times into the barricades that police had built to protect the main entrance of the RTS headquarters. Finally—with the cabin of his bulldozer filled with tear gas and bullets banging against its metal sides—Djokic crashed through the barricades and into the lobby. As the police turned and ran, demonstrators rushed in behind the bulldozer, setting fire to the building and surging through its halls in a brutal hunt for the hated personalities who had sent Milosevic's news over the airways for the past thirteen years. RTS Director Dragoljub Milanovic was severely beaten. Crowds surrounded Ljilja Jovanovic, one of the chief news announcers, spitting on her and shouting, "Milosevic whore." After the attack was over, Jovanovic sat crying on the sidewalk while armed demonstrators deployed to defend the building against possible efforts by Milosevic forces to retake it and others prepared to broadcast the first news from liberated Serbia.

While the RTS building was falling, Legija's special police unit was ordered to leave its headquarters at Banjica on the outskirts of Belgrade and move toward the Assembly. As the column of armored police vehicles approached Slavija circle on the outskirts of downtown Belgrade it came under fire from demonstrators hiding behind metal garbage containers. According to police testimony, the lead vehicle alone was hit by twenty-nine bullets. The police did not return the fire and Legija ordered his column to pull up in front of the RTS building.

Looking out over the blade of his bulldozer at the heavily armed police vehicles, Djokic thought that the game was over. Then, he later recollected, as in a video he watched the men in the vehicles remove their masks and give the three-fingered Serb salute. The crowd went wild.

A few minutes later, Djindjic again met Legija, sitting in an armored jeep. "As far as I am concerned," Legija told Djindjic, "It's over. Milosevic is out. There is no return to the old system, the people have won." Djindjic said he had information that Milosevic's forces were preparing a counterattack. Legija replied, "I will tell them that if they intervene, we will move against them. I have 1,200 fighters."

At 7:00 P.M. the order went out over police radio that sealed the fate of Milosevic's thirteen-year rule: "Give up. He's finished."

The Military Dithers

The DOS leaders were as surprised as everyone else by the speed with which the Milosevic regime collapsed. Their plan for October 5 had been to use Studio B, captured by Captain Dragan, to appeal to the country to come over to their side and to continue with what would have amounted to a nationwide general strike until Milosevic fell.

Instead, after little more than two and one-half hours of action, all of Belgrade belonged to them. While Kostunica and other DOS leaders spoke in Belgrade's Republic Square, the jubilant crowd demanded that Milosevic—ensconced in the White Palace only a few miles away—be arrested. But Kostunica is a legalist and he—almost alone among the DOS leaders—did not want Milosevic arrested. "We will not go to Dedinje," he told the crowd. "We will stay here and defend the national institutions." Later, Kostunica explained that he considered it more important to begin creating the new government than to move against Milosevic, who was guarded by a heavily armed and apparently still loyal unit of bodyguards.

The situation, indeed, remained highly confused.

Even though thousands of jubilant demonstrators celebrated their victory in a massive street party that continued into the early hours of the morning, events behind the scenes had not run their course. Milosevic had not conceded, and the army—although it did not intervene—had not acknowledged its acceptance of the change. Throughout 5 October, the general staff was in permanent crisis session at its headquarters near the center of Belgrade. By about 2:30 P.M., as the crowd was preparing to storm the assembly, the military estimated that three hundred thousand people were in the streets. As the attack on the assembly began, Milosevic made a conference call to Pavkovic and Interior Minister Stojiljkovic. Milosevic demanded that the two put in motion plans for suppressing the demonstration that had been developed a week earlier. In response, ten armored vehicles were dispatched to Milosevic's Dedinje neighborhood. Shortly thereafter, Milosevic called again to say that the head of Belgrade television had just phoned him in a panic to report that there were not enough police present to defend his building. Calmly yet insistently Milosevic demanded, "Pavkovic, television is falling, have you moved yet?" Pavkovic and the general staff assembled a column of tanks and a detachment of paratroopers on the outskirts of Belgrade. Although the unit commanders signaled their readiness to move, Pavkovic never gave the order in time to save the assembly or television building, apparently out of concern that some members of the units were showing sympathy toward the demonstrators' cause.

As the evening wore on, Milosevic continued to call. "Nothing is OK," he told Pavkovic in a resigned though still insistent voice—but the generals continued to hesitate. At about 8:30 P.M., or roughly the time that Kostunica was greeting "liberated Belgrade," Minister of Defense Ojdanic—reportedly one of the "hawks" for action against the crowd—ordered the 63rd Parachute brigade, normally based in Nis but now assembled in the Military Academy on the outskirts of Belgrade, to prepare to move for a "special mission." But the troops refused to listen and some allegedly even sought a reckoning with the military brass. "We are the 63rd, already. Don't f— with us," was their supposed reply to the order.

At around 1:30 A.M., Milosevic phoned again. "Is it still possible to do something?" he asked Pavkovic. "I will do what I can," was the response. Finally, the military brass and police—the head of the secret police, Rade Markovic, had joined the military in their command post—put together a last-ditch plan. Some generals proposed to attack at about 4:30 in the morning, when the crowd in the street—still several hundred thousand-strong at midnight—had dwindled. Pavkovic hesitated and convened another meeting. One general, Aleksandar Vasiljevic, stood to say the military faced a choice between supporting a criminal of shameful biography and honorably joining the people. One after another more generals, even those formerly considered hawks, rose to support him. Milosevic, they convinced themselves, was the former president and their place was with the people. At about 7:30 A.M. on 6 October, the general staff issued an announcement that it would "respect the electoral choice of the people." Milosevic did not call again.[39]

The Russians Are Coming

The next day, 6 October, continued to be full of uncertainty, in part because of the intervention of Moscow and in part because Milosevic did not formally concede defeat. On October 5—even as demonstrations were unfolding in Belgrade—Russian President Putin sought to bring Milosevic and Kostunica to Moscow for what Kostunica's advisers later called "a crazy meeting." Events made such a meeting impossible, but on 6 October, Russian Foreign Minister Ivanov arrived in Belgrade on a mediation mission whose rationale had disappeared during his overnight flight. With Ivanov in town and wanting to meet with both Milosevic and Kostunica, the new president's staff realized they needed a suitable place to receive the Russian foreign minister. A telephone call to the Palace of the Federation, where the FRY president had his office, produced a long silence and then a request from the administrative personnel on the other end of the line for time to get instructions. When Kostunica's people called again, the staff still had no instruction, but bowing to the inevitable, they told the Kostunica team to come over. Twenty minutes before Ivanov arrived, Kostunica and his advisers occupied the president's office in the Palace of the Federation building—one of the cleaning staff crossing herself in disbelief as the new team entered. The Russians—wrong-footed by their prolonged support for Milosevic—had little choice but to go along with the will of the people of Serbia, and Ivanov's meeting passed off with little substance.

Not until 8 P.M. on October 6—more than twenty-four hours after he had lost control of Belgrade—did Milosevic meet Kostunica. A Kostunica adviser told me the initiative for the meeting came from Chief of Staff Pavkovic. A comprehensive and authoritative history of the October events in Belgrade, by contrast, reports that the initiative for the meeting came from Kostunica's office, which sought to use Pavkovic as an intermediary. According to this version, when Pavkovic called Milosevic and suggested that he go to Kostunica's office, Milosevic replied angrily, "Out of the question." Milosevic insisted that Kostunica visit him alone, which Kostunica rejected. After several calls back and forth an exasperated Pavkovic asked Milosevic if he would object if Pavkovic went to Kostunica and begged him to come to Milosevic. "Okay," the now ex-president replied.

When Pavkovic arrived he insisted that Kostunica go alone to meet Milosevic. Kostunica's staff was aghast, but Kostunica—a man of courage and calm presence of mind—climbed into the jeep and disappeared.

The meeting—with only the two men present—lasted one hour. It was the first time Kostunica had ever visited Milosevic and, noting this, Kostunica pointed out that Milosevic had spent far more time with U.S. negotiator Richard Holbrooke than he had with the Serbian opposition. According to Kostunica, Milosevic initially insisted that his term as FRY president would continue until July 2001, regardless of the election. Milosevic also complained about the destruction of his son Marko's perfume shop in Belgrade and of the house of an SPS official in the southern Serbian town of Leskovac. The meeting ended when Kostunica referred to the decision of the Constitutional Court, which had declared him the winner in the September election. Milosevic claimed to be unaware of the court's action and added that it only remained for him to congratulate Kostunica as the new president.

Milosevic's assertion surprised Kostunica—as well it might since it must be classed as one of the most egregious lies in a career notorious for its repeated falsehoods. Later that evening, Milosevic repeated the assertion in a short farewell speech on Serbian television. Announcing that he had just learned that Kostunica had actually won the September 24 elections, Milosevic thanked those who had supported Kostunica for "removing from his soul the great burden of responsibility that he had borne for a full ten years." He welcomed the opportunity to spend more time with his family—"especially his grandson Marko," but in a potentially ominous sign for the future also said he would devote more attention to strengthening his party.[40]

So ended Milosevic's bloody and disastrous rule over Serbia—not with a bang but a snicker.

Waiting

In the six months after Milosevic's fall from power, he and his wife lived a curious kind of twilight existence. The pair remained in Belgrade's official White Palace, where they continued to be guarded by a regular unit of special police, for sometime after the overthrow. They then moved into a luxurious official villa in the prestigious Dedinje section of Belgrade, across the street from the residence that was destroyed by NATO bombs. At the end of January 2001, as pressure mounted at home and abroad for his arrest, Milosevic was said to have gone into "self-imposed house arrest."

Although Milosevic continued to enjoy the same kind of reclusive lifestyle he had adopted during his last years in rule, he also made good the pledge in his departure statement to keep up his position as a leader of the political opposition. He rebuffed efforts by some former SPS leaders who he had ousted over the years, such as former Yugoslav President Jovic and Prime Minister Ratko Markovic, to get him to step down as party leader. When former SPS Vice President Mihajlo Markovic presented an updated party program, which called for a new party chair and for the SPS to distance itself from Mira Markovic's hated JUL party, Milosevic, according to press accounts, tore it up in a rage.

In late November, Milosevic, in his first public appearance since his overthrow, presided over a congress of the SPS party. His performance was aggressive and unrepentant. "Everybody in this hall knows what kind of violence and lawlessness has taken place since the coup on October 5," he said. Continuing the tactic of accusing his opponents—now the rulers of the country—as betrayers of the national interest, he thundered, "Those who defended the country and were in the country during the war are declared as enemies now. The country is in danger. The biggest defender of the state and national interests is the Socialist Party of Serbia, and that's why the party is the main target of the attacks," he said to long applause. Milosevic described the war crimes tribunal as "the new Gestapo in The Hague."[41]

In the 23 December elections to the Serb Assembly, DOS won handily with 64 percent of the vote, gaining 177 seats in the Assembly. But Milosevic's SPS emerged as the largest opposition party with 13 percent of the vote and 35 seats. In a surprise that showed the continuing strength of extreme nationalism in Serbia, Seselj's hard-line SRS won 9 percent and 23 seats, while a party tracing its roots back to murdered paramilitary leader Arkan won 6 percent of the vote and 15 seats.

Milosevic returned to his reclusive lifestyle after the elections, but it appeared that his political and legal maneuvering room was contracting. Although the new government in Belgrade continued to resist handing Milosevic over to the Hague tribunal, there were growing calls among Serbs for Milosevic's arrest. In January, Milosevic held a private meeting with Kostunica, where he reportedly sought guarantees for the safety of himself and his family—including his son Marko, who fled to Russia shortly after his father's ouster. Two officials who had remained with Milosevic to the end were arrested—Customs Director Kertes and head of the secret police Rade Markovic—and another such official, former Interior Minister Zoran Sokolovic, was found dead. A sense was growing in Belgrade that the man who millions of Serbs once hailed as their savior would soon find himself behind bars in his own country.

Dress Rehearsal

The first step on Milosevic's long-delayed road to legal accountability came at the end of March 2001, thanks to pressure from the U.S. NGO community and the Congress, which linked U.S. assistance to progress made by the new government in Belgrade toward compliance with its obligations to the Hague Tribunal. On 31 March, as a U.S. deadline expired, the Serbian authorities arrested Milosevic, after several days of drama during which Serbian police first withdrew in the face of armed resistance by Milosevic's bodyguards and military units who were protecting him threatened to intervene.

Milosevic was eventually taken to jail in downtown Belgrade after emotional negotiations during which Milosevic reportedly waved a gun and threatened to kill himself and his family. His daughter Marija fired several shots as her father was being driven away to prison. A senior Serbian official told Western journalists that Milosevic had only agreed to surrender after receiving guarantees that his family would be protected and could continue to live in their official residence and that he would receive a fair trial in Serbia and not be transferred to the Hague. After Milosevic's arrest, authorities discovered a veritable arsenal in his residence, including two armored vehicles, thirty automatic rifles, three machine guns, and one rocket launcher.

Milosevic was charged with misuse of his official position through the diversion of large sums of money to subordinates and to officials of the SPS party. According to the text of the indictment, which was leaked to the Serbian media shortly after Milosevic's arrest, Milosevic overstepped the limits of official financial authorizations "to secure property to the SPS and other benefits with the aim of preserving his political party in power." The indictment accused Milosevic of organizing the diversion of official funds beginning in 1994 and 1995, including having a part of customs fees collected in cash and other customs fees illegally diverted to a secret account in Beogradska Banka. The indictment also charged that Milosevic gave more than one million dollars to the SPS for its unsuccessful election campaign in September 2000.

Within a few days Milosevic's old combativeness reappeared. He wrote a long appeal, denying any improper use of official funds but acknowledging that he had presided over the secret diversion of money to purchase equipment for special police forces and to support Serb governments and military forces in Croatia and Bosnia.[42]

The End

On 28 June 2001, twelve years to the day after he spoke to a crowd of one million Serbs on the six hundredth anniversary of the battle of Kosovo Polje, Slobodan Milosevic was transferred to the Hague Tribunal to face war crimes charges. June 28—St. Vitus' Day, or Vidovdan in Serbo-Croatian—has a special place in Serbian history. It was, first of all, the day on which the Turks snuffed out the independence of the medieval Serbian empire. It was also the day in 1914 when a young Serb in Sarajevo named Gavrilo Princip assassinated Austrian Archduke Franz Ferdinand, unleashing a world war that claimed tens of millions of victims including, according to some estimates, one-third of the adult male population of Serbia. Nine years later, the first constitution of the new Yugoslav state that emerged after the First World War was proclaimed on Vidovdan, an act which many of Yugoslavia's non-Serb peoples saw as symbolic of how the new state could not make up its mind whether it was an extension of the pre–First World War

Serbian kingdom or a truly equal union of all the south Slav peoples. A few years later, after Tito had recreated a new Yugoslavia on the basis of his wartime Partisan guerrilla movement, Stalin chose 28 June 1948 to publicize his break with the stubbornly independent Yugoslav communists. Stalin—along with many others—thought his blow would end Yugoslav independence but, in fact, it ushered in a period of relative tolerance and prosperity that marked the high point of the joint life of the Yugoslav peoples.

Even after being forced out of office, Milosevic continued to overshadow the Serbian political scene, in large part because of disagreements among the DOS coalition about what to do with him. Kostunica—who described the Hague Tribunal as an anti-Serbian institution—initially took the position that Milosevic should be tried in Serbia. Later, when it became clear that Milosevic would have to go to the Hague, Kostunica insisted that the FRY constitution should be revised before Milosevic could be extradited in a legal fashion. Kostunica's rival in the DOS coalition, Serbian Prime Minister Zoran Djindjic—a pragmatist whose views and actions combined equal does of democracy, nationalism, and pecuniary self-interest—represented the majority of the DOS coalition, which after months of maneuver and increasing Western pressure simply wanted the matter disposed of as quickly as possible.

The discovery in June 2001, as the debate over Milosevic and the Hague was intensifying, of several sites near Belgrade where the bodies of hundreds of victims of Serbian ethnic cleansing in Kosovo had been concealed caused a palpable shift in Serbian opinion. Polls already showed that many had no problem with Milosevic's being sent to the Hague, but the display of the sad and grisly remains—this time not in some faraway field but hidden in the rivers, lakes, and soil of Serbia itself—seemed to bring home to Serbs the ugliness of the crimes that had been committed in their name by the Milosevic regime. The remarks of one Serb man in the street seemed to typify this reaction when he told me, "When I saw the pictures of those corpses I thought that if Milosevic is responsible for what happened to those people he has to go to the Hague immediately."

Difficulties at the top of the DOS coalition also affected the timing and the circumstances of Milosevic's transfer to the Hague. Kostunica's legalistic strategy collapsed when the pro-Milosevic Montenegrin party that Kostunica had been relying on in the FRY Assembly refused its support. Under prodding from Djindjic, the Serbian authorities responded by adopting a decision authorizing Milosevic's transfer through court order. This strategy, in turn, collapsed the morning of 28 June when the Constitutional Court, allegedly under lobbying by Kostunica's staff, sent the decision back for further review.

While Milosevic's lawyers celebrated the decision with toasts of whiskey in the corridors of the court, Djindjic responded by, in effect, simply putting Milosevic on an aircraft and sending him to the Hague, relying ironically on a provision of the 1990 Serbian constitution Milosevic had introduced as part of his strategy to break up Yugoslavia. Once again, U.S. pressure was critical to the timing of the move against Milosevic. As he later described events to foreign reporters, Djindjic decided that he had to honor a pledge given to U.S. Secretary of State Colin Powell, who said the United States would participate in a 29 June conference of international aid donors if Djindjic would promise that Milosevic would be in the Hague before the conference began.

Late in the afternoon of 28 June, Djindjic convened a meeting of the Serbian government, where a decree authorizing extradition to the Hague was adopted by a vote of fourteen to one, with the lone dissenting vote coming from a representative of Kostunica's DOS party.

About two hours later the public prosecutor entered Milosevic's jail cell in downtown Belgrade and spent twenty-five uncomfortable minutes informing Milosevic of his fate. As later described in media accounts, Milosevic sat in disbelieving silence on his bed. An hour later a detachment from the police Special Operations Unit, whose defection on 5 October had sealed Milosevic's fate but whose units had been responsible for some of the worst atrocities against civilians in the Yugoslav wars unleashed by Milosevic, strode past the one bodyguard that Milosevic was allowed in the Serbian prison. "Prepare to leave," the police ordered. When Milosevic asked, "Where am I supposed to be going?" the reply was "To the Hague. So start packing." After a moment's reflection, Milosevic pulled a black leather bag out from under his prison cot, changed his socks, and packed his belongings, taking along with him two books on Serbian history and an Orthodox Bible.

A small convoy of black vehicles drove Milosevic to a secret rendezvous with a police helicopter—bypassing a special aircraft Djindjic had arranged to be sent from Montenegro as a decoy to foil any intervention on Milosevic's behalf by the Serbian military. At the police base an official from the Hague Tribunal read Milosevic his rights and the Tribunal's indictment. Asked if he had anything to say, Milosevic reportedly refused to recognize the Tribunal at all, calling it "a political circus whose aim is to endanger the

Serbian people until it destroys them completely." Milosevic called the Tribunal a "charade" and described his arrest as a kidnapping for which those responsible would one day be punished. After he had made his own speech Milosevic became impatient and urged the group to get going. Walking toward the helicopter, Milosevic waved to the Serb policemen and remarked sarcastically, "Congratulations on a job well done."

Milosevic was flown to the U.S. air base in the Bosnian town of Tuzla. From there, a twin-engined RAF jet flew Milosevic to a Dutch military base at Eindoven, where a police helicopter transferred him to the prison facilities at the seaside town of Scheveningen, next to the Hague. If Milosevic had any inclination for contemplation on what was likely his final flight out of the territory of the former Yugoslavia, he might have reflected that the Tuzla airbase was where thousands of anguished Bosnian women had been taken after the capture of nearby Srebrenica almost six years ago. Here they waited in vain for news about the fate of thousands of their men who they later learned had been murdered by Bosnian Serb forces.

Milosevic's day ended at about 11 P.M., when Dutch television showed pictures of a seemingly handcuffed Milosevic entering prison with a slight stoop and a distracted gaze.[43]

Reaction in Serbia to Milosevic's transfer was relatively muted. A poll taken by a Western agency in May showed that 45 percent of those sampled agreed that Milosevic should be sent for trial to the Hague, while 36 percent said Serbia should not recognize biased foreign courts.[44] The evening of Milosevic's transfer a few thousand supporters gathered in Belgrade's central Republic Square, where they listened to angry speeches, attacked a few journalists, and trashed several cars but dispersed without further incident before midnight.

But Milosevic's transfer provoked an angry confrontation between Kostunica and Djindjic that most Belgrade observers believed would eventually mark the split of the DOS coalition and set the stage for an election battle between Kostunica and Djindjic that many saw as a struggle for Serbia's future. The evening of Milosevic's transfer, Kostunica, who claimed that he had not been consulted regarding the move, made a savage public attack on the transfer, which he charged "cannot be regarded as legal or constitutional," and accused those responsible of "seriously jeopardizing the constitutional order of our country."[45]

Djindjic replied by pointing to the necessity of sending Milosevic to the Hague for Serbia to get on with the business of rebuilding the country on a democratic and market-oriented basis. His supporters also leaked what purported to be a transcript of a conversation between Djindjic and Kostunica in which the latter seemed to assent to the transfer.

Milosevic continued to be defiant when he was formally arraigned a few days after his transfer to the tribunal. His suit immaculate and sporting the same tie he had worn when he spoke to the Serbian nation in June 1999 to announce the end of the NATO bombing, Milosevic refused to enter a plea and declined to have any legal counsel represent him before the Tribunal. Speaking mostly in English, he told the three judges that he considered the court "a false tribunal" that was trying him to justify NATO crimes against the FRY. Urged to appoint a lawyer to represent him, Milosevic responded, "I have no need to appoint counsel to an illegal organ," and when the presiding judge asked if he wanted the indictment read, Milosevic replied, "That's your problem."[46]

Closure

A few days before Milosevic was transferred to the Hague, I attended a meeting with Foreign Minister Goran Svilanovic, a young Serb from Kosovo who in the October 2000 uprising led a column of demonstrators to Belgrade from the southern city of Uzice. Svilanovic, the leader of the moderate Civic Alliance party, complained that he and the other members of the DOS coalition could not proceed with the political and economic reforms they considered their most important task because they were continually forced to deal with issues from the past, which included, in Svilanovic's, view what to do with Milosevic.

Once Milosevic was sent to the Hague, the coalition that overthrew him had the opportunity to show what it could do to build a new Serbia. The transfer also presented an opportunity for evaluating—even if only preliminarily—the consequences of Milosevic's rule.

Kostunica—along with many other Serbs—is fond of saying that Milosevic's worst crimes were committed against the Serbian people, something that the inhabitants of Vukovar, Sarajevo, and Kosovo, to name just a few of the places outside Serbia devastated in the wars unleashed by Milosevic, would find both offensive and incredible. This view of Milosevic reflects the notion of Serbia as a victim, which Milosevic did so much to inculcate during his rule. It is also a consequence of Milosevic's media monopoly, which deprived the Serbian people of objective news about what was happening in the rest of the Balkans for over a decade.

Yet it is true that the thirteen years of Milosevic's rule were a period of almost unparalleled disaster for Serbia. Shortly before the September 2000 elections the group of independent economic experts, G-17, published a short document that revealed in stark terms the truly catastrophic social and economic decline Serbia experienced under Milosevic. Virtually every indicator of social and economic health showed a drop, and the cumulative effect was to turn Serbia from one of the most prosperous and vibrant societies in Eastern Europe in the mid-1980s to one of its poorest and most troubled at the end of the millennium. Real average pay in Serbia by 1999 had fallen to approximately 50 percent of the level in 1987, when Milosevic assumed supreme power in Serbia. Over the same period social production fell to about 40 percent of the 1987 level while industrial production fell to about 30 percent. The rate of natural increase of the population in Serbia fell from a rise of about two per thousand in 1987 to an annual decline of about three per thousand in 1998. The number of murders over the period 1987 to 1997 almost doubled while the number of minor children convicted of crimes rose by about 65 percent.[47]

The NATO bombing of Serbia, provoked by Milosevic's stubborn unwillingness to compromise in Kosovo and the brutal campaign he and his minions unleashed there, also cost Serbia heavily. The G-17 economists estimated that Serbia experienced over $4 billion worth of damage to infrastructure, economic facilities, and to public sector and household facilities.[48]

But the damage to Serbia caused by Milosevic went much deeper than the cost to the economic system. The human destruction that Milosevic inflicted on Serbia may prove to be even more damaging in the long run. War and blighted economic prospects for over a decade led thousands of young Serbs to flee their country, many never to return.

At the beginning of the Yugoslav dissolution a good friend of mine, the foreign editor of one of Belgrade's major papers, passed up an opportunity to become chief editor, choosing instead to become the paper's Washington correspondent because he could see what was coming at home. When Milosevic took over the paper and proclaimed my friend an enemy of Serbia, return became impossible. Now he lives permanently in the United States. His two sons have become American citizens. They graduated with computer degrees from a fine university and have well-paying jobs. This kind of experience, repeated thousands of times under Milosevic, marks an irretrievable loss of human resources for Serbia.

There is another kind of human cost experienced by those who remained in Serbia that could prove even more devastating. The generation of young people who grew up under Milosevic for more than a decade saw no economic prospects other than smuggling and crime. They absorbed the anti-Western messages of Milosevic's media and then experienced the trauma of the NATO bombing, which the Milosevic regime—and his successor, Kostunica—told them was a criminal act that they had done nothing to deserve.

During a visit to Belgrade in the summer of 2001 Serbian friends described to me how the events of the past decade had left its traces in their own children. One prominent editor, who was demoted early in Milosevic's career and who was briefly jailed by Milosevic shortly before his fall, told me his daughters had asked why he was having dinner with an American friend. Another prominent journalist reported that a bitter and resentful younger generation was growing up in Serbia, convinced that its belief in Western values had been betrayed by the 1999 NATO bombing. This journalist told how young people at a Belgrade high school had described the erection of a sign to mark EU aid given to rebuild the school as sickening evidence of the way foreigners were "sucking up" to Serbia.

But the consequences of Milosevic's rule in Serbia—bad as they are—pale in comparison with the sufferings elsewhere in the former Yugoslavia. In Kosovo, as has been already noted, it is estimated that 12,000 Albanians died in the 1998 and 1999 Serbian campaigns against the civilian population. Well over a million people were driven from their homes. The CIA estimated that 81,500 military personnel and 156,000 civilians had died in the Bosnian war, all but 10,000 of the latter in Bosnian or Croatian held parts of the country. Experts attached to the UN Human Rights Commission found evidence of approximately 12,000 rapes, the majority committed by Serbs. The CIA estimated that between 900,000 and 1.2 million people fled Bosnia as refugees and an additional 1.3 to 1.5 million were displaced from their homes but remained within Bosnia. In all, over half of Bosnia's population was driven from its homes.[49]

Nor, unfortunately, is it possible to say with confidence, even with Milosevic finally in the Hague, that the process of violence he helped unleash has run its course in the former Yugoslavia. In the summer of 2001 an insurrection erupted among the Albanians in Macedonia, who had long been treated as second-class citizens by the Macedonian majority of that country. Low-level violence continues in Kosovo against the Serbs remaining in the province and within the Albanian community. The international community, moreover, shows no signs yet of grappling seriously with the future status of Kosovo, where both Albanians and Serbs continue to put forward mutually incompatible claims.

It would, of course, be too much to blame Milosevic alone for all of this. Milosevic had plenty of willing accomplices in Serbia and emulators elsewhere in the former Yugoslavia. Nor can international statesmen escape responsibility for failure to act in a timely fashion to head off the violence that many saw coming.

In the late 1980s, as Milosevic first came to international attention, some senior U.S. diplomats caused considerable controversy by describing Milosevic as a reformer. Time proved that Milosevic was most definitely not a reformer but rather an ugly killer who even now fails to acknowledge the existence of the crimes he committed let alone admitting any personal responsibility for them.

And yet now that it is all over, at least for Milosevic himself, it is hard not to see an element of tragedy in Milosevic's fate. I did not meet Milosevic or have any personal experience with the consequences of his actions until 1987, when he had already launched himself on the dangerous path of nationalism. But many of the people who knew Milosevic before this period have described a very different individual: modest, loving toward his family, and basically seeking to make a career within the relatively tolerant Yugoslav Socialist system created by Tito.

By the time of Milosevic's downfall it had become an element of faith among virtually all Serbs that his wife, Mirjana Markovic, was the true power behind the throne. There is no doubt that Markovic exercised a baleful influence over Milosevic, especially in his later days. Milosevic's almost unnaturally close relationship with his wife and his apparent need for her approval have been explained by some as stemming from Milosevic's need to duplicate a close early relationship with his mother, but these kind of psychological explanations lie beyond the scope of this book. In my view, the tendency of the Belgrade intelligentsia to attribute Milosevic's actions to the influence of his wife represents a lingering unwillingness to come to grips with what Serbs and Serbia did in the 1990s. No one who ever had anything to do with Milosevic, moreover, has ever doubted the man's own innate capabilities and his own role as a prime mover in Balkan events.

In the end, it comes down to personal responsibility. If there is any glimmer of a positive ray in Milosevic's history, it can only be this. For the first time in human history, a head of state was brought to international, legal accountability for crimes committed as a result of his rule. This is a new development and, although Milosevic richly deserves his fate, the resort to an international criminal tribunal raises legitimate questions about scope, fairness, and future applicability.

Nevertheless, bringing Slobodan Milosevic to justice is an essential first step toward helping the people of the former Yugoslavia to put the Milosevic era behind them. It is, of course, too much to expect that Milosevic's fate will, by itself, prevent other rulers from engaging in similar crimes in the future. If, however, his trial adds a measure of deterrence to future crimes it will have served its purpose, and it will provide a reason for remembering the strange and ugly career of Slobodan Milosevic.

Notes

Introduction

1   See Ivan Stambolic, *Put u bespuce* (Belgrade: Radio B-92, 1995), 166–67.

2   This account is drawn from conversations with Vllassi and other participants in the Kosovo Polje event, and from a series of articles published in *Borba* in January 1993 by an eyewitness, journalist Slavko Curuvija, who was murdered under mysterious circumstances at the beginning of the NATO bombing campaign against Serbia. The official text of Milosevic's speech is published in Slobodan Milosevic, *Godine Raspleta* (Belgrade: Beogradski izdavacko-graficki zavod, 1989), 146. In *The Death of Yugoslavia* (London: Penguin, 1996), by far the best account yet to emerge of the Yugoslav collapse, Laura Silber and Allan Little write that Milosevic came secretly to Kosovo Polje four days before 24 April. Vllassi told me in May 2000 that he was aware of and sanctioned Milosevic's 20 April visit.

3   Slavoljub Djukic, *Izmedju Slave i Anateme: Politicka biografija Slobodana Milosevica* (Belgrade: Filip Visnic, 1994), 29. Anyone writing about Milosevic in English must pay tribute to Djukic, Milosevic's Serbian biographer, whose books on Milosevic and his wife—based on a wide range of contacts within the Serbian elite—are an invaluable source of insider information on their lives. Milosevic's notorious wife, Mirjana Markovic, once inadvertently testified to the pungency of Djukic's commentary, angrily commenting to a collection of her cronies that his books read as if he were inside the bedroom she shared with her husband.

4   James A. Baker III. *The Politics of Diplomacy* (New York: G. P. Putnam and Sons, 1995).

ONE. *The Young Milosevic and the Yugoslavia He Destroyed*

1   See Slavoljub Djukic, Izmedju Slave i Anateme: Politicka biografija Slobodana Milosevica (Belgrade: Filip Visnic, 1994), 14.

2   See John Lampe, *Yugoslavia as History: Twice There was a Country* (London: Cambridge University Press, 1998), 235.

3   Ibid., 223–24.

4   See Ivo Banac, *With Stalin against Tito: Cominformist Splits in Yugoslav Communism* (Ithaca, N.Y.: Cornell University Press, 1988), 148.

5   Emily Milich and Tom Walker, "Daughter Returns to Haunted Home of Milosevic Clan," *Sunday Times*, 15 July 2001.

6   Quoted in George Jahn, "Milosevic's Hometown Lauds Freedom," Associated Press, 16 October 2000.

7   Emily Milich and Tom Walker, "Daughter Returns to Haunted Home of Milosevic Clan," *Sunday Times*, 15 July 2001.

8   See Djukic, *Izmedju*, 15.

9   See Laura Silber, "Milosevic Family Values," *New Republic*, 30 August 1999.

10 Quoted in Phil Rees, "Mira Markovic: The Power behind the Throne?" BBC News Online, 26 April 1999.

11 See Slavoljub Djukic, *He, She, and We: A Political Portrait of Slobodan Milosevic and His Wife*, trans. FBIS (Belgrade: Radio B-92, 1997), 7.

12 Quoted in Rees, "Mira Markovic."

13 The anecdote was first reported in Djukic, *He, She, and We*. It has subsequently appeared in many articles, including Alex Todorovic, "Milosevic Wife Bolsters Bid to Stay in Power," *London Times*, 18 September 2000.

14 See Djukic, *Izmedju*, 12.

15 Quoted in ibid., 18.

16 See ibid., 20.

17 See Dennison Rusinow, *The Yugoslav Experiment: 1948–1974* (Los Angeles: University of California Press, 1977), 172–78.

18 Ibid., 198.

19 See Lampe, *Yugoslavia as History*, 286–89.

20 See Dijana Plestina, *Regional Development in Communist Yugoslavia: Success, Failure, and Consequences* (Boulder, Colo.: Westview Press, 1992), 175.

21 See Rusinow, *Yugoslav Experiment*, 223.

22 Interview, 23 June 2001.

23 Interview with Vucic, 23 June 2001.

24 See Lampe, *Yugoslavia as History*, 323.

25 Ibid., 293, 317; see also Plestina, *Regional Development*.

26 See Mihailo Crnobrnja, *The Yugoslav Drama* (Montreal: McGill-Queen's University Press, 1994), 84–87.

27 Quoted in Djukic, *Izmedju*, 31.

28 Latinka Perovic, ed., *The Case of Ivan Stambolic* (Belgrade: Helsinki Committee for Human Rights in Serbia, 2001), 156–61.

29 See Slavko Curuvija, "Godine Zapleta—decenije Slobodana Milosevica," *Borba*, 18–29 January 1993.

30 Quoted in Ivan Stambolic, *Put u bespuce* (Belgrade: Radio B-92, 1995), 138.

31 Quoted in Djukic, *Izmedju*, 37–39.

32 See Stambolic, *Put*, 149.

33 Quoted in Djukic, *He, She, and We*, 23.

34 See Curuvija, "Godine Zapleta."

35 See "Nothing Unexpected Will Happen," *Borba*, 18 April 1991; cited in "Eastern Europe Daily Report," FBIS, 29 April 1991, 35, AU2704145191.

36 Ales Debeljak, *Twilight of the Idols: Recollections of a Lost Yugoslavia* (Fredonia, N.Y.: White Pine Press, 1994), 35.

37 See Susan L. Woodward, *Balkan Tragedy: Chaos and Dissolution after the Cold War* (Washington, D.C.: Brookings Institution Press, 1995), 36.

38 See Andrew Baruch Wachtel, *Making a Nation, Breaking a Nation: Literature and Cultural Politics in Yugoslavia* (Stanford, Calif.: Stanford University Press, 1998), 196.

39 See Woodward, *Balkan Tragedy*, 430.

40 Debeljak, *Twilight*, 68.

41 See Eric D. Gordy, *The Culture of Power in Serbia: The Destruction of Alternatives* (University Park: Pennsylvania State University Press, 1999), 112.

42 Debeljak, *Twilight*, 65.

43 See Lampe, *Yugoslavia as History*, 292.

44 See Wachtel, *Making a Nation*, 184–89.

TWO. *The Rise of Milosevic*

1 Quoted in *New York Times*, 1 September 1991.

2 Quoted in Ivan Stambolic, *Put u bespuce* (Belgrade: Radio B-92, 1995), 175.

3 See Julie A. Mertus, *Kosovo: How Myths and Truths Started a War* (Los Angeles: University of California Press, 1999), 146–56. Mertus has done a thorough, objective job of reviewing the published record in the Yugoslav media, and where possible, interviewing individuals involved in this and a number of other incidents that figured in the rise of Kosovo as a major issue in the 1980s.

4 Branko Mamula, *Slucaj Jugoslavija* (Podgorica: CID, 2000), 102.

5 See Slavoljub Djukic, *He, She, and We: A Political Portrait of Slobodan Milosevic and His Wife*, trans. FBIS (Belgrade: Radio B-92, 1997), 27.

6 Census data drawn from tables in Susan L. Woodward, *Balkan Tragedy: Chaos and Dissolution after the Cold War* (Washington, D.C.: Brookings Institution Press, 1995), 32–35.

7 Cosic's political speeches and writings can be found in Milan Nikolic, ed., *Sta Je Stvarno Rekao Dobrica Cosic* (Belgrade: Draganic, 1995); and Dobrica Cosic, *Stvarno i moguce* (Otokar Kersovani: Rijeka, Croatia, 1983). Discussions of Cosic's political activities and the role of the Belgrade intellectuals can be found in Kjell Magnusson, "The Serbian Reaction: Kosovo and Ethnic Mobilization among Serbs," *Nordic Journal of Soviet and East European Studies* 4, no. 3 (1987): 3–29; and Nicholas Miller, "The Nonconformists: Dobrica Cosic and Mica Popovic Envision Serbia," *Slavic Review* (fall 1999): 515–34. A thoughtful discussion of the role that Cosic and other intellectuals played in the rise of Serbian national feeling and the destruction of an emerging sense of Yugoslav consciousness can be found in Andrew Baruch Wachtel, *Making a Nation, Breaking a Nation: Literature and*

Cultural Politics in Yugoslavia (Stanford, Calif.: Stanford University Press, 1998), 1971–203 (for Cosic).

8   The text can be found in Branka Magas, *The Destruction of Yugoslavia: Tracking the Breakup, 1980–1992* (New York: Verso, 1993), 49.

9   After the leaked draft was published, work on the memorandum ceased and a final version was never formally released. As far as I am aware, it has not appeared in English and the complete text is rather rare even in Serbo-Croatian. The version I used appeared in *Nasih Tema* (Zagreb) 33, nos. 1–2 (1989): 128–63.

10   Stambolic, *Put*, 118.

11   See Milos Misovic, "Od Memoranduma do rata" ("From the Memorandum to War"), *Vreme*, 24 August 1992, part 4.

12   Quoted in ibid., part 5; and *Politika*, 17 February 1987.

13   Quoted in Djukic, *He, She, and We*, 24; and Tim Judah, *The Serbs: History, Myth, and the Destruction of Yugoslavia* (New Haven, Conn.: Yale University Press, 1997), 160. Judah says that Milosevic made his critical remarks on the memorandum to the Security Academy in June 1987—that is, two months after he returned from Kosovo Polje—but Djukic gives no date for the speech. Olivera Milosavljevic gives a complete account of the genesis of the memorandum in the academy, the campaign against it under Stambolic, and the way that the memorandum's arguments moved into the mainstream after Milosevic's victory. She recounts Milosevic's public criticism of the memorandum, but does not mention his speech at the Security Academy. See Olivera Milosavljevic, "Upotrebna autoriteta nauke: Javna politicka delatnost Srpske Akademije Nauke I Umetnosti (1986–1992), *Republika* 1 (31 July 1995): 1–30.

14   Quoted in *Borba*, 14 September 1987; cited in "Eastern Europe Daily Report," FBIS, 49, AU 081152.

15   See Djukic, *He, She, and We*, 28.

16   See *Tanjug*, 20 September 1987; and Belgrade Radio Domestic Service, 20 September 1987; both cited in "Eastern Europe Daily Report," FBIS, AU201456.

17   See *Borba*, 25 September 1987; and Tanjug Domestic Service, 24 September 1987; both cited in "Eastern Europe Daily Report," FBIS.

18   Quoted in Stambolic, *Put*, 258.

19   Latinka Perovic, *The Case of Ivan Stambolic* (Belgrade: Helsinki Committee for Human Rights in Serbia, 2001), 167.

20   See Marko Lopusina, *Ubij bliznjeg svog 1:* Jugoslovenska tajna policija od 1945 do 1997 (Belgrade: Narodna Knjiga Alfa, 1997), 312.

21   See Mamula, *Slucaj*, 117–19.

22   See ibid., 117–21.

23   Quoted in Slavoljub Djukic, *Izmedju* Slave I Anateme: Politicka biografija Slobodana Milosevica (Belgrade: Filip Visnic, 1994), 103.

24   See *Tanjug*, 30 May 1988; and "Eastern Europe Daily Report," FBIS, 1 June 1988, 38.

25   See *NIN*, 3 July 1988, 8–15; no. 1557, cited in "Eastern Europe Daily Report," FBIS, 22 July 1988, 64, AU0907050188.

26   Quoted in *Politika*, 14 July 1988; and *Tanjug*, 18 July 1988; both cited in "Eastern Europe Daily Report, FBIS, 19 July 1988, 62, EEU-88-138.

27   See *Tanjug*, 6 September 1988; cited in "Eastern Europe Daily Report," FBIS, EEU-88-175.

28   "Situation Report," RFE, 9 September 1988.

29   See Lopusina, *Ubij*, 314.

30   See Djukic, *Izmedju*, 108.

31   See *Tanjug*, 6 October 1988; cited in "Eastern Europe Daily Report," FBIS, 7 October 1988, 40, LDO0610224488.

32   Quoted in Djukic, *Izmedju*, 109.

33   See "Situation Report," RFE, 11 October 1988.

34   See *Agence France Presse*, 9 October 1988.

35   Mamula, *Slucaj*, 165.

36   See *Feral Tribune*, April 1994; cited in Mamula, *Slucaj*, 122.

37   See Belgrade radio, 19 November 1988; cited in "Eastern Europe Daily Report," FBIS, 21 November 1988, 72, AU1911132488.

38   See Belgrade Radio, 2 December 1988; cited in "Eastern Europe Daily Reports," FBIS, 7 December 1988, 52, EEU-88-235.

THREE. *Milosevic Takes Kosovo*

1   Quoted in *Politika*, 10 July 1987.

2   Quoted in *Tanjug*, 10 July 1988; and "Kosovo Provincial Committee Session," cited in "Eastern Europe Daily Report," FBIS, 16 July 1987, Y 9.

3   Quoted in Viktor Meier, *Yugoslavia: A History of Its Demise* (New York: Routledge, 1999), 71.

4   Ambassador John D. Scanlan, interview with author, March 2000.

5   See Branko Horvat, *Kosovsko Pitanje* (Zagreb: Globus, 1988), 130.

6   In the rest of this book, whenever I refer to the Serb population of Kosovo, I will also include the Montenegrins. The differences primarily relate to place of historical origin—many of the so-called Montenegrins in Kosovo trace their origins to colonists settled there by the interwar Royal Yugoslav government—but by the end of the twentieth century, the differences were of little consequence for contemporary political developments in Kosovo.

7   Data provided by the FRY Institute of Statistics. Yugoslavia's final census was held in 1991, just as the country was starting to come apart. Albanians in Kosovo refused to participate. Census data for Kosovo in that year, accordingly, are estimates.

8   See Dijana, Plestina, *Regional Development in Communist Yugoslavia: Success, Failure, and Consequences* (Boulder, Colo.: Westview Press, 1992), 181.

9   See Horvat, *Kosovsko Pitanje*, 98.

10   This summary treatment of the battle is largely drawn from Thomas A. Emmert, "The Battle of Kosovo: Early Reports of Victory and Defeat," in *Kosovo: Legacy of a Medieval Battle*, ed. Wayne S. Vucinich and Thomas A. Emmert. (Minneapolis: University of Minnesota Press, 1991), 19–36. Branimir Anzulovic in *Heavenly Serbia: From Myth to Genocide* (New York: New York University Press, 1999) has published a comprehensive and objective account of the way Kosovo myths and

legends "were reinvigorated by the Serbian intelligentsia to fan their compatriots' nationalist passions in the 1980s." My own experience has led me to believe that it is virtually impossible for a foreigner to walk where the Serbs go on Kosovo. In the late 1980s—admittedly the height of the period of Serb national euphoria—my wife and I made a resolution never to bring up Kosovo in our Belgrade home in order to avoid the unpleasant responses from too many of our otherwise decent and intelligent Serb friends.

11   See Svetozar Koljevic, "The Battle of Kosovo in Its Epic Mosaic," in *Kosovo: Legacy of a Medieval Battle*, ed. Wayne S. Vucinich and Thomas A. Emmert (Minneapolis: University of Minnesota Press, 1991), 136. This tradition of oral history through poetry never completely died out in Serbia. In the interwar period, accounts of the debates in the Yugoslav assembly were disseminated in verse sung by a Serb peasant poet. At the end of the war in Bosnia, I witnessed a Serb singer weaving a tale of lament that described the ongoing flight from Serb-held areas around Sarajevo. The singer—not, I believe blind—accompanied himself on the traditional one-stringed gusle while all around him buildings burned and panic-stricken Serbs loaded their families and belongings onto buses, cars, and wagons to flee incoming Bosnian forces.

12   Ilija Garasanin, "Nacertanije," in *Izvori Velikosrpske Agresije*, ed. Boze Covic (Croatia: Tiskarna Rijeka), 67.

13   John Reed, *The War in Eastern Europe* (New York: Scribners, 1919), 39.

14   See Noel Malcolm, *Kosovo: A Short History* (New York: New York University Press, 1998), 194.

15   Vladimir Velebit, "Kosovo: A Case of Ethnic Change of Population," *East European Quarterly* 33, no. 2 (June 1999), 177.

16   See Malcolm, *Kosovo: A Short History*, 230.

17   Ibid., 255; and Leon Trotsky, *The Balkan Wars: 1912–1913* (New York: Pathfinder, 1991), 267.

18   Lenard J. Cohen, *The Socialist Pyramid: Elites and Power in Yugoslavia* (New York: Mosaic Press, 1989), 343. Cohen provides an insightful description of the history of antagonism and a warning of the tensions simmering just below the surface on the eve of Milosevic's appearance.

19   See Malcolm, *Kosovo: A Short History*, 286.

20   See Cohen, *Socialist Pyramid*, 338.

21   When I lived in Belgrade in the late 1980s and early 1990s, Cubrilovic was still alive. His continued advocacy of the ethnic reconquest of Kosovo found a ready audience in the climate of nationalist euphoria that Milosevic unleashed. The Serb plan for ethnically cleansing Kosovo in the 1999 war—called "Operation Horseshoe"—was based, according to media accounts, on re-creating Cubrilovic's vision.

22   See Cohen, *Socialist Pyramid*, 344.

23   Svetozar Vukmanovic-Tempo, *The Struggle for the Balkans* (London: Merlin Press, 1990), 72.

24   See Velebit, "Kosovo," 192.

25   See Cohen, *Socialist Pyramid*, 347; and Marko Lopusina, *Ubij, bliznjeg svog 1: Ju-*

goslovenska tajna policija od 1945 do 1997 (Belgrade: Narodna Knjiga Alfa, 1997), 128.

26 See Cohen, *Socialist Pyramid*, 350, 353.

27 See ibid., 356, 366; and Malcolm, *Kosovo: A Short History*, 326.

28 See Cohen, *Socialist Pyramid*, 361.

29 See Julie A. Mertus, *Kosovo: How Myths and Truths Started a War* (Los Angeles: University of California Press, 1999), 23.

30 Mahmut Bakalli, interviewed with author, 1 July 2000.

31 Ibid.

32 See Mertus, *Kosovo*, 31. In a 1 July 2000 interview with the author, Bakalli, who remains an influential figure within Kosovo to this day—in part because of his decision to resign rather than go along with the harsh measures imposed by Belgrade—gave his version of the 1981 events. Bakalli said that he believed the student demonstrations, which according to some accounts began as a protest over poor living conditions in the dormitories of Pristina University, may have been exploited by individuals close to the Albanian intelligence service, the Sigurimi, which saw unrest in Kosovo as a way to weaken Yugoslavia. The demonstrations began on a small scale, according to Bakalli, and he allowed local police to use only rubber truncheons and not firearms in response. The relatively small number of police in Kosovo, however, had difficulty in fully containing the demonstrations, and Bakalli consented to the dispatch of special federal riot-control police because he thought they would act in a "professional" manner. Yet on the night of 1–2 April, the special police carried out a "rampage" through the dorms, savagely beating every student they encountered and allegedly thrusting a nightstick into the vagina of a female student. When word spread of the police behavior, Kosovo erupted in anger. The Yugoslav collective leadership, facing its first crisis since Tito's death, decided that stronger measures were needed. Under the chair of the Macedonian, Lazar Kolishevski, who Bakalli described as a "Serb puppet," the presidency characterized the upheaval in Kosovo as "counterrevolution" and decided to dispatch JNA troops to the province. When Bakalli learned that Belgrade intended to send in troops, he resigned. Bakalli said that JNA General Nikola Ljubicic, a Serb who later played an influential behind-the-scenes role in Milosevic's rise, was a driving force behind the dispatch of JNA troops.

In his memoirs, published in 2000, Admiral Branko Mamula, who was Yugoslav defense minister at the time of the 1981 demonstrations, seems to indicate that the Yugoslav military decided on its own to send troops to Kosovo. Mamula writes that the situation in Kosovo in early April had passed beyond the ability of the local authorities to control it, and that "from the leadership of the country (that is, Yugoslavia), nothing could be expected" (Slucaj Jugoslavija [Podgorica: CID, 2000], 38). Informed by the country's collective presidency of its expectations for ongoing negotiations with the students, but also aware that the students had been joined by large numbers of protesting citizens in the streets of Pristina, Mamula judged that the situation "would very quickly go beyond political and police control" (ibid., 39). Even though "mass unrest [*nemiri*]" had not yet broken out, the military decided to move forces into Kosovo from nearby garrisons in Skopje, Nis, and other Serbian cities. After the JNA deployed in Kosovo, Mamula describes "armed conflict" in Pristina and other parts of Kosovo (ibid., 40). He asserts that in Podujevo—also a hot spot during the demonstrations of the 1980s and the conflict in the late 1990s—JNA units barely managed to prevent demonstrators from seizing a storage depot containing thousands of weapons. Had the depot fallen, Mamula maintains, armed uprising would have broken out in Kosovo fifteen years before it actually did.

Mamula is silent on the number of casualties in the 1981 Kosovo demonstrations. Bakalli contends that the official number of eleven dead was roughly correct.

33 Thorough accounts of the Martinovic case and its political repercussions can be found in Mertus, *Kosovo*, 100–110; and Kjell Magnusson, "The Serbian Reaction: Kosovo and Ethnic Mobilization among the Serbs," *Nordic Journal of Soviet and East European Studies* 4, no. 3 (1987): 3–29. For the reactions of KOS and the secret police, see Lopusina, *Ubij*, 313.

34 Mertus, *Kosovo*, 107.

35 See ibid., 108.

36 See Plestina, *Regional Development*, 180.

37 See "Yugoslavia: Crisis in Kosovo," *Helsinki Watch*, March 1990, 23.

38 Quoted in Mertus, *Kosovo*, 22.

39 Kacusa Jashari and other participants in the meeting, interview with author, 9 June 2000; see also *New York Times*, 14 October 1988.

40 Scanlan, interview with author, March 2000.

41 *Tanjug* English, 17 October 1988; cited in "Eastern Europe Daily Report," FBIS, 18 October 1988, 81, EEU-88-201.

42 See Belgrade Radio, 17 October 1988; cited in "Eastern Europe Daily Reports," FBIS, 19 October 1988, 48, EEU-88-202.

43 See Slavoljub, Djukic, *Izmedju Slave I Anateme: Politicka biografija Slobodana Milosevica* (Belgrade: Filip Visnic, 1994), 119.

44 See Meier, *Yugoslavia*, 87.

45 Ibid., 89–91. German journalist Viktor Meier, who covered Yugoslavia for many years, based his account of what went on behind the closed doors of the LCY presidency on the former League of Communists of Slovenia's records, which he read in Ljubljana after Slovenia became an independent state.

46 See Belgrade radio, 28 February 1989; cited in "Eastern Europe Daily Reports," FBIS, 1 March 1989, 61, EEU-89-039.

47 See Belgrade radio, 1 March 1989; cited in "Eastern Europe Daily Reports," FBIS, 2 March 1989, 43, EEU-89-040.

48 See Meier, *Yugoslavia*, 92.

49 See "Crisis in Kosovo," *Helsinki Watch*, 14.

50 See *New York Times*, 4 April 1989.

51 See "Crisis in Kosovo, "*Helsinki Watch*, 28.

52 Quoted in *Borba*, 29 June 1989; "Eastern Europe Daily Report," FBIS, 3 July 1989, 84, EEU-89-126.

53 Janez Drnovsek, *Escape from Hell: The Truth of a President* (Ljubljana, Slovenia: Delo, 1996), 60.

54   See Chuck Sudetic, "Albanians' New Way: Feuds without Blood," *New York Times*, 17 April 1990.

55   Ibrahim Rugova, *La question du Kosovo* (Paris: Fayard, 1994), 126.

56   Ibid., 172.

57   See Warren Zimmermann, *Origins of a Catastrophe* (New York: Random House, 1996), 81.

58   See Borisav Jovic, *Poslednji Dani SFRJ* (Belgrade: Politika, 1995), 32.

59   See Eric D. Gordy, *The Culture of Power in Serbia: The Destruction of Alternatives* (University Park: Pennsylvania State University Press, 1999), 57.

60   Slobodan Nedovic, *Izvestaj sa predsednickih izbora u Srbiji Decembar 1997* (Beograd: Dosije, 1997), 94.

61   Quoted in Drnovsek, *Escape*, 198.

62   See Chuck Sudetic, "Serbia Suspends Government of Albanian Region," *New York Times*, 6 July 1990.

63   See Shkelzen Maliqi, "The Albanian Movement in Kosovo," in *Yugoslavia and After: A Study in Fragmentation, Despair, and Rebirth*, David A. Dyker and Ivan Vejvoda (New York: Longman, 1996), 151.

64   See "Yugoslavia: Human Rights Abuses in Kosovo, 1990–1992," *Helsinki Watch*, October 1992: 30.

65   Ibid., 38.

66   Ibid., 42.

67   Quoted in *New York Times*, 6 February 1999.

FOUR. *A New Tito?*

1   Quoted in Henry Kamm, "The Serb Who's Giving Orders," *New York Times*, 14 October 1988.

2   Quoted on Belgrade Radio, 12 April 1989; cited in "Eastern Europe Daily Report," FBIS, 13 April 1989, 37, EEU-89-070.

3   See *Politika*, 26 July 1989; cited in "Eastern Europe Daily Report," FBIS, 2 August 1989, 65, EEU-89-147.

4   See *Delo*, 23 June 1989; cited in "Eastern Europe Daily Report," FBIS, 30 June 1980, 73, EEU-89-125.

5   See Borisav Jovic, Poslednji Dani SFRJ (Belgrade: Politika, 1995), 27.

6   Ibid., 28.

7   Janez Drnovsek, *Escape from Hell: The Truth of a President* (Ljubljana, Slovenia: Delo, 1996), 107.

8   Quoted in Reuters, 14 November 1989.

9   Quoted in *Narodna Armija*, 13 July 1989.

10   Drnovsek, *Escape*, 127.

11   Jovic, *Poslednji Dani*, 41.

12   Drnovsek, *Escape*, 128.

13   See *Tanjug*, 1 January 1990; cited in "Eastern Europe Daily Report," FBIS, 5 January 1990, 90, EEU-90-004.

14 See *Borba*, 21–22 January 1989, 4, cited in "Eastern Europe Daily Report," FBIS, 9 February 1989, 57, EEU-89-026.

15 See *Tanjug*, 19 April 1989; cited in "Eastern Europe Daily Report," FBIS, 20 April 1989, 49, FBIS-EEU-89-075.

16 See *Borba*, 26 October 1989; cited in "Eastern Europe Daily Report," FBIS, 17 November 1989, 85, EEU-89-221.

17 Quoted in *Rilindija*, 22 December 1989; cited in "Eastern Europe Daily Report," FBIS, 3 January 1990, 103, EEU-90-002.

18 Quoted in Slavoljub Djukic, *Izmedju Slave I Anateme: Politicka biografija Slobodana Milosevica* (Belgrade: Filip Visnic, 1994), 142.

19 Ibid., 144.

20 See Lenard J. Cohen, *Broken Bonds: The Disintegration of Yugoslavia* (Boulder, Colo.: Westview Press, 1993), 160.

21 See *Delo*, 8 July 1989; cited in "Eastern Europe Daily Report," FBIS, 14 July 1989, 40, EEU-89-134.

22 Jovic, *Poslednji Dani*, 47.

23 Ibid., 99.

FIVE. *All Serbs in One State*

1 See Borisav Jovic, *Poslednji Dani SFRJ* (Belgrade: Politika, 1995), 72.

2 Quoted in *Tanjug*, 10 May 1990; cited in "Eastern Europe Daily Report," FBIS, 11 May 1990, 49, EEU-90-092.

3 See Belgrade Radio, 25 June 1990; cited in "Eastern Europe Daily Report," FBIS, 26 June 1990, 51, EEU-90-123.

4 See Jovic, Poslednji Dani, 90.

5 Slavoljub Djukic, *Lovljenje Vetra: Politicka ispovest Dobrice Cosica* (Beograd, Samizdat B-92, 2001), 161.

6 Ibid., 72.

7 The publication at the end of the 1980s of Djilas's books for the first time in Yugoslavia in the Serbo-Croatian language, although they had been printed in the millions in other languages around the world, was a major political and literary event. Djilas's remarks are cited in Djukic, *Lovljenje Vetra*, 155.

8 Borisav Jovic, *Poslednji dani SFRJ* (Beograd: Prisma, 1996), 193. Cosic told me in a conversation on 26 June 2001 that he had never drawn up any maps regarding the division of Croatia. He said that he had never favored breaking up Croatia and described Milosevic's concept of "all Serbs in one state" as "crazy and unachievable." Cosic said he had always argued that the majority Serb areas in Croatia should be given broad autonomy, equivalent to what, he said, was enjoyed by the Aaland Islands. Cosic acknowledged that he had always favored the division of Kosovo, with the northern portion and the historic Serb shrines staying with Serbia and the remaining portions being allowed to go their own way.

9 See Slavoljub Djukic, *Izmedju Slave I Anateme: Politicka biografija Slobodana Milosevica* (Belgrade: Filip Visnic, 1994), 164.

10 Ibid., 163.

11 See Paul Shoup, "The Future of Croatia's Border Regions," *Radio Free Europe Situation Report*, 29 November 1991.

12 See Janez Drnovsek, *Escape from Hell: The Truth of a President* (Ljubljana, Slovenia: Delo, 1996), 205.

13 See *Vjesnik*, 9 July 1989; cited in "Eastern Europe Daily Report," FBIS, 12 July 1989, 49, AU1107104289, EEU-89-132.

14 See Jovic, *Poslednji Dani*, 100.

15 See *Radio Free Europe Newsline*, 16 March 2000; Radio Montenegro, Podgorica, 30 April 2000; Radio Zagreb, 16 March 2000; and Tim Judah, "Croatia Reborn," *New York Review of Books*, 10 August 2000, 20. Shortly after Mesic took office in February 2000, he announced that his staff had found a secret hot line telephone between Tudjman and Milosevic. Later accounts made it appear that what had been found was a dead phone, but whether it was actually connected with the Serbian leader and ever worked is open to question. The Mesic team also discovered an archive of approximately 830 tapes and transcripts of about 17,000 conversations, covering almost every meeting Tudjman had after 1991, when the secret taping system was allegedly installed in his office. The Croatian media published transcripts of a number of these conversations, most apparently intended to embarrass the Tudjman regime. As of the end of 2000, no transcripts purporting to come from the Milosevic-Tudjman hot line had been published, and months after the appearance of the initial media reports a senior official in both the Tudjman and Mesic administrations told me that as far as he was aware, there was no Milosevic-Tudjman hot line.

16 Quoted in Marko Prelec, "Franjo Tudjman's Croatia in the Balkans," in *Crisis in the Balkans: Views from the Participants*, ed. Constantine P. Danopoulos and Kostas G. Messas (Boulder, Colo.: Westview Press, 1997), 80.

17 See Robert Bajrusi, "Stipe Mesic o Sarinicevim memoarima," *Nacional*, 10 October 1999.

18 See *Tanjug*, 13 June 1991; and *Borba*, 14 June 1991; both cited in "Eastern Europe Daily Report," FBIS, 14 June 1991, 37, EEU-91-115.

19 Robert Bajrusi, "The Sensational Transcript between Tudjman and Radic: Even in 1999 Tudjman Wanted to Annex Banja Luka," *Nacional*, 1 June 2000.

20 Quoted on Belgrade Radio, 10 July 1990; cited in "Eastern Europe Daily Report," FBIS, 11 July 1990, 72, EEU-90-133.

21 See *Borba*, 1 February 1991; cited in "Eastern Europe Daily Report," FBIS, 6 February 1991, 53, EEU-91-025.

22 Drnovsek, *Escape*, 188.

23 See Jovic, *Poslednji Dani*, 98.

24 See Stipe Sikavica, "The Army's Collapse," in *Burn This House: The Making and Unmaking of Yugoslavia*, ed. Jasminka Udovicki and James Ridgeway (Durham, N.C.: Duke University Press, 1997), 136. Milosevic's toadying may not have done much good. According to a recent history of the Yugoslav secret police, Mamula— who stepped down as minister in 1988—may have been involved in an attempted

coup against Milosevic in 1993 (see Marko Lopusina, *Ubij bliznjeg svog 1: Jugos-lovenska tajna policija od 1945 do 1997* [Belgrade: Narodna Knjiga Alfa, 1997], 311).

25 Jovic, *Poslednji Dani*, 55, 65.

26 Ibid., 86.

27 Ibid., 113.

28 Ibid., 146.

29 Ibid., 145.

30 The Vojna Linija and its RAM plan have a shadowy history. The RAM plan seems to have been first mentioned at a 19 September session of the Yugoslav government, chaired by Prime Minister Ante Markovic, who described contacts among Milo-sevic, Karadzic, and JNA generals as part of the RAM program for a Greater Serbia (see *Vreme*, 30 September 1990, 4). While I was serving in the U.S. embassy in Bel-grade from 1987–1991, I cannot recall ever hearing of either the Vojna Linija or the RAM plan, although the actions of the Serb authorities in providing military and other forms of support to Serbs in Croatia and Bosnia were certainly well-known. At some point during my last year in the embassy, I was shown a covertly obtained document that revealed contingency plans by the military to rapidly carve out a zone of control over an area marked on a map that roughly approximated the areas of then Serb agitation and that later became the so-called Serb Krajina. This may have been the RAM plan or something similar.

Former intelligence community analysts with responsibility for Yugoslavia have confirmed my own recollection that in the period 1990 to early 1991, before the actual outbreak of hostilities, the bulk of the gun running and other forms of covert support for the Croatian Serbs came from the Serbian police and not the JNA. When war actually broke out, the JNA, which never expected to fight a war against its own people, seemed rather poorly prepared both in a logistic and tactical sense.

Writing in the *New York Review of Books*, Mark Danner cites testimony by former Bosnian Minister of Defense Jerko Doko before the Hague Tribunal about the RAM plan. According to Doko, the word RAM refers to the boundaries or frame within which it was intended that the new Serb-dominated lands would be estab-lished. The plan described how artillery, ammunition, and other military equip-ment would be stored at strategic locations in Croatia and Bosnia, and how, with the help of the Serb secret police, shadow police and military units would be armed and trained among the local Serb population. See Mark Danner, "America and the Bosnia Genocide," New York Review of Books, 4 December 1997, 61.

Most discussion of the Vojna Linija has appeared in Western works about Yugo-slavia—for example, see Tim Judah's interesting treatment of the subject in *The Serbs: History, Myth, and the Destruction of Yugoslavia* (New Haven, Conn.: Yale University Press, 1997), 170. *Ubij bliznjeg svog 1*, by Marko Lopusina, a seemingly well-informed but somewhat sensational history of the Yugoslav secret police that appeared in Belgrade at the end of the 1990s describes the Vojna Linija as a group of senior officials within Milosevic's secret police—including its head Jovica Stani-sic, his deputy Mihajlo Kertes, and others—who were responsible for arming Serb paramilitaries in Croatia and Bosnia. This account, however, may also reflect Western information since it appears to cite the *Guardian*, which apparently sourced its story on the Vojna Linija to a "former paramilitary commander and high member of Milosevic's leftist coalition" (see Lopusina, *Ubij*, 388). A hagiographic Serb biography of Mladic makes no mention of the Vojna Linija, although Mladic is cited as calling many of the senior figures in the JNA in 1991 "traitors of the highest caliber," which certainly shows his dissatisfaction with the cautious policy pursued by Kadijevic and Adzic in the run-up to war (see Jovan Janjic, *Srpski General Ratko Mladic* [Novi Sad, Vojvodina: Matica Srpska Press, 1996], 7).

31   Quoted in Djukic, *Izmedju*, 149.

32   Robert Hayden, "Politics and the Media," *Radio Free Europe Situation Report*, 6 December 1991.

33   See Lenard J. Cohen, *Broken Bonds: The Disintegration of Yugoslavia* (Boulder, Colo.: Westview Press, 1993), 156.

34   Quoted in *Borba*, 26 February 1991; cited in "Eastern Europe Daily Report," FBIS, 6 March 1991, 54, EEU-91-044.

35   See Robert T. Thomas, *Serbia under Milosevic: Politics in the 1990s* (London: Hurst and Company, 1999), 99.

36   Jovic, *Poslednji Dani*, 160.

37   Veljko Kadijevic, *Moje Vidjenje Raspada* (Belgrade: Politika, 1993), 113. Jovic (Poslednji Dani, 162) and Drnovsek (*Escape*, 242) seem to agree substantially on what the JNA proposed, but Kadijevic, in his account, does not mention the proposal for democratic elections in six months.

38   The presidency's discussions are drawn from Jovic, *Poslednji Dani*, 167–76; Drnovsek, *Escape*, 235–55; and Stipe Mesic, *Kako Smo Srusili Jugoslaviju* (Zagreb: Globus, 1992).

39   See Jovic, *Poslednji Dani*, 176.

40   Quoted in *Tanjug*, 16 March 1991; cited in "Eastern Europe Daily Report," FBIS, 18 March 1991, 47, EEU-91-052.

41   Quoted in Judah, *The Serbs*, 175.

42   Jovic, *Poslednji Dani*, 181.

43   On 15 April 1991, *Vreme* published excerpts from the stenographic record of Milosevic's meeting with the district leaders. Accounts also appear in *NIN*, 12 April 1991; and Djukic, *Izmedju*, 187. Interestingly, Milosevic had apparently not intended to address the district leaders personally. But when the head of the Serb assembly spoke to them, the district leaders rebelled, claiming that no one was giving them information about what was going on or instructions about what they should be doing in response to the unfolding crisis. They demanded that Milosevic speak to them, and after a brief pause, he was hastily summoned. Milosevic's remarks, which were never intended to be made public, offer an insight into his strategy made in an unusual impromptu setting. The confusion evident among the local leaders was also a sign of the lack of political and psychological preparation for war that quickly became evident in Serbia once armed conflict actually began a few months later in Croatia.

1   Interview with Vucic, 23 June 2001.

2   John Scanlan, interview with author in March 2000.

3   James A. Baker III, *The Politics of Diplomacy* (New York: G. P. Putnam and Sons, 1995).

4   Quoted in Steven Engleberg, "Carving out a Greater Serbia," *New York Times Magazine*, 1 September 1991.

5   Warren Zimmermann, *Origins of a Catastrophe* (New York: Random House, 1996), 5–8.

6   Ibid., 20.

7   Baker, *Politics*, 630–33.

8   See Borisav Jovic, *Poslednji Dani SFRJ* (Belgrade: Politika, 1995), 193.

9   Ibid., 199.

10 Quoted in Zimmermann, *Origins*, 149.

11 Baker, *Politics*, 631.

12 Quoted in "Ratni Memoari General Martin Spegel," *Globus*, 14 and 21 July 1995; cited in Norman Cigar, "Croatia's War of Independence: The Parameters of Conflict Termination," *Journal of Slavic Military Studies* 10, no. 2 (June 1997): 48.

13 Quoted in Zimmermann, *Origins*, 154.

14 See *Washington Post*, 2 September 1991.

15 See *Washington Post*, 7 September 1991.

16 See Henry Wynaendts, *L'engrenage: Chroniques Yougoslaves, Juillet 1991–Aout 1992* (Paris: Denoel, 1993), 125.

17 Senior Montenegrin official, interview with author, 26 September 2000; and Jovic, *Poslednji Dani*, 233.

18 Veljko Kadijevic, *Moje Vidjenje Raspada* (Belgrade: Politika, 1993), 140.

19 Zimmermann, *Origins*, 157.

20 Kadijevic, *Vidjenje*, 136.

21 Ibid., 138.

22 Quoted in Tony Barber, "Yugoslavia in Crisis: Bellicose Milosevic Raises Stakes," *Independent*, 8 July 1991.

23 Milos Vasic, quoted in *Washington Post*, 21 September 1991.

24 See Jovic, *Poslednji Dani*, 221–23.

25 Engleberg, "Carving," *New York Times Magazine*.

26 See Laura Silber, "Milosevic Family Values," *New Republic*, 30 August 1999.

27 Quoted in Jovic, *Poslednji Dani*, 211.

28 See Paul Williams and Norman Cigar, *War Crimes and Individual Responsibility: A Prima Facie Case for the Indictment of Slobodan Milosevic* (Washington, D.C.: Balkan Institute, 1997).

29 See Jovic, *Poslednji Dani*, 233–35.

30 See Norman Cigar, "Croatia's War," 37.

31 Zimmermann, *Origins*, 160.

32 See Cigar, "Croatia's War," 37.

33 Conversation with Ambassador Okun, 1999.

34 Jovic, *Poslednji Dani*, 247–49.

35 See Sead Arnautovic, *Izbori u Bosni I Hercegovini '90* (Sarajevo: Promocult, 1996), 108.

36 Ibid., 154.

37 Alija Izetbegovic, *Islamska Deklaracija* (Sarajevo: Bosnia, 1990).

38 See Zimmermann, *Origins*, 173.

39 Zimmermann, *Origins*, 175. See also Kenneth B. Dekleva and Jerold M. Post, "Genocide in Bosnia: The Case of Dr. Radovan Karadzic," *Journal of the American Academy of Psychiatric Law* 25, no. 4 (1997): 485–96.

40 Quoted in Steven L. Burg and Paul S. Shoup, *The War in Bosnia-Herzegovina: Ethnic Conflict and International Intervention* (Armonk, N.Y.: M. E. Sharpe, 1999), 77.

41 See Smail Cekic, *The Aggression on Bosnia and Genocide against the Bosniacs, 1991–1993* (Sarajevo: Institute for the Research of Crimes against Humanity and International Law, 1995), 45.

42 See Jovic, *Poslednji Dani*, 241.

43 See Milovan Djilas and Nadezeda Gace, *Bosnjak Adil Zulfikarpasic* (Zagreb: Globus, 1995), 189–94.

44 Quoted on Belgrade Radio, 29 February 1992; translated by BBC summary of World Broadcasts.

45 Zimmermann, *Origins*, 180.

46 Conference on Yugoslavia Arbitration Commission, "Opinion No. 4 on International Recognition of the Socialist Republic of Bosnia-Hercegovina by the European Community and Its Member States," R. Badinter, Paris, January 11, 1992.

47 See Burg and Shoup, *War in Bosnia*, 106.

48 Ambassador Okun, telephone interview with author.

49 See Baker, *Politics*, 640–42; and David Binder, "US Set to Accept Yugoslav Breakup," *New York Times*, 12 March 1992.

50 See Burg and Shoup, *War in Bosnia*, 124.

51 Ibid., 171.

52 See Williams and Cigar, *War Crimes*, 8.

53 See Blaine Harden, "Serb Forces Overwhelm Key Town," *Washington Post*, 15 April 1992.

54 See final report of the UN Commission of Experts on Human Rights Abuses in Yugoslavia, S/1994/647, 28 December 1994, annex 5, 19–23.

55 See Belgrade Television, 23 April 1992; cited in BBC summary of World Broadcasts.

56 See Blaine Harden, "Serbia Seen Adopting a New Bosnia Policy," *Washington Post*, 25 April 1992.

57 Quoted in Blaine Harden, "Serbian Leader in Firm Control Despite Protests," *Washington Post*, 10 March 1992.

SEVEN. *Milosevic and the Politics of Power*

1 Quoted in "Otisli su zauvek," *Glas Javnosti*, 22 October 2000.

2 Slavoljub Djukic, *Lovljenje Vetra: Politicka ispovest Dobrice Cosica* (Beograd: Samizdat B92, 2001), 199.

3 Wes Clark, interview with author, Washington, D.C., 13 November 2000.

4 Quoted in "Otisli su zauvek."

5 Warren Zimmermann, *Origins of a Catastrophe* (New York: Random House, 1996), 26.

6 Carl Bildt, *Peace Journey: The Struggle for Peace in Bosnia* (London: Weidenfeld and Nicolson, 1998), 102.

7 See Richard Holbrooke, *To End a War* (New York: Random House, 1998), 135.

8 Bildt, *Peace Journey*, 231.

9 Ivor Roberts, "Why Yugoslavia Died" (lecture at Oxford University, 2 February 1999).

10 The incident appears in General Wesley K. Clark, *Waging Modern War* (New York: Public Affairs, 2001), 110.

11 Interview with Milosevic, TV Palma, 12 December 2000.

12 Interview with Viktor Chernomyrdin, "War in Europe," *PBS Frontline* (http://www.pbs.org/wgbh/pages/frontline/shows/kosovo/interviews/chernomyrdin).

13 Interview with Milosevic, *Washington Post*, 13 December 1998.

14 Interview with Milosevic, TV Palma, 12 December 2000.

15 David Owen, *Balkan Odyssey* (New York: Harcourt Brace, 1995), 173.

16 See William Drozdiak, "How the Kosovo Deal was Reached," *Washington Post*, 6 June 1999.

17 Interviews in June 2001 with Slavoljub Djukic and Dobrica Cosic.

18 Narcissism is one of three Freudian personality types—the others being erotic and obsessive. According to this concept, most people combine elements of all three personality types. Individuals who are said to be primarily narcissists are often characterized by independence, innovation, and self-esteem. They want to be admired, not loved, and are often driven to achieve power and glory. Many leaders have elements of narcissism in their personalities. Narcissism, like any personality trait, has its negative side and can be taken to extremes. Malignant narcissists are said to be self-centered, vain, motivated by self-love, puffed up with themselves, and callous in their treatment of others. Milosevic exhibits many of these traits in spades. But he has crossed the moral line from personality disorder into active evil on a massive scale.

    This discussion of the psychological side of Milosevic's personality is informed by conversations with Dr. Ken DeKleva of the University of Texas Southwestern Medical School and Dr. Jerold Post of George Washington University. I am grateful for their willingness to share their insights with me, but the responsibility for the judgments is mine alone.

19 Roberts, "Why Yugoslavia Died."

20 Slavoljub Djukic, *He, She, and We: A Political Portrait of Slobodan Milosevic and His Wife*, trans. FBIS (Belgrade: Radio B-92, 1997), 15.

21 See *Vijesti*, 28 September 2000.

22 Laura Silber, "Milosevic Family Values," *New Republic*, 30 August 1999.

23 Interview 20 June 2001.

24 Author's interview with Tijanic, in Belgrade, 20 June 2001.

25 Interview 23 June 2001.

26 *Delo*, 22 October 1988, 19; cited in "Eastern Europe Daily Report," FBIS, 28 October 1988, 63, EEU-88-208, AU261014788.

27 Zimmermann, *Origins*, 118.

28 See Djukic, *He, She, and We*, 91.

29 Interview with Vucelic, 23 June 2001.

30 See Eric D. Gordy, *The Culture of Power in Serbia: The Destruction of Alternatives* (University Park: Pennsylvania State University Press, 1999), 71, 41.

31 Ibid., 100.

32 See Milan Milosevic, "The Media Wars," in *Burn This House: The Making and Unmaking of Yugoslavia*, ed. Jasminka Udoricki and James Ridgeway (Durham, N.C.: Duke University Press, 1997), 118.

33 Author's interview with Matic, Belgrade, 22 June 2001.

34 Author's interview with Zivanovic, 27 June 2001.

35 Mladjan Dinkic, ed., *Final Account* (Belgrade: stubovi kulture, 1999), 10.

36 Anonymous, *Financial Needs for Macroeconomic Reforms and the Reconstruction of Post-Milosevic Serbia* (Belgrade: G-17 Plus, 2000), 39.

37 See Irena Guzelova, "Milosevic's Bank Delivers Secrets: Beogradska Banka Funded the Yugoslav Dictator's Cronies and Paid off Potential Foes," *Financial Times*, 7 December 2000.

38 See Radio B-92, daily news, 6 December 2000, citing *Nedelni Telegraf* of same day.

39 See Thomas Brey, "How the Milosevic Clan Robbed Serbia," *DPA*, 27 October 2000.

40 Quoted in Stephen J. Hedges, "The Looting of Yugoslavia," *US News and World Report*, 21 July 1999.

41 See Glenn Kessler, "Milosevic Cronies Took $1 Billion, U.S. Learns," *Washington Post*, 2 December 2000.

42 Interview with Mrgic, 20 June 2001.

43 Interview with Vucic, 23 June 2001.

44 See Hedges, "Looting."

45 See "Serbia's Grain Trade: Milosevic's Hidden Cash Crop," *International Crisis Group*, 5 June 2000.

46 See Tom Walker "Milosevic Builds Two Million Pound Belgrade Villa," *Sunday Times*, 22 October 2000.

47 See Hedges, "Looting."

48 See "Mira and the 165,000 Tip," *London Times*, 21 January 2001.

49 Quoted in Silber, "Family Values," 26.

50 Djukic, *He, She, and We*, 74.

51 See "Batinasi I revolverasi Mire Markovic," *Glas Javnosti*, 7 November 2000.

52 See "Ruska zima," *Glas Javnosti*, 5 November 2000.

53 See Guzelova, "Milosevic's Bank."

54 Quoted in Djukic, *He, She, and We*, 17.

55 See *New York Times*, 6 July 1999.

56 See "German Report on Milosevic's Money," *New York Times*, 17 October 2000.

57 Interview 21 June 2001.

58   See Gordy, *Culture of Power*, 197.

59   Ibid., 184.

60   Ibid., 2.

EIGHT. *Man of Peace*

1   See Robert T. Thomas, *Serbia under Milosevic: Politics in the 1990s* (London: Hurst and Company, 1999), 163–65.

2   Quoted in James Gow, *Triumph of the Lack of Will: International Diplomacy and the Yugoslav War* (New York: Columbia University Press, 1997), 227.

3   Quoted in ibid., 228.

4   John Major, *The Autobiography* (New York: HarperCollins, 1999), 538.

5   David Owen, *Balkan Odyssey* (New York: Harcourt Brace, 1995), 126–29.

6   Quoted in Hrvoje Sarinic, *Svi Moji Tajni Pregovori Sa Slobodanom Milosevicem* (Zagreb: Globus, 1999), 41–45.

7   Ibid. Herceg-Bosna was the Croat entity in Bosnia. It functioned for all practical purposes as a part of Croatia; using Croat money, watching Croat media, and voting in Croat elections.

8   Ibid.

9   The text of Cosic's letter is found in Milan Nikolic, ed., *Sta Je Stvarno Rekao Dobrica Cosic* (Belgrade: Draganic, 1995), 159; and Slavoljub Djukic, *Lovljenje Vetra: Politicka ispovest Dobrice Cosica* (Beograd: Samizdat B-92, 2001), 187.

10   See Slavoljub Djukic, *Izmedju Slave I Anateme: Politicka biografija Slobodana Milosevica* (Belgrade: Filip Visnic, 1994), 222.

11   Ibid., 229–34.

12   Ibid., 244.

13   See Slavoljub Djukic, *He, She, and We: A Political Portrait of Slobodan Milosevic and His Wife*, trans. FBIS (Belgrade: Radio B-92, 1997), 58–59.

14   Ibid., 60.

15   Slavoljub Djukic, *Lovljenje Vetra*, 216.

16   Cosic interview, 26 June 2001.

17   Thomas, *Serbia under Milosevic*, 131.

18   Vladimir Goati et al., *Guide through the Electoral Controversies in Serbia* (Belgrade: Centar za Slobodne Izbore I Demokratiu, 2000), 60–62.

19   Interview, 19 June 2001.

20   Warren Christopher, *In the Stream of History: Shaping Foreign Policy for a New Era* (Stanford, Calif.: Stanford University Press, 1998), 346. Christopher declined to be interviewed for this book.

21   Ibid.

22   Ibid., 347; and Elizabeth Drew, *On the Edge: The Clinton Presidency* (New York: Simon and Schuster, 1994), 152–61. See also Raymond Seitz, *Over Here* (London: Phoenix, 1998), 327–29. Seitz—an experienced career diplomat—says that he suggested Prime Minister Major tell Christopher "straight" that Major would be unable to deliver the "skeptical Cabinet to such a risky proposal," surely one of the

more egregious recent examples of an ambassador confusing which government he was supposed to be providing advice to.

23   See Paul C. Szasz, "The Quest for a Bosnian Constitution: Legal Aspects of Constitutional Proposals Relating to Bosnia," *Fordam International Law Journal* 19, no. 2 (December 1995): 368. Szasz did much of the legal drafting for the international negotiators operating under ICFY auspices during 1992–1995.

24   Owen, *Odyssey*, 105–8.

25   Ibid., 125.

26   Interview with Miloved Vucelic, 23 June 2001.

27   Owen, *Odyssey*, 144–49, 154–55.

28   Interview with Milosevic, TV Palma, 12 December 2000.

29   Owen, *Odyssey*, 173.

30   Ibid., 144.

31   Charles Redman, telephone interview with author, 2000.

32   Quoted in Richard Holbrooke, *To End a War* (New York: Random House, 1998), 106, 114.

33   Ivor Roberts, "Why Yugoslavia Died" (lecture at Oxford University, 2 February 1999).

34   Interview with Wes Clark, "War in Europe," *PBS Frontline* (http://www.pbs.org/wgbh/pages/frontline/shows/kosovo/interviews/clark).

35   Interview with Viktor Chernomyrdin, *PBS Frontline*.

36   Holbrooke, *To End a War*, 273, 285; and Roberts, "Why Yugoslavia Died."

37   Interview with Klaus Naumann, "War in Europe," *PBS Frontline* (http://www.pbs.org/wgbh/pages/frontline/shows/kosovo/interviews/naumann).

38   Wes Clark, interview with author, 13 November 2000.

39   Roberts, "Why Yugoslavia Died."

40   Holbrooke, *To End a War*, 285.

41   Michael Rose, *Fighting for Peace: Bosnia 1994* (London: Harvill Press, 1998), 46.

42   Ibid., 66.

43   Testimony by Ambassadors Peter Galbreath and Charles Redman before a special congressional committee investigating the affair.

44   Roberts, "Why Yugoslavia Died."

45   Ibid.

46   See Thomas, *Serbia under Milosevic*, 202–4.

47   See Roberts, "Why Yugoslavia Died."

48   Interview with Milosevic, TV Palma, 12 December 2000.

49   See Thomas, *Serbia under Milosevic*, 193.

50   Quoted in Sarinic, *Tajni Pregovori*, 187–89.

51   Roberts, "Why Yugoslavia Died."

52   See "Surrender and Blame," *New Yorker*, 19 December 1994, 44–51, and Michael Gordon, "Conflict in the Balkans," *New York Times*, 4 December 1994.

53   See Ivo H. Daalder, *Getting to Dayton: The Making of America's Bosnia Policy* (Washington, D.C.: Brookings Institution Press, 2000), 33–36.

54   See Steven L. Burg and Paul S. Shoup, *The War in Bosnia-Herzegovina: Ethnic Conflict and International Intervention* (Armonk, N.Y.: M. E. Sharpe, 1999), 312.

1 Quoted in *Washington Post*, March 7, 1995; cited in Steven L. Burg and Paul S. Shoup, *The War in Bosnia-Herzegovina: Ethnic Conflict and International Intervention* (Armonk, N.Y.: M. E. Sharpe, 1999), 322.

2 See Charles G. Boyd, "Making Peace with the Guilty: The Truth about Bosnia," *Foreign Affairs* (September/October 1995): 29. General Boyd, the deputy commander in chief of the U.S. European command from 1992 to 1995, cites a senior UN official.

3 See Hrvoje Sarinic, *Svi Moji Tajni Pregovori Sa Slovodanom Milosevicem* (Zagreb: Globus, 1999), 203–56.

4 Ivor Roberts, "Why Yugoslavia Died" (lecture at Oxford University, 2 February 1999).

5 See Steven Greenhouse, "US Makes a New Offer to Serbian," *New York Times*, 18 May 1995; and Roberts, "Why Yugoslavia Died." Frasure reported to Assistant Secretary for European Affairs Richard Holbrooke. In his account of the Dayton peace agreement, Holbrooke does not refer to Frasure's deal but it was common knowledge among diplomats involved in Yugoslavia at the time and is mentioned in numerous sources. British charge Roberts said that Frasure briefed him on the agreement the day of its conclusion, after a long telephone report to Holbrooke in Washington.

6 Quoted in Misha Glenny, "Washington Will Miss Skilled Envoy Whose Bosnia Mission was Repudiated," *London Times*, 21 August 1995, cited in Jan Willem Honig and Norbert Both, *Srebrenica: Record of a War Crime* (New York: Penguin Book, 1997), 168.

7 See Carl Bildt, *Peace Journey: The Struggle for Peace in Bosnia* (London: Weidenfeld and Nicolson, 1998), 65.

8 See ibid., 64–68. Bildt's memoirs say that Kinkel agreed with his plan, which may have happened later. My account is based on my notes of the meeting.

9 Quoted in Roberts, "Why Yugoslavia Died."

10 See Ibid.

11 See Burg and Shoup, *War in Bosnia-Herzegovina*, 329.

12 General de la Presle, Bildt's military adviser and therefore a colleague of mine, met with Mladic during the crisis. He told me there was no deal on release.

13 See Honig and Both, *Srebrenica*, 65.

14 See Misha Glenny, *The Fall of Yugoslavia: The Third Balkan War* (New York: Penguin Books, 1994), 272.

15 See Charles Lane and Tom Shanker, "Bosnia: What the CIA Didn't Tell US," *New York Review of Books*, 9 May 1996, 14.

16 See Honig and Both, *Srebrenica*, 179.

17 Bildt, *Peace Journey*, 60–62.

18 Roberts, "Why Yugoslavia Died."

19 See Robert T. Thomas, *Serbia under Milosevic: Politics in the 1990s* (London: Hurst and Company, 1999), 237; and Honig and Both, *Srebrenica*, 179.

20 Bildt, *Peace Journey*, 55.

21 See Charles Truehart, "War Crimes Trial Starts with Grisly Images," *Washington Post*, 18 March 2000.

22 Eric Schmitt, "Fortunes of War Ease US Military Tasks," *New York Times*, 21 August 1995.

23 See John Darnton, "Accord in London," *New York Times*, 22 July 1995.

24 Croatian actions in Krajina were well documented by diplomatic and UN observers at the time, and by reports from international human rights organizations, such as the International Helsinki Federation. See "Report to the OSCE: The International Helsinki Federation for Human Rights Fact-Finding Mission to the Krajina, August 17–19, 1995." See also Mark Danner, "Operation Storm," *New York Review of Books*, 22 October 1998, 73.

25 Sarinic, *Tajni Pregovori*, 270.

26 Bildt, *Peace Journey*, 76. Also, Vucelic interview, 23 June 2001. Vucelic, who as RTS director had access to information from world media reports that ran counter to Milosevic's optimistic portrayal of the situation in Krajina, believes that Milosevic was lying and that the Serb leader was not surprised by Krajina's subsequent fall.

27 See Slavoljub Djukic, *He, She, and We: A Political Portrait of Slobodan Milosevic and His Wife*, trans. FBIS (Belgrade: Radio B-92, 1997), 91.

28 Ibid., 95.

29 Thomas, *Serbia under Milosevic*, 239.

30 Sarinic, *Tajni Pregovori*, 278–82.

31 See Bob Woodward, *The Choice* (New York: Simon and Schuster, 1996), 257, 266; and General Wesley K. Clark, *Waging Modern War* (New York: Public Affairs, 2001), 52.

32 See Richard Holbrooke, *To End a War* (New York: Random House, 1998), 74; and Bildt, *Peace Journey*, 82. Holbrooke and Bildt publish two quite different versions of the seven points. See also Ivo H. Daalder, *Getting to Dayton: The Making of America's Bosnia Policy* (Washington, D.C.: Brookings Institution Press, 2000), 112.

33 Quoted in Bildt, *Peace Journey*, 86.

34 Quoted in Sarinic, *Tajni Pregovori*, 297.

35 See Holbrooke, *To End a War*, 105.

36 See Roberts, "Why Yugoslavia Died."

37 See Bildt, *Peace Journey*, 94.

38 Many questions were raised at the time about this incident, in part because of the Serb disinformation campaign, in part because of ingrained suspicions of the Bosnians among many internationals in Sarajevo, and in part because the shelling seemed to come at a convenient time to allow NATO to begin the bombing that it had clearly been intending since the 21 July London conference. Questions focused on the fifth shell, which caused most of the casualties and which appeared to follow a different trajectory from the others. The UN investigation concluded, however, that this shell probably hit a nearby building before exploding on the pavement. There is no reason to think that the fifth shell had a point of origin different from the others. In any case, it is hard to believe that the Bosnians could have

somehow managed to fire this fifth shell at the same time as the others—of undoubtedly Serb provenance—and with such pinpoint accuracy, even if one were prepared to believe—which I do not—that the Bosnians would have been willing to slaughter their own people in order to provoke international outrage and begin the bombing. For more discussion of the questions about this incident, see Burg and Shoup, *War in Bosnia-Herzegovina*, 167–68.

39 See Daalder, *Dayton*, 131.

40 Ibid., 135.

41 Bildt, *Peace Journey*, 102.

42 Holbrooke, *To End a War*, 147–52.

43 Information on the Geneva conference is from Holbrooke, *To End a War*, 133–41; Bildt, *Peace Journey*, 99–100; and my own recollections.

44 See Bildt, *Peace Journey*, 121.

45 Quoted in Holbrooke, *To End a War*, 243.

46 Bildt, *Peace Journey*, 145, 123; and Holbrooke, *To End a War*, 233.

47 Bildt, *Peace Journey*, 126.

48 Holbrooke, *To End a War*, 245.

49 Ibid., 264.

50 Ibid., 291.

51 Ibid., 308–9; and Bildt, *Peace Journey*, 158.

52 Quoted in Bildt, *Peace Journey*, 155; see also Holbrooke, *To End a War*, 302.

53 Bildt, *Peace Journey*, 160.

54 Roberts, "Why Yugoslavia Died."

55 Interviews with Aleksandar Tijanic and Milorad Vucecic, in their offices in Belgrade, June 21 and 23, 2001, respectively, and with several other Belgrade journalists or former associates of Milosevic, who do not wish to be named.

56 Warren Christopher, *Chances of a Lifetime: A Memoir* (New York: Scribners, 2001), 259.

57 Richard Holbrooke, *To End a War* (New York: Random House, 1998), 74.

58 Milosevic's remarks on the sanctions were made during his preelection interview with TV Palma on 12 December 2000. In *Getting to Dayton*, Daalder's insider account of the U.S. policy process that led to the Dayton Peace Agreement, the author, an official in the National Security Council during the negotiations, states that one element of the U.S. Endgame Strategy was the "complete lifting of sanctions once the agreement had been implemented" (113).

59 See Mladen Lazic, *Protest in Belgrade* (Budapest: Central European Press, 1999), 10–23.

TEN. *Milosevic Loses Kosovo*

1 See Henry Wynaendts, *L'engrenage: Chroniques Yougoslaves, Juillet 1991–Aout 1992* (Paris: Denoel, 1993), 118–31.

2 See James Gow, *Triumph of the Lack of Will: International Diplomacy and the Yugoslav War* (New York: Columbia University Press, 1997), 75–77. Gow believes

that the Kosovo Albanians might have enjoyed greater success had they constructed their arguments on the basis of the colonial treatment by the Serbs.

3   See Stefan Troebst, *Conflict in Kosovo: Failure of Prevention* (Flensburg, Germany: European Center for Minority Issues, 1998), 37.

4   Quoted in *Washington Post*, 18 April 1999.

5   David C. Gompert, "The United States and Yugoslavia's Wars," in *The World and Yugoslavia's Wars*, ed. Richard H. Ullmann (New York: Council on Foreign Relations Press, 1996), 137. Gompert was a senior official at the National Security Council with responsibility for Yugoslavia during the Bush administration.

6   Warren Zimmermann, *Origins of a Catastrophe* (New York: Random House, 1996), 57.

7   David Owen, *Balkan Odyssey* (New York: Harcourt Brace, 1995), 129.

8   Interview with Klaus Naumann, "War in Europe," *PBS Frontline*.

9   Interview with Wes Clark, "War in Europe," *PBS Frontline*.

10   Zimmermann, *Origins*, 22.

11   Kai Eide, interview with author, Pristina, 28 April 2000.

12   Mahmut Bakalli, interview with author, 1 July 2000.

13   See Robert Bajrusi, "Stipe Mesic o Sarinicevim memoarima," *Nacional*, 10 October 1999.

14   Wes Clark, interview with author, 13 November 2000, Washington, D.C. This incidence and other talks Clark had with Milosevic also appears in Clark's memoirs, *Waging Modern War*. See also Ivo H. Daalder, *Getting to Dayton: The Making of America's Bosnia Policy* (Washington, D.C.: Brookings Institution Press, 2000). Drenica was the center of both the post–World War II and 1998–1999 uprisings against Serb rule.

15   See International Crisis Group, *Kosovo Spring: The International Crisis Group Guide to Kosovo* (Brussels, 1998), 62.

16   Interview with three KLA soldiers, "War in Europe," *PBS Frontline* (http://www.pbs.org/wgbh/pages/frontline/shows/kosovo/interviews/kla).

17   Quoted in Robert T. Thomas, *Serbia under Milosevic: Politics in the 1990s* (London: Hurst and Company, 1999), 297.

18   Ibid., 410.

19   Ibid., 403.

20   Information on U.S. policy comes from interviews with U.S. officials. See also Bob Woodward, *The Choice* (New York: Simon and Schuster, 1996), 258. For the Bildt speech, see "Address by the High Representative, Mr. Carl Bildt, to the Netherlands Association of International Affairs, Europe and Bosnia: Lessons of the Past and Paths for the Future," The Hague, 27 May 1997 (accessed through the OHR Web site, 28 December 2000).

21   Clark, *Waging Modern War*, 109.

22   Quoted in Chris Hedges, "Kosovo's Next Masters," *Foreign Affairs* (May/June 1999): 29.

23   See *Radio Free Europe Newsline*, 5 November 1997.

24   Adem Demaci, interview with author, Pristina, 14 May 2000.

25 Bardh Hamzaj, *A Narrative about War and Freedom: Dialogue with the Commander Ramush Haradinaj* (Pristina: Zeri, 2000), 26.

26 See International Crisis Group, *Kosovo Spring: The International Crisis Group Guide to Kosovo* (Brussels, 1998), 70–71.

27 See Chris Hedges, "Serbian Forces Reportedly Bombarding Ethnic Albanian Villages," *New York Times*, 7 March 1998.

28 See *Radio Free Europe Newsline*, 27 February 1998.

29 Quoted in *Radio Free Europe Newsline*, 23 February 1998.

30 See Ivo H. Daalder and Michael E. O'Hanlon, *Winning Ugly: NATO's War to Save Kosovo* (Washington, D.C.: Brookings Institution Press, 2000), 282; and Elez Biberaj, "The Albanian National Question: The Challenges of Autonomy, Independence, and Separatism," in *The New European Diasporas: National Minorities and Conflict in Eastern Europe*, ed. Michael Mandelbaum (New York: Council on Foreign Relations, 2000), 284.

31 Demaci, interview.

32 Quoted in Georgie Anne Geyer, "Kosovo Countdown: Any Plans after Bombs?" *Washington Times*, 5 October 1998.

33 Quoted in Elaine Sciolino and Ethan Bronner, "How a President, Distracted by Scandal, Entered Balkan War," *New York Times*, 18 April 2000.

34 Interview with Ivo H. Daalder, "War in Europe," *PBS Frontline* (http://www.pbs.org/wgbh/pages/frontline/shows/kosovo/interviews/daalder).

35 Richard Holbrooke, telephone interview with author, 14 July 2000.

36 Interview with Richard Holbrooke, "War in Europe, *PBS Frontline* (http://www.pbs.org/wgbh/pages/frontline/shows/kosovo/interviews/holbrooke).

37 Holbrooke, interview.

38 See Steve Erlanger, "Allies Are Confused by Another Change in US Policy on Kosovo," *New York Times*, 28 May 1998.

39 Bakalli, interview.

40 For Holbrooke's promise to Rugova, see Daalder and O'Hanlon, *Winning Ugly*, 38. See also Steve Erlanger, "Clinton Encourages Kosovo Leaders in Peaceful Settlement," *New York Times*, 30 May 1998; and Sciolini and Bronner, "Distracted by Scandal."

41 Interview with Samuel "Sandy" Berger, "War in Europe," *PBS Frontline* (http://www.pbs.org/wgbh/pages/frontline/shows/kosovo/interviews/berger); and interview with Daalder, "War in Europe."

42 For an outstanding discussion of the relationship between Russia and Milosevic see Oleg Levitin, "Inside Moscow's Kosovo Muddle," *Survival* 42, no. 1 (spring 2000), 130–40. For Primakov on Milosevic, see Yevgeniy Primakov, *Gody v bolshoi politike* (Moskva: Soveshenno Sekretno, 1999), 171–78 and 338–59.

43 Boris Yeltsin, *Midnight Diaries* (New York: Public Affairs, 2000), 265.

44 Oleg Levitin, "Inside Moscow's Kosovo Muddle," *Survival* 42, no. 1 (spring 2000): 132–35.

45 Quoted in Daalder and O'Hanlon, *Winning Ugly*, 33.

46 Interview with Naumann, "War in Europe."

47   Ibid., 47; Holbrooke, interview; and interview with Holbrooke, "War in Europe."

48   See Daalder and O'Hanlon, *Winning Ugly*, 46–48. After a long debate in which, according to U.S. NATO Ambassador Alexander Vershbow (interview with author, Brussels, 12 July 2000), the nineteen NATO members expressed nineteen different points of view on the bombing, Solana summed up the session by stating, "I conclude from this discussion that there is consensus."

49   Richard Holbrooke, telephone interview with author, 24 July 2000.

50   See *New York Times*, 13 October 1998.

51   See Timothy Garton Ash, "Kosovo: Was It Worth It?" *New York Review of Books*, 21 September 2000, 53.

52   Clark, *Waging Modern War*, 137.

53   Quoted in *New York Times*, 18 April 1999.

54   Wes Clark, interview with author, in Washington, D.C., 14 November 2000.

55   Interview with Vucelic, 23 June 2001.

56   See Jane Perlez, "Serbia Shuts Two More Papers Accused of Stirring up Fear," *New York Times*, 15 October 1998.

57   Quoted in *New York Times*, 11 October 1998.

58   Quoted in *Radio Free Europe Newsline*, 20 October 1998.

59   Quoted by Beta news agency, 28 October 1998.

60   Quoted in Radio Free Europe–Radio Liberty *Newsline*, November 1998.

61   The open letter—and much other material on Markovic—is found in Predras Popovic, *Oni ne prastaju: Poslednje ispovest Slavko Curnvija* (Beograd: Info Orfej, 2001), 445. The meeting with Markovic is described in Jane Perlez, "Milosevic's Purges Hint at Violent End for the Regime," *New York Times*, 29 November 1998.

62   See "U sredu dokazi za krivicnu prijavu," *Glas Javnosti*, 1 November 2000, and "Batinasi I revolverasi Mire Markovic," *Glas Javnosti*, 7 November 2000.

63   Quoted in "U sredu dokazi za krivicnu prijavu"; Hamzaj, *Narrative*, 115–20; Ash, "Kosovo," 53.

64   See "KLA Marks Kosovo Date," Associated Press, 29 November 1998.

65   Quoted in Daalder and O'Hanlon, *Winning Ugly*, 64; and *Washington Post*, 23 January 1999.

66   Wes Clark, interview with author, 15 July and 13 November 2000; interview with Clark, "War in Europe"; and interview with Naumann, "War in Europe."

67   Quoted in Steve Erlanger, "US Hardens Stance on Yugoslav Leader," *New York Times*, 14 December 1998.

68   1991 Census, FRY Institute of Statistics.

69   See Biberaj, "Albanian National Question," 84; and Blerim Shala, interview with author, Pristina, 24 August 2000.

70   Daalder and O'Hanlon, *Winning Ugly*, 82.

71   Quoted in Michael Hirsh, "At War with Ourselves: In Kosovo America Confronts Its Own Ideals," *Harpers* (July 1999): 63.

72   Conversations with members of the Albanian delegation.

73   Quoted in Daalder and O'Hanlon, *Winning Ugly*, 83.

74   Interview with U.S. and European participants; and Daalder and O'Hanlon, *Winning Ugly*, 84.

75   Holbrooke, interview; and interview with Holbrooke, "War in Europe."

76   Quoted in Daalder and O'Hanlon, *Winning Ugly*, 299.

77   Quoted in *New York Times*, 24 March 1999.

78   Quoted in *New York Times*, 2 July 1999.

79   Ibid.

80   Holbrooke, interview.

81   Quoted in Daalder and O'Hanlon, *Winning Ugly*, 94; and Ash, "Kosovo."

82   Quoted on BBC News, 1 May 1999.

83   See Daalder and O'Hanlon, *Winning Ugly*, 91. One exception to this was Holbrooke, according to Daalder.

84   Author's interview with Draskovic, Belgrade, 21 June 2001.

85   Author's interview with Pentagon officials, March 2000.

86   See Dana Priest, "Target Selection was Long Process: Sites were Analyzed Again and Again," *Washington Post*, 20 September 1999.

87   Interview with Short, "War in Europe."

88   Clark, *Waging Modern War*, 202.

89   See Robert Suro and Thomas E. Ricks, "Pentagon Acknowledges Leaks of NATO Kosovo Air War Data," *Washington Post*, 10 March 2000.

90   Clark, *Waging Modern War*, 175.

91   See *London Times*, 9 April 1999, and Jeffry Smith and William Drozdiak, "Serbs' Offensive was Meticulously Planned," *Washington Post*, 11 April 1999. Some figures involved in the diplomacy of the Kosovo conflict believe that the "Horseshoe" plan did not exist. I have spoken to members of the U.S. diplomatic and intelligence community who say they saw it, and they have described it as a detailed operational plan. Some, however, have questioned its provenance. According to Ivo H. Daalder and Michael E. O'Hanlon (*Winning Ugly*, 58), the plan took its name from the proposed coordinated attack of a horseshoe-shaped swath of territory along the Albanian and Macedonian borders with Kosovo, aimed at emptying large parts of Kosovo of its Albanian population to isolate KLA fighters and change the ethnic balance of the province. Whether or not there was actually a plan called "Horseshoe" is, in any case, somewhat irrelevant since it is obvious that Serb actions against the Albanian civilian population in Kosovo were well planned in advance and carried out with clear political as well as military objectives.

92   Interview with Naumann, "War in Europe." The Belgrade daily *Danas* claimed that Milosevic told Naumann and Clark in Belgrade before NATO's bombing campaign began that he intended to "solve the Kosovo problem once and for all," but this may be a report of the same Naumann conversation phrased slightly differently. See *REFRL Newsline*, 8 September 1999.

93   Department of State, "Erasing History: Ethnic Cleansing in Kosovo," Washington, D.C., May 1999.

94   See International Crisis Group, *Reality Demands: Documenting Violations of International Humanitarian Law in Kosovo, 1999* (Brussels, 2000), 68–74.

95 Investigators from the Atlanta Center for Disease Control (CDC) calculated that approximately 12,000 Albanians were killed in the Kosovo conflict, over the period February 1998 to June 1999. In September 1999, the CDC researchers conducted a door-to-door survey of almost 12,000 households comprising more than 8,000 people to come up with their data. They also found that an estimated 3,900 people were still missing as a result of the conflict. See Alan Mozes, "Elderly Men Target of Ethnic Cleansing in Kosovo," Reuters, 26 June 2000. On 26 October 2001, the respected international group Human Rights Watch released a massive 593–page report, which explicitly documented 3,453 killings by Serb forces in Kosovo. The report notes that its data on killings, based on interviews with over six hundred survivors, is only partial. Documenting in detail the atrocities committed by Belgrade's forces during the 1998–1999 conflict in Kosovo, the report makes it clear that Milosevic and other senior Serbian officials—some, such as Chief of Staff Nebojsa Pavkovic, still serving in responsible positions in post-Milosevic Belgrade—were responsible for serious war crimes and atrocities. Serbian actions included three distinct waves of killings, systematic rape, expulsions, burning and looting of homes and villages, in pursuit of a carefully planned and implemented operation that fit into the Belgrade government's strategic aims. Unfortunately, the report was released too late to be included in this book.

96 Yeltsin, *Diaries*, 264.

97 See William Drozdiak, "How the Kosovo Deal was Reached," *Washington Post*, 6 June 1999.

98 Quoted in Daniel Williams and Bradley Graham, "Milosevic Notes Troop Casualties; NATO Proclaims Air War's 'Best Day Yet,'" *Washington Post*, 13 May 1999.

99 See Daalder and O'Hanlon, *Winning Ugly*, 144.

100 Ibid., 152; and Hamzaj, *Narrative*, 153.

101 See *New York Times*, 1 May 1999.

102 Ibraahaim Rugova, interview with author, Pristina, April and August 2000.

103 Martti Ahtisari, *Misija u Beogradu* (Beograd: Filip Visnic, 2001), 173–80. This is a Serbian language version of Ahtisari's memoirs of his involvement in the Kosovo crisis. An English translation from Ahtisari's Finnish original was not available at press time.

104 Interview with Viktor Chernomyrdin, "War in Europe," *PBS Frontline*.

105 Qouted in Michael Dobbs and Daniel Williams, "For Yugoslav President, Peace Deal Signals End of War and Start of Internal Battle," *Washington Post*, 6 June 1999, A23.

106 Interview with Vuk Draskovic, Belgrade, 21 June 2001.

107 Clark, *Waging Modern War*, 405.

108 Quoted in Daalder and O'Hanlon, *Winning Ugly*, 160. See Steve Erlanger, "NATO Was Closer to Ground War Than Is Widely Realized," *New York Times*, 7 November 1999, and Dana Priest, "A Decisive Battle That Never Was," *Washington Post*, 19 September 1999, A1.

109 Quoted on BBC News, 1 May 2000.

110 Quoted on "Why Did Milosevic Give Up?" *PBS Frontline* (http://www.pbs.org/wgbh/pages/frontline/shows/kosovo/fighting/giveup).

111   Interview with Strobe Talbott, "War in Europe," *PBS Frontline* (http://www.pbs.org/wgbh/pages/frontline/shows/kosovo/interviews/talbott).

112   Clark, *Waging Modern War*, 325.

113   See Ivo H. Daalder and Michael E. O'Hanlon, "Unlearning the Lessons of Kosovo," *Foreign Policy* (fall 1999): 132; and Steve Erlanger, "Serbs in Milosevic Government Know When to Quit," *New York Times*, 6 June 1999.

114   Yeltsin, *Diaries*, 257.

115   Ibid., 264.

116   Clark, *Waging Modern War*, 377.

117   Ahtisari, *Misija*, 220–24.

118   Yeltsin, *Diaries*, 266.

119   Interview with Strobe Talbott, "War in Europe," *PBS Frontline.*

120   Clark, *Waging Modern War*, 375–96, and interview, November 2000.

ELEVEN. *War Criminal*

1   See "The Prosecutor of the Tribunal against Slobodan Milosevic et al.," 27 May 1999; and "President Milosevic and Four Other Senior FRY Officials Indicted for Murder, Persecution, and Deportation in Kosovo," press release, The Hague, 27 May 1999, JL/PIU/403-E.

2   Quoted in Charles Trueheart, "A New Kind of Justice," *Atlantic Monthly* (April 2000): 87.

3   Some observers criticized the tribunal for slowness in reacting to the atrocities committed by Serb forces against the Kosovo Albanian civilian population in the summer of 1998, when over 250,000 people fled amid killings, burning homes, and the theft or destruction of other property. But the tribunal's mandate is limited to crimes committed in time of war. Its investigators had to establish that an organized military conflict existed in Kosovo. This meant, according to Arbour and Blewitt, that much of the tribunal's activity in 1998 was actually connected with investigating the KLA to establish whether it could be considered a genuine military force with sufficient organization and command structure to allow the hostilities in Kosovo to be classified as an armed conflict between two militaries, rather than a low-level insurgency or terrorist campaign, which would be outside the tribunal's mandate. See also Ed Vulliamy, Rory Carroll, and Peter Beaumont, "How I Trapped the Butcher of the Balkans," *The Observer*, 1 July 2001.

4   Statement by Justice Louise Arbour, The Hague, 27 May 1999, JL/PIU/404-E.

5   Louise Arbour, telephone interview with author, 1 August 2000.

6   Graham Blewitt, interview with author, The Hague, 13 July 2000.

7   Arbour, interview. I have no information to substantiate Arbour's remark about a deal with Milosevic regarding war crimes and peace negotiations in Bosnia.

8   Interview with Strobe Talbott, "War in Europe," *PBS Frontline.*

9   Blewitt, interview.

10   See Tim Judah, *Kosovo: War and Revenge* (New Haven, Conn.: Yale University Press, 2000), 280.

11   Quoted in Trueheart, "A New Kind of Justice," 89.

12   Blewitt, interview.

13   Arbour, interview.

14   Bob Graham and Tom Walker, "Milosevic Ordered the Hiding of Bodies," *Sunday Times*, 1 July 2001.

15   Marlise Simons, "The Case against Milosevic Not Simple to Prove," *New York Times*, 2 July 2001.

16   Quoted in Paul Williams and Norman Cigar, *War Crimes and Individual Responsibility: A Prima Facie Case for the Indictment of Slobodan Milosevic* (Washington, D.C.: Balkan Institute, 1997), 10; citing an interview with Sljivancanin in "The Order Came from Dedinje," *Sviet* (Ljubljana), 25 April 1996, p. 20.

17   Ludwig Boltzmann Institute for Human Rights, *Ethnic Cleansing Operations in the Northeast Bosnian City of Zvornik from April through June 1992* (Vienna, 1994), 16–17.

18   Blewitt, interview.

19   Quoted in Robert T. Thomas, *Serbia under Milosevic: Politics in the 1990s* (London: Hurst and Company, 1999), 97; citing Seselj interview by Mirjana Bobic-Mojsilovic, *Glas Javnosti*, 1994, 76–77.

20   Quoted in Hrvoje Sarinic, *Svi Moji Tajni Pregovori sa Slobodanom Milosevicem* (Zagreb: Globus, 1999), 46.

21   Interview with Milosevic, TV Palma, 12 December 2000.

22   See Thomas, *Serbia under Milosevic*, 137.

23   See Blane Harden, "Serbia's Treacherous Gang of Three," *Washington Post*, 7 February 1993.

24   Beta News Agency, 28 October 1998.

25   See Williams and Cigar, *War Crimes*, 7–8.

26   Quoted in ibid., 20; citing an interview with Seselj, "I Would Suggest to All Serbs from Croatia to Leave."

27   See Williams and Cigar, *War Crimes*, 20; citing interview by Predrag Popovic, "Trebalo je da slusamo Tudjmana," *Intervju*, 10 March 1995, 10.

28   Ibid., 54.

29   Quoted in Williams and Cigar, *War Crimes*, citing "Ubod kobre rusi stara gledanja," *Ilustrovanna Politika*, 4 November 1991.

30   Ibid., 11; citing Gajic-Glisic, Srpska Vojska, 110.

31   The International Criminal Tribunal for the Former Yugoslavia, Case no. IT-01-50-I, the prosecutor of the tribunal against Slobodan Milosevic; and Marlise Simons, "Milosevic, Indicted Again, Is Charged with Crimes in Croatia," *New York Times*, 10 October 2001.

TWELVE. *The End*

1   Quoted in *New York Times*, 31 October 1999.

2   Quoted on BBC, 10 June 1999.

3   Quoted in *New York Times*, 19 August 1999.

4   Poll conducted by Penn, Schoen, and Berland Associates, 24 October 1999; results were also cited in *Blic*, 26 October 1999.

5   See *New York Times*, 31 October 1999.

6   Quoted on BBC, 11 October 1999.

7   Quoted on BBC, 22 July 1999.

8   Quoted in Steve Erlanger, "Former Yugoslav Army Chief Denounces Milosevic," *New York Times*, 23 July 1999.

9   Quoted on BBC, 10 March 1999.

10 Quoted on BBC, 17 October 1999.

11 Quoted in *Vijesti*, 27 October 1999.

12 Quoted in Eve-Ann Prentice, "Milosevic Hand behind Arkan Shooting," *London Times*, 18 January 2000.

13 See *Washington Post*, 30 July 2000.

14 Quoted in Gordana Filipovic, "Queues are a Pre-poll Privilege in Topsy-Turvy Serbia," Reuters, 19 September 2000.

15 See Beta News Agency, 5 July 2000.

16 See Steve Erlanger, "Informal Talks Reported on Exit Terms for Milosevic," *New York Times*, 19 June 2000.

17 See "From Inside Milosevic's Camp," *Jane's Intelligence Digest*, 18 September 2000.

18 For a discussion of Pribicevic and the DS, see Ivo Banac, *The National Question in Yugoslavia: Origins, History, Politics* (Ithaca, N.Y.: Cornell University Press, 1984), 178–89.

19 See Steve Erlanger, "Reluctant Revolutionary: Vojslav Kostunica," *New York Times*, 9 October 2000.

20 See "Milosevic Far behind Opposition Candidate," Reuters, 9 September 2000.

21 Quoted in Tom Walker and Alex Todorovic, "Milosevic Critic Vanishes on Morning Run," *Sunday Times*, 27 August 2000.

22 Quoted in "When in Trouble, Milosevic Turns to His Wife," Associated Press, 19 September 2000.

23 Quoted in Steve Erlanger and Carlotta Gall, "As Election Nears, Yugoslavia's Main Rivals Lash Out," *New York Times*, 21 September 2000.

24 Interview with Matic, 22 June 2001; and Matthew Collin, *This Is Serbia Calling: Rock 'N' Roll Radio and Belgrade's Underground Resistance* (London: Serpent's Tail, 2001), 200–201.

25 Author's interview with Dereta, Belgrade, 18 June 2001.

26 Author's interview with Homen, Belgrade, 19 June 2001.

27 Collin, *This Is Serbia Calling*, 210.

28 Interview 22 June 2001.

29 Interview 19 June 2001.

30 Interview 18 June 2001.

31 Data on the results of the election can be found in *Oko Izbora 4: Izvestaj sa parlementarnikh i predsednickih izbora u SFRJi pokrajinskih izbora u Vojvodini septembar–oktobar 2000* (Beograd: CESID, 2000), 56–57, 64–66. (There remains a certain amount of mystery about the final results of the election, although there is no doubt that Kostunica won convincingly. On October 7, two days after Milosevic's fall, the Central Election Commission, which only a few days earlier had obligingly manipulated the results to favor Milosevic, announced that Kostunica had

won 2,470,304 votes, or 50.24 percent of the total votes, to 1,826,799, or 37.15 percent, for Milosevic. Representatives of CESID told me in June 2001 they believed that after eliminating the votes from Kosovo, which were subject to significant manipulation by the Milosevic authorities, Kostunica had won at least 52 percent of the total but CESID's report on the election does not give a complete, final tally of the vote totals.

32 Quoted in Steve Erlanger, "Yugoslavia's Opposition Leader Claims Victory over Milosevic," *New York Times*, 26 September 2000.

33 Quoted on Radio B-92, 28 September 2000.

34 See Radio B2-92, 29 September 2000.

35 Quoted in Steve Crawshaw, "In Slobodan Milosevic's Hometown, You Can Smell the Fear Now Gripping His Brutal Regime," *Independent*, 3 October 2000.

36 See "Milosevic's Final Days: From Arrogance to Panic to Disgrace," Associated Press, 7 October 2000.

37 See *New York Times*, 29 September 2000.

38 My summary account of the events of October 5 is drawn from a number of sources, including discussions with some of the participants, Serbian and foreign news stories, and a book containing a minute-by-minute account of the uprising that several participants told me was an accurate depiction of the fast-moving events of that day. The book I refer to is Dragan Bujosevic and Ivan Radovanovic, *5 Oktobar: Dvadeset cetiri sata prevrata* (Beograd: Medija centar, 2001). Western press stories include Julius Strauss, "Henchmen Betrayed Milosevic in Revolt," *Daily Telegraph*, 20 October 2000; and Steve Erlanger and Roger Cohen, "How Yugoslavia Won Its Fight for Freedom," *New York Times*, 15 October 2000; and "Milosevic's Final Days," Associated Press, 7 October 2000.

39 See "Sta se u kriticnim trenucima demonstracija desavalo u Generalstabu," *Glas Javnosti*, 17 and 18 October 2000.

40 Quoted in "civilizovana smena vlasti," *Glas Javnosti*, 7 October 2000.

41 Quoted in Carlotta Gall, "Milosevic Wins Re-Election as Leader of Socialist Party," *New York Times*, 26 November 2000.

42 The account of Milosevic's arrest is based on articles by Steve Erlanger and Carlotta Gall, "Milosevic Gave Up After Vow He'll Get A Fair Trial," *New York Times*, 2 April 2001; and by Jeffrey Smith, "Details Milosevic Arrest," *Washington Post*, 2 April 2001. A partial text of the indictment appears in "Milosevic Accused of Creaming Customs Dues," Reuters, 1 April 2001. The text of Milosevic's rebuttal is in *Glas Javnosti*, 3 April 2001.

43 In the days after Milosevic's transfer the Belgrade and international media carried a number of articles with detailed witness accounts of Milosevic's transfer. This account is drawn from the following: Bob Graham and Emily Milich, "Unrepentant Milosevic Faces Charges of Muslim Genocide," *Sunday Times*, 1 July 2001; Carlotta Gall, "Premier of Yugoslavia Resigns in Protest," *New York Times*, 30 June 2001; and Jeffrey Smith, "Milosevic Reaction and Donors' Conference Aid Pledges," *Washinton Post*, 30 June 2001.

44 The poll was taken between May 14–20, 2001, by the SMMRI Agency on behalf of the U.S. International Republican Institute.

45 "Special Bulletin on Milosevic extradition," Radio B92, 28 June 2001.

46 "Milosevic Court Appearance," Associated Press, 3 July 2001.

47 G-17 Plus, *Bela Knjiga Milosevicve Vladavine*, Beograd, 2000.

48 Mladjan Dinkic, ed., *Final Account: Economic Consequences of NATO Bombing: Estimate of the Damage and Finances Required for the Economic Reconstruction of Yugoslavia* (Belgrade: Stubovi Kulture, 1999), 9.

49 Steven L. Burg and Paul S. Shoup, *The War in Bosnia-Herzegovina: Ethnic Conflict and International Intervention* (New York: M. E. Sharpe, 1999), 169–71.

Bibliography

Books

Ahtisari, Marti. *Misija U Beogradu*. Beograd: Filip Visnjic, 2001.

Anzulovic, Branimir. *Heavenly Serbia: From Myth to Genocide*. New York: New York University Press, 1999.

Arnautovic, Sead. *Izbori u Bosni I Hercegovini '90*. Sarajevo: Promocult, 1996.

Baker, James A., III. *The Politics of Diplomacy*. New York: G. P. Putnam and Sons, 1995.

Banac, Ivo. *The National Question in Yugoslavia: Origins, History, Politics*. Ithaca, N.Y.: Cornell University Press, 1984.

——. *With Stalin against Tito: Cominformist Splits in Yugoslav Communism*. Ithaca, N.Y.: Cornell University Press, 1988.

Basiouni, Cherif, et al. *Final Report of the United Nations Commission of Experts on the Evidence of Grave Breaches of the Geneva Convention and Other Violations of International Humanitarian Law Committed on the Territory of the Former Yugoslavia* (S/194/647), December 28. New York: United Nations, 1994.

Begic, Kasim I. *Bosna I Hercegovina Od Vanceove Misije Do Daytonskog Sporazuma (1991–1996)*. Sarajevo: Bosanska Knjiga, 1997.

Bela Knjiga Miloseviceve Vladavine. Beograd: G 17 Plus, 2000.

Biberaj, Elez. "The Albanian National Question: The Challenges of Autonomy, Independence, and Separatism." In *The New European Diasporas: National Minorities and Conflict in Eastern Europe*, edited by Michael Mandelbaum. New York: Council on Foreign Relations, 2000.

Bildt, Carl. *Peace Journey: The Struggle for Peace in Bosnia*. London: Weidenfeld and Nicolson, 1998.

Bokovoy, Melissa K., Jill A. Irvine, and Carol S. Lilly. *State-Society Relations in Yugoslavia, 1945–1992*. New York: St. Martin's Press, 1997.

Bujosevic, Dragan and Radovanovic, Ivan; *5 Oktobar: Dvadeset ceteri sata prevrata*: Beograd: Medija centar, 2001.

Burg, Steven L., and Paul S. Shoup. *The War in Bosnia-Herzegovina: Ethnic Conflict and International Intervention.* Armonk, N.Y.: M. E. Sharpe, 1999.

Cekic, Smail. *The Aggression on Bosnia and Genocide against Bosniacs, 1991–1993.* Sarajevo: Institute for the Research of Crimes against Humanity and International Law, 1995.

Christopher, Warren. *In the Stream of History: Shaping Foreign Policy for a New Era.* Stanford, Calif.: Stanford University Press, 1998.

———. *Chances of a Lifetime: A Memoir.* New York: Scribners, 2001.

Cigar, Norm. *Genocide in Bosnia: The Policy of Ethnic Cleansing.* College Station: Texas A&M University Press, 1995.

Clark, Wesley K. *Waging Modern War.* New York: Public Affairs, 2001.

Cohen, Lenard J. *The Socialist Pyramid: Elites and Power in Yugoslavia.* New York: Mosaic Press, 1989.

———. *Broken Bonds: The Disintegration of Yugoslavia.* Boulder, Colo.: Westview Press, 1993.

Collin, Matthew. *This Is Serbia Calling: Rock 'N' Roll Radio and Belgrade's Underground Resistance.* London: Serpent's Tail, 2001.

Conference on Yugoslavia Arbitration Commission. "Opinion No. 4 on International Recognition of the Socialist Republic of Bosnia-Hercegovina by the European Community and Its Member States." Paris. 1992.

Cosic, Dobrica. *Stvarno i moguce.* Otokar Kersovani: Rijeka, 1983.

Covic, Boze, ed. *Izvori Velikosrpske Agresije.* Rijeka, Croatia: Tiskarna Rijeka, 1989.

Crnobrnja, Mihailo. *The Yugoslav Drama.* Montreal: McGill-Queen's University Press, 1994.

Daalder, Ivo H. *Getting to Dayton: The Making of America's Bosnia Policy.* Washington, D.C.: Brookings Institution Press, 2000.

Daalder, Ivo H., and Michael E. O'Hanlon. *Winning Ugly: NATO's War to Save Kosovo.* Washington, D.C.: Brookings Institution Press, 2000.

Danopoulos, Constantine P., and Kostas G. Messas, eds. *Crisis in the Balkans: Views from the Participants.* Boulder, Colo.: Westview Press, 1997.

Debeljak, Ales. *Twilight of the Idols: Recollections of a Lost Yugoslavia.* Fredonia, N.Y.: White Pine Press, 1994.

Dinkic, Mladjan, ed. *Final Account: Economic Consequences of NATO Bombing: Estimate of the Damage and Finances Required for the Economic Reconstruction of Yugoslavia.* Belgrade: Stubovi Kulture, 1999.

Djilas, Milovan, and Nadezeda Grace. *Bosnjak Adil Zulfikarpasic.* Zagreb: Globus, 1995.

Djukic, Slavoljub. *Izmedju Slave i Anateme: Politicka biografija Slobodana Milosevica.* Belgrade: Filip Visnic, 1994.

———. *Lovljenje Vetra: Politicka ispovest Dobrice Cosica.* Beograd: Samizdat B92, 2001.

———. *He, She, and We: A Political Portrait of Slobodan Milosevic and His Wife.* Translated by FBIS. Belgrade: Radio B-92, 1997.

Doder, Dusko, and Louise Branson. *Milosevic: Portrait of a Tyrant.* New York: Free Press, 1999.

Drew, Elizabeth. *On the Edge: The Clinton Presidency.* New York: Simon and Schuster, 1994.

Drnovsek, Janez. *Escape from Hell: The Truth of a President.* Ljubljana, Slovenia: Delo, 1996.

Emmert, Thomas A. "The Battle of Kosovo: Early Reports of Victory and Defeat." In *Kosovo: Legacy of a Medieval Battle,* edited by Wayne S. Vucinich and Thomas A. Emmert. Minneapolis: University of Minnesota Press, 1991.

Garasanin, Ilija. "Nacertanije." In *Izvori Velikosrpske Agresije,* edited by Boze Covic. Rijeka, Croatia: Tiskarna Rijeka.

Glenny, Misha. *The Fall of Yugoslavia: The Third Balkan War.* New York: Penguin Books, 1994.

Goati, Vladimir, et al. *Guide Through Electoral Controversies in Serbia.* Belgrade: Centar Za Slobodne Izbore I Demokratiju, 2000.

Gompert, David C. "The United States and Yugoslavia's Wars." In *The World and Yugoslavia's Wars,* edited by Richard H. Ullmann. New York: Council on Foreign Relations Press, 1996.

Gordy, Eric D. *The Culture of Power in Serbia: The Destruction of Alternatives.* University Park: Pennsylvania State University Press, 1999.

Gow, James. *Triumph of the Lack of Will: International Diplomacy and the Yugoslav War.* New York: Columbia University Press, 1997.

Gutman, Roy. *A Witness to Genocide.* New York: Macmillan, 1993.

Hamzaj, Bardh. *A Narrative about War and Freedom: Dialogue with the Commander Ramush Haradinaj.* Pristina: Zeri, 2000.

Helsinki Watch. *Yugoslavia: Human Rights Abuses in Kosovo, 1990–1992.* New York, October 1992.

Helsinki Watch and International Helsinki Federation. *Yugoslavia: Crisis in Kosovo.* New York, March 1990.

Holbrooke, Richard. *To End a War.* New York: Random House, 1998.

Honig, Jan Willem, and Norbert Both. *Srebrenica: Record of a War Crime.* New York: Penguin Books, 1997.

Horvat, Branko. *Kosovsko Pitanje.* Zagreb: Globus, 1988.

International Crisis Group. *Kosovo Spring: The International Crisis Group Guide to Kosovo.* Brussels, 1998.

———. *Reality Demands: Documenting Violations of International Humanitarian Law in Kosovo, 1999.* Brussels, 2000.

Izetbegovic, Alija. *Islamska Deklaracija.* Sarajevo: Bosna, 1990.

Janjic, Jovan. *Srpski General Ratko Mladic.* Novi Sad, Vojvodina: Matica Srpska Press, 1996.

Jovic, Borisav. *Poslednji Dani SFRJ.* Belgrade: Politika, 1995.

Judah, Tim. *The Serbs: History, Myth, and the Destruction of Yugoslavia.* New Haven, Conn.: Yale University Press, 1997.

———. *Kosovo: War and Revenge.* New Haven, Conn.: Yale University Press, 2000.

Kadijevic, Veljko. *Moje Vidjenje Raspada.* Belgrade: Politika, 1993.

Kandic, Natasa, ed. *Human Rights Violations in the Territory of Former Yugoslavia, 1991–1995.* Belgrade: Humanitarian Law Center, 1997.

Koljevic, Svetozar. "The Battle of Kosovo in Its Epic Mosaic." In *Kosovo: Legacy of a Medieval Battle*, edited by Wayne S. Vucinich and Thomas A. Emmert. Minneapolis: University of Minnesota Press, 1991.

Lampe, John. *Yugoslavia as History: Twice There was a Country*. London: Cambridge University Press, 1998.

Lazic, Mladen. *Protest in Belgrade*. Budapest: Central European Press, 1999.

Lopusina, Marko. *Ubij bliznjeg svog 1: Jugoslovenska tajna policija od 1945 do 1997*. Belgrade: Narodna Knjiga Alfa, 1997.

Magas, Branka. *The Destruction of Yugoslavia: Tracking the Breakup, 1980–1992*. New York: Verso, 1993.

Major, John. *The Autobiography*. New York: HarperCollins, 1999.

Malcolm, Noel. *Kosovo: A Short History*. New York: New York University Press, 1998.

Maliqi, Shkelzen. "The Albanian Movement in Kosovo." In *Yugoslavia and After: A Study in Fragmentation, Despair, and Rebirth*, edited by David A. Dyker and Ivan Vejvoda. New York: Longman, 1996.

———. *Kosovo: Separate Worlds, Reflections, and Analyses, 1989–1998*. Pristina: Dukagjini, 1998.

Mamula, Branko. *Slucaj Jugoslavija*. Podgorica: CID, 2000.

Mazowiecki, Tadeusz. *The Situation of Human Rights in the Territory of the Former Yugoslavia* (A/48/92/s/25341). New York: United Nations, February 26, 1993.

Meier, Viktor. *Yugoslavia: A History of Its Demise*. New York: Routledge, 1999.

Mertus, Julie A. *Kosovo: How Myths and Truths Started a War*. Los Angeles: University of California Press, 1999.

Mesic, Stipe. *Kako Smo Srusili Jugoslaviju*. Zagreb: Globus, 1992.

Milosevic, Milan. "The Media Wars." In *Burn This House: The Making and Unmaking of Yugoslavia*, edited by Jasminka Udovicki and James Ridgeway. Durham, N.C.: Duke University Press, 1997.

Milosevic, Slobodan. *Godine Raspleta*. Belgrade: Beogradski izdavacko-graficki zavod, 1989.

Muller, Stephan, et al. *Ethnic Cleansing Operations in the Northeast Bosnian City of Zvornik from April through June 1992*. Vienna: Ludvig Bolzmann Institute of Human Rights, 1994.

Nedovic, Slobodanka, ed. *Oko Izbore 2: Izvestaj sa predsednickih izbora u Serbijii (decembar 1997)*. Beograd: Centar Za Slobodne Izbore I Demokratiju, 1997.

———, ed. *Oko Izbora 4: Izvestaj sa parlamentarnih I predsednickih izbora u SRJ I pokrainskih izbora u Vojvodini (septembar–oktobar 2000)*. Beograd: Centar Za Slobodne Izbore I Demokratiju, 2000.

Nikolic, Milan, ed. *Sta Je Stvarno Rekao Dobrica Cosic*. Belgrade: Draganic, 1995.

Owen, David. *Balkan Odyssey*. New York: Harcourt Brace, 1995.

Pavkovic, Aleksandar. *The Fragmentation of Yugoslavia*. New York: St. Martin's Press, 1997.

Perovic, Latinka, ed. *Case of Ivan Stambolic*. Belgrade: Helsinki Committee for Human Rights in Serbia, 2001.

Pipa, Arshi, and Sami Repishti, eds. *Studies on Kosovo*. New York: Columbia University Press, 1984.

Plestina, Dijana. *Regional Development in Communist Yugoslavia: Success, Failure, and Consequences.* Boulder, Colo.: Westview Press, 1992.

Popovic, Predrag. *Oni ne prastaju: Posledna ispovest Slavko Curuvija,* Beograd: Info Orfej, 2001.

Poulton, Hugh. *The Balkans: Minorities and States in Conflict.* London: Minority Rights Publications, 1993.

Prelec, Marko. "Franjo Tudjman's Croatia in the Balkans." In *Crisis in the Balkans: Views from the Participants,* edited by Constantine P. Danopoulos and Kostas G. Messas. Boulder, Colo.: Westview Press, 1997.

Primakov, Yevgeniy. *Gody v bolshoi politike.* Moskva: Sovershenno Sekretno, 1999.

Ramet, Sabrina Petra. *Balkan Babel: The Disintegration of Yugoslavia from the Death of Tito to Ethnic War.* Boulder, Colo.: Westview Press, 1996.

Reed, John. *The War in Eastern Europe.* New York: Scribners, 1919.

Rose, Michael. *Fighting for Peace: Bosnia 1994.* London: Harvill Press, 1998.

Rugova, Ibrahim. *La Question du Kosovo.* Paris: Fayard, 1994.

Rusinow, Dennison. *The Yugoslav Experiment: 1948–1974.* Los Angeles: University of California Press, 1977.

Sarinic, Hrvoje. *Svi Moji Tajni Pregovori Sa Slobodanom Milosevicem.* Zagreb: Globus, 1999.

Seitz, Raymond. *Over Here.* London: Phoenix, 1998.

Sekelj, Laslo. *Yugoslavia: The Process of Disintegration.* New York: Columbia University Press, 1993.

Shoup, Paul. "The Future of Croatia's Border Regions." *Radio Free Europe Situation Report,* 29 November 1991, 26–33.

Sikavica, Stipe. "The Army's Collapse." In *Burn This House: The Making and Unmaking of Yugoslavia,* edited by Jasminka Udovicki and James Ridgeway. Durham, N.C.: Duke University Press, 1997.

Silber, Laura, and Allan Little. *Yugoslavia: Death of a Nation.* New York: Penguin, 1997.

Stambolic, Ivan. *Put u bespuce.* Belgrade: Radio B-92, 1995.

Stojanovic, Svetozar. *Avtoritet Bez Vlasti: Dobrica Cosic kao sef drzave.* Belgrade: Filip Visnic, 1993.

Tanner, Marcus. *Croatia: A Nation Forged in War.* New Haven, Conn.: Yale University Press, 1997.

Thomas, Robert T. *Serbia under Milosevic: Politics in the 1990s.* London: Hurst and Company, 1999.

Troebst, Stefan. *Conflict in Kosovo: Failure of Prevention.* Flensburg, Germany: European Center for Minority Issues, 1998.

Trotsky, Leon. *The Balkan Wars: 1912–1913.* New York: Pathfinder, 1991.

Vasic, Milos. "The Yugoslav Army and the Post-Yugoslav Armies." In *Yugoslavia and After: A Study in Fragmentation, Despair, and Rebirth,* edited by David A. Dyker and Ivan Vejvoda. New York: Longman, 1996.

Vllasi, Azem. *Majstori Mraka: Zatvorski Zapisi.* Zagreb: Globus, 1990.

Vukmanovic-Tempo, Svetozar. *The Struggle for the Balkans.* London: Merlin Press, 1990.

Wachtel, Andrew Baruch. *Making a Nation, Breaking a Nation: Literature and Cultural Politics in Yugoslavia*. Stanford, Calif.: Stanford University Press, 1998.

Williams, Paul, and Norman Cigar. *War Crimes and Individual Responsibility: A Prima Facie Case for the Indictment of Slobodan Milosevic*. Washington, D.C.: Balkan Institute, 1997.

Woodward, Bob. *The Choice*. New York: Simon and Schuster, 1996.

Woodward, Susan L. *Balkan Tragedy: Chaos and Dissolution after the Cold War*. Washington, D.C.: Brookings Institution Press, 1995.

Wynaendts, Henry. *L'engrenage: Chroniques Yougoslaves, Juillet 1991–Aout 1992*. Paris: Denoel, 1993.

Yeltsin, Boris. *Midnight Diaries*. New York: Public Affairs, 2000.

Zimmermann, Warren. *Origins of a Catastrophe*. New York: Random House, 1996.

Articles

"Ako ne umemo dobro da radimo, bar cemo znati dobro da se tucemo." (Notes from Milosevic secret meeting with Serbian local leaders, March 1991.) *Vreme*, 15 April 1991.

Allain, Marie-Francoise. "Kosovo: L'Energie Du Despoir; Entretien avec Ibrahim Rugova." *Politique Internationale* 81 (fall 1998).

Ash, Timothy Garton. "Kosovo: Was It Worth It?" *New York Review of Books*, 21 September 2000, 53.

Bajrusi, Robert. "Stipe Mesic o Sarinicevim memoarima." *Nacional*, 10 October 1999.

——. "The Sensational Transcript between Tudjman and Radic: Even in 1999 Tudjman Wanted to Annex Banja Luka." *Nacional*, 1 June 2000.

Banac, Ivo. "Historiography of the Countries of Eastern Europe: Yugoslavia." *American Historical Review* (October 1992): 1084–104.

Barber, Tony. "Yugoslavia in Crisis: Bellicose Milosevic Raises Stakes." *Independent*, 8 July 1991.

Binder, David. "US Set to Accept Yugoslav Breakup." *New York Times*, 12 March 1992.

Bougarel, Xavier. "Yugoslav Wars: The 'Revenge of the Countryside' between Sociological Reality and Nationalist Myth." *East European Quarterly* 33, no. 2 (June 1999): 157–75.

Boyd, Charles G. "Making Peace with the Guilty: The Truth about Bosnia." *Foreign Affairs* (September/October 1995): 22–38.

Brey, Thomas. "How the Milosevic Clan Robbed Serbia." *DPA*, 27 October 2000.

Cigar, Norman. "Croatia's War of Independence: The Parameters of Conflict Termination." *Journal of Slavic Military Studies* 10, no. 2 (June 1997): 34–70.

Crenshaw, Steve. "In Slobodan Milosevic's Hometown, You Can Smell the Fear Now Gripping His Brutal Regime." *Independent*, 3 October 2000.

Curuvija, Slavko. "Godine Zapleta—decenije Slobodana Milosevica." *Borba*, 18–29 January 1993.

Daalder, Ivo H., and Michael E. O'Hanlon. "Unlearning the Lessons of Kosovo." *Foreign Policy* (fall 1999): 132.

Danner, Mark. "The US and the Yugoslav Catastrophe." *New York Review of Books*, 20 November 1997.

——. "America and the Bosnia Genocide." *New York Review of Books*, 4 December 1997, 61.

——. "Operation Storm." *New York Review of Books*, 22 October 1998, 73.

Darnton, John. "Accord in London." *New York Times*, 22 July 1995.

Dekleva, Kenneth B., and Post, Jerrold M. "Genocide in Bosnia: The Case of Dr. Radovan Karadzic." *Journal of the American Academy of Psychiatry Law* 25, no. 4 (1997): 485–96.

Drozdiak, William. "How the Kosovo Deal was Reached." *Washington Post*, 6 June 1999.

Engleberg, Steven. "Carving out a Greater Serbia." *New York Times Magazine*, 1 September 1991.

Erlanger, Steve. "Allies Are Confused by Another Change in US Policy on Kosovo." *New York Times*, 28 May 1998.

——. "Clinton Encourages Kosovo Leaders in Peaceful Settlement." *New York Times*, 30 May 1998.

——. "Serbs in Milosevic Government Know When to Quit." *New York Times*, 6 June 1999.

——. "Former Yugoslav Army Chief Denounces Milosevic." *New York Times*, 23 July 1999.

——. "Ignoring Scars, Milosevic is Stubbornly Pressing On." *New York Times*, 30 October 1999.

——. "NATO was Closer to Ground War Than is Widely Realized." *New York Times*, 7 November 1999.

——. "Informal Talks Reported on Exit Terms for Milosevic." *New York Times*, 19 June 2000.

——. "Yugoslavia's Opposition Leader Claims Victory over Milosevic." *New York Times*, 26 September 2000.

——. "Reluctant Revolutionary: Vojslav Kostunica." *New York Times*, 9 October 2000.

Erlanger, Steve, and Roger Cohen. "How Yugoslavia Won Its Fight for Freedom." *New York Times*, 15 October 2000.

Erlanger, Steve, and Carlotta Gall. "As Election Nears, Yugoslavia's Main Rivals Lash Out." *New York Times*, 21 September 2000.

Evans, Michael. "Swedish Role in Kosovo Peace." *London Times*, 9 March 2000.

Filipovic, Gordana. "Queues are a Pre-poll Privilege in Topsy-Turvy Serbia." *Reuters*, 19 September 2000.

Gall, Carlotta. "Milosevic Wins Re-Election as Leader of Socialist Party." *New York Times*, 26 November 2000.

Geyer, Georgie Anne. "Kosovo Countdown: Any Plans after Bombs?" *Washington Times*, 5 October 1998.

Glenny, Misha. "Washington Will Miss Skilled Envoy Whose Bosnia Mission was Repudiated. *London Times*, 21 August 1995.

Gordon, Michael. "Conflict in the Balkans." *New York Times*, 4 December 1994.

Greenhouse, Steven. "US Makes a New Offer to Serbian." *New York Times*, 18 May 1995.

Guzelova, Irena. "Milosevic's Bank Delivers Secrets: Beogradska Banka Funded the Yugoslav Dictator's Cronies and Paid off Potential Foes." *Financial Times*, 7 December 2000.

Harden, Blaine. "Serbian Leader in Firm Control Despite Protests." *Washington Post*, 10 March 1992.

——. "Serb Forces Overwhelm Key Town." *Washington Post*, 15 April 1992.

——. "Serbia Seen Adopting a New Bosnia Policy." *Washington Post*, 25 April 1992.

——. "Serbia's Treacherous Gang of Three." *Washington Post*, 7 February 1993.

Hedges, Chris. "Serbian Forces Reportedly Bombarding Ethnic Albanian Villages." *New York Times*, 7 March 1998.

——. "Kosovo's Next Masters." *Foreign Affairs* (May/June 1999): 29.

Hedges, Stephen J. "The Looting of Yugoslavia." *US News and World Report*. 21 July 1997.

Helm, Toby, and Julius Strauss. "Yugoslavia 'Milked of Millions' by Milosevic." *Daily Telegraph*, 18 October 2000.

Hirsh, Michael. "At War with Ourselves: In Kosovo America Confronts Its Own Ideals." *Harpers* (July 1999): 60–69.

Hnuhtanen, Matti. "Former Peace Envoy Claims Russian Military Had Secret Pact with Milosevic." Associated Press, 26 October 2000.

Ignatieff, Michael. "Balkan Physics." *New Yorker*, 10 May 1999, 69–80.

Judah, Tim. "Croatia Reborn." *New York Review of Books*, 10 August 2000, 20.

Kamm, Henry. "The Serb Who's Giving Orders." *New York Times*, 14 October 1988.

Kaplan, Richard. "International Diplomacy and the Crisis in Kosovo." *International Affairs* 74, no. 4 (1998): 745–61.

Kelly, Michael. "Surrender and Blame." *New Yorker*, 19 December 1994, 44–51.

Kessler, Glenn. "Milosevic Cronies Took $1 Billion, U.S. Learns." *Washington Post*, 2 December 2000.

Lancaster, John. "$77 Million Helps Foes of Milosevic." *Washington Post*, 19 September 2000.

Lane, Charles, and Tom Shanker. "Bosnia: What the CIA Didn't Tell US." *New York Review of Books*, 9 May 1996, 14.

Levitin, Oleg. "Inside Moscow's Kosovo Muddle." *Survival* 42, no. 1 (spring 2000): 132–35.

Maccoby, Michael. "Narcissistic Leaders: The Incredible Pros, the Inevitable Cons." *Harvard Business Review* (January–February 2000): 66–77.

Magnusson, Kjell. "The Serbian Reaction: Kosovo and Ethnic Mobilization among the Serbs." *Nordic Journal of Soviet and East European Studies* 4, no. 3 (1987): 3–29.

Markovic, Ante. "Deset Dana Koji Su Srusili Jugoslaviju." *Slobodna Dalmacija*, 3–28 September 1992.

Miceta, Luka. "Ja verujem Milosevicu: Intervju sa Adilom Zulfikarpasicem." *NIN*, 9 August 1991.

Miller, Nicholas. "The Nonconformists: Dobrica Cosic and Mica Popovic Envision Serbia." *Slavic Review* (fall 1999): 515–34.

Milosavljevic, Olivera. "Upotrebna autoriteta nauke: Javna politicka delatnost Srpske Akademije Nauke I Umetnosti (1986–1992)." *Republika* 1 (31 July 1995): 1–30.

Misovic, Milos. "Od Memoranduma do rata" ("From the Memorandum to War"). *Vreme*, 24 August 1992.

Mozes, Alan. "Elderly Men Target of Ethnic Cleansing in Kosovo." *Reuters*, 26 June 2000.

Newhouse, John. "Dodging the Problem." *New Yorker*, 24 August 1992, 60–71.

Perlez, Jane. "Serbia Shuts Two More Papers Accused of Stirring up Fear." *New York Times*, 15 October 1998.

———. "Milosevic's Purges Hint at Violent End for the Regime." *New York Times*, 29 November 1998.

Popov, Nebojsa. "Srpski Populizam: Od marginalne do dominantne pojave." *Vreme*, 24 May 1993.

Popovic, Predrag. "Trebalo je da slusamo Tudjmana." *Intervju*, 10 March 1995, 10.

Post, Jerrold M. "Searching for New Enemies, Reviving Old Enmities: The Psycho-Politics of Hatred in Central and Eastern Europe." *International Affairs Review* (fall 1993): 13–21.

Prentice, Eve-Ann. "Milosevic Hand behind Arkan Shooting." *London Times*, 18 January 2000.

Priest, Dana. "A Decisive Battle That Never Was." *Washington Post*, 19 September 1999, A1.

———. "Target Selection was Long Process: Sites were Analyzed Again and Again." *Washington Post*, 20 September 1999.

Ramet, Sabrina P. "Serbia's Slobodan Milosevic: A Profile." *Orbis* 35, no. 1 (winter 1991): 93–105.

Roberts, Ivor. "Why Yugoslavia Died." Lecture at Oxford University, 2 February 1999.

Schmitt, Eric. "Fortunes of War Ease US Military Tasks." *New York Times*, 21 August 1995.

Sciolino, Elaine, and Ethan Bronner. "How a President, Distracted by Scandal, Entered Balkan War." *New York Times*, 18 April 2000.

Serbian Academy of Arts and Sciences. "Memorandum o aktuelnim drustvenim pitajima u nasoj zemlji." *Nasih tema* (Zagreb) 33, nos. 1–2 (1989): 128–63.

Silber, Laura. "Milosevic Family Values." *New Republic*. 30 August 1999.

Smith, Jeffry, and William Drozdiak. "Serbs' Offensive was Meticulously Planned." *Washington Post*, 11 April 1999.

Strauss, Julius. "Henchman Betrayed Milosevic in Revolt." *Daily Telegraph*, 20 October 2000.

Sudetic, Chuck. "Albanians' New Way: Feuds without Blood." *New York Times*, 17 April 1990.

———. "Serbia Suspends Government of Albanian Region." *New York Times*, 6 July 1990.

———. "Blood and Vengeance: One Family's Story of the Massacre at Srebrenica and the Unending War in Bosnia." *Rolling Stone*, 28 December 1995, 91.

Suro, Robert, and Thomas E. Ricks. "Pentagon Acknowledges Leaks of NATO Kosovo Air War Data." *Washington Post*, 10 March 2000.

Szasz, Paul C. "The Quest for a Bosnian Constitution: Legal Aspects of Constitutional

Proposals Relating to Bosnia." *Fordham International Law Journal* 19, no. 2 (December 1995): 363–07.

Traynor, Ian. "Milosevic Ally Linked to Heroin Stash." *Guardian*, 16 March 2001.

Truehart, Charles. "War Crimes Trial Starts with Grisly Images." *Washington Post*, 18 March 2000.

——. "A New Kind of Justice." *Atlantic Monthly* (April 2000): 87.

U.S. Department of State. "Erasing History: Ethnic Cleansing in Kosovo." Washington, D.C., May 1999.

Vasic, Milos. "The Yugoslav Army and the Breakdown of Yugoslavia." *Vreme*, 27 August 1995.

Velebit, Vladimir. "Kosovo: A Case of Ethnic Change of Population." *East European Quarterly* 33, no. 2 (June 1999): 177–94.

Walker, Tom. "Milosevic Builds Two Million Pound Belgrade Villa." *Sunday Times*, 22 October 2000.

Walker, Tom, and Alex Todorovic. "Milosevic Critic Vanishes on Morning Run." *Sunday Times*, 27 August 2000.

Williams, Daniel, and Bradley Graham. "Milosevic Notes Troop Casualties; NATO Proclaims Air War's 'Best Day Yet.'" *Washington Post*, 13 May 1999.

Index

Louis Sell served twenty-seven years with the U.S.
Department of State, including eight in the former
Yugoslavia. From 1995–1996 he served as political adviser
to Carl Bildt, the first High Representative for Bosnian
Peace Implementation. In that capacity he attended the
Dayton Peace Conference and participated in the first
year of implementation of the Dayton accords. In 2000
he served as Kosovo Director of the International Crisis
Group. He speaks Serbo-Croatian, Russian, and French.
He is currently an adjunct professor at the University of
Maine at Farmington. He lives on a Christmas tree farm
in Whitefield, Maine, with his wife, children, three cats,
and one large dog.

Library of Congress Cataloging-in-Publication Data
Sell, Louis.
Slobodan Milosevic and the destruction of Yugoslavia/
Louis Sell.
Includes bibliographical references and index.
ISBN 0-8223-2855-0 (cloth : alk. paper)
1. Milosevic, Slobodan, 1941–. 2. Politicians—
Yugoslavia—Biography. 3. Yugoslavia—History—1992–.
DR2053.M55 S45 2002 949.7103/092 B 21 2001055581